THE GREAT CAULDRON

THE GREAT CAULDRON

A History of Southeastern Europe

MARIE-JANINE CALIC

Translated by Elizabeth Janik

HARVARD UNIVERSITY PRESS

Cambridge, Massachusetts
London, England
2019

Library of Congress Cataloging-in-Publication Data
Names: Calic, Marie-Janine, author. | Janik, Elizabeth, translator.
Title: The great cauldron : a history of southeastern Europe / Marie-Janine Calic;
translated by Elizabeth Janik.
Other titles: Südosteuropa. English
Description: Cambridge, Massachusetts : Harvard University Press, 2019. |
Includes bibliographical references and index.
Identifiers: LCCN 2018043583 | ISBN 9780674983922 (alk. paper)
Subjects: LCSH: Balkan Peninsula—History. | History, Ancient.
Classification: LCC DR37 .C3513 2019 | DDC 949.6—dc23
LC record available at https://lccn.loc.gov/2018043583

Contents

Maps

All maps © Peter Palm, Berlin, Germany

THE GREAT CAULDRON

Southeastern Europe in 2018

Introduction

ALL POWERFUL EMPIRES are alike; every poor land is poor in its own way. The Romans and Byzantines, followed by the Venetians, Habsburgs, and Ottomans, dominated and shaped southeastern Europe for centuries in imperial style. The peoples of southeastern Europe have many shared experiences, and even today their fates remain closely intertwined. Nevertheless, Albanians, South Slavs, Romanians, and Greeks responded quite differently to foreign domination. Southeastern Europe has maintained a unique sociocultural diversity, and a common identity remains elusive.

This book reinterprets the evolution of southeastern Europe from the perspective of transcultural relations and global history. It explores the interrelationship between southeastern Europe and distant continents and cultures, as well as how border-transcending processes and interactions were perceived, shaped, and socially constructed. Relationships of exchange between people, ideas, and things played a much larger role in the past than familiar historical narratives and representations have often depicted. An understanding of these historical relationships offers insight into the many facets of globalization.

Many scholars of southeastern Europe have focused on the development of nations and nation-states. For most people today, nations represent a primary source of shared identity. However, before the nineteenth century—and to some degree, even in the twentieth century—things were different. Most southeastern Europeans still lived in great multiethnic, multireligious, and multicultural empires—conglomerates of loosely connected territories populated by members of different faiths with very different ways of life. Social groups, milieus, and networks had not yet grown into nations. Some histories have assumed the establishment of the nation-state to be the logical culmination of a supposedly linear process. Broader European and global processes, and experiences that are common to more than one region, have too easily slipped from view.

Other scholars have viewed southeastern Europe as a distinct historical region, defined by certain internal structural characteristics like geography, demography, economics, culture, or even mentality. Because the West generally serves as the model and standard in a worldwide process of modernization, other countries and regions can suffer in comparison—through the apparent absence of a Renaissance or Enlightenment, for example, or simply in socioeconomic backwardness. This interpretive approach tends toward Eurocentrism: processes that transcend borders are too often presented only in terms of the transfer and diffusion of Western ideas and inventions. Phenomena that do not fit within the framework of Western modernity can disappear from sight. Moreover, it can be difficult to understand the connections and interrelationships between countries, regions, and continents in southeastern Europe if too much emphasis is placed on spatial boundaries. The frequent shifting of borders, the fluidity of border regions, and the massive movement of peoples defies such analysis.

Approaching the history of southeastern Europe through imperial studies, by contrast, brings us to literature that views the region from the perspective of the great imperial centers. Sources from Venice, Istanbul, or Vienna tended to gloss over the harsher realities of the periphery. From these sources, we learn most about how the empires saw themselves—namely, as good and just hegemons—rather than how relations between the metropolises and provinces actually functioned, how people in the regions experienced imperial authority, or how certain centrifugal dynamics emerged. Hence, the myth arose that multiethnic empires promoted a greater degree of tolerance than nation-states did. The bloody dissolution of Yugoslavia rekindled this nostalgia for empire and narrowed perspectives on southeastern Europe to investigations of nationalism and violence.

Neither nation, region, nor empire dominates this narrative. Rather, I focus on translocal, transregional, and transnational relationships of exchange. Trends in the study of history have challenged the traditional conception of space as a receptacle of culture, social formation, and identity, thereby exposing supposedly objective characteristics of space as a cultural construct. Inspired by the groundbreaking works of Edward Said and Maria Todorova, numerous scholars have subsequently investigated how Western travelers, writers, and scholars conceptualized and imagined "the Balkans" from the eighteenth century on. Their work shows how romantic ideals and scholarly prejudices about supposedly essential spatial characteristics continue to shape perceptions and discussions about southeastern Europe into the present day.[1]

The new global history and research on translocality and transnationalism have encouraged scholars to look beyond the paradigm of nation-states, thereby touching off a veritable historiographical revolution.[2] Investigating relationships of exchange has taken precedence over the search for internal explanations, and synchronous developments and global constellations are now more likely to be studied than linear processes. Borders of historical regions are now considered as contact zones and transitional spaces. These approaches have become so influential that we can now speak of a "new consensus" in the study of history, one that identifies interactions between societies as a driving force of change.[3] As Christopher Bayly concludes, "all local, national, or regional histories must, in important ways, therefore, be global histories."[4]

There are advantages in telling the history of southeastern Europe from the unfamiliar perspective of worldwide interdependence. Many phenomena cannot be fully understood when considered solely within a regional or national framework, particularly in an age of increasing global connections. By focusing on interactions, interrelationships, and experiences that transcend borders, a new, multifaceted picture of southeastern Europe can emerge, in contradiction to the popular images and stereotypes of a backward and violence-ridden "European other." In a global context, what was once thought to be exceptional becomes the regional expression of overarching processes. This book describes and explains the dark sides of history, too, but offers a more complete picture by including intellectual, scholarly, and cultural achievements, proposals for political reform, and not least, the agency of historical actors. These emphases necessarily lead to new questions and topics of study. How did processes that transcend borders, including globalization in the narrower sense, manifest themselves in southeastern Europe? Who and what promoted integration and exchange? How did the region fit within the structures of the world economy, and what were the political and cultural consequences of the world growing closer? How strong were the forces of resistance, and how influential were those who shunned entanglement in overarching relationships?

Defining "southeastern Europe" is an insuperable task. It is difficult enough to determine the territorial boundaries of "Europe," as its meaning and significance can be understood in so many different ways. Likewise, there are opposing views as to precisely which countries and regions ought to be considered part of southeastern Europe. Definitions abound, but no boundaries are entirely persuasive, whether geographic or political, cultural or historic. Some historians argue that southeastern Europe should include only those areas once under Byzantine or Ottoman influence. They exclude the former Habsburg territories, which structurally resembled the lands of central Europe. Their argument is not unreasonable, but the borders of the great empires changed constantly over the centuries, and many regions shifted back and forth between the spheres of influence. Thus, anyone writing a history of southeastern Europe ultimately must make a pragmatic decision as to which countries will be covered and which will not. This book includes the historic regions that became part of Yugoslavia, Bulgaria, Romania, Albania, and Greece in the twentieth century. All of these territories look back to a formative, though not exclusive, Byzantine and Ottoman heritage. Hungary, which is also sometimes considered part of southeastern Europe, fits better structurally and historically within the group of central (eastern) European states that includes today's Czech Republic, Poland, and Slovakia. Strictly speaking, Slovenia, Croatia, and Transylvania also belong to this group because of their predominantly Western Christian and Habsburg influences. However, because of their ethnic makeup and recent political history, they are very closely linked with parts of southeastern Europe once associated with the Eastern church and Ottoman Empire. Categorically excluding them from the narrative would lead to omissions. In any event, this troublesome question about what to include or exclude becomes less urgent if by analyzing transnational processes and worldwide connections, southeastern Europe is treated as part of a larger, perhaps even global, whole. Southeastern Europe appears here as a hub of transregional connections that are themselves the product of social practices and worldviews that change over time. Thus, boundaries in this history sometimes shift, depending upon the chosen time frame and the particular issues under discussion.

The words we choose for this region must also be considered carefully. Should one speak only of "southeastern Europe," or is "the Balkans" also acceptable? In the region itself, there is a clear distaste for the Balkan label because of the many negative stereotypes it invokes. The concept of "Balkanization"—shorthand for political fragmentation and irrational, internecine warfare—developed alongside the Ottoman Empire's violent separation from its southeastern European periphery in the nineteenth century, and the term is still used today. By 1900, scholars from the region were already pleading on behalf of "southeastern Europe," a less burdened term that indicated common cultural ties and political cooperation. Shortly thereafter, this term was tainted by the National Socialists, who used "southeastern space" *(Südostraum)* to describe the area they sought to reorganize along racial lines and exploit economically. So "southeastern Europe" is likewise freighted with negative connotations, although these are often unconscious. No neutral identification for the region exists, thus I have used both "southeastern Europe" and "Balkans" to refer to the same region, although "Balkans" tends to refer to the area that was under Ottoman influence.[5]

How can the history of southeastern Europe be written from the perspective of global connections? This book is informed by four overarching sets of questions and objectives.

First, I seek to place events, processes, and experiences within their global contexts. From this perspective, for example, we can see how the warriors who fought the Turks in the fifteenth century depended upon the emerging merchant capitalism of the Mediterranean world. We can also see how strongly the scholars and rebels of the nineteenth century were influenced by the global age of revolutions, and how political Islam could spread to the Balkans in the twentieth century.

A second objective is to reconstruct global interrelationships and interactions in space and time as concretely as possible. This involves familiar topics of study like trade, migration, and the history of empires, as well as processes that have been less widely investigated, such as the dissemination of knowledge and global challenges like human trafficking, epidemics, and humanitarian disasters. Relational narratives inspired by global history tend to focus on particularly mobile groups such as travelers, pilgrims, and traders. Transimperial and transcultural subjects and mediators, such as scholars, emigrants, and interpreters, also figure prominently.

Sites of trade, port cities, and even monasteries receive special attention as the hubs of boundary-crossing networks and processes of exchange.

As a third consideration, I investigate the position that southeastern Europe assumed in the emerging global connections—from a political, economic, and cultural perspective. This involves tracing the evolution of the world economy, and asking when and why the lands of southeastern Europe fell victim to the "great divergence."[6] Why, after a certain point, were they unable to expand their wealth as dramatically as the West? What potential for change did the Balkan societies possess, and how did cultural resources affect their participation in the modern globalized world? Why have persistent socioeconomic disparities not yet been overcome?

Finally, I examine differing views of the world and how they changed over time. When, and through whom, did attitudes toward global connections develop? How was globality experienced, interpreted, explained, and discursively constructed—in different historical eras, and in different cultural contexts and spaces? And how did global connections influence self-perception and political action?

While this book seeks to adopt a global historical perspective, it is likewise intended as a broad overview of southeastern Europe. Thoroughly depicting all parts of southeastern Europe would be impossible in one volume, thus the narrative draws upon representative examples in order to make sense of its immense subject matter and to highlight broad trends. To provide space for microhistory as well as macro-level processes, I punctuate the chronological and systematic narrative with sections that depict a specific place in a certain key year. These sections are historical interjections, intended to capture the various perspectives of the past. Using a magnifying glass, we can reconstruct how contemporaries experienced history, as well as how specific internal and external conditions influenced their thoughts and actions—as in Istanbul in 1683, Plovdiv in 1876, and Sarajevo in 1984. How did historical changes manifest themselves in a particular time and place? What did the people who lived then and there understand about the world? How did certain groups and individuals come in contact with others? These magnified snapshots illuminate sociocultural diversity and historical change.

Global history becomes more vivid when it is approached as a story of human lives.[7] Biographies of men and women who typified the lifestyle and spirit of their times are included here as a means of introducing readers to contemporaries' habitus and ways of thinking. We will meet, among others, an Albanian astronomer, a Croatian bishop, a Greek revolutionary, a Bulgarian trader, a Romanian foreign minister, and a female Serbian entrepreneur—representatives of very different life experiences and intellectual horizons. Above all, these biographies demonstrate that humans everywhere have always considered alternative courses of action; without their curiosity, courage, and desire for adventure the course of history would be very different. In this book I emphasize how historical developments have been strongly informed by open-endeddness and contingency. Here and elsewhere, the supposedly decisive historical power of culture and structure is revealed to be a myth.

The book covers an expansive time frame, from late antiquity to the present day. It is impossible to speak of a single, interrelated world before the European voyages of discovery around 1500, when the first signs of "archaic globalization," followed by "proto-globalization," developed.[8] However, already in ancient and medieval times there were spaces of intensive communication with the external world, and mobile groups that promoted cultural contacts and interacted across great distances. World economies that linked far-flung territories, and a "hierarchy of compartmentalized 'worlds,'" were already developing in this early period.[9] But only in the second half of the nineteenth century can we speak of globalization in the stricter sense of an integrated world economy. It was likewise in this era that transnationalism—engagement across borders for universal causes—gained its first foothold.[10] Nevertheless, we should be wary of a linear narrative of steadily increasing global integration. Phases of more intensive exchange have alternated with phases of disengagement and isolation. Moreover, even as the world grew together, new kinds of fragmentation emerged. Political, economic, and cultural globalization have rarely proceeded in unison. Finally, some regions and social groups avoided these overarching processes altogether, or at least remained unaware of them.

A book of this chronological depth and thematic breadth cannot cover all topics of interest, nor can it acknowledge all relevant scholarly controversies and secondary literature, thus annotation has been kept to a minimum in the interest of the general reader. Adopting broad brushstrokes necessarily means that some interesting details must be omitted.[11] In this book I do not seek to test or apply one of the numerous theories and definitions of globalization and globality. Some historians, economists, and political scientists, for example, have drawn general conclusions about "world systems" and unequal relationships between world powers and their former colonies. Others have either emphasized a general pattern of "moderniza-tion," or, on the contrary, challenged the idea that all industrial societies would converge. Instead, they put forward the concept of "multiple mo-dernities" as well as "entangled" and "global" modernities in order to ad-equately describe the contemporary world. Additional impulses for global history have come from research on empires, and on how imperial control was effected or failed. Last but not least, important contributions have emerged from the broad field of postcolonial studies, which concentrates on cultural relations between former colonizers and the colonized. Such approaches offer important impulses and insights for historical analysis, but they certainly cannot provide a general explanatory framework for all of the different, and sometimes contradictory, phenomena and processes that occurred over the course of so many centuries. Although no general theory is tested in this book, by the end it will be possible to draw some fundamental conclusions regarding the history of southeastern Europe.

1

Southeastern Europe before 1500

In the beginning, there was Alexander the Great. No other leader, no other commander has so sparked the imagination of his successors to a similar degree. The history, life experiences, and even the future of the Greeks, Slavs, Turks, Romanians, and Albanians became projections of his magnificent deeds: war and conquest, empire and wealth, power and glory. Hellenes and Romans, Byzantine emperors and Ottoman sultans, Albanian, Serbian, Bulgarian, and Romanian princes and opponents of the Turks, even Greek and Turkish revolutionaries and modern statesmen—all have hoped to inherit the mantle of the storied Macedonian hero of war. For centuries, those in power restyled Alexander's marvelous, idealized image so that it might better fit themselves. Today, both Greece and the Republic of Macedonia see themselves as the successor of Alexander's ancient empire, which has been the source of bitter political dispute.[1] Groups and societies that have for centuries been threatened or dominated by outsiders yearn to have had a glorious history in the distant past, a desire that corresponds to the degree of uncertainty they feel in the present. The ancient era is a reliable standby in the Balkan peoples' repertoire of identity construction, so it is surprising that most recent surveys of southeastern European history do not cover this period.[2] Scholarly research has refuted mythic interpretations of national history, along with the familiar depiction of perpetually barbaric Balkans as the European other. When viewed in the distant mirror of ancient and medieval historical times, southeastern Europe becomes an integral part of a continent that was formatively shaped by Greco-Roman and Christian tradition.

Southeastern Europe and Its Inhabitants

"Of all the lands in Europe, our knowledge of [European] Turkey alone is still very incomplete or deficient," wrote the geographer Ami Boué in 1840. The few of his contemporaries who had ventured to travel there painted an alarming picture. They were not interested "in freeing the European public from the falsehood . . . that the place was teeming with bands of robbers and murderers."[3] Boué was the first Western scholar to travel to the interior of the Balkan Peninsula with the aim of depicting every corner.[4] The result was an impressively rich and detailed geographic and ethnographic work, an introduction to the region and its inhabitants for Western readers.

Before the nineteenth century, when scholars discovered the independent value of all folk cultures through Romanticism, only archaeologists were interested in southeastern Europe. Because of ancient Greece, the area was referred to as the "Hellenic," "Greek," "Byzantine," "Illyrian," or "Moesian" Peninsula. The local cultures were not a source of much interest for the Ottomans, either. The Orientalist Joseph von Hammer-Purgstall commented that "the Turks do not recognize Macedonia, Serbia, Bulgaria, Dobruja, etc. as geographic categories," but instead were familiar only with Ottoman administrative units.[5] They simply called their European possessions "Rumelia," meaning the "land of the Romans," which they had taken from Byzantium.[6]

Only over the course of the nineteenth century did the southeastern European peninsula receive the name "Balkan." At the time, it was common practice to name regions after prominent geographic features.[7] Because geographers wrongly envisioned the Balkan Mountains as a range that connected the Black Sea with the Alps, separating southeastern Europe from the rest of the continent (similar to the way that the Pyrenees demarcated the Iberian Peninsula), the name "Balkan Peninsula" took hold. Classically trained Europeans had previously called these mountains by the ancient name "Haemus." There was a Balkan mountain range in Bulgaria, although its length and location did not correspond to widespread conceptions. Ami Boué, who discovered the error, preferred to speak of "European Turkey." But the more the borders of the Ottoman Empire receded over the course of the nineteenth century, the more popular the "Balkan" label became, referring not only to the broad geographic region but also to its notoriously turbulent political conditions and endemic violence. In 1917 a standard history of the Eastern Question explained that "the name generally given to that segment is 'the Balkan Peninsula' or simply, 'the Balkans.'"[8]

Because no natural barriers exist between southeastern Europe and the rest of the continent, it has participated in supraregional processes and interactions since ancient times. Exchange with other lands and regions was encouraged by its geographic openness toward central Europe and proximity to the Mediterranean and Black Seas, its function as a bridge between two continents and, above all, the human drive to explore. Individual travelers and entire populations moved along the great roads that connected distant regions, giving rise to a diverse and constantly changing ethnographic map. Migrations brought different tribes and cultures into contact with one another, communities disbanded and reconvened, names were passed down or disappeared. Conversions and assimilations, both religious and cultural, created hybrid or even completely new identities. These processes of exchange continue today. Peoples, languages, and cultures are constantly evolving; they are not materially, spatially, or temporally fixed.

Nevertheless, the question of ethnogenesis is uniquely contentious. Since the Renaissance, and particularly during the age of nationalism, scholars looked to antiquity as the cradle of European civilization, seeking their own cultural origins in the distant past. They searched for ancient continuities in ancestry, history, language, and customs, in order to prove a timeless existence that could outlast the Ottoman era. Teleological narratives emerged, describing how developments in the ancient past necessarily led to the founding of a nation-state. Conceptions of a supposedly timeless national existence remain popular today, even though contemporary scholarship has corrected many of these cherished myths.[9]

If we wanted to identify the individual historical layers of ethnogenesis up through the Ottoman era, they might roughly correspond to the following scheme. The oldest substrate of today's population would be the Indo-European peoples, who migrated to southeastern Europe over very long periods of time, beginning around 3000 BCE. These peoples were the source of many different ancient Balkan tribes and cultures. After the third century BCE, when the Imperium Romanum expanded into southeastern Europe, the tribes assimilated with colonists from Italy and other parts of the empire. Between the fifth and ninth centuries, they were joined by migrants from several different language families: Slavs, Turkic Proto-Bulgars, and Finno-Ugric Magyars. In addition, nomadic tribes such as the Goths, Avars, Huns, and other steppe peoples left traces behind as they passed through the region. The Indo-European Roma came to southeastern Europe from northwestern India beginning in the eleventh century, "Saxons" from Germany in the thirteenth century, and Sephardic Jews from the Iberian Peninsula beginning at the end of the fifteenth century. Migration, expulsion, colonization, and assimilation have continuously reshaped the ethnocultural landscape in later eras as well.

According to current research, although many uncertainties remain, the Balkan Peninsula was populated by different tribes throughout the ancient period. Which groups survived the passage of time and which parts of their cultures were passed down to others remain subjects of debate. Because written records from the period are rare, scholars have had to rely on more ambiguous archaeological, linguistic, or epigraphic sources and artifacts. It seems clear, however, that mostly Greek-speaking groups lived south of an invisible border that ran toward Constantinople through Albania, Macedonia, and Thrace. North of this line were the tribes that have become known as Illyrians, Thracians, and Dacians. All belonged to the Indo-European language family; excavations show that their cultures were highly developed.

Some of the oldest settlements in southeastern Europe are found on the Greek peninsula. In the ninth century BCE, a system of autonomous, culturally and politically sophisticated Greek city-states emerged under the influence of the Mesopotamians, Egyptians, Phoenicians, and others. The Greeks dominated the eastern Mediterranean Sea in the Classical period. To secure additional economic opportunities, they founded colonies throughout the entire Mediterranean region and along the Black Sea, as well as in Anatolia and northern Africa. These included Byzantium, Korkyra (Corfu), Odessos (Varna), Melaina Korkyra (Korčula), Pharos (Hvar), and Issa (Vis). From the islands along the Adriatic coast, Greek traders penetrated deep into the interior of the Balkan Peninsula, selling goods such as pottery and purchasing amber, salt, and metals in return.[10]

To the north of the fragmented world of the Greek city-states, the kingdom of Macedonia rose to prominence in the fourth century BCE. Most likely, the Macedonians were originally Greeks, although they later assimilated with Illyrian, Thracian, and other tribes. Philip II established a centralized imperial authority before he and his son Alexander conquered

Greece, Egypt, and the Persian Empire. The gigantic Macedonian Empire fell apart after Alexander's death, but his legendary victories would become an aspirational example for many rulers, in southeastern Europe and beyond. As the Slavs began to settle in Macedonia in the sixth century CE, the Greek identity of the area waned until only its name remained. The identification as "Macedonian" became part of the Slavic idiom.[11] The complex process of amalgamation continues to be the source of bitter controversies today. Greek historiography is premised on a continuity between the Greeks and Macedonians, whereas Macedonian historians emphasize the role of early (not Greek) inhabitants who assimilated with the Slavs.[12] Both interpretations arise from constructions of history that have been colored by nationalism and a certain disinterest in empirical evidence. Since the dissolution of Yugoslavia, a political battle has raged between Skopje and Athens over who can rightfully claim the name "Macedonia" and the symbols from the time of Philip II and Alexander.[13]

But back to the past. The Illyrians settled farther west—in northern Greece, Albania, and the territory that later became Yugoslavia. They separated into many different tribes and cultures. In addition to the "real Illyrians," these included the Dalmatae, Liburnians, Iapodes, and Pannonians. The Illyrians lived in pile dwellings and sustained themselves through agriculture, fishing, and piracy. Today there is no known text that was written in an Illyrian script. Our knowledge about the Illyrians derives primarily from their coins and burials. They were apparently well versed in shipbuilding, geography, navigation, meteorology, and astronomy. In the third century BCE, an Illyrian kingdom thrived under the reign of King Agron. Pirates from the kingdom created uncertainty throughout the Mediterranean, which irritated the Greeks as well as the Romans.[14] During the Renaissance a theory arose that the Slavs were descendants of this ancient tribe. In 1525 the Dominican Vinko Pribojević from Hvar described the Illyrians as ancestors of the Croats and all other Slavs in his work *On the Origins and History of the Slavs*. His thesis was repeated by the religious scholars Mauro Orbini and Juraj Križanić in the seventeenth century, and it became the founding idea of the pan-Slav movement, which reached its pinnacle in the nineteenth century.[15]

Thracians inhabited territory that now belongs to Bulgaria and eastern Macedonia; the Dacians lived to the north, in present-day Romania. It is possible that in ancient times they formed a single people—but that, like so much else, is a point of contention.[16] In the first century BCE, King

Burebista created a powerful Dacian empire, including Getae and Thracians, in the Danube-Carpathian region. Today, nationally minded Romanians still consider this the first Romanian empire. Excavations have revealed evidence of sophisticated tools and building methods, as well as coins, pottery, and valuable handicrafts. Because of their riches, the Dacians maintained close trade relations with the Greeks and Romans.[17]

At the end of the third century BCE, the Romans began to overtake the Balkan Peninsula. It took several centuries before they had subdued all of Illyria, Macedonia, Greece, and finally, Dacia, around 100 CE. Illyricum, as the Romans called southeastern Europe, was divided into provinces and incorporated within the Imperium Romanum. As in all their newly acquired territories, the conquerors began a systematic policy of Romanization.[18]

The Romans uprooted and enslaved the native population, destroyed their cities, and brought in colonists from the Latin West and Asia Minor, heightening the intermingling between many different populations. They constructed fortresses and military bases, and they built streets, ports, mines, and border fortifications called *limes*. Romanization proceeded from the cities, which coalesced around military camps like Singidunum (Belgrade) and veterans' settlements like Scupi (Skopje). Traders, craftsmen, and soldiers introduced Roman culture and traditions, and Latin became the region's common language. Colonists brought oil lamps and medical instruments from northern Italy, glass and mirrors from the Rhineland, and jewelry and cosmetics from the Orient. They built baths, theaters, and temples in the Roman style, as well as forums and basilicas, market halls and aqueducts.[19] Roman rule functioned as did every other colonial regime, with precious resources such as salt, iron, copper, lead, silver, and gold—along with wool, lumber, and other provisions—brought from the outlying provinces to the imperial center.[20]

Latin influences spread fastest along the Dalmatian coast, beginning in the first century CE, whereas the older cultures were more enduring in Bosnia, Croatia, Slavonia, Pannonia, and Dacia. These lands were Romanized only in the second and third centuries CE. Structures that still exist today recall the era of Roman rule—including the arena in Pula and Diocletian's palace in Split, and archaeological sites like Gamzigrad (in present-day Serbia), Ratiaria (Bulgaria), and Stobi (Macedonia).[21] Latin language and Roman culture reshaped older ways of life, although excavations show that older languages, names, gods, and rites did in part survive the Roman occupation.[22] Latin influence was weakest in the southern, Greek-speaking regions of the Balkan Peninsula. Roman colonization here was sparse, thus allowing Hellenistic culture, Greek language, and urban living patterns to remain in place.

As Goth invaders increasingly threatened the Imperium Romanum in the third century, the Romans had to give up their Dacian province so that the Danube became the empire's external border. A topic of debate is whether the Romanized Dacian population remained in Dacia after the Romans retreated (as many Romanian historians assert) or the original inhabitants left the province alongside their occupiers and returned at a later time (as Hungarian research proposes). The broader question is whether or not Romanian settlements have been a permanent presence in the region, which would suggest a Daco-Romanian continuity from the ancient to the modern eras. Based on place names and archaeological evidence such as funerary objects, tools, and jewelry, it seems plausible that some of the original Dacian inhabitants upheld their own traditions, and that these traditions in turn informed the new Latin-speaking culture brought by Romanization. This does not, however, demonstrate linear continuity.[23] For example, archaeological excavations of a necropolis in Brateiu indicate the coexistence of Roman and Dacian traditions; funerary objects such as coins, glass, pottery, and weapons were Dacian, whereas the burial ritual was Roman. Through the migrations that occurred in subsequent centuries, additional population groups such as the Slavs likewise contributed to Daco-Romanic culture and language. Historical sources typically spoke of Vlachs before the name "Romanians" first appeared in the ninth and tenth centuries.[24]

Still other Romanic peoples, collectively referred to as Vlachs or Aromanians, lived south of the Danube, particularly in Bulgaria, Serbia, Macedonia, Albania, and Greece. Nomadic shepherds and the Latinized urban population spoke dialects that were related to, but distinct from, Romanian: Aromanian, Istro-Romanian, and Megleno-Romanian. These groups may have broken away from the Daco-Romanic culture north of the Danube or they could have been Romanized farther south. Later, nomadic shepherds who spoke Slavic, Albanian, or Greek dialects were also called Vlachs. Some eventually settled in one place. Thus, "Vlach" can be an ethnic or socioprofessional identification.[25]

Similar to the Daco-Romanian and Illyrian-Slavic continuities, an assumed Illyrian-Albanian continuity is also controversial. Its advocates are nationally minded Albanians who consider the Dardanians, native to the territory of Kosovo, to be part of the Illyrians. Albanian belongs to the Indo-European language family, but it is not closely related to any other branch, even if it does share many idioms (for example, with Romanian). Linguists believe that the Albanian language existed long before the Romans expanded their empire, and it continued to thrive in certain mountainous regions despite Roman rule. It might have evolved from Illyrian, Thracian, or another ancient Balkan idiom, but there is no consensus here, either. Today, Albanian is divided into two dialects: Gheg is spoken in northern Albania, Kosovo, and Macedonia, and Tosk is prominent in southern Albania, Greece, and Italy.[26]

It has not been conclusively determined whether today's Albanians descended from the Illyrians or from the Thracians or another ancient Balkan people. Their ancestors might have migrated from elsewhere, but evidence is insufficient to prove any of the numerous theories of origin. The Albanians are first mentioned in written sources from the eleventh century; however, sources written by Albanians themselves do not appear until the sixteenth century. The priest Gjon Buzuku, who lived in Rome, wrote the first Albanian-language book in 1555. In the Middle Ages, Albanians called themselves "Arvanites" or "Arbarësh," which possibly derived from the ancient Albanoi tribe, although the precise origins of the name are unknown. The name "Shqiptar," which is still used by Albanians today, did not take hold until around the year 1700.[27]

The Goths came to southeastern Europe in the late ancient period. The Romans drove them out of Dacia in the third century, but their periodic incursions into the region continued until the fifth century. They pushed into Macedonia, Thrace, Greece, and Asia Minor, and they even laid siege to Thessaloniki and Byzantium. An anonymous medieval chronicle asserted that the Goths were ancestors of the invading Slavs, and that they had originally come from Scandinavia before migrating to eastern and southeastern Europe. Around 1600, Mauro Orbini, a Benedictine monk from Dubrovnik, took up the somewhat improbable thesis in his famous work *The Kingdom of the Slavs*. His thesis has been periodically cited ever since, although never proven.[28]

The Goths eventually moved on toward Italy, but nomads on horseback from the steppes of central Asia appeared soon thereafter—first the Huns and Avars, followed by the Slavs and Proto-Bulgars. The "barbarian" onslaught finally obliterated the Roman defense system in southeastern

Europe in the seventh century. The Avars settled in the Carpathian Basin, where they established a khaganate that lasted more than two hundred years and dominated much of southeastern Europe. It was powerful enough to demand tribute from the Byzantine and Frankish Empires. The Avars laid siege to Thessaloniki and Byzantium before Charlemagne crushed the empire at the beginning of the ninth century.

As allies of the Avars, Slavic tribes also crossed the Danube. They fought in the Avar army and built streets, bridges, and fortresses that later became permanent settlements. The precise relationship between the two tribal groups can only be speculated on. Contemporary observers saw the Avars and Slavs as separate peoples who worked cooperatively.[29] A Roman commander had little good to say about the Slavic arrivals: "They live far apart from one another, in miserable huts, frequently changing their place of residence. When they go to battle, it is usually on foot. They only carry shields and lances; they do not wear armor. Some do not even own a shirt or a cloak, but just wear breeches covering their loins, and they attack their opponents in this way."[30] Byzantium seemed powerless to oppose the Slavic conquest, as noted by John of Ephesus: "They [the Slavs] overran all of Greece, the area around Thessaloniki, and all of Thrace, conquering many cities and forts. They devastated and set them ablaze, they took prisoners, and became masters of the land. They established their dominion without the slightest fear, as if the land were their own."[31]

Because archaeological evidence and historical documents are lacking, the original homeland of the Slavs is unknown. It must have been somewhere in eastern Europe, probably within Ukrainian territory. The many hypotheses about their name may have derived from the Slavic words for glory *(slava),* word or language *(slovo),* or swamp *(slova).*[32] Ancient sources describe two main tribal groups that came to Byzantium: the Slaveni and the Antes. Historians later surmised that the Croats and Serbs evolved from the Slaveni and that the Bulgarians and Slavic Macedonians came from the Antes.[33]

Beginning around 580, the Slavic tribes settled in large numbers on the Balkan Peninsula, intermingling with the existing population. They settled throughout most of Greece, Macedonia, Thessaly, Albania, Serbia, Bosnia, and Dalmatia, and then moved farther into Croatia and Slovenia. One century later, the Byzantine emperor Justinian II encouraged Slavic free peasants and soldiers to settle within his imperial territory.[34]

In one way or another, the older population—descendants of the Illyrians, Romans, Goths, Avars, and others—was mostly absorbed by the

Slavs; ancient and migrant cultures combined to form a new habitus, which contemporary observers identified as "Slavic."[35] The mostly egalitarian social order of the Slavic warrior-peasants made it easy to integrate other population groups. Only in the South did the Greek language hold strong. Slavs who settled there became Hellenized, in part through a systematic policy that was initiated by Byzantium two centuries later. Jakob Philipp Fallmerayer, a nineteenth-century historian and Orientalist from Munich, went so far as to say that "not a single drop of old Hellenic blood flows undiluted within the veins of the modern Greeks."[36] That was, however, an oversimplification of a highly complex historical process.

Historical sources identified the Slavic settlements collectively as the "Slavinia" or "Sclavinia"—regions within the territory of Byzantium, but where imperial authority had no real influence. At first the tribes possessed no fixed territory and had hardly any internal organizational structure beyond a chief and an assembly. The tribes were made up of clans or lineages, which were themselves made up of brotherhoods and individual families. The idea of a common ancestry fostered solidarity, a feature that the tribes shared with the Roman *gens,* the Albanian *fis,* and the Scottish clan. As necessary, closer family ties could be consolidated not only through kinship but also through ritual brotherhood and adoptive sponsorship.[37] The tribes only gradually took possession of fixed territories, where they adopted simple methods of farming and raised cattle. The multiple-family household called the *zadruga,* which nineteenth-century observers took to be an ancient Slavic institution, probably developed at a later time.[38]

At first, only one name was used to identify all the Slavs. "Croats" and "Serbs" began to be recognized as independent groups only around 630. Since the Croats' own name for themselves (Hrvati) is not a Slavic word, many different origin theories have been proposed, although none have been proven definitively. The name may have come from Iranian nomads, who first encountered the Slavs in the steppe regions to the east. The name "Serb" comes from the Slavic word root "srb," which is common to many Slavic languages, originally meaning "relative" or "ally." In any case, it has been clearly shown that the Serbs and Croats share the same group of Slavic ancestors who migrated together to southeastern Europe before ultimately settling in different areas. Both peoples were first mentioned by name in ninth-century historical sources.[39]

Around the same time, Turkic-speaking Proto-Bulgars migrated to the Danube and Balkan region. After 680, they established a well-organized state structure. The khan was at its pinnacle, presiding over a society of warriors that was composed of various clans. He was the deputy of their most powerful god, Tangra.[40] The kingdom possessed a competent and mobile ruling class, experienced in waging war. Agriculture flourished in its core territory, which was compact and easy to defend. The remaining descendants of the Thracians, as well as Slavs who had settled in the area more recently, became part of the new regime. By 900, the Turkic Proto-Bulgars had become Slavic-speaking Bulgarians, and their state had become a great power that controlled half the Balkans.[41]

At the end of the ninth century, another new group of nomadic tribes settled in southeastern Europe—an equestrian people led by the Magyars. They had migrated westward from the steppe lands of Eurasia alongside the Turkic peoples, with whom they shared many cultural similarities. However, they spoke a completely different, Finno-Ugric language. The members of one of the tribes called themselves "Magyars," and the name was later used for the entire heterogeneous group. Westerners associated them with a Turkic people called the Onogurs, who had settled in the Carpathian Basin alongside the Avars; the name "Hungary" derived from this connection. Led by the Árpád dynasty, the Hungarian tribes first settled in the Black Sea region, later moving on to Transylvania and elsewhere in the Carpathian Basin. From here, the horseback warriors launched legendary invasions of conquest and plunder, pushing farther into western Europe until halted by a devastating defeat at Lechfeld (near Augsburg) in 955. After their conversion to Christianity and the coronation of the first Hungarian king, Stephen I, in the year 1000, Hungary became the most important regional power in central Europe.

In addition to these regional powers, the great empires that dominated southeastern Europe for centuries did much to assert their own cultures within the southeastern European mélange of peoples. The Imperium Romanum—followed by Byzantium, Venice, the Ottoman Empire, and the Habsburg Monarchy—desired the Balkan region for three reasons: its strategic location, its transportation network, and its abundance of workers, foodstuffs, and raw materials. The peoples of southeastern Europe became subjects of imperial culture, which facilitated their governance and exploitation—practical considerations that were reinforced by universal claims to leadership and a sense of cultural superiority and a *mission civilisatrice*. No clear boundaries existed between civilizations: Balkan, Roman, Byzantine, Venetian, Ottoman, and central European cultures intersected, overlapped, and combined. When historians later spoke of "cultural spaces" or "cultural zones," they were usually referring to ideal types.[42]

Because the peoples of southeastern Europe, their languages, and their cultures developed over very long periods and under very different circumstances, the quest for original peoples and homelands is never-ending. The ancient Balkan people were Romanized or Hellenized, whereas in later eras, some groups were Slavified, others Graecized, or—even later—Islamized. "Croats," "Serbs," "Bulgarians," "Greeks," "Romanians," and "Albanians" were not constant, transhistorical entities. Rather, they were culturally similar groupings that established their present-day identities only over the course of many centuries, not least as the consequence of migrations and foreign rule.

The "antiquating" of folk and national histories is a familiar means of identity construction. Being able to invoke a powerful and culturally sophisticated past bolsters national pride and self-assurance in times of fundamental dislocation and uncertainty. Today passions continue to flare over questions of ancestry, homeland, and migration. Identities are refined with the help of imagined continuities, and whoever was on the scene first can claim an advantage in territorial disputes. Feeling superior to one's opponents is that much easier with a glorious past. Political goals seem legitimate when they are associated with the renewal of a bygone "golden age." Today the ancient era provides a screen onto which national identity, territorial claims, and political self-awareness are projected, offering a useful means for distinguishing the self from the other.[43]

Civilizations and Religions between Rome and Byzantium

Since the invasion of the Goths in the third century, the Roman Empire (which at that time encompassed all of southeastern Europe) was constantly threatened along its external borders in Pannonia and Asia Minor. As the situation in the Southeast became increasingly unstable, the empire's focus shifted in that direction; Illyrian troops were indispensable for the empire's defense. These changes were likewise reflected in the backgrounds of Rome's political and military elite, the "Illyrian emperors" and generals who governed the Imperium between the second and fifth centuries. Emperor Diocletian, the great reformer of the provinces, came from Dalmatia. Decius and Maximian were Pannonians. Aurelian, Constantine, and Galerius were born in Moesia. Justinian the Great, later known for his comprehensive law code, was Macedonian.

Emperor Constantine transformed the old world more profoundly than had any of his predecessors. The successful military leader, statesman, and imperial reformer from Naissus (Niš) paved the way for a new religious age, acknowledging Christianity's burgeoning influence and proclaiming it a tolerated religion in 311. Seventy years later, his successor Theodosius made Christianity the official state religion. Estranged from the "Eternal City," the unbaptized Constantine decided to build a new, Christian capital. In 330 he moved his official residence to the old Byzantion, a comparatively insignificant provincial city with an outstanding strategic position. He wanted the "New Rome" to become the greatest, most splendid, and most important metropolis in the world.[44]

The Roman Empire had become ungovernable because of its sheer size. In 395 it was divided administratively into two parts. Beginning at the Danube, the border followed the Drina River southward and entered the Adriatic Sea south of Salona. Croatia and Bosnia were in the western half, and Serbia and Montenegro were in the East. Constantinople, the capital of eastern Rome, governed the eastern Mediterranean region, including northern Africa, Asia Minor, Syria, Palestine, Egypt, and the Black Sea coast.[45]

When the last western Roman emperor fell in 475, eastern Rome claimed the mantle of the Imperium Romanum. The emperor, church, and elites of Constantinople called themselves "Rhomaioi" (Romans); the name Byzantium was a creation of the Renaissance. By the sixth century, however, the eastern Roman Empire was overwhelmingly Greek and Christian, with few lingering connections to Latin culture. The size and splendor of the empire gave it unique standing among the states of the early medieval era. Constantinople ("the glory of the Greeks, rich in fame, and even richer in wealth," as a crusader later stated) became a symbol of universal Christian civilization because of the size of its population, its geography, and its grandeur.[46]

The Byzantine emperor, who saw himself as Christ's deputy on earth, also ruled over the church. He had the right to intervene in its internal affairs and to select its leaders. In contrast to the Latin West, the spheres of church and state in Byzantium were organically bound to one another through the ideal of symphony, or mutual agreement. Although the principle was never fully realized, it did not mean that the church was completely subordinate to the state.[47]

The Bishop of Constantinople originally occupied a tier in the church hierarchy second to Rome, but after the collapse of the western empire he claimed leadership over all believers, Latin and Greek. This authority was evident in the title "Ecumenical Patriarch," as well as the monumental architecture of the Hagia Sophia, built in sixth-century Constantinople. It remained Christendom's largest and most impressive basilica for around one thousand years, until the construction of Saint Peter's.[48]

The church in Constantinople believed its mission was to uphold and interpret the one true faith, or "orthodoxy," that had been passed down for centuries, although the precise contents of this faith were intensely debated at ecumenical councils. In the eighth century, a dispute over icons plunged the church hierarchy into a deep crisis. The core of the conflict between supporters and opponents of the veneration of icons involved whether or not Jesus Christ ought to be depicted visually and whether or not icons could be used in prayer. The conflict between emperors and church leaders lasted for more than a century before the veneration of icons was definitively permitted in 843. The date of the decision has since been celebrated as the Feast of Orthodoxy.

The Byzantine emperors considered all of southeastern Europe as the legitimate territory of their empire. They established a kind of imperial commonwealth around the center of Constantinople—a belt of neighbors who were favorably disposed toward the empire, if not fully dependent on it. Byzantine foreign policy was informed not only by the Roman idea of universal empire but also by the Hellenistic concept of a barbarism in need of taming and the Christian missionary impulse. Constantinople pushed forward with missionizing the Slavs, using alliances, payments of tribute, and military power to create political satellites and spheres of influence that recognized (or at least no longer challenged) the emperor's political and religious supremacy.[49]

In late antiquity the residents of southeastern Europe had already come into contact with Christianity as it spread outward from the Roman Empire. Evidence of Christian congregations, sacral buildings, necropolises, and frescos has been found in sites such as Singidunum, Scupi, and Diocletiana (in Kosovo). However, the sixth-century migrations of the Avars, Slavs, and Proto-Bulgars upended the structures of church and state alike in Roman Illyricum; in some cases, the process of Christianization was reversed.[50]

Before the spread of Christianity, the region's older as well as newer inhabitants believed that the world was populated by many gods, or even that the world itself was godly. They packed their understanding of the world into ancestral and cosmological myths. There was a diversity of religious expression, with local cults, objects of veneration, and the intensity of faith varying widely from place to place. The early Slavic pantheon included multiple high deities, who appeared in different guises in the regional and local cultures. Lord of the earthly world was the four-headed Vid, or Svetovid, who rode on horseback dressed in a white garment. Responsible for protecting warriors and arable land, he represented the sun, light, and good fortune.[51] Perun, the god of lightning and thunder, ruled the heavens. He rode his chariot across the firmament, armed with a powerful axe that he could throw at evil spirits. His rival, Veles, presided over the waters and the underworld, and he was also the protector of horned animals. In contrast to the many male gods, Mokoš (goddess of the solstice) and Roda (goddess of childbirth) were female.[52]

The Slavs also believed in demigods, who could take the form of a mouse, bear, or wolf, and in demons and evil spirits. Magical fairies called vilas, who took the form of women or animals, were thought to be present in springs, caves, and mountains. Like the Germanic Valkyries, they were warriors; they killed their enemies with bows and arrows or danced them to death.[53] Belief in vampires, the idea that the undead can rise from their graves and wreak havoc among the living, dates back to the earliest times. Fear of ghosts and werewolves was widespread in many cultures. The Turkic Proto-Bulgars believed that the dead could rise again in order to run around committing evil. Thus, the feet of deceased individuals who might still be dangerous were amputated before burial.[54]

Life was primarily experienced through the cyclical progression from day to night and the passing of the seasons. People in many pre-Christian cultures believed that things held magical power, that many objects within nature had souls, and that the world was governed by ancestral spirits. Different cults paid homage to natural phenomena, particularly the sun, moon, and stars, as well as to holy places like rocky cliffs, or to trees, plants, and animals. People took special care to maintain a relationship with their ancestors by bringing them sacrifices such as wheat, honey, nuts, and wine.[55]

The monotheistic religions, Judaism and Christianity, first introduced the concept of transcendence—the idea of creation by an all-powerful God who existed beyond the real world, giving humans a certain freedom within accepted cultural norms. This encouraged a more rational and ethically grounded understanding of the world. Yet for many believers, the earth remained populated by magical powers, spirits, and demons, which could be tamed by the old cults. Belief in vampires, for example, continued into the modern era.[56] In the nineteenth century, Slavs still believed in the *vukodlak,* that is, "in the dead who leave their graves in order to torment the living, or even to strangle them and suck out their blood," as reported by the geographer Ami Boué. "One can become such a monster through the hand of fate, or as punishment for past sins or godlessness."[57]

The Christian God and saints were expected to protect believers from natural disasters, diseases, and curses, and more broadly, to give their lives meaning. The old cults and new religion complemented one another; folk wisdom and magical practices helped to explain forces of nature and to defend against all kinds of afflictions. Through prayer, one could ask God for help with a good harvest, for the healing of sicknesses, and for good fortune in battle. Wanting to be saved from earthly suffering, many people adopted a pious demeanor oriented toward the afterlife.[58]

The point when Christianity irreversibly asserted itself in the Balkan region cannot be precisely determined. The missionizing process lasted for centuries, spreading throughout the southeastern European lands at different times. Croats, Serbs, and Proto-Bulgars first came into contact with the new religion when they arrived in the sixth century. However, Christianity's breakthrough began only in the ninth century, helped by the missions of the Franks, Romans, and Byzantines. Before the new faith spread throughout the populace, the Slavic princes and nobles first had to be baptized. There was a close symbiosis between paganism and Christianity for a very long time.

By the seventh century, Rome and Constantinople had increasingly become rivals in the missionizing of southeastern Europe. As part of the movement for eastward colonization, Bavarian missionaries from the bishoprics of Freising, Salzburg, and Passau set off for Carinthia, Slovenia, and Pannonia, while Dalmatia and lands south of the Drava were missionized from Aquileia. In the ninth century, a growing number of monastic orders came to the region as missionaries. The Benedictines arrived first, followed by the Franciscans, Dominicans, and others from the twelfth century onward.[59] Around 600, Pope Gregory I had already explained the strategy of conversion: "The temples of the idols . . . should not be destroyed, but only the idols within them. Let the temples be purified with holy water, build altars, and place relics within them. For if the temples are well built, the worship of demons will naturally give way to service of the true God."[60] In the place of the old cultic sites, the missionaries built Christian churches, and instead of animal sacrifices, they honored the birthdays of martyrs. Over time, the old Slavic gods merged with the new saints. Perun became Saint Elijah, Veles became Saint Blaise, and Svetovid was transformed into the figure of Saint Vitus. Today, numerous toponyms, folktales, and idiomatic expressions still refer back to the old deities, although their powers have moved on to new heroes. The legendary Kraljević Marko, for example, took on some of the old Slavic god Svetovid's distinguishing features, and Vidovdan (the feast day of Saint Vitus) became the Serbs' most important celebration.[61]

From Thessaloniki and Dyrrhachion (Durrës), Constantinople worked to spread Christianity into the eastern parts of southeastern Europe that it called "Slavinia." The mission to the Slavs received new energy in the second half of the ninth century, when the Moravian prince Rastislav invited missionaries into his kingdom in order to strengthen his position among the Christian states. The patriarch sent the brothers Methodius and Constantine (Cyril), who came from Thessaloniki. These well-spoken sons of a Byzantine military officer had studied theology and taught philosophy at the emperor's palace in Constantinople. They were experienced in the disputation of other religions.[62] As Apostles to the Slavs, they made innovative use of the Slavic vernacular instead of Latin, and they also developed the new Glagolitic alphabet. The Bible and other religious texts could henceforth be translated into Old Church Slavonic and disseminated much more easily.

Bitter disputes with the Latin Church and Frankish missionaries, who feared losing influence and therefore objected to the Slavic liturgy, resulted in the Byzantine missionaries' expulsion from Moravia after only a few years. Some fled in the direction of the Adriatic, and others headed toward Bulgaria and Macedonia.[63] The Glagolitic script moved into the Balkan and Adriatic regions, along with the missionaries. In Bulgaria, it incorporated numerous Greek letters and developed into the Cyrillic alphabet, while in Bosnia, a regional variation called *bosančica* emerged. The original form was preserved in scattered locations throughout Croatia,

Saint Demetrius with the secular and sacred founders of
the church named in his honor, seventh century. Hagios
Dimitrios, Thessaloniki.

Dalmatia, and the Adriatic islands, where variations of the Latin, Cyrillic,
and Glagolitic scripts coexisted, overlapped, and combined with one another for centuries.[64]

After the expulsion of the Eastern Christian missionaries from Moravia,
in the seventh century the Bulgarian Empire became the center of Old
Slavic high culture. Khan Boris wavered between the rival Christian
churches but eventually sided with Constantinople, which (in contrast to
Rome) allowed him to have a national church with its own archbishop. In
864 he was baptized according to the Eastern rite.[65] Before the end of the
ninth century, Kliment and Naum (disciples and former colleagues of
the Apostles to the Slavs) had built up the Bulgarian bishopric of Ohrid
as a school of Slavic orthodoxy. Here clerics were trained in Old Church

Slavonic, enabling them to translate theological, hagiographic, and liturgical literature from Byzantium. The most important works of Old Bulgarian literature were associated with the "School of Ohrid." The Bulgarian Church, which declared itself autocephalous, was a driving force in missionizing neighboring lands, and in promoting Byzantine theology, liturgy, and church governance among the Serbs and the Romanians.

Since the fifth century, the Western and Eastern Churches had begun to grow apart from one another, both theologically and institutionally. Their rivalry intensified in the second half of the eighth century, as the Roman patriarchate increasingly oriented itself toward the Kingdom of the Franks and introduced new doctrines of faith. Theological differences of opinion concerned most urgently the divinity of Jesus Christ and the *filioque,* the Latin doctrine according to which the Holy Spirit proceeds from the Father and the Son. The appropriate understanding of the Trinity was at stake—was the Holy Spirit sent only by God or by Jesus Christ as well? Since Orthodox theologians believed that there could only be one source of the divine, they denounced the *filioque* as heresy. Additional points of contention were the pope's claim to primacy and the mission to the Slavs—issues that directly affected spheres of influence in southeastern Europe. The final rupture came in 1054, brought on by a dispute over hegemony in southern Italy. A legate of the Roman pope and the patriarch of Constantinople excommunicated one another simultaneously. In the ensuing years crusades were mounted against eastern Rome. The pope triumphed when western Crusaders conquered and plundered Constantinople in 1204, establishing a Latin kingdom and patriarchate there. The Byzantine emperor and his church leaders were forced to flee, and Byzantium broke apart into the successor states of Nicaea, Epirus, and Trebizond. A greatly weakened Byzantine Empire and its capital Constantinople were not restored until 1261, a half century later.

The *filioque,* papal authority, and the legitimacy of ecumenical councils (the Eastern Church recognizes only seven) remain the most important points that divide the Orthodox and Catholic Churches today. Differences in theological interpretation also exist. Both Churches celebrate mass differently, with a special emphasis in the East on liturgy, ritual, song, and prayer as expressions of true faith. Religious services that last for hours (to be attended while standing), incense, candles, and brilliant gold icons create a holy spectacle for believers. Other differences concern the church year and calendar, days of fasting, the sacraments, and the veneration of icons.

Only Orthodox Christians accept icons as an expression of divine revelation, comparable to the biblical word of God.[66]

In Orthodoxy, the monasticism of hermits and anchorites, itinerant and mendicant monks, ascetics and stylites, and many other forms of solitary living played a prominent role. In contrast to the Latin Church, Orthodoxy had no orders or congregations, and each monastery possessed its own rule, or typikon. As in the West, convents not only served a religious mission but also fulfilled social, intellectual, and cultural functions.[67] In both parts of Europe, they attained great wealth through the possession of seigneuries (called *metochia* in the East). The medieval Dečani monastery, for example, owned forty Serbian villages and nine Vlach pastoral communities *(katuns)*.[68]

Mount Athos, located on the Greek peninsula of Halkidiki, became the center of Byzantine monasticism in the tenth century. The Greek Megisti Lavra, the Serbian Hilandar, the Bulgarian Zograf, and the Russian Saint Panteleimon are among the renowned monasteries that claimed the "Holy Mountain" as their home. Through their scriptoria and libraries, they became centers of learning and exerted a formative influence on culture, theology, dogma, and liturgy.[69] Today, Athos continues to attract pilgrims and charitable donors from all over the world. Many thousands of names appear in the monasteries' historical records, including the names of members of royal families and clerics, as well as cobblers, tailors, salt merchants, and soap makers. Even today, however, women remained barred from Athos.[70]

Christianization was an immense political undertaking. Princes were baptized first, effectively claiming God-given authority, before the broader population embraced the new faith. Thus, Christianization became a driving force in the development of normed societies and state authority. Externally, it demonstrated a kingdom's acceptance within the Christian Western world, signaling membership within a political culture and opening dynastic connections through marriage. Internally, it had an integrating and stabilizing effect on young states by promoting cohesion and a common cultural identity.[71] Membership in either the Latin or Byzantine cultural sphere also created better economic opportunities. Not least, Christianity guaranteed access to scholarship and architecture, literature and luxury goods, as well as to a certain understanding of time and the world at large. Serbia, Bulgaria, and the Danubian Principalities used the Byzantine calendar, for example, which began to count time with the creation of the world in 5509 BCE. Bosnia and Dalmatia, by contrast, adopted the Latin practice of counting time from the birth of Christ.

Throughout the Middle Ages, no clear boundary existed between the spheres of influence of the Western and Eastern Churches. The Latin and Slavic-Orthodox rites were both present in many areas, particularly in Croatia, Dalmatia, Albania, Bosnia, and Herzegovina. In the tug-of-war between the churches, Rome had the upper hand in Croatia, although it encountered local resistance. Around 900, for example, Bishop Gregory of Nin protested against the papal ban of the Slavic liturgy, advocating instead for a unified church structure.[72] Hybrid rituals and religious and cultural practices developed wherever the influence of the Western and Eastern Churches overlapped. In Dalmatian towns that nominally belonged to the eastern Roman Empire, but that also fell within the jurisdiction of the Roman Church, Easter prayers were offered in the eleventh century on behalf of both the Byzantine emperor and the Latin Croatian king. Because of the cultural synthesis between East and West, the Saint John Vladimir monastery (near the Albanian town of Elbasan) contains an inscription in Greek, Slavic, and Latin.[73] Beyond the Adriatic region, the influence of the Roman Church must have remained strong in Bulgaria, Montenegro, and Serbia before their leaders decided in favor of Byzantium later in the Middle Ages.[74] The Serbian king Stefan Nemanjić accepted his royal crown from the pope in 1217. Only after the Serbian Church declared its independence two years later was the coronation repeated in a Byzantine ceremony.[75]

In a sense, southeastern Europe became the point of intersection between the Latin West and the Greek East, the site where their distinguishing cultural features intermingled. Most people, including the clergy, remained unaware of the underlying schismatic arguments. They embraced parts of both cultures, upheld some traditional patterns of thought and behavior, and combined the disparate influences into something new. Even high-ranking clerics sampled from the religious contents of both great churches, developing their theology and worldviews on the basis of Latin, Greek, and even Middle Eastern intellectual traditions.[76]

Amid this background, the Balkans became part—and possibly the source—of a pan-European heretical movement that was fed by a widespread desire for religious change across the continent.[77] Although the Western and Eastern Churches battled one another fiercely, they were of one mind about the question of heresy: every deviant expression of faith

Southeastern Europe in 1200

had to be eliminated, root and branch. The rivalry over spheres of influence provided fertile ground for all kinds of unorthodox spiritual teachings. The hierarchies fought a particularly bitter struggle against the remnants of dualism, a religion of salvation that had become influential in the first millennium BCE in different parts of the world, in the West as well as in China, India, and Iran.[78] In the Early Middle Ages, dualism lived on in the form of Gnosticism, Paulicianism, Manichaeism, and other variations. Its core belief was the opposition of two powers from the time of creation—the good God and evil Satan, invisible spirit and visible material world, the contradiction between light and dark. Dualism existed in the Balkans in many different varieties and hybrid forms; syncretic doctrines of faith developed alongside Christianity. Many people believed in the eternal struggle between God and Satan, although this view was condemned by the official church.[79]

In Bulgaria, where the Latin and Greek Churches' battle for preeminence was especially bitter, the tenth-century priest Bogomil created an uproar with his interpretation of dualism. He saw himself as Christian, although he radically opposed the Greek Orthodox Church. He preached that God ruled over the heavens, whereas Satan had created all earthly things, and therefore humans as well. He repudiated the Old Testament as an evil revelation, and he rejected the veneration of icons and the crucifix.[80] In accordance with these teachings, the Bogomils lived a nomadic life of poverty and prayer. They rejected church pageantry and the sacraments, following a simple rite that especially appealed to the poorer classes. The priest Cosmas, who was loyal to the church, reported that the heretics "teach their own people not to obey their masters, they revile the wealthy, hate the Tsar, ridicule the elders, condemn the boyars, regard as vile in the sight of God those who serve the Tsar, and forbid every serf to work for his lord."[81]

There were numerous reasons for the Bogomils' success and their expansion as a significant religious movement. Christianity was still young, Paulician teachings and popular superstitions continued to thrive, and established church structures did not exist. Slavic village priests eyed the Greek-speaking higher clergy with mistrust, all the more once Byzantium sought to destroy the Bulgarian Empire. Grave social problems and growing poverty alienated the peasants of higher standing, including the clergy. Dualism could apparently address the spiritual needs of the age better than the official churches.[82]

After the Byzantine emperor destroyed the Bulgarian Empire at the beginning of the eleventh century, forcing the Bogomils to flee, their teachings spread throughout the other lands of southeastern Europe. They divided into regionally distinctive dogmas and churches, including the "Bulgarian Church," the "Church of Dragovica," the "Bosnian Church," and the "Dalmatian Church."[83] Merchants, crusaders, pilgrims, and missionaries carried the Bogomil faith westward. The Cathars in Italy and France embraced it in nearly unaltered form, presuming the Balkan teachings to be the most authentic form of their faith.[84] In order to learn more, the Cathar Jacob Bech even hoped to travel to Bosnia himself at the end of the fourteenth century. When called before the Inquisition, he praised the land as a model for his faith.[85]

After Bulgaria, Bosnia had become the home of dualism by the end of the twelfth century. Although dualism is often thought to have inspired the doctrine of the independent Bosnian Church, its degree of influence is uncertain. Both the Latin and Orthodox Churches claimed the diocese of Bosnia for themselves. Although Bosnia was formally subordinate to Hungary, the powerful leader Ban Kulin decided to pursue greater independence, establishing an autonomous Bosnian Church around the year 1200 as a bulwark against outside influence. The Byzantine historian John Kinnamos noted that "a neighbouring people with its own customs and government" lived here.[86] The new Bosnian Church saw itself as Christian, but it was accused of heresy by both Rome and Constantinople. Because almost no primary sources still exist that can illuminate the Bosnian Church's origins, beliefs, religious practices, social makeup, or attitudes toward authority, the established churches' polemics against heresy—which sought to demonize and denounce the new faith—are the most important source of information that remains.[87] Roman and Byzantine sources assert that the Bosnian Church rejected the doctrine of the Trinity and the Old Testament, which it viewed as the legacy of Satan. It was also said to deny the authority of the official hierarchy and to reject the church, images of the saints, relics, and the ordination of priests—instead promoting celibacy and ascetic morality.[88]

Given the many inconsistencies and contradictory sources, scholars have sometimes identified the Bosnian Church as an offshoot of the Bogomils, sometimes as a variation of Orthodoxy, and sometimes as its own breakaway Christian sect. None of the interpretations can be proved definitively. It seems most likely that different hierarchies and doctrines of faith coexisted in Bosnia. At first, there were the three Christian churches (Bosnian, Orthodox, and Latin), each of which claimed support among part of the nobility and other believers. Existing alongside these churches—and possibly within them as well—were dualistic faith practices that Rome and Byzantium derided as "heretical."[89] The fifteenth-century will and testament of the Bosnian cleric Gost Radin, for example, demonstrates how all kinds of religious traditions and ideas intermingled. The document features a cross and identifies ordained priests and Christian holidays within Radin's church. Radin apparently also believed in the Last Judgment.[90]

Immediately after the founding of the Bosnian Church, Rome began to pursue the suspected heretics with particular fervor. In 1203 Ban Kulin and his church's followers, the *krstjani,* had to renounce their faith before a papal legate and pledge their loyalty to Rome. When this measure had only limited success, Rome sent Franciscan missionaries to Bosnia around 1300 as inquisitors and evangelists. They were to promote Catholic principles and dogma, while consigning the theological texts of "heretics" to flames—a pattern that resembled past persecutions of the Patarenes and Cathars. Because they initially preached in Latin, they had difficulty connecting with the local population. As time passed, a class of native Slavic monks emerged and gained the ear of merchants, craftsmen, and mineworkers in the towns.[91] As both the threat of Ottoman conquest and pressure from Catholic allies increased, the Bosnian king decided to ban the Bosnian Church in the mid-fifteenth century. It disappeared soon thereafter, as did the Bosnian state. It is often said that the followers of the Bosnian Church were the first to convert to Islam after the Ottoman conquest, becoming the ancestors of Bosniaks today, but this is a myth. Members of all different faiths accepted the religion of the new leaders.[92]

Today tens of thousands of medieval tombstones recall a time when distinctions between religious practices were still fluid. The famed *stećci* were once thought to typify the Bosnian Bogomil heritage, but adherents of the established Christian churches also erected them in the fourteenth and fifteenth centuries. They can also be found in Dalmatia, Serbia, and Montenegro. They belonged to a time of economic prosperity, lively trade relations, and courtly high culture. Their motifs and inscriptions show that they were symbols of status in all faith communities, but the idea that these impressive stones could prove the existence of an early Bosnian culture was highly seductive for later generations.

On the eve of Ottoman conquest, southeastern Europe had been shaped by the heritage of Greek and Roman antiquity and by Christianity. These influences defined a common civilization across the European continent, which was shared by Albanians, Slavs, Romans, and other peoples. The schism between the Western and Eastern Churches created internal divisions. The "first Rome" lived on in Bohemia and Moravia, Hungary, Croatia, and Dalmatia; the "second Rome" asserted itself in Bulgaria, Serbia, Montenegro, Romania, and Macedonia. In between were hybrid and transitional zones in Bosnia, Herzegovina, Albania, and also Dalmatia. The religious spheres of influence were not delineated by stable or airtight cultural boundaries, for a variety of reasons. Some cultural characteristics emerged in different eras; cultural spaces were socially, intellectually, artistically, and biographically intertwined; and in many regions, the two official churches coexisted with other faith traditions. Because of this historical background, a "clash of civilizations" between western Christianity and eastern Orthodoxy was not predetermined. These civilizations and religious systems were not bound to clearly defined states or centers of cultural authority; they should not be understood as geopolitical units that could have pursued such warlike aims.

Sovereignty, Knowledge, and Comprehending the World

After the great Slavic wave of migration in the sixth and seventh centuries, in the eighth century Byzantium succeeded in reincorporating Thessaloniki, Greece, and the Peloponnese into its sovereign territories through military might. Thrace and the Dalmatian towns and islands were also brought into the empire. However, the Slavinia of the western and central Balkan Peninsula (which had once belonged to Byzantium) remained permanently out of the reach of eastern Rome. Independent sovereign territories had begun to emerge here in the seventh century. Tribes claimed territory, formed provinces, and began to differentiate socially, enabling the formation of a ruling caste. The sources speak of *župans, archons, bans,* and *duces* whose power depended on military leadership, and who lived from plunder and tributes. Christianization enabled a further consolidation of power. Through baptism, the Slavic ruling class joined the Christian ecumene and civilization. The tenth-century emperor Constantine Porphyrogenitus mentioned the leaders of the Croats, Serbs, Zachlumians,

Terbounians, Diocletians, and Paganians in his work *De administrando imperio.*[93]

The Byzantine emperors worked to bring the new state entities under their influence. They plied the princes with gifts or backed their own pretenders to the throne.[94] As proof of their loyalty, regional leaders had to travel regularly to Constantinople and prostrate themselves before the emperor in the submissive act of *proskynesis.* They were also obliged to perform military service. In return, they received imperial titles, privileges, gifts, or even a Byzantine princess bride.[95] France, the Bulgarian Empire, the Kingdom of Hungary, the Crusaders, the Republic of Venice, and finally the Ottomans later competed for hegemony over these local princedoms. Depending on the political climate, Slavic, Albanian, Greek, and Romanian princes had to recognize one of these suzerains. The princes' loyalty could be fleeting, depending on whomever promised the greatest advantages at a given moment. Individual principalities were not able to assert their self-sufficiency for more than a short period. Rivalries and tribal feuds hindered consolidation into more influential and independent state entities before the twelfth century.

These medieval principalities' model of sovereignty corresponded to that in western and central Europe. Personal ties, mutual dependencies, and loyalty were decisive, not institutional rules. The power of local princes depended on the military allegiance they could command, mostly from relatives and vassals—that is, dependent and allied noble families. Fixed territories and unified polities did not yet exist. Princes did not have a permanent residence, but rather moved back and forth between palaces, castles, and estates. Their foremost responsibility was to lead their army into battle. Allied nobles were obligated to answer a prince's call to service, bringing along their own horses and military contingent. Warriors on horseback, archers, and foot soldiers—armed with lances, swords, and maces—entered into battle accompanied by the fanfare of trumpets. Waging war included taking enemy prisoners, plundering and burning their homes to the ground. In addition to these campaigns of plunder, princely incomes were supported by tributes as well as taxes and levies on the population.[96]

Away from the battlefield, the prince surrounded himself at court with loyal followers, high-ranking advisers, and other dignitaries. Medieval sovereignty always depended on the consent of those who held positions of influence—warlords, nobles, and church officials. Important decisions about issues such as succession, church governance, laws, and peace treaties were made at regional assemblies. One such gathering, the Croatian Sabor, lasted for days and brought together hundreds of participants with horses and tents; papal emissaries and representatives of other lands sometimes attended as well.[97]

Sovereignty was also demonstrated through acts of ritual. Alongside the regional assemblies, other acts of representation—including receptions, festivals, banquets, processions, and awards ceremonies—provided the stage on which social roles, loyalties, and the greater political order were affirmed. The ruling classes took care to maintain personal relations not only with the sovereign but also with relatives and other useful acquaintances. For this reason, territorial sovereignty in the Middle Ages was generally short-lived and unstable. Marriages between ruling houses and other families of influence could solidify political relations. So, for example, the wives who married into the Serbian Nemanjić dynasty included Byzantine, Venetian, French, Hungarian, and Bulgarian princesses.

Byzantium's attention to the Slavic principalities increased after the Bulgarian and Frankish kingdoms emerged as contenders for hegemony in southeastern Europe in the ninth century. Prince Simeon I received the title of Bulgarian emperor in 913. He had initiated a military campaign of unprecedented success, conquering Belgrade, Syrmia, and Macedonia, and he subsequently established a powerful and culturally sophisticated Byzantine-Bulgarian empire.[98] Simeon's successors likewise ensured that Bulgaria remained a constant threat to Byzantium. It was not until the beginning of the eleventh century that the Byzantine emperor Basil II succeeded in subduing his rival, earning him the dubious title of "Bulgar-Slayer." The great Slavic empire was crushed, and Bulgaria and Macedonia were subsumed within the Byzantine administration. Constantinople once again controlled the greater part of southeastern Europe, extending its borders to the Danube and all the way to Istria.[99]

Byzantium also faced a threat from the West. In 800 Charlemagne was crowned emperor of the Frankish kingdom, thereby challenging the exclusive sovereignty of eastern Rome. Charlemagne claimed the Latin-dominated, former western half of the Imperium Romanum. The division between the Western and Eastern Churches now also extended into the political sphere. The establishment of a Latin empire divided the Christian ecumene into two parts, separated by language, culture, politics, and religion. Effects of the division were also evident in southeastern Europe.[100] Charlemagne defeated the Avar kingdom and established Frankish sovereignty in Carantania, Istria, Croatia, and Dalmatia, with only the coastal towns and islands remaining under Byzantine control. Local leaders were not always cooperative, however. Around 850, the Trpimirović dynasty expanded its influence within and beyond Croatia, disregarding Frankish suzerainty. King Tomislav conquered large parts of Dalmatia, Bosnia, and Slavonia in the tenth century, creating an illustrious kingdom that the Croats hearken back to proudly today. He also sealed Croatia's integration within the Latin Church.[101] Disputes over succession subsequently allowed the Kingdom of Hungary, which had already subdued Transylvania and Slavonia, to attack Croatia. Hungary became the largest central European power, and had the strongest army. The Croatian nobles feared for their privileges and decided to compromise with their power-hungry neighbors. Through the *Pacta Conventa,* the Hungarian royal house accepted the Croatian crown in 1102—and kept it until 1918. Because the original text of the agreement no longer exists, scholars continue to debate whether Croatia retained, or effectively relinquished, its statehood within Hungary. The Kingdom of Croatia (later, Croatia-Slavonia) did retain special regional status, an assembly of nobles, and an executive called a *ban*.[102] The Croatian national movement of the nineteenth century interpreted these elements as evidence of "historic statehood," and the constitution of present-day Croatia is premised on a continuity that reaches back to the Middle Ages.

Although privileged social classes were not an original feature of the early Slavic tribes, by the eleventh century a differentiated feudal order had emerged throughout southeastern Europe. Croatia, Bosnia, Hungary, and the Danubian Principalities developed a hereditary nobility that upheld a certain independence from their rulers; noble families possessed large estates that were passed down through the generations. In Serbia and Bulgaria, as in Byzantium, economic power was overwhelmingly concentrated among an imperial elite. Here, the ruler granted nobles parcels of land in return for military service. Before this point, peasants had been free members of village communities, which were legally recognized entities for taxation and other purposes. Social differentiation brought new kinds of dependency on landowners (princes, nobles, and the church). In most parts of southeastern Europe, the rural population was obligated to lifelong service and the payment of rents, although legal arrangements varied widely. As a holdover from the Roman era, forms of tenant farming *(colonatus)* continued in the coastal areas; church estates possessed both field and house slaves. The institution of slavery did not originate with the Slavic tribes, but was brought to the region by other groups.[103]

Ongoing social differentiation and the regional powers' increasing economic might began to tip the balance of power away from Byzantium by the second half of the twelfth century. The South Slav principalities of Zeta (Duklja) and Raška renounced their ties in response to internal Byzantine tensions. In Bulgaria, the Asen dynasty rose to power and restored the Bulgarian Empire, withdrawing it once more from the eastern Roman alliance. After Bulgaria, Serbia and Bosnia also developed into powerful kingdoms. State and empire formation in southeastern Europe received an additional boost when Byzantium fell to the Crusaders in 1204.[104]

In Serbia, the grand *župan* Stefan Nemanja successfully united the principalities of Raška and Zeta—encompassing central Serbia and the adjoining coastland—and established a supraregional kingdom in the middle of the twelfth century. The founder of the Nemanjić dynasty then abdicated his throne in order to live the rest of his life as a monk, and he was sainted after death.[105] His son Stefan Nemanjić completed the process of Serbian state-building when he was crowned "King of all Serbian lands and the coastland" and declared his independence from Byzantium in 1217.[106] Stefan's brother Rastko, who took the name of Sava after his time on Athos, persuaded the patriarch to recognize an autonomous Serbian Orthodox archbishopric, and thus an independent church. The first Serbian bishop is still honored today as the patron saint of Serbia.[107] The Nemanjić state reached the height of its power and territorial expansion under Stefan Dušan in the mid-fourteenth century. In addition to Serbia and Montenegro, he acquired Macedonia, Albania, and northern Greece. In 1346 he was crowned "Emperor of the Serbs and Greeks," and the Serbian archbishopric in Peć was elevated to a patriarchate. Kosovo, the site of the most important Serbian cultural monuments, became the cultural and religious center of the Nemanjić state. The region is still recognized today as the cradle of Serbian culture, as a "Jerusalem" for the Serbs.[108]

Disputes over inheritance weakened the Serbian empire after Stefan Dušan's death. A potential successor as hegemonic power in the Balkans was Serbia's western neighbor, the kingdom of Bosnia. Formerly dependent on Byzantium—and then Croatia, Hungary, Bulgaria, and Serbia—Bosnia was subject to Hungarian sovereignty in the twelfth century. This was the source of the title *banus,* or *ban,* that distinguished Bosnian princes.

Life of Saint Sava, sixteenth century. Morača monastery, Kolašin.

Under Ban Kulin and his successors, Bosnia began to expand rapidly at the end of the twelfth century. In order to solidify its power, the ruling house established a Bosnian state church. In 1377 Tvrtko I was crowned "King of Serbia, Bosnia, the coastland, and the western lands." As a vassal of Hungary, he adorned his coat of arms with the fleur-de-lis of Anjou, which is still depicted on the Bosnian flag today. It was a symbol of the dynasty of Louis the Great, King of Hungary, Croatia, and Poland at that time.

Although the rulers of Bulgaria and Serbia liberated themselves politically from Byzantium, they continued to uphold its spiritual traditions in their ceremonies, coronation rituals, and understanding of sovereignty. According to Greek precedent, they never spoke of "we" or "I," but rather of "my kingdom," "my empire," or "my dominions," since they saw themselves as the personification of their empire. They likewise desired to emulate Byzantium's claim to universal sovereignty, with the Bulgarian Simeon declaring himself "Emperor of the Bulgarians and Greeks" in the tenth century, and the Serb Stefan Dušan taking the title "Emperor of the Serbs and Greeks" in the fourteenth century.[109] In the Byzantine style, they bedecked themselves with imperial crown, scepter, robes, and purple shoes.[110] Elsewhere, the situation was less straightforward. In Croatia and Dalmatia—and to a certain extent, also in Bosnia, Albania, Montenegro, northern Greece, and the Danubian Principalities—Byzantium was not the only model. The Italian Principalities, Hungary, and the Holy Roman Empire served this function as well. The princes of Moldavia and Wallachia were sometimes called *voivode* (as in Hungary), and sometimes *gospodar* (as in Byzantium), which was one sign of the complex political relationships in the region.[111]

As in the Latin West, the conception of empire in Byzantium (which was also embraced by Balkan rulers) assumed a religious character. The ruler was Christ's representative, crowned and legitimated by God.[112] He could become a saint himself—like Saint Stephen in Hungary or Stefan Nemanja in Serbia. The notion of the state merged with church tradition, and worldly power simultaneously assumed sacred meaning. Members of the Nemanjić dynasty commissioned depictions of their distinguished family members' life stories in monastery churches, as with the frescos at Studenica and Sopoćani. Like the Byzantine emperor, the tsars of Bulgaria and Serbia at once possessed both secular and sacred authority.

Castles and courtly architecture, coins, seals, and miniatures demonstrated that southeastern European rulers and nobles saw themselves as part of a European secular culture of nobles and knights. They supported chancelleries, saw that official documents were written in different languages and scripts, and maintained diplomatic relations with other royal houses and courts. They were well versed in the arts of conversation and etiquette, and they passed the time with archery, tournaments, and sword dancing.[113] Traveling musicians, actors, and artists provided entertainment. Clowns, jugglers, magicians, acrobats, pantomimes, and musicians from Germany, Russia, and Italy toured the courts of southeastern Europe. In Serbia, for example, a bagpiper named Kunz performed in 1379, a flute player named Hans in 1383, and a piper from Cologne named Peter in 1426.[114]

Wherever a strong central power developed, economics, culture, and intellectual life thrived. Soon after embracing Christianity, princes typically summoned painters and builders to their courts, thereby affirming their membership in the western cultural community through art and architecture. Later, this was also the reason for the Adriatic territories' orientation toward humanism and the Italian Renaissance. By contrast, many buildings in the countries' interior demonstrated close cultural ties with Byzantium. In all these locations, the highest purpose of medieval art was the expression of spirituality. Builders and painters were not merely artists but also interpreters and transmitters of biblical truth, as conveyed in frescos and other forms. Their identities were usually kept hidden; only in exceptional cases did their names become known.

Some of the most beautiful and sublime works of Byzantine art and architecture were created in the Balkans, including in Preslav, Ohrid, Mileševa, Sopoćani, and Gračanica.[115] Architectural design and iconographic programs conveyed the idea of a godly universe with Christ Pantocrator, judge of the world, at its pinnacle; his image adorned the domes of cross-shaped churches. On the walls and pillars below—in a descending hierarchy from heaven to earth—one could view scenes from the Bible and the lives of saints and martyrs.[116] Western and eastern influences frequently intertwined. Builders from southern Italy used both Romanesque and Byzantine forms in the Church of the Virgin at the Serbian monastery in Studenica. The Dečani monastery, designed at a workshop in Kotor, features colorful ashlar stones in the Italian style, and Gothic influences are apparent in the Gradac monastery and the monastery church of Gračanica.[117] In the Romanian monasteries of Moldavia and Wallachia, situated at the crossroads of the great empires and religions, brilliant iconographic programs and other unique creations took shape.

In philosophy, literature, and cultures of knowledge, Latin and Byzantine traditions likewise overlapped. In Byzantium, which did not have its own universities or a distinct scholarly tradition, ancient texts were copied and commented on again and again. Works of Islamic, Latin, and Hebrew literature were translated as well.[118] Almost everything that was widely read in Byzantium eventually found its way to southeastern Europe, where intellectually curious Bulgarians, Romanians, and Serbs copied, edited, and added to the texts.[119] The cultural centers of Preslav, Ohrid, Thessaloniki, and Athos led the way, although culture also thrived at smaller courts like Serres, Ioannina, and Mystras. From the twelfth century on, literatures and early written languages that had once been shaped by a single Cyrillo-Methodian, Old Church Slavonic tradition began to follow different paths of development, alongside the new state entities.[120]

Many different kinds of texts made the journey to, and around, southeastern Europe in the Middle Ages. The most extensive body of work consisted of liturgical texts, lives of saints, and historical chronicles. Comprehensive anthologies like the "Belgrade collection" brought together translations of ancient and Byzantine texts that were relevant to philosophy and theology. Florilegia, aphorisms, and other literary collections—as well as the Tales of 1,001 Nights, heroic tales of Troy and Alexander the Great, and the Arthurian and Charlemagne legends—were also widely read.[121] The Apocrypha—creation stories that were not recognized by the church—traveled from Palestine, Syria, Egypt, and Asia Minor to Byzantium, and then on to southeastern Europe. Apocryphal texts such as the *Sibylline Oracles,* the *Razumnik,* and noncanonical accounts of Jesus's death and resurrection were translated and adapted further in Bulgaria, Serbia, and Russia, providing an important source of inspiration for dualistic faith teachings.[122]

Renaissance humanism came from the West and spread to Hungary, Transylvania, Croatia, and Dalmatia.[123] The fifteenth-century court of Matthias Corvinus, King of Hungary and Croatia, was renowned for its patronage of scholarship in medicine, natural philosophy, astronomy, logic, and geometry. Scholars from all over Europe came to Buda, where the Croatian bishop Johannes Vitez became a patron of astronomy and founded the university in Posonium (Bratislava).[124] The Croatian Janus Pannonius (Ivan Česmički), the Istrian Pier Paolo Vergerio (Petar Pavao Vergerije), the Bosnian Giorgio Benigno Salviati (Juraj Dragišić), and the Albanian Johannes Gazulus (Gjon Gazulli) are just a few of the region's many outstanding Renaissance scholars. Humanists in the Byzantine cultural sphere included the Bulgarian Constantine the Philosopher, and the Greek John Kantakouzenos. The new intellectual movement did not, however, exert the same degree of influence as in western Europe.[125] But the Byzantine emperors also brought renowned scholars and philosophers to their court. In the eleventh century, a doctor, astronomer, and astrologer from Antioch named Symeon Seth brought scientific discoveries and theories of government from the Far East to Constantinople, and these subsequently made their way to the Slavic world.[126]

Even in the Middle Ages, cultural and religious barriers could not restrain the human desire for knowledge; this was particularly apparent in the field of medicine, which drew on centuries of discoveries made by the ancient Greeks and medieval Arabs. New sites of medical research began to flourish in eleventh-century Italy, and the new knowledge spread from there throughout the rest of Europe. In Salerno, the Muslim herb trader Constantine the African, who engaged in business throughout the Mediterranean, translated specialized medical literature from Arabic into Latin. And Burgundio from Pisa traveled to Constantinople to acquire medical texts from ancient Greece.[127]

The field of medicine developed in the Adriatic coastlands and Croatia in close communication with Italian sites of learning. Monasteries became centers of medical practice and instruction; Benedictines and Franciscans collected remedies and specialized literature, grew medicinal plants, mixed medications, and treated the sick in their monasteries. The eleventh-century medical practitioner and monk Gregor from Split earned a far-reaching reputation for his healing talents, as did the Franciscans in Dubrovnik, who opened the first pharmacy at the beginning of the fourteenth century. Monks and surgeons received training in Salerno, Bologna, and Padua, and some went as far as Paris, Vienna, Prague, or Kraków.[128] This medical knowledge extended into Bosnia and Serbia, where rulers often invited doctors from towns along the Adriatic, especially Dubrovnik and Zadar, to serve at their courts. In 1330 the outstanding eye doctor Draga Slava, a woman from Croatia, was even allowed to practice in Venice.[129]

Common ties between East and West were apparent in all areas of knowledge and ways of thinking about the world. Among both Latin and Byzantine scholars, the astronomer and mathematician Ptolemy's depiction of the world prevailed. Moon, sun, planets, and stars revolved around the Earth, which was the center of the universe. Jerusalem, where the three continents of Europe, Africa, and Asia supposedly converged, was thought to be at the center of the world.[130] Among the broader population, however, such views were hardly common. Less educated Europeans saw the Earth as a flat disk, surrounded by the sea. According to this conception of the world, which remained influential even into the modern era, Earth was at the center of the cosmos, with heaven above and the underworld below.[131]

Eastern and western Europeans thought of history as a linear story of salvation that began with creation and progressed toward the awaited return of Christ sometime in the near future.[132] The idea that the world periodically collapsed in chaos and then rose again, according to God's predetermined plan, originated in ancient thought traditions. Catastrophes and cataclysms would precede the state of perfection and mythical end of days that was envisioned as a "golden age," "cosmic spring," or "heavenly kingdom." New calculations were constantly undertaken to determine the beginning and end of the world. After the Ottoman conquest of Constantinople, for example, Patriarch Gennadios Scholarios predicted that the end of the world would occur in 1493 / 94.[133]

For many people in southeastern Europe, the inexorable advance of Islam seemed to signal that end times were nigh. At the end of the eleventh century, nomadic Turkish tribes from Central Asia had already migrated westward and settled in Asia Minor, most likely in search of a more favorable climate. Byzantium was no longer able to drive the intruders away from its sphere of political influence. By the thirteenth century, Osman had established an emirate less than one hundred miles away from Constantinople; the dynasty that he founded soon initiated a campaign of conquest without parallel. In the borderlands next to the Christian-controlled territories, Osman built up his Islamic empire and assumed the title of "frontier lord," or "leader of the *gazi*," as he presided over the frontline soldiers in holy war. Turkish warriors occupied European soil for the first time around 1350. One century later, they had conquered Constantinople and most of southeastern Europe.[134]

Neither Byzantium nor the Balkan states offered much resistance to the Ottomans. The Serbian empire began to collapse after the mid-fourteenth century, and soon thereafter the Bosnian and Bulgarian Empires broke apart into rival principalities. The Byzantine emperors still claimed nominal hegemony over southeastern Europe, but they no longer had means to enforce it. Rivalries between the Balkan noble families hindered the formation of strong central powers and a common military defense. Many princes saw that they were more likely to protect their sovereignty and privileges by accepting Ottoman suzerainty, rather than by waging war.

On June 28, 1389, the celebrated Day of Saint Vitus, one more alliance came together to battle the Ottomans. Led by the Serbian prince Lazar, his son-in-law Vuk Branković, and King Tvrtko of Bosnia, the Christian armies met Sultan Murad I on the Kosovo Polje, or Field of Blackbirds. Much about the course of the battle remains unknown, except that both commanders (Lazar and Murad I) perished, and there were devastating losses on both sides. The size and composition of the armies, and even the winners and losers of the battle, remain shrouded in uncertainty.[135] In Serbian popular culture, however, the event is recognized as a historic turning point that marked the end of medieval statehood.

Prince Lazar was sainted by the Serbian Church, and hagiographic texts and epic poetry embellished the Kosovo legend so that it resembled religious myth. Archetypal figures, reminiscent of those in biblical stories, made it a durable fixture of Serbian memory culture. On the night before the battle, Prince Lazar was said to have sworn an oath that he would choose death over living in shame, which led him to embrace the heavenly kingdom. Lazar's son-in-law Vuk Branković assumed the role of the devious traitor who collaborated with the Ottomans. The legendary Miloš Obilić, meanwhile, appeared as the national savior who sacrificed his life to murder the sultan, compelling the Ottoman armies to retreat. For the Serbs, the Kosovo myth evolved into a central, identity-affirming narrative that depicted timeless virtues like courage and righteousness as well as values like freedom and unity.

Although the Battle of Kosovo did not yet erase the weakened state of Serbia from the map, it did signal the inexorable decline of the small Christian states in southeastern Europe. Subsequent efforts of the pope, the Hungarian kings, and individual Western princes to subdue the Ottomans all ended in failure. The princes of Moldavia and Wallachia, and the Albanians under Skanderbeg, offered military support, but to no avail. The Crusade movement was defeated in Varna in 1444, and in the Second Battle of Kosovo in 1448. Constantinople fell in 1453.[136]

Of the powerful, economically prosperous, and culturally sophisticated empires of the Middle Ages, all that initially remained was a memory. In a history that was later distorted by Ottoman rule, these empires stood out as pinnacles of a bygone golden age. Before the rise of the Ottomans, southeastern Europe had belonged to the sphere of Christian civilization, which—in all its different variations—enduringly shaped the political, legal, cultural, and intellectual life of the region. Although the subsequent period of foreign rule marginalized or supplanted certain traditions, the medieval era lived on. It provided a home for central sites of memory with great identity-affirming power, and a stage for the performance of historical self-awareness by heroes and saints. In response to the Ottoman threat, the peoples of southeastern Europe developed a clearer understanding of their own Christian-Western identity, in opposition to the Islamic "other."[137]

Grounded in real historic events and experiences, this culture of memory, which was primarily upheld by the churches, created explanatory narratives and myths that remain influential today. Over the centuries, the Middle Ages became a cipher of national identity, which the Ottomans suppressed but never entirely eliminated. In the age of national awakening, activists emphasized continuities with the medieval past in order to justify contemporary political goals and foster a sense of tradition. This was apparent in the nineteenth-century "Megali Idea," a vision for unifying Greeks that was based on Byzantine hegemony. In the same time period, the Kosovo myth became a national ideology for Serbs, and Illyrianism brought together Croats and other South Slavs. Even today, invoking a distant past can help to strengthen group cohesion, legitimate power and authority, shape norms and values, and mobilize the masses on behalf of political ideas.

Medieval World Economies

On the morning of September 8, 1298, the Genoese and Venetian fleets engaged in battle off the coast of the Adriatic island of Korčula. For decades, the two city-states had competed for hegemony over the port cities and trade routes of the Aegean, and especially over connections to the Levant and Black Sea. This time, the Venetians suffered a devastating defeat. Their admiral and other commanders were captured, including the forty-four-year-old Marco Polo.[138] While imprisoned in Genoa, he dictated the world-famous account of his travels to the Mongol Empire, Persia, China, and Indonesia to his cellmate Rustichello da Pisa. Scholars today continue to debate the veracity of his *Description of the World,* which can be read as a guide for merchants, a travelogue, or an adventure tale. His depiction drew on authentic observations, outside sources, and literary embellishments.[139]

Marco Polo came from a well-to-do family of traders who resided in Constantinople and other locations throughout the Mediterranean and Black Sea regions.[140] Because medieval Venetian histories reported that the Polo family moved from Dalmatia to the famed city of canals, some Croatian and Italian historians developed the thesis that Marco came from there, too. On Korčula, where historical documents mention a Polo or Depolo family, one can visit the supposed site of his birth. Marco Polo's Croatian heritage cannot be definitively proved or disproved. In any event, the community sponsored a reenactment of the historic sea battle on its seven hundredth anniversary in 1998.[141]

The controversy over whether the famed explorer and travel writer was actually Croatian or Venetian recalls the dispute over astronomer Nicolaus Copernicus, whom both Germans and Poles claim as their own. Such debates are anachronistic because ethnicity did not yet play a role for people who lived in a prenational age. During Marco Polo's lifetime, citizens of the maritime republic were identified as "Venetians," independent of their place of birth or native language.

Marco Polo's interest in the unknown was atypical for the Middle Ages, placing him almost a century ahead of his time. In his *Description of the World,* the merchant reported on the rise of the Tatars and on the regime of the Mongolian Great Khan and Emperor of China, Kubilai, whom he served for some time. He extolled the magnificence of cities and marveled at the population's unusual customs. Not least, he recorded detailed observations of previously unknown plants and animals. Marco Polo may well have influenced early Orientalist stereotypes in his depictions of the Islamic world, but these were not entirely pejorative.[142] Contemporaries who expected to read about the barbarism and brutishness of the East even denounced him as a liar.[143]

Marco Polo's experience of the world occurred within the context of the rise of the Venetian republic as a colonial power, the emergence of merchant capitalism, and the linking of world economies, which even in this era was substantially larger than often assumed. Population growth, innovations in agriculture, and the dynamism of trade, cities, and transportation networks had encouraged the formation of two distinct economic regions in Europe since the eleventh century. In the North, a commercially oriented hub of economic activity emerged in the Netherlands and the lands around the North and Baltic Seas, while trade dominated the Italian and Mediterranean lands of the South.[144]

Since ancient times, the Mediterranean Sea had been the Old World's motor of development. Even after Islam established itself in Anatolia, the Levant, and northern Africa, the Mediterranean basin still functioned as an economic unit.[145] Irrespective of cultural differences, trading ships connected the port cities and coastal regions of the Iberian Peninsula, Italy, northern Africa, the Balkans, and Constantinople. Christian and Muslim merchants shipped flax from Egypt, and textiles from Greece, Tunisia, Sicily, and Spain, and they engaged in all kinds of business dealings with one another, trading with animal hides, olive oil, soap, and wax. The trade in products from the Orient was especially lucrative: pepper, cinnamon, ginger, and cloves, as well as rosin, essential oils, medicinal herbs, dyes, pearls, and semiprecious stones. As early as 1050, a Levantine trader who worked throughout the Mediterranean carried more than 280 different items in his inventory.[146] Trade relationships necessitated the adoption of standard coinage; the gold currency of the Arab world circulated alongside the silver and copper that was still widely used throughout the Mediterranean.

The economic boom of the twelfth century led Venice to construct trading posts along the Mediterranean coasts and on the islands where merchants, government officials, and soldiers settled. These outposts extended to the Black Sea basin, where Italian and Greek merchants conducted business with their Armenian, Jewish, Turkish, Caucasian, Arab, and "Frankish" counterparts. Marco Polo's family, too, established a base in the Crimea. From there, father, uncle, and son embarked on their ultimately twenty-four-year journey in 1271. They first sought to acquire gems in Central Asia and subsequently were compelled to travel farther eastward.

Venice competed with Genoa for economic hegemony over the Black Sea, which (like the Mediterranean) functioned as an economic unit, providing vital connections for long-distance travel. Access to the Dardanelles became a main source of conflict.[147] Already in the early Middle Ages, enterprising Vikings from Novgorod and Kiev had brought wax, amber, and the pelts of martens, sables, and ermines to trade at the Black Sea ports. Now, cotton products from Anatolia, woolen clothing from western Europe, pelts and hides from Poland and the Russian steppes, grain from the Balkans, Ukraine, and Crimea, and pepper and spices from Asia were traded in all directions through the port cities of Caffa, Maurocastro (Akkerman), and Licostomo.[148]

Since ancient times, however, the most important branch of the economy was the slave trade. In Caffa "they sell more slaves, both male and female, than anywhere else in the world," a Spanish traveler remarked at the beginning of the fifteenth century. Venetian traders picked up Russians, Tatars, and Circassians on the eastern coast of the Black Sea, transporting them through the Bosporus and Dardanelles into the Mediterranean, so they could be resold in Constantinople, Venice, Egypt, or the Levant.[149] The slave trade was one more reason that the sea powers of Venice and Genoa fought for centuries to control the straits.

In the thirteenth and fourteenth centuries, Venice managed to outmaneuver its Genoese rival and significantly expand its territorial holdings so that it came to preside over a far-reaching maritime colonial empire. After the Fourth Crusade and the conquest of Constantinople in 1204, the maritime republic took possession of parts of the imperial city and eastern Roman territory so that it controlled the straits as well as the old trade routes of the Byzantine Empire. At the height of its expansion, the Venetian *dominio da mar* encompassed Istria, Dalmatia, and the

Albanian-Montenegrin coastland all the way to the Peloponnese, and to Crete, Corfu, and the Ionian Islands. The Venetians underscored their imperial claims by building up ports and fortresses. The Greek ports of Modon and Coron were known as the "eyes and ears" of the republic because sailing vessels brought news from the entire known world when they landed here.[150]

In the late Middle Ages, Venice was the center of an expansive zone of economic activity that encompassed western Europe, the Mediterranean basin, Constantinople, and the Black Sea, with connections for long-distance travel to Asia and Africa.[151] The Venetians conducted a substantial portion of their European trade through the hub of Constantinople, which had linked Europe and Asia since the late ancient period. They brought spices and luxury goods from the Mediterranean and the Orient, and grain and slaves from the Black Sea region. Trade routes extended from Trebizond into Persia and Arabia; the Dnieper, Don, and Volga Rivers provided access to the Baltic and far northern lands. Venice also controlled trade routes to Flanders, and to Augsburg, Nuremberg, Prague, and Vienna.

The trade in Oriental luxury goods was immensely lucrative, and the import of grain, salt, animal hides, and wood was essential to Venetian prosperity. Convoys regularly transported people and goods from the imperial capital to Venice, and from there they were sold throughout Europe. Venetian traders opened up trade routes to the Azores, the Canary Islands, and to western Africa and India.[152] Besides commodities, practical knowledge came to the West from Asia, Egypt, and Byzantium—for example, regarding the production of silk and cotton fabrics, glass-blowing, rice cultivation, and the processing of sugar cane, which Venice introduced to its colonies on Crete and Cyprus.[153] Never before had there been such a far-flung and complex system of trade, connecting regions in Europe, northern Africa, and Asia.[154]

The rise of the Mongol Empire in the thirteenth century simplified trade relations with the Far East, which had existed since ancient times. The Polo family, too, profited from the newfound ease of transporting luxury goods along the Silk Road from China and India, to the ports of the Black Sea.[155] Marco reported stations no more than thirty miles apart on the main road, where travelers could refresh themselves and spend the night. Horses stood ready, "so that all of the Great Khan's messengers and all emissaries can stop as needed and exchange their horses." In addition, the Mongol

Empire maintained a dense network of postal runners for delivering letters and packages: "Because many small bells hang on their belts, their arrival can be heard at a great distance. The runner in the next village stands at the ready, so he can take the package and dash off with it."[156] After the collapse of the Mongol Empire at the end of the thirteenth century, the Central Asian land route to Beijing became more dangerous to travel. An Italian travel guide from this era recommended that merchants grow a long beard, hire a good interpreter, and bring along provisions for twenty-five days.[157]

As hubs of international commerce, Venice and the northern Italian cities became the nuclei of early merchant capitalism. The city of canals assumed responsibility for organizing, promoting, and protecting overseas trade—by having state-owned galleys patrol the waters to deter pirates and unwanted competitors, for example, or by providing merchants with cog vessels.[158] The Great Council was an assembly of patricians, members of the city's most influential and well-to-do families, who held a monopoly on political and economic power and acted according to the motto "honorem et proficuum" (for honor and profit).[159]

The nautical revolution, advances in shipbuilding, new sailing manuals and maps, and the invention of the compass made traveling easier and less risky. Even greater fortunes could now be made through overseas trade. The accumulation of commercial capital stimulated credit and insurance markets, partnerships and corporations, as well as new methods of business administration.[160] The Polos, for example, possessed a *fraterna compagnia,* a new form of family partnership in which the brothers shared liability and rights of inheritance. Marco, who resided in Venice after his three years of Genoese imprisonment, died a wealthy man.

The genesis of the world economy and the beginnings of "archaic globalization" belong to this era. Even before Europeans' discovery of the Americas rapidly accelerated the pace of globalization, mobile groups connected the known continents. Diplomats, commanders, traders, pilgrims, monks, and artists traversed great distances, driven by the idea of universal sovereignty, military expansionism, missionary zeal, desire for material gain, and the quest for medical remedies.[161] It was still a multipolar world, divided into five large transregional and continental subsystems: Europe, the Silk Road, and the Indian Ocean basin (which communicated with one another), and the sub-Saharan and Central American / Mexican regions (still isolated from the others).[162] An economically interconnected world system had not yet emerged, although porous interfaces between the economic subsystems of Europe, Asia, and Africa brought mobile humans into contact with one another and enabled the exchange of goods.[163] Jewish, Armenian, and other merchants established footholds in the Balkans and around the Black Sea, as well as in western Europe, northern Africa, Central Asia, and Indonesia.[164]

Southeastern Europe participated in the flows that connected the subsystems of the world economy along the Silk Road and throughout the Mediterranean and Black Seas. In this era, the Republic of Ragusa (Dubrovnik) achieved prosperity through overseas trade, excelling in its function as a hinge between Balkan and overseas trade routes. In the mid-fourteenth century, Ragusa freed itself from the control of Venice, which had served as its role model in many respects. Like La Serenissima itself, the Croatian merchant city had an aristocratic constitution that enabled a few wealthy patrician families to control all economic and government affairs. They elected their head of state, or Rector, for terms of only one month. The official government language was Latin, but most of the population and the nobility spoke a South Slavic dialect.[165] The Ragusans founded merchant colonies throughout the entire Mediterranean region, all the way to the Black Sea. Trading ships transported precious metals, ores, leather, salt, wax, wool, honey, wine, and Oriental spices across the Adriatic; caravan roads connected the port, which was protected by heavy city walls, with important markets and sites of production in southeastern Europe.[166] Slaves from Bosnia, the Levant, the Black Sea region, and Africa were also sold in Dubrovnik. In the mid-fifteenth century, around the same time as Venice, Ragusan merchants began to produce cloth in larger quantities for export to the Balkan lands, thereby building up another lucrative branch of the economy.[167] Similar to the northern Italian cities of this era, merchant capitalism flourished in Dubrovnik.

The Ragusans followed Venice, Genoa, Pisa, and Florence in adopting innovations like banking and insurance, noncash loans, bill transactions, and ad hoc corporations, which significantly increased the likelihood of turning a profit. Between 1280 and 1400, more than two million Venetian ducats were loaned in Dubrovnik; two-thirds of the creditors were local patricians, and one-fifth were outsiders. Many traders from Bosnia and Serbia borrowed money in Dubrovnik to invest in their businesses in other Balkan lands.[168] In 1440 the teacher Filip de Diversis poked fun at the city's predominant business ethic, oriented toward profit. The local nobles believed that "happiness consists in wealth and that virtue is in its acquisition and avid accumulation."[169] A merchant and economist from Dubrovnik, Beno Kotruljević (Benedetto Cotrugli), invented double-entry bookkeeping, an important instrument of early capitalism. He outlined the new method of accurately tracking debits and credits in his four-volume economic treatise, *Of Commerce and the Perfect Merchant.*[170] He also wrote *De navigatione liber,* one of the oldest sailing manuals for navigating the Mediterranean. Three decades before Columbus "discovered" America, he recommended sailing westward to reach India.[171] Thanks to its riches acquired through trade, Dubrovnik developed into an important center of science, culture, medicine, and law in the early Renaissance era. Distinguished scholars such as the economist Beno Kotruljević and the theologian John of Ragusa brought their knowledge, and entire libraries, to the city. In this era, specialized literature could already be acquired from book dealers on Dubrovnik's main street.[172]

Regional economic conditions varied considerably throughout southeastern Europe, but the different patterns of living and working complemented one another and encouraged specialization. On the coasts of Croatia, Albania, and Greece, farmland and precipitation were scarce, but conditions were favorable for fishing, cultivating wine and olives, and growing figs, pomegranates, almonds, lemons, oranges, and melons—products that had thrived in the Mediterranean region since ancient times. Thanks to the continental climate, agriculture was more successful on the plains of Pannonia, Moldavia, Wallachia, eastern Thrace, and Thessaly. People had settled here for centuries, transforming the river valleys into one great breadbasket. Peasants grew wheat, rye, millet, barley, and oats, along with hemp and flax, which not only provided for the local population but also yielded surpluses for trade. Raising livestock, beekeeping, and cultivating silk were other important economic activities with supraregional significance. Fertile land in the interior of the Balkan Peninsula and dense forests that stretched across Transylvania, Serbia, Bosnia, and northern Albania, all the way to the Adriatic, provided wood and food for livestock. In the nineteenth century, these landscapes appeared so romantic to the geographer Ami Boué that he compared them to the Ardennes, the Harz, and the Viennese woods.[173]

The southern part of the peninsula, by contrast, was dominated by mountains. Fertile farmland was scarce, and precipitation was rare. Residents of the dry, craggy highlands typically raised sheep and goats.

Traversing the rutted terrain of the Dinarides and Rhodopes, and the Pindus, Balkan, and Carpathian Mountains took considerable effort; communication was slow. "There are landscapes here, with their barren and weathered karst cliffs, that are as bleak as the moon," wrote the historian Konstantin Jireček.[174]

Over the centuries, the impassable terrain provided refuge from intruders, and from the hand of state authority. Archaic ways of life lingered on here with relatively little disruption. But even nomadic mountain herders did not live in isolation from the world. Already in the Middle Ages, trails were forged across the steep mountain ranges so that caravans could transport cargo between the coast and the interior. Pack horses could be rented from the chieftains of the mountain tribes. Wares were loaded onto wooden pack saddles in bales, sacks, or leather saddlebags. Armed with bows and arrows to protect against thieves, merchants made their way to the fairs and markets throughout southeastern Europe. In exchange for provisions, they traded cloth and silks from northern Italy and Flanders, cotton from Syria and the Mediterranean islands, and weapons, armor, glass, and leather goods from central Europe.[175]

Southeastern Europe was rich in ores and precious metals, some of which had already been exploited in the ancient period. For centuries, silver, gold, copper, and lead had been important commodities of trade. Salt mining played a significant role in Transylvania, and later in Moldavia, Wallachia, Bosnia, and Dalmatia.[176] To extract the desired raw materials, miners from Germany, Flanders, and Wallonia were brought to Hungary and Transylvania in the twelfth and thirteenth centuries. The Hungarian king granted these so-called Saxons extensive privileges and administrative autonomy. Before the European discovery of America, one-third of all gold and one-fourth of all silver produced in the world came from Hungary.[177]

Bosnia and Serbia were also rich in ores and precious metals—particularly Srebrenica and Novo Brdo, where privileged "Saxon" miners also settled.[178] Merchants from Dubrovnik took up residence here, seeking to invest their capital as profitably as possible. A significant portion of the city's wealth came from the trade in silver, which was first sold in Venice and then elsewhere in Europe. In the first half of the fifteenth century, an average of twelve tons of silver per year was mined in Serbia and Bosnia; forty-seven tons per year were mined in central Europe.[179]

With the emergence of trade corporations, lending institutions, and a supraregional market for agricultural products, prosperity radiated outward from the mining towns to the hinterlands. In the Middle Ages, the silver-mining town of Srebrenica minted its own coins, and its urban infrastructure (including a sewage system) was likewise advanced for its time. The work of miners, gold washers, metal workers, blacksmiths, pewterers, swordsmiths, and goldsmiths developed into specialized trades. Rising incomes elevated cultural life, as prosperous and well-read individuals brought their libraries of classical literature to Srebrenica.[180] Merchant capitalism enhanced the wealth of Mediterranean port cities along the Croatian, Montenegrin, and Albanian coasts, allowing culture to flourish. In Zadar in 1385, for example, the cloth dealer Mihovil Petrov not only kept gold, pearls, gems, and silver in his locked wooden chests; he also possessed a copy of Dante's *Divine Comedy,* pictures on his walls, and a decoratively painted house chapel.[181]

People of all social classes in the Middle Ages embarked on journeys for a variety of reasons. Next to the Danube, which centuries earlier had ensured the Romans' access to the Balkan passes, the great Via Militaris (leading from the fortress of Belgrade to Constantinople) remained the most important transportation route since ancient times. Setting out from Belgrade, a traveler could reach the transportation hub of Niš after several days' journey through the Morava valley. The road then wove through mountains, passing the Iron Gates of the Danube, before arriving in Serdica (Sofia), where a stone plaque still reminds visitors today that Emperor Trajan once "conquered mountains and river and constructed this road."[182] The road continued on to Philippopolis (Plovdiv), Adrianople (Edirne), and finally, Constantinople. A typical traveler needed thirty days to complete this journey; a courier might take half as long. Beginning in the nineteenth century, the Orient Express steamed along this route.[183] Another central east–west route with various branches followed the ancient Via Egnatia from Durrës, past Ohrid and Thessaloniki, across Thrace and ending in Constantinople. Numerous arteries crossed the Balkan Peninsula in a north–south direction, connecting the Danube with the Adriatic Sea.[184]

In addition to craftsmen and traders, who traveled for business, beggars and lepers were also on the move, hoping for alms. Monks, priests, and other believers covered great distances to reach churches, monasteries, and other sacred destinations. They made pilgrimages to Rome, Santiago de Compostela, and the holy sites of Jerusalem, Egypt, and the Sinai Peninsula. Diplomats who served the royal courts also traveled long distances. A representative of the Serbian king, for example, visited southern Italy in

1281 and the French court in Paris in 1308.[185] Scholars who disseminated knowledge across great distances can also be counted among the mobile groups of the medieval era.

Traveling on land and sea was strenuous and dangerous. Dark, dense forests and impassible mountains might harbor wild animals or evil spirits. Thieves and highwaymen were on the prowl, and every few miles tolls and duties had to be paid. Only the wealthy traveled by horse, or at least by donkey, since the roads were usually not suitable for journeys by carriage. Most travelers went on foot, carrying water and provisions in blazing heat or freezing snow, and otherwise relying on the hospitality of villages and rural settlements. Sea voyages were generally more comfortable, but no less risky, as there were storms and shipwrecks to be feared. In good weather, one could sail from Kotor to Dubrovnik in two days, and from Durrës to Venice in one week.[186]

With the exception of tolls, no political barriers restricted mobility. Around 1050, for example, one could travel all the way across the Byzantine Empire from Anatolia to Alexandria, with stops in Constantinople, Chios, and Rhodes, without any bureaucratic obstacles. One Levantine trader at this time moved back and forth between Palermo, Genoa, Marseille, Thessaloniki, and the Arab territories—writing a letter home at every stop. Pious individuals of different faiths used postal delivery. Jews and Muslims, for example, sent donations to academies in Jerusalem and Baghdad, and they queried religious scholars about matters of faith.[187]

A dark side of long-distance travel was the spread of previously unknown diseases. In 1347 the bubonic plague came to Europe for the first time, from Asia by way of Crimea, as a new era in world trade brought more and more people and goods into contact with one another across great distances. The Mongolian army, which laid siege to Caffa in 1346, may also have carried the plague westward. Ships with infected cargos sailed from continent to continent; caravans spread the infection throughout the Orient. Within ten months of the first outbreak, the plague wiped out three-quarters of the population of Crimea, and other colonies as well. Trading ships carried the plague to Constantinople, and from there to Alexandria, Sicily, and throughout the Mediterranean. Denser networks of travel and trade relations shortened the intervals between epidemics.[188] Starting in the fourteenth century, the plague periodically raged throughout southeastern Europe, decimating the population and devastating entire regions. Well into the nineteenth century, traders, soldiers, diplomats, and pilgrims carried the pathogens along the great connector roads that led from Istanbul to Edirne, Sofia, Belgrade, and then into Hungary and northern Europe—or by ship to Rhodes, Smyrna, Messina, Marseille, and other Mediterranean metropolises.[189]

In the late Middle Ages, only Dubrovnik was largely spared. There, as in Venice, the role of long-distance trade in spreading infection was recognized early. Street cleaning and sewage disposal were supposed to hinder the spread of infectious disease, although attempts at prevention were not always successful. After a devastating outbreak, city officials in the fourteenth century introduced a strict quarantine. To stop the spread of infection, in 1590 they built a modern lazaretto outside the gates of the city, where travelers, pilgrims, and traders from the Ottoman Empire had to wait with their goods for forty days. The Turkish traveler Evliya Çelebi, who visited Dubrovnik in 1664, was impressed by the beautiful stone walls, the spacious accommodations and storerooms, regretting only that one could not leave the facility at will, as it was guarded by soldiers.[190] Other Adriatic cities, such as Zadar and Split, also established lazarettos around this time.[191]

Epochal changes confronted the lands of southeastern Europe in the mid-fifteenth century: the intellectual developments of humanism and the Renaissance, merchant capitalism and the beginnings of an archaic world economy, and not least, the rise and expansion of the Ottoman Empire, which fundamentally challenged Europe's political, social, and religious self-image. The Balkan lands were part of this Western Christian world. Ancient Balkan, central European, Mediterranean, and Asian cultural influences all flowed together here, creating a unique microcosm of life worlds and cultures that combined and interacted in a variety of ways. The competition of Rome and Byzantium for political and spiritual hegemony, along with their efforts to compel the people of the Balkans to adopt their respective cultural, religious, and civilizational norms, resulted in richly diverse symbioses with many regional variations. Even so, the people remained open to future encounters with distant worlds and to experiences unknown. They also participated in far-reaching processes of change. Clerics and scholars shared and enriched the world's recognized forms of knowledge, its conceptions of truth, and descriptions of reality. Regional princes asserted and oriented themselves toward forms of legitimation, sovereignty, and representation that prevailed throughout Europe. Artists adopted diverse aesthetic standards and developed them further. Traders, craftsmen, and pilgrims accommodated the thought patterns and ways of life of the different milieus that they encountered. Not least, people in the region came into contact with distant places and cultures by participating in the flows of the medieval world economies. Merchants, cities, and entire regions profited from the growing division of labor and the exchange of goods, people, and knowledge. Although many people were not aware of these relationships, few were unaffected by them.

Krujë, 1450

In 1450, the Albanian uprising was entering its seventh year. The strategically important fortress city of Krujë was surrounded by Ottoman troops, and the sultan had already conquered Epirus and central Albania. The civilian population had been evacuated and soldiers of the rebel leader George Castriot Skanderbeg were holding their position in the castle overlooking the city. Skanderbeg himself was hiding with more of his troops elsewhere in the mountains. Atop the awe-inspiring castle, more than sixteen hundred feet above sea level, one could survey the plains of Albania all the way to the sea, spot faraway enemies, and warn lowland peasants of their approach with a signal of fire. Viewed from above, the "myriad white tents" that the Ottomans pitched on the plains "appeared to hover above the ground like a bank of fog."[192]

In March 1444, Albanian nobles had established the League of Lezhë, an alliance against the Turks, in Venetian Alessio. Under Skanderbeg's leadership, they proceeded to occupy strategically important strongholds in the area. In the spring of 1450, Sultan Murad II and his crown prince Mehmed, accompanied by tens of thousands of soldiers, personally took to the battlefield to crush the pocket of resistance around Krujë. Their military advance was terrifying enough that numerous princes who were once allied with Skanderbeg abandoned him for the enemy. The irregular soldiers known as *akinji* first raided, plundered, and abused the population, creating confusion and panic. Once they had prepared the way, a long procession of horsemen, archers, artillery, foot soldiers, and auxiliary troops rolled through the Albanian lowlands. The auxiliaries were lightly armed Christians, as described in one chronicle of the fighting: "In open battle . . . they were sent out as cannon fodder for the enemy, to distract attention and exhaust his energies."[193] A seemingly endless train of supply, medical, and maintenance units accompanied the army, along with religious scholars.

Pack camels and oxcarts transported provisions, tents, drums, battering rams, weapons, shields, and armor, as well as bronze and iron, so that artillery could be cast on site.

The attackers used gigantic cannons to fire balls as heavy as six centners at the fortress walls. The Albanian historian Marin Barleti described how they stormed the castle and used giant ladders to scale its walls, as "the noyse and clattering of their armour, did resound on all sides, the sound of the drummes and trumpets continually redoubling in the ayre." The surrounded soldiers hurled arrows, stones, and hot pitch at their attackers through the merlons that punctuated the castle's battlement. Thousands lay dead or wounded on the battlefield. Ottoman miners later dug underground tunnels beneath the castle walls to drain away its moat. The besiegers and the besieged fired animal cadavers at one another, seeking to spread disease throughout enemy lines during the heat of the summer.[194]

Skanderbeg did not have an organized army, countering his opponents instead with nimble horsemanship and wild resolve. According to a contemporary observer, Skanderbeg's men were "good for looting and plundering, but useless for warfare according to the Italian style, and helpless against our swords and our spears."[195] They could do little more than ambush the Ottoman camp and replenish urgently needed supplies. No prisoners were taken, but instead enemy soldiers were gruesomely slaughtered. Soon the Ottoman army ran out of provisions. After a final great assault on the fortress failed in the fall of 1450, Sultan Murad grudgingly gave the order to retreat at the end of October. News of Krujë's miraculous rescue and Skanderbeg, its victorious hero, rapidly spread throughout Europe.

Skanderbeg's story is that of a feudal order in decline on the Balkan Peninsula, as well as the rise of a new world empire. George Castriot was the son of an Albanian noble from the region around Krujë. As the Ottomans advanced, his father became a vassal of the sultan. He was allowed to keep a remainder of his lands, but he had to give up his sons as hostages. His talented youngest son, George, trained as a page at the sultan's court in Adrianople, which had become the Ottoman Empire's new capital in 1365. He converted to Islam and later rose to become a general in the cavalry. He received the honorary title Skanderbeg ("Lord Alexander"), recalling

Alexander the Great, because of his skill with weapons. The Ottomans, too, saw themselves as heirs of Alexander.[196] When Skanderbeg was only eighteen, the sultan appointed him as *sancak bey,* or district commander. The sultan later sent him back to the fortress of Krujë as governor, but did not restore his father's title and lands. Embittered and humiliated, Skanderbeg forged secret contacts with Venice and Naples, and with the Hungarian military leader John Hunyadi, who led a crusade against the Ottomans in the fall of 1443. Skanderbeg used a Turkish defeat as a pretense to leave the sultan's army. He occupied the Krujë fortress with his troops and declared independence on November 28, 1443, demonstratively converting back to Christianity.

Skanderbeg assumed the command of the anti-Ottoman league. He established his reputation as a military leader when he and ten thousand men, although vastly outnumbered, defeated the Ottomans at Torviolli on June 29, 1444. Seven thousand Turkish soldiers lost their lives in this great battle, and five hundred were taken prisoner. The league lost only half as many men.[197] The crusaders suffered a heavy defeat in Bulgaria and retreated to Hungary in November 1444; Skanderbeg conquered back the principality of his father. After another failed advance in Kosovo in 1448, the crusaders conceded defeat. Skanderbeg, however, defended his independent territory for a quarter century, longer than any other leader in the Balkans.[198]

Albanians today still celebrate Skanderbeg as a popular hero. Within his lifetime, he earned Western renown as a Christian prince who had courageously resisted the advance of Islam, inspiring the pope to laud him as Athleta Christi. Numerous myths, legends, and historical controversies still surround his biography, including whether or not he was driven only by revenge.[199] George Castriot Skanderbeg was, in any event, a charismatic leader—tall, attractive, and athletic. His biographers described him as a gifted fighter and captivating speaker, courageous on the battlefield and skilled in politics. In addition to the Albanian and South Slavic tongues of his homeland, he mastered the diplomatic languages of Italian and Greek, as well as Turkish and Arabic, which he had learned at the sultan's court. On the battlefield, he wore armor and a helmet with the head of a horned goat. In civilian life, the secularly oriented noble liked to wear an Italian beret, along with fine clothes and weaponry, although he was also seen in Rome "with a few horses and as a poor man," as one eyewitness reported.[200]

George Castriot Skanderbeg, attributed to
Antonio Maria Crespi, seventeenth century.
Veneranda Biblioteca Ambrosiana, Milan.

Skanderbeg irritated Sultan Murad with his successful campaign of resistance, until the sultan decided in 1450 to settle the score with the rebels.
The fortress of Krujë survived the months-long onslaught, but the land
around it was bled dry. Thousands died, and allies defected to the sultan.
The fortress and town lay in ruins; the land was devastated. The Catholic
world that celebrated Skanderbeg as the defender of Christianity offered
only halfhearted support. In the fall, Skanderbeg attempted to offer the
fortress to Venice. The following year, he sought protection as a vassal of
the King of Naples, to whom he formally gave the castle in the spring of
1451.[201]

At the beginning of the fifteenth century, "Albania" referred to the region
that is central Albania today, and to the coastlands from Kotor (Cattaro)
to Lepanto. The term had more than one meaning; it could describe the
area where Albanians settled, or the diocesan territory beyond Durrës

(Durazzo). At this time, there was no Albanian state and no clearly defin-able Albanian culture. The name of the "Albanos" is layered with ambiguities because it could refer to geographic origin, ethnic identity, the legal status of the land's residents, or to mountain-dwelling nomads who raised cattle.[202]

Greek, Roman, Byzantine, and then Venetian rule played a role in shaping the architecture, culture, and social makeup of the Albanian-Montenegrin coastland, as in many southeastern European regions. Latin, Greek, Italian, and Slavic influences intermingled. The origins and ethnic identities of the population were highly diverse. The most frequently spoken languages were Albanian, South Slavic, Vlach, and Greek. Venetian served as a lingua franca in the North, and Greek in the South.

Because Albania was exactly situated at the intersection between Roman and Byzantine spheres of influence, the land was Christianized twice, by the Western and then the Eastern Church. The Catholic faith eventually prevailed in the North, and the Greek Orthodox faith in the South. Both confessions coexisted in many areas. Durrës, for example, had a Latin and a Greek archdiocese.[203] The churches possessed considerable political and economic power before the arrival of the Ottomans. Clerics assumed important positions and offices in both urban and rural society, acting as diplomats and judges. Bishoprics and monasteries owned manors, fishing rights, and mills, which were sources of wealth. Because the Catholic Church supported Skanderbeg and his allies in their ongoing struggle against the Turks, its bishoprics, monasteries, and parishes became targets of Ottoman attacks. By the mid-fifteenth century, the dioceses of central Albania were destitute and empty.[204]

Albania was composed of three different, but closely interrelated cultural zones: the Mediterranean coast, the rural hinterlands, and the mountainous regions occupied by herders. Along the coast were highly developed cities including Durazzo (Durrës), Scutari (Shkodra), Antivari (Bar), Alessio (Lezhë), and Dulcigno (Ulcinj), with their administrative and judicial buildings, churches and chapels, business districts and markets. Nobles lived in *palazzi,* and burghers in stone or wooden houses with gardens. In Rome and Byzantium, cities had had different legal statuses. For this reason, Dubrovnik, Budua, and Cattaro had legally documented freedoms and their own organs of communal self-government, while Krujë and the southern Albanian cities had no such statutes and, therefore, no autonomy.[205] The former Byzantine cities and central locations that developed into commercial centers and mines after the thirteenth century were sometimes autonomous.

In the outlying areas, peasants cultivated fields, vineyards, and olive groves, which provided the city residents with food. A mixture of different agricultural and legal arrangements regulated the ownership of land. Most land belonged to territorial lords, private owners, churches, and communities; property could also be given as a grant *(pronoia)* in return for military service. Landlords lent or rented their fields to peasants so the peasants could work the land. Peasants were usually free, but they had to pay tributes and tithes and sometimes perform labor services. Villages, which were often ethnically mixed, assumed collective responsibility for taxes. A native chief presided over each community, in accordance with ancient law.

The plains, cities, and countryside were ruled by local noble houses, including those of the Thopia, Castriot, Balsha, Muzaki, and Dukagjin families. Their privileged status was acquired through noble birth. They possessed estates, resided in castles, maintained armed retinues, and oversaw chancelleries that engaged in written correspondence. They oriented themselves culturally toward Byzantium, Venice, or Serbia, adopting the corresponding titles of leadership. Some notables served as diplomats for one of the empires, or received monetary payments for their loyalty. Otherwise, their income came from tributes and tithes, tolls, and the trade in salt, wood, and grain. As the Ottomans drew closer, numerous princes (like Skanderbeg's father) became vassals of the sultan, seeking to hold on to a remainder of status, power, and property. They changed religion for political reasons, as new opportunities arose.[206]

The dominion of George Castriot Skanderbeg, who called himself "Lord of Albania," stretched across (and for a time, beyond) the mountainous landscapes of Krujë, Dibra, and Mati. His power flowed from supporters who were bound to him through personal dependence and loyalty, not through his control over a modern territorial state. Two thousand cavalrymen belonged to his troop, and other men who were fit for battle could be called on as necessary. He and his allies were said to have mobilized up to ten thousand soldiers at a time. His entourage also included clerks, merchants, and clerics. They corresponded with powers such as Venice, Dubrovnik, and Hungary, and they obtained money and weapons from the West in their function as emissaries and diplomats.[207]

Like other princes in the region, Skanderbeg saw himself within the tradition of Christian-Byzantine rulers. His coat of arms, the black two-headed eagle on a red background, recalled the church and state of eastern Rome. He ensured the loyalty of the most powerful families in the region through a series of strategically arranged marriages. His wife was from the influential Araniti family of southern Albania; his son's wife was from the Brankovići. His daughters married into the Crnojević, Araniti, Balsha, and Thopia families. For a time, Skanderbeg was one of the most powerful men in the region, but the nobles who were his allies never entirely submitted to his authority. They fought not for a unified Albanian state but against the sultan's infringement on their personal power. Depending on circumstances, a brotherhood of arms could turn into enmity, betrayal, or a family feud at any time.

Anyone who waged war in the Middle Ages needed a substantial income of money and natural resources to arm and compensate his troops. Loyal followers also expected a share of the booty and gifts. During his campaign against the Turks, Skanderbeg received considerable financial support from Dubrovnik, the Italian city-states, and the Catholic Church. The trade in grain, livestock, salt, and other goods yielded profits, as did tributes and tolls. Skanderbeg brought in additional income through his raids of Venetian and Ottoman territory. His men plundered, took prisoners, demanded ransoms, and requisitioned masses of cattle, usually in winter. In the spring, when the Ottomans returned for another season of battle, they retreated back into the mountains.[208]

The Adriatic coast and lowlands were open to the influences of the Mediterranean world, whereas the less accessible mountain regions of northern and central Albania were dominated by tribal societies organized according to seemingly archaic social rules. They functioned largely as self-sufficient communities. The economy there was pastoral, as in the high-altitude regions of eastern Herzegovina and Montenegro. People covered great distances with their sheep herds, moving back and forth between summer pastures in the mountains and winter pastures in the plains. Some produced just as much as was necessary for themselves; others sold cheese, wool, and sheepskins at markets and fairs. The mountain dwellers needed to purchase salt and grain when they could not produce enough for themselves. This kind of seasonal migration, or transhumance, existed through the entire Mediterranean region, from the Iberian Peninsula to Anatolia and northern Africa.[209] The herders probably began to occupy fixed territories in response to the Ottoman incursion. They joined together to form *katuns,* pastoral communities with their own leaders. The approximately thirty Albanian tribes were not all structured alike, although they were usually composed of clans, which in turn were composed of extended families. They traced their lineage back to a common ancestor, whose name they assumed—for example, the Hoti, Kuči, and Berisha, as well as the Pamalioti, Paštrovići, and Duraševići. The tribes were governed by a patriarchal code of honor and a set of common laws known as the *kanun,* which enabled blood feuds through the concept of *besa,* or "word of honor." It was believed that a murder victim's soul could find peace only through an act of atonement, and it thus became a holy duty to avenge every murder. Some tribes presented themselves as leagues of warriors, agreeing to serve the region's changing rulers or accepting their protection. Later, the Ottomans often employed the herders to watch over mountain passes, exempting them from taxes and other duties.[210] Turkish accounts from the fifteenth century describe the region's inhabitants as brutal and violent. The barren, craggy landscape could be unnerving as well: "No birds fly in these mountains. No animals run, no crows hop; the devil needs a stick to reach the summit. . . . Even the chickens need horseshoes."[211]

In the regions surrounding Albania, political conditions around 1450 were extremely messy. After the Fourth Crusade and the defeat of Constantinople in 1204, the once-mighty Byzantine Empire had sunk to the status of a regional power, divided into multiple successor kingdoms and despotates. In 1453 the Ottomans not only conquered the old capital city, but swallowed up all of the Byzantine Empire's remaining territorial possessions.[212]

The Republic of Venice was likewise ineffective in resisting the Ottomans militarily and signed treaties with them instead. Its "Albania Veneta" was an administrative area that encompassed the Montenegrin coastland and territories south and east of Lake Scutari. The Venetian governor resided in Cattaro (Kotor). Venetian Albania was one of the bases within the maritime empire that was supposed to secure trade routes to the Levant. It was at war with Skanderbeg for a time. Only after the Ottoman threat could no longer be avoided did La Serenissima rally its fleet, mercenaries, and local support troops to defend its colonial territories. Venice nevertheless forfeited all its Albanian possessions to the "infidels" in 1479.

From the Balkan lands, Skanderbeg could at best expect only occasional military assistance. The once-influential empires of Bosnia, Bulgaria, and

Serbia had fallen apart, and more than twenty different principalities were competing for land and power. A unified front of Western and local princes never coalesced, even if some of them did support the Albanian war hero for a time.

By the 1440s, Bosnia had split into two territories. The northern part oriented itself toward the Hungarian-Polish kingdom and became Catholic, and the Bogomil South pledged fealty to the sultan. In 1448 the regent took the title of *herceg* (duke) and was thus said to govern Herzegovina, or the "land of the *herceg*." Although linked together for a time through marriage, the rulers of Bosnia and Herzegovina remained hostile toward one another. Bosnia finally lost its independence to the Turks in 1463, and Herzegovina followed in 1485.[213]

Serbia did not entirely disappear from the political map after the battle on the Field of Blackbirds in 1389, but all that remained of the once-mighty Nemanjić state was a despotate led by Prince George Branković. He did lend Skanderbeg military and financial assistance, but the prince, too, lost his territory to the sultan in 1459.[214] Things went more favorably for the principality of Zeta (Duklja), located in the Albanian-Montenegrin borderland, which frequently shifted its allegiances. In the North, the Crnojević dynasty and the bishop of Cetinje maintained a degree of independence by becoming Ottoman vassals at the end of the fifteenth century. A theocratic system developed in the sixteenth century, wherein an Orthodox bishop was elected by tribal leaders. The arrangement can be seen as the nucleus of Montenegro.[215]

Farther north, the principalities of Moldavia and Wallachia, the predecessors of Romania, provided occasional assistance in the struggle against the Turks. Around 1350, these local powers developed into independent feudal states.[216] One century later, the Moldavian *voivode* Stephen the Great and his Wallachian counterpart Vlad II gained reputations as courageous fighters against the Turks. As a member of the Order of the Dragon, Vlad was commissioned with defending Christianity against the Hussites and the Ottomans. Thus, his sobriquet was "Drăcul," or "the Dragon."[217] Vlad II supported the Hungarian-led crusades alongside Skanderbeg before changing sides and becoming a vassal of the sultan, like so many others.

His son Vlad III, who claimed the Wallachian throne after his father's death, was known as "Drăculea," or "the Little Dragon." He, too, was a fickle ally. He withdrew his tribute and fealty to the Ottomans, but he kept his reputation as a brute. Seeking economic privileges for himself, he laid waste to the town of Brașov and brutalized the rebellious Romanian boyars. As a deterrent, he filled entire forests with the impaled bodies of his victims, which is how he received the sobriquet "Țepeș," or "the Impaler," after his death. Already during his lifetime, a pamphlet campaign that began in Hungary tagged him with the image of a savage despot. Adopting a scorched-earth strategy, he tried in vain to stop the advance of the Turks. He was imprisoned and executed. Because of his legendary cruelty, Vlad III provided the inspiration for Bram Stoker's world-famous vampire, Dracula, four hundred years later.[218]

The prosperous merchant republic Ragusa (Dubrovnik) was an important neighbor and benefactor to Skanderbeg. In December 1450 the famed war hero—whom the patricians affectionately called "frater et amice noster carissime"—visited the independent city in person. The pope cordially requested that the local patricians offer Skanderbeg their financial support.[219] Skanderbeg arranged for his other allies to send their gifts of coins and silver to Florentine and Ragusan banks in the city-state, where his agents accepted them on his behalf. Like other princes from Croatia, Bosnia, Serbia, and Montenegro, he was an honorary citizen of the republic, an honor that guaranteed political asylum should the military situation demand it.[220]

The Albanian Johannes Gazulus (Gjon Gazulli), one of the famous scholars who resided in Ragusa, was a trusted ally of Skanderbeg. The Dominican had earned his doctorate in Padua, and he was recognized throughout Europe for his achievements as a mathematician and astronomer. Now around fifty years old, he represented Dubrovnik on diplomatic missions to European courts. For Skanderbeg, he traveled abroad to ask for financial assistance in the fight against the Turks, receiving weapons and donations on behalf of the rebels.[221]

The Albanian Gazulus was a typical thinker of the early Renaissance. He belonged to the humanistically trained generation of astronomers, mathematicians, and natural philosophers whose investigations prepared the way for a new conception of the world, their influence extending throughout Europe.[222] The ancient theories of Aristotle and Ptolemy, which viewed the Earth as a godly creation at the center of the universe, were still broadly accepted. Contemporary thinkers used the terms *mundus* and *universum* to describe the cosmos, which they understood to be a gigantic but finite sphere filled with matter. Beneath the outermost celestial sphere, they believed, planets, elements, and solid bodies occupied additional spheres that nested within one another like the layers of an onion. In the late Middle Ages, scholars began to more precisely investigate the movements of the celestial bodies. Humanism and the Renaissance initiated a movement away from primarily religious explanations of the world, toward experimental ones.[223]

While studying in Italy, Gazulus collected important manuscripts from the fields of theology, law, and natural philosophy. He copied foundational literature in astronomy by hand and built upon its ideas. His *De directionibus,* which was frequently cited at the time, expanded on the work of Campanus of Novara. Novara's division of the zodiac into twelve houses provided a basis for Gazulus's own astronomical calculations of the movement, dimensions, and distances between the planets, and for the expansion of the universe. Gazulus also likely authored a text on the use and construction of the astrolabe, which was based on the writings of the astronomer Jean Fusoris. This astronomical device could determine direction, local time, and the position of the stars. Astrolabes were increasingly used aboard ships in this era, and they were also manufactured in Dubrovnik.[224]

Gazulus was an independent producer of contemporary European knowledge, not merely an interpreter of what was already known. He was invited to the court of Matthias Corvinus, a center of European humanism. Matthias's chancellor, Johannes Vitez, wrote to Gazulus that his book was "so eloquent and rich in knowledge; we found reading it to be as delightful as its contents were useful"; Gazulus should by all means continue his research and writing, for the benefit of science and personal renown.[225] At the end of his life, Johannes Gazulus bequeathed his valuable book collection to the church, on the condition that it would be made available to all "who wanted to see and read something in the aforementioned books." And so the first public library was established in the merchant republic of Dubrovnik, even earlier than in Venice.[226]

After the Turks conquered Constantinople in 1453, Skanderbeg's situation grew more precarious. He could no longer count on the Christian powers' support, and he became increasingly entangled in the feuds and rivalries of local princes. For decades, Albania had been in a near-constant state of war. In 1466 the sultan made one more attempt to break the Albanian resistance once and for all. His troops scorched the earth, and entire villages disappeared from the map. Peasants were abducted and forced into servitude, and anyone who could fled to the cities as soon as smoke signals from the Krujë castle warned of imminent danger. Fior Jonima from Scutari later recalled that "this landscape was brought to a state of almost complete devastation."[227]

Every advance made by the Ottomans touched off great waves of migration, as the sultan's troops searched for rebels valley by valley, terrorizing the population. Thousands crowded into the ports, attempting to save life and limb by escaping to Italy. Corrupt Venetian civil servants, like the chamberlain of Alessio, took money from the refugees before smuggling them to the port of Durrës. Shipowners and smugglers amassed fortunes as desperate travelers scrambled for the few available openings to cross over to Venice or Apulia. In 1467 Piero Zane described the scene after Mehmed II "destroyed and left everything in rubble and ashes in a span of three months." Only the privileged had an opportunity to escape. They "hurried to rid themselves of the animals they brought along; . . . they sold cattle for a sum of money that was worth less than the price of the hides alone."[228] Tens of thousands made their way to Italy, where today their descendants belong to the ethnic community of the Arbëreshë.[229] Broken by war and betrayed by his allies, Skanderbeg died from a fever in 1468. Krujë fell in 1478, and Albania became a possession of the Ottoman Empire for more than four centuries.[230]

2

Rise of the Ottoman Empire

IN THE SECOND HALF of the fifteenth century, the last principalities, city-states, and dominions that could have held their own between the fronts of the Ottoman, Venetian, and Habsburg Empires lost their independence. All southeastern Europe found itself within the great empires' spheres of control. The empires were vast multiethnic and multireligious political communities, composed of many different kinds of territories that were acquired through conquests and treaties. They were organized hierarchically. The ruling dynasties or noble classes governed from the center, holding together their conglomerated lands with a universalistic ideology and the threat of violence, and exploiting the periphery to the best of their ability. The tone was set by the elites of the dominant people—Austrians in the Habsburg Monarchy, and Turks and Muslims in the Ottoman Empire. Only in exceptional circumstances did "subalterns" from the provinces ascend the ranks of leadership. Although the symbolism of empire was intended to foster unity, a common imperial culture was, at best, a superstructure imposed upon otherwise completely heterogeneous lands. An integrated society, which later characterized the nation-state, did not yet exist.[1]

Empires that claimed to rule the entire known world, like the empire of Alexander or the Romans, had existed since ancient times. Only in the age of European exploration at the end of the fifteenth century, however, did it become possible to navigate the entire globe and link together previously unknown continents and cultures. The Ottomans extended their circle of

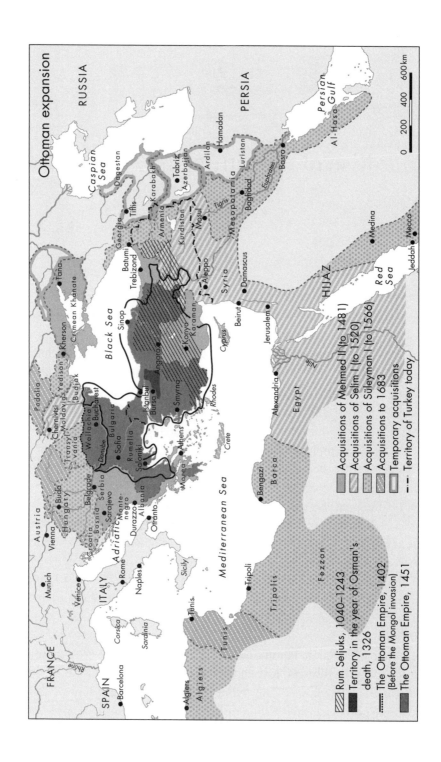

Ottoman expansion

Acquisitions of Mehmed II (to 1481)
Acquisitions of Selim I (to 1520)
Acquisitions of Süleyman I (to 1566)
Acquisitions to 1683
Temporary acquisitions
Territory of Turkey today

Rum Seljuks, 1040–1243
Territory in the year of Osman's death, 1326
The Ottoman Empire, 1402 (Before the Mongol invasion)
The Ottoman Empire, 1451

0   200   400   600 km

influence by subduing the Balkan peoples, destroying the Mamluk Empire, and pushing back the Safavid rulers of Iran. They established political ties to the Islamic world, and by claiming the caliphate at the beginning of the sixteenth century, the sultan asserted his hegemony over the entire *umma*, the community of all believers in the known world. Through military force, the Ottomans built an empire that stretched across three continents and brought together "the might of the whole East," to borrow the words of humanist Ogier Ghiselin de Busbecq.[2] The era was further distinguished by the rise of the Catholic Habsburg Empire, which rose to world power status after the European discovery of the Americas, and also by the two great empires' competition for universal dominion over the entire globe.

Although the world empires functioned as separate political entities with different civilizations, they were not closed units. The discovery of new continents and cultures brought worldviews closer together, and these new contacts allowed geographers, scholars, and explorers to recognize and reflect upon global relationships. Conflicts and wars, on the other hand, demonstrated how foreign civilizations could threaten cultural identity, as Christendom and Islam increasingly defined themselves as ideological opposites. Imperial rule and mass migrations encouraged new kinds of intermingling, appropriation, and cultural transformation. Economic expansion into distant continents became an increasingly influential means of exerting hegemony, alongside imperial ideology and military power. Rivalry over access to human and material resources became a driving force of worldwide exploration, and more broadly, historical change. Conceptions of imperial sovereignty informed not only the mobility of people, goods, and ideas but also the way that the world grew together. As trade relations expanded, networks of interdependence became more closely interwoven, and a transcontinental division of labor emerged.[3]

The Ottoman Empire's Rise to Power

No other event influenced the world of the Balkan peoples as decisively as the Ottoman conquest. Islamization, imperial rule, and waves of migration touched off groundbreaking sociocultural changes. The first steps in this process commenced around 1300, when "frontline soldiers in holy war" first emerged from the Ottomans' small emirate in northwest Anatolia. In 1302 Osman, the dynasty's founder, defeated a Byzantine army of mercenaries. In 1326, after further victories, he moved his capital to the former imperial city of Bursa. Osman's son Orhan continued the process of expansion on European soil. In 1354 he occupied the Byzantine fortress of Gallipoli along the Dardanelles, allowing the Turks to advance across the Balkan Peninsula nearly unchecked. In less than one century, the sultans extended their dominion across the majority of southeastern Europe. In 1361 Murad I captured the city of Adrianople (Edirne) in eastern Thrace, making it the capital of his empire. Turkish armies quickly overran Plovdiv, Niš, and Sofia. They fought the Serbs on Kosovo Polje, and they overtook Macedonia, Epirus, and Albania. They expanded eastward through Anatolia at the same time. By the time Turkish troops captured the imperial city of Constantinople in 1453, the West was in shock.

Sovereignty and Governance in Rumelia

In the historical memory of the Greeks and the entire Western world, the fall of Constantinople became a source of trauma like the Serbs' experience of the battle on Kosovo Polje. After a fifty-four-day siege by Ottoman forces on land and water, Sultan Mehmed II successfully overcame the metropolis on the Bosporus at the end of May 1453. The historian Oruç wrote that the soldiers breached the city's fortifications "with guns as big as dragons." They entered "by force on every side . . . and put the infidels in the fortress to the sword. . . . They looted and plundered . . . and made their sons and daughters slaves."[4] By the end, the proud city lay in ruins, gutted and burned to ashes as if a firestorm had swept through. The emperor had fallen, his armies had fled, and the churches were ransacked. Men, women, and children were chained together in long rows and brought to the slave market in Adrianople. The Western world gazed in horror at the loss of the former Byzantine imperial capital. After the Christian armies' miserable defeat near the Bulgarian city of Varna in 1444, any plans for new papal Crusades found little support. The idea of *Christianitas,* the unity and superiority of the Christian world, had been deeply wounded.[5]

Mehmed the Conqueror, as he was now called, moved the capital of his empire to Constantinople, which he renamed Istanbul. Located at the intersection between Asia and Europe, it was a strategically ideal site for the further expansion of Ottoman power. Mehmed soon sent out messengers to all of his lands, saying, "Whoever wishes, let him come, and let him become the owner of houses, vineyards, and gardens in Istanbul!" Families from across the entire empire were taken from their homes and resettled in the city. "They began to build mosques," one historian noted. "Some of them built dervish convents, some of them private houses, and the city returned to its previous state."[6] The Hagia Sophia, once a proud symbol of Christianity, was converted into a mosque. From their new imperial center on the Bosporus, the Ottomans continued their expansion unabated. They took Morea, the last part of the Greek lands, in 1458, followed by the remainder of Serbia (1459), Bosnia (1463), Albania (1479), and Herzegovina (1483). The principalities of Moldavia and Wallachia became vassal states (1504). Afterward, the sultan governed practically all of the Balkan Peninsula south of Belgrade and the Danube. The Ottomans called this territory Rumelia, or the "land of the Romans," which had once belonged to the Byzantines. In this same period, the Ottomans broke the supremacy of the Venetian fleet in the Mediterranean and conquered Anatolia. The Ottoman Empire ascended to great power status, with two nearly symmetrical halves in Europe and Asia.[7]

The Ottoman sultans sought universal sovereignty, and with it, an imperium that would continue the legacy of Rome and Byzantium. Strategic considerations aside, the conquest of Constantinople, the center of the (eastern) Roman Empire, held enormous symbolic meaning. The Ottomans saw it as their holy duty to bring Islam and Islamic governance to the lands of Europe—and so, too, civilization, justice, prosperity, and peace.[8] In their view, the world was divided into Muslim and non-Muslim spheres, the House of Islam *(Dar al-Islam)* and the House of War *(Dar al-Harb)*. The House of Islam comprised the entire Muslim community, or *umma,* which included all believers, regardless of place of residence, ruler, or family background. In addition to the empire of the sultans, this also included Sunni dominions like the Uzbek khanates and the Indian Mughal Empire. Non-Muslim state entities that paid tribute likewise belonged to this camp. The other half of the world belonged to the "infidels," who were either identified as "Rûm" (Romans), meaning Byzantine and Orthodox—or else as "Franks," meaning Latin and Catholic. Non-Muslims were considered inferior and generally described in a disparaging way. Historical sources spoke of them as "accursed," or "foreordained to hellfire."[9] According to this worldview, the Ottoman Empire theoretically existed in a permanent state of war with the non-Muslim world. It took centuries to develop an appreciation for coexistence, and a culture of orderly relations with the outside world. When necessary, the Ottoman government, the Sublime Porte, later entered

Southeastern Europe in 1475

POLAND   LITHUANIA   Kiev

Elbe   Oder   Dnieper

Prague

HOLY
ROMAN
EMPIRE

Krakow   Lviv

Bug

Vienna

Košice

Dniester

Graz

Esztergom   MOLDAVIA   Suceava   Bender

Buda   Oradea   Bistrița   Vaslui

Ljubljana   Pécs   Akkerman

KINGDOM OF HUNGARY   Cluj

Tisza

Fiume   Zagreb   Mohács   Mureș   Sibiu   Brașov   Chilia

Venice   Slavonia   Srem   Brăila

VENICE   Croatia   Sava   Belgrade   Târgoviște

Zara   Srebrenica   Wallachia   Dristra

Spalato   Vidin   Danube

PAPAL
STATES

Adriatic   Mostar   Niš   Nicopolis   Shumen   Varna

Ragusa   Peć   Tarnovo

Rome   Cattaro   Sofia   Burgas

Prizren   Skopje   Philippopolis

Durrës   Adrianople

Bari   Ohrid   OTTOMAN EMPIRE   Istanbul

Naples   Kastoria   Thessaloniki

Taranto   Vlora   Veria   Athos

KINGDOM OF NAPLES

Kerkyra   Ioannina   Larissa   Lesbos   Pergamon

Palermo   Messina   Arta   Aegean   Smyrna

Reggio   Negroponte   Chios (to Genoa)   Ephesos

Sicily   Patras   Corinth   Athens

Syracuse   Glarentza   Nauplia   KNIGHTS OF ST. JOHN

Mystras   Rhodes

Modon   Malta   Coron   Monemvasia   DUCHY OF THE ARCHIPELAGO

Canea   Candia

Rethymnon   Crete

Mediterranean Sea

Controlled by Venice
Approximate area of Skanderbeg's
rebellion (1443–68)

0   100   200   300 km

into peace agreements with the "infidels." The agreements were usually limited to a certain time period, however, and were readily violated.[10]

According to Ottoman theories of governance, an absolute sovereign, the Padishah, was the highest authority within the empire. His imperative was holy war.[11] Although older scholarship has asserted that the political drive for conquest was motivated by the Islamic faith, newer research has questioned this finding, emphasizing the purely imperial logic behind the desire to found an empire that was as large and as prosperous as possible. An empire constantly demanded new resources, including access to farms, mines, and forests, as well as additional income from taxes and customs. Controlling the Balkans' military roads, or gold and silver mines, carried great economic importance. Ottoman elites did, of course, use religious rhetoric to intimidate enemies, motivate their own army, and mobilize broader support for their campaigns. In the end, it is impossible to determine how pious they actually were.[12]

The Ottoman conquest was a centuries-long process. New subjects had the opportunity to recognize Islamic sovereignty, even if they did not want to convert. When the Ottomans conquered new territories, one of their first steps was to attract regional lords as their vassals. Those who accepted the offer had to recognize the supreme authority of the sultan, agree to pay tribute, participate in military campaigns, and even send their sons as hostages to the Ottoman court. To protect their own sovereignty, already in the thirteenth and fourteenth centuries numerous Bulgarian, Serbian, Albanian, and Greek lords swore fealty not only to the Byzantine emperor but also to the sultan, as Skanderbeg's father had done. The Ottomans also sought to establish family ties with Christian royal houses. In the early stages of Ottoman expansion, several sultans took the daughters of Christian rulers as wives. A Serbian and a Byzantine princess were among the several wives of Osman's son Orhan.[13]

At the beginning of their rule, the Ottomans demonstrated a certain goodwill toward the natives, as long as local elites supported the new authorities' military campaigns and taxation of the provinces. Loyal nobles, churches, and monasteries could keep property that they had acquired in the Byzantine era, and village traditions of self-governance were upheld.[14] Christian mercenaries participated as *martolos* or *voynuks* in Ottoman campaigns, local tribal leaders kept their authority in mountainous regions and monitored the passes, and on the Greek island of Lemnos there was even a troop of several hundred Christian soldiers who served as an Ottoman occupation force. Likewise, those who practiced trades initially experienced few disadvantages. In fifteenth-century Serres (a town in eastern Macedonia), for example, Christians continued to work as traders, furriers, goldsmiths, and producers of silk; Muslims took over just the production of textiles and leather goods.[15]

Only later, after the Ottomans had consolidated their rule over the acquired territories, were the old dynasties disempowered and their lands swallowed up by a tightly centralized administration.[16] According to Ottoman legal tradition, nearly all land belonged to the sultan, who granted plots called timars to local landlords in return for military service. As in other Middle Eastern states, land remained the property of the sultan and could not be passed down to future generations. The timariots were, however, entitled to income from their plot's farmland and forests, as well as certain taxes. In return, they had to serve as *sipahis,* or cavalrymen, in the sultan's campaigns and bring along additional armed troops according to the size of their land. Judges, clerics, and even Christians could also receive benefices in exceptional cases. In Albania and Thessaly, for example, many local nobles were able to transform their property into timars. Peasants who resided on these estates received a hereditary lease on a small parcel of farmland *(çiftlik),* which they could work with a team of oxen. They were obligated to pay taxes and rents and to perform services in return for the use of the land. Although they were legally free, they remained bound to the land in practice. A timariot had no personal or legal authority over the peasants on his land. The hand of the sultan protected them, discouraging the emergence of a landowning hereditary nobility. Until the sixteenth century, the Ottoman sultan was much more powerful than the monarch of a European feudal state; his absolute personal sovereignty had no counterweight. In contrast to the West, no power struggles took place between the crown and the aristocracy.[17]

The Ottomans' understanding of their empire began to change around 1500—from European power to world power. In the fourteenth century, they had settled on the Balkan Peninsula and established their capital there, signaling their ambitions as a European empire and seeking to dominate as much of the continent and its economy as possible. In the sixteenth century, a new phase began. Sultan Selim I conquered the Shia Safavids in Iran (1514), and the Mamluks in Syria (1516) and Egypt (1517), including the holy cities of Mecca, Medina, and Jerusalem. With Constantinople, he inherited the Roman Empire's claim to universal dominion, and in 1517 he took the title of Muslim caliph, ruler over all believers in the world. The Ottoman Empire now covered the core territories of Sunni Islam—from Andalusia and Morocco in the west, to India and Indonesia in the east—and so the tectonics of the empire shifted. An immense Arab territory joined the core regions of Anatolia and Rumelia, so that Muslims, not Balkan Christians, now made up the majority of the empire's population. Differentiation between Muslims and non-Muslims became a determining social principle, and the push for Islamization increased. Expansion into the Arab world brought powerful economic advantages, since Egypt was a crossroads not only for the Ottomans' trade in gold with Ethiopia and Sudan but also for the spice trade between Europe and the Far East. The imperial center of Istanbul profited from the vast farmlands for cultivating wheat, rice, and beans.[18] Finally, the empire's strategic position improved. Sultan Süleyman I successfully drove the Knights of Saint John from the island of Rhodes, consolidating Ottoman control over the entire eastern Mediterranean. The long-standing conflict between the region's Muslim and Christian powers in the Mediterranean region, simmering since the Middle Ages, intensified from this point forward.

The House of Habsburg, united through numerous marriages, emerged as the Ottoman Empire's greatest rival in southeastern Europe, the Mediterranean, and northern Africa at the end of the fifteenth century. Habsburg armies overtook the Islamic emirate of Granada in 1492, completing the Christian Reconquista of the Iberian Peninsula. The Catholic Habsburgs first expelled the Jews from Spain and Portugal, and then the Muslim Moors. Under the leadership of Charles V, who styled himself as a new Alexander the Great, the Habsburgs sought to assert their great power status within the sixteenth-century world by recalling the Roman Empire's glory and geographic reach. Charles became King of Spain in 1516, and he was chosen as Holy Roman Emperor in 1519. One year later, his rival Süleyman I assumed the throne of the Ottoman sultan. In fact, Charles did not rule the world. Instead, he presided over a diverse conglomeration of kingdoms, duchies, and principalities—including the kingdoms of Aragon, Castile, Naples, Sicily, and Sardinia, the Spanish colonies in America and Africa, and the Austrian hereditary lands. His imperial authority was far weaker than the sultan's. The papacy, nobility, and towns formed a significant counterbalance to the emperor, and competed for privileges. Catholicism served as the Holy Roman Empire's unifying ideology, a defense not only against Islam but also (after Martin Luther) against the Protestant Reformation. In contrast to the sultan, the Christian emperor was perpetually engaged in complex dynastic negotiations with various noble houses.[19]

Sultan Süleyman I, called "the Magnificent," rejected the Habsburgs' claim to world power, believing that it was rightfully his. He instituted fundamental economic, social, and religious reforms that strengthened his reign. Then he sent his armies westward, with the goal of depriving the "Spanish king Carlo" (as he taunted Charles V) from the title of "last emperor" by uniting the world under his imperial rule and a single religion.[20] During the conquest of Constantinople, the metaphor of the golden apple had stood for the idea of a universal empire and also acted as a justification for war. Since then, an emblem of the pursuit for fortune and power had come to represent the claim for world dominion. The Ottoman golden apple and the western European imperial orb may well have shared the same origin. Turkish prophecies foretold the acquisition of the golden apple as a final act before the Day of Judgment. In concrete terms, this now meant the conquest of Vienna. According to the Ottoman worldview, the subjection of Habsburg-led Hungary and Austria was an essential step along the path toward universal dominion.[21]

Since the early fifteenth century, the Republic of Venice had been entangled in a series of wars against the Ottoman Empire, resulting in its loss of hegemony in the eastern Mediterranean. For the Habsburgs, the era of Ottoman wars began in the sixteenth century. With a revolving set of allies, they fought seven larger wars against the Ottomans through the end of the eighteenth century. Süleyman I conquered Belgrade in 1521 and Rhodes in 1522, before defeating the Hungarian armies at Mohács in 1526. King Louis II of Hungary and Bohemia lost his life while fleeing. The Archduke of Austria and future Emperor Ferdinand I assumed the throne of Bohemia, Croatia, and Hungary, allowing the empire of the Habsburgs to extend into central and southeastern Europe.

As the battle for Hungary continued, the Ottoman army unsuccessfully laid siege to Vienna in 1529, and then again in 1532. Although the sultan's attempts to capture the capital city failed, he succeeded in making central Hungary and Budapest an Ottoman province, and Transylvania a vassal state. Only the northwestern territory of "Royal Hungary" remained under Habsburg control, with Pressburg (Bratislava) as its capital.[22] Süleyman I embarked on a further campaign against the Habsburgs in 1566, but the advance came to a halt. During the siege of the southern Hungarian fortress of Szigetvár, the aged sultan died in his camp. However, large parts of Hungary, Croatia, and Slavonia had already fallen to the Ottoman Empire. In 1568 the Peace of Adrianople sealed Hungary's division into three parts. A fortified border between the two great empires ran through Croatia. It was guarded by mercenaries and peasants and financed by "Turk taxes," which were levied by the emperor to support the fight against the Turks.

The sixteenth century witnessed the political dismantling of not only Hungarian but also Croatian areas of settlement—a source of considerable bitterness for Croatian poets and scholars of the time. Having lost all but its core territories around Zagreb, Karlovac, and Varaždin, Croatia henceforth belonged to the Habsburg Empire. Because Hungary and Croatia had shared a common ruler since the Middle Ages, the defeat at Mohács meant that the Croatian nobles had to recognize Ferdinand I as King of Croatia. Slavonia, Bosnia, and Herzegovina also fell to the Ottoman Empire, whereas Istria and Dalmatia remained under Venetian control. In the following centuries, the Croats lived under extremely varied conditions. No other people in southeastern Europe has been divided between so many different political, administrative, and economic regimes.

The Ottoman advance touched off massive waves of migration that dramatically altered patterns of settlement. Between the fourteenth and sixteenth centuries, hundreds of thousands of Christians on the Balkan Peninsula fled to Austrian, Hungarian, and Venetian territories. Slavic Catholics emigrated to the Austrian Burgenland, which still has a Croatian minority today. Orthodox Slavs and Vlachs fled from the Ottomans into Dalmatia, Bosnia, and Herzegovina, or farther northward across the Danube. They were strategically resettled in the area of the military frontier. Many people retreated to the mountains of Albania, Greece, and Montenegro, where, as migratory shepherds, they remained largely untouched by Ottoman rule.[23] Greeks from the Peloponnese, Cyprus, and Crete moved to new homes in Venetian territory, southern Italy, central Europe, southern Russia, and Ukraine. Venice, Vienna, and Odessa became new hubs in the network of the Greek diaspora that spread across Europe in this era.[24]

Religion and imperial ideology encouraged the expansion of the Ottoman Empire, but its rapid military successes could be attributed to the power of its army. Whereas the Habsburg Empire depended on the

Mehmed II at the Siege of Belgrade, 1456. Topkapi Palace Museum, Istanbul.

goodwill and support of individual monarchs, princes, and their merce-
nary armies in the time of war, the Ottoman Empire possessed a permanent and tightly organized military force. It was composed of the Porte's
standing army, which stood under the personal command of the sultan,
as well as provincial troops that could be mobilized in time of war. The
elite corps of janissaries, who also served as the sultan's personal guards,
were an important pillar of the central army. Provincial troops were com-
manded by regional governors in Anatolia and Rumelia. In peacetime
they were responsible for guarding the empire's borders and fortress garrisons. The *sipahis,* recipients of the sultan's beneficence who were obligated
to perform military service, fought in the provincial troops as heavy cavalrymen. Additional contingents came from lands that owed tribute, especially those of the Crimean Tatars and Danubian Principalities. Thousands
of Christians served as auxiliaries to the Ottoman troops—as guards of
mountain passes and bridges, garrison suppliers, armorers, miners, and
transport workers. The guerrilla tactics of the *akinji* light cavalry were especially notorious. They raced ahead of the army, attacking, plundering,
and setting fire to their surroundings as a means of spreading panic in
advance of a battle.[25]

The Ottoman army owed its remarkable success to excellent training,
rigid discipline, and superior morale. Experienced commanders perfected
their strategy and tactics in open battle, frontal and flank attacks, en-
circlements, and sieges. They used all available weapons—bows and arrows, spears, scimitars, sabers, maces, muskets, pistols and firearms, mortars,
cannons, and explosives. Their colorful equipment and uniforms seemed
impressively exotic, and the battle cry "Allahu akbar" (God is great) sent
Western armies into a state of panic and fear. Until the late seventeenth
century, the Ottoman army seemed to be almost invincible. In the 1540s
the historian Francisco López de Gómara described the two rivals, Emperor Charles V and Sultan Süleyman I, in this way: "Each worked to become the king and lord of the world. . . . Both of them had about the
same age but different fortunes; both gave themselves over equally to war,
but the Turks succeeded better at fulfilling their projects than did the
Spanish; they devoted themselves more fully to the order and discipline of
war, they were better advised, they used their money more effectively."[26]

Since the invention of the printing press in the mid-fifteenth century,
"Turkish prints" by Western scholars and court and military officials had
spread news about the Ottomans' advances. These texts reported on the

Ottomans' barbarism on the battlefield and warned readers to fight back against the "Turkish peril." Pamphlets, humorous poems, and songs created the topos of a barbaric and brutal Islam, which the West had to combat in holy war. They also encouraged discussion about conditions and abuses within the Western Church.[27] The age of the Reformation and the Wars of Religion was a time of great upheaval. On one hand, political thinkers of the Renaissance admired the sultan's strong central authority; on the other, they characterized it as "despotic" and "tyrannical." Perceptions softened only as trade relations continued to expand during the era of absolutism, allowing the still-expanding Ottoman Empire to be seen as a political partner in concert with the European powers.[28]

By 1600, the Ottomans dominated not only the Balkans, but the entire area between Morocco and Iran, including the Mediterranean and Red Seas. How were the sultans able to hold together such a vast and heterogeneous empire? In addition to the threat of military force, the Ottomans relied not only on their own governors to administer their provinces but also on local elites. Depending on their particular situation, local elites who accepted the legitimacy of the sultan's rule were able to negotiate various arrangements with the capital. The sultan tolerated very different leaders, legal arrangements, and living conditions throughout the parts of his empire, creating a dominion that was hierarchically ordered, according to pragmatic considerations.[29]

Within the Ottoman Empire, one can distinguish between four different kinds of status areas as ideal types. All were centrally oriented toward the capital, with practically no institutional relations between them. First, there was a core region that included western Asia Minor and large parts of southeastern Europe, where the Ottoman system of taxation and administration was fully in place. Conditions were similar in well-connected regions of the Arab world, such as Egypt, Damascus, and Aleppo. A second group comprised vassal states surrounding the imperial core, such as Dubrovnik, Moldavia, Wallachia, and the Crimean khanate. They recognized Ottoman suzerainty and paid tributes, but continued to maintain their own local structures of leadership. Third, there were the outer peripheries, including the coasts of northern Africa and the desert regions of the Arabian Peninsula, which were bound to the Ottoman dominions in a looser tributary relationship. A fourth type consisted of remote, agriculturally unproductive

mountain regions, which Ottoman state authority had difficulty penetrating. Tribes in Mount Lebanon, Montenegro, Albania, and parts of
Kurdistan were obligated to pay an annual tribute, but otherwise left mostly
to themselves.[30]

The Balkans, or Rumelia, thus belonged to the core territory of the Ottoman Empire. At first the region was treated as one large province. This
was later divided into several administrative areas, which were overseen by
the sultan's deputies and exploited with the help of tax registers. The largest
divisions were called *eyalets* (later *vilayets*), which in turn, were composed
of *sancaks* and other smaller units. Magistrates called kadis played an important role in the provincial administration, administering religious law
(sharia), customary law *(örf)*, and government decrees *(kanun)*. They were
chiefly responsible for Muslims because Christians and Jews had their own
judicial authorities for civil affairs.[31]

Incorporating the Balkan Peninsula within the administrative structures
of the empire was so important because the region formed a strategic,
cultural, and economic bridge between Europe and Asia. Its roads and
rivers, cities and castles extended Ottoman influence beyond the empire's borders.[32] It also provided an important reservoir of human capital,
foodstuffs, raw materials, and tax income. In 1527, for example, 37 percent
of all Ottoman imperial revenues came from this region. Of these revenues, 42.3 percent came from the head tax on non-Muslims, and the rest
from tolls and other duties on trade, agriculture, and industry. About half
of this income flowed to the central treasury. A small percentage was given
to pious foundations, and the rest went to the timariots.[33]

At first the duties were not too burdensome, but in the sixteenth century
they gradually increased. The Danubian Principalities likewise suffered
from a growing burden of imperial tributes, although these did buy certain freedoms. Between 1503 and 1593, the tributes paid in Wallachia grew
from 8,000 to 155,000 ducats, and in Moldavia, from 10,000 to 65,000
ducats. In addition, there were expensive gifts for the sultan and his entourage, costing tens of thousands of ducats each year, along with levies
on products like honey and wheat. In addition, the principalities had to
cover the costs of military installations.[34] The vassal states of Transylvania
and Dubrovnik also paid tribute, although they enjoyed greater political
independence and a lighter burden of payments.

Beginning in the sixteenth century, a strict differentiation between Muslims and non-Muslims informed all levels of the state, administration,

and society. As Peoples of the Book, Jews and Christians enjoyed a special protective status as *dhimmi;* they could practice their own religion, maintain their own houses of worship, and manage certain affairs independently, as long as they accepted the primacy of Islam. In all important functions, however, Muslims took precedence. Non-Muslims could only occupy certain niches, like the Jewish palace doctors of the sultan, or his Greek Orthodox interpreters, the dragomans.[35]

The Ottoman social order further distinguished between taxpaying subjects *(reaya)* and the sultan's officeholders *(askeri)*. Regardless of religion, the *reaya* had no political influence. They were organized according to profession, with clearly delineated rights and obligations. Alongside the guilds, religious communities and local institutions served as important pillars of the imperial administration and its tax-collecting procedures. Members of the privileged class of court officials, military officers, and clerics were called *askeri;* they were exempt from paying taxes. Although the sultans exercised absolute power within the empire, and continued to direct government affairs personally until the mid-sixteenth century, the *askeri* were later able to attain significant influence as the sultans' advisers. In contrast to the nobles of Western nations, however, these "professional Ottomans" possessed no formal rights. They attained their position through individual achievement, not through birthright or their status as landlords. The sultan could appoint, dismiss, or even execute them at will.[36]

Non-Muslims, too, could rise up to become members of this class, which performed all important political and administrative functions within the empire. Most came from influential Muslim families, but some dignitaries, military officials, and the elite troops and personal guard of the sultan were recruited through the *devshirme,* the so-called child levy. Since the fifteenth century, sons of Christian peasants had been forcibly taken from their homes in Anatolia, the Balkan Peninsula, and along the Black Sea coast every one to five years. Most were boys between the ages of eight and fourteen years, but older teenagers were drafted as well. After converting to Islam, they received thorough educations as soldiers or pages. The janissary Konstantin Mihailović reported in the fifteenth century that "whenever the Turks invade foreign lands and capture their people an imperial scribe follows immediately behind them, and whatever boys there are, he takes them all into the Janissaries."[37] Thus, the sultans could rely on a loyal class of servants within the palace who attained their position through individual achievement, not through noble lineage or inherited rights. For parents, however, the abduction of their Christian sons was a fate worse than death, as a Greek source from the sixteenth century recounted. It would have been better "if they had died, and we had buried them in our church . . . they separate us in life, taking you away and turning you into Turks."[38]

Particularly talented young men, like Skanderbeg, were sent to serve at the sultan's court. In practice, they were state and military slaves *(kul)* and not allowed to marry during their active service. Once they were freed, however, they could serve in the most prestigious state offices as court officials, provincial administrators, and clerics. Some even rose to the position of grand vizier, head of the government and deputy to the sultan. Between the fifteenth and seventeenth centuries, when the child levy was discontinued, twenty-five of ninety-two grand viziers alone came from Albania.[39] Native-born Turks frowned on this form of elite recruitment. In the sixteenth century, the poet Veysi complained how strange it was "that those who enjoy rank and power are all Albanians and Bosnians, while the people of the Prophet of God suffer abasement."[40]

In addition to the male servants and military slaves acquired through the child levy, there were women in the Ottoman Empire who lived as house slaves in the harem of the sultan, or in the harems of other dignitaries. All female members of the household, as well as children, were part of the harem—including up to four wives, and any number of concubines and house servants. Female slaves could attain a certain social status, be set free, or become an official wife. Their sons who were fathered by the sultan were potential successors to the throne. To avoid disputes over inheritance, half brothers of the chosen heir were murdered, a harsh custom that was not renounced until much later.

Unfree people not only served the sultan but also worked in upper-class households and estates. In contrast to American and other overseas colonies, unfree laborers in the Ottoman Empire did not work primarily on farms or plantations, but rather as house and personal servants. Slavery was thus an essentially urban phenomenon.[41] Children who came from a relationship with a female slave were considered freeborn. Because there was not a hereditary class of slaves that reproduced itself, the empire had to obtain slaves from outside its borders. Islamic law forbade enslaving the dependents of protected subjects who were resident within the empire, so the Ottoman army took prisoners from enemy territory on its campaigns of plunder and conquest. In 1666 an Ottoman traveler observed how residents of Kanije (Kanizsa), a fortress city on the Hungarian-Ottoman border, cheered an incoming parade of soldiers with their prisoners. They were brought to market the next day. Male and female slaves—along with their clothing, weapons, and other plundered items—were sold off in an auction that lasted for five days. One-fifth of the proceeds and the prisoners went to the sultan; the remainder was divided up in the mosque among the plunderers and their helpers. Seventy-five thousand women and children were taken during the siege of Vienna in 1683; another fifty thousand were taken at Klausenburg in 1788. The slave trade thus flourished in the border provinces.[42]

The Ottoman Empire drew its strength from different sources. It successfully incorporated regional structures and cultures within the sultan's dominion, giving rise to an enormous imperial space that was governed from Istanbul. The Ottomans controlled lands and seas, cities and ports through sophisticated networks that extended beyond their empire's borders. Useful groups—such as Jewish, Armenian, and Greek traders—received protection. In contrast to the Habsburg monarchs, the sultan presided over a centrally administered empire. He did not have to contend with forces of opposition within the nobility, church, or bourgeoisie. Most significant, there was no Ottoman aristocracy defined by hereditary landownership or independent armed forces that could potentially undermine his imperial rule. The sultan maintained his nearly unassailable personal power by fathering children within the harem and by selecting his high-ranking officials from the ranks of converted Christians. In the provinces, he could count on timariots' loyal, capable service.[43] Finally, religion served as a central mechanism for legitimating and exercising imperial sovereignty, as well as for affirming the internal social order.

Islamization, Confessionalization, and Identity Formation

From the mid-sixteenth century on, religious institutions and central doctrines of faith became inseparable from the state and social order of the Habsburg and Ottoman Empires. Religion, or confession, became a dogmatically defined and exclusionary statement of identity, enabling the early modern empires to broaden their scope of power to include all aspects of life—culture, social order, values, and state institutions.[44] This also affected the lands of southeastern Europe, which the empires dominated in no small part through the power of the religious systems they espoused. In both empires, the personnel and institutions of faith communities defined themselves more clearly over the course of the sixteenth century. Dogmas and rituals became more rigid, alongside the thoughts and actions of believers. Although Habsburg and Ottoman rule lasted for different periods of time in the individual regions of southeastern Europe, assuming different forms and sometimes switching back and forth, confessionalization had an enduring cultural and social influence on all of these regions. For this reason, some of these lands today share historically conditioned structures, experiences, and cultural identities with the Catholic or Orthodox Christian universe, while others have a greater affinity with the former Ottoman world.[45]

At the beginning of the Ottoman conquest, the population of southeastern Europe was overwhelmingly Christian.[46] Because the Ottomans believed that they held a divine mission to spread their religion among non-Muslims, they sought to systematically Islamize the population through holy war. This process occurred in very different ways, depending on time and place, and scholars continue to debate how exactly it began. To generalize very broadly, Turkish historians have tended to assert that the drive for Islamization coincided with the migration and colonizing efforts of Muslim population groups, while those in southeastern Europe have more often emphasized forced conversion. There is no doubt that both phenomena occurred at various times.

Beginning in the thirteenth century, Turkish Muslims spontaneously settled on the Balkan Peninsula.[47] The sultans also systematically colonized areas of strategic importance, particularly near cities, following successful conquests. In the second half of the fourteenth century, for example, Tatars and Anatolian Turks were resettled in Filibe (Plovdiv) and Üsküb (Skopje). Volunteers were recruited to replenish the population of Istanbul, although prisoners of war and peasants from Serbia, Albania, Greece, and Crimea were forcibly deported. A gradual pattern of resettlement from Anatolia to the Balkans became apparent in the fifteenth and the first half of the sixteenth centuries. The entire lower Danube region to the east of Bulgarian Nicopolis and Kavala, and also the southern half of Macedonia, attracted Muslim residents who altered the territories' ethnic and religious structure.[48]

Islamization primarily occurred as the Ottomans expanded their social order and structures of governance to the conquered lands. Until the mid-sixteenth century, the centers of this process were larger cities, where

Muslim officials, soldiers, traders, and craftsmen settled and strategically constructed religious infrastructure after the Ottomans took power. The Ottomans transformed Christian churches into Islamic houses of prayer; they built mosques, madrasas (Islamic schools), *hans* (hostels), *hamams* (baths), *türbes* (mausoleums), and other culturally representative structures. Pious foundations *(waqfs)* supported Islamic worship services and charitable causes, including schools, libraries, poorhouses, and other infrastructure.[49] The provincial town of Vrhbosna, for example, became a typical Ottoman city in the fifteenth century. The Turkish governor established his headquarters there, ordering the construction of a seraglio, or palace *(saray)*—which is why the city was subsequently called Sarajevo. Bosnia's new seat of government received a bazaar called the Baščaršija, and a large number of mosques, foundations, caravansaries, hostels, and foundations. As early as the sixteenth century, Sarajevo had become an overwhelmingly Muslim city.[50] Many other locales changed their physiognomy according to the same pattern.

Conversions were an important part of Islamization, although how and when they occurred is highly controversial. In the fourteenth and fifteenth centuries, the Ottomans had already coerced conversions in isolated circumstances, but without a comprehensive strategy. The Ottomans razed entire Christian villages to the ground as they conquered new territory. In Bulgaria, for example, hundreds of thousands were killed, enslaved, or expelled.[51] In 1493 the Catholic bishop of Nin, Juraj Divnić, wrote that the Ottomans had "an insatiable appetite for the slaughter of the faithful and the avid desire to seize power over the entire world."[52] Initially, however, the pace of conversion was not that urgent. At the end of the fifteenth century, only about 2.5 percent of the subdued population had accepted the new faith. The Ottomans placed greater emphasis on Islamization in the sixteenth century—after they had conquered additional Muslim territories and assumed the caliphate, after their internal consolidation of state power, and not least, within the context of their wars with Christian powers. By 1530, 22.2 percent of households in Rumelia were Muslim—although it is unclear how many of these had converted and how many had migrated to the region. In general, city dwellers were more likely to convert to Islam. After the mid-sixteenth century, however, the movement for conversion also spread to the countryside, and the pace of Islamization quickened, especially in multireligious lands like Bosnia, Herzegovina, Albania, and parts of Bulgaria. Within a century, the Catholic-influenced regions of northern and central Albania, as well as Kosovo, had become majority Muslim. Even so, some of the converted Muslims in these regions were crypto-Christians who continued to practice their old faith in secret.[53]

Differentiation between Muslims and non-Muslims became a defining principle of the social order in the sixteenth century, in tandem with the expansion of state structures and the desire for greater internal integration within the empire. There were many different motivations for converting to Islam. According to Ottoman understanding, it was a state responsibility to tolerate and protect nonbelievers in the conquered territories—insofar as they embraced Judaism or Christianity, the other Religions of the Book. The Ottomans believed that these faiths were likewise based on holy scripture and divine revelation. The three religions shared the same origins, but Islam was the newest and most perfectly developed. The *dhimmi,* or protected people, were allowed to practice their religion, but they were also subject to discriminatory rules about what they could wear, and where they could travel and live. They could not ride horses in the city, wear the color green, or build tall churches. They had to pay a head tax and higher rents. Only believers of the true faith were allowed to perform important state and administrative duties, and after a certain point in time, only they could acquire hereditary estates. Christians usually experienced active persecution and harassment only in conjunction with rebellions and campaigns of conquest. As long as things stayed quiet, they lived in a state of toleration but lesser privilege. In contrast to the *dhimmi,* polytheists were ruthlessly persecuted, and anyone who renounced Islam could be punished by death.[54]

Given the inferior legal status of non-Muslims, the Ottoman leadership did not necessarily have to use physical force to move them to convert. Upper-class Christians in the provinces often adopted the new creed voluntarily—so that they might convert their property into a timar, for example. Muslim peasants, meanwhile, could avoid the head tax and the child levy. In the northern Bosnian district of Bijeljina, two-thirds of the population became Muslim within eighty years of the sixteenth century because property was taken away from Christians and transferred only to Muslims. It was usually young people who converted, while their parents were more likely to remain loyal Christians. As a result, many families had mixed religious affiliations in this era.[55] Elsewhere, there is evidence of nonmaterial motivations. Many converts emphasized the role of religion, such as the Orthodox priest from Athens who accepted Islam at the beginning of the seventeenth century and took the name Mehmed. He saw Islam as spiritually and theologically superior to Christianity, and he believed the West was doomed.[56]

The mystical dervish orders, particularly the Bektashi, played an important role in the spread of Islam. They settled in cities as well as rural areas, building monasteries (tekke) near known cultic sites. Because they incorporated elements of folklore and the miraculous in their doctrines and practices, the Christian population often found them more approachable than official Islam. The Bektashi believed in the trinity (of God, Muhammad, and Ali), as well as the Twelve Imams (in lieu of the Apostles). They also practiced confession and venerated saints. For religious people, the mystical and sometimes ecstatic practices of the dervishes could feel more compelling compared with the sober, official Islamic ritual. Nearly every larger Balkan city had a branch of one of various dervish orders, enabling well-connected networks that linked Sufi brotherhoods across the European and Arab provinces of the empire.[57]

Because the Slavs converted to Islam in such large numbers, entirely new group identities emerged across the Balkans—including the Bosnian Muslims, the Gorani in Kosovo, the Torbeshi in Macedonia, and the Pomaks in Bulgaria and Greece.[58] Although it was once believed that followers of the Bogomils were the chief converts to Islam in Bosnia and Herzegovina, we now know that people from all faiths and classes adopted the new religion.[59] As the centuries progressed, religious membership contributed to the definition of independent national identities. Religious affiliation informed social roles, norms, and values, as well as cultural practices and traditions. The faith communities' administrative and legal organization also contributed to the separation between members of different religions, even when they spoke the same language.

Beginning in the mid-fifteenth century, the *millet* system regulated the status of the monotheistic Religions of the Book. The term *millet* takes on different emphases in historical sources; it could mean "religion," "community," "nation," or simply, "rite." In practice, the concept involved the officially recognized self-administration of the religious communities. Each *millet* formed a religious-political entity with certain legal, economic, and administrative capacities. It provided a framework for settling religious and cultural questions, maintaining schools and hospitals, regulating civil affairs, and collecting taxes. Beginning in the mid-fifteenth century, Greek Orthodox, Armenian, and Jewish *millets* existed alongside the Muslim one; others were added in later centuries.[60] *Millets* created not only distinct legal milieus but also social ones, since people lived overwhelmingly with members of their own religious community in neighborhoods known as *mahalles*.[61] In the cities, *mahalles* were enclosed by walls. Each *mahalle* had its own leader, as well as religious infrastructure, fountains, and a market, depending on its size. Sixteenth-century Thessaloniki, for example, had twelve Jewish, ten Orthodox, and forty Muslim *mahalles*. Nevertheless, communal life continued to thrive in many places—in public spaces, marketplaces, and in certain guilds.[62]

Ashkenazi Jews, who had emigrated from the Rhineland, Venice, Hungary, and Poland, had lived in the Balkans since the Middle Ages. The Jewish population grew significantly after 1492, when the Spanish Sephardic Jews were driven from the Iberian Peninsula as a result of the Reconquista. The sultans saw many advantages in accepting the prosperous, well-educated Jews from Spain, Portugal, and later, Italy, particularly since the newcomers could help to colonize the capital and the Balkans. They were granted unprecedented freedoms, leading the rabbi Samuel de Medina to praise the "sovereign who imposes no restrictions on travel or on commercial activities on any of his subjects."[63] Thousands of doctors, artists, printers, scholars, weapon makers, and tradesmen fled across the Mediterranean, settling in Istanbul and many other cities in the Levant and in southeastern Europe. In Thessaloniki, where Jews were granted a monopoly on producing uniforms for the Ottoman army, they were already in the majority by 1520. Substantial Jewish communities also arose in Sofia, Sarajevo, and Skopje.[64]

The *millet* system allowed Jews and Christians to practice their faith and also to uphold their group identity. The Jewish *millet* was led by the chief rabbi, and its Christian counterpart by the ecumenical patriarch in Constantinople. The latter was the spiritual head of Ottoman Christians, responsible for settling doctrinal questions, administering church property, and exercising judicial authority over clerics. He also collected his church members' taxes and forwarded them to the sultan. The patriarch was formally responsible for all Christians in the empire, not only ethnic Greeks but also Bulgarians, Macedonians, Vlachs, Serbs, and Albanians. In contrast to the Greek Orthodox Church, the Latin Church did not have its own institutional structure within the Ottoman Empire. Only in Bosnia did the Franciscans manage to uphold a remnant of church and monastic autonomy.[65]

The patriarch saw himself as the head of a universal church, a kind of Greek Orthodox commonwealth, which stretched across the entire territory once under Byzantine rule. He tolerated no exceptional structures; soon after his appointment he dissolved the autocephalous Serbian patriarchate in Peć and placed it under the jurisdiction of the archbishopric of Ohrid. For about one century, the patriarchate in Constantinople held jurisdiction over all Christians in the Balkans, before an Ottoman vizier reversed this practice in the mid-sixteenth century. With a tradition of independence dating back to the thirteenth century, the Serbian Church reclaimed its spiritual and political leadership of the South Slavic Orthodox believers. Between 1557 and 1766, the Serbian patriarchate was the only institution that constituted a link to the pre-Ottoman era. The patriarchate kept alive the Serbs' memory of their illustrious medieval empire, along with its historic and cultural center of Kosovo, hoping that it would one day rise again. Serbian kings were venerated as saints, and the memorable battle on the Field of Blackbirds was commemorated in religious texts and prayers. Hagiographic depictions created a myth that has persisted to the present day.

In the mid-eighteenth century, the ecumenical patriarch in Constantinople dismantled the autonomous church structures in the Balkans once again. This time, the Bulgarian archbishopric of Ohrid and the Serbian patriarchate lost their independence. Discontent with the Greeks and the Greek-dominated Orthodox Church hierarchy grew among the Serbian and Bulgarian clergy. The church increasingly seemed to act on behalf of the people of an emergent Greek nation.[66]

A special situation arose in the *sancak* of Montenegro, where the Ottomans had never been able to fully assert their authority over local tribes. Prince-bishops had held power there since the sixteenth century, and during the Great Ottoman War at the end of the seventeenth century, the Ottomans retreated from the area altogether. Under Vladika (Bishop) Danilo Petrović, also known as Danilo Šćepčević, the small land began to assert its religious and political independence.

Although the ecumenical patriarch was able to uphold the institutional existence of the Orthodox Church within the Ottoman Empire, its potential for expansion was limited. Everything depended on good relations with the sultan; the patriarch and bishops had to purchase their offices. Because the church's involvement in education was limited to training new priests, scholarly traditions withered, and the influence of folk religion grew.[67] "Since we lost the [Byzantine] Empire, we have also lost wisdom," an Orthodox theologian complained in the seventeenth century. "Through our long dealings with the barbarians, we have become barbarians ourselves."[68] Only a very small minority engaged themselves in secular fields of knowledge such as philosophy and the natural sciences, which Orthodoxy and Islam alike strictly distinguished from theology.[69] In 1612 the Croatian Jesuit Bartol Kašić was astounded by the ignorance of Orthodox clerics in Syrmia who were unfamiliar with the Ten Commandments and prayers, let alone the significance of the cross.[70] Many clerics, such as the seventeenth-century Greek priest Synadinos from Serres, took no issue with living in the Ottoman Empire and calling the sultan "basileus," in the Byzantine tradition. He did not even object to the child levy.[71]

The Western Church was dominant within the Habsburg and Venetian Empires, and thus within Slovenia and much of Croatia. All bishops and priests were responsible to the Vatican, which presided over a single hierarchy centered in Rome. A few territories temporarily fell under Ottoman control, but not the dioceses of Split, Šibenik, Zadar, Senj, and Zagreb.[72] Within Latin Christendom, however, confessional divisions loomed. In 1517, the very year that the Ottoman sultan claimed the title of caliph, head of the *umma,* Martin Luther published his theses that sparked internal conflict within the church. As soon as the first princes adopted the new confession, the old church was under threat. Within the Habsburg Empire, the Reformation spread first to Austria, Bohemia, and Moravia. In the 1530s it moved on to Hungary, Slovenia, and Croatia, where the power of the nobility had weakened after the defeat at Mohács. Numerous magnates adopted the new faith, and by the end of the sixteenth century, Hungary and Transylvania were overwhelmingly Protestant. The teachings of Luther and Calvin appealed to Magyars and Saxons, whereas Romanians and Serbs stayed loyal to Orthodoxy, and Croats overwhelmingly remained Catholic. The Protestants nevertheless worked to expand their influence throughout Europe and the Mediterranean basin.[73]

Because the Reformation threatened to destroy the internal unity of the Western Church, the integrating ideology of empire, and the Habsburgs' universal claim to sovereignty, it was opposed with particular vehemence in Austria. Protestant clerics were driven away, and non-Catholics were forced to choose between conversion and exile. Only in 1781 did Emperor Joseph II guarantee the toleration and freedom of the Protestant churches and Orthodox Christians.

But first, in 1545, Emperor Charles V asked the Council of Trent to clarify church doctrine and clearly distinguish it from the ideas of the Reformation. He and his successors decisively advanced the Counter-Reformation in southeastern Europe and elsewhere—by forbidding Protestant practices, promoting Catholic missions, and working toward greater cooperation between the Western and Eastern Churches. In the mid-sixteenth century, Ferdinand I called on Spanish Jesuit missionaries to defend and spread the "true faith" throughout the Croatian lands.[74] They settled in Zagreb, Varaždin, Dubrovnik, and other cities, becoming the leading supporters of the Counter-Reformation and Catholic missions across the region. In 1576 the pope had the Roman Catholic catechism translated into Greek and disseminated twelve thousand copies throughout the Ottoman Empire.[75] He founded seminaries in Rome to educate Orthodox Greeks and South Slavs in the Catholic faith. A half-century later, in 1622, the papal Sacra Congregatio de Propaganda Fide began its campaigns to spread the Roman Catholic faith throughout Bosnia, Albania, the Greek islands, and the rest of the world. Missionaries, Jesuit priests, and Capuchin and Franciscan monks fanned across southeastern Europe, seeking to convert Orthodox Christians, Armenians, and Maronites and to advance the authority of the pope. They usually operated under the protection of France. As an important Ottoman trading partner, France had been granted freedom of worship and permission to employ priests and hold services for its traders and diplomats within the empire.[76]

Relations between the Catholic and Orthodox clergy in the Ottoman Empire deteriorated as missionizing intensified during the Thirty Years' War. A Franciscan complained that "a Serbian pope would sooner see a Greek as his brother than a Catholic monk, and the monk would rather see an Italian as his brother than . . . a Serb."[77] The standardization of rites and doctrines also meant ridding the peasants of old folk traditions. Belief in vampires still thrived in many areas. On the island of Šipan, for example, peasants believed that the dead were still living and climbed out of their graves at night to kill. "Deceived by Satan," the peasants dug up graves and mutilated the corpses inside them, doing "what we would not do even to the greatest criminal in the world."[78]

Throughout Croatia, Dalmatia, and Dubrovnik, the clergy and nobility sided with the Counter-Reformation in the final third of the sixteenth century. According to a 1604 law, which remained in place until the mid-nineteenth century, Protestants were not even allowed to reside on

Habsburg lands.[79] Because the Ottoman wars drove many Orthodox Christians, particularly Serbs and Vlachs, to flee to Habsburg territory, the fifteenth-century idea of uniting the Western and Eastern churches under papal authority was revived once more. The idea attracted few proponents, however, and the number of Uniate Christians in Croatia remained small.[80] Only in Transylvania did a Greek Catholic Church emerge. After reconquering the land at the end of the seventeenth century, the Habsburgs refused to recognize the Orthodox Church, compelling the clergy to accept these eastern Catholics.

After the Catholic Reformation, a close symbiosis emerged between a renewed Catholicism and Croatian identity, significantly influencing the literature, architecture, and music of the Baroque. Translations and Catholic reformist texts became the cornerstone of the Croatian written language. A sense of communal awareness developed in waging war against the Ottomans, and in competition with the Serbian Orthodox Church. War against the Turks politicized Christian self-awareness. Croatian nobles, clerics, and scholars saw the Christian Catholic faith as a bulwark against Islam in their vulnerable borderlands. Ivan Gundulić's epic poem *Osman,* which depicted the struggle between Christianity and Islam, was a paradigmatic expression of this sentiment.[81] The religious argument not only encouraged militancy but also became a (pre-)national symbol of unity. Catholicism was the most important element connecting a Croatian population spread across so many different lands.

Certain clerics and scholars believed that uniting the Christian churches in the fight against Islam was absolutely essential. Slavic language and culture became an important vehicle in the movement toward greater cooperation and a potential alliance. In 1525 the humanist Vinko Pribojević addressed "the Slavs"—including Russians, Poles, and South Slavs—in a sermon on the island of Hvar. The Benedictine Mauro Orbini, who authored a history of the Slavs, and the Jesuit Juraj Križanić, who advocated for a union between the Russian and Roman Catholic Churches, further developed the (pan-)Slavic idea. Križanić, who traveled to Moscow in 1658 without the approval of the pope, developed a common Slavic language and a program for uniting all Slavs under the tsar, as a means of counteracting the Islamic threat.[82] This was somewhat unusual for a Catholic cleric, although Serbian, Bulgarian, and Romanian Orthodox monks traveled frequently to the Muscovite empire, collecting donations or seeking moral support against the Ottomans. In 1626 the abbot of the Hilandar monastery on Athos even offered a prayer that God might empower the tsar to overtake the Ottoman Empire and "seize Constantine's throne."[83] Centuries before modern nationalism took off, a communal feeling based on religion and Slavic culture had already begun to develop.

In the Romanian lands, by contrast, the Orthodox Church divested itself of Old Church Slavonic, the language of liturgy and scholarship. The Romanian metropolitanates were formally subordinate to the patriarchate, but in practice they managed themselves. Slavic literature had long been composed and copied within the monasteries. With the completion of the first Bible translation in the second half of the seventeenth century, Romanian became the official language of the church, thus allowing it to reach a wider audience. The Romanian language established itself, alongside Greek, as a means of poetic and scholarly communication. The pan-Orthodox commonwealth fell apart. A century later, Transylvanian clerics began to use the Latin alphabet, instead of Cyrillic.[84]

Under growing pressure from the Protestant and Catholic Reformations, both the Catholic and Orthodox Churches worked to achieve spiritual renewal. Established in Zagreb in 1578, a college with a humanist school sought to train new priests in the spirit of the Catholic Reformation and to provide instruction not only in theology but also mathematics, physics, and philosophy. Additional religious academies followed in subsequent decades, including a Jesuit college in Dubrovnik in 1658. The Orthodox Church was likewise compelled to study the new teachings and to clarify doctrines that had gone unchanged for centuries.[85] Between 1620 and 1638, Kyrillos Loukaris from Crete—a Venetian citizen who sympathized with some Protestant ideas—served as the patriarch of Constantinople. He opposed the pope's efforts to reunite the Catholic and Orthodox Churches, seeking instead to forge an Orthodox-Reformed alliance against the "Catholic peril," even seeking to unite the Ottoman Empire and Russia in a military pact against Poland. His efforts to reform and strengthen the Orthodox Church against its opponents ran aground; he fell from the sultan's favor and was strangled.[86] His friend, the Orthodox humanist Theophilus Korydaleus, opened up the Patriarchal Academy to fields of study beyond theology.[87] Ancient philosophy, natural history, geography, and astronomy entered the curricula in all forty or so of the Greek Orthodox sites of education—on Mount Athos, as well as in Edirne, Athens, Ioannina, Chios, Thessaloniki, Jerusalem, Jassy, Bucharest, Moscow, and

Kiev. A close relationship of exchange with the University of Padua enabled the teachings of Copernicus and Galileo to work their way into the Orthodox world of ideas in the 1680s. A new network of scholarly activity in philosophy and the natural sciences emerged, linking together the Latin and Greek academic worlds.[88] Catholic and Orthodox clerics struggled with the new teachings, which threatened to diminish the church's geocentric conception of the universe to the point of absurdity. Michael Mitros (a later metropolitan of Athens), for example, did not suppress the newest astronomical discoveries, but—like many of his Catholic colleagues—he sought refuge in the ideas of the Danish scholar Tycho Brahe, who continued to hold that the sun orbited the Earth, even as the other planets orbited the sun.[89] Nevertheless, the academies became a driving force in the conception of a rational universe, and in the gradual marginalization of theology as the dominant science.

Sunni Islam also faced new challenges in the sixteenth and seventeenth centuries, as new religious movements raised doubts about longstanding dogma. Pantheistic and radical Sunni sects, and even atheists, spoke out in greater numbers. Within Judaism, the mystical and messianic movement of Sabbateanism sowed discord.[90] In response, there was a growing need to standardize rites and doctrines and to place public morality under tighter control. Conservative Islamic scholars, followers of the Kadizadeli movement, gained influence at the sultan's court. They argued on behalf of a renewed, Salafist piety that could cleanse Muslim society of dangerous influences, heresies, and atheistic tendencies. Escalating rivalry between these scholars and the mystical Halveti brotherhood erupted in a bitter controversy over the consumption of coffee and tobacco—defended by the dervishes, but condemned by the orthodox conservatives, along with music and dancing.[91] The last third of the seventeenth century became a phase of rising intolerance. Heretical movements were opposed with greater vigor, and new rules regulated the attendance of religious services and other matters. Public ceremonies were held to circumcise converts, and countless new mosques were constructed. Sects were suppressed, and their followers forced to convert. Even the Jewish palace doctors had to accept Islam at the end of the seventeenth century.[92]

The more the new teachings challenged the religious foundations of the sultans' power, the more bitterly the sultans presented themselves as the executors of divine law. More than ever before, the sultans took the conversion of non-Muslims as an expression of their personal piety and legitimation of their sanctified rule. On the Balkan Peninsula, this was expressed through more aggressive, and sometimes violent, Islamization.

The historiographical paradigm of confessionalization—the effort to achieve political and sociocultural integration through the standardization of faith practices—originally applied to the Christian lands of central Europe after the Reformation, but it is also helpful for explaining some developments within the Ottoman Islamic world.[93] As religious practices, dogma, and lifestyles became more uniform, a new understanding of the modern state emerged. Church and state authorities developed new means of governance and control, and religious intolerance became an instrument for asserting territorial sovereignty, disciplining subject populations, and expanding state institutions.[94]

Islamization and confessionalization brought far-reaching sociocultural changes that are still felt today. First and foremost, there was the transformation of southeastern Europe's ethnic and religious structure through migration and conversion, as new groups made the region their home or, like the Balkan Muslims, emerged for the first time. Membership in a particular cultural sphere and belief system was expressed through architecture, music, popular culture, cuisine, and other aspects of everyday life. Typical "Balkanisms" developed in the languages spoken in the Ottoman-controlled lands, and Albanian and Bosnian authors composed literature in Persian, Turkish, and Arabic until the beginning of the twentieth century. Others wrote their native language with an Arabic alphabet that was modified to fit their own phonetic system.[95] New cultures were not simply imposed on the peoples of southeastern Europe, but were appropriated and embraced by these peoples in a variety of ways.

As with all European lands and peoples, confession building and cultural-political identity formation went hand in hand. The idea of *societas christiana* and universal empire had already been shattered in the Middle Ages, along with the division of the church. The Reformation destroyed whatever remained of the aspiration for religious unity in the Latin West. As in other European lands, confessionalization—which also involved erecting barriers against external worldviews—acted as a catalyst for early modern nation-building. Scholars and opinion leaders frequently came from religious communities whose church structures gradually gave shape to "confessional nations" that were grounded in a collective self-awareness (and distancing from outsiders) based on religion. War against the Muslim Ottomans played a significant role in shaping religious, and then (pre-)national consciousness among members of Christian religious communities.

Thus, a premodern differentiation based on cultural identities had already become apparent in the sixteenth and seventeenth centuries. For Croats, Serbs, and Slavic Muslims, who shared a common language, this differentiation was overwhelmingly informed by religion. A renewed Catholicism became the defining factor of community building, and distancing from outsiders, among Slovenes and Croats. Orthodoxy assumed this role for Greeks, Romanians, and Serbs. Religion and the church became the core of collective identity because the Balkan peoples remained politically and territorially fragmented into the modern era.[96] Only in the nineteenth century did secularized national awareness replace formalized religion as the source of communal belonging.

Ottoman World Power in the Age of Exploration

Under Süleyman the Magnificent, the Ottoman Empire's universalistic ideology of sovereignty and projection of imperial power reached their zenith. Competition with European rivals to divide up the world demanded a better understanding of its still-isolated spaces. Around 1500, the Ottomans, too, were seized by an unprecedented fever to explore. Like the European West, they profited from new advances in maritime technology and from more effective methods of market development and customs management. Muslim travelers gave eyewitness accounts of their experiences in distant lands, and scholars translated works of geography from Arabic and other languages. Maps, atlases, and scientific treatises expanded the perspective of Ottoman decision makers.[97]

The territory and spheres of influence of the great empires, including the Spanish and Portuguese kingdoms, expanded immensely between the fifteenth and eighteenth centuries. Given the Ottomans' supremacy over the eastern Mediterranean and land routes to Asia, the other empires sought alternative trade routes by sea. The accidental discovery of America in 1492, followed by the first sea voyage to India via the southern tip of Africa in 1498, created new constellations of power and redistributed the spheres of influence in what was the known world at that time. The relationship between Europe and the Islamic world of the Ottomans shifted dramatically. The Spanish and Portuguese conquered vast expanses in Central and South

America, while the French and British claimed the northern American hemisphere. The new colonial powers acquired the ability to exploit valuable precious metals and to cultivate enormous quantities of raw materials like cotton and sugar as monocultures on plantations. By 1600, wealthy and powerful transoceanic empires had emerged.

Asia also presented the Europeans with opportunities for expansion, not least because the new sea route around the Cape of Good Hope freed them from their dependence on Ottoman middlemen, who had until this point transported the desired spices, medicines, dyes, and textiles to Europe by sea, or with camels over land. The new sea route set the stage for the Portuguese trading empire's expansion into Asia.[98] Immediately after landing in India, the Portuguese began to forge agreements with local leaders. They built and fortified trading posts, levied tariffs, and erected naval blockades, seeking to control all maritime trade throughout the Indian Ocean and, in particular, to secure a monopoly on the import of pepper, an immensely profitable commodity. In fact, Lisbon temporarily became the central point of distribution for spices from Asia and Africa.

The Ottomans lost access to trade routes that were essential to their survival, including the route from India to the holy sites of Islam. Because every adult Muslim was supposed to undertake a pilgrimage (hajj) once in his life, and Mecca was an important point of distribution for Eastern goods, the need for action was great. The scholar Omer Talib aptly summarized the dilemma in 1625: "Now the Europeans have gained knowledge of the entire world, send their ships in every direction and take possession of the most important ports. . . . Only the things they do not consume themselves reach Istanbul and the other Islamic countries, and even then are sold at five times their original price. . . . If nothing is done, before too long the Europeans will become lords even of the lands of Islam."[99]

The Ottomans were, moreover, annoyed that they had not discovered America themselves. After all, Columbus had not sailed westward to discover new continents, but rather to find an alternative sea route to India. Since the Ottoman Empire already controlled a short route from the Mediterranean to India, it had focused its attention on the Red Sea and the Persian Gulf. It had not occurred to the Ottomans to sail westward.[100]

In light of these changes on the world stage, the Ottomans had to maintain their control over existing spheres of influence and also acquire new ones. They worked toward this goal with neighboring states. In the

Danubian Principalities and the khanates in Crimea and Georgia, they built up political spheres of influence through goodwill gestures, negotiations, and threats. These territories became buffers that kept Hungary, Poland, and Russia away from the strategically important Black Sea. As caliphs, or rulers over all believers and protectors of Islam's holy sites, the sultans also sought to expand the Ottoman Empire's religious claim to power over Muslims in Africa and Asia.[101] Here, the strategic goal was to create an Ottoman commonwealth that stretched from Morocco to Sumatra. Islamic entities beyond the territory of the empire could continue to function autonomously, since their loyalty was assured through their dependence on the prestige, legitimacy, and authority of the sultan in Istanbul. Thus, the Ottomans did not seek to acquire overseas colonies.[102]

The architect of Ottoman foreign policy in the sixteenth century was Sokollu Mehmed Pasha, the son of a lesser noble from the area near Bosnian Višegrad. The child levy brought eighteen-year-old Bajica (as he was then called) to the court of Sultan Süleyman I.[103] He became Muslim and changed his name to Mehmed, serving as chief taster and gatekeeper after an extensive training period. He later participated in campaigns against Austria and Iran, and he rose to become governor *(beylerbey)* of Rumelia and admiral of the Ottoman fleet. His father, like many Bosnian family members, likewise embraced Islam in order to ensure a position of leadership at a pious foundation.[104]

As a close confidant to the sultan, Sokollu Mehmed served in the divan and married the daughter of the future sultan, Selim II. In 1565 the Bosnian was named grand vizier. European diplomats admired the "great pasha," whom they described as attractive and well groomed. They valued the courtly demeanor and mental acuity of the tall man with the gray beard, although they were perplexed by his hints of arrogance and his avarice for gifts. However, these weaknesses paled alongside his legendary boldness in dangerous wartime situations.[105] He was also held in high regard by his former countrymen. The Croatian writer Marin Držić wrote that because the vizier "is part of our language and people . . . and our Bosnian blood, we ought not to hesitate . . . to keep him as our friend."[106]

Sokollu Mehmed Pasha was a gifted politician who had mastered the contemporary art of statecraft, assuring his unassailable position within the Ottoman government apparatus. The "grand vizier is the actual leader of Turkey," remarked the Venetian Marion Cavalli. "No other minister in this state has ever held such power."[107] Understanding the limits of Ottoman military power, Sokollu Mehmed warned against military adventurism. He preferred to seek diplomatic solutions with potential opponents of the empire (the House of Habsburg, the Republic of Venice, and the Russian tsar), while simultaneously expanding imperial power vis-à-vis Iran and the Islamic world in the East through agreements, threats, and economic incentives. He cultivated friendships with influential Venetian, Jewish, and Greek families as well. The Austrian envoy in Istanbul could not stop "praising . . . the sobriety of his reason and judgment, his skill and finesse in governing."[108]

The Ottoman grand vizier with Bosnian roots had an imperial biography that was typical for his time. The empire shaped his personal experiences, providing a space for action that transcended borders.[109] His primary objective was the expansion of Ottoman power, but he remained sensitive to the well-being of his homeland. In 1565 and 1566 Sokollu Mehmed orchestrated war against the Holy Roman Empire, but within this context he also reinstated the Serbian patriarchate in Peć and probably appointed a relative as its leader. During the campaigns in Croatia and Hungary, he sought to win the favor of the Serbs in both regions. In 1568 Emperor Maximilian II had to accept the division of Hungary and the payment of an annual tribute in the Peace of Adrianople.

Since the European powers already controlled North and Central America at this time, advancing into new territory and pursuing global politics appeared possible only in Africa and Asia. Alongside political, strategic, and religious motivations, Sokollu Mehmed sought to win back control over the lucrative spice trade as well as the import of dutiable luxury goods into Europe, in order to break the monopoly that the Portuguese had only recently acquired. He built a clever, empire-wide customs system for skimming off a portion of the exorbitant profits of Western long-distance trade for the Ottoman state. He sold weapons, muskets, gunpowder, and cannonballs to the leaders of Sumatra so that they sent desirable goods including silk, pepper, cinnamon, and cloves back to his empire on favorable terms.[110]

Diplomacy and intrigue went hand in hand. Sokollu Mehmed sent agents provocateurs to foment a pan-Islamic rebellion against the Portuguese maritime empire in India, Ceylon, Sumatra, and elsewhere, and also to create unrest on the western coast of Africa. With the help of Muslim missionaries and Islamic propaganda, he sought recognition of the universal caliphate in the Indian Ocean. In Indian Calicut, he rewarded preachers with gold from the state's coffers for saying Friday prayers in the name of the sultan, insofar as they had not (as in Fez, Ceylon, and Aceh) already done this on their own. He sent soldiers and weapons to the sultan of Aceh to affirm their relations. "You must make your best effort to carry out your responsibilities to religion and to our Imperial State," he wrote to the sultan. "With the help of God Almighty, you must cleanse those lands of the infidel filth, so that under our Imperial rule . . . the Muslims of that land may live in a state of tranquility and, free from anxiety, may busy themselves with earning a livelihood."[111]

Sokollu Mehmed, recognizing that hegemony in the Indian Ocean depended on controlling the sea and transport routes that largely lay in the hands of the Portuguese, directed the governor of Egypt and his best architects and builders to plan a canal across the Isthmus of Suez. From the port of Suez, the Ottoman fleet would be able to beat the Portuguese in India and safeguard routes of pilgrimage to the holy sites. Because Muslim merchants and pilgrims also complained about the advance of the Safavids in Iran and Russia, he planned an additional canal between the Volga and the Don. From Bukhara and Samarkand, one could then travel by ship from the Caspian Sea along the two great rivers, all the way to the Black Sea. From there, a sea route would connect to the Mediterranean Sea, the Suez canal, and the holy sites, by way of the Red Sea. For the time being, however, his bold plan for artificial waterways that would create a direct connection between central Asia and Mecca and Medina, and from there to the Indian Ocean and back, remained a dream for the future.[112]

By contrast, new mosques, madrasas, pious foundations, and baths did become a reality, all built by the grand vizier to demonstrate and reinforce Ottoman sovereignty throughout the empire. He was particularly fond of roads, bridges, and caravansaries, which facilitated the empire's consolidation and the blossoming of trade. Hundreds of architectural masterpieces in the Balkans were built in this era.[113] Among other projects, he had the Ottoman chief architect Sinan construct a stone bridge with eleven arches across the Drina River in Višegrad, in his Bosnian homeland. Construction of the six-hundred-foot-long span across the turbulent river lasted six years. The monumental bridge, which later became world famous, completed the final leg of the route between Edirne and Sarajevo. In the twentieth century, Ivo Andrić immortalized the legendary "Bridge on the Drina" in his Nobel Prize–winning novel.

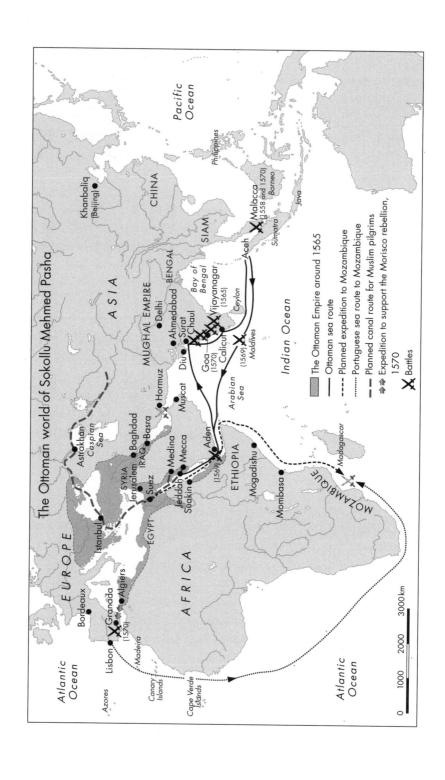

The Ottoman world of Sokollu Mehmed Pasha

Legend:

The Ottoman Empire around 1565
Ottoman sea route
Planned expedition to Mozambique
Portuguese sea route to Mozambique
Planned canal route for Muslim pilgrims
Expedition to support the Morisco rebellion, 1570
Battles

Place names and labels:

Atlantic Ocean
Pacific Ocean
Indian Ocean
Arabian Sea
Bay of Bengal
Caspian Sea

EUROPE
ASIA
AFRICA
CHINA
SIAM
BENGAL
MUGHAL EMPIRE
SYRIA
IRAQ
EGYPT
ETHIOPIA
MOZAMBIQUE

Khanbaliq [Beijing]
Delhi
Ahmedabad
Surat
Chaul
Diu
Goa (1570)
Vijayanagar (1565)
Calicut
Ceylon
Maldives (1569)
Aceh
Malacca (1558 and 1570)
Philippines
Borneo
Sumatra
Java

Hormuz
Muscat
Baghdad
Basra
Medina
Mecca
Jeddah
Suakin
Aden (1569)
Suez
Jerusalem
Istanbul
Astrakhan
Algiers
Granada (1570)
Bordeaux
Lisbon
Azores
Madeira
Canary Islands
Cape Verde Islands
Mogadishu
Mombasa
Madagascar

0 100 2000 3000 km

Sokollu Mehmed's sharp intellect made him a key patron of the arts and sciences in his era. He employed painters from Verona and imported Venetian glass. He lobbied for the opening of an observatory in Istanbul, and for the translation of a world history from the Mughal Empire in India. The Bosnian supported and subsidized geographers and historians, and he commissioned a history of Ottoman conquests in the Indian Ocean. With the translation of specialized terminology, Turkish was increasingly used for imperial representation, taking its place alongside Italian, Greek, and Church Slavic as an official language of diplomacy.[114]

Sokollu's expansionist plans suffered a blow when Sultan Selim II decided to engage Venice and the Holy League on Cyprus, against the measured advice of his grand vizier. In 1571 Don Juan of Austria dealt the Ottoman fleet a crushing defeat near Lepanto on the Gulf of Corinth. On a single day, tens of thousands of Ottomans lost their lives.[115] The military disaster not only ended Ottoman hegemony in the Mediterranean but also halted the expansion of the Ottoman commonwealth. From this point forward, Sultan Selim II directed his military ambitions against the Shiite Safavids of Iran, who had already been an irritant to his predecessors. By this time, the aging grand vizier Sokollu Mehmed Pasha had only limited influence on the foreign policy of the empire. War with the Safavids entangled the sultan for years, consuming all of his energy and attention.

On October 11, 1579, a supplicant appeared at the house of the more than seventy-year-old grand vizier, as he was receiving afternoon visitors. A French eyewitness saw how the Bosnian visitor, who was dressed as a dervish, suddenly pulled a dagger from his robe and "stabbed Sokollu so forcefully in his chest that he cut through the arteries to his heart."[116] A surgeon who came running could not do anything to help the bleeding victim. The grand vizier passed just as the muezzin's call to prayer sounded from the Hagia Sophia. The assassin, who may have sought revenge for the loss of his timar or because he was a member of a persecuted sect, was publicly drawn and quartered on the streets of Istanbul the next morning.[117]

A fundamental transformation in the production of knowledge, and in comprehending the world, occurred at the beginning of the sixteenth century, as the empire sent famous admirals like Piri Reis and Seydi Ali Reis into Arabia and Asia on journeys of conquest and discovery. These men created important material for maps, along with drawings and reports of their travels, which depicted the new imperial visions in a concrete way. Empirical evidence played a growing role, and religion was no longer the

Observatory on the Galata Tower in Istanbul, Ottoman miniature, sixteenth century. Istanbul University Library.

only measure for explaining the world.[118] The Mediterranean Sea became a central focus of study; its possession was considered one of the keys to world dominion. The Habsburg rulers Charles V and Philip II also promoted cartography as a means of apprehending their territorial acquisitions.[119] Southeastern Europeans, too, caught the fever of discovery—for example, the Croatian shipowner Blas Francisco Conich, who settled in Peru, as well as his countrymen who served as captains in the armada of Philip II. The adventurer Melek Jasa from Ragusa (Dubrovnik) converted to Islam and later worked for the Portuguese in India, and the Greek Constantine Phaulkon became a favored adviser to the King of Siam.[120]

A century of exploration and discovery fed the desire for new geographic knowledge. Before this point, Ottoman scholars had simply repeated information from the Middle Ages that had been passed down by the Arabs. This included translations of ancient thinkers like Aristotle, Hippocrates, Ptolemy, and Galen, as well as astronomical and medical texts from India and Iran. This canon of essential knowledge had been thought to be best left undisturbed by new findings or developments.[121] Now, however, dealers were granted permission to sell Arabic, Persian, and Turkish printed works within the Ottoman Empire, including the Arabic geography book *The Garden of Wonders of the World and Its Peoples,* which was published in Venice in 1585. Works of geography translated from Arabic, portolans with nautical information, and European maps and globes all sold briskly.[122] As Ottoman merchants, sailors, clerics, and diplomats increasingly made their way to Asia, their curiosity about the history, geography, and culture of the Pacific world grew as well. The extensive travelogue of Admiral Seydi Reis, which offered a detailed portrait of the Indian, Iranian, and central Asian royal courts, became an early modern best seller.[123]

But how did the discovery of new continents change perceptions of history and the world as a whole? As the Ottoman Empire approached the height of its power and territorial expansion, there was a desire to document its rapid rise and to place recent history within the broader context of the past thousand years. Government officials, judges, and poets all contributed to an upsurge in historical writing. More people from the lower classes, too, recorded their thoughts on world events.[124] In *The Essence of History,* the polymath Mustafa Ali placed the Ottoman Empire and its rapid expansion in global historical perspective. Underlying his account was a reflection on the conditions of the present, which he sought to explain through the past. Did it not seem as if growing military pressure, economic problems, and inner instability threatened to destroy the divinely sanctioned world order? The historical search for meaning fit the spirit of the era; according to the Muslim calculation of time, the thousandth year was 1590/91, and there were fears that the world might end with the new millennium—which Mustafa Ali, however, refuted.[125]

Within the framework of his world history, Mustafa Ali—who came from Gallipoli himself—created a kind of European ethnology. The Ottomans had long shown no particular interest in individual countries; they did not even have a name for most of them.[126] Mustafa Ali described the people of Rumelia for the first time, and he also reported on the language and ethnography of Albanians, Croats, Hungarians, Vlachs, and other groups. He believed that the Ottoman Empire's cultural diversity represented an advantage over other imperial entities such as Iran or Arabia. The child levy enabled those with physical, moral, and intellectual talents to become members of the elite; the strength and beauty of the Balkan people joined with the intellectual energy and piety of the core Ottoman territories. He sometimes resorted to superficial stereotypes, as when he described the Serbs as competent and pious, or the Croats and Bosnians as courteous, intelligent, and virtuous.[127]

Mustafa Ali also wrote *Public Instructions for the Distances of Countries,* in which Istanbul—not Rome or Jerusalem, as in the West—appeared to be the center of the universe. Thus, Islamic universalism and Ottoman imperialism functioned as sources of a worldview that was typical of the era.[128] Comparatively speaking, however, Mustafa Ali's ideas were ahead of his time—as can be seen in the travelogues of Mehmed Asik, who did not yet have a clear understanding of the cultural or physiographic identity of other regions when he wrote his universal cosmography in 1598. The categories of "self" and "other" were not yet familiar to him. He mostly acknowledged what was already known, as he reported on the strange occurrences and amazing things that he experienced in foreign lands. Opponents of war interested him only as a source of vast quantities of gold and silver coins, pelts, and silks to be plundered, and prisoners to be exploited.[129]

Like most scholars of his day, Mustafa Ali still stood within the intellectual tradition of cosmography. As in the West, Islamic teachings on creation sought to explain all phenomena, both natural and miraculous, from a religious perspective. Cosmography developed out of two different movements that existed parallel to one another in this era, although they were combined in many texts. First, there was Islamic religious tradition, based on the revelation of the Koran, which taught that God had created the world and its inhabitants out of nothing, and also that he possessed the power to destroy them at will. Earth was thought to be a disk, with the vault of heaven arching above it. Angels and demons governed the surrounding cosmos.[130] The second intellectual tradition came from Greek antiquity and was grounded in secular philosophy, natural philosophy, and mathematics. Almost all Aristotelian and Ptolemaic philosophy had been translated into Arabic, becoming part of Islamic civilization. As in the Latin West, this tradition envisioned a finite universe with the Earth at its center, with multiple heavenly spheres arching above it, like the layers of an onion.[131]

Cosmographies usually began by describing the spheres and heavenly bodies, followed by the earthly world with its four elements—fire, air, water, and earth. According to the cosmographies' narrative logic, the world was divided into three parts. At its center was the authors' own, familiar milieu. It was surrounded by foreign lands, beyond which lay an unknown world of fabulous monsters and other creatures. Cosmology associated certain parts of the Earth with heavenly bodies, thereby explaining the variety of human races, geophysical features, plants, and animal species in existence.[132]

An anonymous author, who published a comprehensive work about the discovery of the New World in Istanbul in 1580, also situated his assertions within the context of cosmography. As long as the Ottomans' attentions were focused on Arabia and Asia, self-produced knowledge about the New World on the other side of the Atlantic remained fragmentary. Information about America first appeared on two world maps that Admiral Piri Reis created in 1513 and 1528, drawing on materials from Columbus. He later authored a voluminous *Book of Navigation,* featuring updated information about the New World.[133] Few other sources were available, so the anonymous author set out to fill this gap in Ottoman scholarship by translating excerpts of recent Italian books and maps. His *History of the West Indies* told of the fascinating discoveries made in North and South America since 1492. "Until this moment, no one in this region [the Ottoman Empire] has visited that area [the New World] nor has anyone given any information on its description," he explained.[134]

The anonymous author began by describing the universe as a collection of concentric spheres. The larger spheres covered the smaller ones "like the pages of a book." The lowest layer was the Earth, which was round; anyone who kept walking straight ahead would eventually come back to where he started. The author also recognized the poles and both hemispheres. He described the travels of Christopher Columbus and the invasion of Mexico and Peru, as well as the flora and fauna, and the landscape and people, on the opposite side of the Atlantic. From the standpoint of Istanbul, America lay between the western and eastern oceans. It could be divided into New Spain in the north, and Peru in the south, and it possibly touched the western coast of China—which was also thought to be true in the Christian West. The author advised halting the Iberian states' expansion so that Islam could spread to the New World, which ought not to be left to the infidels. Numerous copies of his book soon circulated widely. Over the next three centuries, it remained the only source of its kind.[135]

Although the Ottomans did not intend to participate in the exploitation of the American continent, they were nevertheless sensitive to its consequences. The massive influx of precious metals from overseas, especially silver, increased inflation, devalued the Ottoman currency, and sent many people into financial ruin. The Ottomans were also introduced to tobacco, corn, and turkey. It would have been difficult to predict how much the discovery of the New World ultimately transformed their natural environment. The typical flora of the Mediterranean region and large parts of southeastern Europe today are the result of exchange with foreign cultures from overseas—eucalyptus from Australia, cypresses from Persia, tomatoes, paprika, corn, and tobacco from America, and cotton from Egypt.[136]

The sixteenth century was a transitional phase characterized by hybrid conceptions of the world. On one hand, sailors, geographers, and historians turned to empirical-rational methods for describing distant lands, preparing maps, and accurately charting the constellations. On the other hand, archaic ideas about the cosmic energy of heavenly bodies and the nature of the universe persisted, as seen in the writings of Mustafa Ali and the anonymous depiction of the discovery of America. This leads to a key point: worldviews were informed by a mixture of religious doctrine and existing knowledge, but also by new experiences and individual reflection. New insights were always embedded within culturally anchored conceptions and prejudices that evolved over time.[137] New discoveries and experiences did encourage residents of the Ottoman Empire to think more closely about unexplored territories and cultures, as well as about their own geographic, political, and intellectual position within the new global framework. Scholars began to interpret the changing relations between continents, peoples, and cultures according to European categories of thought. Conceptions of the Earth and the universe were no longer abstract and imaginary, but took concrete shape as a result of interactions with new continents and cultures. Western / European and Eastern / Islamic worldviews grew much closer together.[138] There was a growing convergence in the religions' understanding of the world, although they still promoted different ideological and interpretative systems. Uniform, spatially concrete conceptions of global relationships began to coalesce.

Archaic Globalization

In the era of European exploration and discovery, the polycentric world economies of the Middle Ages began to grow together, ushering in the first signs of "archaic globalization," a closer networking of continents and seas.[139] At the beginning of the sixteenth century, the Ottomans still controlled the eastern Mediterranean region, the Black Sea, and Arabia, as well as the most important trade routes to India and China. They earned tremendous profits through the trade in pepper and spices, silk and porcelain, and also cotton fabrics. Now, however, the Turks and Arabs lost control over the maritime route to Asia to European competitors, and over numerous ports and outposts along the way.[140] The Europeans simultaneously forged economic ties with North and South America, working to consolidate their control over the new global trade networks between Europe, southeast Asia, India, western Africa, and the Americas. In this pursuit they adopted different strategies—including subduing newly discovered lands with military force and appropriating foreign land, entering into agreements with distant rulers, and enslaving great numbers of people to acquire cheap labor. Trade companies supported complex business dealings and introduced new financial instruments to enable the transfer of capital and goods across great distances. South American empires were plundered for gold and silver, in order to finance wars in Europe and to penetrate Asian markets. Precious metals became the currency of international monetary transactions.[141]

The background of these developments was the escalating competition between Europe's absolute monarchies in the late sixteenth century. It was driven by mercantilism, which taught that states had to create favorable conditions for industry and trade. Since a country's prosperity depended substantially on its surplus of trade, raw materials had to be imported cheaply and processed within the country so that the finished products could then be exported at high prices. The state was supposed to promote domestic industries and protect them from foreign competition. Stable state institutions and a favorable climate for business, innovations in waging war, and more effective military organization gave the Europeans additional advantages compared to other regions of the world, but also led to military conflicts between the trading powers over raw materials and markets.[142]

Around 1600 the archaic world economy's center of gravity shifted to the Atlantic, where a transcontinental, triangular trade pattern emerged. Trade companies, merchants, shipowners, and captains sold textiles, metal goods, weapons, and other European products to the western coast of Africa. From here, they shipped slaves to the plantations of Brazil, the Caribbean, and North America. The merchants then transported sugar, tobacco, cotton, and other goods back to Europe. A large proportion of trade in England, France, and Holland no longer depended on Europe, but rather on overseas colonies. The new division of labor based on slavery enabled immense profits and encouraged large-scale investments in business. Commercial capital laid the foundations for the later Industrial Revolution in Great Britain, although it is still debated whether this revolution could have occurred at all—or perhaps only later or more gradually—without slave labor. In any case, colonialism fundamentally transformed economic structures and ways of life in northwestern Europe.[143]

The Netherlands and England became the center of a global economy, while northern Italy, the Iberian states, south-central Germany, and the Baltic and North Sea region lost some of their economic importance. Antwerp, Amsterdam, and later London became the powerhouses of this new world economy that stretched from China to Peru; they replaced older trade capitals like Venice, Genoa, Florence, Augsburg, and Lübeck.[144] In the new global context, the Flemish-Hanseatic trade network established closer ties to the Mediterranean region. Additional relationships developed with Poland and territories east of the Elbe River, where northwestern Europeans could obtain agricultural surpluses, particularly grain.[145]

These processes gave shape to the early modern world economy, with defining features that are still present today: a global market, an interregional division of labor and relationships of exchange between differently developed economic areas, and, not least, competition for hegemony within the new system.[146] The polycentric medieval "world economy" developed into a unipolar global trade system that was dominated by Europeans, paving the way for the "great divergence" of the late eighteenth century.[147]

Alongside the world trade system, western European merchant capitalism expanded from the Atlantic into much of the rest of the world in the following three centuries. The new trade companies were largely able to build on the established commercial relationships of earlier eras, reorganizing them to bring in ever greater profits. A race to economically integrate and exploit additional territories outside of Europe commenced at the same time. The Dutch established a colonial empire in southeast Asia in the seventeenth century; the French and English competed for influence in North America and Africa. In 1500, the European powers controlled about 7 percent of the world's territory; by 1775, they controlled 35 percent.[148] The volume of goods exchanged between Africa, Asia, and America was initially small, limited to precious metals and luxury goods like silk, porcelain, coffee, tea, spices, and opium, but as time progressed, large quantities of everyday goods were traded as well. Capitalism and its main elements—competition, pursuit of profit, dynamic expansion, and willingness to assume risk—came into their own in this era at an astounding speed.[149]

The emergence of a global economy dominated by Europeans, and the reorientation of world trade toward the Atlantic, did not initially present the Ottoman Empire with any visible disadvantages. It continued to build its own "world economy"—a geographically limited, autonomous market that supported itself through complex relationships of exchange between various internal subcenters and external peripheries. The empire profited from its immense territorial expanse and from large surpluses in the production of cattle, wheat, leather, and even textiles. In addition, it possessed numerous industries and trades and transcontinental routes of long-distance trade. The transport of goods was tightly organized and closely supervised, contributing significantly to the strength of the Ottoman economy.[150] Relations between the metropolises of Izmir, Aleppo, and Thessaloniki and their hinterlands were economically more significant for the empire than transcontinental commerce. These internal relationships were barely affected by Western colonial trade.[151]

In this era, the Ottoman Empire experienced a phase of unprecedented prosperity. The lucrative Mediterranean and Red Sea trade in spices,

Trader from Dubrovnik, around 1700.

medicinal herbs, dyes, Indian cloth, opium, and coffee continued to thrive despite—and alongside—growing Portuguese competition. Southeastern Europe profited from this trade. Pepper, ginger, and other spices made their way to Wallachia, Transylvania, Hungary, and even Vienna. Goods were transported along traditional routes in the Levant, through the Crimean port of Caffa, and over land via Belgrade. Caravans carried Chinese and Indian wares through the Balkans, along centuries-old transport routes between Asia and Europe. From Istanbul, their cargo continued its journey to the Mediterranean ports.[152] In addition to land routes, the Ottomans still controlled the Black Sea, along with the Bosporus, Dardanelles, and the mouth of the Danube, providing them with access to grain from Moldavia, Wallachia, and Crimea. Trade thrived all around the Black Sea, as substantial quantities of goods were transported back and forth between Caffa, Akkerman, Kilya, Trebizond, Sinop, Istanbul, and the smaller port cities, and then shipped to the Mediterranean. Alternatively, goods traveled along the Danube, Dniester, and Don Rivers, or by caravan into the Ottoman interior.[153]

Southeastern Europe profited from the larger and more uniform economic area that came from its integration within the Ottoman Empire. Rumelia and the Aegean provided foodstuffs and raw materials for the Ottoman market, particularly the imperial capital of Istanbul. No longer hindered by the economic barriers associated with many small kingdoms, Dubrovnik's merchants extended their reach far into the territory surrounding the Black Sea and the interior of the Ottoman Empire. They were protected by the sultan and allowed to trade freely within the empire in return for an annual tribute. At the height of the economic boom in the sixteenth century, the total value of goods handled by the city-state each year ranged between 400,000 and 500,000 gold ducats. It possessed one of the largest trading fleets in the world.[154]

In the sixteenth century, the Ottoman Empire still seemed immune to the rise of northwestern Europe, although the beginnings of an interregional division of labor that became significant in later centuries were already apparent. Muslim, Armenian, Greek, and Jewish merchants exported mostly agricultural products and raw materials—especially grain, silk, and cotton—to Europe, while introducing European manufactured goods into the Ottoman Empire. From France, England, Venice, and the Netherlands, for example, they imported woolen clothing, metal goods, and weapons.[155]

The slave trade, which was subject to duties and taxes imposed by the sultan, continued to be a lucrative source of income for the Ottoman state. It consisted of two branches: the import of white slaves from the Caucasus across the Black Sea, and of black slaves from Africa across the Mediterranean. The Muslim Tatars acquired people by "harvesting the steppes"— abducting men, women, and children from Russia, Ukraine, and Poland and selling them in the Ottoman Empire. In the sixteenth century, 29 percent of Ottoman tax revenues in the Crimean ports came from the slave trade. A slave cost between twenty and forty gold pieces, which was about the cost of living for an adult for two to three years.[156] Italian traders who brought slaves from the Black Sea into Egypt and the Levant profited handsomely. Between 1500 and 1650, about ten thousand people were trafficked annually across the Black Sea.[157] However, the mass of slaves came from sub-Saharan Africa, Ethiopia, and Sudan. They were brought by caravan to the northern African port cities, and from there were shipped to the Ottoman Empire via Crete and Ioannina. They were sold at large slave markets, particularly in Istanbul, to European traders who brought the men, women, and children to Europe. The traders also sold imprisoned Christians to Spain, northern Africa, and Egypt.[158]

The expansion in trade called for new diplomatic and legal arrangements. The Ottoman Empire regulated its political and economic relations through the agreements between states known as capitulations (ahdname). In the fourteenth century, Genoa and Venice were the first to receive the right to trade and sail within the waters of the empire. In the sixteenth century, France—and then England, Holland, the Habsburg Empire, Prussia, Russia, and Spain—could grant their merchants trade licenses, which gave them freedom of travel, diplomatic immunity, and favorable terms of customs. In addition, these merchants were allowed to hire Ottoman subjects as interpreters and protégés, who in turn enjoyed the same privileges.[159] The former Islamic taboo against signing treaties with "infidels" was circumvented by declaring the treaty partners to be subjects worthy of protection. The Ottoman Empire guaranteed Christian powers and trade groups corresponding legal status, and Christian powers entered into agreements with Muslim rulers to establish trading posts in Asia and elsewhere. Foreign consulates thus acted at the juncture of trade, diplomacy, politics, and espionage.[160]

As Ottoman, Venetian, and western European trading ships competed for influence in the Mediterranean, and interactions between Muslim, Greek Orthodox, and Catholic sailors increased, there was likewise a growing need to regulate sea travel and particularly the handling of crews. The Bosnian grand vizier Sokollu Mehmed had a strong interest in formalizing the status of English and Dutch traders, who had become active in the Levant after the turn of the sixteenth century.[161] People were no longer seen as individual adherents of other religions, but rather as subjects of foreign empires. People now "belonged" to their state, which protected their interests and conducted relations with other states.[162]

The dynamism of trade in and around the Mediterranean, in addition to economic connections with the Atlantic world, brought the cities and regions of southeastern Europe many advantages in the fifteenth and sixteenth centuries. Merchants not only from Dubrovnik but also from Bosnia and Albania—where salt, animal hides, wool, wax, and grain were produced—profited from the growing trade between Italy, Europe, and the

Ottoman Empire. Sarajevo, which was once a small town, boomed spectacularly in the sixteenth century because it was the end of the caravan road that led from Bursa, Istanbul, and Edirne toward the Adriatic Sea. An extensive merchant infrastructure—including numerous caravansaries, hostels, storehouses, and cloth halls—arose in the city of forty thousand inhabitants. Foča and Novi Pazar, market towns on the same route, also flourished. Bosnian traders became Dubrovnik's fiercest competition, after Venice built up the Adriatic city of Split (Spalato) as a central hub of Balkan commerce in the Mediterranean, opening up new trade routes.[163] The Venetian Nicolò Contarini described how suddenly "there began to arrive in Venice from Spalato . . . silks, spices of various sorts, carpets, wax, wool, hides, camlets [*ciambelolotti*], cottonstuffs, and all the things that are produced or made for men's use by the lands of the East."[164] In addition to Split, Dubrovnik, and the Mediterranean port cities, towns on the caravan roads also prospered from the cattle, grain, wax, honey, wool, hides, and pelts from Transylvania, Bosnia, Thrace, and Macedonia that were transported to the fairs and Mediterranean ports. The Danube ports of Brăila, Smederevo, Vidin, Nicopolis, and Ruse, as well as the Carpathian city of Brașov (Kronstadt), emerged as central points of exchange for goods from the entire Black Sea region, Hungary, and Poland. Powerful price increases in sixteenth-century Europe further enhanced agricultural exports' potential for profit.[165] A large part of the trade to Italy, Austria, and the Mediterranean was conducted through Croatia and Slovenia. Even when the Turks conquered parts of these lands, trade relations were not initially disrupted.[166] Between 1450 and 1650, all southeastern Europe experienced a continuous increase in prosperity that was evident through population growth, expansion of trade, and the flourishing of industry and skilled trades.

Long-distance and transit trade were lucrative for merchants and moneylenders, and for anyone who earned a living through the transport of goods—including shipowners and sailors, as well as camel and donkey drivers. New opportunities arose for specialized groups such as Greek, Armenian, and Jewish merchants and their networks. Since traders wanted to take their wares where they could get the best price, they needed information. The Cretan Theodoro Taulari sailed with his olive oil and honey to Chios in 1687, so he could find out where profits were greatest. The island was a favored site of trade and a first-rate location to hear the latest news.[167] In the sixteenth century, crossing the Mediterranean from north to south took an average of one to two weeks; an east–west passage took two to three months.[168]

Piracy became a great disruptor of maritime trade at the end of the fifteenth century. Corsairs from Spain, Sicily, Sardinia, and Corsica, who sailed under the flag of Christian lands—like Muslim pirates from the Barbary states of Tripoli, Tunis, and Algiers—lived from raiding coastal regions and ships at sea in search of plunder. They not infrequently served one of the great empires. State authorities tolerated or even expressly permitted the pirates' operations by issuing letters of marque. Prisoners who were taken during raids were forced to row on galleys from the pirates' homelands or were sold as slaves. Captains from France and Venice assembled their crews from slaves whom they purchased at the markets of Livorno, Messina, Malta, and Crete; many came from the Balkans. "Slavs and Greeks," wrote Cristoforo Canale in his ship manual from the mid-sixteenth century, "are outstandingly suited for work at the oars; they seem to be naturally created for all labors on board."[169]

In the Adriatic coastal areas, the Uskoks also fomented unrest. They were refugees of various ethnic backgrounds who had fled from the Ottoman Empire to Habsburg and Venetian lands around 1530. From their stronghold at Senj, they officially served as protectors of the Christian powers at sea, but they also raided Ottoman territory and seized all manners of trading ships. These pirates threatened the security of the entire Croatian coast, and Venice attempted to subdue them repeatedly, with little success. They were brought under control only in the seventeenth century, when Austria resettled them as peasant soldiers in the area of the military frontier.[170]

After a phase of impressive economic prosperity, around 1650 world economic conditions changed dramatically for the Ottoman Empire in general and for the Balkan lands in particular. First, transatlantic trade had begun to outstrip the exchange of goods within Europe and around the Mediterranean Sea. The quantity of items sold decreased so that shippers, carriers, and producers all suffered losses. Traditional trade routes and cities went into decline as merchants opted to use the new sea routes instead. Second, the volume of trade decreased, as new crops from the overseas colonies, particularly corn and potatoes, lowered demand for grain imports to Europe. European traders shipped more finished goods like clothing overseas, instead of to eastern and southeastern Europe. The new international division of labor meant that trade with and through southeastern

Europe became less significant compared to the booming markets and sites of production in the New World. And third, agricultural prices sank alongside the volume of trade all across Europe in the second half of the seventeenth century, because increases in productivity stoked a crisis of overproduction in wheat. Grain and cattle prices fell faster than the prices of textiles and finished goods, so the terms of trade worsened for southeastern European producers. They had to export their commodities cheaply, while paying higher prices to import the foreign goods that they needed. Long before the Industrial Revolution, regions dependent on the export of agricultural produce and raw materials suffered under disadvantageous structural and developmental conditions.[171]

The economic downturn of the seventeenth century prompted very different reactions within Europe. On the western side of the continent, it reinforced mercantilism and an emphasis on commercial production. In the east and southeast, it led to systemic changes in the organization of labor and agriculture. To compensate for the loss of income from the shrinking export trade in agricultural produce and cattle, landlords increased rents and services for peasants. This helped to boost production and to reduce its costs through cheap labor, enabling a greater margin of profit. Peasants were compelled to invest more of their time in involuntary, unpaid labor, especially hauling and transporting commercial goods. These changes affected peasants in Croatia and Slavonia, just as in Hungary, Wallachia, and Moldavia.[172] Thus, world market forces of the early capitalist era created a "second serfdom," as peasants lost their freedom of movement, faced greater rents and services, and became personally dependent on landlords.[173]

Growing concentration in land ownership could be observed throughout eastern and southeastern Europe. From Livonia and Poland to Bohemia, Hungary, Romania, and Croatia, ever greater shares of farmland shifted away from peasants and into the hands of estate owners and landlords.[174] There were particular consequences in the Danubian Principalities, where the noble boyars claimed ever greater rights at the peasants' expense. Expropriation heightened the concentration of landownership and bound peasants to the soil, dramatically worsening social conditions. While there were still free peasants in the eighteenth century, serfdom spread widely. Landlords and peasants no longer produced for themselves or the local market, but became part of a supraregional division of labor that was oriented toward maximizing profits. Grain was the most important export of the Romanian lands, which—like much of eastern Europe—became an economic periphery that relied on monocultural production. To compensate for falling prices, more land was farmed.[175]

The painful effects of the worldwide economic downturn were likewise apparent in the core territories of the Ottoman Empire. The seventeenth-century influx of American gold and silver debased the coinage and led to inflation, and growing financial needs contributed to a massive budget deficit. Economic productivity remained low, although state expenditures for new military ventures grew exponentially. The loss of territories in the Ottoman wars had additional economic consequences, since former recipients of benefices expected compensation for giving up their land. To stave off financial crisis, the sultan raised taxes again and again, and ultimately introduced a new system of lifelong tax farming *(malikane),* whereby the authority to collect taxes was auctioned to the highest bidder.[176] Meanwhile, the Ottomans' long-distance trade with Asia had also fallen apart, since nearly all spices were now shipped by sea to Antwerp and London. Even Istanbul acquired its spices this way.[177]

For all these reasons, the Ottoman timar system that had evolved over centuries now found itself in crisis. Available land grew scarce, and it had to be divided among a growing number of supplicants. Many parcels were too small to remain profitable. As in many parts of eastern Europe, landlords sought full legal possession of their benefices. In many parts of Albania, Bosnia, Serbia, Bulgaria, Thessaly, and Macedonia, a new form of private estate with dependent peasants began to produce for the commercial market. These estates first appeared in the sixteenth century and became more widespread in the centuries thereafter. Timars that had once been granted at the sultan's discretion became inheritable property. If the term "çiftlik" initially described a small parcel of farmland that could be worked with a team of oxen, it now referred to entire estates (with their dependent villages) that produced for the commercial market. Village traditions of self-government broke down, as landowners pressed the rural population into serf-like conditions with minimal income. As common lands were usurped and brought under cultivation within larger estates, many residents lost their means of existence. They often had to serve three masters—the landowner, the tax farmer, and the Ottoman civil servant, all of whom continuously invented new duties to be paid. Many impoverished peasants fled the land altogether.[178] The rural population suffered from periodic famines that were exacerbated by rising prices, an overall shortage of food, and a growing tax burden. Peasant uprisings broke out repeatedly in Romania, Croatia, Bosnia, Albania, and Serbia.[179]

In contrast to the West, an early capitalist economic system did not develop in the Ottoman Empire in this era, due to both internal and external factors. Traders had to cover long and dangerous routes, so they invested less and drew smaller profits from their business than their European competitors. The financial and banking system was underdeveloped. Merchants were subject to the whims of state authorities, who raised taxes and duties at will. The insatiable state treasury of the sultan skimmed off a significant portion of their profits. Although there was a very wealthy trading class, powerful merchant dynasties comparable to the Medici or Fugger families did not develop, nor did any great trading companies that could keep pace with their Dutch and English counterparts.[180]

One on hand, the despotic power of the sultan made it possible to steer the economy with tributes and taxes and to exploit the peripheries for the benefit of the center. On the other hand, all this required an elaborate bureaucracy and military force, which were expensive to maintain and overwhelmed the state's finances. Peasants, traders, and businessmen had little incentive to earn more, as long as the state could skim off their profits at will. Taxes and tributes increased constantly, and then there was the loss of population from war, famine, and migration.[181]

In summary: after 1500, the great empires not only claimed universal sovereignty, but to some extent (and with different geographic accents), they actually exercised it. Exploration and colonialism led, on one hand, to a fundamental reconfiguration of power and the economy, and on the other, to new global constellations. The empires' enormous territorial expansion across the globe correlated with growing central control over economic resources and long-distance trade, and thus with the emergence of early modern statecraft. New nautical and military technologies—and economic innovations such as trade companies, trade monopolies, factories, and plantations—became instruments of the global projection of power. At the same time, innovations in diplomacy and early forms of international law were introduced within the zones of contact and conflict between empires, offering new means of creating order and legitimacy in a world that was increasingly difficult to comprehend.

If the Ottoman Empire and southeastern Europe did not yet experience economic disadvantages in the first 150 years after Europeans began exploring the globe, this situation changed after the mid-seventeenth century. Structural asymmetries deepened, as did the division of roles between centers and peripheries in a European-dominated world economy, and between capitalist industrial regions and "feudal" agricultural regions. As the rise of home industry and proto-industrialization in the eighteenth century ushered in the transition to mass production, Ottoman and southeastern European spinning and weaving mills faced growing competition. Cheap textiles from western Europe and India flooded the Ottoman market. Key factors that determined developmental opportunities and disadvantages were set in this era.

Istanbul, 1683

In March 1683, Sultan Mehmed IV set off on a great campaign toward Vienna. The Protestant Kurucs in Royal Hungary, who had revolted against Habsburg absolutist rule, provided the immediate motivation for attack. After years of war against Austria, their leader Imre Thököly appealed to the sultan for help. Mehmed IV recognized a favorable opportunity to reach for the "golden apple" one more time, hoping at last to conquer the remainder of Hungary, and then Austria.

Ottoman messengers rushed to the most distant corners of the empire, summoning cavalry from the provinces. With units from the Balkans, Anatolia, and Egypt, as well as from the Tatars, the army and its followers grew to 250,000 men under the command of Grand Vizier Kara Mustafa. All this demanded sophisticated logistical coordination. Streets and bridges had to be put in order before the troops' arrival, and march times calculated precisely. An enormous army, plus herds of sheep and cattle, needed to be fed. Albert Caprara, an Austrian envoy who accompanied the campaign, estimated that thirty-two thousand pounds of meat and sixty thousand loaves of bread were consumed each day. Some of the military equipment and provisions were shipped by boat along the Danube.[182]

The Ottoman forces provided a fearsome but colorful spectacle. The main army, which marched behind the advance guard and the janissaries, was composed of three columns—the cavalry from Anatolia was on the right, European cavalry on the left, and infantry and artillery in the middle. Every regiment had its own colorful uniforms and special weapons; some of the decorations and costumes were highly elaborate.

Supply units came next, and finally the rear guard. A military band accompanied by drummers performed "janissary music" during attacks.[183]

As he approached Vienna on July 14, 1683, Kara Mustafa dictated a summons for the city to surrender: "Accept Islam, and live in peace under the Sultan! Or deliver up the fortress, and live in peace under the Sultan as Christians; and if any man prefer, let him depart peaceably, taking his goods with him! But if you resist, then death or spoliation or slavery shall be the fate of you all!"[184] Wanting to avoid war, the Habsburgs had long ignored the impending danger. Emperor Leopold I and many residents fled only just before the Ottoman army marched on Vienna. Only eleven thousand soldiers and a citizen militia of five thousand men remained behind in the city, which was strongly fortified with trenches, ramparts, and bastions. Kara Mustafa applied every tactic in the Ottomans' military palette in order to take the city. The artillery began a ferocious bombardment, and miners dug tunnels and blasted gaps in the city walls. The besieging army kept up the assault. "From the artillery and guns of the army of Islam, such fire was unleashed upon the enemy of our faith that the earth and the vault of heaven reverberated with the sound," the Ottoman master of ceremonies recorded in his diary of the campaign. "The enemies, with their shattered nerves, had no chance to take any initiative.[185]

The encircled Viennese withstood the attacks for two months, until the Polish king Jan III Sobieski arrived with his Bavarian, Saxon, Austrian, and Polish relief army. The grand vizier received the message "that the godless giaours were attacking the fighting bands of Islam like pigs gone wild." At Kahlenberg, they dealt the Ottoman troops a crushing defeat. "Ammunition from the artillery and guns of the enemy poured down upon the army of Islam like rain," the campaign diary stated. "The Muslims recognized that all was lost. . . . Most fled to their tents straightaway and thought only of saving their lives and possessions." Kara Mustafa also took flight. That same year, he was strangled to death as punishment for his armies' loss. "It was a defeat and a catastrophe unlike any the empire had ever suffered!"[186]

Hundreds of miles away, the people of Istanbul gradually realized that the defeat near Vienna represented a turning point. With 700,000–800,000 residents, the Ottoman capital was the most important Eastern metropolis of the seventeenth century. The center of the Islamic world united a surfeit of power with artful sophistication, religious piety with reverence for learning. Covered bazaars, hostels, and caravansaries all contributed to the character of the city, as did magnificent complexes of buildings (including mosques, madrasas, libraries, kitchens, and baths) that were built by charitable foundations.[187] Although the Ottoman Empire did not have the same kinds of municipal statutes, privileges, and institutions as in Europe, a specific urban identity did exist. It drew on the capital's grandeur and prosperity, its unique position at the intersection of two continents and seas, and its extraordinary diversity of different peoples, languages, religions, and cultures.[188]

All kinds of people mixed in Istanbul—including Arabs, Greeks, Slavs, Vlachs, and gypsies, and a substantial "Frankish" colony of traders and diplomats from the western European lands. All lived side by side, without blending together. There were flashes of east-west cosmopolitanism, like the "Marchand Franc," with his unusual blend of Ottoman-European dress.[189] The most commonly used language in the city was Turkish, but on the streets one heard Greek, Slavic, Armenian, Ladino, Persian, Arabic, and countless other dialects. Christians and Jews were not allowed to ride on horseback within the city walls. On sidewalks they were expected to step aside whenever a Muslim approached. Their head coverings and clothing indicated their religious affiliation.[190] Nevertheless, as the seat of the chief rabbinate, and of the Greek and Armenian patriarchates, Istanbul was still an important cultural center for the non-Turkish population, too.[191]

Istanbul was divided into four administrative districts. The first of these was the city center, which was enclosed by the Theodosian Walls, on the peninsula between the Golden Horn and the Marmara Sea. The districts in the greater Istanbul area encompassed the suburbs of Eyüp, Üsküdar, and Galata and the surrounding Bosporus villages.[192] Even at this time, Istanbul was too large to traverse by foot. Only the upper class owned horses and carriages. Most people walked within the city, or else they boarded one of the many barges to the suburbs.

As the administrative, military, religious, and economic center of an enormous empire, Istanbul employed a large number of court officials, judges, soldiers, and civil servants. The administrative and military elite, the sultan's entourage, was recruited in part from well-established families, and in part from the ranks of former slaves and civil servants from the provinces. The urban elite resided in the best neighborhoods, in palaces and well-appointed villas with gardens.[193] The majority of the population, by contrast, was concentrated within local communities, or *mahalles*. Women and children spent most of their lives here. Business districts with their hostels, covered markets, workshops, and other businesses formed the broader public sphere, which was reserved for men.[194]

Trade was overwhelmingly dominated by Greeks, Jews, and Armenians, although state authorities oversaw the markets and set prices. Ensuring adequate provisions for such a large city was a daily challenge. This task was important enough that the grand vizier visited the bazaar each week to monitor the price and quality of bread.[195] The supply of drinking water was precarious, although the city maintained numerous wells and even long-distance water conduits. Hundreds of uniformed carriers dragged heavy hoses made from goat or ox leather into neighborhoods, offering cups of water to passersby. There were about 220 public baths where one could participate in ritual cleansings, meet other people, or find young male prostitutes.[196]

Large quantities of food, particularly grain, had to be imported from distant provinces all the time. Shepherds drove enormous herds from the Balkans into the city. Overland transport flourished, but most provisions arrived by sea; a large portion of imported foodstuffs came from the Black Sea region. Woven fabrics came from Europe, grain and tobacco from the Balkans, sugar, spices, and rice from Egypt, currants and figs from Izmir, carpets from the Caucasus, and pearls and dyes from India. "The port is the most beautiful and secure port I have ever seen," a French traveler reported. "It is so deep that however large the ships, they may present their prow to the shore." Garbage thrown carelessly into the sea by the city's inhabitants collected here as well. Only the tides brought occasional relief.[197]

From the port, it was a short distance to the great covered bazaar in the center of the city and to the thousands of shops that stretched along the waterfront. Weapons and luxury goods were sold in the Bedestan, a massive cloth hall; money and valuable documents were held in its safes.[198] Half of the capital's male residents were traders or craftsmen, organized in guilds according to their fields of specialty. Most guilds were segregated by religion, but some brought together members of different faiths. Each of the approximately 140 organizations had its own statute and elected a governing board that represented its interests.[199]

The sultan once ordered that all of the trades be mustered for a three-day procession. After the court officials, the parade was led by members of low-status professions such as the collectors of dog feces and gravediggers. Then came the group of security forces, janissaries, and hangmen, as well as the pickpockets, pimps, and male prostitutes. The scholarly professions formed a block: imams, judges, *mollas,* interpreters of the Koran, reciters, booksellers, public storytellers, astrologers, and students of religion, followed by doctors and surgeons. Finally, all of the other professions, along with their carts: bakers of bread, filo pastry, sesame rings, and zwieback, followed by butchers, meat cutters, and cattle breeders, *boza* brewers and cheesemakers, saddlers, shoemakers, blacksmiths, and all the rest of the trades marched by, including the (ill-smelling) Armenian sewage workers, and at the very end of the procession, Jewish barkeepers. On this day, however, they carried only sugar water instead of wine.[200]

Istanbul was a central point of exchange for news from all over the world. All the information that Ottoman diplomats and spies systematically collected in Vienna, Paris, and Moscow—and later Saint Petersburg—and Iran came together here. Janissary spies kept their ears open at marketplaces and bazaars, in coffeehouses and taverns, so they could compose reports for the grand vizier. Provincial authorities and vassal states like Dubrovnik also provided sensitive information.[201] Envoys to the sultan's court from Venice, France, and Holland, and later envoys from the Habsburgs, were another important source.[202]

Beyond these official channels, information and knowledge were primarily disseminated through informal channels in the seventeenth century. In upper-class circles, established forms of sociability provided regular opportunities for the exchange of ideas between natives and foreigners across cultural and linguistic divides. Politicians, state officials, and scholars in Istanbul, London, and Paris maintained personal contacts with one another; they collected information and brought news to their homelands. In the 1680s, for example, the British envoy William Trumbull mingled with Greek-, Turkish-, and Arabic-speaking merchants, state officials, clerics, and scholars. Gifts such as sought-after salves, balms, and oils, or free treatment by his personal doctor, opened the door to Ottoman officeholders, whom Turnbull met in public audiences or one-on-one, inviting them to embassy dinners and other festivities. Technical devices including clocks, telescopes, and barometers were likewise welcome presents.[203]

Procession of the guilds in Istanbul in 1720, Surname-i Vehbi, eighteenth century. Topkapi Palace Museum, Istanbul.

Communication across borders was also facilitated by the regular postal and courier service that had connected Istanbul with Venice, France, and England since the sixteenth century. Letters, consular reports, books, gazettes, and newsletters all reached the capital city in this way. Depending on the weather and current affairs, mailing a letter from Venice to Istanbul could take between fifteen and eighty-one days.[204] Spectacular news traveled faster; reports of the Battle of Lepanto, which occurred on October 7, 1571, reached Venice on October 18, and Paris on October 31.[205]

Religious and legal scholars, merchants, preachers, dervishes, Orthodox priests, doctors, and naturalists communicated with foreign colleagues and brought news and information from Europe and the Arab world into the Ottoman Empire, and vice versa.[206] The English merchant and geodesist Dudley North, the Italian botanist Count Luigi Ferdinando Marsigli, and the French Arabist Antoine Galland were all active in cosmopolitan scholarly circles. Galland was a particularly eager collector of books, maps, and manuscripts, which he acquired from traders and colleagues in exchange for Western literature.[207]

But even people who did not occupy this elite stratum acquired firsthand information from afar, especially at the port, where ships from the entire Mediterranean and Black Sea regions moored. News about droughts and failed harvests, wars, and other upheavals spread quickly. Servants, translators, and workers at the embassies in Istanbul picked up interesting news at work, relaying it to friends and family. Rumors accompanied migrants, travelers, preachers, priests, mercenaries, soldiers, prisoners of war, slaves, and appellants from the provinces to the city.[208]

Travelers carried information away from the capital, too, passing it along from person to person into the empire's farthest corners. People waited impatiently for news at markets, fountains, churches, mosques, and inns.[209] Of course, the nature of personal contacts meant that this information was obtained in a haphazard way. Encounters tended to be coincidental and sporadic. With a dearth of reliable sources, even the most outrageous story could attain the status of incontrovertible truth.

The official interpreters known as dragomans played a central role as mediators of information, ideas, and worldviews between East and West. Many European converts from Poland, Austria, or Hungary, as well as native Greeks and other minorities within the empire, served as interpreters and translators for the Ottoman government. Many of the dragomans were actually poets, theologians, or scientists. As "transimperial subjects," they were at home in many cultures; their own knowledge informed their work. They were translators not only in the technical sense; they also rendered content and ideas into local idioms and served as mediators of knowledge.[210] The dragomans' abilities "determine the success of every mission," a Venetian envoy confirmed. "A consul can make a supreme effort to present impeccable arguments in the negotiations with the Ottomans. But his labor is futile unless a dragoman interprets it convincingly and skilfully."[211]

The most important and influential dragomans came from the city district of Phanar (Fener), where the Orthodox, mostly Greek, population was concentrated. The Phanariots, descendants of old Byzantine noble families, had acquired wealth and political influence through trade. As new foreign policy challenges arose with the ascendance of Russia and the Habsburg Empire in the last third of the seventeenth century, they frequently assumed important positions within the state bureaucracy as court interpreters and diplomats. They were often well educated in the Western diplomatic languages of Italian and French, which were less familiar to Muslim scholars. The Phanariots were closely linked with the Orthodox patriarchate, which was likewise located in the Greek part of the city. The Patriarchal Academy trained new priests from all over southeastern Europe. It also became a central pipeline for the Ottoman bureaucracy. Many Phanariots held church and state offices at the same time. Thus, Istanbul was the most important cultural center of all Orthodoxy.[212]

Kara Mustafa was accompanied by a Phanariot—the sultan's head interpreter, Alexander Mavrokordatos—on his campaign to Vienna in 1683. Alexander had studied medicine in Padua, and then he became the physician of the grand vizier and taught at the Patriarchal Academy. He was later sent on diplomatic missions to Austria and other locations. Held partially responsible for the Ottomans' defeat, he was thrown in prison for two years and released only after paying a large sum of money. He resumed his travels with the sultan, and in 1699 he led the negotiations for peace at Karlowitz.[213] At the beginning of the eighteenth century, the sultans installed Phanariots as princes *(hospodars)* in the Danubian Principalities because they were more loyal than the Romanian boyars. The first Phanariot *hospodar* of Moldavia was Nicholas Mavrokordatos, the son of Alexander. Other descendants of the influential family subsequently assumed the thrones of Moldavia and Wallachia, although not always to the advantage of those who lived there. For more than a century, Greek families from Istanbul determined the fate of the two Romanian lands.[214]

Istanbul was an outstanding center of the arts and sciences—calligraphy, poetry, logic, medicine, religion, spirituality, and law. The metropolis drew artists, writers, and scholars from all corners of the empire, and the most important Ottoman libraries were located here.[215] The ruling family and others systematically collected books from all over the world; the shelves of private scholars might hold as many as seven thousand volumes. Foreign literature and maps could be acquired in bookstores or purchased or traded from merchants, consuls, priests, monks, and scholars.[216] The French Orientalist Antoine Galland admired the importance of books in Ottoman cultural life—a rich source of erudition.[217]

The center of artistic and intellectual life was the sultan's palace. Sultan Mehmed IV, who attacked Vienna, was in fact less interested in the art of war than in music and painting. He was also a patron of the sciences. He summoned geographers and historians to his court, and he commissioned the production of maps and medical reference works on the basis of Western sources.[218] Just to be safe, he continued the old tradition of employing a court astrologer, whose tabulations supposedly provided exact predictions for each day and year. The sultans also sought the advice of fortune-tellers. Horoscopes, oracles, dream interpretation, and prophecies informed the predictions that were made before important battles and other life events. If predictions were bad, one hoped that prayers, talismans, and magic might offer a measure of protection.[219]

As in Christian Europe, theology continued to provide an essential explanation of the world that prevailed over all else. Worldly authority and spiritual authority complemented one another. Islam was the state religion, and Istanbul one of its important intellectual centers. Allah was the undisputed, wise, and all-powerful creator who guided the passage of time, shaping the past and future alike. The rule of the sultan was thought to be the pillar of a divinely sanctioned order. Religious scholars, the class of ulema, held a position of great influence. It was their responsibility to interpret the Koran, formulating dogmas and rules of behavior for Muslims, and—within certain limits—to interpret the world in its entirety. Islam did not draw a distinction between law and faith, since the entire world order was subject to God's will. Thus, religious scholars were not only clerics but also legal authorities. They belonged to a privileged class that was exempt from taxes, and they were allowed to bequeath their profession to future generations. The highest-ranking legal and religious scholar was the *molla*.[220]

The Muslims' holy book shaped their ideas about the history of the world. The Koran depicted the world's divine creation and its subsequent development. As in the West, Islamic historians told world history exclusively as the history of salvation. Therefore, history was subordinate to theology. The classical narrative began with Adam and led directly to the Ottoman Empire. Prophets and revelations were the central focus, from Adam through Abraham, Moses, and Jesus, and finally Mohammed. After a summary of the various Islamic dynasties, one came to the most magnificent, fairest, and wealthiest of all the sultanates—namely, the Ottomans, who had fought tirelessly against the infidels and received God's sanction. Other forms of history writing, however, sought to entertain as well as instruct, by combining cultural-historical and religious narratives.[221]

Scholarly culture had continued to evolve after the sixteenth-century voyages of discovery, and empirical observation assumed greater significance. This became evident, for example, in the writing of history. New discoveries in geography and astronomy meant that the Ottoman Empire could no longer be described without reservation as the center of the universe, or as the endpoint of historical development. The linear telling of history gave way to a comparative narrative of progress that was arranged in stages. Other lands, empires, and historical actors became subjects of interest, and the Ottoman Empire lost its privileged position as a "chosen state" in the writing of world history. The writer Hüseyin Hezarfenn, known as a man of many talents, served as Mehmed's court historian and also belonged to his inner circle of favorites and trusted advisers. He struck a new tone with his detailed analysis of the events of 1683. More than seventy years old, he may have personally experienced the siege of Vienna. He blamed the unlucky grand vizier Kara Mustafa for the Ottomans' defeat, pointing to his greed, overconfidence, unwillingness to heed advice, and insufficient piety. Hezarfenn's interest in the present drove him to explore new themes, ways of thinking, and narrative styles. He wrote a history of Istanbul based on Latin and Greek sources, and a compendium of world history that covered not only Ottoman but also Roman and Byzantine history, describing

The Mediterranean Sea, author unknown. Portolan chart, 1652 (anonymous)—
Bavarian State Library Manuscripts collection, Cod. Turc. 431.

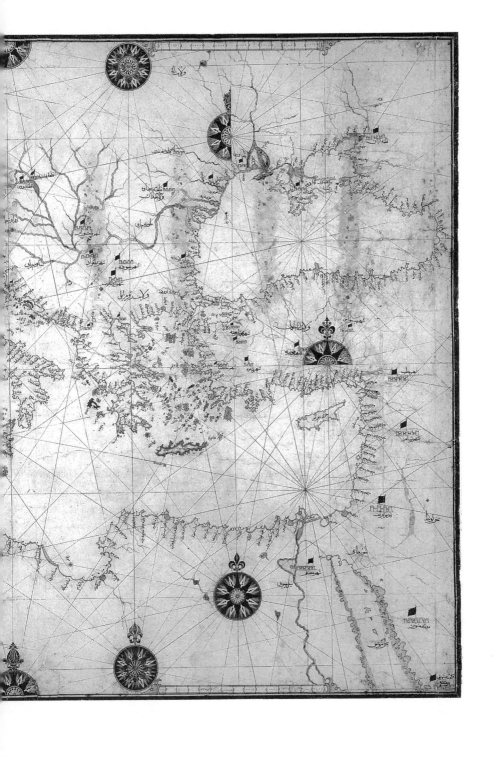

China, India, and America as well. He drew information from his own observations and from his contacts with European scholars. After visiting Yemen, for example, he wrote a treatise on the cultivation, preparation, and effects of coffee.[222]

Disciplines other than history also demonstrated how a closed religious worldview had become porous by the seventeenth century. There was, for example, a renewed interest in old Greek and Arabic medical texts. Leading physicians translated the historic works, moving away from a religious understanding of medicine, toward a natural scientific approach. As more Jewish and Orthodox converts entered the service of the sultan, different medical traditions blended together. The Jewish Moshe ben Raphael Abravanel, who converted to Islam and became the sultan's personal physician, reformed medical training at the madrasas. Students began to read the ancient philosophers and perform chemistry experiments. The Greek doctors who came to Istanbul after the Ottoman conquest of Crete in 1669 brought along new medical knowledge. Many of them had trained at the University of Padua, the most renowned school of medicine at this time.[223]

How did residents of Istanbul understand the geography of the world? In the seventeenth century, cartographic production multiplied and its quality improved. This can be seen in the portolan chart of the Mediterranean Sea, created by an unknown author. In contrast to older representations, the map shows topographic details, identifies cities by their exact names (including Belgrade, Sofia, and Vienna), and shows the administrative borders of the *vilayets* for the first time.[224]

The century's most important geographer, Katib Çelebi, wrote entirely from the perspective of the capital city; he saw the Balkans as its natural extension. Although traveling between the two cities took thirteen days, he remarked that Selanik (Thessaloniki) could "be seen as part of Constantinople in many respects."[225] He followed old cosmographic traditions by reporting on wondrous phenomena, but in his geography *Cosmorama (Cihannüma),* he took pains to describe the physical features of the earth and its natural laws scientifically. He also included information about the politics, institutions, religion, culture, and economy of Europe and the New World. At the end, he addressed the classic themes of climate, flora, and fauna. Katib Çelebi wanted to provide an orientation that was based on facts; the religious and cosmographic dimensions had, at best, symbolic significance for him. "If someone knows . . . rules and maps . . . he will have learned more than someone else . . . in several thousand years of travel."[226] In any case, new knowledge and ways of thinking about geography spread slowly. When a Russian fleet appeared in the Mediterranean Sea more than one hundred years later, the Ottoman government protested to a diplomat from Venice. The Ottomans believed that the Venetians had allowed the Russians to travel through Venetian waters, along a channel shown on medieval maps that was thought to connect the Baltic and Adriatic Seas.[227]

More than anyone else, Evliya Çelebi, the most productive and famous travel writer of the seventeenth century, influenced Istanbul residents' conceptions of foreign lands. Born in Istanbul and raised in the sultan's palace, he traversed the vast Ottoman Empire for forty years as a secretary, imam, courier, and associate of diplomats and pashas. He traveled from Morocco to Azerbaijan, by way of Crimea. From Russian Azov, he journeyed to Iran and Nubia. He wrote ten detailed volumes, called the *Seyahatname,* about his travels.[228] Evliya's perspective was that of the Ottoman Empire, with Istanbul as the center and measure of all things. When he visited the island of Crete not long after it had been conquered, he vividly described its mosques, minarets, religious schools, and dervish monasteries. By contrast, he resorted to brittle clichés when writing about Christian churches and ancient structures. He extensively described Hungary and Austria, including the fortifications around Vienna. In his estimation, however, the Nemçe (Austrians) were "like the Jews: They have no stomach for a fight and are not swordsmen and horsemen." In Vienna, he was impressed by the organ of Saint Stephen's Cathedral, and by the skill of doctors and surgeons. But, "everywhere in the land of the giaours" there was "the disgusting custom" of women moving freely in public. He had friendlier words for the Hungarians. They "have fine tables, are hospitable to guests, and are capable cultivators of their fertile land. . . . They do not torture their prisoners as the Austrians do. They practice swordplay like the Ottomans."[229] He was disgusted by unusual foods such as horsemeat that were eaten by the Egyptians, Iranians, and Tatars, and he was shocked by unfamiliar customs like female circumcision. The farther he traveled from his homeland, the more fantastic his narrative became.[230] In seeking to entertain and surprise his readers with his depictions of wondrous events, he adhered to longstanding tradition. He seemed to enjoy telling tales, and it is unclear whether or not he personally visited all the sites that he mentioned. He may have drawn on written sources and stories that he came across somewhere in Istanbul.[231]

Evliya's view of the world was informed on one hand by theology, and on the other by his curiosity for detail. His travelogues were notable not only for their length but also—like the writings of Katib Çelebi—for their attention to concrete objects and events. His depiction of personal experience, his incorporation of subjective viewpoints, and his simple, often emotional, writing style were unusual,[232] although the written testimonials of other city residents also reveal a stylistic and intellectual shift toward individualism.[233]

The travel writer Evliya Çelebi, the geographer Katib Çelebi, and the historian Hezarfenn were not only confidants of the sultan but also close acquaintances who exchanged ideas regularly. Together, they represent a thought collective that was typical of their era. Religion and cosmography still defined their writing and thinking, but new elements also began to inform their spatial, historical, and spiritual interpretations of the world—a more rational understanding of time, individualized observation, and an empirically grounded view of the world.

3

Challenges of the Ancien Régime

THE OTTOMAN EMPIRE reached the height of its territorial expansion with the siege of Vienna in 1683. After the Ottomans' devastating loss at Kahlenberg, they began their involuntary retreat from central Europe. Imperial overextension, the deterioration of its system of governance through corruption and nepotism, disintegrative tendencies in the provinces, financial problems, and failed reforms all impaired the great empire that had once seemed invincible. The shifting of international trade toward the Atlantic took away the special economic advantages of its central position amid Europe, Asia, and Africa. Shrinking revenues limited the army's ability to acquire supplies and equipment and to produce new weapons, just as Christian Europe was making great strides to catch up with advances in military technology. Through a coincidence of world economic, military, and political changes, the difficulties besetting the Ottoman Empire mounted steadily. How did the sultans nevertheless hold on to power for another two and a half centuries? Recent historical research suggests that the sultans of the eighteenth and nineteenth centuries still understood how to balance their own interests with those of local elites, as well as how—despite ethnic, religious, and social disparities—to create sufficient legitimacy within their "negotiated" state.[1] In the long run, however, the sultan had few options for countering the Habsburg Reconquista or Russian expansion. Ruptures within his empire became increasingly evident. New worldviews and ways of thinking continued to spread, and elites took advantage of opportunities outside of Ottoman borders. Social and economic

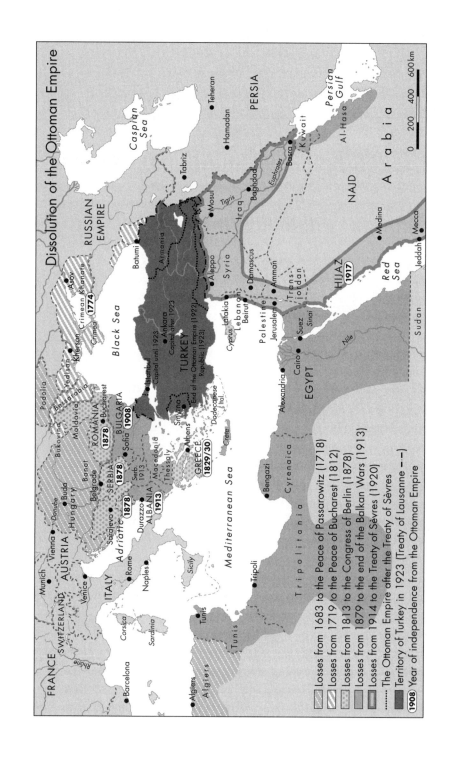

Dissolution of the Ottoman Empire

Losses from 1683 to the Peace of Passarowitz (1718)
Losses from 1719 to the Peace of Bucharest (1812)
Losses from 1813 to the Congress of Berlin (1878)
Losses from 1879 to the end of the Balkan Wars (1913)
Losses from 1914 to the Treaty of Sèvres (1920)
The Ottoman Empire after the Treaty of Sèvres
Territory of Turkey in 1923 (Treaty of Lausanne ‒ ‒)
1908 Year of independence from the Ottoman Empire

FRANCE
SWITZERLAND
Munich
Vienna
AUSTRIA
Venice
ITALY
Rome
Naples
Corsica
Sardinia
Barcelona
Algiers
Algiers
Tunis
Tunis
Sicily
Mediterranean Sea
Tripoli
Tripolitania
Cyrenaica
Bengazi
Rhône
Hungary
Buda
Danube
Banat
Belgrade
SERBIA **1878**
Sarajevo
Bosnia
Durazzo
ALBANIA **1913**
Adriatic
Serb. 1913
Macedonia
Thessaly
Athens
GREECE **1829/30**
Crete
Bukovina
Podolia
Bessarabia
Moldavia
Wallachia
ROMANIA **1878**
Bucharest
BULGARIA **1878**
Sofia **1908**
Kherson
Crimea **1774**
Crimean Khanate
Asov
RUSSIAN EMPIRE
Caspian Sea
Black Sea
Istanbul
Capital until 1923
Smyrna
Dodecanese (Ital.)
TURKEY
Ankara
Capital after 1923
End of the Ottoman Empire (1922)
Republic (1923)
Batumi
Armenia
Tabriz
Teheran
Hamadan
PERSIA
Aleppo
Mosul
Tigris
Euphrates
Baghdad
Iraq
Basra
Kuwait
Persian Gulf
Al-Hasa
NAJD
Arabia
Antakia
Lebanon
Beirut
Damascus
Syria
Amman
Trans- jordan
Cyprus
Palestine
Jerusalem
Sinai
Suez
Cairo
Alexandria
EGYPT
Nile
Sudan
Red Sea
HIJAZ **1917**
Jeddah
Medina
Mecca
Arabia

0 200 400 600 km

changes in the peripheries set centrifugal forces in motion that were difficult to control. In eighteenth-century southeastern Europe, foreign rule encountered a variety of challenges that paved the way for the revolutionary stirrings of the following century and the transformation to modernity.

Habsburg and Russian Expansion

The year 1683 ushered in a century of change for the Ottoman Empire, marked by military defeats and reconquests and an increasingly aggressive rivalry with the Habsburg Empire and Russia. After the abdication of Charles V in 1556, the house of Habsburg had divided into separate Spanish and Austrian lines, so the court at Vienna depended entirely on its central European possessions. These included the Archduchy of Austria and its surrounding territories, as well as the lands of the Bohemian and Hungarian crowns. Now a favorable opportunity for expanding the empire, at least toward the southeast, had finally emerged.

In the Great Ottoman War (1683–1699), Austria and its allies in the Holy League—including the pope, Poland-Lithuania, and Venice—succeeded in reconquering the lands of Hungary, Transylvania, Croatia, and Slavonia after about 150 years of Ottoman rule.[2] After retaking Buda in 1686 and achieving other impressive victories, in 1687 the Hungarian estates awarded the Crown of Saint Stephen to the young Joseph I, heir to the Austrian throne. For the first time, the nobles agreed that the Hungarian kingdom would be linked to the house of Habsburg by blood. On this basis, Austria could assert its status as a hegemonial power in southeastern Europe, thus gradually outgrowing the confines of the Holy Roman Empire. In 1688, the imperial armies conquered the border fortress of Belgrade and pushed farther toward Kosovo and Macedonia. Beforehand, the commanding general of the Holy League had entered into an agreement with the Serbian patriarch and the Albanian Catholic archbishop, seeking to encourage popular revolt against the Ottomans.[3] When the military operation failed near Kačanik in 1690, the sultan's troops wrought terrible revenge. The papal envoy in Vienna reported that they were "burning and ruining the country," and later that they had "barbarously butchered those poor inhabitants and taken a great number of them away into slavery."[4] That same year, tens of thousands of Orthodox Christians, led by the Serbian patriarch Arsenije III, fled to Habsburg territory to escape further retribution. So that the migrants could be resettled in southern

Hungary and along the military frontier, Emperor Leopold I issued three diplomas that guaranteed them privileged legal status. These included (as in the Ottoman Empire) the free exercise of religion, religious self-administration, and tax relief—but not territorial autonomy or political representation within the Habsburg Empire.

The Ottoman troops mounted a fierce resistance, but they could not halt the Habsburgs' advance. Margrave Louis William of Baden and Prince Eugene of Savoy distinguished themselves in numerous battles—including at Slankamen in 1691 and Zenta in 1697. They, too, left behind a scorched earth. In 1690 they nearly razed Skopje to the ground. When the city of Sarajevo refused to surrender to the "noble knight" Prince Eugene in October 1697, he had it plundered and set afire. "We burned the city and its surroundings to the ground," he wrote in his war diary. "Our troops, who hunted down the enemy, brought in booty, including women and children."[5] He laid waste to magnificent mosques, Koran schools, and the entire city center. The mercantile city, once known for its splendor and prosperity, never fully recovered from the devastation. An Ottoman counteroffensive foiled the permanent capture of Bosnia and Herzegovina. Along with Prince Eugene, thousands more Serbs and Vlachs retreated to Habsburg territory. In turn, masses of Albanians and other groups migrated northward, seeking to lay claim to areas that had been partially abandoned. The Ottoman wars of the early modern era had already touched off other large-scale population movements. Historians in the age of nationalism turned these events into a political issue. The question of when Kosovo became mostly Albanian, for example, and which group can claim Kosovo as its historical territory, continues to be fiercely debated today.[6]

In 1699, the Great Ottoman War ended with the Peace of Karlowitz. Hungary, Transylvania, and Slavonia were liberated by the Habsburgs, and Venice expanded its territory at the Ottomans' expense. Although the European balance of power shifted away from the Ottoman Empire, at the peace negotiations the Phanariot Alexander Mavrokordatos, the sultan's talented dragoman, successfully pushed back against Austrian demands for the Danubian Principalities, and against Russian claims to strategic sites on the Black Sea coast. Back home in Istanbul, the sultan rewarded him generously—until this was frowned upon by Islamic religious scholars. They blamed Alexander Mavrokordatos for surrendering Muslim territory to the "infidels."[7]

The new Catholic leadership drove the entire Muslim population out of its newly acquired lands. Most traces of Islamic culture were destroyed. The Habsburgs constructed fortresses and cities in Baroque architecture, impressive representations of courtly and Catholic Church culture. Hungarian and Croatian nobles took over the great Ottoman estates. The Habsburgs also enhanced the economy. They declared Fiume (Rijeka) and Trieste free ports, and they encouraged shipping along the Danube in order to expand their trade into Serbia and Romania. Beginning in 1689, an imperial decree offered favorable terms of settlement to German colonists in southern Hungary. In the eighteenth century, up to 400,000 peasants and craftsmen migrated from Austria and southwestern Germany to the Batschka, Baranya, and Banat regions, as well as to Slavonia, Syrmia, and Szatmár. Czechs, Slovaks, Ruthenians, Romanians, Bulgarians, Slovenes, Croats, and Serbs were also recruited. The colonists were exempt from taxes, and they received leases for inheritable plots of land. Additional measures encouraged the development of agriculture, mining, and industry. Model settlements were even designed for the Banat and Batschka regions. When the Austrians took possession of Bukovina in 1775, German colonists were sent there, too.[8]

A guarded border that clearly delineated the Venetian, Habsburg, and Ottoman Empires did not come into being until 1699, after the Peace of Karlowitz. In the age of absolutism, the fortified frontier that had existed since the sixteenth century became a tightly controlled military border. The Habsburgs successively expanded this border along the Sava and Danube Rivers and the Carpathian Mountains, from Slavonia to Transylvania. Already in 1630, the emperor had issued the *Statuta Valachorum,* which granted certain freedoms to Vlachs fleeing the Ottoman Empire, so they could be resettled and obliged to perform military service. Since then, there had been a steady influx of new refugees. The frontier was directly administered by Vienna and had its own patriarchal-militarized social order. The colonists generally lived in extended family units called *zadrugas,* which were presided over by the oldest family member. A judge or a commanding *voivode* oversaw the villages that comprised multiple *zadrugas.* All able-bodied men were obliged to serve in the border troops. The military frontier's special administrative status was dissolved only between 1871 and 1881.[9]

On the Bosnian side, the Ottomans maintained a border regime *(serhad)* that was overseen by captains and janissaries; the peasant population was also enlisted to protect the border as necessary. The Venetians, too, relied on the military service of Orthodox peasants, the Uskoks and Morlachs, in the Adriatic coastal areas. Northwest of Knin, the territories of Venice, the Habsburg Monarchy, and the Ottoman Empire came together at a point known as the *Triplex Confinium*.[10] The borders between the empires could be porous, and not only for the resident herders. The *haiduks,* former Hungarian cattle drovers and border soldiers who had been released from service, also caused trouble around the military frontier. On either side of the borders, robbers and highwaymen frequently committed murder and assault.[11]

After their conquests in the historical territory of Hungary, the Habsburgs and their empire appeared to be satiated at the beginning of the eighteenth century. For the time being, they did not pursue further military action against the Ottoman Empire, but rather looked westward in setting their foreign policy priorities. The War of the Spanish Succession, which the Habsburgs fought against France, had made the Spanish crown seem attainable once again. Internal reforms were impossible against the will of the estates, and victory over the Turks had increased the complacency of a political system that depended on close cooperation between the crown, nobility, and church. Only in the mid-eighteenth century, after losing to Prussia in the Silesian Wars, did the Habsburg Monarchy demonstrate greater interest in the Prussian model of cameralism and Enlightenment.[12] Austria began to consolidate the legal order of its diverse empire of many peoples, moving it further in the direction of a centralized state.

The Habsburg Empire, with its Magyars, Croats, Serbs, Romanians, and other groups, was relatively stable. In contrast to the Ottoman and British Empires, there were no fundamental religious or ideological contradictions between the ruling house and its subjects in the peripheries. Roman Catholicism was dominant, as was the understanding of the church-state relationship that had emerged from the Counter-Reformation, which held the empire together. Because the Habsburgs had acquired nearly all their territories through marriage, inheritance, or signing treaties—and only rarely through military conquest—their rule appeared more legitimate than that of the Ottomans. Previous legal norms and institutions remained intact in their basic features.[13]

Nevertheless, neither the Hungarian nor the Croatian nobles were satisfied with their subordinate role within the empire. In the 1660s, an anti-Habsburg conspiracy of Hungarian and Croatian magnates failed, and beginning in the 1670s, the noble, mostly Calvinist, Kurucs of Transylvania and Upper Hungary rose up repeatedly against the emperor. They fought against absolutism and centralism, and against re-Catholicization and religious intolerance. The last of these uprisings was not put down until 1711. The peace agreement granted Hungary a certain degree of autonomy—its Diet continued to meet regularly until 1764, and nobles were exempted from paying taxes. Restitution of the nobles' lands and freedom of religion were guaranteed as well. Apart from the usual disagreements about succession, these occurrences highlighted the urgent need to more firmly bind together the accumulated Habsburg lands (which now extended from the Upper Rhine all the way to Romania and Serbia) in a revitalized union. In the Pragmatic Sanction of 1713, Emperor Charles VI established the fundamental legal principle that all parts of the Habsburg Empire were indivisible and inseparable, along with the responsibility of the lands to provide mutual military support. The succession of female descendants was permitted in the absence of a male heir. On this basis, Maria Theresa assumed the throne in 1740. Because all of the crown lands had to approve this bundle of laws, the Pragmatic Sanction can be considered the constitutional foundation and charter of the Habsburg Monarchy. It remained in effect until 1918.[14]

In the meantime, war continued in the southeast. The Habsburgs won the fortress of Belgrade and parts of Serbia and Bosnia in the Peace of Passarowitz in 1718, but they were later forced to retreat and lost most of these territories again in the Peace of Belgrade in 1739. This is how the Croatian lands came to assume their familiar crescent shape. In 1745 Croatian nobles established the "Triune Kingdom of Croatia, Dalmatia, and Slavonia" within Hungary, if only on paper. In reality, only the partial kingdoms of Croatia and Slavonia had a representative assembly, and a viceroy, the *ban*. Because the military frontier ran between them, however, Croatia and Slavonia were not a single contiguous territory. The two lands also enjoyed very different rights. Dalmatia still belonged to Venice, and the Ottoman Empire kept its access to the Adriatic Sea at Neum, in the middle of Croatian territory. This short portion of the coast still belongs to Bosnia and Herzegovina today.[15]

The processes of confessionalization, which had begun during the Reformation, and the formation of a prenational awareness continued to solidify at the end of the seventeenth century. The Serbian patriarch, who had fled Peć in 1690, was granted freedom of religion and church autonomy under Habsburg rule, but no assembly or diet. In the years that followed, the Serbian Orthodox metropolitanate established itself in Karlowitz (Sremski Karlovci), in the Vojvodina region. Because it assumed both spiritual and political leadership in representing the interests of the Orthodox community, the metropolitanate developed into a quasi-political institution. Because there was no diet, the church assembly effectively functioned as an ersatz parliament. Learned church leaders helped to make Karlowitz an intellectual and political center of the Enlightenment. The city became the nucleus of a crystallizing Serbian national movement that crossed imperial boundaries.[16]

The Habsburgs also did not allow the Orthodox Romanians of Transylvania to have their own representative assembly. Only the Hungarians, Saxons, and Szeklers (who had arrived in the Middle Ages to serve as frontier guards) were considered privileged nations, while the Romanians were merely "tolerated." In contrast to the Serbs, they did not even receive church autonomy. The "received" religions were limited to Catholics, Calvinists, Lutherans, and Unitarians. The Habsburgs had founded the Greek Catholic "Uniate" Church to integrate their acquired territories more firmly within their union of states. Some Romanian Orthodox clergy were forced to join the Uniate Church, if they wanted to remain active at all. In the ensuing years, more and more Romanian Uniate and Orthodox clerics began to protest their lack of rights. Beginning in the 1730s, Bishop Ioan Micu-Klein advocated for the equal legal recognition of the Romanian nation. Only at the beginning of the 1790s, however, did Orthodox Romanians receive full citizenship rights. Archbishops and bishops received a seat and voting rights in the Transylvanian Diet. The Romanian confessional nation in Transylvania—like its Serbian counterpart in Vojvodina—became a catalyst for the national movement and political nation of Romanians.[17]

On both sides of the Danube and Sava Rivers, Orthodox elites were frustrated by the Catholicization policies of the Habsburg Empire, and they began to look toward Russia with greater interest. The Muscovite Empire had grown since the mid-sixteenth century by conquering the khanates of Kazan and Astrakhan, as well as substantial territories between the Volga, Don, and Caspian Sea. Driven by strategic and economic motivations, Russian soldiers, merchants, adventurers, and Cossacks pushed into the vast territory of Siberia all the way to Okhotsk. In this process of expansion, Russia transformed itself into a polyethnic, multireligious empire. Its territory tripled in the seventeenth century, from 2.1 to 5.9 million square miles.[18]

A half century earlier than Austria had, Tsar Peter I ("the Great") began to transform his empire into a centralized, absolutist state, seeking to expand Russian power in Europe in the first half of the eighteenth century. He used his power as an autocrat to institute Westernizing reforms; he modernized the state and economy, created secular institutions of education, and broke with old Russian cultural traditions. In the Great Northern War, Peter I secured Russian hegemony in the Baltic. He also sought access to the Caspian and Black Seas, so he could eventually push through the straits to the Mediterranean.[19]

In the last third of the seventeenth century, Russia began to engage the Ottoman Empire militarily. Russia did not succeed in its campaign against the Crimean Khanate, an Ottoman vassal state, in the Great Ottoman War, but it did conquer the strategic fortress city of Azov, as well as Taganrog on the Sea of Azov. When the sultan declared war on Russia in 1711, threatening to open up a second front in the south in the Great Northern War, the Russian army crossed the Dniester River to attack the Ottoman Empire. The tsar counted on a revolt of Christians in the Danubian Principalities and throughout the empire, which he hoped would tie up the Ottoman troops.

For the elites of southeastern Europe, Peter the Great and his expansive, enlightened empire represented the era's greatest hope. Serbs, Croats, and Romanians in the Habsburg Monarchy and the Ottoman Empire were frustrated by political and religious discrimination. They had repeatedly appealed to Peter as "their tsar," pleading for his support in their struggle for rights, or even asking to become Russian subjects. The tsar was not only a potential liberator; he also embodied reforms that the Habsburg Monarchy and Ottoman Empire stubbornly refused to enact.[20] As Peter began his southward march, he called on Balkan Christians to revolt.

The noble Sava Vladislavich Raguzinsky was the tsar's adviser and the author of a manifesto to all Christians in the Ottoman Empire. Sava's wealthy family of Orthodox merchants originally came from Herzegovina and later settled in Dubrovnik. After studying in Venice, Spain, and France, Sava moved to Istanbul so he could concentrate on business with Russia. The Herzegovinian, who traded pelts, grain, wood, cloth, copper, and potash, attracted the attention of a Russian secret agent. The Russians hoped that the Ottoman subject with the noble title from Dubrovnik could help not only with their trade around the Black Sea but also with diplomacy. When the forty-year-old businessman moved to Saint Petersburg, tsarist Russia offered him special trading privileges. The "Illyrian Count Vladislavich"—who spoke Latin, Greek, Italian, and Turkish, in addition to his native tongue—became one of the wealthiest and probably most influential men in Russia, rising to become a close adviser and envoy of Peter the Great. He became an intercultural mediator par excellence. He forged economic connections with the Ottomans, opened political channels to the Balkan Christians, negotiated on Peter's behalf with France and the pope, and bought art in Venice for the court of the tsar. Peter also asked him to create a Russian translation of the Dubrovnik monk Mauro Orbini's early seventeenth-century history of the Slavs, which became a founding text of pan-Slavism. At the slave market in Istanbul, he purchased a young boy named Ibrahim, whom he gave to Peter as a gift. Abram Petrovich Hannibal, as he was named after his baptism, later served as an officer in the Russian military and as the governor of Reval. He was also the great-grandfather of the poet, playwright, and novelist Alexander Pushkin.[21]

Sava Vladislavich's "transimperial biography" was typical of many in this era. Local elites still pursued careers within the social and political structures of the empire where they coincidentally lived, but a growing number also began to seize opportunities that arose outside their empires of origin. In so doing, they crossed political, cultural, religious, and other kinds of borders. In the name of Peter the Great, Sava Vladislavich composed his manifesto to all "Greek and Roman" Christians in Serbia, Slavonia, Macedonia, Bosnia, Herzegovina, and Montenegro in 1711. He called them to "fight for faith and fatherland," and for their freedom, alongside the Russians. Together, he promised, they would send the descendants of Mohammed back to the Arabian Desert.[22] The manifesto spread among Catholic and Orthodox South Slavs via the patriarchate in Constantinople, and even became a folk song. Its message—like the cult of the tsar—continued to resonate into the era of the French Revolution.[23]

The prince of Moldavia, the Romanian Dimitrie Cantemir, held out particularly great hope for Peter's arrival. As prince, Cantemir was actually supposed to have pursued an imperial career with the Ottomans. Like so many others before him, he spent his youth and adolescence as a hostage of the sultan at the court in Istanbul. While Cantemir was still in Moldavia, a Cretan monk (who had studied theology in Cambridge and Leipzig) introduced him to Western scholarship, and at the court he learned

Greek, Latin, Italian, and Russian, as well as Ottoman, Persian, and Arabic. His gift for playing the tambura endeared him to Turkish court officials, who gave "little Cantemir" *(Küçük Kantemiroğlu)* access to the library of the seraglio, with its books, pictures, and handwritten documents that had accumulated over centuries. He studied neo-Aristotelian philosophy at the Patriarchal Academy, while continuing to learn Islamic theology and Ottoman history.[24] Broadly educated and curious about a wide range of fields, he wrote tracts on ethics as well as on science and musicology, and he conversed with Western diplomats, politicians, theologians, and philosophers in Istanbul's cosmopolitan milieu.

The sultan placed such trust in Cantemir that he appointed him as prince of Moldavia when he was not yet forty years old, in 1710, as war with Russia was on the horizon. But Cantemir betrayed the sultan and signed a treaty with the tsar, believing that Russian forces would soon enter Moldavia. He promised military assistance, placed Moldavia under Russian sovereignty, and declared his own family the Moldavian royal dynasty. When Peter personally accompanied his troops as they marched into Jassy, Cantemir, as promised, gave the signal for revolt. He and the Russians were counting on support from neighboring Wallachia, but its prince chose to side with the sultan. The battle on the Prut River against the much larger Ottoman army ended in fiasco. Cantemir was forced to flee, following the tsar's troops into Russian exile.[25]

Cantemir, who for the rest of his life dreamed of reclaiming the Moldavian throne, now dedicated himself to his studies. As a polymath, composer, historian, Orientalist, and philosopher, he was readily accepted into the society of enlightened Russian nobles. A French brigadier remembered the "small, delicate man with fine features, a nobleman, serious and with such a pleasant demeanor as I had never before experienced."[26] He put aside his Turkish robes so he could receive his visitors "without a beard in the Russian style, dressed as a Pole." He greeted the Austrian Baron Franz von Tiepolt in Latin, "which he spoke with an excellent accent."[27]

Cantemir's writings were voluminous and encyclopedic, corresponding to the spirit of his time. They promoted a secular image of the world and humanity, and an early expression of the national idea. He committed himself to the pursuit of scientific truth, which he sought to grasp through the study of primary sources and rational thought. His close confidant, the diplomat Johann Gotthilf Vockerodt, attested that Cantemir was "at heart . . . a pure deist."[28] In *The Divan or the Sage's Dispute with the World,* he fiercely criticized despotism and the Ottoman feudal system. In *Historia Hieroglyphica,* he used the then-familiar genre of animal allegory to pillory current affairs. He was personally acquainted with many European thinkers of the Enlightenment, and he was accepted into the Academy of Sciences in Berlin, which was led by the philosopher and polymath Gottfried Wilhelm Leibniz. Cantemir later became president of the Russian Academy.[29]

Cantemir wrote in Romanian as well as Latin. In his *Romano-Moldavo-Wallachian Chronicle,* he emphasized the ancient Roman origins of the Romanian people, and he denounced the alien influence of Old Church Slavonic—themes that would become popular many years later, with the rise of nationalism. His best-known works were an Arabic grammar book, a treatise on the *System of Mohammedan Religion,* and the *History of the Growth and Decay of the Ottoman Empire,* which was translated from Latin into many other languages in the eighteenth century.[30] From the perspective of "enlightened" Russia, he developed his theory of the decline of the sultan's empire, which influenced the emerging discourse of Orientalism. He regarded Islam as "bestial," and Mohammed as a "pseudo-prophet." Western intellectual leaders such as Edward Gibbon and Voltaire praised and cited his Ottoman history, which also became an important reference work for scholars in southeastern Europe. The pioneer of the Bulgarian national movement, Bishop Sofroniy Vrachanski, translated it into Bulgarian a century later.[31]

Cantemir's way of thinking was typical of many early Enlightenment figures, although he preceded most of them by decades. To this point, only a few others had caught the same intellectual fever—including the Phanariot and dragoman Alexander Mavrokordatos, who wrote a well-received dissertation on the circulation of the blood, and Archbishop Meletios of Athens, whose *Old and New Geography* was frequently cited in Europe. Other groundbreaking thinkers of this era included the Croatian Andrija Kačić Miošić and the Greek Kyrillos Loukaris. They worked to popularize useful knowledge decades before the Enlightenment influenced broader scholarly circles in southeastern Europe, in the last third of the eighteenth century.

Dimitrie Cantemir's hopes of returning to the Moldavian throne remained unfulfilled. After 1711, the sultan only installed loyal Phanariots as princes *(hospodars)* in the Danubian Principalities. They oversaw tax collection, administration, and the export of grain and meat. They also had to guard the borders to Russia and the Habsburg Monarchy, and provide the sultan with troops in case of war. No Romanian noble occupied the throne here again until 1821, when the "Phanariot period" ended with the Greek uprising. The members of many non-Greek families of this era who wanted to become part of the upper class—for example, the Wallachian Moisiodax and the Albanian Ghica—adopted Greek language and customs.[32]

A contradictory system of rule developed in Moldavia and Wallachia. On one hand, a base culture of corruption and exploitation spread as the century progressed; *hospodars* paid the sultan dearly for their title, which they usually had to relinquish within a year. One traveler learned firsthand, "with all candor," from the prince's commissioner that the prince and his officials "sought to enrich themselves in all possible ways, whether through robbery, plunder, or other kinds of extortion."[33] On the other hand, the state academies that were founded around 1700 became important centers of southeastern European intellectual life. In contrast to other parts of the Ottoman Empire, in Moldavia and Wallachia one could study Greek language and literature, logic, rhetoric, physics, philosophy, and astronomy largely undisturbed by the Sublime Porte and the Ecumenical Patriarchate. In the eighteenth century, Constantine Mavrokordatos stood out among the Greek *hospodars*. Constantine, grandson of the great dragoman Alexander Mavrokordatos, alternated between the thrones of Wallachia and Moldavia. He not only commissioned translations of Molière and Voltaire but also distinguished himself by promoting economic development and legal reform. In this era, great libraries could be found at the royal courts as well as in monasteries and the villas of educated boyars. Traders, consuls, travelers, and monks constantly brought new additions to the shelves. Relative intellectual freedom, material security, and close contacts with Austria, Poland, and Russia contributed to a lively cultural atmosphere that attracted scholars from all over southeastern Europe and extending into the nineteenth century.[34]

The time had not yet come for casting aside Ottoman rule, so the South Slav Sava Vladislavich and the Romanian Dimitrie Cantemir directed their energies toward the expansion of Russian imperial power. In 1722, Cantemir served as Peter the Great's adviser and dragoman on his expedition to the Caucasus and Iran. Cantemir brought along a printing press, and he composed Peter's manifestos to the local residents, reassuring them that "whichever faith and nation they may be, not the slightest harm will befall them."[35] Three years later, Sava, too, embarked on a journey in service to the tsar. He was supposed to negotiate a series of peace, border, and trade agreements with China. Because much was still unknown about the distant parts of the empire, Sava became a pioneer of Siberian cartography. "The Russian agent Lang gave me a map of some neighboring countries, but it was unusable," he complained. On a border that was thousands of versts long, the only feature depicted was the Amur River.[36] Through skilled negotiation, flattery, threats, bribes, and even the deployment of Russian border troops, the Herzegovinian succeeded, at long last, in concluding a long-term agreement of peace and friendship with (as he saw them) the stubborn, arrogant, and wily Chinese.[37] The Treaty of Kyakhta, which fixed the previously undefined, nearly 4,000-mile-long Russian-Chinese border in Siberia and Mongolia, was a diplomatic masterstroke.[38] Both men, Vladislavich and Cantemir, were highly decorated and promoted to the uppermost echelon of imperial advisers.

Enlightenment? Enlightenment!

On July 7, 1753, Patriarch Kyrillos of Constantinople made a courageous decision. He appointed the Greek scholar Eugenios Voulgaris as the director of a new academy of philosophy on the "Holy Mountain" of Athos, at the Vatopedi monastery. Voulgaris was to teach philosophy, mathematics, theology, and ethics, and to fundamentally reform the training of Orthodox clergy. He had made a name for himself as a professor of philosophy and scientific theory in Ioannina and Constantinople. He was the earliest and most prominent, if not the most influential, proponent of Enlightenment in southeastern Europe. In just a few years, the scholar from Corfu, who was in his late thirties, transformed the small seminary into a well-respected, modern academy with about two hundred students. In addition to ancient philosophers, they studied the works of Descartes, Leibniz, Wolff, and Locke. This was intolerable to conservative clerics, who continued to defend the Aristotelian universe. In 1759, Voulgaris had to leave Athos. His successor, Nikolaos Tzertzoulis, a natural philosopher who had been influenced by Newton, also did not remain for long. The experiment with enlightened ideas on Athos came to an end, but Voulgaris's influence did not. He translated Voltaire and wrote *Logic,* his most important work. He disparaged medieval scholasticism and held reason as the only source of knowledge.[39]

While Voulgaris was still serving as the academy's director, the monk Paisi sat in the library of the Hilandar monastery, just a short distance away on Mount Athos. He pored through documents and leather folios, working on an undertaking of great personal importance: the first written synthesis of Bulgarian history. Unlike Voulgaris, Paisi was not an intellectual; he had no higher education. But the knowledge he had acquired as a now forty-year-old monk was sufficient for combing through monastery libraries, searching for additional sources in Bulgaria and Austria, exchanging ideas with Serbian historians, and finally, publishing the first *Slavo-Bulgarian History* in the Bulgarian language in 1762.[40] Paisi was a forefather of the Bulgarian national movement; he traced the origins of the Bulgarian people back to biblical times and reported on the glorious achievements of the Bulgarian Empire in the Middle Ages. His heroic tales of tsars and saints were meant to encourage Bulgarians to take pride in their own past. Paisi, who came from the Bulgarian town of Bansko, was not an Enlightenment thinker in a philosophical sense, nor was he driven by the national idea that took off much later. He was unfamiliar with Rousseau, Voltaire, and their compatriots. He was, however, concerned about the Bulgarians' lack of education and the deficiencies of their language. His worries about the decline of his own people and about the disproportionate influence of the Greek language and Greeks in the Orthodox Church found an outlet in his descriptions of a glorious historical past.

The *Slavo-Bulgarian History* is full of legends and hardly holds up to the standards of contemporary scholarship. It did, however, embody a new intellectual spirit. It was the product of diligent research and drew on all kinds of sources, including the writings of Mauro Orbini and Caesar Baronius. Paisi's history did not dwell on the contemplation of eternal truths, but instead focused on worldly events. Its central narrative concerned the rise and fall of the Bulgarian people, rather than the universal Christian story of salvation. Paisi used the past as a mirror for reflecting the bleakness of the present because he had a political mission: creating a better future by awakening the language and historical awareness of the people. "Why are you ashamed to call yourself Bulgarians, why do you not read and speak your own language?"[41]

By the mid-eighteenth century, the Holy Mountain of Athos was no longer a site of seclusion, inner retreat, and spirituality oriented toward the afterlife. The monasteries began to open themselves to the outside world, sending out better educated monks to collect donations, receive confessions, and lead pilgrimages. The Zograf and Hilandar monasteries owned sites in Vidin, Ruse, Sofia, Bansko, Kotel, and Veles, where traveling monks could stop to rest. They returned to the Holy Mountain with money, clothing, furniture, and pack horses as well as new experiences and acquaintances.[42] The monk Paisi was one of the men who set out to collect donations in the 1760s. In 1765 he arrived in Kotel in central Bulgaria, with his *History* in tow. A writer and cleric—the later Bishop Sofroniy Vrachanski—made the first copy of the later world-famous work, touching off a chain reaction. Vrachanski was also the first bishop to address Bulgarian believers in their vernacular language.[43]

The Greek Voulgaris and the Bulgarian Paisi were very different representatives of a time in which new ideas and methods of thinking had begun to take hold. Some people took inspiration from European philosophers of the Enlightenment, interpreting conditions around themselves on the basis of empirical observation and rational thought. Others developed their own methods, themes, and ideas, depending on their individual political, religious, and social context. Perceptions, needs, values, and concepts changed alongside social reality.

The Balkan lands' participation in the European "century of Enlightenment" has been evaluated in very different ways. Western historiography has overwhelmingly argued that there was no "authentic" Enlightenment in the Balkans, and if there was, then only as the reception of Western ideas.[44] This assessment is grounded in purely normative assumptions about the Enlightenment as a uniform phenomenon that occurred within a particular era, defined by French radical-skeptical philosophy that tended toward atheism. But even contemporaries did not agree on the significance of the new intellectual attitudes. And newer research has shown that a broad spectrum of different national, regional, and confessional "Enlightenments" existed within Europe and the world.[45] In the historiography of the countries of southeastern Europe, by contrast, Enlightenment is often equated with national awakening. These phenomena were closely related, but they were certainly not identical.

The Enlightenment developed under very different conditions in the lands of the Habsburg Monarchy and the Ottoman Empire. Rationalism gained a foothold in Austria under Emperor Joseph I and Maria Theresa.[46] But the Catholic Habsburgs worried about the spread of Protestant and radical Enlightenment writings. In 1751 a Book Commission was established as a central censorship authority in Vienna. The books of Voltaire,

Rousseau, Hume, Machiavelli, Hobbes, and others were deemed anti-Catholic or antireligious, and then banned. Joseph II was the first to loosen the rules, although many classics, including works by Goethe and Lessing, remained forbidden.[47] Nevertheless, enlightened absolutism established the essential preconditions so that different variations of the Enlightenment could spread among the peoples of the monarchy, especially through public school reform. This reform set educational standards by harmonizing teaching plans and methods and by introducing schoolbooks in the languages of the nationalities.

Conditions were less favorable in the Ottoman Empire than in the Habsburg Monarchy because schooling was not supported to the same degree. Scholars continue to debate whether an autochthonous Enlightenment existed at all within eighteenth-century Turkish and Islamic culture. Clearly, some Muslim scholars were well versed in Western religion, philosophy, and recent scientific discoveries. The ideas of deists and Freemasons were well received in certain circles, and individuals with a higher education harbored doubts about the sharia. But all this occurred in private because a bourgeois public sphere did not yet exist. Reception of the Western Enlightenment was not fully realized in Turkey until the last third of the nineteenth century, when greater support for schooling encouraged a broader audience of readers, a larger book and newspaper market, and a modern public sphere. The classics of Enlightenment literature were also translated and studied at this time.[48]

Enlightened absolutism in Russia was particularly influential in spreading the new philosophy among Christians in the Ottoman Empire. During the Russo-Ottoman wars, Empress Catherine II—at the time, still a devoted follower of Voltaire—had his pamphlets translated into Greek so they could be distributed by Russian troops in the occupied territories, stirring up local discontent against the rule of the sultan.[49]

By the last third of the eighteenth century, a transformed intellectual climate was palpable in southeastern Europe—identified as *prosvjetiteljstvo* by the Croats, *prosvećenost* by the Serbs, *prosvetlenie* by the Bulgarians, *iluminism* by the Romanians, and *iluminizëm* by the Albanians. The new ideas were first articulated among the Magyars, Romanians, Greeks, Croats, Slovenes, and Serbs. The Bulgarians, Albanians, and Turks came later, but they, too, were influenced by the new ideas.[50] Centers of the Croatian Enlightenment included the cities of Zagreb, Osijek, Split, and Dubrovnik, which had a longer tradition of scholarship and learning as well as an emerging bourgeoisie. The poet and lexicographer Matija Petar Katančić and many others were active here. The doctor and polymath Julije Bajamonti lived and worked in Dalmatia, and the writer Matija Antun Reljković in Slavonia. For the Serbs, the Habsburg-controlled region of Vojvodina became the intellectual nucleus of the new movement. Three of the most influential Serbian thinkers of the Enlightenment came from Vojvodina—the historian Jovan Rajić, the philosopher Zaharije Orfelin, and the language reformer and politician Dositej Obradović. The influence of their work also extended into Ottoman-controlled Serbia. The "Transylvanian School" assumed a similar function among Romanians. Among others, Samuil Micu-Klein, Petru Maior, Ion Budai-Deleanu, and Gheorghe Șincai investigated the origins of the Romanian people and their language, and they wrote grammars and schoolbooks as well as works of history in the spirit of the Enlightenment. They became an important source of intellectual activity in the Danubian Principalities.[51] The Ionian Islands, and the philosophical schools in Thessaloniki and Athens, Ioannina and Moscopole (Voskopojë), in western Macedonian Kozani, and on Mount Athos continued to play a central role for Greeks and for Albanian, Serbian, Bulgarian, and Vlach Orthodox scholars. Likewise, Bucharest and Jassy became renowned for their enlightened cosmopolitanism and sites of academic training in the Phanariot era. In southeastern Europe as in other parts of the world, the Enlightenment stood for a new way of using reason—rather than faith, superstition, or revelation—to understand and grapple with problems.

All over southeastern Europe, educated people became interested in new scientific discoveries and philosophical literature. The books of German-speaking authors Christian Friedrich Baumeister and Christian Wolff, "moderate" proponents of Enlightenment who sought to reconcile theology and logic, found a wide readership. But even the more "radical" French philosophers Voltaire, Montesquieu, Rousseau, and Fontenelle—and the encyclopedists Diderot and d'Alembert—were popular, too. Locke, Bayle, Newton, and many other authors from the fields of literature, science, philosophy, history, and geography entered the repertoire of widely read texts.[52] Voltaire favored enlightened monarchy, Montesquieu supported a strong constitution and parliament, and Rousseau anticipated the emergence of new popular movements. The bookshelves of the educated classes give us a sense of how widespread these writings actually were. The Moldavian noble, diplomat, and writer Antiochus Cantemir, a close friend of

Voltaire and Montesquieu, owned a library of more than 1,700 classical titles. The son of the exiled prince Dimitrie Cantemir collected books by Christian Wolff, Samuel von Pufendorf, Thomas Morus, Francis Bacon, Thomas Hobbes, John Locke, Descartes, d'Alembert, and other philosophers. The Serbian legal scholar Sava Tekelija, meanwhile, possessed more than 5,000 works of Enlightenment and other world literature.[53]

For example, Voltaire's writings were well known in educated circles throughout southeastern Europe and were taught at the Greek academies. Despite Habsburg censorship, Voltaire's works were still present—in the original French or in translation—in a Serbian bookstore in Novi Sad, and also in numerous private and monastery libraries in southern Hungary and Transylvania.[54] The reading public engaged intensively with his ideas, without accepting them word for word. Readers discussed, criticized, adapted, and expanded upon them, as illustrated by the example of Eugenios Voulgaris. The Greek philosopher, who translated Voltaire's text on Polish dissidents in 1768, developed his own defense of religious tolerance, which departed significantly from the original. Even in less rarified academic circles, Voltaire was considered a benefactor of humankind. In 1776, the Comte de Choiseul-Gouffier was astounded when he climbed to the monastery on the island of Patmos and met a monk who asked him in Italian what had happened in Europe in the past seven years. His most urgent question: "Can you tell me if Voltaire is still living?"[55]

A common characteristic of the southeastern European Enlightenments is their close association with the churches. There were Enlightenment thinkers in all confessions and religions—Catholics, Protestants, and Jews, and Orthodox and Uniate Christians. They saw philosophy and science as a means for overcoming outdated thinking in the church and state, for legitimizing authority, and for reforming political conditions in favor of greater freedom, prosperity, and happiness. In the great empires, high-ranking clerics were the only representatives of the people and their religious communities who were recognized by the courts. Clerics often held secular leadership positions, too, because the noble and bourgeois educated classes were still very small in the eighteenth century. The well-known figures who advocated for Enlightenment-inspired reforms included Catholic bishop Maksimilijan Vrhovac from Zagreb, Serbian Orthodox archbishop Pavle Nenadović from southern Hungary, and bishop Sofroniy Vrachanski from Bulgaria. Archbishops Leon Gheuca and Jacob Stamate and bishop Chesarie of Râmnic were active in the Danubian Principalities. The Serbian bishop of Timișoara, Peter Petrović, went so far as to write the Austrian chancellor, Count Kaunitz, that as a philosopher, he "rejected as prejudices the truths of the catechism itself."[56] Within this group, the earliest forms of national awareness began to form contemporaneously with the ideas of Enlightenment.[57]

A typical representative of the church Enlightenment was the Croatian bishop Ivan Dominik Stratiko. He was born into a well-to-do Greek immigrant family in Zadar, and he was considered a prodigy. His parents sent him to school in Rome and Florence. In Italy, he joined the Dominican order. He later taught theology and philosophy at the universities in Siena and Pisa, and he earned renown as an author and translator. In the liberal climate of Tuscany, Stratiko gained access to the works of contemporary Enlightenment thinkers. He admired Voltaire and the French encyclopedists, studied Montesquieu and Rousseau, and supported the physiocrats. The tall cleric in his mid-thirties was not terribly handsome, but he was witty, well educated, and thoroughly charming. He was able to take certain liberties because of his fame and popularity, and his success with women astonished even the Venetian Giacomo Casanova. In 1770 he promised Casanova "every pleasure of the heart and the mind." Casanova rhapsodized that "in Pisa, the monk initiated me into the charming society in which he delighted. He had chosen two or three well-born girls who combined beauty with talent, so that he could teach them to sing improvisations in which he accompanied them on the guitar."[58] Casanova found this somewhat unusual for a monk, but he set aside his astonishment in the company of the entertaining Croat. Despite his unconventional views, speeches critical of the church, and assorted love affairs, Stratiko was anointed bishop.

When Stratiko came to the small Istrian diocese of Novigrad, and later the island of Hvar, he was shocked by the degree of poverty, illiteracy, and superstition, which seemed incomprehensible to him within an enlightened Europe. In many parts of Dalmatia, the rural population survived on porridge and onions; agriculture and livestock farming were poorly developed. Drought and wind regularly destroyed the harvests, and large stretches of land had been abandoned by their starving inhabitants. Those who remained had usually lost all hope for a better future.[59] A typical thinker of the Enlightenment, the philosopher-bishop (as he was called) developed concrete projects to accompany his ideas. He was less concerned with eternal bliss than with instituting improvements in the here and now. He encouraged village priests to acquire additional training, worked to improve his followers' living conditions and nutrition, translated standard works on public health, built poorhouses and village schools, and organized music and theater performances. Like many of his contemporaries, he praised bourgeois virtues such as achievement and hard work, in contrast to the idleness of peasants.

Stratiko did not content himself with fighting poverty and underdevelopment. He also wrote about the equality of the sexes, argued against censorship, torture, and the death penalty, and reflected on the foundations of a democratic social order in the spirit of Montesquieu. In lectures and sermons he openly criticized arbitrary and despotic rule, aiming his remarks at the "enlightened" Archduke Leopold.[60]

Rationality and religion were not at odds with one another in the eyes of clerics such as the Greek Orthodox Eugenios Voulgaris and the Roman Catholic Ivan Dominik Stratiko. So why did radical atheism, deism, or anticlericalism fail to take hold in southeastern Europe in this era? For one, the educated elites who promoted Enlightenment were almost exclusively clerics who had been socialized by the churches. Religion was closely associated with collective (later national) identities. Under foreign rule, the church was the only place where communal awareness could be promoted and group interests expressed. The church was seen as a space of protection against cultural and religious alienation, Germanization, Magyarization, and Islamization all at once. Since intellectuals directed their criticism primarily toward foreign rulers, not local institutions, the Enlightenment did not represent a serious danger—at least for the Orthodox Church—until the outbreak of the French Revolution. The church did not recognize the subversive power of the new ideas until after 1789.

In all southeastern European lands, the new thinking expressed itself first in the study of the past. The people of these lands were regarded as historical subjects for the very first time.[61] Translations of works like Montesquieu's *Considerations on the Causes and Greatness of the Romans and Their Decline* encouraged readers to apply the republican theory of corruption, despotism, and degeneration to their own situation—whether it concerned serfdom in Transylvania or tax farming in Thessaly. Greeks and Romanians looked back to ancient times; Serbs, Croats, and Bulgarians, to the Middle Ages. History became a guide for the present, a surface onto which new structures of meaning could be projected. For the Greeks, ancient Hellas became a source of inspiration for cultural development and a new political order. Proponents of the Transylvanian School deepened their convictions in a direct continuity between the Dacians of the Roman classical age and present-day Romanians. Awareness of past national grandeur shaped collective identity, and self-confidence grew.[62] After the monk Paisi, Jovan Rajić from Karlowitz became a role model for Slavic historians. After decades of research, in the 1790s he published a four-volume *History of Various Slavic Peoples, Particularly the Bulgars, Croats, and Serbs*.

Historical and spatial awareness developed in tandem. Scholars began to organize geographic data according to empirical and systematic criteria, in order to gain a better understanding of humans' natural environment and civilization. This kind of inventory naturally drew attention to social grievances. The *New Geography* by Daniel Philippidis and Grigorios Konstantas contained not only information about Greece but also a biting critique of despotic rule in the Ottoman Empire.[63]

The necessity of engaging with language and education seemed to be a logical outgrowth of Enlightenment ideas. Until this point, Latin had been the language of theology, philosophy, and scholarship in the Catholic lands, whereas ancient Greek and Church Slavic were favored in Orthodox regions—but all these tongues were understood by only a small educated elite. Since enlightened thinkers sought to uplift the standards of civilization, to promote science and literature, and, increasingly, to bring this message to average people, almost every enlightened scholar raised the issue of language. Even Father Paisi intentionally distanced himself from all signs of scholarly elitism: "I wrote for the simple Bulgarians simply."[64] Above all, native languages became a medium for experiencing and conveying progress. Dositej Obradović emphasized that "when scholars record their thoughts in a language that is shared by all of the people, then intellectual enlightenment does not only reach those who understand the language of old books, but also the peasants."[65] Obradović—who in addition to his native Serbian language, also knew Latin, Greek, Church Slavic, Romanian, Italian, French, German, and English—was not the only one promoting the use of vernacular language. Zaharije Orfelin was likewise active in Serbia, and Iosipos Moisiodax, Dimitrios Katartzis, Rhigas Velestinlis, and Adamantios Korais promoted the vernacular in Greece. After 1800, language reformers began to appear in other lands; they included Naum Veqilharxhi in Albania, and Petar Beron and Neofit Rilski in Bulgaria.

The Enlightenment could not have thrived in southeastern Europe without the social changes that accompanied the new intellectual discourses. New social groups had the education, material well-being, and self-awareness to interpret the world according to criteria that had not been used in the past. These new groups included a younger generation who had studied in Germany, Italy, or France—many Croatian, Greek, Serbian, and Romanian doctors, for example. Teachers, scholars, merchants, military officers, lawyers, writers, and artists joined the growing ranks of the educated bourgeoisie. The Greek diaspora played an important role, particularly in the Danubian Principalities, as did the intelligentsia in Vienna and Paris; Adamantios Korais was its best-known representative. In these (early) bourgeois groups, education was an important instrument for keeping up with Jewish, Armenian, and other traders. Merchants founded schools for advanced training, attracted qualified teachers, invested money in books and instruments, and arranged for the translation of up-to-date learning materials. The settlements of Bulgarian, Aromanian, Serbian, and other merchants in areas controlled by the Ottomans served as a transmission belt for education and Enlightenment.[66] Wars, too, played a role in establishing new connections. The Croatian officer and writer Matija Antun Reljković, who fought for Austria in the Seven Years' War, gained an appreciation for French Enlightenment literature as a prisoner of war. Like many others involved in the war, he smuggled banned books back to his Slavonian homeland. His popular educational work, *The Satyr,* encouraged peasants to give up their Turkish customs and manners.[67]

The early bourgeois classes developed new forms of communication and social interaction that demonstrated a fundamental transformation in the character of the public sphere. New kinds of sociability and social relations were no longer primarily defined by birth, religion, or profession, but instead brought together like-minded individuals in intellectual exchange. Educational standards, lifestyles, and values provided a common basis for interaction, while ethnic identity was unimportant. The Serb Obradović had been steeped in the traditional Greek canon and the fundamentals of Orthodox theology at the Serbian Hopovo monastery and on Athos. He also studied rationalist philosophy in the university towns of Leipzig and Halle, and he experienced modern Western living in London and Vienna. He described himself as a rational being whose origins were inconsequential; it was the knowledge he acquired throughout the different phases of his life that eventually made him a well-educated person.[68] The Wallachian Iosipos Moisiodax oriented himself toward Hellenic language and culture, and Daniel Philippidis wrote in Greek while he lived in the Danubian Principalities. These scholars did not ask whether they belonged to the Greek or Romanian Enlightenment because national intellectual traditions in the contemporary sense did not yet exist. They and their colleagues interacted and got to know one another in private circles and salons, in reading and patriotic societies, and in Masonic lodges and scientific academies. All across Europe, a specific group identity and independent cultural practice emerged, later defining itself as "cosmopolitan." Southeastern European contacts and correspondence reached from Bucharest to London and Paris, from Belgrade to Saint Petersburg and Vienna, from Smyrna to Venice.[69] Adamantios Korais alone left behind thousands of letters, in which he exchanged philosophical, scientific, and political ideas with scholars, writers, and politicians from all over Europe. Enlightenment: in addition to new ideas and ways of thinking, it was a changed cultural system of discourses, values, social practices, and representations.

From the mid-eighteenth century on, academies and "patriotic," "charitable," and "economic" societies became important institutions of the enlightened public sphere throughout eastern and southeastern Europe. Their goal was to promote the sciences and make them useful for agriculture, fishing, commerce, and other trades. The academies played an important role in anchoring the ideas of Enlightenment within the value system of their societies.[70] Masonic lodges also served as forerunners of Enlightenment and the idea of tolerance; they could be found in Trieste, Vienna, Budapest, Osijek, and Hermannstadt as well as within the territory of the Ottoman Empire. Catholic, Protestant, and Orthodox clerics—for example, Bishop Vrhovac of Zagreb, Archbishop Stratimirović of Karlowitz, and Bishop Petrović of Timişoara—were active in various kinds of associations.[71]

All this notwithstanding, enlightened ideas remained the privilege of a small, cosmopolitan elite in the second half of the century. Even members of the privileged classes—like the Croatian feudal nobility, Ragusan patricians, and Romanian boyars—remained overwhelmingly loyal to traditional worldviews and ways of life. In this, they were no different from their western European contemporaries.[72] Courtly sociability, European clothing, newer styles of architecture and horticulture, and the pastimes of dance, music, and playing cards only gradually made inroads among the upper classes. A half century later, the Wallachian boyar and enlightened thinker Dinicu Golescu complained about his fellow aristocrats' lack of education: "Many of the bursars and state secretaries, whose decisions and actions affect the affairs of the entire population of the Wallachian principality, are not capable of composing a report."[73]

Despite the work of charitable and economic societies, it was even more difficult for Enlightenment thinkers to reach the rural population. The overwhelming majority could neither read nor write; instead of a signature, they simply made a cross. When the Croatian intellectual Imbro Tkalac looked back at his youth, he recalled that "no glimmer of eighteenth-century European culture" had enlightened the peasants.[74] On the other hand, the ability to read and write was not an absolute requirement for absorbing new ideas, since books, calendars, almanacs, pamphlets, and newspapers were also intended to be read aloud. Bishop Stratiko, for example, used rhymes in folk songs and illustrated calendars to inform his followers about rational methods of farming.[75]

Scribes in the Romanian lands had translated and copied foreign works since the Middle Ages, a tradition that continued even after the first printing presses.[76] The scribes were monks as well as laypeople, often self-taught, with varying levels of education. "My dear brothers," one copyist noted in 1777, "to whomever may pick up this book—may he love and read it to others, and whenever someone asks you, give it to him with a joyful heart, so that he may copy it, too." But not everyone could transcribe correctly; some people omitted or added new passages. In 1829 one reader from Wallachia recorded his displeasure on the copied text itself: "I have not found a single correct word; everything is turned around and distorted; in this confusion . . . it is impossible to understand anything, and one loses the desire to read at all."[77]

The diversification and desacralization of the written word, and the growing use of vernacular languages in print, helped to create a new kind of public sphere in the last third of the eighteenth century. Alongside oral communication, print media multiplied the transmission of new ideas through text and image. There was a transformation in understanding and in the ways that writing was disseminated as well as in the value of reading alone and to others. If texts had previously affirmed eternal truths in histories and the lives of saints or served a purely utilitarian purpose in legal and administrative documents, now they sought to reach a broader audience by entertaining, informing, and spreading new knowledge. "What a fine thing printing is," wrote the merchant Ioannis Pringos, who donated eight hundred books to his hometown of Zagora in Thessaly in 1762. "Reading opens the eyes of the reader and makes him a learned man."[78] Dositej Obradović recommended techniques of reading that were physically relaxing, so that farmers and herders would also learn to appreciate books. The central concern was enlightening and educating the public, thereby encouraging ethical behavior. Adamantios Korais hoped that reading would spark a "moral revolution."[79]

Because the Ottoman Empire had few presses for books in the languages of the Balkan peoples, Greek, Serbian, and Bulgarian books were usually printed in Venice, Paris, Vienna, Halle, Leipzig, Buda, and Pest, or in the Danubian Principalities. The first Serbian and Greek-language newspapers appeared in the 1790s, also in Vienna. Hungary, Croatia, Slavonia, and Dalmatia, by contrast, had numerous presses.[80] The printing industry boomed. In the first quarter of the eighteenth century, 107 Greek-language books were published; in the last quarter, 749.[81]

Book publishing underwent a qualitative as well as quantitative transformation. The proportion of scientific and literary texts grew as the relative significance of religious and theological literature declined. Grammar and instructional books were published, alongside works about history and geography. New genres of popular literature such as novels, satire, and poetry also emerged. Books of wisdom and instructional guides on etiquette, good behavior, and ethical questions were in high demand.[82] Even after the turn of the century, books were still considered very precious. In 1826, a Romanian soldier immortalized himself on the pages of one volume, writing: "I found this book with a Turk who was about to throw it into the fire; after I asked many times, he gave it to me for 5 paras. I wrote this down so it will always be remembered."[83]

Do intellectual revolutions bring about transformations in values, attitudes, beliefs, and ideas, or can a new philosophy emerge only from a social context that has itself fundamentally changed? This academic question has inspired much discussion. Without a doubt, both phenomena—society and ideas—are mutually reinforcing.[84] The ideas and ways of thinking, social practices, values, and representations that characterized the "century of Enlightenment" first appeared in the scholarly circles of southeastern Europe around 1750. Initially limited to a small group of mobile, intellectual elites, after the 1770s these new ideas increasingly spread among the early bourgeois classes as well. The contours of an enlightened civil society first became apparent in salons, reading societies, Masonic lodges, and academies, and later in secret societies. As perspectives and issues changed over time, they reinforced one another and heightened awareness about the historic conditioning of the present. Secular categories replaced religious categories for understanding the world, sharpening awareness about this very transformation. The desire for cultural renewal and social progress would ultimately bring the political order in southeastern Europe, as elsewhere, to the point of collapse. Without this fundamental upheaval, the main goals of Enlightenment could not be attained. Intellectual and cultural changes thus paved the way for the later revolutions of the nineteenth century.

Exploring the World

As scholars and educated Europeans began to observe natural phenomena empirically and seek rational explanations, their conceptions of the world underwent fundamental transformation around 1750. The points of departure for these changes were new concepts, including Descartes's strict rationalism (which introduced systematic doubt as the basis for reaching scientific certainty), Newton's analytical method (which explained diverse natural phenomena with simple laws), and Locke's theory of knowledge (which was based on human perception and understanding, instead of divine creation). Through the influence of rationalism and empirical philosophy, new forms of knowledge—the sciences—began their emancipation from theology.

In the mid-eighteenth century, science in the modern sense did not yet exist. Science was considered an integral part of philosophy, and those who investigated nature were called natural philosophers. Individual disciplines had not yet taken shape. Knowledge came from empirical observations, and from theoretical and philosophical discussions, and thus from conceptions and ideas that had evolved over very long periods of time. The epistemological methods of the Enlightenment challenged this understanding of the world in the second half of the century, as seen in the biographies of the most renowned southeastern European natural philosophers.

Ruđer Bošković, the son of a prosperous trader from Dubrovnik, was a Jesuit and priest, physicist and astronomer, poet and philosopher, and a world-renowned polymath. When he was fourteen, he began his religious training in Rome. He taught mathematics at the Jesuit Collegium Romanum, where he also became acquainted with astronomy and physics. He was a typical scholar of his time; his ideal was the *respublica literaria,* the cosmopolitan republic of scholars and artists, where ethnic or national background was not important. Participants in the republic of letters communicated in Latin, and they were committed to universal educational ideals.[85]

Ruđer Bošković's intellectual personality was full of contradictions. As a man of the church, he was committed to the world of faith and tradition, although natural observations, calculations, and empiricism raised doubts about the old religious dogmas. Like many pious scholars of his time, Bošković struggled with the idea that Earth was not the center of the universe. Copernicus, Kepler, and Galileo had proved long before that the planets orbited elliptically around the sun. But the heliocentric universe was heresy to the church, and so the Jesuit Ruđer initially remained skeptical that the Earth revolved around the sun. Only after the Vatican withdrew its ban on the teachings of Copernicus in 1757 did his internal conflict between religion and science begin to ease.[86] He saw no contradiction between religion and science per se. Like his great role models Isaac Newton and Gottfried Wilhelm Leibniz, Bošković proceeded from the notion that the universe was divinely created. Unlike Newton and Leibniz, he no longer saw time and space as the creations of an almighty God, but rather as quantities that could be mathematically understood. In contrast to Leibniz, he rejected the notion that God had created "the best of all worlds." Rather, the world could be improved—a belief shared by the Enlightenment thinkers of his time.[87] The conservatism of the Jesuits eventually drove Bošković from Rome; he complained that "anyone here who speaks about a material object having a particular effect, force, or property is immediately suspected of heresy."[88] He found new academic homes in London, Paris, and Vienna, and he was invited to participate in the most important European scientific societies. The Royal Society in London, which had just sent Captain Cook to explore the southern seas, even wanted him to go to California to observe the constellations there.

Bošković wrote groundbreaking works about matter. His most famous book was the *Theoria Philosophiae Naturalis,* published in Vienna in 1758, which traced all physical occurrences back to calculable forces between the smallest particles. His model of the atom prefigured modern quantum physics, his "points of matter" returned much later in the study of elementary particles, and his conceptions of space and time prepared the way for the theory of relativity. In addition, Bošković was known for his expertise in the applied sciences. He assessed cracks in the dome of Saint Peter's Basilica for the Vatican, and the stability of the Imperial Library in Vienna for Maria Theresa. He built an observatory, and he invented optical, astronomical and geodetic instruments. At last, when he was seventy-six years old, he complained to his sister that his head had "become weaker and no longer does what I want."[89]

Several trends of the eighteenth century came together in Bošković's scientific career—including the gradual recognition of mathematics and the observation of nature as central methods of acquiring knowledge, and the emerging division between philosophy, science, and theology into separate, if still interconnected, intellectual spheres. Bošković stood at the threshold of a new age, but he never stepped all the way across it. Although he gradually moved away from an Aristotelian and scholastic interpretation of the world, his thoughts on space and time remained within the confines of classical cosmology. The Greek Eugenios Voulgaris, who never embraced the idea of a heliocentric universe throughout his lifetime, likewise remained a transitional thinker. He clung to the ideas of Tycho Brahe, who in the sixteenth century had tried to reconcile the traditional biblical interpretation of Earth as the center of the universe with new astronomical knowledge. Along with Brahe, Voulgaris asserted that the sun and moon circled Earth, while the other planets moved around the sun. Voulgaris's students could no longer accept this interpretation. One of them, Iosipos Moisiodax, wrote one of the most clearly formulated criticisms of Aristotelian logic. A disciple of Newton, Moisiodax taught his courses in astronomy with the assistance of a globe and a reflecting telescope. He was a confirmed empiricist who pleaded for the strict separation of science and religion, which he believed was essential for progress. He argued that the Holy Spirit could instruct initiates of the Bible, but not architects or mathematicians.[90] Around the same time, in 1783 the Serb Zaharije Orfelin became the first southeastern European to publish a handbook for physics and astronomy, the *Eternal Calendar,* which popularized the conception of a heliocentric universe. Demand for the book was so great that it had to be reprinted several times.[91]

Nevertheless, no one conception about the nature of the universe or the origin of knowledge prevailed at the end of the eighteenth century. Confirmed opponents of Galileo, Copernicus, and Newton continued to populate Orthodox and Catholic Church circles. Older depictions of the universe and early modern cosmographies still circulated widely, and Romanian and Slavic translations of medieval Byzantine literature continued to be reprinted into the first third of the nineteenth century. One genre envisioned the Earth as resting on the backs of four whales, while three hundred angels carried the weight of heaven. The authors had calculated the distance between heaven and Earth at exactly 349.92 kilometers. Romanian, Serbian, and Bulgarian translations of early Christian teachings about nature continued to be copied and distributed. The *Physiologus*, a popular work from the Middle Ages, allegorically described stones, plants, and animals, including the unicorn and phoenix. It presented creation as the result of a universal Christian plan for salvation. One can only conclude that southeastern Europeans had very different ideas about the world, depending on their background and level of education.[92]

In the 1790s the Orthodox Church responded to the French Revolution by launching an ideological campaign against the rationalist view of the universe. In Vienna, theology professor Sergios Makraios published *Triumph* (1797), a polemical text that castigated heliocentrism and the theory of multiple worlds as a creation of the devil. The church hierarchy distributed the text wherever it could.[93] In 1798 the patriarchate of Constantinople published a *Christian Apology* that denounced the French philosophes in general, particularly the "godless" Voltaire.[94] The Kollyvades monastic movement sought reforms in the spirit of an Orthodox counter-Enlightenment.[95] Subscription lists demonstrate, however, that the denounced books still spread rapidly, particularly after the turn of the century. Conservative men of the church, and even the patriarch in Constantinople, acquired books that popularized the Copernican worldview.[96]

As the new worldview gradually penetrated the different classes of society, the dissolution of medieval universalism first became apparent in historical writing. Works of history began to reflect a secularized understanding of time that was no longer cyclical, but oriented toward a linear depiction of human progress. Natural phenomena had previously shaped perceptions of history and time. Heavenly constellations ordered the calendar of saints; biological inheritance determined the succession of rulers.[97] In the 1830s the philosopher Constantine Michael Koumas published a twelve-volume history of the world from ancient times to the present, an encyclopedic synthesis of existing historical works. Koumas assumed that the world's origins were divine, but his narrative of progress was otherwise oriented toward humanistic and early historicist models and values.[98] Likewise, calendars and maps now provided a concrete, rather than mythic, awareness of time and space. Cadastral authorities began to measure parcels of land and to record data precisely. Official documents noted exact dates and years, a departure from peasant communities' traditional orientation around religious festivals and agricultural cycles of planting and harvesting. Even among the uneducated and illiterate classes, a gradual transformation of worldview had begun.[99]

A new culture of travel contributed to broader horizons of awareness. The construction of new streets and waterways meant that longer distances could be covered more quickly, and organized postal delivery facilitated communication. Goods, people, and news all traveled faster. At the end of the seventeenth century, a letter from Vienna could reach Venice in about one and a half weeks. By the mid-eighteenth century, it took only five days—and with express delivery, one day less.[100] Denser and speedier transportation networks improved opportunities for communication, changed contemporaries' experiences and perceptions, and created the conditions for travel to become its own form of knowledge.

Travelers from southeastern Europe set out to collect new experiences, preserving their impressions in books and reports. They got to know the developed West as well as more backward parts of the continent. Foreign lands could be a blank surface for projecting travelers' own desires, hopes, and fears. At the same time, their encounters with unfamiliar places made them more critical observers of conditions at home. By engaging with the "other," the contours of their own self-image became more distinct. One of these travelers was Ruđer Bošković, who accompanied the English envoy from Istanbul on a journey to Poland through Thrace, Bulgaria, and Moldavia in the spring of 1762. He wanted to go to Saint Petersburg for professional reasons. Covering long distances was a logistical, wearying challenge that could take many weeks—particularly within the Ottoman Empire, which had no organized means of transportation for people, money, or goods, or even way stations for changing horses. Travelers relied on the goodwill of Ottoman authorities, who assigned a state official to accompany foreign diplomats. A *firman* from the sultan meant that his subjects had to provide travelers with lodging, horses, cattle and wagon, and provisions. Since Turkish officials used the opportunity to skim off money to line their own pockets, outsiders were not well received. In Moldavia, the streets were completely barren because of "the barbaric custom . . . of seizing everything that one finds along the way . . . and without paying anything for it, whether oxen, horses, or wagon. They are taken away from peasants in the villages, and travelers along the road."[101] Travelers were often delayed for days, waiting for the Ottoman officials to coerce peasants with a wagon.

Bošković was hot-tempered by nature, but he recorded his travel impressions with sobriety, attention to nature, and—thanks to his rich knowledge of languages—a certain sympathy for the people he conversed with. Although he had lived in Italy for decades, he always emphasized his Slavic and Ragusan identity. He made his observations from the perspective of an educated outsider whose heritage facilitated his access to the Balkan lands that he visited. He observed the "barbaric" customs of the natives with horror, and he was shocked by their uncleanliness and lack of education. In Bulgarian Kanara, for example, he met a twenty-five-year-old priest. "He said his liturgy in Greek, but his ignorance, and the ignorance of his parishioners, was unbelievable. They know nothing about their religion other than the days of fasting and celebration; they make the cross, pray to their icons, which are quite repulsive, and call themselves Christians. They do not know the Creed or the Lord's Prayer, and they know nothing about their religion's noblest secrets." He recounted all of this in an anecdotal, not condescending, tone. He expressed genuine disgust only for the caprices of Ottoman authority, which had subjected these lands to "the most horrible despotism." He consistently described the Turks as haughty, greedy, and heartless. And in the Moldavian town of Galaţi on the Danube River, he observed Muslims who otherwise acted piously "enjoying days of freedom, visiting loose women, and drinking as much wine as they could."[102]

The problem of good governance likewise occupied the Romanian Dinicu Golescu, who traveled through Russia, Germany, Switzerland, and Italy a few decades later. The son of a Wallachian boyar, Golescu had received a good education in Bucharest and participated in enlightened Greek society. Of his own volition, he had already freed the Roma who were once bound to his land. By traveling through Europe, he sought to experience what was "good," so that he could pass it on to his own countrymen— "because it is clear that we have fallen behind all peoples."[103]

In Vienna, he was impressed not only by the architecture and transportation infrastructure but also by the hospitals, schools, and poorhouses. Seeing the prosperity, he could not help thinking "about the poverty of the inhabitants of the Romanian land, about the miserable, tattered clothing, but especially about those [people] on the far side of the Olt, who walk around, blackened, like animals that have made it through the winter, exhausted and emaciated." The Viennese must have dropped their jaws when the stout boyar from Wallachia exited his carriage, with his dark skin, dense beard, and bushy brows, clothed in a long Oriental robe and sable fur hat. A doctor in Vienna stopped him from entering a hospital "because [he] was wearing Turkish clothing, and everyone would become so excited by [his] appearance that the whole hospital would be in an uproar."[104]

Golescu's report is evidence that people began to reflect critically on their own situation—an important characteristic of modernity. New impressions elsewhere drew attention to unfavorable circumstances back at home—including legal uncertainty, wastefulness, injustices in taxation, nepotism, and the sale of offices. Thus, Golescu had "[his] own fatherland before [his] eyes and in [his] thoughts" throughout his entire journey. The practice of "good law" tugged at his conscience, for example, because as a district commissioner he had previously "exacted unlawful taxes from this [his] people, who could not even afford their daily bread."[105]

Bošković, Golescu, and other educated southern Europeans—like Dimitrie Cantemir before them—saw the Ottoman Empire as the antithesis of the civilized continent. "Europe" (which included Russia), by contrast, was the cultural paragon of reason and progress. "Greece needs Europe," asserted the scholar Iosipos Moisiodax, "because while Greece lacks everything, Europe has everything in abundance."[106] Individual opportunities and experiences shaped the authors' differing perceptions of the world, and their own place within it. In his 1783 autobiographical novel *Life and Adventures*, the Serb Dositej Obradović described the different stations of his life in southeastern Europe and elsewhere, and how he became an educated person. He—and other like-minded authors—did not develop ideas that were specific to his homeland. "The character of the Serbian people differs in no way from that of the English or Saxons," he wrote. "Nature bestowed it with the same advantages of body, heart, and spirit. It lacks only one thing, but the one thing is worth more than half: education."[107]

In contrast to educated Serbs, Croats, Romanians, and Greeks, the worldview of Muslims remained largely closed until the mid-nineteenth century. The Bosnian kadi Mustafa Muhibbi from Sarajevo left behind an expansive library of handwritten documents around the year 1850. His notes, marginalia, and collected texts reveal his disappointment and anxiety about an empire that was falling apart, its intellectual horizons limited by Islamic civilization. Muhibbi was an intellectually curious sharia judge, although he engaged exclusively with Islamic sources and networks—namely, the Sufi brotherhoods and ulema (clerics). He read only Arabic, Turkish, and Persian texts, which he borrowed and copied, or acquired from book dealers and estate auctions. His interests were wide-ranging—literature from his fields of specialization, law and religion, as well as mystical poetry, grammar, geography, medicine, and astronomy. In this intellectual system, knowledge was acquired in a traditional manner, usually by receiving what was already known, instead of firsthand investigation. This included the certainty that the world was the center of the universe, and that the heavenly bodies influenced fate. The kadi took countless notes, recording important events, medical remedies, poems, and necrologies. He often simply wrote down whatever someone had told him, especially medical advice, because at this time no trained doctors lived in Sarajevo. He also wrote about miracles.[108]

By the end of the eighteenth century, Western scholars had already discovered southeastern Europe as an object of study. Philosophers searched for the natural state of being, physiocrats worked to uncover natural economic laws, educational reformers sought ideal methods of upbringing, and anthropologists investigated early stages in the history of civilization. Jean-Jacques Rousseau introduced the paradigm of the "noble savage" who lived in a supposedly ideal state of nature. Rousseau's call to "return to nature" reflected the longing for an unspoiled paradise—and a reaction against the growing social complexity that had destabilized many eighteenth-century lives. The Italian priest and researcher Alberto Fortis projected longing for the "noble savage" onto the Slavs, introducing European readers to a side of the continent that was wholly unfamiliar to them. He published his *Travels into Dalmatia* in Venice in 1774. The book attracted great interest and was translated into German, Swedish, English, and French. Fortis drew on the work of a Franciscan monk from Ragusa, Andrija Kačić Miošić. Fortis's chapter on the "customs of the Morlachs"—an ethnographic study of primitive traditions among residents of the Dalmatian hinterlands—found particular resonance. The precise identity of the Morlachs is still disputed by scholars today. They were sometimes identified as the direct descendants of ancient peoples, sometimes as Romanized Vlachs, and sometimes they were equated with Slavs. Mountain herders in the Ottoman-Habsburg-Venetian borderlands were originally called "Morovlachi," but over the centuries the term's meaning changed many times. The term first referred to a Slavic-speaking, ethnically and religiously mixed rural population with distinctive customs and traditions.[109]

Fortis's exotic discoveries were made within the political context of Venetian imperial expansion. In the Great Ottoman War at the end of the seventeenth century, Venice had acquired new territories in Dalmatia with ethnically and culturally foreign populations. He described the Morlachs as primitives who lived in filth "like the Hottentots," who practiced all kinds of curious customs, and who angrily resisted any improvements to their desolate living conditions. At the same time, they demonstrated "natural" virtues like hospitality, courage, solidarity, and a sense of honor. Fortis described the "nobles from the sea" as trustworthy, sincere, and honest, "in daily life as well as in their treaties."[110]

The Morlach discourse provided a justification for subduing and taming the Slavic population, but it had a cultural subtext as well. It contrasted the nobility of nature with decadent civilization, untainted innocence with moral decay, noble virtue with extravagance and vice. In his travelogue, Fortis included the text of the classical Bosnian ballad "Hasanaginica." At a time when European writers were searching for ancient poetic folk traditions, the seventeenth-century Bosnian mourning song of the noble wife of Hasan-Aga sparked great attention. Goethe translated the Italian version into German, and Herder included it in his collection of European folk literature. Walter Scott, Alexander Pushkin, and Adam Mickiewicz were all enthusiasts of the epic poem. The "Illyrian bards," who sang of tragic heroes while playing the single-stringed instrument called the *gusla,* seemed to be the direct descendants of Homer, natural poets with an authentic and highly regarded aesthetic. For years thereafter, Fortis's travelogue inspired countless literary treatments of the Morlach theme.[111]

In Dalmatia, reactions to Fortis's revelations were mixed. The Croatian medical student Ivan Lovrić responded bitterly to Fortis's depiction of noble savages. Lovrić saw the Morlachs as descendants of the ancient Illyrians, who were distinguished by their hospitality, sense of freedom, and courageous heroism. They were morally superior to the ancient Romans and other civilized peoples, lacking only the education to overcome their old superstitions. As an alternate narrative, Lovrić introduced the life story of Stanislav Sočivica, the heroic *haiduk* and slayer of Turks, to Romantic folk song research. Sočivica was the Croatian version of the noble brigand, a popular figure in European literature; the character of Karl Moor in *The Robbers* by Friedrich Schiller is a prominent example.[112] Lovrić did, however, recognize the need for improving the socioeconomic conditions of the population. He lamented the Morlachs' mistrust of the new in their stubborn insistence that "whatever our ancestors didn't do, we won't either." Because of their warlike traditions, they viewed agriculture as an inferior pursuit. "There is nothing else that they neglect more," Lovrić complained.[113]

Bishop Stratiko, too, participated in the discourse about the natives. In the seventeenth century, Venice had systematically resettled mainland refugees fleeing the Turks on the Dalmatian islands, and Stratiko felt that Hvar was his own "Morlachia" within his diocese. "I don't know why writers always mention Canada and Madagascar when they are looking for examples of barbarism," he wrote to a friend, "when these [Dalmatian] . . . islands offer us the same thing, at a much closer distance."[114] Stratiko believed, however, that the savage islanders could be educated and properly socialized. "Some fools say that our Morlachs are lazy by nature. . . . This lie can only be dignified by someone who doesn't know the facts. Only the oppressed are lazy. Once they are freed from servitude, diligence is there."[115]

Contemporaneous with the Morlach discourse, other fundamental changes were reorganizing the cognitive map of Europe. Since the Renaissance, philosophers and travelers had distinguished between the "civilized" South as the cradle of European culture, and the "barbarian" North. The rise of new economic and cultural centers like Paris, London, and Amsterdam shifted this perspective in the eighteenth century. During the Enlightenment, the center of civilization moved westward, and backwardness went east.[116] In this context, the image of the Orient also became more clearly defined. The Ottoman wars reinforced the topos of a threatening, despotic, and cruel Ottoman Empire, which had been in place since the Renaissance.[117]

Postcolonial studies have shown how travelogues, scholarly treatises, and novels from the Enlightenment and Romantic eras cultivated stereotypes of an exotic Arabian culture that was defined by backwardness, violence, and eroticism. This culture was mysterious and alluring on one hand, but inferior and repugnant on the other. Orientalist discourse reflected a way of thinking that defined the "Orient" and "Occident" as asymmetrical opposites. It underscored the superiority of Western culture and defined

European and Occidental identity. With its pejorative stereotypes, Orientalism reinforced colonialism by suggesting the necessity of Western cultural dominance and imperial hegemony over less developed parts of the world.[118]

As artists, journalists, scholars, and adventurers began to travel more frequently to "European Turkey" in the eighteenth century, these stereotypes extended to southeastern Europe. The Duke of Richelieu, who traveled to Bukovina and Moldavia in 1774, remarked that "here is precisely where Europe stops, because the customs of the provinces . . . share a much greater resemblance with those of Asia."[119] Around the same time, Edward Gibbon wrote in his *History of the Decline and Fall of the Roman Empire* that the lands of Croatia and Bosnia were "still infested by barbarians."[120] European travelers and philosophers constructed images of otherness that informed thoughts and attitudes about southeastern and eastern Europe, and southeastern European authors themselves contributed to the exotic portrait of Ottoman conditions. The negative image of the Ottoman Empire colored emerging Orientalist stereotypes of the dangerous and wild, but also romantic, Balkans. These stereotypes would mature fully in the nineteenth century.[121]

Trade and Transformation during Protoglobalization

Global trade began to expand dramatically around 1750. Population growth, early industrialization, and the opening of new trade routes increased demand and revenue, so that the Ottoman Empire and its provinces become more closely integrated within the world economy. Southeastern Europe continued to serve as a hub between Europe, the Ottoman Empire, and parts of Asia. Ever since the discovery of America and the sea route around the Cape of Good Hope, trading nations were no longer compelled to use the traditional caravan routes. Nevertheless, until the beginning of the twentieth century silk, coffee, cotton, cloth, wheat, wax, camel hair, and leather continued to be transported through the Balkans from China and India to Gibraltar, and from Arabia and Asia Minor to Astrakhan and Kazan.[122]

The Ottoman Empire's most important trading partner in the eighteenth century was France, followed by the Habsburg Empire, Holland, Venice, and England. In the busy port cities of Istanbul, Smyrna, and Thessaloniki, the "Franks"—meaning Catholic Europeans—had an established presence with numerous consulates and trade offices. They purchased grain, cattle, cotton, silk, leather, oil, wax, wood, and tobacco at the Ottoman ports. In return, luxury goods were imported from Europe, especially valuable textiles, mechanical devices, porcelain, medical supplies, and clocks. In the meantime, the Ottoman Empire also received colonial goods that were imported by Europeans through the Atlantic triangle trade, especially coffee, sugar, cotton, and tobacco. Cheap slave labor on plantations pushed prices so low that even classic Levantine products like sugar and coffee were imported into the Ottoman Empire because of cheap overseas competition.[123]

Trade expanded within Europe as well after the Peace of Passarowitz opened the Adriatic Sea and Danube River for the international transport of goods in 1718. The Austrian emperor subsequently granted privileges to traders from the Orient, allowing numerous "Greek" merchants to settle in Trieste and Fiume, Vienna and Zagreb, Hungary and Transylvania. They established trade agencies along the Danube and other navigable rivers—for example, in Vidin, Belgrade, Novi Sad, Osijek, Pressburg (Bratislava), Buda, and Pest.[124] In the aftermath of a new Ottoman war and the Peace of Küçük Kaynarca in 1774, Russia compelled the opening of the Black Sea—including the Bosporus, the Dardanelles, and the Danube—to international trade. Christian traders from the Ottoman Empire were henceforth allowed to sail under the Russian flag and participate in the lucrative Ukrainian grain trade. A lively, transimperial triangle trade developed between the Anatolian Trabzon, the (new) Russian Odessa, and the Romanian cities of Brăila and Galați.[125]

The peace agreements of the eighteenth century sharpened competition among the great powers for access to economic resources and potential markets for commercial products. Because of transport routes to India, the Balkans were strategically important to the colonial powers. For two centuries, capitulations had provided the Ottoman Empire with a means of regulating the legal status of its foreign trading partners, but in the meantime they had also become instruments of economic penetration.[126] French, English, Dutch, and Russian envoys interpreted the privileges ever more broadly. They distributed and sold a great number of diplomas of appointment (berat) to Greek, Armenian, and Jewish traders, although these were originally intended only for interpreters and other local personnel. The traders acquired the protection of a foreign power and avoided Ottoman taxes, while the powers bolstered their own economic and political interests.[127] At the beginning of the nineteenth century, Russia alone had about 120,000 "protected" residents of the Ottoman Empire, who became a useful pretense for meddling in the empire's domestic affairs.[128]

In the early stages of industrialization, cotton was the commodity in highest demand on world markets. Producing, transporting, and processing the white fibers became the heart of the expanding capitalist system. Capital, specialized knowledge, institutions, and labor from all across the globe came together to build the "empire of cotton"—the driver of technological and material progress that created the modern world.[129] When the American War of Independence cut off these colonies from world trade flows in 1775, the aspiring European textile industries needed new sources of cotton, so the Ottoman Empire became one of the raw material's most important exporters. The amount of cotton sent to Marseille, the largest European transshipment port, increased twentyfold in the eighteenth century. Of this cotton, 22 percent went through the port of Thessaloniki alone.[130]

Because cotton was in such high demand, entire regions in southeastern Europe changed their patterns of cultivation accordingly. In Macedonia, cotton production tripled between 1720 and 1800.[131] Forty percent of all harvested cotton, grain, and tobacco flowed to Europe.[132] "The city of Sérès is the common market, to which the peasants repair every Sunday, during the winter, out of the whole valley," the French consul observed. "Some come to offer cottons, the growth of their own fields. Others . . . come to seek dupes for the cottons, which they have purchased in small quantities, and which they want to sell again by wholesale." Wholesalers and middlemen often purchased goods sight unseen. "It is thus that immense transactions are commenced."[133] Merchants acted within networks that connected capitalists, wholesalers, manufacturers, and consumers across vast distances, enabling great profits. In the nineteenth century, Turkish cotton was again pushed from the market by American cotton, which was better and cheaper.[134]

While export and import markets expanded significantly in the second half of the eighteenth century, domestic trade remained decisive for the Ottoman Empire around 1800. Farmers, craftsmen, textile and weaving mills, shipyards, and armories served a market of twenty-five million to thirty-two million consumers, which was immense for its time. As before, a large portion of southeastern European products were marketed within the Ottoman Empire—for example, grain from the Danubian Principalities, cotton from Macedonia, tobacco from Bulgaria, and leather goods from Bosnia and Kosovo. Domestic demand was at least as important as the export market for the development of trade and industry—and thus for the early stages of industrialization—within the Ottoman Empire.[135]

The explosion of foreign trade allowed a growing class of Christian traders and suppliers to emerge. Many a "Greek trader" found new wealth and social recognition, whereby all Orthodox Christians (including Serbian, Bulgarian, Albanian, and Wallachian merchants) were counted as "Greeks." This new commercial class could be found in diverse regions of the Ottoman Empire. Its members included Phanariots from Istanbul and the Danubian Principalities, as well as Greek traders and shipowners from the Aegean islands, who entered into long-distance trade agreements with the European states and founded commercial outposts in the Habsburg Empire and Russia. Others who demonstrated their aptitude for business included Greek Albanian traders from the Adriatic, Wallachian and Slavic mule drivers from Macedonia, Epirus, and Thessaly, Greek and Bulgarian wagon drivers from the Rhodope and Balkan Mountains, and Serbian cattle traders from Pannonia and the Šumadija.[136] Established Muslim trading families from Bosnia also got involved in the business of long-distance European trade.[137]

Given the potential profits of trading in and with the great empires, prosperous colonies of merchants arose in Russia and the Habsburg Monarchy. Traders from southeastern Europe created centers of education and culture—as in Vienna, where the first Greek- and Serbian-language newspapers appeared in the 1790s, and where a "Greek National School" was even established after the turn of the century. Orthodox, Jewish, Armenian, and Protestant migrants became part of an aspiring economic middle class in Trieste. The Herzegovinian shipowner Draga Todorović, for example, had his fourteen galleons set sail to America and southeast Asia from Trieste.[138] In 1786 the port city's chief of police confirmed that longtime residents and newcomers were striking advantageous business deals with one another, regardless of religion. The wealthy merchant Nikolaos Plastaras from Ioannina sat down to dine with the Austrian governor Karl von Zinzendorf.[139] "Those who are not Catholic may be, and often are, honest men, with the same moral values, who have learned their customs and felt the same needs."[140] Greeks, Serbs, and Albanians also settled throughout the Black Sea region—for example, in Taganrog, Sevastopol,

Kherson, and Odessa. The Serb Sava Tekelija, who visited Odessa in 1811, "was amazed to hear mostly Serbian in the streets and coffee houses. Even the burgomaster was then Petrović, a Serb from Novi Sad. . . . After the Serbian language, Italian was most audible; then Greek, Russian, and Turkish. And there were many Jews."[141]

The growth of international trade remained strong after the end of the eighteenth century, and businessmen covered ever greater distances to create systems of manufacturing and sales that were based on the division of labor. Family and business ties as well as a common outlook linked overseas markets and central locations within the Ottoman Empire, the Habsburg Monarchy, Russia, and other states. The Greek Ralli family from Chios owned one of the most important companies in the international cotton trade. The Rallis gradually opened offices in London, Liverpool, Manchester, Istanbul, Odessa, Calcutta, Karachi, Bombay, and the United States over the course of the nineteenth century. They purchased the desired raw material in the United States, processed it in English factories, and finally sold the finished goods in India. Each part of this global system of production and distribution remained in the hands of just one family. Bulgarian merchants from Plovdiv who maintained a large site of operations in Calcutta followed a similar model.[142]

Even merchants who did not establish a foreign office maintained contacts with other parts of the world through business relationships, travel, and correspondence. The Macedonian cotton trader Marko Teodorović, for example, conducted business with thirty-four different correspondents in the 1790s. From Serres, he sent goods all the way to Vienna and Pest, traveling back and forth constantly between the different locations.[143] The twenty different types of money in one Bulgarian merchant's till illustrate the diversity of trade relationships in southeastern Europe at the beginning of the nineteenth century. The Ottoman kurus, Brandenburg brandabur, Venetian ducat, and Russian moskovski were among the coins he collected.[144]

Professional specialization was still incomplete around 1800. Traders were businesspeople in the broadest sense. Anyone who sold goods for profit might also serve simultaneously as a transporter, moneylender, tax farmer, commercial agent, or manufacturer. Linguistic and ethnic identities were still in flux. In a world of business that straddled many cultures, Greek was the lingua franca, interspersed with local idioms and words in Turkish,

Arabic, and Slavic. Despite their diverse backgrounds, the new merchant class formed a cosmopolitan community that developed similar interests, views, and ways of life. Its members often lived thousands of miles apart.[145]

Hristo Račkov was a typical merchant of his time. Born in Bulgarian Gabrovo in the mid-eighteenth century, this furrier's son kept a business register for thirty-five years. He noted the details in Bulgarian and Greek—what he sold and to whom, how much he earned, and where he invested his profits. Hristo engaged in both wholesale and retail trade in his native region, but he also supplied more distant markets within and outside the Ottoman Empire, including Thessaloniki, Istanbul, Bucharest, and even Moscow. He imported linen from Egypt and buffalo leather from Russia. His lists included 122 different articles, among them foodstuffs and live-stock, wooden goods and textiles, silver and jewelry, tobacco and rose water. An expansive, supraregional network of business partners of all different backgrounds supported him and profited alongside him. This enterprising businessman—who was already familiar with specialized terms such as capital, copy, and commission—eventually redirected his efforts toward investing in a profitable cottage industry. He purchased large quantities of raw silk at favorable prices from large estate owners in the region around Tarnovo and Gabrovo so that the silk could be spun and processed by wage earners. At the end of his life, Hristo owned a house, two shops, a bakery, an inn, two water mills, plus numerous other properties and a consider-able sum of money.

Hristo was not only skilled in business, but also pious, charitable, and politically engaged. He donated money for two public wells in his home-town of Gabrovo, gave to the church and the poor, and remembered or-phans in his will. Despite a booming business, he nevertheless undertook a pilgrimage to the Holy Land to earn the title of *haji*. This increased his social standing and sales. He secretly gave part of his fortune to the Greek underground organization Filiki Eteria, which sought to overthrow Ot-toman rule. Ethnic or national identity did not appear to play a role for him. Fearful of being exposed after the outbreak of the Greek uprising in 1821, he took his own life.[146]

A new generation of entrepreneurs advanced protoindustrialization in other parts of southeastern Europe, too. Petko Stoianov supervised the manufacture of overgarments in Bulgarian Kalofer, selling his products as far away as Istanbul and Anatolia. And Anatas Gümüşgerdan and his sons, who came from Plovdiv, employed peasant homeworkers in the Rhodope Mountains to supply the Ottoman army.[147]

The greater the potential for profit on the markets, the faster a capitalist economic mentality developed, as illustrated by the example of the Macedonian Gjurčin Kokaleski. The long-distance merchant, cattle trader, publisher, and employer of about 150 wage earners wrote an autobiographical narrative—a kind of early modern advice book for businessmen—that shared his experiences and tips for getting rich.[148] The virtues that inspired capitalism, such as thrift and hard work, did not depend on the religion of those whose personal initiative brought economic success. A specific "Protestant ethic," as proposed by Max Weber, was not essential. Most economic historians now refute the connection between religious orientation and a capitalist work ethic.[149]

Rising demand, better chances for making money, and a profit-oriented economic mentality encouraged specialized commercial landscapes with supraregional significance at the end of the eighteenth century—for example, in Plovdiv, Serres, Thessaloniki, Shkodër, and Trnovo. Spinning mills and dye works expanded because henna-red "Turkish yarn" was so popular in European markets. About 2,500 bales were exported annually from the Thessalian town of Ambelakia and the surrounding villages to the Habsburg Monarchy and Germany. "All arms, even those of children, are employed in the dyes of Ambélakia," one observer marveled.[150] The residents founded cooperative associations and trade offices in cities like Thessaloniki, Istanbul, Smyrna, Vienna, Amsterdam, London, and Odessa.[151]

In addition to manufactured products, special handcrafted items from southeastern Europe were also in high demand. Dye workers from Thessaly found work elsewhere in Europe, as did tailors from Epirus. They produced rustic work clothes for sailors and peasants, the beloved *capotti alla greca*. Austrian and French entrepreneurs hired Greeks to show their own workers how to create products in the "Levantine style." In return, southeastern European traders and merchants embraced Western fashions, decorative objects, and styles of design, which became new status symbols in the Balkans. In the town of Zagori in the Pindus Mountains, for example, a merchant decorated his house with a mural of Napoleon and Josephine.[152]

Like the Bulgarian Hristo Račkov, other businessmen wanted not only to turn a profit but also to change the world. Businessmen distinguished themselves as patrons of literature, book publishing, and newspapers for the Balkan peoples, and as sympathizers, supporters, and even instigators of revolutionary movements. Half of the members of the Greek secret society Filiki Eteria, which was founded in 1814, had mercantile backgrounds. An increasingly self-confident and internationally well-connected early bourgeoisie arose from the ranks of traders and capitalists, their economic success now inspiring political demands. The leaders of nineteenth-century Serbian and Romanian uprisings, Djordje Petrović Karadjordje and Tudor Vladimirescu, earned their wealth as cattle traders.[153]

As in many places around the world, potential profits through the sale of raw materials led to new means of controlling labor and land. Cost-effective mass production for the supraregional market was achieved by concentrating land in the hands of powerful estate owners. They determined what crops were cultivated—grain for the Ottoman domestic market or high-profit cotton for export. Commercialization and worldwide economic integration hastened the transformation of the old agrarian order that had begun in the seventeenth century. In the eighteenth century, the sultan gave in to pressure to privatize state lands. Given the empire's shortage of funds, he apparently decided that profit-oriented large estate owners were preferable to the old feudal lords who were most concerned about status and privileges. Former timariots, state officials, and janissaries purchased property or took estates by force, frequently driving peasants from their farms. The Romanian boyars were particularly aggressive in seizing ever more land from free peasants, village communities, and markets, often in the guise of phony sales contracts. Tenant famers on the resulting latifundia had to pay high rent and perform mandatory labor services. Between the 1760s and 1830s, the labor requirement rose from three to sixty-eight days per year.[154]

The northern Bulgarian region around Vidin illustrates the close relationship between rising supraregional and global demand, and the emergence of commercially profitable large estates. The transformation of lands into private estates with dependent peasants (*çiftliks*) that had once been temporarily granted by the sultan began when the Danube was opened for trade in the eighteenth century, and the value of arable land shot up suddenly. The state profited considerably from the sale of its land to private owners, which now occurred on a large scale. The new property holders were exclusively Turkish, although the previous peasant farmers were mostly Bulgarian. From this point forward, they earned a wage to grow grain, fruit, vegetables, cotton, and other produce on estates of thirty to five hundred hectares for supraregional markets. Newly established trade companies provided ships and storehouses for transport along the Danube. In just a few decades, Vidin became part of a far-reaching economic network. The region not only profited from trade, but later from industry, too.[155]

The general decline of Ottoman institutions, which had been apparent since the seventeenth century, picked up speed everywhere in the eighteenth century. Property, along with administrative and military offices—such as those of provincial administrators, tax collectors, and janissaries—were sold to the highest bidder, no longer awarded on the basis of skill or accomplishment. The state auctioned off the right to collect taxes and duties in the provinces, typically to relatives of Istanbul elites, for great sums of money. In turn, these elites employed local tax farmers to collect the money on site. Becoming a tax farmer often entailed taking on a great amount of debt, so the position was seen as a legitimate source of personal enrichment and was ultimately impossible for others to oversee. Competition among landlords, janissaries, provincial administrators, merchants, governors, and local notables for the lucrative office was correspondingly fierce.[156]

The system was disadvantageous for many because taxes were no longer levied per head, but collectively from villages and city districts. The Ottoman financial officer Süleyman Penah Efendi complained that, in practice, tax farmers simply collected what they wanted, keeping the lion's share for themselves. The population had to pay head and land taxes, import and market duties, and contributions to landlords, governors, state officials, and the church. Illegal taxation and embezzlement were everyday occurrences, as was violent extortion. Men were imprisoned and held in chains "to extort even more *akçe* [taxes] out of them." The new system created growing dissatisfaction among subjects of the Ottoman state. The people "no longer knew their way in or out; or . . . which tyrant they had to pay first."[157] In addition, tax farmers in the capital city withheld a significant portion of taxes and goods. As a consequence, less grain reached Istanbul; despite strict bans on exports, merchants preferred to sell their grain abroad. Tax farmers became a rich, powerful, and self-confident class of local elites, a counterweight to central authority that was hard to control.[158]

Economic power was increasingly concentrated in the hands of Muslim *ayan,* or local notables. The Ottoman state had long used the *ayan* to administer its provinces more effectively. These respected personalities had traditionally served as intermediaries between the bureaucracy and the local population. In the eighteenth century, the position of the *ayan* could also be purchased, and its powers grew correspondingly. Many *ayan* served in multiple capacities at once—for example, as tax farmers, provincial administrators, landlords, and traders. Other responsibilities included upholding public order and safety, fighting against smuggling, and regulating postal and messenger service. They also oversaw mobilization and supply of the army. In return, they were allowed to collect additional payments from the population.[159]

The *ayan* formed a new elite that held political, economic, and military power in the Ottoman provinces. Supported by family networks, tribal structures, and militias, they exercised nearly unlimited power in certain parts of Rumelia, Anatolia, Syria, and Egypt. They were at once despots, magnates, and warlords. In the Balkans, for example, Ali Pasha from Ioannina, Osman Pazvantoğlu from Vidin, and Ismail Pasha from Ruse became self-sufficient local power brokers and agents of military power. Around 1800, at least thirty-nine territories in the region were effectively autonomous, controlled by *ayan*.[160]

In certain areas, the Ottoman state also relied on Christian notables who were involved in local government, such as village elders and other community leaders who came from well-known families. At first they were responsible for maintaining order and security and for implementing certain administrative duties. In the eighteenth century, they developed into a Christian social elite who were comparable to the *ayan*—called *kocabaşı* on the Peloponnese, and *çorbacı* in Bulgaria and Macedonia. They lived from their land, tax farming, trade, and moneylending.[161] A Greek revolutionary attested that Greek landowners and elites on the Peloponnese were no different from the Muslim *ayan*. The "only difference is their name; one was called Gianni instead of Hasan, and he went to the church instead of the mosque."[162] They extorted the peasants, enriched themselves at the cost of the state, and undermined the legitimacy of the sultan, gutting the Ottoman system of rule. These elites, who were derided as "Christian Turks," increasingly competed with the Muslim *ayan* over property and income from taxes, as well as over political influence and upward mobility. Dissatisfaction grew because the Ottoman social order largely excluded members of the Christian elite from any further social or political advancement. Many later supported the fight for independence.

The great economic, social, and legal changes that began in the early seventeenth century and increased rapidly in the second half of the eighteenth

Dubrovnik, eighteenth century. Liber Viridis.

century profoundly transformed the social order. The revolution in trade reinforced the worldwide division of labor, which assigned the lands of southeastern Europe—and the entire Ottoman Empire—the role of raw materials and foodstuffs supplier. At the same time, this revolution created new wealth and economically aspirational social groups. The expansion of the world economy hastened the commercialization of agriculture and the creation of large private estates. Peasants became poorer and more dependent, and the Ottoman state lost revenue and control over new regional elites. Among the Balkan Christians, groups emerged that positioned themselves as rivals to the old Ottoman elites. They had contacts that transcended state borders, sufficient capital, and often a higher education, allowing them to bring about fundamental changes in structures of power. They were driven by socioeconomic interests and by idealistic and political motivations.

Ragusa (Dubrovnik), 1776

When the British colonies in North America declared independence on July 4, 1776, Ruđer Bošković was in Paris. Three years earlier, he had taken French citizenship and accepted a position as "director of optics," so that he could develop nautical instruments for the navy of Louis XV. At heart, however, he remained loyal to his "first, true home," sending newspaper articles and current reports to the government of the Republic of Ragusa, called Dubrovnik in the language of the people. Bošković was enthusiastic about the new America, and a few years earlier he had almost traveled to California himself for astronomical observations.[163] For his sister Anica, a writer who lived in Dubrovnik, America was a mystery; she wrote to him, "We did not know what or how it was, nor where, this wonderful place was located."[164] For Ruđer, however, the world had become a smaller place. He became reacquainted with his colleague in physics Benjamin Franklin, whom he had met years ago in London, as the American ambassador at the French court.[165]

Dubrovnik's consul in Paris, Francesco Raimondo Favi, also recognized the international political significance of the Americans' declaration of independence. He complained about the "unjustly begun and so poorly waged war" of the British, predicting the United States' economic dominance in the future. International recognition would come, and Dubrovnik should not lag behind. "Their ports are open to practically anyone," Favi reported. The only requirement was a good sense for business.[166] This raised sensitive questions for the patricians of Dubrovnik. Wouldn't diplomatic contacts with the revolutionary government provoke a conflict with the British? The city's representatives did not give the go-ahead until the middle of 1783, when a formal peace agreement between Great Britain and the United States was imminent.[167]

Trade relations with the United States were a pressing matter because competition from Holland, England, and France had reduced Dubrovnik's share of Mediterranean trade. With 190 sailing vessels, the Ragusan merchant fleet was larger than that of Venice or Prussia, providing a source of income for about 2,200 sailors as well as 400 shipowners and shareholders. Fourteen different types of vessels were built in twelve shipyards. Because of their enormous carrying capacity and solid construction, the three- and four-masters, naves and galleons, were favored even in the old seafaring nations of Italy and England.[168] A contemporary remarked that "the seas are full of ships from Dubrovnik and . . . the flag of Saint Blaise is accepted and welcomed all over the world."[169] Hundreds of workers, carpenters, joiners, builders, masons, fishermen, as well as divers for corals and sponges depended on shipbuilding. In addition, there were the employees of trade agencies, port authorities, consulates, and insurance companies. Together, the navy, sea trade, and the port constituted the most important pillar of tax revenue.[170]

To support its trade relationships around the world, the city-republic maintained eighty-five consulates in the second half of the eighteenth century, in sites such as Vienna, Rome, Paris, Lisbon, Madrid, Cádiz, Marseille, Venice, Naples, Palermo, Mallorca, Tunis, Tripoli, Alexandria, and Istanbul.[171] "Stick a finger in the sea, and you are in touch with all the world!" went a familiar saying.[172] Consuls were tasked with collecting information and reporting back to the Ragusan Senate with the "greatest accuracy and candor." For their reports, they used a special, secret diplomatic script. To ensure the goodwill of other powers, Dubrovnik served as an unofficial hub of foreign intelligence. Informants reported regularly to the Roman Curia, Austria, and other interested states about happenings in the Ottoman Empire.[173] At the same time, the "loyal tributary"—as Dubrovnik styled itself—also informed the Sublime Porte about the Christian powers' plans.[174]

For residents of Dubrovnik around 1776, the great changes of the era were barely visible. The social order continued to be defined by seemingly insurmountable barriers—between nobles and burghers, men and women, natives and foreigners, Catholics and "infidels." About 4,000 people lived in the city. Another 31,000 were spread throughout the rest of the state's territory, which stretched from Neum to the Bay of Kotor, and included several islands.[175]

The highest echelons of society were occupied by nobles, who effectively held a monopoly on political power and economic resources in the republic at the end of the eighteenth century. Only twenty-four elite families, including the Bona, Ghetaldi, Gondola, Ragnina, and Sorgo, dominated positions of leadership in public life, state service, and the church. This was not more than one hundred people in all. Even so, the nobility could be divided into more than ten different levels of status.[176] The clergy and urban bourgeoisie belonged to the other traditional estates, along with the majority of the population—marketeers and sailors, craftsmen and laborers, peasants and beggars. Only the nobility spoke Italian, the language of public life. The burghers and common people exclusively spoke a dialect that was sometimes called "Illyrian" or "Slavic," or else simply "naški" (our language).

Noblemen were shipowners and merchants, or else large landowners. The former made their fortunes through trade, the latter through agriculture. Their large estates were located outside the city, which they supplied with food. Free peasants were rare; most worked as serfs or *kmets* to secure the landlords' income. In return for the use of house and land, they had to pay rents and perform services. At the end of the eighteenth century, this might be up to ninety days of labor per year. To escape these high burdens, many young men fled the land and joined the crew of a ship. Peasant daughters, by contrast, were compelled to become domestic servants for wealthy urban families. If they pleased the head of the household, they were also expected to serve him at night.[177]

Because the status of the nobility was defined by inheritance, marriages were only permitted among social equals. Patricians distinguished themselves through their lifestyle, clothing, demeanor, values, and not least, through an arrogance that was insufferable to outsiders. An Austrian spy, who spent five weeks in the city in 1776, noted that "the patricians view their subordinates as slaves, and everyone outside their class as inferior." Their haughtiness and hypocrisy deeply repulsed him. "But even the burghers look disdainfully at foreigners and those of a lower class."[178] The social distance between families was great, and it was entirely insurmountable between classes. "In public places, on the main square, in the churches, at the theater . . . each class keeps its distance from the others," remarked the French consul Le Maire.[179] At large celebrations, balls, and salons, at tournaments and regattas, in the theater or at the renowned Carnival, the different social groups kept to themselves.[180]

In elite society, the sexes were strictly segregated. Only married women were allowed to appear in public, at church, at social events, or on the street. As in France, ladies wore expensive dresses of velvet or brocade, with large hoop skirts decorated with lace and pompons.[181] Women who could be seen in everyday life were almost exclusively from the lower classes—bakers, market-women, servants, washerwomen, seamstresses, weavers, and innkeepers.[182]

The nobility and bourgeoisie upheld a strict sexual morality—although only outwardly. "It is a crime and a scandal merely to visit women during the day, even with honorable intentions," Consul Le Maire noted with indignance, "but creeping into their homes at night hardly shocks anyone."[183] Covering up affairs with a cloak of silence was an accepted convention of elite society. Unwanted children could be left anonymously in a "baby hatch." They remained in the care of the state until they were six years old, when they were given to adoptive families.[184]

The city-republic's aristocratic constitution followed Venice's example. On reaching adulthood, patricians' sons wore long black robes that distinguished them as nobles and as members of the political class that governed the city through three bodies. The general assembly of the nobles was the Great Council, which elected the city rector, or *knez*. As first among equals, he directed the affairs of the republic for a term of one year, supported by his ministers, the Small Council. The Great Council also elected the members of the powerful Senate, which was responsible for all domestic and foreign policy decisions. Forty-five patricians, including the *knez,* sat in the eighteenth-century Senate.[185] After a terrible earthquake decimated the ranks of the nobility in 1667, the patricians decided to accept four particularly wealthy and well-respected bourgeois families into the noble class that same year. Since then, the values, interests, and ambitions of the nobility had begun to diverge. Tensions between the old and new nobility, wealthier and poorer patricians, landlords and shipowners had become apparent by the end of the eighteenth century.[186] In addition, new elites began to challenge the old order, particularly members of the bourgeoisie who had acquired great wealth through trade and now sought a political voice. Intellectual movements that questioned the supremacy of the aristocracy also played a role. With respect to foreign policy, patrician society splintered into Franco-, Austro-, and Russophile factions.[187]

Almost entirely surrounded by Ottoman territory, the small city-republic had managed to preserve its *libertas* through diplomatic cunning, strict neutrality, and various tribute payments. In the city center, not far from the rector's palace, a statue of Roland had embodied the city's will for liberty since 1419. The legendary hero from the time of Charlemagne, whose adventures were immortalized in the *Song of Roland,* had supposedly freed the city from Arab attack. For three centuries, Orlando—as he was affectionately called by the city's residents—had carried the white flag bearing the image of the city's patron, Saint Blaise. The statue was probably erected during the reign of Sigismund (King of Hungary and Bohemia, and then German emperor), under whose protection Ragusa stood at that time. In Dubrovnik, freedom and repression went hand in hand; the Roland statue also served as a "pillar of shame."[188]

Dubrovnik in the eighteenth century was the Catholic outpost that lay farthest to the south and to the east, a small *antemurale christianitatis*. It had been the seat of an archdiocese since the Middle Ages, and few cities could claim so many churches, chapels, and monasteries within such a small space. Catholicism was the state religion. The papacy had always paid special attention to the diocese because of its position on Christianity's front lines. Foundations and endowments were established to help spread the true faith, whether in opposition to the Bogomil heretics in Bosnia, or later the Muslims in the Ottoman Empire. Because the Senate did not permit local nobles to serve as bishop, most church leaders (and the clerics who accompanied them) came from Italy, ensuring close ties with the Holy See in Rome. The old law was abolished in 1680, and the first native archbishop was appointed in 1721.[189] In contrast to western Catholic lands, the church in Dubrovnik was completely subordinate to politics; it did not represent a true counterbalance to the government. The archbishop was explicitly forbidden to interfere in the city-republic's domestic and foreign affairs.[190] The Senate had affirmed that only the republic was "master over all worldly and spiritual questions."[191] According to the French consul, under these circumstances it was "better to be a complete idiot, like the current office-holder," than to be disturbed by the lack of independence.[192]

The monasteries played an important role in the city's social and political life. Franciscans, Dominicans, and Benedictines had begun to settle here in the thirteenth century. The monks served as the "eyes" of the republic because they not only preached and attended to spiritual matters, but were also active in science, diplomacy, and social affairs. It was typical for sons of the nobility to join one of the orders, and only men of their standing could become abbot.

The monks also promoted medical knowledge. For centuries, they had traveled to Italy and elsewhere to collect the latest remedies and specialized literature. Thousands of folios with pharmaceutical, chemical, and anatomical literature filled monastery libraries. In 1775, the Dominican Vitale De Santis completed a monumental reference work on 604 medicinal plants.[193] At this time, the monks knew more than two thousand remedies, both "secret" and everyday. They grew medicinal plants such as sage, coltsfoot, lungwort, and speedwell in monastery gardens, and they purchased sulfur, cone sugar, and animal specimens. They mixed tinctures and extracts to treat infectious diseases and fight parasites, and also to promote longevity, memory, and even marital harmony. They procured large quantities of leeches and kept poisonous snakes.[194] Franciscans and Dominicans operated pharmacies that attracted patients from great distances. The Benedictine pharmacy that Brother Martin and a Florentine doctor turned into a joint-stock company *(societas)* in 1690 became so profitable that by 1776, it gave every monk a stipend for clothes and even loaned money to people outside the monastery.[195]

At the request of the archbishop, the Jesuit order came to the city at the beginning of the seventeenth century to missionize the Orthodox and Muslim population in the Ottoman Empire, and to fight the remnants of heathenism.[196] The Jesuits had been an influential force since the Counter-Reformation, and also in the Baroque period. In the mid-seventeenth century, the order established a college that Ruđer Bošković later attended. The power of the Jesuits within the church had since become so strong, the cleric Đuro Matijašević wrote, that every archbishop who sought to make a name for himself in Dubrovnik was advised "to stay on their good side."[197] The pope suppressed the order in 1773.

In the patriarchal society of the eighteenth century, nuns were expected to lead a strictly ordered life of contemplation and seclusion. At best, they could take up a social mission by caring for the sick and the poor. Convents for women served primarily to stabilize the strict social hierarchy. Among the upper classes, only prospective brides with a generous dowry could expect to attract a husband. If the family's wealth was only enough for one daughter, the others had to enter a convent. Hundreds of young women involuntarily disappeared behind high walls and barred windows because they could not find an appropriate husband. Even the Dominican Bazilije Gradić was moved when virgins were forced to enter a convent "completely against their will . . . crying and wailing" over their misfortune, or submitting mutely to a fate of obedience, silence, denial, and pain.[198]

The first fruits of women's scholarship, and formal Croatian writing of any kind, arose in the nuns' convents. Since there was little religious literature in the vernacular, the sisters began to compose pious poetry, prayer books, and psalms in the "Slavic or Illyrian language."[199] With the permission of the prelate, theatrical performances were even held in the convents, and masked singers appeared underneath the nuns' windows during Carnival. One cleric described the tradition of "young brides who are related to a nun bringing their entire wedding party to the convent" as "one of the greatest absurdities. . . . Love songs are performed to musical accompaniment, and there is even dancing and food."[200]

The priesthood primarily recruited from the lower classes and held little social cache. Clerics were often uneducated, and the office was sometimes held by former fortune-tellers. The relationship between archdiocese and priesthood was fraught. The latter organized itself in a brotherhood *(confraternitas)* with its own rules, largely removing itself from church oversight. "The native clergy closed itself off, as in a fortress, taking aim at the seat of the archbishop."[201] Other professional classes also organized in brotherhoods—including artists, craftsmen, and members of social professions. There were twenty-eight such professional associations in all, sacred and secular. Among other responsibilities, they oversaw hospices for the poor and other charitable institutions.

Religion played a dominant role in both public life and popular culture of the eighteenth century. The city honored its patron, Saint Blaise, who was ensconced above the western city gate; many churches and chapels bore his name. Each year on February 3, his relics were carried through the city in a great procession. People crowded into the streets to kiss them, or merely to steal a glimpse. The power of faith and the Catholic Church was nearly unrivaled. Despite all efforts, however, traces of pre-Christian beliefs remained among the common people, who—as one cleric complained— had "heads full of devils, witches, vampires, snakes, and a thousand other idiocies."[202]

Catholic society functioned according to strict rules of religious inclusion and exclusion. Religious participation was allowed for non-Catholics only in niches. Twelve to fifteen Orthodox families, who had emigrated from Bosnia and were mostly active in trade, were allowed to practice their faith. But the city fathers decisively opposed the construction of an Orthodox church.[203] The Jews, by contrast, were allowed to maintain a synagogue and brotherhood.[204] Otherwise, they were subject to similar discrimination. As was the case everywhere else in the Catholic world, they had to tie a yellow ribbon around their hats. The city had a ghetto, but because it did not have room for the city's approximately two hundred Jews, they were also permitted to live nearby. Jews could own houses and ships, but they were not allowed to walk on the streets at night.[205] The Catholic diocesan synod forbade its believers to work or spend the night in Jewish households. Any physical interaction "with them and the Turks" was outlawed.[206] Any close contact between Christians and Muslims was likewise strictly proscribed. In 1774 the Senate ordered punishment by public shaming for every Christian woman who became involved with a Turk.[207]

In Dubrovnik, too, there were people who did not—or did not any longer—believe in the omnipotence of God and the church, although both church and state authority zealously guarded the true faith. On December 23, 1776, the archbishop interrogated the twenty-five-year-old Nicollò Remedelli: "Do you know a heretic, a blasphemer . . . or anyone who owns or reads banned books of any kind?" Multiple witnesses had confirmed statements made by the accused that there was no God, no hell, and no paradise, and that a sin did as little harm as a dog howling at the moon. Remedelli was said to own banned books by Rousseau, and to refuse confession and worship. In addition, he sinned with women. Although he denied everything ("falso falsissimo!"), the Holy Curia pronounced him guilty. The Senate sentenced him to six years in prison. One council member's suggestion—to put the delinquent in a sack and throw it far out to sea—was not approved by the majority. Before the sentence could be carried out, Nicollò fled to Bologna. Only years later was he pardoned in his home city.[208]

At the end of the eighteenth century, the Ottoman Empire's decline in power sharpened rivalry among the great powers over political influence, market access, and the protection of trade routes to the Near East and Asia. England and France competed to expand their colonial empires, while Austria and Russia fought over political influence and military strongholds in southeastern Europe, which became a focus of the new tensions in international relations.

Despite its dramatic decline, the Ottoman Empire was still Dubrovnik's most important—and most dangerous—neighbor. Since the sultan had wrested away Hungary's sovereignty over the city-republic in 1526, it was expected to pay a tribute called the *haraç*. At the end of the eighteenth century, this was a sum of 12,500 ducats, to be paid every third year. If there were problems with payment, Ottoman soldiers appeared before the city walls. The Bosnian pasha who was responsible for Dubrovnik unambiguously announced: "If our master . . . is enraged by a Christian leader who treats him like an enemy, his people will be . . . subdued. You must

understand that . . . his commands are to be obeyed."[209] The city's representatives thus preferred not to question the tribute payments. In return, the
sultan guaranteed protection from attack—from his own forces as well as
from corsairs in the Mediterranean who were his allies. On April 24, 1776,
all Ottoman officeholders were reminded to "protect and defend" those
who lived in the city, who had "long depended on Ottoman protection. . . .
No one may hinder them when they travel or engage in trade."[210]

In their interactions with the sultan, whom they called the "Great Lord,"
the people of Dubrovnik relied on a mixture of subservience and cunning.
The envoys, consuls, and dragomans of the city brought not only payments
of tribute but also a wealth of presents for the sultan's family and court.
Sometimes the services of a doctor helped to soothe the absolute ruler. For
concerns of a practical nature, they consulted the pasha of Bosnia. Emissaries from the city journeyed regularly to Travnik to bring gifts of money,
cloth, clocks, writing paper, medical supplies, chocolate, and tropical fruits
to the pasha, as well as to his relatives and friends.[211]

The envoys took pains to present themselves with the utmost modesty,
so as not to awaken any jealousies. The Senate ordered that "neither here
nor anywhere else, and certainly not at the Porte, should there be any *gran-
dezza* on display." On their missions to Travnik and Istanbul, representatives of the city rode only their oldest horses and stayed in the most humble
lodgings. The envoys were supposed to appeal to the grand vizier in Istanbul
"with plenty of real tears," that he might "describe our misery to the sultan
and ask for his benevolence." This took dramatic flair. "Be humble and be-
lievable at the same time. Throw yourselves, one after the other, at the feet
of his majesty with fervent ardor. Cry and wail, and tell him that his protection is our last resort!"[212] It is unknown whether the Sublime Porte took
the Ragusans' performances seriously, or simply viewed them as a face-saving
ritual. In any event, the quasi-independent status of the city-republic was
advantageous for the sultan in many respects. The city conducted a large part
of Levantine trade with the West, brought additional income into state coffers, and provided intelligence from Europe.

Russia emerged as a new challenger to Ottoman supremacy in the Adriatic in the last third of the eighteenth century. In February 1770, the Russian navy found its way to the Mediterranean under the command of Count
Orlov. His mission was to encourage revolt in Greece. Near Nafplio, he
met the fleet from Dubrovnik, which had to transport reinforcements for
the Ottomans, and he declared the city-republic an enemy power. The

Russians confiscated the ships and further demanded the construction of an Orthodox church in Dubrovnik—to the horror of the Catholic city leaders. They argued that this would provoke "a terrible conflict with the Great Lord," the sultan. In fact, they feared an influx of Orthodox Christians, "and since we won't be able to suppress them, they will eventually be the actual masters in the state. And because they are allied with the Russians in spirit and faith, Russia will try to use them to acquire power and sovereignty over our city." After difficult negotiations, Count Orlov accepted a reparation payment of 20,000 ducats in 1775. It was agreed that a Russian consul would be sent to Dubrovnik, and an Orthodox chapel built in his garden. In return, Dubrovnik could engage in trade throughout the Black Sea region.[213]

The conflict with Russia forced the Senate to reconsider its relationship to Austria. Since the defeat of the Turks outside Vienna in 1683, the Viennese court had tried to expand its political, economic, and military sphere of influence in southeastern Europe. Empress Maria Theresa even sent an informant to Dalmatia; he traveled around the region for more than a year, seeking to obtain an impression of local conditions that was as comprehensive as possible.[214] Part of Austria's strategy in southeastern Europe was to encourage Dubrovnik once again to accept Hungarian sovereignty (and the accompanying financial obligations), which had lapsed after Hungary's defeat by the Ottomans in 1526. The Senate did not want to pay, but good relations with Austria were important for counterbalancing the expanding influence of Russia. Representatives from Dubrovnik continued to string the Viennese court along until the conflict with Russia was resolved. In the spring of 1776, the ambassador from Dubrovnik let Maria Theresa know "with all candor" that despite the most careful research, no document could be found confirming Hungarian sovereignty—an outright lie.[215]

The situation in France came up less often in diplomatic correspondence, even after the revolution of 1789. Here, too, economic relations were most important for the city. France was primarily concerned about the disruptive competition that Dubrovnik brought to Mediterranean trade. In January 1776 alone, more than one hundred ships arrived to exchange goods in French ports.[216] Because the ships were considered to be from the Levant, they were subject to a strict quarantine and high tariffs. The Dubrovnik Senate asked the city's most famous son, Ruđer Bošković, to intervene. Thanks to his efforts, the conflict was resolved. A bilateral trade agreement was signed on April 2, 1776, bringing Dubrovnik certain economic advantages and greater diplomatic prestige. The city-republic was subsequently counted as part of the West.[217]

After the papal suppression of the Jesuits, the new ideas of the encyclopedists and other Enlightenment thinkers also gained a foothold in Dubrovnik. The conservative Senate complained to the French government about their consul Le Maire because he loaned out scandalous Enlightenment texts like Voltaire's satire *The Maid of Orleans,* which mocked belief in miracles and the cult of saints.[218] But even without Le Maire, the city's scholars began to engage with the language and culture of their homeland, to collect folk songs and proverbs, and to research their own history and literature. The lexicographer Joakim Stulli was tireless in his search for sponsors of his Croatian-Latin-Italian dictionary. He found supporters not only in his hometown of Dubrovnik but also in Rome, Venice, Dresden, Vienna, Saint Petersburg, Budapest, and Zagreb. He worked on the monumental undertaking for half a century before the first volume of the complete work, which defined 80,000 words, appeared in 1801. Dubrovnik's first press was established in 1783; the schoolteacher Francesco Maria Appendini published a Croatian grammar book and a two-volume history of Dubrovnik.[219] And in 1793, the noble Miho Sorkočević and other proponents of "democratic ideas" founded a Patriotic Society to discuss how best to increase prosperity, institute state reform, and abolish seigneury.[220]

In the palazzo of noblewoman Marija Giorgi Bona, meanwhile, writers, composers, doctors, and diplomats regularly gathered in a salon—a form of sociability that was imported from France and typical of the Enlightenment, a great attraction for educated men and even women. They discussed philosophy and literature, the sciences and Greek classics, texts by the encyclopedists and other Enlightenment thinkers. The library of this highly educated lady held the works of famous authors: Boccaccio, Machiavelli, Montesquieu, Orbini, Newton, Condorcet, Locke, von Pufendorf, Christian Wolff, and many others. Banned works of literature were here, too, including *The Memoirs of the Comtesse Du Barry* and Jean-Jacques Rousseau's socially critical novel *Julie, or the New Heloise.* The Italian cleric and scholar Alberto Fortis was a frequent visitor to the house of Giorgi Bona. He fell in love with the lady of the house—who was intelligent, beautiful, and unhappily married—and he wrote her passionate letters for years there-after.[221]

While the Austrian spy gathered information, the archbishop interrogated the heretic, and the monks mixed their medications, men and women of the lower classes amused themselves in the city's wine cellars and taverns. "Among the residents of Ragusa," a contemporary remarked, "they spend their time in the most enjoyable way."[222] Others played soccer, handball, and tennis—outdoor amusements that had come to Dalmatia during the Renaissance, via Florence and Venice. The monk Faganeo, later bishop of Korčula, liked to kick a ball in front of his church, to the enthusiasm of the natives. Nevertheless, the incessant hooting and hollering disturbed clerics in Dubrovnik so much that the city threatened harsh punishments for playing in front of houses of God. Since 1597, graffiti on a church wall warned: "Pax Vobis. Memento mori qui ludetis pilla" (Peace be with you. To those who play ball here, remember that you, too, are mortal).[223]

4

The Age of Global Revolutions

Two KEY EVENTS marked the transition from the old political order
to the modern age: the British colonies' declaration of independence in
North America in 1776, and the French Revolution in 1789. France and
the United States accepted republican constitutions, becoming the model
of democratic, secular statehood for the entire world. From this point on,
a century of global revolution and upheaval began. The first states in Latin
America and the Ottoman Empire earned their independence, and then a
great revolutionary wave swept across much of Europe in 1848.[1] Uprisings
in southeast Asia, civil wars in Spain, Portugal, and Lebanon, peasant revolts in Mexico, the Middle East, and Japan, and anticolonial resistance
in Ireland, Egypt, and Asia occupied the entire century until the fundamental dislocations of the First World War, which led to the dissolution of
the old European monarchies with their outdated political orders, based
on dynastic interests. Long, bloody wars destroyed the great multiethnic
empires, creating an order of European nation-states and a new international system.[2]

In a field of tension between the impulses of revolution and Enlightenment, orientation toward the past and resistance against change, and proposals for reform that were sometimes contradictory, southeastern Europe
participated in the transition to modern statehood that lasted more than a
century. Here, too, the new era began with the revolutions on opposite sides
of the Atlantic, coming of age in 1848 and the Great Eastern Crisis of the

1870s, and finally culminating in the decade of Balkan wars between 1912/13 and 1923. Only then did an order of nation-states sweep aside the last traces of the Ottoman Empire from the European continent.

The Dissolution of the Old Order, 1770–1830

No other event influenced modern southeastern Europe as decisively as the French Revolution. Political, social, and cultural transformations in France drove the revolutionary movements and uprisings, and also the liberal political cultures that took root over the course of the nineteenth century.[3] The French Revolution and Napoleonic dictatorship brought groundbreaking changes to structures of government and society, which eventually led to the formation of nation-states and to a fundamental re-orientation of political thought and the experience of time. After a longer period of social change, contemporaries broke with the tradition of the ancien régime. They experienced the collapse of foreign rule, the construction of new social orders, the spread of national ideologies, and finally, the most comprehensive reorganization of the political landscape in the entire modern era.[4] The nature of political thought underwent a fundamental transformation, moving away from a religiously determined worldview and toward the values and sense of order that distinguished the early bourgeoisie. Many intellectuals came to see equality and responsible governance as the measure of social coexistence. The peoples of southeastern Europe entered the first phase of nation- and nation-state-building, which was initially shaped by a small circle of religious and secular elites. The ideas of universal liberty and human rights combined with an early patriotic nationalism.

The opposition between revolutionary, or Bonapartist, models of leadership and those of monarchical restoration stoked new conflicts, resulting in the formation of a new international system. The classic ministerial politics of the ancien régime gave way to new forms of collective security. Russia emerged as the most dangerous threat to Ottoman power in southeastern Europe, with political competition and hegemonic rivalry intensifying wherever revolutionary events compelled the Ottoman Empire to withdraw. The Eastern Question, with the Balkans at its heart, became the European governments' most sensitive foreign policy problem in the "long nineteenth century."

The American and French Revolutions

In the first days of December 1797, Rhigas Velestinlis was readying crates of printed materials and personal belongings for transport from Vienna to Trieste. The Greek merchant and author packed 2,785 copies of his pamphlet *The New Political Constitution,* thirty-three reproductions of a self-made "Map of Hellas," and seventy-seven lithographs of Alexander the Great. Rhigas, who was almost forty years old, intended to send the cargo from Habsburg-occupied Trieste to the Peloponnese. His plan was to incite an uprising against Ottoman rule.[5]

Rhigas, who was also called Rhigas Pheraios after his hometown in Thessaly, was a poet and polymath. A priest had taught him how to read and write. In the mid-1780s, he entered into the service of influential Phanariots in Istanbul and Bucharest, where he established contacts with European intellectuals and members of the Greek diaspora. His network came to include more than one hundred scholars, writers, traders, and students in Vienna, Pest, Trieste, Zemun, Istanbul, Smyrna, Bucharest, Jassy, Ioannina, and Preveza. He had additional connections throughout Italy and Greece, as well as in Leipzig, Bern, Brussels, Amsterdam, and Paris. Rhigas's calling was education and enlightenment; his passion was revolution.[6]

Rhigas's biography represented the transformation in philosophical discourse that occurred in the years after the French Revolution in southeastern Europe and elsewhere. The Enlightenment became political. The poet, composer, geographer, and scholar became a constitutional theorist and revolutionary. The hopes that the Greek Voulgaris, the Serb Orfelin, and the Romanian Samuil Micu-Klein had once held for enlightened absolutism in Austria, Prussia, and Russia gave way to disillusionment and disappointment. A younger generation complained that the new philosophy served merely to disguise the great powers' imperialist designs on the Balkans. Those who lived here began to develop theoretical justifications for independent statehood. The Enlightenment did not necessarily have to end in revolution, but if one accepted the existence of universal human rights, one also recognized the necessity of removing a despotic, exploitative regime that excluded large parts of society from political and social participation.[7]

In 1797 Rhigas published his *New Political Constitution* in Vienna. The pamphlet addressed all "Christians and Turks" who were victims of Ottoman tyranny, regardless of religion, and passionately called for an uprising to topple the degenerate Ottoman regime. Its contents included a declaration of human rights, a 124-article "Constitution of the Hellenic Republic," and the future national hymn "Thourios," which Rhigas had written and composed himself. "Better to have lived one hour in freedom than forty years in slavery and prison!" the lyrics proclaimed.

Rhigas intended to enact the new constitution on May 1, 1798, following the successful overthrow of the Ottoman regime. The model for his "Greek democratic republic" was the Jacobin constitution of 1793. As in France, the goal was to realize the principles of revolution—popular sovereignty, human rights, and representative government. Privileges and feudal entitlements would be eliminated; the rule of law, separation of powers, freedom of the press, and civil rights guaranteed. "All residents . . . without exceptions for religion or language, Hellenes, Bulgars, Albanians, Vlachs, Armenians, Turks, and any other kind of race" were to have equal rights. "Primary assemblies" throughout the country would directly elect parliamentary representatives, and these would in turn appoint the executive (called the Directory). Boys and girls alike would attend school; women would also perform military service.[8] Like France, the Greek republic would be "unified and inseparable"; despite its diversity and geographic expanse, including the entire Balkan Peninsula and parts of Asia Minor, it was to become a unitary centralized state. Although Montesquieu and Rousseau had reflected on the virtues of a federal constitution, Rhigas did not consider this solution, emphasizing the principle of solidarity instead: "The Bulgarian must be moved to act when the Greek suffers; and in the same way, the Greek for the Bulgarian, and both for the Albanian and the Vlach."[9]

The monarchies viewed with consternation the enthusiasm for revolution that had seized the European continent. In Austria, where Maria Theresa had already introduced enlightened reforms, now steps were taken backward toward restoration. Emperor Joseph II—who had introduced equality before the law, abolished serfdom, and instituted religious tolerance in the 1780s—encountered bitter resistance from the old estates when he sought to create a uniformly administered, secular, and modern state. More problems arose as he sought to execute his plans. In 1784 Romanian peasants in Transylvania rose up against the Hungarian nobility. Their revolt was defeated. Additional resistance developed in the Habsburg Netherlands, especially in Belgium. In 1790 the weakened monarch had to take back many of his reforms.[10]

After the French Revolution, "confessional nations" felt empowered to demand greater political rights. In 1790 under the leadership of Metropolitan Stefan Stratimirović, the Serbs of Banat gathered in Timişoara for a Serbian-Illyrian National Congress, demanding an autonomous territory within the Habsburg Monarchy with independent leadership. The Croatian nobility also sought greater independence, emphasizing that Croatia was not a subordinate territory of Hungary, but instead that Hungary and Croatia were allied kingdoms with equal rights. In a 1791 petition, prominent Romanians demanded greater recognition for Transylvania's Romanian majority, which had to date been merely "tolerated." The *Supplex Libellus Valachorum* cited central revolutionary concepts like equality, the social contract, and human and civil rights to demand representation in political and public life proportional to the Romanians' share of the population.[11]

With the outbreak of war against France in 1792, Austria entered a phase of fanatic, counterrevolutionary politics under Emperor Francis II. Alongside Prussia and other European powers, it fought multiple wars with changing coalitions to contain the French Republic and later subdue the Napoleonic Empire. In 1793, the execution of Louis XVI and his wife, the Austrian Marie Antoinette, upended and shattered the self-image of the Habsburg Monarchy. In response, the emperor tarred numerous clerics and philosophers as atheists and insurrectionaries, banning their works. He tightened censorship and expanded the secret police within the notorious Polizeihofstelle to intimidate the adherents of revolutionary ideas in all of his lands. Schools, newspapers, associations, and foreigners were closely monitored, and Freemasonry was banned. When the authorities uncovered a "Jacobin conspiracy" in Austria and Hungary in 1794, the suspects were sentenced to death or imprisonment.[12]

Rhigas, too, became a victim of the Austrian secret police when he was betrayed by a spy. Caught in Trieste with "extremely revolutionary texts" on his way to Greece at the end of 1797, he was interrogated for months. The authorities accused him of inciting rebellion against the legitimate ruler of the Ottoman Empire and of seeking to establish a popular government on the French model. Rhigas and seven compatriots were bound in chains and delivered to the sultan. They were strangled in the Turkish fortress of Belgrade on a June night in 1798.[13] Today Rhigas's portrait adorns the Greek ten-cent coin; he is renowned as a martyr and the earliest visionary of a free Greece.

The ideals of the French Revolution, however, could no longer be suppressed. This was evident in the work of leading scholars, such as Adamantios Korais, one of the outstanding political philosophers of his time. The son of a merchant from Smyrna, Korais was supposed to work for his father in Amsterdam, but the intellectually curious young man preferred reading books over doing business. He went to France to study medicine and later wrote a prizewinning dissertation about Hippocrates. Like many scholars of his day, he had a well-rounded education and was interested in many fields. His well-received, twenty-six-volume *Hellenic Library* brought together ancient Classical authors from Homer to Strabo. He became known as one of the best ancient philologers of his time, and he was also respected as a serious political philosopher.

Korais, who is best known to us today as a linguistic reformer and an advocate of the national idea, was also an early theorist and champion of modern statehood. Natural law and the idea of reason led him to the concepts of freedom, justice, and humanity. When he was forty years old, he became an eyewitness to the French Revolution. He met with influential revolutionaries in Paris, and he eventually followed the thinkers of the Directory with enthusiasm.[14] When Napoleon occupied the Ionian Islands in 1797 and attacked Ottoman Egypt in 1798, Korais called the people of his country to a *levée en masse* in his *Brotherly Instruction* and in the pamphlet *Military Fanfare*. A Greek republic should promote freedom and equality, he explained to European readers in his *Report on the Present State of Civilization in Greece*. Later, after the outbreak of the Greek revolution, he reflected on the foundations of democracy and a modern constitution, which he sought in revolutionary France and the United States. He wrote to Thomas Jefferson, his old friend from Paris, for advice in 1823. What would the best possible constitution look like for revolutionary Greece? Jefferson recommended human rights and freedom of the press, and a representative form of government in a centralized, not federal, order. Korais was flattered that the former president of the United States mostly agreed with his own ideas about a modern constitution.[15] And the American model appealed to him more than the French because he mistrusted the European powers. He wrote to Jefferson in 1823 that he feared they would "grant liberty to Greece only in so far as it is compatible with their interests." The United States, by contrast, he saw as an altruistic power.[16]

Dositej Obradović, a priest and enlightened thinker from Timişoara, played a comparable role for the Serbs, who were scattered across three different empires in the revolutionary era. In his bildungsroman *Life and Adventures,* the polyglot Obradović depicted the pleasures of learning and the necessity of a respectable education. These values turned the former cleric into a resolute critic of the church, which he denounced as hopelessly backward. He would have liked to convert all monasteries into schools and universities.[17] He saw the standardization of the Serbs' vernacular language as one of his most important missions. Like the Greek Korais, Obradović believed that linguistic reform was necessary to reach, educate, enlighten, and finally, to liberate the masses. He was also interested in the workings of the judiciary and constitutional law.[18]

In this era of transition between eighteenth-century enlightened rationalism and the more emotional nationalism of the nineteenth century, political thinkers throughout southeastern Europe—including the Romanian Ion Budai-Deleanu and the Croatian Count Janko Drašković—grappled with the foundations of modern statehood. Like Rhigas, they thought less about nationalism than about universal rights and liberties, as formulated by the Enlightenment. They sought an appropriate constitutional framework for guaranteeing these rights. The forefathers of the southeastern European revolutions understood themselves as citizens of the world, especially since the Enlightenment taught that all people (regardless of social, religious, or linguistic differences) were reasonable beings. But the seed of patriotic, and later national, thinking had already been planted. Although the rights of the individual were the focus of the new political philosophy, there could only be free people within a free polity. Thus, national self-determination appeared to be an indispensable precondition for any kind of social progress. Throughout Europe this generation was characterized by both a cosmopolitan and patriotic sensibility; this combination of rationalism and sentimentalism gave rise to the era's *esprit révolutionnaire*.[19]

The transition to the national idea could be seen, for example, in Ion Budai-Deleanu's gypsy ballad of 1812. The *Țiganiada* took place in the fifteenth century during the reign of the fearsome despot Vlad Țepeș. However, it was really about the contemporary regime of the Phanariots in the Danubian Principalities. The satire of existing conditions contained a clear plea for social reform, national awareness, and cultural progress—the quintessence of later national thought.[20] The writings of Voltaire, Rousseau, and Condorcet were well known in Wallachia and Moldavia, and the French Declaration of the Rights of Man and of the Citizen of 1789 was translated here, too. The French consul encountered "many boyars who clearly speak in favor of our revolution, and many who are no less supportive, but do not dare to speak openly about it."[21] There was a strong class of nobles who still wanted to maintain their social privileges over the peasants. Thus, many Romanian reformers—like those in Russia, Poland, and Hungary—sought a constitution less radical than the French. They preferred an aristocratic republic under the protective leadership of an enlightened monarch.[22] In 1802 Dimitrie Sturdza designed a republican constitution that would operate according to democratic principles, with a separation of powers, but would nevertheless be dominated by the boyars.[23]

In France, meanwhile, Napoleon rose to become the republic's First Consul in 1799, and he proclaimed the empire in 1804. The power-hungry general conquered and annexed much of Europe. At the height of his power, he governed not only France but also Belgian, Dutch, Rhineland, Hanseatic, Italian, and "Illyrian" (South Slav) *départements* as well as a chain of satellite states. Sweeping aside the old political order, Napoleonic rule prepared the way for modernization according to the principles of the French Revolution. Particularly in the Ottoman Empire, many observers placed great hope in the conquering dictator, who had invaded Ottoman Egypt in 1798. Both the Greek revolutionary Rhigas Velestinlis and the Serb leader Karadjordje sought Napoleon's support for an anti-Ottoman uprising. The Moldavians sent him a memorandum requesting that he establish an independent state called "Dacia" or "Greater Wallachia." "All the Christians of the Near East prayed to God that France should wage war against the Turks, and they believed that they would be freed," a Greek revolutionary recalled.[24]

But Bonaparte had other plans. Following the War of the First Coalition, France and Austria divided Venice's possessions between themselves in the 1797 Treaty of Campo Formio. Vienna received Dalmatia, while Paris took possession of the Ionian Islands and the nearby mainland. Shortly thereafter, the Russians and Ottomans took the islands from the French, founding a "Septinsular Republic" with the capital city of Corfu in 1800. Its aristocratic constitution was modeled after Dubrovnik, and it was obligated to pay tribute to its formal sovereign, the Ottoman state. Russia was supposed to guarantee its independence. In 1807 France reconquered the Ionian republic and established a military government there. Two years later the British attacked. In 1814 they took possession of

Corfu, the last of the islands to fall. Although Napoleonic rule had lasted only a few years on the islands and was geographically limited, it laid the foundation of modern statehood by abolishing feudalism, freeing the peasants, and modernizing the educational and legal systems. "The attempts of the French to poison the minds of the Peasants of Corfu, were not altogether unsuccessful," the British consul summarized. Until 1864, the island republic remained a British protectorate.[25]

In the South Slavic region, too, Napoleonic rule acted as a catalyst for the modern nation-state. In the 1805 Treaty of Pressburg, Austria had to cede the Venetian, Istrian, and Dalmatian territories it had won at Campo Formio in 1797 to Napoleon's kingdom of Italy. Control over the Adriatic coast brought France significant strategic and economic advantages because Austria and England lost access to the Adriatic ports and could not circumvent the Continental System instituted by Napoleon in 1806. Moreover, France secured important transport routes from the Ottoman Empire, including for Macedonian cotton, which was in high demand.[26] In 1808 Napoleon dissolved the Republic of Dubrovnik and added its territory to Italy, too.

In 1809, after another lost war, Austria also had to cede Carinthia, Carniola, Croatia, and the southern military border to France. Napoleon united these territories, together with Dalmatia and Istria, as the "Illyrian Provinces"—a name that recalled the ancient empire of the Romans. From the capital city of Ljubljana, the French governor-general enacted a series of reforms. He introduced the Code Napoléon and established the basis for a modern administration and school system. For the first time, the Slovenian and Croatian populations were placed together in a single *département,* with South Slavic "Illyrian" as an official language. Since many reforms only existed on paper and the burden of taxes was high, many residents were nevertheless relieved when the Austrians and British drove the French away from the coastland in 1813/14.[27] French imperial rule lasted only a few years, but it laid important foundations for a modern bureaucracy and modern social order. Not least—as soon became apparent—it also encouraged the development of national awareness.

On Ottoman territory, where the old imperial powers were faltering, some renegade local elites *(ayan)* approached Napoleon on their own, seeking international recognition for their leadership. The most famous of these was Ali Pasha of Ioannina, called the "Lion," who styled himself as the "Bonaparte of the Balkans." Ali was Muslim, his native language Albanian, his character larger than life. He began his career as the leader of a band of outlaws, later changing over to the side of the state. Responsible for policing mountain passes, he brought wider areas under his control and attracted the attention of the sultan, who named the power-hungry Ali Pasha of Ioannina in 1787. He built up his own small empire, in which he exercised unlimited power, with the help of relatives and mercenaries and the use of brute force. He amassed tremendous riches by laying claim to local taxes, assuming personal control of large estates, and taking wealthy citizens hostage so he could extort ransoms from their families. He conquered more and more territory with his army and fleet. At the height of his power, he controlled southern Albania and large parts of Macedonia and Greece.[28]

Contemporaries described the "Lion" as avaricious and cruel. "I have never followed any road previously travelled by Ali Pasha, without seeing some newly filled-up grave, or some wretches hanging on the trees," the French consul noted with disgust. "His footsteps are stained with blood, and . . . to display the extent of his power, he orders executions equally terrible and unexpected."[29] Ali's tyrannical behavior formed a disturbing contrast to his self-portrayal as a benefactor who built streets and public buildings, promoted trade and industry, and subdued fearsome bands of Albanian brigands. He surrounded himself with well-known intellectuals and founded a Greek academy. Ioannina and Moscopole thrived as centers of supraregional trade and production and of Greek education, philosophy, and high culture. The British poet Lord Byron immortalized Ali in his epic poem *Childe Harold's Pilgrimage,* thus helping him to become the most popular figure of nineteenth-century Oriental literature. For years, the power-hungry Ali entangled the sultan's troops in military conflicts, tying up forces that the Ottomans could have deployed elsewhere to combat unrest and rebellion. After approaching the French, he offered himself as an ally to the Russians and English, seeking to extract their recognition of his regime.[30] But an alliance with the Christian powers did not emerge. In 1820, five years after the conclusion of the Napoleonic Wars, Ali Pasha was stripped of all his offices, and he was killed in 1822.[31]

Farther east, Osman Pazvantoğlu, Pasha of Vidin, built up his local rule. His father was a janissary aga, whom the sultan had executed for conspiracy years before. Like Ali of Ioannina, Osman antagonized the Sublime Porte and terrorized the population, confiscating taxes and large estates. Osman likewise proposed a military alliance with the French against the sultan, and he negotiated the possibility of an uprising with Rhigas Velestinlis.

He provided a safe haven for renegade janissaries, whom the Sublime Porte sought to disempower. The once elite fighting force, which was supposed to protect the external borders of the empire, had become an underpaid and unruly militia. From Vidin, they fought against the modernizing reforms that Selim III had introduced in 1789; his "New Order" was supposed to make the state more efficient and more competitive. The sultan wanted to build a modern army, adopting the European model of training and equipment.[32] From Vidin, Osman's troops and the janissaries launched repeated raids into Serbia and Bulgaria. The sultan denounced him as a rebel and bandit, and placed a bounty on his head. Multiple attacks on his territory failed, and he likely died of tuberculosis in 1807.[33]

The overall legal uncertainty became one of the Ottoman Empire's greatest problems, as it encouraged a climate of violence in many parts of southeastern Europe and inflamed revolutionary passions. In his memoirs, the Bulgarian bishop Sofroniy Vrachanski wrote about the ceaseless kidnappings, beatings, and executions in the region around Vidin: "Every day, some of the Arnauts [Albanian mercenaries] were impaled before our eyes." Then the Ottoman authorities approached Sofroniy and other bystanders "and threatened to impale [them], too."[34] Fear and terror spread even among those who had committed no offense, and immense sums of money were extorted wherever possible. It was hard to say which armed groups represented the greatest danger: the "outlaw hordes" of Osman Pazvantoğlu who plundered villages and cities, the armed Muslim fighters who besieged communities on behalf of local warlords, the janissaries who rebelled against the sultan, or the soldiers of the Ottoman army who were quartered in Christian homes, devastating and plundering the land to root out resistance. Every few days, Sofroniy recalled, the marauding bands of another leader stormed through his eparchy.[35]

The highwaymen, robbers, and deserters who preyed on traders, travelers, and money carriers brought further unrest. Men of different backgrounds joined the armed bands of Greek *klephts,* Serbian *haiduks,* and Montenegrin Chetniks—including former members of the Christian support troops (the *armotoloi* or *martolos*), marauding mercenaries, as well as impoverished herders and peasants. Their growing numbers made assaults so common that it was almost impossible to travel in some areas. After his capture by Greek brigands, the traveler David Urquhart was told: "Look at those men, some of them barefoot, with clothes of string rather than cloth, with empty tobacco bags, and empty stomachs."[36]

Even at the time, it was unclear how the militia-like Christian bands might position themselves in case of a rebellion against Ottoman state authority. *Klephts* and *haiduks* tended to see themselves not as bandits, but as resistance fighters against state authority. As Christian avengers against the Turks, they acquired a mixed reputation as savage heroes in popular literature.[37] In 1818 the philologist and folklorist Vuk Stefanović Karadžić noted that it was the "greatest disgrace" for a *haiduk* to be told he was "a common thief and a despicable robber."[38] And if one can believe the recollections of the revolutionary Theodoros Kolokotronis, "The prayer of a father for his sons was that he might become a *klepht*."[39] Their courage and heroism were regaled in countless folk songs, and in the Romantic era they were seen (usually incorrectly) as the earliest fighters for national independence. They continued to be a disruptive influence throughout the entire nineteenth century.[40]

By 1800, a mixture of internal and external factors had created a revolutionary stew in southeastern Europe. The Habsburg Monarchy forfeited legitimacy because of its counterrevolutionary course, while throughout much of the Ottoman Empire, completely unsustainable conditions of capriciousness and legal uncertainty created a revolutionary climate that was permeated by violence.[41] Allegedly good and just imperial power eroded. Abuse of power, nepotism, and corruption were everyday occurrences, old institutions disintegrated, and provincial governors, tax farmers, and landlords bled the peasants dry with onerous rents. New, self-assured elites began to challenge traditional power holders; they could count on stronger support from a broader cross-section of the population, including the armed bands in some cases. Within this context, the American and French Revolutions served as a guide for converting general dissatisfaction into concrete political demands, translating them into the language of revolution. They served as role models, fed the awakening democratic consensus, and popularized the ideals of tolerance, equality, and solidarity. For this reason and others, the power of the Ottoman state was increasingly unable to keep the situation under control.

From Revolution to Statehood

At the beginning of the nineteenth century, Ottoman sovereignty began to fray at the seams. Between 1804 and 1815, the Serbs fought for their own principality in two uprisings. A Romanian rebellion failed in 1821, and that same year the Greeks began their own uprising, which led to the establishment of an independent kingdom. The Bulgarians' anti-Ottoman conspiracies, by contrast, were suppressed before they could gain steam. In 1830 the great powers recognized the first independent states in southeastern Europe: the Principality of Serbia, the Kingdom of Greece, and the mostly autonomous Danubian Principalities. The uprisings of the Balkan peoples have often been viewed either as purely national historical turning points or as the reactionary revolts of peasants. In fact, they were not Western bourgeois national revolutions. Nevertheless, intentionally or not, they marked the dawning of a new age that was shaped by political modernity. And for all their regional particularities, the uprisings occurred within the context of a worldwide era of insurrection and revolution.

Despite their global context and numerous transnational connections, the revolutions in southeastern Europe—as everywhere in the world—rose up from local roots. They were the result of a chronic crisis of imperial rule. Social grievances created internal unrest, new elites challenged old power holders, external military threats heightened insecurity, new subversive ideas and discourses undermined existing loyalties, and disruptive political movements turned violent. Like most revolutionaries, the Serbs, Greeks, and Romanians did not have clearly formulated programs as their uprisings began. Their rhetoric was contradictory. On one hand, rebels demanded a return to the good old days; on the other, they placed their hopes in a radical new beginning. The peasants, in particular, may initially have sought a more just order, not necessarily an entirely new one.[42] As time progressed, however, political goals changed and became more concrete, new groups of supporters came to the fore, and the international situation transformed. The unrest developed a dynamic of its own, leading to the violent overthrow of existing conditions by new elites, and finally to a fundamental transformation in the structures of society and power. In the end, these were no mere uprisings, but actual revolutions.[43]

The first people to rise up successfully against the Ottomans were the Serbs in the Belgrade *pashalik,* with a population of 300,000 to 400,000 residents. This border region to the Habsburg Monarchy was sparsely populated, its agricultural economy largely isolated. Most households produced just enough for their own consumption. But here, too, social changes became evident in the 1790s, as demand for agricultural products in the Habsburg Monarchy grew, and the export of cattle became more lucrative. Because of communal self-government, there was a respected, self-assured, and in some cases, prosperous class of village elders and district leaders (*knezes*) whose responsibilities included collecting taxes and recruiting soldiers.[44]

Hopes for regime change materialized more concretely between 1787 and 1792, when Russia and Austria temporarily occupied Belgrade and Bucharest during another Ottoman War. Many Serbs volunteered to fight for the Austrian emperor. At the war's end, however, the allies were compelled to give back the territories. Although Serbia remained in Ottoman hands, Sultan Selim III agreed to concessions in light of his regime's military defeats and the growing calls for revolution. The sultan granted amnesty to the Serbian irregulars, gave more rights to the *knezes,* and promised to uphold trade and religious freedoms. He also expelled the hated janissaries, who had been assigned to protect the border but increasingly acted like a "state within the state," terrorizing the population. The janissaries retreated to the neighboring territory that was controlled by the renegade local ruler, Osman Pazvantoğlu of Vidin, but they returned to Belgrade at the beginning of 1801 to stage a coup against the Ottoman governor. Their leaders, the *dahije,* displaced the *knezes,* extorted taxes and rents, and forcibly turned the land of free peasants into landlord-owned estates, or *çiftliks.* Until 1804, they upheld a regime of terror that was effectively independent of Ottoman central authority.[45]

Resistance in the Belgrade *pashalik* had brewed since the *dahije*'s military coup. *Knezes* and clerics wanted their old rights back; merchants and wealthier peasants wanted to go about their business without interference. The rural population, which had been forced into serfdom, suffered from exploitation, poverty, and the unpredictability of the new leaders. "The spark of insurrection, which has to this point been smoldering under the ashes, may soon burst into flame in Turkey," an Austrian eyewitness reported from Serbia in 1801. "Everyone is preparing in secret for this decisive moment." Although the Christians were not allowed to own weapons, "it is well known that they have buried a large store of weapons in the ground, and even directed their ten- and twelve-year-old sons to take up arms."[46]

When the *dahije* heard that the Serbs were preparing to revolt, they publicly executed seventy *knezes,* priests, peasants, and traders at the beginning of 1804. To deter the rebels, the severed heads were put on public display. The outrageous and frightening "slaughter of the *knezes*" was the final straw that led local leaders to call for an uprising against the *dahije*'s regime of terror, in Orašac in the Šumadija, in February 1804.[47] The chief instigator was the charismatic cattle trader and *knez*, Djordje Petrović, called Karadjordje (Black George). Under his leadership, approximately 25,000 armed fighters liberated the entire *pashalik* and its surrounding regions from the janissaries in just a few months. The *dahije* were executed.[48] "He despised splendor and magnificence," the young historian Leopold Ranke wrote about Karadjordje in his 1829 book about the Serbian Revolution. "He was always seen in his old blue trousers, in his worn-out short pelt, in his famous black cap." It would have been easy to mistake him for a peasant, if not for his mighty aura and reputation. "Wherever he appeared, the Turks trembled in fear. One had to believe that victory was his."[49] The leader of the Serbs did, however, resort to threats and coercion to keep his troops together. If a *knez* did not mobilize every man who was able to carry a weapon to fight against the *dahije*, Karadjordje promised he would die in agony: "Whomsoever they find at home they will kill him and break him on the wheel and burn his house."[50]

Over the course of 1805, the rebellion against the janissaries' tyrannical *dahije* turned into a broader revolution against Ottoman foreign rule. The sultan was prepared to negotiate over autonomy, but he rejected the Serbs' demands for a guarantee of protection by Russia or Austria. So the rebels fought on, forming their first government in August 1805. In the meantime, they no longer sought merely to restore local self-government, but to establish their own state. A new order emerged in the regions controlled by the Serbs. The new Serbian leaders expelled the Turks, destroyed their homes, and broke up the large estates, or *çiftliks,* redistributing land among the peasants. Taxes and rents were no longer paid to the treasury of the Ottoman state. *Knezes,* military leaders, clerics, and village elders formed a national assembly (Narodna skupština) and a new government. Karadjordje became head of state. "Serbia considers itself an independent state," the prime minister, Sima Marković, declared in 1807. "It will not voluntarily pay tributes or take up arms against allies or brothers in faith."[51]

Karadjordje and his compatriots understood that they would need external support to build an independent state. Although the new head of state could neither read nor write, there were educated, respected, and well-connected personalities among the land's *knezes,* clerics, and merchants. They communicated with clerics and scholars in southern Hungary such as the metropolitan Stefan Stratimirović and the Enlightenment thinker Dositej Obradović. Obradović collected donations for the revolution, and then—deeply moved—he relocated to Belgrade in the summer of 1807, personal library in tow. He helped to write the Serbian constitution and he served as Serbia's foreign minister as well as its first minister of education.[52]

Since the beginning of the uprising, the cleric and writer Prota Matija Nenadović had served as its chief diplomat. His father was one of the *knezes* who had been executed in the *dahije*'s great raid. Nenadović, who was in his late twenties, was one of the uprising's most prominent leaders and commanders, and he later became the first prime minister of Serbia. Assigned by Karadjordje to maintain contacts with the Austrians and Russians, he and a small delegation even traveled all the way to Saint Petersburg in the fall of 1804. With luck and persistence, he obtained an audience with the Russian foreign minister so that he could ask for his country's support of Serbian autonomy. "Good, but Serbia and Russia are very far apart and we are in friendship with the Turks," the minister responded drily.[53] Russia, like the other great powers, feared an Ottoman alliance with Napoleon and another great war. Above all, the monarchs were afraid that the goals of the French Revolution would spread to the rest of the continent.

In the meantime, Napoleon—"Emperor of the French" since 1804—had subdued and reorganized half of Europe after breathtaking campaigns in Italy and Egypt. In December 1805 he dealt the Russian-Austrian army a crushing defeat. The sultan, who temporarily allied with France, felt emboldened to recover lost terrain in southeastern Europe and closed the Dardanelles—an affront to the Russians. The tsar's army seized the opportunity to occupy the Danubian Principalities in 1806. The new Russo-Ottoman War allowed the Serbs to continue their uprising and even undertake shared military actions. Numerous Bulgarians and Greeks volunteered to fight alongside the Serbs and Russians.[54] Envoys of the tsar continued to negotiate with the Bulgarians about a popular uprising. But as Napoleon prepared to invade Russia in 1812, Russia pulled its troops out of southeastern Europe, dimming the prospects for a Bulgarian uprising. In the Russian-Ottoman Treaty of Bucharest that same year, Russia acquired Bessarabia, which was part of Moldavia, and ended its support for the Serbs. In October 1813, after eight years of war, the First Serbian Uprising collapsed under the weight of the Ottomans' superior military force.

The uprising was defeated, and its leader Karadjordje exiled, but Serbia was not yet ready to give in. The rebels' initial military successes were not forgotten, and Serbia had acquired its first state-like institutions and constitution. After Napoleon's military fiasco in Russia in 1812 and the central European wars of liberation between 1813 and 1815, the international climate shifted back in favor of the rebellious Balkan peoples. In April 1815 the Serbs began a second uprising under Miloš Obrenović. Belgrade was reconquered. With Russia again threatening military intervention, the Sublime Porte began to renegotiate the issue of autonomy with the Serbs in the summer of that same year. In the meantime, Prota Matija had made a name for himself as a tireless advocate of an independent Serbia at the Congress of Vienna in 1814/15. Miloš Obrenović entered into an agreement with the sultan's representatives in November 1815, which granted Serbia structures of self-government and the right to levy taxes. The military hostilities of the Second Serbian Uprising came to an end. Miloš Obrenović, having had his rival Karadjordje (who had recently returned from exile) murdered, was installed as ruler in 1817. Only in 1830, however, did the Ottomans formally recognize an independent Serbia.[55]

The Serbian principality covered only the small territory of the former Belgrade *pashalik* and had no certified legal status, but the two uprisings had an immense effect on nearby Greece. To begin, the revolutions' intellectual forefathers, the Enlightenment thinkers Dositej Obradović and Adamantios Korais, communicated with one another directly. In 1806 Trieste, an anonymous Greek author composed a call for revolution that explicitly referred to Serbia's "new and great" example.[56] And one year later in Vienna, Triantafyllos Doukas published a *History of the Slaveno-Serbians,* the first comprehensive depiction of the Serbian uprising, which offered a positive example to the Greeks.[57]

There had already been a Greek uprising in the Peloponnese during the Russo-Ottoman War of 1768–1774. In 1770 the Orlov brothers sailed with the Russian fleet to the Mediterranean Sea, seeking to stir up the Balkan Christians in the name of the tsar. After some initial military victories, the Ottomans brutally put down the rebellion with the help of Albanian mercenaries. The Greek leaders of the uprising were impaled and thousands of civilians massacred. Much of the Peloponnese was devastated and burned to the ground. Nevertheless (and particularly after the Serbs' successful uprising), Russia was still seen as a potential protector of the anti-Ottoman struggle for liberation. Many Phanariots and other Greeks had followed in the footsteps of Dimitrie Cantemir and Eugenios Voulgaris and emigrated to the tsarist empire. The Ypsilantis brothers and members of the Soutso, Ghica, Cantacuzino, and Sturdza families were among those who came from the Danubian Principalities. They pursued successful careers in the Russian army and diplomatic service. From 1809, Count Ioannis Kapodistrias from Corfu served the Russian tsar as a diplomat, head of the chancellery, and even foreign minister. He later became the first president of liberated Greece.

The opportune moment for an uprising in Greece appeared to draw closer in the years following the Congress of Vienna. Its supporters— whether we identify them as rebels, freedom fighters, or revolutionaries— represented an even broader cross-section of society than in Serbia. They included merchants and shipowners from the mainland and the islands, and members of the Greek diaspora who had become rich through long-distance trade, funneling their money into subversive activities. They already possessed a military-like force because they had armed their trading ships to protect against pirates during the years of the Napoleonic Wars and the continental blockade. On the eve of the Greek uprising, 615 Greek trading ships with about 6,000 cannons were sailing the Mediterranean.[58]

On land, too, political sentiments grew more radical. The formation of *çiftliks* had impoverished masses of peasants in the Peloponnese, and discontent was heightened by a rapidly growing population. The thin stratum of Greek landowners felt unfairly treated and the small circle of Turkish estate owners faced a mass of Greeks who possessed little or no land at all. About 40,000 Turks owned 940,000 acres of land on the Peloponnese, while the 360,000 Greeks together owned only half as many acres. On average, Turks possessed eighteen times more land than the Greeks.[59] Christian elites, the archons or *kocabaşi,* represented an unpredictable source of unrest. They pushed for change to improve their social standing and economic opportunities.[60]

The *armatoloi* or *martolos,* Christian militiamen who had originally guarded roadways and passes for the Ottomans, were a further disruptive influence on land. They coexisted in a fluid relationship with the thieves and highwaymen known as *klephts,* who were tolerated by Ottoman authorities and controlled entire regions. On the eve of the Greek uprising, the *klephts* formed a tightly organized military aristocracy. The most famous revolutionary heroes originally came from their ranks.[61]

Thus, the Greek merchants who founded the secret "friendly society," Filiki Eteria, in Russian Odessa in 1814 hoped to attract a broad base of support. Their goal was a general uprising to "liberate the fatherland" and restore the Greek Empire, with Constantinople as its capital. However, the political organization and territorial borders of the future state remained undefined. The Filiki Eteria was organized along the same lines as the Carbonari in Italy, or the League of Virtue in Germany, with rules and rites resembling those of the Freemasons.[62] Upon the outbreak of the uprising in 1821, it had more than one thousand members—mostly merchants and scholars, Phanariots and *klephts*. The greatest number of members lived in Russia and the Danubian Principalities. By contrast, the society was only weakly represented in majority Greek areas, with the exception of the Peloponnese and the Ionian Islands. Substantial impetus for the struggle for liberation came from the diaspora.

The Eterists were led by the Phanariot Alexander Ypsilantis, who served as a general in the Russian military. Like their revolutionary predecessor Rhigas Velestinlis, they hoped that the Serbs and Bulgarians would join the armed struggle for liberation under Greek leadership. With this goal in mind, they sought contact with Karadjordje, and later with his rival and successor, Miloš Obrenović. Miloš was sympathetic to the Greek cause but reluctant to get involved, insofar as Russia's foreign minister, Ioannis Kapodistrias, had suggested to him that the uprising's prospects were dim. After fighting broke out in the spring of 1821, the Greeks unsuccessfully appealed to Serbia and Montenegro for military support.[63] The Eterists received a warmer response in Bulgaria, where wealthy merchants coordinated money and weapons for the rebels, and tens of thousands of volunteers stood ready to fight. It did not take long, however, for the Turks to suppress all Bulgarian support for the rebellion. They disarmed the Bulgarian population and executed the movement's leaders.[64]

Conditions were more favorable in the Danubian Principalities. After being occupied by Russia during its war with the Ottoman Empire between 1806 and 1812, the principalities were demilitarized and effectively became a Russian protectorate. For Romanians, the empire of the tsar became their greatest hope. The Eterists thus decided to use the Danubian Principalities as their revolutionary springboard. They hoped for the support of the boyars, who were burdened by onerous tributes. Parallel to an uprising in Greece, the revolutionaries wanted to strike in Moldavia, Wallachia, and Istanbul as well.

In fact, the Romanian elites hoped that Russia would restore the "old rights" of self-government in the Danubian Principalities, thereby ending Ottoman suzerainty. In 1818 the great boyar and Moldavian treasurer Iordache Rosetti-Roznovanu sent a new memorandum on this subject to the

Russian ambassador in Istanbul.[65] However, the revolutionary sentiment brewing in the Danubian Principalities was not only directed against the Ottomans; the oligarchy of the Greek Phanariot princes and some Romanian boyars attracted the greatest opposition. Demographic revolution and immigration had created a shortage of land, and the practice of enclosure disenfranchised and impoverished the peasants. The mass of the rural population was bound to the land and suffered under a high burden of rents.

Tudor Vladimirescu—a minor boyar, militia officer, and local administrator from Oltenia—made the most of this social discontent. In January 1821 he formed a parliament-like People's Assembly and a pandour army. He sought not only to overthrow Ottoman "tyranny" by initiating an armed rebellion but also to dispossess the large estate owners and introduce a constitution. This produced a dangerous conflict with the Phanariots and great boyars, who feared for their privileges.[66]

Alexander Ypsilantis, a leader of the Filiki Eteria, crossed the Prut River with about five hundred volunteers in February 1821, seeking to proclaim a general uprising of all southeastern European Christians. He and his Sacred Band captured Jassy. Hundreds of fighters joined him—including Greeks, Russians, Ukrainians, Albanians, Serbs, Poles, Germans, French, Swiss, and Italians. He marched on to Bucharest with this army, intending to join up with the troops of Tudor Vladimirescu.[67]

The military campaign of the Filiki Eteria ended in fiasco. Ypsilantis and Vladimirescu fought over the leadership, strategy, and goals of the continued rebellion. Ypsilantis had the Romanian leader imprisoned and then executed as a traitor. Russia did not come through with the military support that the Eterists had hoped for. Fearful of revolutionary subversion, the Russian tsar even allowed the sultan's troops to enter the Danubian Principalities. In June 1821, the Ottoman army dealt the rebellious Holy Company a crushing defeat at Drăgășani.[68] Ypsilantis fled the country before being captured and imprisoned by the Austrians.[69]

The Ottoman occupation of the Danubian Principalities was brief. Under international pressure, the sultan decided to end Phanariot rule in the Danubian Principalities, placing their crowns in the hands of the local nobility instead. In July 1822, the sultan named Ioan Sandu Sturdza Prince of Moldavia, and Grigore Ghica Prince of Wallachia. In the Convention of Akkerman in 1826, the sultan was compelled to accept Russia's special role as protector of the principalities' autonomy. The old order was largely restored, but Vladimirescu's revolutionary demands for self-government, agricultural reform, and the promotion of domestic trade were not forgotten.[70]

In Greece, by contrast, the Filiki Eteria had greater success. In March 1821 a general uprising broke out in the Peloponnese and central Greece. The rebels quickly gained ground, capturing Athens and Nafplio and brutalizing the Muslim population. They rarely took prisoners, instead sacrificing the lives of Turks as "bloody atonement for their murdered brothers."[71] Upon taking the besieged city of Tripolitsa, the rebels massacred between six thousand and eight thousand people. The living and the dead were stripped of all their clothing and valuables. Rebels were paid a bounty for severed heads—common practice among the Ottomans as well.[72] Thousands of volunteers—Serbs, Bulgarians, Romanians, Albanians, Montenegrins, Vlachs, and even a few Muslims—rushed to the aid of the Greek insurgents.[73] Among the best known was the Bulgarian Hadži Christo.[74]

The Turks responded to the revolutionaries with the greatest possible brutality. Believing that Gregory V, the aged patriarch of Constantinople, had not distanced himself sufficiently from the uprising, they had him dragged from church and hanged in his full regalia on Easter Sunday of 1821. His corpse hung in front of the patriarchal church for two days, then was dragged through the streets and thrown into the Bosporus. The execution provoked great outrage across the Balkan Peninsula. In a *firman* dated May 3, 1821, Sultan Mahmud II proclaimed to the commanders of the Ottoman troops, the kadis, and the *ayan:* "The laws of the holy sharia demand that the infidels meet the blade of the saber; their women and children must be enslaved and Islamized, their fortune divided among the victorious Muslims, and their houses surrendered to flames." Not even the crow of a rooster was still to be heard.[75]

The rebels nevertheless succeeded in bringing large parts of the Peloponnese, the Aegean Islands, Thessaly, and southwestern Macedonia under their control. Even as the fighting raged on, the first Greek national assembly met at the end of 1821. On January 1, 1822, Phanariots, clerics, archons, and *klephts* declared Greek independence and the political rights of citizens in the provisional constitution of Epidaurus. Alexander Mavrokordatos was elected as the first president of the republic.

However, in the first year of fighting, various revolutionary governments emerged. The diverse regional factions and social milieus, including the landowners of the Peloponnese, the mainland *klephts,* and the maritime traders of the Aegean Islands became increasingly entangled in struggles amongst themselves. Members of the diaspora who returned to Greece also joined the fray. In 1823 and 1824, the anti-Ottoman uprising evolved into two successive civil wars. Differences in social background were compounded by conflicting worldviews, attitudes, and values. Oligarchical interests, regional traditions, political and social conflicts, clientelism, and greed undermined consensus over the future state, its constitution, and potential social reforms.[76] It took international diplomatic and military interventions to pacify the country and enable the formation of an independent Greek state.

Can the anti-Ottoman uprisings in southeastern Europe be considered part of a broader European or transatlantic phenomenon? The uprisings were rooted in the intellectual world of the European Enlightenment, and they were influenced by the crisis of the ancien régime that touched all of Europe.[77] There were, moreover, concrete biographical connections; some southeastern European intellectuals experienced the revolutionary era in America and France, and thousands of volunteers fought in Italy, Egypt, and the Mediterranean on the side of the great powers during the Napoleonic Wars. Demetrios Ypsilantis participated in the American War of Independence, Adamantios Korais witnessed the French Revolution, and Theodoros Kolokotronis served in the British military.[78] They and others with similar experiences brought revolutionary ideas, symbols, and personal contacts back to their homelands. They saw the Atlantic revolutions as an important signal and as a role model for the establishment of freedom and democracy. They adapted familiar discourses on liberty, developed their own constitutions, forged contacts with the great powers, engaged in diplomatic correspondence, and traveled to European capitals for international meetings and conferences. Within southeastern Europe, too, revolutionaries stayed in close contact. Serbs, Bulgarians, Greeks, Romanians, and others maintained personal contacts, planned common initiatives, and found allies and compatriots across ethnic and political boundaries. In so doing, they transmitted ideas (sometimes only unconsciously) about a new international order, in which their native lands might be recognized as equal, sovereign members of the community of states.

In contrast to the West, these upheavals were not the result of "national" or "bourgeois" revolutions. Neither the Industrial Revolution nor bourgeois nationalism had yet become evident in this era. Influential actors such as the Serb Prota Matija and the Greek Theodoros Kolokotronis never mentioned the national idea. It was, at best, an indirect presence in the discourse of freedom. But socioeconomic transformations created social classes that pushed for radical change—new elites seeking opportunities for advancement, but also an impoverished, land-deprived, and rebellious underclass. While drawing inspiration from the ideals of the French Revolution and the American revolutionary model, the new elites had genuine motivations of their own that were sometimes quite contradictory. The revolutions and the prospect of independent statehood did, however, create the political, institutional, and social preconditions for social and economic developments that reached much further. Above all, there was now a chance to replace the outdated Ottoman feudal system with a social order based on private property, free trade, legal certainty, and modern institutions—an order that would promote modernization and economic growth.

Thessaloniki (Salonica), 1821

"My God, how great was my surprise when I stepped through the Vardar Gate," Molla Hayrullah Efendi reported to the sultan. "Your highness can be proud that Thessaloniki is among the many cities in your possession," he averred. The twenty-eight-year-old had arrived in Thessaloniki in September 1820 to serve as the city's highest-ranking legal and religious scholar. "What should be admired first? The mosques? The *tekkes?* The bazaars?"[79] For centuries, the capital of Macedonia had held special significance because of its favorable location. In front of the city, a gulf opened to the Mediterranean Sea. Forested hills and mountains blanketed the city's hinterlands, and rivers ran through the fertile plain that extended westward. Major transportation routes and a protected harbor encouraged Thessaloniki's role as a hub of supraregional trade and an administrative and cultural center. The Roman Via Egnatia, which connected Italy with Anatolia, ran through the center of the city. Viewed from afar, the city provided a picturesque tableau: massive city walls from the Byzantine era, including a citadel, gates, and towers; behind them, minarets and domes, interspersed with cypresses and olive trees, small gardens, and vineyards. Before the Macedonian metropolis fell to the Ottomans, it had been successively governed by the Greeks, Romans, and Byzantines. In historical sources, the city was known by seventeen different names: Selanik, Salonicco, Solun, Salonika, and others, until a royal decree made "Thessaloniki" official in 1937.[80]

At the beginning of 1821, rumors began to spread that the Greeks were planning an uprising. The deputy governor *(mütesellim)* who oversaw the city administration, Yusuf Bey, had a particularly despotic and fearsome reputation. To intimidate the rebels, he took more than four hundred hostages, including one hundred monks from Mount Athos. Suspects were sent to the White Tower for even the smallest infractions. Murderers, thieves, smugglers, and other criminals were normally detained in this prison, but now political suspects joined them in ever greater numbers. "Many of them were completely stiff from dampness and hunger," Molla Hayrullah reported to the sultan. One day, the deputy governor's henchmen brought in the half-dead Eterist Aristides Papas, a compatriot of Alexander Ypsilantis, who had been traveling through the Danubian Principalities. "Just as he was about to enter the palace of the bishop, he was seized by two irregulars, and they dragged him by force to the governor's palace. They dealt him one hundred lashes of the whip, without even giving him a chance to speak."[81] He was executed three days later.

The situation escalated after May 16, when Greeks in Polygyros sought vengeance by murdering a Muslim administrator and his soldiers. In response, Yusuf Bey had two hundred hostages executed in Thessaloniki. So horrified was Molla Hayrullah by these events that he recounted them to the sultan after his departure—leaving behind a remarkable historical source. The governor "ordered his spies to strike every infidel they met on the city streets, showing no mercy. . . . Every day and every night one heard nothing from the streets but screams, cries, and moans. Saloniki . . . was transformed into a giant slaughterhouse." The shocked *molla* locked himself in his room and prayed for the salvation of their souls. "Almighty sultan, what my eyes were forced to see!" Pregnant women and children, too, were not spared. Yusuf Bey even executed Bishop Makarios and other notables. The church leader was literally ripped into pieces at the great Kapani marketplace. "They cut off the legs and hands . . . of another cleric. And then they took the severed hands and scratched out his eyes with the fingers."[82]

After Istanbul, Thessaloniki was the largest and most important Jewish city of the Ottoman Empire. Of the approximately 60,000 to 70,000 residents of different linguistic, ethnic, and religious backgrounds, about half were Jewish. The remainder of the population was largely composed of Turkish Muslims and Orthodox Greeks. Countless other groups lived here as well, including Slavs, Albanians, Roma, Armenians, Vlachs, Caucasians, Africans, and western European "Franks."[83]

Although the Jews constituted a relative majority in the city, they did not form a homogenous group. Most were descendants of the Sephardim, Spanish Jews who were driven from the Iberian Peninsula after the Reconquista of 1492, settling throughout the Mediterranean, northern Africa, and the Levant. In the sixteenth and seventeenth centuries, they were followed by the Marranos, Iberian Jews whose ancestors had converted to Catholicism, but who had kept their Jewish names and traditions. Francos were the Sephardic traders who, through capitulations, were considered the protected subjects of European powers, and therefore exempted from taxes.

The Sephardic émigrés were so numerous that they changed the entire Mediterranean world of the Jews. Jews who previously spoke Greek now acquired Judeo-Spanish, or Ladino, which became so widespread that one could almost get by without Greek or Turkish in everyday life. Thessaloniki became an important center of Jewish education and culture. It was home to the Talmud Torah school, which shaped Jewish public and intellectual life for four hundred years. In addition to educating theologians from all over the Mediterranean, the school levied special taxes and collected donations, and it maintained its own printing press and charitable organizations. Later in the century, it served as a nucleus of Jewish nationalism.[84]

Jews were particularly active in the commercial life of Thessaloniki, as the British consul noted: "The Bankers, Cashiers, Buyers and Sellers of imports and exports are Jews, the Porters, Boatmen and persons necessary to employ in preparing wools, cotton, silks, grain and seeds of all Kinds for exportation are all Jews, and very many of the Shops, where all the necessities of life are to be purchased, are kept by Jews."[85] Thousands of Jewish stevedores, fishermen, porters, and laborers nevertheless lived in miserable conditions. They scraped out a living in the ramshackle, dirty alleys near the port, which relied on them for its operations. This is why the port was closed on the Sabbath.

By contrast, the Dönme (apostates), descendants of members of the Jewish Sabbatean sect who converted to Islam in the seventeenth century, were counted as Muslims. These "turncoats" adhered to a mystical Islam, which was enriched by various faith practices, including Talmudic and Sufi influences. They had Turkish names, although they spoke Ladino at home. Although they celebrated Ramadan, and some even made pilgrimages to Mecca, they also revered the eighteen commandments of the sect's founder, Sabbatai Zvi. After a mass conversion in 1683, Thessaloniki became their center. Over the centuries, the Dönme developed their own ethnic and confessional identity. They maintained their own cemeteries, schools, sites of prayer, and voluntary associations, as well as a separate religious administration. But neither the Turks nor the Jews regarded them as equals.[86]

In Thessaloniki and elsewhere in the empire, the *millet* system allowed faith communities a loose form of self-government under their respective religious leaders. Each community possessed its own institutions, professional associations, schools, and sanctuaries. The city had not only thirty-four mosques but also twelve Orthodox churches, seven synagogues, and several dervish monasteries.[87]

The religions erected social barriers that prevented close personal relationships, and certainly marriage, between members of different faiths. The leaders of the *millets*—imams, rabbis, and bishops—watched closely to ensure that cultural and social lines of separation held fast. At this point in time, one could not yet speak of a unified urban society. Instead, multiple religiously defined societies existed in parallel, each with its own jurisdiction, privileges, and informal power relations. Religious traditions, social practices, and legal regulations separated the faith communities, even when they lived side by side. Prejudices and rivalries abounded, and a fight between neighbors could easily grow into an interreligious conflict. Civil disagreements were usually handled informally, but sometimes the authorities were compelled to intervene. The sultan once decided that the Jews had to give up a piece of their cemetery because Muslims wanted to build a promenade there.[88]

In private and sometimes public spaces, clearly demarcated boundaries between the religious communities were constantly renegotiated. One traveler remarked that only a superficial observer could imagine "a kind of melting together of the different peoples," or "a happy convergence of the races." "The nature of faith and differences in family background" tended to keep these groups apart.[89] As in all Ottoman cities, there were primarily Muslim, Jewish, and Christian neighborhoods, the *mahalles*. The Muslims lived near the fortress in the privileged, more spacious upper town, the Jews near the port and to the west, and the Greeks in the city center and to the east. Only in the mid-nineteenth century did these spatial divisions gradually begin to break down.

Even after the great massacre, however, there was no deep-seated hatred between the peoples. "We all belong to God," emphasized Mehmed Ali

Efendi, the wise dervish leader. "Christians, Turks, Jews, etc." Only God could know why he created the world with so many different religions. "But we must be good to one another, and not hate."[90] And despite the religious lines of division, cultural connections existed in everyday life. Saint Demetrios, patron of Thessaloniki and "Deum intercessor," had, since the Byzantine era, been revered for his acts of kindness and reconciliation and for his protection of the city. At the end of the fifteenth century, his church was converted into a mosque. However, the shrine continued to be venerated by Christians and Muslims alike.[91] Other common ties arose from ancient folk customs and calendar holdovers that made their way into the Orthodox, and later Muslim, canon of faith. Two holidays that predated Christianity, originally marking the change of the seasons, came to structure the official church year: Saint George's Day on April 23, and Saint Demetrios Day on October 26. The Muslims later used these dates to honor the saints Kasim and Hizr. These adaptations gave the official hierarchy greater control over popular religious movements and encouraged more homogeneity in religious practice.[92]

For the three world religions that made their home here, Thessaloniki was a hub that brought together believers from many different regions. For centuries, Muslims from the Balkans traveled to the port of Thessaloniki so they could sail to Aleppo or Alexandria, and then join a pilgrimage caravan to Mecca. Sufi mystics likewise set out from Thessaloniki, usually on the way to Anatolia, Egypt, or Iran. Thessaloniki also served as a way station for Christian travelers. Before continuing on to Mount Athos, thousands of monks from Russia and Ukraine came to collect donations and visit one of the city's countless charitable organizations.[93] Finally, both Catholic and Protestant missionaries established bases here for spreading Christianity throughout the Ottoman Empire.[94]

A unified city government with the corresponding services did not yet exist in 1821. Each of the fourteen city districts had its own administrative structure. Only the distribution of drinking water, supervision of the markets, public safety, garbage removal, and construction were centrally administered. Molla Hayrullah Efendi noticed just the imperial splendor, not the miserable conditions of rundown neighborhoods where the lower classes resided. By contrast, another traveler remarked that "Thessaloniki could be a charming city. But it is rotting away in neglect and filth; its winding streets are stuffed with garbage, the houses are crumbling . . . plague-like vapors poison the air."[95] The French consul, too, complained that the city was like a labyrinth, "with none but narrow crooked streets, houses badly built, and not one square . . . that was paved." Even the famed Via Egnatia was just a dusty, swampy trail. Since there was no sewage system, residents simply dumped their wastewater in the streets. Animal cadavers lay outside for days; mountains of trash piled high. "One of the finest cities of Turkey," the consul remarked, "has the appearance of one of our villages."[96]

The two- and (only rarely) three-story houses were typically made from wood, not stone or brick. Dark, airless, and unhygienic, they were a breeding ground for infectious diseases like leprosy and the plague. About 15,000 people had died in the most recent outbreak of the plague in 1814.[97] "It is inconceivable how people can decide to live in such a cesspool!" Anton Prokesch von Osten remarked with disgust.[98] Clean drinking water—or any kind of fresh water—was scarce. Two Roman-era aqueducts supplied the public fountains in the neighborhoods, where people had to wait in long lines. Only a very few wealthy families enjoyed the luxury of running water in their homes. Fire was a chronic danger that was difficult to avoid. There were small fires almost every day; the larger ones periodically wiped out entire neighborhoods. In 1840, 1,500 houses succumbed to flames; eight years later, 640 shops burned down in the marketplace. "Everything that was in them fell prey to the fire," an eyewitness lamented.[99]

As elsewhere in the empire, Jews and Christians who had "protected" status were required to pay a head tax. This was levied on adult men who were fit to work, and boys eight years and older—but not on women, the elderly, or the sick. Leaders of the city districts and guilds and firefighters were also exempt. We do not know why, but the 1835 census recorded taxpayers according to the color of their moustaches—black, black-brown, chestnut brown, blonde, and gray. Grown men without whiskers were listed separately. Only priests, monks, and old men had full beards and thus fell into a separate category. There was, moreover, the usual impenetrable confusion of all kinds of taxes, rents, duties, and tithes. These were collected by tax farmers and authorities, who could increase them at will.[100]

Because cities in the Ottoman Empire did not have independent legal status, Thessaloniki was administered by the sultan's appointed governors. The highest-ranking officials in the city were the pasha, who represented secular legislative and executive authority, and the *molla,* the top spiritual leader who was responsible for criminal justice as well as oversight of the markets, including prices and exports. The aga of the janissaries and the chief of police, who were responsible for public safety, also assumed an influential role, as did the spiritual dignitaries of the ulema.

Because of the city's importance, the sultan appointed only members of influential families to its high-ranking posts. The highest bidder received the office of pasha, although the title was sometimes given away as an act of beneficence. New arrivals, whether foreign consuls or Turkish functionaries, were expected to pay their respects to the pasha and ply him with gifts. He was also entitled to a tithe from the surrounding villages. "If he is covetous and rapacious," Félix Beaujour reported, "he devours the country." In some circumstances, the pashas would "strike off, or cause to be stricken off before them, the head of a man, with as much coolness as a butcher slaughters an ox."[101]

Under—and in some cases, alongside—the pasha was a complicated web of various legal and dependent relationships, which were not ordered in any clear hierarchy. According to long-standing tradition, independent bodies within every religious group participated in local administration. These included councils of elders, who were responsible for civil concerns, and clerics, who presided over religious matters. Guilds that brought together craftsmen and merchants also exercised certain legal authority. In practice, informal relations dominated public life—the exchange of favors and sanctions, patronage, corruption, clientelism, personal whims, and violence. The pasha, too, had to negotiate with the influential families of the large Turkish landowners.[102]

The head rabbi was the leader of the Jewish community, and his position was practically unassailable. "This Grand Kakam [Grand Rabbi] is usually placed . . . under the protection of France or of England," the French consul reported, "and, his person becoming thus inviolable by the Turks, he rules with regal authority over the Jews."[103] Two influential families of rabbis, the Nahmias and the Covos, competed for this high office in Thessaloniki. All others had to hope that they remained on good terms with the dominant clan, so they might receive access to influential positions and material resources.[104]

Jewish life took place within the synagogue community, the fate of which was likewise determined by a small, wealthy oligarchy. From cradle to grave, the Jews kept to themselves—whether at home or at work, in charitable organizations or the synagogue. Anyone who broke away from these narrow social confines was punished—with fines, public warnings, or excommunication *(herem)*, which was ceremonially proclaimed in the synagogue.[105] Although criminal law remained the preserve of Ottoman judges, civil disputes were ruled on by the heads of the religious communities, whose decisions were binding, with no possibility for appeal. The French consul wrote that the terror of being excommunicated by the chief rabbi was so great "that I have seen parents, abandoned by their children, and wives, forsaken by their husbands, come to implore my intercession against his terrible tyranny."[106]

Sa'adi Besalel a-Levi, a Sephardic Jew, was just one year old when the uprising broke out in 1821. His family had worked in publishing for generations, and Sa'adi himself later became the influential editor of *La Epoka,* the first and most important newspaper in the Ladino language. Sa'adi frequently came into conflict with the city's conservative Jewish leaders, whom he described as corrupt and fanatic. They later excommunicated him from the Jewish community.[107] In his memoirs, Sa'adi denounced the gruesome punishments of the "fanatic" religious leaders of his youth, which included lashes with a whip or cane on the souls of the feet *(falaka),* as well as torture presses for women who became pregnant outside of marriage. He also criticized the rabbinical oligarchy for squeezing the poor with taxes on kosher meat, wine, and other foodstuffs. Anyone who advocated for reform was threatened with excommunication. The rabbis once sentenced Sa'adi to two hundred lashes to his feet because he sang *à la turka*—in Turkish. Only the pasha's intervention stopped the execution of his punishment. "This is how our ancestors suffered in the olden days due to their ignorance and fanaticism."[108]

Like the Jews, Christians were allowed to govern themselves through their own religious and secular institutions. The highest-ranking leader of the Orthodox community was the metropolitan, who was formally subordinate to the patriarch in Constantinople. A council of bishops ruled on religious matters, while civil affairs were the domain of a council of elders, whose members were elected for one year by representatives of the different professions. The Orthodox system of education was less developed than its Jewish counterpart; there was only a single Greek school and no printing press.[109] Since the chief of police was easily bribed, wealthy Greeks were able to enjoy all kinds of liberties.[110] Molla Hayrullah observed the self-assurance of the "infidel Rûm" with astonishment. Although it was forbidden, they rode through the streets on horseback, decked out in their finest apparel. "And even worse: they do not leave the sidewalk when they encounter a believer."[111]

The Greeks had never fully accepted that the once so splendid Byzantine city had fallen to the Turks. In the meantime, subversive ideas had begun to spread among the circles of prosperous, well-educated Greeks. Notables gathered regularly to discuss politics in the Agios Minas church. "The daily ringing of the church bells upset me very much," the *molla* admitted.[112] The rebellious intellectuals received support from the wealthy diaspora in the economic and cultural centers of central and western Europe, including many Greeks who originally came from Thessaloniki. This was one of the reasons that the secret society Filiki Eteria established an organizational foothold in the city in 1818.[113] Saint Demetrios, whose cult had survived nearly four hundred years of Ottoman rule, became both a symbol and a projection of the struggle against the Turks. The Greeks of Thessaloniki also helped to popularize the revolutionary song "Thourios" by Rhigas Velestinlis. But anyone who sang it was punished harshly, Molla Hayrullah reported.

Thessaloniki was home to one of the largest ports in the Ottoman Empire. The fleets of all the great trading nations moored here, up to three hundred ships at a time. Different groups profited from the activity at the port. Greeks, Jews, and Ragusans dominated the European trade, while Muslims conducted business with Egypt, and Armenians with Iran. North Africans dominated the slave trade.[114] Important land routes intersected here as well. The city was a conduit for practically all exports from European Turkey, and it sent goods to at least nine supraregional trade fairs.[115] Commensurate with the city's significance for international trade, all larger European countries maintained a presence here with consuls, branch offices, and trading houses.[116]

The value of Thessaloniki's external trade multiplied by a factor of ten over the course of the eighteenth century, the result of favorable economic trends. The city especially profited from the consequences of the Napoleonic Wars. Because there were shortages of many different commodities, the price of wheat (for example) increased tenfold between 1780 and 1813, and profits rose as well.[117] When Napoleon's continental blockade disrupted supply routes between Great Britain and the European mainland, the English began to ship their colonial goods through the port of Thessaloniki, rather than across the English Channel. Local trade agents then transported the goods into central Europe. Convoys of 150 to 300—and sometimes more than 1,000—horses and mules regularly traveled north, their wooden pack saddles laden with bales, sacks, and leather bags. Reaching Vienna in this way took an average of thirty-five days.[118]

Wares of all kinds were bought and sold under the vine-covered roofs of the city's bazaar, which was located in the long, narrow alleys of the lower town, not far from the wharves. A colorful, bustling crowd filled the tight streets by day, until the city walls closed at sundown to enforce nighttime quiet. Saddlers, shoemakers, bakers, millers, masons, carpenters, and other craftsmen kept shops in the business district alleys. The economic boom continuously attracted people from all over the Balkans who were looking for work as porters, laborers, or servants, which is why the city had grown so dynamically in recent decades. In addition to traders, pilgrims, and travelers, the port attracted suspicious characters, too: criminals, smugglers, refugees, and political activists, whom the authorities would have liked to apprehend or expel from the city right away.[119]

Alongside the port and trade, which employed many people, textile manufacturing was another important branch of the economy. Thessaloniki had been a center of textile production in the eastern Mediterranean since the sixteenth century, when the sultan had commissioned the city's Jews to produce the janissaries' uniforms. Jewish traders purchased wool and cotton, which was spun, dyed, and woven into cloth, and then they sold the finished materials at markets in the Ottoman Empire and beyond.[120] The city became famous for the production of rough woolen cloth *(aba)*, silk, cotton fabrics, and tapestries, as well as for its dyers, printmakers, and tailors. They sold their creations all over the Balkans and Anatolia.[121]

Peasants and agricultural laborers also lived in Thessaloniki. They either worked their own land, or labored on the estates of Turkish agas and beys and their powerful families in the outlying areas.[122] Agriculture thrived within the walls of the city throughout the entire nineteenth century. Gardens, orchards, and vineyards covered one-third of the city's area. Its residents kept chickens, goats, and even cows. Foodstuffs like milk, butter, and yogurt were mostly produced and consumed at home.[123]

The peninsula of Athos, with its twenty monasteries and numerous hermitages, belonged to the *sancak* of Thessaloniki—as did Serres, Veria, and other central sites. In the spring of 1821, Emmanuel Pappas (a wealthy trader and banker from Serres) and his compatriots set up headquarters at the Esphigmenou monastery on the Holy Mountain. They had been tasked by the Filiki Eteria to organize the uprising throughout Macedonia.[124] The region's population was as diverse as Thessaloniki's, and no one knew exactly which language groups resided here. The land was comparatively prosperous and well developed—with large commercial estates, cotton fields, vineyards, and fruit orchards, as well as the rich spoils from salt, gold, and silver mines. The monks, too, traded grain, chestnuts, hazelnuts, wine, and schnapps with people in other regions. The Holy Mountain's evident economic prosperity came from the monasteries' landholdings and the offerings and donations they received. A four-person administrative council managed the business affairs of the monastery community, which—like all Christians—had to pay a head tax to the responsible aga.[125]

There were numerous members and sympathizers of the Filiki Eteria among the monks on Athos. The sultan's governors viewed them with suspicion. In fact, the Holy Synod not only sheltered revolutionaries but also helped to recruit new fighters among the peasants and armed bands. They even signed a treaty with local pirates. The privateers were supposed to protect the coast from the Turks, and in return they received financial compensation as well as the right to attack and plunder Turkish villages and ships.[126]

When the uprising broke out in the spring, the Holy Synod called to arms all monks who were able to fight. They commissioned the doctor Dionysius Pyrros to make gunpowder according to his personal recipe, although he complained that "there was no saltpeter and no sulfur . . . we worked as hard as we could to make cannons from wood, with wheels of iron, but we didn't accomplish that either."[127] A delegation from Athos traveled to Alexander Ypsilantis, the leader of the uprising, to ask him for gunpowder. Given the overall shortage of munitions, he reminded them "that the riches of the monasteries in that district were not supposed to take care of just one site, but also the surrounding area." Nevertheless, as one veteran recalled, he gave them 4,000 piastres to take along.[128]

In the end, about 1,200 battle-ready monks marched down the Holy Mountain with 40 cannons, ready to support the rebels' campaign. Greeks in the Peloponnese gained control of larger areas, but after initial military successes the fighting monks were overcome by superior Ottoman forces just outside of Thessaloniki. All of the Greek units were defeated or had to flee. The Turks marched to Athos at the end of December 1821, and the monks formally surrendered at the start of the new year.[129] According to old tradition, the monasteries were plundered and burned to the ground. Four-fifths of the monks fled the mountain. The monastic community was depleted for years to come.[130]

The vengeance of the Turks against the rebels was bitter. They devastated Greek villages and burned down churches and monasteries throughout the surrounding area. Men were executed, and long, miserable trains of women and children were brought to Thessaloniki to be sold as slaves. In July 1821 an English missionary observed how 550 women and children were auctioned off in Thessaloniki—older women for 40 to 60 piastres, and others for 200 to 300 piastres.[131] People were impaled in the public squares. A horrified consul reported that "in all, 120 heads were skewered" at the Vardar Gate alone.[132] Fearful of retribution, thousands of Greeks left the city, and their property was repossessed. It took the city decades to recover from the wave of terror.

European Answers to the Eastern Question

The Eastern Question took on a new dimension after the uprising in Greece. In the last third of the eighteenth century, it had become the most stubborn problem on the agenda of international diplomacy.[133] What would happen to the Balkans if the Ottoman Empire could no longer maintain order? How should the powers respond to growing instability and mass violence? The basic constellation of dangerous rivalry that came to characterize the entire nineteenth century was fully evident: Russia's drive to control the straits and extend its influence into the Mediterranean, England's and France's concern that this would interfere with trade routes to their colonies, and Austria's desire to establish a colonial backyard in southeastern Europe.

Since the time of Peter the Great, the tsarist empire had been determined to expand southeast. It had won three wars against the Ottoman Empire (1768–1774, 1787–1792, and 1806–1812), and each peace settlement brought the country a more favorable strategic position and greater influence. Already after the Russo-Ottoman War of 1768–1774, the sultan was forced to accept a humiliating peace. The Russians marched into the Danubian Principalities, annihilated the Ottoman fleet near Çeşme, conquered Crimea, crossed the Danube, and pushed into Bulgaria. The Peace of Küçük

Kaynarca compelled the sultan to cede the port of Azov to Empress Catherine II and to give up strategic territories on the Black Sea coast and in the steppeland. Russia's trading ships gained free passage on the Black Sea and through the Dardanelles and Bosporus. Russia could now trade freely within the Ottoman Empire and also sail the Danube. The sultan also had to accept the independence of the Muslim khanate in Crimea. The strategically important peninsula now fell within the Russian sphere of influence. The tsarist empire further received a formidable payment of reparations. Finally, it secured rights of protection for Orthodox Christians in the Ottoman Empire, which were to be enforced by the Russian envoy in Istanbul. This became an important lever for intervening in domestic Ottoman affairs. The Danubian Principalities formally remained under Ottoman suzerainty, but they received greater autonomy.[134] The outcome was not merely disadvantageous, it was also demeaning, for the Ottoman Empire. It was forced to vacate strategically important parts of Europe, while Russia's economic, military, and political might grew substantially. The Ottoman Empire never regained the momentum to turn around its military and strategic decline. In 1783 the empress annexed Crimea and additional territories around the Black Sea and the Caucasus. Soon thereafter, she installed a consul and vice-consul in Bucharest and Jassy, who forwarded Russian instructions to the ruling *hospodars*.

Empress Catherine II continued to advance her expansionist policies by presenting a "Greek Plan" to Austrian Emperor Joseph II at the beginning of the 1780s. Her proposal was essentially a partition of the Ottoman Empire. Serbia, Montenegro, Bosnia, Herzegovina, and Albania would go to Austria; Russia would be allowed to take possession of the Danubian Principalities, the Caucasus, and the northern coast of Asia Minor, including the straits. A restored Byzantine Empire that was allied with Russia would arise in Bulgaria, Macedonia, and Greece (including Constantinople).[135]

War broke out again in 1787, and Joseph II himself joined the Russians on the battlefield, seeking to drive "the barbarians of the Orient" from Europe.[136] The Austrians conquered Belgrade and Bucharest, and the Russians occupied Moldavia. But because of Austria's growing rivalry with Russia, it declined to dismember the Ottoman Empire completely. The peace of 1792 brought Russia only small territorial gains, although these were of considerable strategic interest. It took possession of the territory between the Bug and Dniester Rivers, and thus the area bordering Moldavia.

After 1806, when the tsar was engaged in another war against the sultan, the Russians sounded out the possibility of dividing up the Ottoman Empire with Emperor Napoleon. The Russian army occupied the Danubian Principalities but was forced to retreat from the region because of an impending attack by the French. In the 1812 Treaty of Bucharest, Russia acquired only Bessarabia and the mouth of the Danube. The rest of Moldavia and Wallachia remained with the Ottoman Empire. The tsar did, however, secure the right to issue directives to the *hospodars,* and to have a voice in negotiations should they be deposed. Ottoman troops were not allowed to remain in the Danubian Principalities. In effect, an informal Russian protectorate was established.

Over the course of the Napoleonic Wars, southeastern Europe increasingly found itself at the center of the great powers' conflicting economic and political interests and their active military engagement. The Russians, British, and French unabashedly pursued their ambitions in the eastern Mediterranean, each occupying the Ionian Islands in turn. In the end, the Ottoman Empire profited indirectly from the great powers' rivalry, because they recognized that the empire's continued existence guaranteed the maintenance of equilibrium in the question of the straits and the eastern Mediterranean. The empire was so large and strategically important that any one-sided adjustment to the status quo that favored an external actor threatened to provoke an extended war over territories and spheres of influence.[137]

This became a key recognition at the Congress of Vienna in 1815, as England, Russia, Austria, and Prussia laid the foundations of a new territorial and political order in Europe, which was necessitated by Napoleon's defeat in Russia and the collapse of his rule. Territories that had been reorganized by revolutionary and / or Napoleonic France stood at the top of the agenda: German-speaking central Europe, Poland, Italy, and the Netherlands. Only the margins of southeastern Europe were affected. From the mass of French possessions, Austria acquired Venice, Lombardy, Galicia, and the "Illyrian provinces" (including Dubrovnik), while Russia secured Finland, Bessarabia, and much of Poland for itself. A special treaty established the "United States of the Ionian Islands" as a free and independent state under British protection. The Eastern Question as such was not a focus of the negotiations. Thanks to Russian advocacy and military threats, the Serbian delegation managed to wring partial autonomy for the Belgrade *pashalik,* the later Principality of Serbia, from the Ottoman Empire in extra negotiations.

The European order of 1815 was based on the idea of a balance of power between England, Russia, Austria, and Prussia. After a three-year waiting period, France was recognized as an equal member of the group. The powers wanted to resolve future foreign policy problems in concert, including the Eastern Question. The goal of the international system created in Vienna was to balance interests fairly, and thus to uphold a stable and peaceful European order. Smaller and medium-sized states also had a place in the system. It was grounded in the rejection of hegemonic ambitions, and accepted rules of conduct in responding to crises. The powers renounced their right to wage wars or support revolutions that would change the territorial status quo. If an international question directly affected the vital interests of a state, the state was entitled to participate in the matter's resolution. Confrontations and direct threats were discouraged, and participation in international conferences was mandatory if larger conflicts did arise. At a time when institutionalized forms of intergovernmental cooperation did not yet exist, international conferences served as the most important diplomatic instrument, allowing the Pentarchy to safeguard peace and stability on the continent until the Crimean War in 1853.[138]

On one hand, the order created by the Congress of Vienna promoted ideals of restoration, but on the other, it was fundamentally modern. Following Napoleon's territorial reorganization, for example, the Holy Roman Empire was superseded by a new federative system of states, the German Confederation.[139] Although the powers did not intend to fully restore pre-revolutionary conditions, they did want to build a dam against systemic changes that could not be controlled. Russia, Austria, and Prussia forged the Holy Alliance to defend the principle of monarchical, dynastic legitimacy against future revolutionary movements. They made religion the foundation of their politics, and they agreed to intervene forcefully against revolutionary states. But the drive for political emancipation was difficult to contain. In the 1820s, uprisings erupted in Spain, Portugal, Italy, Russia, and Greece.

After 1821, the new guidelines of international diplomacy were put to the test in Greece. Although the powers had managed to set the Serbian problem aside, now the escalation of violence demanded a response. Since the Ottoman Empire was not an equal partner in the concert of powers, the Viennese rules of conduct had only limited application. On the other hand, because the Eastern Question represented a special situation, the crisis could be managed by jettisoning older principles and forging an entirely new political direction.[140] The Greek uprising marked the beginning of a new approach in international conflict management: the "humanitarian intervention."

The grounds for military intervention were the startling atrocities perpetrated by both the Greek rebels and the Ottoman military against the civilian population. Among other acts of violence, the Greek rebels massacred thousands of Turkish men, women, and children, burning fortresses and houses to the ground. They slaughtered the residents of Kalavryta and Kalamata, although these had already surrendered to the rebels. Massacres also took place in Laconia, Tripolitsa, and other locations. Ottoman military and police forces, and the infamous special units, responded with brute force against those suspected of subversion. They executed hostages, impaled and beheaded prisoners, and devastated large swaths of land. A nineteenth-century historian spoke of a "war of annihilation," which was "conducted with barbaric rancor on both sides."[141] A succession of reports on pogrom-like persecutions of the Christian population mobilized the European public. A key turning point was the Ottomans' reconquest of the island of Chios in the spring of 1822, when thousands of Greeks were vengefully murdered, expelled, or enslaved. In the end, only one-fifth of more than 100,000 Greeks remained. When the British ambassador protested to the Sublime Porte, he was met with scorn and derision.[142]

The European powers treated crimes against the Muslim population in Greece as an internal affair of the Ottoman Empire (and therefore ignored them), but the accumulating reports of Turkish atrocities against the Greeks—from sites like Istanbul, Thessaloniki, and Smyrna—served as a clarion call. Russia, the declared protector of Christians in the Ottoman Empire, pursued humanitarian—but also self-seeking strategic—interests in compelling the Western powers to provide military support to the Greek rebels. Although Russia was otherwise insistent on the principle of monarchical legitimacy, in June 1821 it sent a message to the Sublime Porte that "continued coexistence" with Turkey would require "that the Porte not threaten the Christian religion with war and abuse." Russia did "not intend to allow the destruction of an entire people."[143]

In western Europe, too, the Serbian and Greek revolutions attracted enormous attention in the liberal intellectual climate of the *Vormärz* era. In educated humanist circles, they became a touchstone for protests against restrictions on freedom at home. In his *Serbian Revolution,* the young historian Leopold Ranke was primarily taking aim against restoration and reaction within his own country. Events in Greece, the supposed birthplace of European culture and democracy, were even more unsettling. Scholars, philanthropists, and adventurers founded philhellenic societies in Germany, England, France, Switzerland, Russia, Italy, Spain, and the United States. They collected monetary donations and weapons, printed pamphlets and books, and sent relief supplies to the Balkans. Young men, often of aristocratic background, turned the rebirth of ancient Hellas, and thus the Greek struggle for freedom, into a personal mission. The Munich professor Friedrich Wilhelm Thiersch even wanted to form a German legion of volunteers to support the Greek freedom fighters. Thiersch and the Bavarian crown prince, the later Ludwig I, were the most prominent advocates of philhellenism in Bavaria. Ludwig sent Bavarian officers to the Balkans to train Greek troops, and he transferred money "to buy back the freedom of women and children who had fallen into Turkish hands after the catastrophe of Missolonghi."[144] The fortress on the Gulf of Corinth had fallen after months of siege. The British poet Lord Byron, who embarked for Greece in 1823, became the icon of philhellenes all over Europe. He organized a small fighting force and collected large sums of donations. Many volunteers returned from Greece disillusioned. One English philhellene described the Greeks as "debased, degraded to the lowest pit of barbarism." They treated the Muslims and Jews "like animals to be exterminated."[145] Byron did not let this disturb him. There was great mourning in Greece when he died of a fever in 1824. The poet became a hero of the Greek struggle for freedom and a martyr of philhellenism.[146]

Enthusiasm for the Greek cause inspired new artistic representations that were intended to spark empathy for Christian victims and sympathy for the Greeks' political struggle. Operas and *Singspiele* by composers like Rossini and Berlioz took up the theme of Greek liberty. The painter Eugène Delacroix translated the appeal to aid the violated Hellenes into eye-catching visual images. His allegory *Greece on the Ruins of Missolonghi* depicts a desperate woman, in tears and a torn dress, kneeling on ruins and surrounded by corpses. With open arms, the woman pleads for sympathy—not from an otherworldly god, but instead from her fellow humans in the here and now. The dichotomy between good and evil, civilization and barbarism, Christianity and Islam, is immediately evident in the painting, which was emblematic of a new discourse about intervention that developed amid the backdrop of the Greek War of Independence.[147]

Greece on the Ruins of Missolonghi, Eugène
Delacroix, 1826. Museum of Fine Arts, Bordeaux.

In the end, it was not humanitarian motives, liberalism, or an outraged
public that drove the great powers to intervene militarily in the Greek uprising, but rather concrete political, military, and economic interests. Opportunity was provided by the Egyptian governor, Mehmed Ali Pasha, who
rushed to the aid of the Ottoman troops in 1824. Mehmed Ali, a native
Albanian, had driven Napoleon's troops out of Alexandria and assumed
its Ottoman governorship in 1801. Now he, or his son Ibrahim, sought to
become governor of the Peloponnese after triumphing militarily over the
Greeks. The European powers were unsettled by the threat of a criminal
Muslim state on European soil, which might follow the example of northern
Africans on the Barbary Coast, living primarily from piracy, kidnapping,
and the slave trade. After the shock of Missolonghi in April 1826, the Athe-
nian Acropolis fell in the summer of 1827.

As these events unfolded, in October 1825 the Russian ambassador in London had already floated a rumor about an Ottoman "barbarization plan"—which was supposedly to deport, enslave, and Islamize the entire Greek population. The Sublime Porte denied that such a plan had ever existed, but the European public was scandalized. It was later revealed that the Russians had intentionally spread the rumor in order to persuade the British to intervene. Aside from concern for their Christian brothers in faith, the Russians felt that their strategic advantages from the Peace of Küçük Kaynarca were under threat. England, on the other hand, feared that Russia might attempt to start a new war against the Ottoman Empire, expanding its influence in southeastern Europe and possibly endangering British trade interests in the eastern Mediterranean. In the British view, therefore, it seemed more sensible to follow Russia into a military intervention against the sultan's empire so that British interests could then be accommodated as well. At the beginning of 1826, therefore, foreign minister George Canning concluded that "the selling into slavery—the forced conversions—the dispeopling of Christendom—the recruiting from the countries of Islamism—the erection in short of a new Puissance Barbaresque d'Europe—these are . . . facts new in themselves, new in their principle, new and strange and hitherto inconceivable in their consequences, which I do think may be made the foundation of a new mode of speaking if not acting."[148]

The purported "barbarization plan" provided a moral argument for joint Russian-British action that was easy to present to the public. In the spring of 1826, both powers agreed on their terms for a peace settlement in the Protocol of Saint Petersburg, which France later joined as well. According to the protocol, Greece was to become a tributary state of the Ottoman Empire, and Turks who lived there would be resettled.

The Austrians viewed these proceedings with concern, as Russia was effectively displacing them from their role as protector of the Balkan Christians. The festering rivalry over hegemony in the Balkans could be papered over as long as all parties agreed that the Ottoman Empire should be preserved as a buffer, despite—or because of—its internal weaknesses. Years earlier, Joseph II had already told one of his envoys that "the turban will be a less dangerous neighbor for Vienna than the hats."[149] The existence of the Habsburg Empire, a loose federation of states and peoples, depended significantly on a stable peace. The upsurge of revolutionary nationalism in Greece threatened to spread to the Habsburgs' own multinational empire. The activism furthermore created an imbalance in the European system of alliances. For all these reasons, the Austrian chancellor Prince Metternich did not want to join the British-Russian alliance on behalf of the Greeks. Austria's junior partner, Prussia, also stayed away.[150]

Thus, in July 1827, only Russia, France, and England negotiated the terms of the Treaty of London. For humanitarian reasons and the protection of regional stability, they offered to mediate an armistice and more extensive peace settlement between the warring parties. The Ottoman Empire would recognize the autonomy of Greece, which would in turn pay tribute and remain under the suzerainty of the sultan. To achieve the "complete separation" of both nations, Turkish property was to be transferred to the Greeks. If the Sublime Porte did not accept the allies' offer within a month, a secret passage in the treaty provided for initiating formal relations with the as-yet unrecognized Greek government. The treaty partners affirmed their intent to continue "the work of pacification" and to "determine the future measures which it may become necessary to employ."[151]

In April 1827 the different Greek factions that had become entangled in civil war had already agreed on a constitution through international mediation. The constitution introduced the protection of civil rights, strict separation of powers, and a centralized state apparatus. Count Ioannis Kapodistrias, the former Russian foreign minister, was named the first regent.[152] He immediately initiated an ambitious state-building program. He centralized the administration, instituted uniform legal practices, and built up a tightly organized system of military defense. He also worked to modernize agriculture, banking, and maritime trade.[153]

The allies instituted a naval blockade to prevent the Ottomans from receiving military reinforcements. When the Sublime Porte did not respond to the London ultimatum, the two sides clashed at Navarino in October 1827. The allies destroyed the Ottoman and Egyptian fleet in a three-day sea battle, and six thousand sailors lost their lives. France moved to occupy the Peloponnese, and Russia marched through the Danubian Principalities into the Ottoman Empire. Nineteenth-century experts treated Navarino as a precedent for later international humanitarian interventions, as it demonstrated how discourses of moral responsibility could be translated into military action. Of course, the ostensibly humanitarian undertaking applied only to Christians and not to Muslims, and it happened

Battle of Navarino, Panagiotis Zografos, nineteenth century. Private collection.

to correspond to other national interests—restoring peace and security, combating piracy and slavery, securing the trade routes to Asia, and containing the hegemonic ambitions of rival powers.[154]

Ongoing Greek resistance against the Ottomans, and the sultan's refusal to compromise, led Russia to declare war against him in April 1828. Russian troops advanced deep into Ottoman territory in the Caucasus and the Balkans, and after seventeen months of fighting the sultan was forced to surrender. In the 1829 Peace of Adrianople, he was compelled to recognize the Greek state under Ottoman suzerainty, as had been demanded by the great powers. Russia emerged from the armed conflict with large territorial gains near the mouth of the Danube and in Armenia. Its ships were guaranteed free passage on the Black Sea and through the Dardanelles, an important condition for advancing into the Mediterranean and penetrating the Caucasus.

The uprisings in Serbia and Greece set dynamics in motion that would eventually drive the Turks completely out of Europe. Already in 1821, the Leipzig professor Wilhelm Traugott Krug asserted that "Turkish rule in Europe can in no way be seen as lawful (legitimate) . . . it arose through a war of outright aggression and conquest."[155] The consequences of this position seeped gradually into broader diplomatic circles. In 1824, the British ambassador Stratford Canning expressed his hope that the Turks could be expelled from Europe, "bag and baggage"—even before William Gladstone openly supported "gentle euthanasia" for the Ottoman Empire in 1858. In France, too, many intellectuals looked forward to the "triumph of humanity" when the Ottomans departed.[156]

It was within the context of the Greek uprising that political leaders came to embrace the idea that problems between nationalities might be solved through ethnic disentanglement.[157] With French troops' occupation of the Peloponnese between 1828 and 1833, forced population transfer became a recognized instrument of conflict resolution under international law. In one of the first collectively mandated peacekeeping missions, soldiers were supposed to monitor the retreat of the Egyptian and Ottoman military, as well as the return of Greek expellees and displaced persons. In addition, they were supposed to organize the compulsory resettlement of Muslims. Foreign minister Auguste de La Ferronnay bluntly stated that the objective of the intervention was "to chase the Turks out of Greece." The French subsequently transported about 2,500 Muslims to Smyrna on their ships. Halting the spread of the uprising to western Greece was not, however, part of their mandate.[158] Forced expulsion and resettlement, and the exchange of unwanted population groups, have since belonged to the standard repertoire of international conflict management.[159]

To counteract the growing influence of Russia, France and Great Britain agreed to an independent Greek kingdom in the London Protocol of 1830. The new state encompassed the Peloponnese and nearby islands, with a total population of about 800,000. It agreed to uphold "equal treatment of the non-Orthodox population," an early form of legal protection for minority rights. Thessaly, Epirus, Macedonia, Crete, and numerous islands remained within the Ottoman Empire, as did the majority of the Greek population in the Balkans.[160] Serbia, too, was granted far-reaching autonomy in the Peace of Adrianople. In the Hatt-i Sharifs of 1830 and 1833, the sultan recognized Serbia's status as an independent principality led by a hereditary prince. Serbia still owed tribute, but the Ottoman feudal system was dismantled. The only military presence that remained was limited to a few border fortresses, and these were given up entirely after a Serbian attack in 1867. Moldavia and Wallachia, too, were granted autonomy under the regency of native princes. Russia secured the right to participate in the

French troops in the Peloponnese during the collectively mandated humanitarian intervention, 1828. *The Capture of Morea Castle* (detail), Jean-Charles Langlois, 1836. MV 1802, Château de Versailles.

hospodars' appointment and the administration of their countries. Until 1834, the two principalities were subject to Russian occupation, and they effectively remained under its protection until 1854. Russia brought a modern constitution, the *Règlement organique,* to the principalities as well.[161]

In dealing with the Greek struggle for independence, the European powers established a pattern that they later repeated under similar circumstances. Because of the prevailing view that the Balkan peoples were not yet ready for self-rule and that their complete independence would destabilize the region, the powers developed a hierarchical system of international oversight, administration, and regency.[162] After an extended search for a suitable monarch, sovereignty in Greece was transferred to the younger son of the Bavarian king Ludwig I, who had supported the Greek uprising. The appointment reaffirmed the Holy Alliance's principle of legitimacy, and also gave its members a controlling influence over the new state. The future King of Greece, seventeen-year-old Prince Otto I of Wittelsbach, stepped onto Greek soil for the first time in early 1833. He was accompanied by a three-member council of regents who led the government until Otto came of age. He was determined that Greece should become a "model kingdom." Since this time, the state has possessed a white and blue flag.[163]

The turbulent decades between the French Revolution and the revolutions in southeastern Europe led to the formation of a modern international system and new forms of (more or less) cooperative conflict management. Southeastern Europe became the testing ground for the great powers' developing identities, interests, and foreign policy roles. The weaknesses of the Viennese system soon became evident. It excluded the situation in the Balkans and in the Levant, inviting the egoistic interests of the great powers to fill the political vacuum left by the shrinking Ottoman Empire. The region became a playing field for economic, political, strategic, and cultural competition and projections of power.

For the European great powers, the Greek revolution became paradigmatic for a new means of dealing with international crises. It introduced concepts and justifications for "humanitarian interventions" that have since become part of the permanent repertoire of collective security. At the same time, it established the (not so humanitarian) idea that regional stability can be attained through forced population transfers—a view that has had great historical influence up through the present day. Not least, the Greek example demonstrated how the great powers hoped to deal with movements of secession. They did not immediately consider new states to be subjects of equal legal status. The journey toward full independence (typically not the intended destination) wound through several different stages, including international administration and the appointment of foreign monarchs. The Balkan Question was linked to the beginnings of a new international system and accompanying methods of conflict resolution, the basic features of which remain in place today.

Pirates, Plague, and Other Global Challenges

The reordering of the international system brought collective security issues into ever sharper focus. Revolutions and large-scale atrocities motivated humanitarian interventions because—as stated in the 1827 Treaty of London—the "sanguinary struggle . . . daily causes fresh impediments to the commerce of the States of Europe," demanding "measures which are burthensome for their observation and suppression."[164] Dangers that transcended borders, emanating from Ottoman territory and particularly its European possessions—most of all, plague, piracy, and slavery—were understood as threats to the well-being and the values of "civilized" nations. Efforts to combat infectious diseases, crime, and human trafficking in this era became a shared undertaking among the great powers. The first international initiatives to address global challenges developed out of bilateral diplomatic activities in these fields.

The plague was a danger believed to have been overcome in western Europe and Russia in the seventeenth century. In the Ottoman Empire and on the Balkan Peninsula, however, it still appeared regularly even into the nineteenth century, periodically spilling over into neighboring lands. There may have been a connection between the sultan's declining military fortunes and the occasional decimation of his population by the plague, which seriously disrupted the chain of supply. Between 1700 and 1850, there were fifty-four years when the plague was recorded in northern Albania and Epirus. There were fifty-nine years of plague in Macedonia and Thrace, sixty in the Danubian Principalities, and ninety-four in Istanbul.[165] Up to one-fifth of the population was lost during each epidemic; in the cities, it was often more. Bucharest, Split, Sarajevo, and Istanbul shrank by 30 to 50 percent during larger outbreaks.[166] All economic activities came to a standstill once the fatal disease claimed its first victims. Famine often followed on the heels of the plague. "Waves of devastation like those now caused by the plague . . . have not existed in human memory," the Venetian consul in Thessaloniki reported in 1781. "When three hundred or more die each day, a city of 80,000 soon turns into a wasteland."[167]

The narrow, winding, dirty streets of the Balkan cities, and the filthy, poorly ventilated hostels and caravansaries where long-distance travelers took shelter, were ideal breeding grounds for rats and fleas, which transmitted the pathogen to humans. The vermin leaped from the sick to the healthy, and they could survive for an extended period of time in clothes, bedding, and carpets, so infection threatened not only the homes of the sick but also public squares, inns, and the changing rooms of public baths. Unhygienic living conditions and clothing increased the risk of transmission, as did hunger and fasting. "During especially severe plague epidemics, corpses can lie in the houses for many days before they are buried or attended to." The heirs "hurry to put on the clothes of the deceased, sometimes even without washing them."[168]

Europeans realized that the plague was carried from the Ottoman Empire, the Levant, and northern Africa in the eighteenth and nineteenth centuries. In fact, in Egypt and Syria, in Anatolia and Istanbul—the "kingdom of rats"—there were multiple, relatively stable plague foci where the pathogen permanently reproduced. Southeastern Europe also had two areas of chronic infection. One was the mountainous region encompassing hundreds of square miles from the Dalmatian hinterland to Thessaly, Macedonia, and Kosovo. The second was in the Danubian Principalities.[169] From here, the plague periodically spread across the Balkan Peninsula and threatened neighboring regions. It could spread up to 250 miles in one year. In the years between 1701 and 1716, for example, it crossed the borders of Moldavia and Wallachia into Transylvania, moving farther toward Austria and Poland, reaching Nuremberg and even Hamburg. In later years, too, it repeatedly crossed into the Habsburg Monarchy.[170]

The Austrian health commissioner Joseph Franz Müller described the last great plague outbreak in Rumelia in 1837 and 1838. The first symptoms were an insatiable thirst and a painfully distended stomach. A growth later formed near the lymph nodes "up to the size of an onion, the shape of which it acquired as well; quickly festering and breaking open, it released a liquid that was thick at first, later becoming thin and bloody."[171] This was followed by gangrenous boils on the back and thighs, bloody diarrhea, and an array of other painful symptoms before the sickness either passed or led to death. At least half of all infected people, but usually a much higher proportion, died within four to five days.

The authorities of the European nations tried to contain the disease by blockading affected regions, issuing rigid travel restrictions, and isolating the sick. Throughout the Mediterranean, ships were kept at a distance from the harbors, and—as in Dubrovnik—they were initially held for weeks in quarantine, along with their crew and cargo. Ships that already had the plague on board were out of luck, because no one was willing to take in the sick or even give them food and water. In desperation, ships sailed aimlessly for months. Those who died from the plague were often simply thrown overboard. In 1743 Venetian officials found an actual phantom ship off the coast of Piran—its hold full of olive oil, but without a single living soul on board.[172]

The plague brought terror, panic, and sometimes resignation wherever it appeared. Before the plague bacillus and its means of transmission were scientifically established at the end of the nineteenth century, lots of people believed that heavenly constellations or movements within the earth were responsible for the epidemics. Many contemporary authors still assumed that the sickness spread through contaminated air.[173] Scholars did, however, already possess more accurate knowledge about the spread of infection. Julije Bajamonti was a Croatian doctor, musicologist, and polymath, the son of a bourgeois family from Split. He wrote a history of the plague in 1786, shortly after it had spread through Dalmatia. He described how merchants, horse traders, border guards, and cattle herders carried the sickness from the Ottoman Empire. Convinced that the plague could be contained and treated medicinally, he wanted to persuade the Venetian Senate to improve its preventive health measures. Bajamonti had studied medicine in Padua, and he condemned superstition and religious ritual as expressions of paralyzing fear that prevented rational thought and action.[174] Bajamonti, who admired Voltaire and the "learned bishop" Stratiko, attracted the ire of the bourgeois establishment in his hometown of Split for his criticisms of feudalism and the authority of the church. Many supporters of the church were not interested in heeding his medical advice.[175]

Instead of fighting the plague, the religious communities ascribed their own meanings to it. Christians believed that God wanted to punish them for their sinful behavior. The Austrian emperors and the Catholic Church agreed. Clerics in Slavonia and the Batschka recommended moral behavior and prayer to the faithful, and they built churches and chapels to Saint Roch, protector against the plague.[176] Orthodox Christians, too, hoped for salvation through religious rituals and, especially, relics. In 1816 the French consul observed a procession of fifty-two priests, followed by a bishop, in the Greek town of Arta. "The relics were placed at all crossroads, while the few remaining residents of the town knelt at the doors of their houses, faces turned to the ground, pleading for God's mercy."[177] Muslims tended toward fatalism, seeing death by the plague as divine providence. They prayed, too, but otherwise accepted martyrdom as an act of fate, without wholly neglecting the sick. Jews believed that a person's sins were written on his forehead, and if Satan saw someone marked in this way, he would punish the offender with death by the plague. "Many of these fanatics covered their foreheads with a scarf, so that the devil would not see the writing on their foreheads," the Jewish publisher from Thessaloniki, Sa'adi Besalel a-Levi, wrote in his diary. "As early as 6 P.M., the men cloistered themselves in their homes, covered their windows with black fabric, ate dinner, and went to bed in the dark around 7 P.M., for fear that the devil might peek through a window."[178] But in the end, people of all faiths took flight in panic wherever the disease appeared, as in Prizren in 1837: "It was a sad sight, the deserted streets of the city that was otherwise so lively with commerce, and those of the nearby villages, overgrown with thorn apple and henbane, while the villagers, who had left the sick to their fates, took refuge within lightweight reed huts in the middle of the fields."[179]

Although effective disease prevention measures had already been introduced in western Europe and Russia in the seventeenth century, the Ottoman sultans remained indifferent to the problem into the nineteenth century. Instead, Ottoman authorities engaged in a flurry of activity on the day that the epidemic appeared. In 1813 they ordered all homes in Bucharest to be mopped, smoked out, and aired. Beggars, gypsies, and traveling salesmen were expelled from the city. Jews, too, fell under suspicion as carriers of the plague.[180] Fear of the disease was so great that in 1837 the pashas from Üsküb (Skopje) and Prizren threatened people with punishment of death if they were coming from plague-stricken areas.

At the beginning of the eighteenth century, the Habsburgs erected a cordon sanitaire to protect against infection in Transylvania, Slavonia, and Croatia. Crossing the border from the Ottoman Empire was only permitted at certain quarantine stations. Health inspectors known as the "sanitatis exploratores" monitored the situation in endangered lands, but simultaneously used their position to act as spies for all kinds of other purposes.[181] The Russians also introduced strict health controls and quarantine measures, since the disease repeatedly moved from the Danubian Principalities into Poland and Russia. Only during the Tanzimat period of reforms, when the Ottoman Empire fundamentally modernized its institutions and system of law beginning in the late 1830s, did it systematically introduce mechanisms to combat disease.[182] In this decade the new Balkan states—Serbia, Greece, and the Danubian Principalities—likewise made efforts to protect against infection. Thanks to state health authorities and new quarantine procedures, the plague was finally conquered in southeastern Europe. In Istanbul, the disease broke out for the last time in 1836; in the Balkans, between 1837 and 1838. With cholera, however, a new itinerant disease appeared throughout Europe.[183]

Alongside epidemics, criminality at sea was another threat from the past that had not yet been vanquished. If piracy in the Mediterranean Sea had been largely contained at the beginning of the eighteenth century, it underwent a massive revival during the Napoleonic Wars.[184] Albanian and

Greek privateers who had fought for the English, French, and Russians in various wars now turned their attentions to the eastern Mediterranean. Anti-Ottoman rebels entered into formal agreements with the pirates, whose military power could not be ignored.[185]

In contrast to the privateers from southeastern Europe, corsairs from the Barbary states of Tripoli, Tunis, and Algiers also trafficked in humans. Since the fifteenth century, they had attacked ships and raided coastal cities throughout the Mediterranean. Tens of thousands of Christians were enslaved and sent to northern Africa. In 1814 the British admiral Sidney Smith complained that "Turkish pirates . . . not only oppress neighboring populations, but carry them off or buy them as slaves to be used in armed corsair ships." This "shameful banditry" created a serious obstacle for international trade because sailors were "haunted by the fear of being captured by pirates and taken to Africa as a slave."[186] The European maritime powers and even the U.S. Navy repeatedly threatened the corsair states with military retaliation. The north African pirates were compelled to give up privateering only after the French military's devastating invasion of Algiers in 1830.[187]

Since the end of the eighteenth century, abolitionists who called for the elimination of slavery had attracted ever broader support in Europe, America, and Russia. A religiously motivated, humanitarian idea developed into a social movement and eventually an international norm. The driving force was Great Britain, which had lost its American colonies, and thus a large portion of the slaves within its empire, in 1783. Slaves were employed in large numbers only on the sugar-producing islands of the Caribbean. The monopolistic system of the British colonial economy, which had been grounded in the intercontinental division of labor within the empire, fell apart after the founding of the United States. Trade with other states grew significantly in volume and importance. In addition, ongoing industrialization—which was based largely on the production of textiles, rather than colonial trade—shifted the economic center of the British Empire toward India. The transition from commercial to industrial capitalism, on one hand, meant that Great Britain no longer depended on slave labor. On the other, it meant that Britain had an interest in eliminating slavery wherever the practice led to competition over prices on the world market.[188] "As long as America was our own," the abolitionist Thomas Clarkson wrote in 1788, "there was no chance that a minister would have attended to the groans of the sons and daughters of

Africa."[189] Whether free labor was actually more profitable than unfree labor—as asserted by free market theorist Adam Smith—remains a subject of debate, but Smith's economic liberalism gained ever more followers in the political classes of this era.

Beginning in 1805, Russia, Great Britain, and France declared the international slave trade illegal based on economic, ideological, and humanitarian reasons. The great powers claimed the right to search the ships of other powers and to stop the transport of slaves with the force of their navies. At the Congress of Vienna in 1815, the European monarchies finally agreed to combat the slave trade. The Final Act of the Congress included a statement of intent to abolish the trade in black Africans altogether. However, this and subsequent agreements applied to the Atlantic, but not the Mediterranean. Just the Atlantic slave trade was a factor of production that affected competitive relations in international trade. The Mediterranean did not attract the attention of Great Britain, the leading proponent of abolishing the slave trade, until after 1850, once the transport of Africans to America had significantly declined.[190]

Even after the introduction of the great Tanzimat reforms, Ottoman leaders continued to uphold slavery. They invoked the old traditions of military slavery and the harem, which were deeply rooted in the sociocultural order, and they forbade outside interference. The practice of the child levy for procuring state and military slaves came to an end over the course of the seventeenth century. The last of these probably took place in Greece in 1705. Male and female house slaves did, however, continue to serve Ottoman dignitaries. Even grand viziers of the Tanzimat era kept slaves, whom they considered indispensable to their households. The unfree men and women served as cheap labor (they were usually house servants), as concubines, and also as status symbols. Slavery was a predominantly urban phenomenon. In contrast to the overseas colonies, unfree laborers in the Ottoman Empire did not work primarily on farms or plantations, but in upper-class households. And unlike in the Americas, the children of slaves were born free.[191] In contrast to the West and Russia, abolitionism was rarely discussed, so slaveholding remained legal in the Ottoman Empire until the First World War.[192]

Slaves came to the Ottoman Empire in various ways. Throughout the entire nineteenth century, at least 11,000 to 13,000 slaves—and at times, significantly more—were brought from Africa and the Caucasus each year.[193] The mass of slaves came from the Sudan and sub-Saharan Africa.

They were brought by caravan to the north African port cities, and then transported to the great slave markets by way of Crete and Ioannina. Others came to the Ottoman Empire from Ethiopia by crossing the Red Sea. A large number of the captives did not survive the miserable journey. Even so, the trade in humans was a lucrative business. Despite international condemnation, Europeans received a share of the profits. The Austrians, who possessed no colonies themselves and participated in all the conventions against human trafficking, averted their eyes when Austrian Lloyd steamships ferried slaves from Alexandria to Istanbul. In September 1851 the British foreign ministry informed the embassy in Vienna that "Her Majesty's government have . . . learned with much surprise and regret . . . that it is notorious that slaves are frequently conveyed on the steamers belonging to the Austrian company of Lloyd."[194] Ship captains did their best to cover up the illegal transports, feigning astonishment if they were ever caught during a routine inspection. How could one possibly know that these were not normal passengers?

There were slave markets in the Balkans—in Sarajevo and Thessaloniki, for example, and on Chios and Crete—but the largest market was located in Istanbul, close to the poultry market. A large wooden gate opened onto a filthy, rubbish-filled courtyard that immediately appeared to one European observer as a breeding ground for disease. The space contained a building for holding the slaves, a coffeehouse and a mosque, and seats for dealers and potential customers. At the market, one could bid or make a down payment on white and black slaves, men and women alike, slaves who were newly imported, and those who were previously owned. Charles White, a British citizen living in Istanbul, watched as brokers who were followed by female slaves walked up and down a narrow alley, calling out prices. "Purchasers, seated upon the platforms, then examine, question, and bid, as suits their fancy, until at length the woman is sold or withdrawn."[195] Insubordinate and criminal slaves were kept in chains in dark, stinking cells. Newly arrived Africans could be thoroughly inspected, observed, and tried out in a household for two days before their purchase was final.[196]

Slaves continued to be mustered from the Balkan provinces. Jews and Christians, who enjoyed the sultan's special protection as *dhimmi,* were not allowed to be enslaved, but the protective relationship was rendered invalid in the case of an uprising. In 1821, a fatwa decreed that Greek rebels were to be punished by death, and their wives and children enslaved. Thousands were subsequently abducted and sold.[197] During the April Uprising of

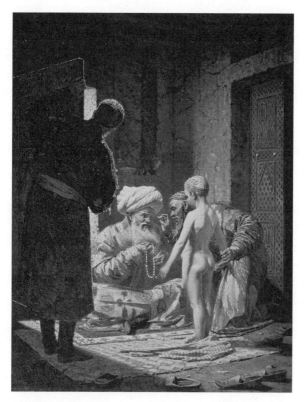

The Sale of the Child Slave, Vasily Vereshchagin, 1871/72.
Tretyakov Gallery, Moscow.

1876 in Bulgaria, the sale of women and children at the Istanbul slave market was an ordinary occurrence. Thousands of Bulgarians were sold off to sites from Beirut to Alexandria for 10,000 to 15,000 groschens apiece.[198]

A Greek orphan from the island of Chios, who was sold as a slave in Istanbul in 1822, experienced an exceptionally fortunate twist of fate. A childless grand vizier adopted the boy and raised him like a son, later sending him to study in Paris. Ibrahim Edhem ultimately served as ambassador in Berlin and Vienna, as foreign minister, and finally as grand vizier himself. The family of another young Greek slave, Alexander Paspates, bought his freedom and sent him on a ship to America. He was taken in by an American family in Boston, and he received a scholarship to study medicine in Paris and Pisa. He became a prominent doctor at the Greek hospital in Istanbul, and he authored works on Byzantine history and archaeology.[199]

As the Atlantic slave trade dwindled, the British placed greater pressure on the Ottoman Empire to give up human trafficking. The slave market in Istanbul was abolished in 1846, the trade in black Africans was forbidden throughout the empire in 1857, and a British-Ottoman convention against human trafficking was signed in 1880.[200] To foreign observers like the British general consul in Tripoli, however, these measures seemed to be "a mere fiction."[201] Long-standing social tradition and a shortage of labor meant that the scope of human trafficking did not noticeably recede until the end of the nineteenth century.

The more British opposition complicated the transport of African slaves across the Mediterranean into the Ottoman Empire, the more urgently dealers sought new sources of slaves. The focus of human trafficking now shifted toward the Caucasus. International condemnation did not extend to the trade and possession of white slaves from the Russian sphere of influence, who were of lesser interest to the British. Although leading Ottoman officials agreed to end the trade in black Africans in 1857, trafficking in white women—mostly Circassians and Georgians—remained common practice. Many members of the upper class were themselves children of white slave mothers.

For the peoples of the Caucasus, the slave trade provided an important source of income. Agriculture was not very productive in the barren steppe regions; sheep and goats were raised instead. A source of income was needed to acquire essential commodities such as salt, iron, and textiles. Entire societies made a living by taking prisoners in warlike raids, and then selling them across the Black Sea—a lucrative business for the very poor. The Circassians were led by a caste of warriors; the Georgians, by a feudal elite. The trade in humans was a privilege of these elites and their followers, who acquired with their earnings not only necessities for survival but also luxury goods, including expensive weapons, saddles, and carpets. In 1823 a Russian study concluded that the slave trade of the Caucasus peoples did not primarily draw on unfree members of their own societies, as the Ottomans believed, but on prisoners of war. The utmost goal of the ceaseless raids and military campaigns was "to take as many prisoners as possible. Later the prisoners are taken to Poti, to Anaklia, to Anapa or other ports of sale."[202]

After the Russians conquered and began to colonize the Caucasus in the 1860s, at least a half million Muslims from the region resettled in the Ottoman Empire.[203] Thousands lost their lives during the crossing because of disease and other misfortunes. Young girls fell into the hands of slave traders, who waited for them "like hunters," a Russian observer wrote. They waited for the ships, "to get excellent merchandise at cheap prices. How many young and beautiful girls did they get at that time!"[204] To double or even triple their value, white female slaves were not usually sent directly to the bazaar, but were first instructed in housework and sewing in the private homes of brokers. Then they were sold into upper-class harems. "They readily thrust out their tongues, extended their wrists, and submitted to other scrutiny," Charles White reported in a firsthand account. "They are aware that many of their countrywomen . . . have been and are married legitimately to influential and wealthy men; and, if similar good fortune be their lot, that they shall be happier than could possibly be the case in their mountain fastnesses."[205]

Circassians and Tatars from Russia resettled in Anatolia and the Balkans, including up to 250,000 along the Danube in Dobruja, in Bulgaria, Macedonia, and Thrace, as well as in Serbia and Kosovo.[206] Because they brought along the institution of slavery, human trafficking became an internal Ottoman problem. The imperial authorities thought the new settlers should serve in the Ottoman military, guard important roads and passes, and form special units to fight against rebels. But the Circassians began to attack Bulgarians, Greeks, and Tatars, seeking to abduct their women and children and sell them to slave traders. This created dangerous disruptions in economic life and public order. Although the sultan decreed that the captured women were no longer "only a commodity" on imperial territory, the trade in humans continued until after the turn of the century.[207]

Thus, a chain of economic and social effects that began with the American Revolution reached into the farthest corners of the Caucasus and the Balkans. After the former North American colonies broke free from Great Britain and founded the United States, they increasingly competed with their mother country on the world markets. As industrial capitalism expanded, slavery began to be perceived as superfluous or as a distortion to competition. Because slaves in the Ottoman Empire were overwhelmingly employed in households, not in the production of global commodities, they were not seen as disruptive to European competition. Only belatedly did Great Britain push to end the slave trade in the Ottoman Empire. In fact, a new niche for human trafficking opened up there as soon as the transatlantic slave trade was contained.

5

Toward the Nation-State

In 1830 THE political order in southeastern Europe was differentiated and fragile. Only Greece was on its way to becoming a sovereign state—albeit one governed by a foreign dynasty. The autonomous principality of Serbia, like the Danubian Principalities, formally remained under the suzerainty of the sultan. Albanians and Bulgarians, by contrast, had not yet taken steps toward national self-government. Only the Montenegrins had an independent, if officially unrecognized, political existence under their prince-bishops. Slovenes and Croats, Serbs, Romanians, and other nationalities lived in various territories of the Habsburg Monarchy without any prospects for self-determination. Although circumstances were very different throughout southeastern Europe, supraregional processes began to smooth out differences between the European lands in an asynchronous way. The modern nation, nationalism, and the nation-state steadily gained influence as models of political order on the Balkan Peninsula, and religion lost its primacy in defining collective identity. Reforms and socioeconomic changes created the foundations of an early bourgeois society and public, along with ways of life and economic organization that were oriented toward industrial production.

Nationalism and National Movements before 1848

The French Revolution and Napoleonic dictatorship set into motion the collapse of the ancien régime, the establishment of a new social order, the spread of nationalism, and the founding of the first bourgeois republics in Europe. Although—or perhaps because—the forces of restoration initially regained the upper hand, the central demands of 1789 did not go away. In July 1830 the Bourbons fell in France, and a new wave of revolutions gripped Europe. In southeastern Europe, too, modern nationalism assumed a new guise, with broader popular support. The cosmopolitan patriotism of well-educated, enlightened elites evolved into political movements for freedom and national unity that were supported by the middle classes. In the Habsburg Monarchy and the rest of Europe, the call rang out for "one nation—one state."

At the beginning of the nineteenth century, however, most thinkers and activists in the southeastern European national movements were not yet able to clearly define who belonged to a national group. In a multicultural space that had been ruled for centuries by foreign powers, different linguistic, religious, and historic traditions overlapped and intertwined. Although there was plenty of discussion about "the nation," no firm understanding emerged about what it meant to be a "Croat," a "Serb," or a "Romanian" in the national sense. Because collective identity might be based on language, religion, or different criteria altogether, concrete national characteristics had to be defined, and in some cases invented. A "Croat," for example, could also identify himself as "Slavonian," "Dalmatian," or "Istrian." As late as 1911, the Croatian scholar Julije Benešić complained that "even in Croatia, the work of uniting the Croats is not yet finished."[1] Around the same time, the Swedish professor Rudolf Kjellén described the Macedonian population as "a flour, from which one can bake every kind of cake, but only after the question of citizenship is settled."[2]

Scholars today still disagree about the concept of the nation, its substance, and how it emerged.[3] Older theories were based on primordial categories and a timeless, linguistically and culturally defined existence of the peoples of the world. More recent scholarship recognizes the identity of ethnic communities, but also emphasizes the social, communicative, and cultural factors that shaped them into modern nations through longer processes of change. Today there is a general consensus that modern nations emerge through various combinations of linguistic, historic, territorial, economic, religious, political, and other ties between their members, and not through essential or binding characteristics. Communication and subjective factors also play a role. To think and act as members of a collective, people first have to develop a sense of belonging together. From this perspective, nations appear as historical entities that evolve over time, or even as political and ideological constructions.[4]

Although nationalism took shape only over the course of the nineteenth century, in the Balkans it built on established traditions of communal awareness. The differentiation of "confessional nations" based on cultural identity had been apparent since the Renaissance, and particularly since the sixteenth and seventeenth centuries. For Slovenes and Croats, Catholicism became a factor that reinforced communal identity while simultaneously excluding outsiders. Orthodoxy fulfilled this role for Greeks, Romanians, and Serbs, as did Islam for Balkan Muslims. The new development of the nineteenth century was that national solidarity no longer derived primarily from faith, but rather from a secularized collective identity. For Dositej Obradović, for example, it was essential that inhabitants of the South Slav lands spoke "one and the same language." He argued that religious diversity made no difference because "faith can change, but origins and language never do."[5] And a Bulgarian primer from 1868 instructed students that outside of faith, nationality was "most sacred for man": "What is your nationality?—I am a Bulgarian.—Why? Because my parents are Bulgarians and I speak Bulgarian.—Cannot man change his faith and nationality?—There are such people who change their religion and nationality but they commit the gravest sin and they are considered traitors by the world."[6]

Nationalism was at first a logical outgrowth of Enlightenment and liberalism, given its attention to human rights and representative forms of government, as formulated in the American and French Revolutions. Foreign rule, coupled with linguistic and cultural discrimination, contradicted the ideal of a society of citizens, in which all men—and only much later, all women—were considered political and legal equals. As dynastic, feudal, and patriarchal relations dissolved and the idea of equal citizenship spread, the notion of an organic people's community that was oriented toward the new values began to take off. No longer just a narrow elite, but the middle classes too, came to embrace "the nation" as the highest source of identity and measure of conduct, as a foundation of society that could not be questioned.[7]

As in Germany and Italy, national movements in southeastern Europe focused on the *Kulturnation,* that is, on common linguistic and cultural ties. A *Staatsnation* that derived its legitimacy from historical tradition and existing state boundaries (as in France), did not yet exist. Bringing members of the nation and the areas where they lived into a still-to-be-defined body politic was a natural next step.[8]

Three broad endeavors were common to all the various nationalisms. A first priority was to develop an independent and well-rounded national culture. Vernacular language had to be standardized, so it could become the norm in education, public administration, and business. Setting linguistic standards was an important tool for the cultural integration of nations that were fragmented into many dialects and regional identities; this was no less important for the Croats than (for example) the Greeks. A second undertaking was the realization of civil rights and political self-determination. At first, this often meant political autonomy, but sooner or later reformist proposals began to include independent and sovereign nation-states—with policy to be set by national, rather than foreign, elites. Third, the chains of feudalism were to be cast aside to create a more egalitarian society, with a modernized economy and educational opportunities for all.

The national movements in southeastern Europe underwent three phases, which we can identify as ideal types.[9] The period from 1770 to around 1830 can be seen as nationalism's "scholarly" phase, which was influenced by the Enlightenment. Clerics and intellectuals brought geography and history to the center of scholarly discussion and emphasized the independent value of languages and cultures. In addition, they worked to define certain national features, such as important historic events, folk songs, and epic poems, as well as a uniform national language. The centers of these movements were sometimes located outside the core areas of settlement—in Vojvodina for the Serbs, Transylvania for the Romanians, and Italy for the Albanians. Accelerated by the French Revolution, universal ideals like liberty, human rights, and equality under the law gained new influence. The topos of national "awakening" also emerged at this time. The Italian Risorgimento found a counterpart in the "rebirth" of the Balkan peoples—for example, in the *preporod* of the Croats, the *rilindja* of the Albanians, and the *văzraždane* of the Bulgarians.[10] Likewise, a new kind of patriotic discourse took hold. Terms like "fatherland" and "love of fatherland" appeared frequently in Romanian writings of this era. National pride was permitted and encouraged.[11]

Only after 1830, the year of a new wave of bourgeois revolutions throughout much of Europe, did this abstract linguistic patriotism develop into a national movement that was supported by broader groups. By embracing new issues and bolder forms of action, nationalism sought to encourage broader social mobilization. Members of the educated middle classes—such as teachers, priests, and the new economic bourgeoisie—now played a formative role. They founded newspapers, reading societies, and voluntary associations, and they constructed academies and schools. Their goal was to win over as many people as possible, from all social classes, to the national cause.

Nationalism received new energy through the spirit of Romanticism, which was characterized by a greater emotionality than the Enlightenment, with its admiration for abstract reason. Doubts about the omnipotence of reason and a distaste for atheism arose from the failure of the European revolutions and the subsequent era of restoration. This led to a rehabilitation of religious faith and historical myths. Abstract explanations of the world gave way to a search for origins. Contemporaries came to believe that the cause of humanity was best served by fighting collectively for the nation, not for the individual alone. Nationalism was altruistic, but the older cosmopolitanism had idealized only the individual. Nationalism elevated the human spirit through solidarity and collective action; it offered a morally superior alternative to individual self-interest.[12]

Only around 1870 did nationalism finally transform into a true mass movement. It also fanned out in different ideological directions. Self-styled nationalists included not only liberal republicans who envisioned a nation of citizens but also advocates of an early bourgeois Romantic patriotism and (later) proponents of an exclusionary, ethnic and racial chauvinism. There will be more to say about these groups in Chapter 6.

The Balkan lands underwent the phases of nationalism at different times. By the end of the eighteenth century, Serbs, Romanians, and Greeks had already begun to call for their own state, but Croats, Slovenes, and Bulgarians voiced these demands only after 1830. Albanians, Macedonians, and Bosnian Muslims did not articulate similar claims until 1870 or later. Nationalism developed earliest among peoples who could build on territorial continuity, past statehood, or a literary tradition in their national language. "Non-historical" peoples, on the other hand, first had to generate the nuclei of institutional nation-building.[13] The Croatian national movement, similar to that of the Czechs, grounded its legitimacy in historical statehood. According to this argument (which is still used today), Croatian nobles of the Middle Ages recognized the sovereignty of the Hungarian king, but they never gave up Croatia's autonomous statehood.[14] In fact, even under Hungarian sovereignty Croatia-Slavonia did continue to exist as a separate political entity, although it had few rights. The Serbs and Bulgarians could hearken back to illustrious medieval empires, although none of their institutions survived the Ottoman conquest. Thus, their claims to national territory had to be entirely constructed from history. Nations that had never had their own state in the past—like the Slovenes, Albanians, Romanians, and Macedonians—had the hardest time. Culture, language, and ethnicity assumed greater importance because their nationalisms could not use historical grandeur or continuity as bases of identification. Discourses about homelands, settlements, ancestry, and migration created feelings of community and legitimated claims to contested territory. Since clear geographic and ethnic boundaries existed neither in the past nor in the present, conflicts among the national movements were foreordained. Disparate points of departure notwithstanding, individuals' identification with the nation became the established norm everywhere by the end of the nineteenth century.

In the *Vormärz* era between the revolutions of 1830/31 and 1848/49, southeastern European peoples (similar to Italians, Poles, and Czechs) in the Habsburg Monarchy began to espouse a cultural nationalism motivated by the ideals of freedom and unity. The immediate point of contention was language policy. Calls to allow the languages of the people in parliaments, government offices, and schools arose so that full participation in society could no longer be tied to ancestry or competence in an official language.[15] The Croatian Count Janko Drašković, for example, argued that Hungarian and German should not be the only languages publicly spoken in Croatia. He emphasized that each nation has "the desire and the right to speak its own language, to write it, and to publish in it, so that every native can understand it."[16] The Diet agreed to accept the regular use of Croatian only in 1847.

At the beginning of the nineteenth century, popular languages everywhere still lacked the terminology to describe contemporary ideas or observations of reality. Dinicu Golescu, who traveled to different European countries in the 1820s, was literally speechless in the face of Western accomplishments "because all too often I encountered things we haven't named in our own language." Thus, he was compelled to write in Greek.[17] All cultures struggled with the same problem. New words had to be coined, alphabets adapted, and orthography simplified, in order to create a uniform medium of communication that could function across regions.

Two kinds of sociolects coexisted in Greece, Bulgaria, and Serbia. On one hand, there was the official language of the churches, the wealthy, and the educated; on the other, simple popular dialects that everyone understood. How could these become a uniform national language? In an emotionally charged dispute, Adamantios Korais decided on a middle way between Attic Greek and the popular *dimotiki*. In Bulgaria, Neofit Rilski likewise opted for a hybrid of Old Church Slavonic and modern Bulgarian. The Serbs, by contrast, discarded the elite Slaveno-Serbian language altogether. Vuk Stefanović Karadžić developed a new linguistic standard based on popular dialect. Karadžić came from a family of peasants and was largely self-taught. He served as secretary to the Serbian government during the Second Serbian Uprising, and he later traveled to Vienna, where he met the Slovene Jernej Kopitar, who worked at the Imperial Library as a censor for Slavic, Greek, Albanian, and Romanian books. Kopitar had written a book on Slovenian grammar, and he encouraged Karadžić to consider his own native tongue more closely. Karadžić subsequently authored a Serbian dictionary and works on Serbian grammar and orthography. Guided by the phonetic principle "Write as you speak!" he sought to provide as many people as possible with access to written culture. Karadžić became the founding father of the common Serbo-Croatian written language, which Croatian and Serbian Slavicists agreed on in Vienna in 1850. Its foundation was the Štokavian dialect that was common to both peoples.[18]

The Albanian language question was particularly contentious because it involved not only two different dialects (Gheg and Tosk) but also multiple alphabets. To this point, Albanian intellectuals had used either Latin, Greek, or Arabic letters. In 1844 Naum Veqilharxhi, an enthusiast of Enlightenment ideals, formulated the first serious proposal for an Albanian alphabet and standard language. He argued that the Albanians had to stop being a "laughingstock" without a proper language. However, the alphabet remained a bone of contention throughout the rest of the century.[19]

The press became the fetish of the national movements and their most important instrument, allowing national literature with a uniform linguistic standard to be spread among the people—even if few could initially read and write. When Serbia gained autonomy in 1830, only about 1,000 of its 670,000 inhabitants were regular consumers of printed material. After the principality obtained permission to operate its own presses, the state introduced the first Serbian newspaper, *Novine Srbske*. Prince Miloš Obrenović, leader of the Second Serbian Uprising, declared that all civil servants, schools, monasteries, inns, and parents of schoolchildren had to treat the newspaper as an instrument of popular education because "by reading the newspaper, the Serbian people will see . . . what is happening in the world."[20] Intellectuals in the Danubian Principalities also lauded the press. Dinicu Golescu called it the "benefactor of mankind," while editor Gheorghe Asachi described it as "the practical method of cultivating the nation."[21] More poems, fables, novels, works of history, and political tracts were published in the Danubian Principalities between 1830 and 1850 than in all previous years. Forty-three journals and newspapers appeared regularly, and hundreds of translations were published in every field, in order to provide the nation with access to world literature and scholarship.[22]

Slovene, Croat, Serb, and Romanian activists in the Habsburg Monarchy founded newspapers, reading societies, economic associations, and theaters to "nationalize" public life. Academies that published schoolbooks, newspapers, and fine literature in the languages of the people also played a key role—including Matica Ilirska (later Matica Hrvatska) in Zagreb, Matica Srpska in Pest, and Slovenska Matica in Ljubljana.[23] Like-minded individuals joined together in a growing number of choirs, reading rooms, and gymnastics and cultural associations. More people of different classes began to assemble in national spaces of communication—an important precondition for forming collective identities, spreading new ideas, solidifying social ties, and creating an emotional national bond.

Thanks to the press and book market, as well as voluntary associations and political parties, a new (early) bourgeois public sphere coalesced in the Balkan lands. Historical writing, theater and literature, satire and caricature, and other forms of artistic expression played a contributing role. Conditions were difficult at first. The middle classes of society were thin, press censorship and political persecution were commonplace, and only a minority of the population could read and write. For this very reason, however, writers, poets, and publishers became opinion leaders in the national discourse. Among the Croats, their ranks included Ljudevit Gaj, Stanko Vraz, Ivan Mažuranić, and Petar Preradović; among the Slovenes, France Prešeren, Matej Cigale, and Anton Janežič; among the Romanians, Ion Heliade, Gheorghe Asachi, and Mihail Kogălniceanu; among the Bulgarians, Petar Beron, Ivan Seliminski, and Ljuben Karavelov; and among the Albanians, Sami and Naim Frashëri as well as Faik Konica.

As publishing and education networks matured and the reading public expanded, information and opinions spread faster, over a wider distance, and among different social groups. Reading materials and schooling in the national languages accelerated social integration—beginning with the middle classes of society, which were still quite heterogeneous.[24] Certain kinds of content, including knowledge about the nation, acquired greater authority. The new forms of social communication were an important precondition for nationalism to spread among the masses.[25]

Scholars of the era insisted that the nations had developed from ancient peoples. They found confirmation in the writings of the philosopher Johann Gottfried Herder, and the "Slavic chapter" of his 1791 *Ideas for the Philosophy of the History of Humanity.* Herder recognized the intrinsic value of all peoples *(Völker),* and he lauded the special cultural accomplishments and humanity of the Slavs. His works were translated into many languages. Herder did not, however, invent the search for national cultural roots, nor was he the first to encourage it in southeastern Europe. Rather, his work underscored the people's own views, experiences, and needs, and they received and adapted it in a variety of ways.[26]

The search for forgotten folk traditions, which had begun during the Enlightenment, gained additional momentum in the nineteenth century. Long-buried examples of folk art, music, poetry, and literature awaited recovery, like sunken treasure. Vuk Stefanović Karadžić earned renown throughout Europe as a linguistic reformer, but he was also noted for his comprehensive collections of fairy tales and proverbs. Serbian epic poetry was translated into English and Russian, and also into German by the enthusiastic Brothers Grimm. Herder attributed special aesthetic and moral power to folk poetry, and he included the Bosnian "Hasanaginica" and other "Morlach songs" in his famed collection of European folk songs. Other literary figures were also active in this field. Elena Ghica (Dora d'Istria), for example, collected Albanian, Greek, Romanian, and South Slav folk songs; Ivan Bogorov and Lyuben Karavelov gathered Bulgarian examples.

For an entire generation of poets from the Karawanken Mountains to the Peloponnese, this folk heritage became a key inspiration for the new national literature. It often took up historical themes, especially the war against the Turks as an interpretation of the contemporary struggle for freedom and independent statehood. Bulgarians, Serbs, Croats, and Slovenes loved Petar Preradović's heroic drama about the fourteenth-century Serbian Prince Marko (Kraljević Marko), an icon of righteousness in the fight against the Turks. Literary works by Georgi S. Rakovski *(The Forest*

Traveler), Petar II Petrović-Njegoš *(The Mountain Wreath)*, Ivan Mažuranić *(The Death of Smail-aga Čengić)*, and Jeronim de Rada *(The Unlucky Skanderbeg)* created a universe of symbols, metaphors, and myths that gave meaning to ideologies of liberation by solidifying communal identity, legitimating national existence, and transmitting collective values.

Historical myths achieved new popularity by speaking to people on an emotional level. Often cloaked in religion, they depicted the shared, historically transcendent fate of the nation. The Kosovo cycle, a poetic rendering of the famous Battle of Kosovo on June 28, 1389, wove an almost biblical tale of heroes, sacrifice, and betrayal. It depicted the fateful battle of the Serbian Prince Lazar against Sultan Murad I, in which the Serbian monarch met his death and his medieval empire collapsed. The Kosovo legend, passed down through the centuries in hagiographic texts and folk epics, became the subject of historicist art genres that inspired almost cultic reverence. In Croatia and Bosnia, too, the Kosovo myth became a code for the national struggle for liberation. In this era, it shifted from being a religious myth to a secular national one, placed in service of the resistance against Ottoman and Habsburg foreign rule. "Kosovo" embodied the identity of not only the Serbs, but all South Slavs and their foreign policy ambitions.[27]

In addition to national myths, sacred sites of memory such as battlefields, graves, memorials, and statues of heroes received new attention. In this way, the Bulgarian national movement discovered the ninth-century Slavic apostles Cyril and Methodius, who invented the precursor to the Cyrillic alphabet and popularized Old Church Slavonic. Days of remembrance, icons, prayers, and hymns to the two saints were "nationalized" and co-opted as symbols of the struggle for liberty. Beginning in the mid-nineteenth century, Plovdiv, Kalofer, Shumen, and other towns introduced holidays honoring the saints and their script—symbolic calls for national mobilization and integration that could now be heard and seen within the public sphere.[28]

In all national movements, history was among the main arguments for national mobilization. Only history provided a comprehensive narrative from the origins of a community to the present day—proof of a historically continuous existence.[29] In this sense, the Romanians presented themselves as "true descendants of the Romans," as the historian Petru Maior wrote in 1834.[30] And nothing angered the Greeks so much as the thesis of the Orientalist Jakob Philipp Fallmerayer, who asserted in 1830 that their people had so thoroughly intermingled with the Slavs and Albanians that they could no longer be seen as direct ethnic descendants of the ancient Hellenes. Selection and interpretation helped to filter positive information from the past, so that it fit within a national narrative. Even so, the nations were not entirely "imagined"; before embracing a grand national narrative, people first had to orient themselves toward what they already knew. There could be a vast difference between the concrete past and how it was translated into history books, folk epics, or family narratives by the culture of memory. Nevertheless, it would be an exaggeration to view the nations as pure ideological constructs.[31]

The territory where a nation's history had actually (or purportedly) unfolded, and the territory where members of the nation currently lived, were nationalist concerns of great consequence to nineteenth-century state-building. After 1830, once the view that all Romanians shared a common Dacian-Roman heritage was broadly accepted, the great ancient empire of Decebalus became the focus of territorial claims. "The nation," wrote Moise Nicoară (who was from the Banat), extended "from the Tisza to the Black Sea, from the Danube to the Dniester."[32] In the same vein, in 1838 Alexandru G. Golescu proposed the establishment of a "Greater Dacia," which would include Transylvania as well as Moldavia and Wallachia.[33]

Around 1830, a Croatian national movement coalesced under the banner of "Illyrianism," which traced the lineage of the South Slavs back to the ancient Illyrians. This idea, along with the concept of the "Illyrian language," had been around since the Renaissance. The new ideology promoted the cooperation of Serbs, Croats, and Slovenes, as realized briefly in Napoleon's Illyrian Provinces. At the time, "Illyrian" could mean either "Croatian," or "South Slav" in the broader sense. The head of the movement was Ljudevit Gaj, who established the Illyrian national newspaper *(Ilirske narodne novine)* in Zagreb. Gaj viewed Croats, Serbs, Slovenes, and Bosnians (and potentially Montenegrins and Bulgarians) as members of the "Slavic," or "Illyrian," nation, independent of religion, and he wanted to forge their cultural unity through a common written language.[34] In 1835 he edited *Danica,* the first literary and cultural review in the Štokavian dialect that most Croats and Serbs shared. In this decade, Illyrianism also inspired a state-building project. In his *Disertatia,* Count Janko Drašković called for the unification of lands inhabited by South Slavs (Croatia, Slavonia, Dalmatia, Slovenia, and Bosnia) into an autonomous "Greater Illyria," and also for democratic and social reforms. It was the first political manifesto written in Croatian, not Latin or German.[35]

Greek nationalism, too, unfurled a grand historical panorama. The prime minister and former revolutionary Ioannis Kolettis had classical antiquity and Orthodox Byzantium before his eyes when he proclaimed the "Megali Idea" in a speech before the National Assembly in 1844. Understanding Greece to be the standard-bearer of universal values, he called on the delegates to view themselves "as representatives of the whole of Greece, not merely the population of the Greek kingdom."[36] This included territory outside their own state's borders, and also—as previously suggested by Rhigas Velestinlis—all Christian inhabitants of the former Byzantine and Ottoman Empires. Concrete foreign policy plans to gain back these lands did not immediately coalesce; instead, Greeks became increasingly aware of their historic mission to civilize the supposedly backward Balkan peoples. Only decades later did an explicitly irredentist, nationally exclusive program develop.[37]

Nationalism in Serbia was articulated in a similar way. The statesman Ilija Garašanin dedicated himself to the revival of Serbian grandeur from the medieval past, convinced that other South Slavs would be drawn to this vision as well. His 1844 foreign policy draft, *Načertanije,* advised Serbia to "strive to encompass all the Serbian peoples that surround her."[38] This included Bosnia and Herzegovina, Montenegro and northern Albania; in addition, a union with Croatia and Bulgaria could be arranged under Serbian leadership. These proposals were significantly influenced by the Polish émigré Adam Czartoryski, whose emissaries advised Garašanin with corresponding suggestions.[39] However, the Serbian situation was more complex than that of partitioned Poland. For this reason, Garašanin emphasized that Serbia needed to recognize the Illyrianists' idea "that Serbs and Croats are one and the same people, and that they speak the same language, only writing with two scripts," and he wanted Serbia to use this idea for nationalist purposes.[40] In the 1860s, he developed a political program for Serbia to become the "Piedmont" of South Slav national unification, which was later viewed as a plan to establish a greater Serbia.

On closer observation, there were numerous parallels between the Croatian-Illyrian and Serbian-South Slav programs. Habsburg authorities already suspected that they were cooperating across political boundaries. Fearful of nationalist "infection," they banned the Croatian *Danica* shortly after the appearance of the Serbian programmatic text *Načertanije*.[41] Even so, the South Slav, or Yugoslav, idea—the cooperation of Serbs and Croats— began to take concrete shape in the last third of the nineteenth century.

Across Europe, nationalism revealed itself to be an emancipatory ideology with tremendous suggestive and mobilizing power. It offered new definitions of statehood, guiding social principles, values, and norms. It also created an emotionally charged communal awareness through national symbols, flags, and emblems, as well as through monuments and museums, holidays and celebrations, music and artworks. Volunteer paramilitary forces came later, interweaving the different nation-state projects and providing a collective experience of the nation through battle. By combining the idea of the nation with a summons for participation, nationalism proved to be much more effective at establishing popular legitimacy than the old ruling dynasties, which sought to uphold class distinctions and abstract notions of empire. It was only a matter of time before the multinational empires broke into pieces.

Peasants, the Bourgeoisie, and Nineteenth-Century Social Change

Southeastern Europe, like the rest of the continent, experienced a noticeable economic upturn and far-reaching social changes in the years after 1830. National state institutions, efficient bureaucracies, and legal reforms set the parameters for this great transformation. Financial revolution, liberalization of world trade, and modernization of transport systems invigorated the economy. Cities grew, middle classes coalesced, protoindustrial trades expanded, and the market economy gradually displaced the traditional economy of subsistence. The spread of nationalism could not have occurred without these fundamental socioeconomic changes, which created the preconditions for closer-knit social communications and a bourgeois public sphere, providing space for mass mobilization and articulation of the national idea.

The establishment of modern state institutions, and the reforms that enabled them, are foremost among the influential structural processes that shaped the "long nineteenth century," the period between the French Revolution and the First World War. The centralization of state administrations, the introduction of equality under the law, national systems of education and jurisprudence, and the liberation of the peasants from feudal dependencies created the preconditions for modernization and social transformation.

After 1830, Europe-oriented elites gave the Principality of Serbia a constitution based on the separation of powers, and they established schools, a legal system, and a bureaucracy based on Western models. "Strange," the historian Leopold Ranke mused in 1844, "which ideas from Europe's constitutional movement seek to penetrate this entity that is still half Oriental: human rights, which have mostly to do with the security of individuals and property; and ministerial responsibility, so the prince is finally subject to the law."[42] Freedom of trade and religion, the elimination of feudal obligations, and the establishment of contemporary property law were also introduced. In practice, however, the constitution had decidedly autocratic features. Civil and parliamentary liberties could be restricted arbitrarily.

The Greek-Bavarian "model kingdom" also laid the foundations of modern statehood. However, King Otto of Greece (from the Wittelsbach family of Bavaria) rejected constitutionalism and parliamentarianism, establishing a neo-absolutist regime. In the Danubian Principalities, Russian protectorate authorities introduced a quasi-constitutional order with the Organic Statute, and also a legislative assembly that was reserved for the boyars.

In Greece, Wallachia, and Moldavia, institution building and professionalization created the nucleus of an administrative and educated bourgeoisie, which was shaped by European norms. Ministers, civil servants, and military officials assumed responsibilities that had previously been held by village elders, district councils, tribal leaders, and priests in patriarchal society. The new state elites secured access to power and resources, evolving into an influential national oligarchy.[43]

Fundamental reforms were introduced in the multinational empires, too—although the nationalities' political participation was not guaranteed. In the era of Tanzimat, or "auspicious reordering," that began in 1839, the sultan reorganized the government bureaucracy according to ministerial principles and modernized the judiciary, military, and financial systems. The legal equality of all male subjects was affirmed, independent of religion. Tax farming and the thicket of special taxes were eliminated, and private property was secured.[44] Private schools and printed materials in the languages of the nationalities were permitted for the first time, and non-Muslims began to participate in local administration. Although many changes existed only on paper, the first institutional steps were taken to support greater rights for the nationalities. After the revolutions of 1848, the Habsburg Monarchy also began to modernize its systems of administration, education, and taxation. The "imposed" March Constitution of 1849 was, however, retracted at the end of 1851. Legal equality and the security of private property were affirmed—but smaller minorities still had no political rights.[45]

The irrevocable transformations experienced by these societies over the course of the nineteenth century were evident even in the lifeworld that was supposedly most resistant to change: the village. For centuries, local communities had managed important political, administrative, tax-collecting, and military responsibilities on their own. Communities functioned on the basis of neighborly solidarity, mutual assistance, and invitations to family celebrations and holidays, irrespective of religion. Values, norms, and customs were passed down from generation to generation, and villagers relied on common law. But the reach of the modern state, and the monetary and market economy, increasingly undermined the rural social order. Modern laws permeated public life, with reforms supporting private property at the expense of traditional rights. Landowners, entrepreneurs, and wholesalers dictated working conditions and prices, while civil servants, teachers, and gendarmes conveyed new values and norms.

The most important precondition for these changes, agricultural reform, was introduced all over Europe, in different guises and at different speeds, eliminating old feudal dependencies and mobilizing private property and labor. Agricultural and legal conditions within southeastern Europe remained extremely diverse. By the early nineteenth century, it had already been an important goal of the Serbian and Greek revolutions to transfer ownership of the land to the people who worked it. A free, but very poor, class of small farmers had emerged after the abolition of Ottoman feudalism. Within the Ottoman Empire, too, the Tanzimat included agricultural reform. The practice of granting land in return for military service came to an end, and Christians were allowed to acquire real estate. A class of small peasant landowners gradually emerged in the regions inhabited by Bulgarians, Macedonians, and Albanians. However, remainders of the large estates, or *çiftliks,* persisted until the twentieth century.[46] Agricultural reforms were introduced in Habsburg Slovenia and Croatia-Slavonia after 1848, and in Romania after 1864. Seigneury was abolished, and large parts of the latifundia were redistributed to free peasants. However, farmers frequently had to accept unfavorable leases or work as wage earners on large estates. In Istria and Dalmatia, feudal dependencies in the form of the Byzantine-era *colonatus* or the corvée lingered on.[47]

The Romanian Roma, a slave class, lived under medieval legal conditions until the mid-nineteenth century. Since their arrival in the fourteenth century, "gypsies"—a synonym for "slaves" in the Danubian Principalities—had been the property of princes, boyars, or the church; they could be sold, given as gifts, pawned, or inherited. By the 1830s, there were about 200,000 Romanian Roma, about one-third of all Roma in Europe.[48] In contrast to serfs, they were bound not to the land but to their owners. Until the mid-nineteenth century, they labored in fields and forests, and also worked as weavers, servants, gold washers, bear tamers, wood carvers, blacksmiths, and masons. Only a minority stayed in one location; many moved from place to place. Most camped in tents in the summer, and in forest dugouts in the winter. The boyars treated them like cattle, whipping them as punishment or forcing them to wear a barbed iron collar if they tried to escape.[49] They were not freed until the 1860s.

Formalized schooling played a decisive role in the establishment of modern states—and the upsurge of nationalism. With the exception of some city dwellers, traders, and clerics, few people could read and write in 1800. Before the nineteenth century, the Ottoman administration had tolerated only religious sites of education; higher knowledge and universities could cause "great danger for the empire" by giving subjects "the idea to question our leadership and encouraging them to rebel."[50] Thus, the expansion of schooling on a larger scale was first possible only within the context of independent statehood.

The Serbs had already begun to build schools during their uprising. "We have enough arms for the defense of Serbia," Karadjordje declared at the opening of a secondary school in Belgrade in 1808, "but we do not have enough skillful men to govern her."[51] Only in 1830 did the Ottomans officially permit the principality to establish a national school system. The Serbian state also provided scholarships for young men to study abroad. In the lands where national structures did not yet exist, popular education was left to private initiative. Since Petar Beron had written his renowned *Fish Primer* in 1824, and Vasil Aprilov founded the first school in Gabrovo in 1835, the Bulgarian national movement worked to establish private elementary and secondary schools where modern subjects were taught in Bulgarian (not Greek). Because of an acute teacher shortage, schools often utilized the method developed by English educators Bell

Students at the secondary school for girls in Sofia, late nineteenth century. Photograph by Dimitar Anastasov Karastoyanov. Regional State Archive, Plovdiv.

and Lancaster, which encouraged students to tutor one another. About two thousand schools were established by 1878, including one hundred schools for girls, in locations such as Svishtov, Koprivshtitsa, Plovdiv, Veles, Sofia, Tărnovo, Tryavna, Kotel, Ruse, and Skopje.[52] The Albanian national movement developed later; only in 1887 did the brothers Sami and Naim Frashëri open the first private Albanian elementary school in Korçë.[53] Other nationalities likewise saw education as the engine of freedom and progress. In Monastir (Bitola), for example, by 1900 there were eleven Greek, thirteen Bulgarian, and three Jewish schools, in addition to individual Aromanian, Serbian, Protestant, and (later) Albanian schools. All were private and mostly financed by emigrants.[54]

The introduction of compulsory schooling was a much longer and more laborious process. Greece began to require school attendance in 1834, Romania in 1864, Croatia in 1868, Bulgaria in 1878, Serbia in 1882, and Albania in 1921. Money, teachers, and instructional materials were in short supply everywhere in southeastern Europe, so the rate of illiteracy was slow to decline. On the eve of the First World War, about 66 percent of the Bulgarian population did not know how to read; in Romania, Serbia, and Bosnia-Herzegovina, it was between 70 percent and 80 percent.[55]

The new states embraced an additional dimension of the "civilizing process" by introducing the Napoleonic Civil Code and humanizing criminal justice. In the Danubian Principalities, archaic punishments such as dismemberment, branding, torture, and the death penalty were abolished in 1829.[56] In the Ottoman Empire, by contrast, it was still common practice to place decapitated heads on public display as a deterrent against rebellion—a custom that one British traveler described as "shocking to humanity." In 1851 the Montenegrin Prince-Bishop Danilo Petrović-Njegoš outlawed decapitation and the practice of blood feuding.[57]

Following the Montenegrin prince-bishops, Ottoman special commissioners introduced a set of policies to stop blood feuds in northern Albania in 1857. In the future, only organs of the state were allowed to prosecute and sentence murderers. The payment of damages, rather than revenge murders, would compensate for lost honor.[58] But ending the outdated practice of self-administered justice proceeded slowly in the Albanian tribal areas. Even after the turn of the century, Lajos Thallóczy, an adviser to the Habsburg court, asserted that "no executive organ of the government (court officials, gendarmerie, or police) could enter its jurisdiction to take any administrative action."[59] In the Toplana tribe, for example, 42 percent of male deaths could be attributed to blood feuds.[60]

State power holders often struggled to respond adequately to the urgent socioeconomic challenges they confronted, beginning with dynamic demographic growth. Between 1800 and 1910, the population of Greece, Romania, Serbia, Montenegro, and Bulgaria about doubled, to nearly thirty million people.[61] Improved security, economic growth, and more favorable living conditions contributed to higher birthrates. "Demographic transition" reinforced population growth after the midpoint of the century. Birthrates remained high as deaths decreased because of better health and nutrition, so the total population grew.[62]

The pace of this growth put new pressure on traditional extended families. The *zadruga*, an economic collective of households under patriarchal leadership, still prevailed in parts of Croatia, Serbia, Montenegro, and Albania.[63] According to long-standing tradition, sons and grandsons and their families continued to live with their parents, while daughters married into other extended families. On average, ten to thirty people lived together in this kind of collective. Extended families were likewise dominant in Romania, Bulgaria, and Greece, albeit with very different social rules and practices of inheritance. For example, in some areas property was divided among all sons after the death of their parents, so landholdings were divided into ever smaller pieces.[64] Population growth, the market economy, and modern property law accelerated the dissolution of traditional family communities. Greater mobility was possible, but poverty increased at the same time. By 1850 the nuclear family predominated almost everywhere. Only a few large *zadrugas* survived into the twentieth century.[65]

Growth in productivity did not keep pace with the population, so agrarian overpopulation became a pressing problem after the middle of the century. A growing number of people shared or divided ever smaller parcels of land—or they had no property at all. Around 1900, in Croatia-Slavonia, Bosnia-Herzegovina, Transylvania, and Romania, about four-fifths of all farmers owned less than twelve acres of land; in Bulgaria, it was two-thirds of farmers. Wherever there were large estates, extreme social inequality prevailed. In Croatia-Slavonia, 1 percent of property owners owned 31.7 percent of the land; in Romania, 48.3 percent of landholdings were in the hands of just 0.6 percent.[66]

Authorities in Croatia-Slavonia, Serbia, and Montenegro attempted to halt the impoverishment of the rural population by forbidding the division of extended families, or by limiting division to properties that met a minimum size requirement. In Serbia, 2.84 acres (later, 8.53 acres) of land—including living quarters, cattle, and furnishings—were exempted from mortgages and could not be forcibly sold if the owner was in debt. But this was generally far too small to support an extended family. The family and mortgage law was supposed to protect peasants from destitution, but it also slowed down the mobilization of land and labor, the spread of the market economy, and the differentiation of social and property structures in rural areas. Thus, in many respects the project of social reform remained incomplete.

Preconditions for an agricultural revolution, as had occurred in the West in the eighteenth century, were not auspicious. Nearly everywhere, peasants owned insufficient land to feed their large families, let alone to produce surpluses or modernize operations. Many people worked the land by hand, with primitive wooden plows or hoes, and were too poor to acquire work animals. Land use and cultivation techniques were unvaried. Farmers either did not know about fertilizer or could not afford it. Only around 1900 did peasants in some regions begin to acquire more iron and steam plows, tractors, and threshing machines.[67]

Bitter poverty prevailed in many regions. Harvests were small, and peasants faced an oppressive burden of rents. In nineteenth-century Ottoman Bulgaria, 20 to 30 percent of farm output was used to pay tithes, rents, and taxes; peasants could barely live on what remained.[68] In Moldavia and Wallachia, 90 percent of peasants had to part with at least a third of their harvests; 60 percent gave up more than half.[69] The effects on motivation were devastating. "The Wallachian is idle," one observer wrote, "because he knows he could not enjoy the fruits of industry, since they would be extorted from him under the name of tithes."[70]

To produce more food, farmers in Romania, Serbia, and Bulgaria switched from raising cattle to growing crops in the second half of the nineteenth century. They enclosed forests and meadows for planting grain, adjusting their diets accordingly. Peasants who had once consumed generous amounts of meat and other animal products now "literally survived on bread alone," as one health expert described.[71] Poverty escalated dramatically during the world economic crisis of the 1870s, which sent agricultural prices crashing downward. Each year, 28 percent of Serbian peasant households faced regular shortages of food by October; another 49 percent joined them by January or February.[72] Croatia-Slavonia and Dalmatia faced regular outbreaks of hunger into the early twentieth century. Poor nutrition worsened overall health, and vitamin deficiencies and tuberculosis spread.[73]

Chronically underemployed, land-poor peasants were forced to find additional income, often through seasonal migration as laborers or craftsmen. Cottage industry became an alternative source of added income for many peasants and shepherds. Protoindustrial production—the manufacture of commercial products from self-produced raw materials—had developed from traditional home-based production in the eighteenth century in poorer, more densely settled areas. In Serbia, for example, protoindustrial trades included spinning, cloth and carpet weaving, pottery, woodwork, masonry, rope making, and food processing. Entire towns and their outlying areas—including Užice, Vranje, Kruševac, Pirot, and Niš—supported themselves this way.[74] Commercial activity in Bosnia, by contrast, primarily developed from mining. In addition to salt production in

Tuzla, smiths crafted items from iron, copper, silver, and mercury in Kreševo and Srebrenica, and from iron ore in Zvornik, Vareš, and Kraljeva Sutjeska. Macedonia, Greece, and Bulgaria all had typical textile-producing regions. In the Bulgarian Rila and Balkan Mountains—for example, in Samokov, Karlovo, Kalofer, Sopot, and Gabrovo—women spun and wove wool, while the men made braid (gajtan) and heavy cloth (aba), often for the Ottoman army. Resident Bulgarians bred some of the sheep that provided the raw material, while other sheep were bred by nomadic shepherds. Other households produced silkworms, winding the silk fibers around spools and spindles.[75]

Spinning and weaving were done in the winter; men left in the summer to pursue a trade. Tailors, stocking- and shoemakers set out from Koprivshtitsa; Tryavna, the "Bulgarian Nuremberg," was renowned for its builders, woodcarvers, and icon painters. The town was also home to dye workers, tanners, and other craftsmen.[76]

People from many other poor regions periodically left their homes to find work as seasonal laborers or craftsmen, including the Bulgarian gurbetçi and the Serbian pečalbari. In some villages, more than two-thirds of the men, and some women, were on the move from the spring to the fall. Bricklayers, confectioners, tailors, gardeners, church painters, and spinners headed to cities, while rural laborers journeyed to distant estates. "We set out on Saint George's day, and along the way the men banded together in groups of 500 to 1,000 souls," reported a Macedonian who was looking for work. "Travel was unsafe because of the robbers and haiduks, so we traveled in groups."[77] Mitre Trajkovski, from the Macedonian village of Capari, journeyed to sites as distant as Turkey, northern Greece, and Bohemia.[78] Those who roamed were usually destitute. When they set out in the spring they were "real mummies, they're so weak," one contemporary complained. Once they were on the road, they were able to "regenerate . . . despite bad food and hard work," so that when they returned home in the fall, they looked "very good."[79]

Emerging nation-states, demographic growth, a thriving economy, and expanding trade promoted the development and social differentiation of cities, despite rural poverty. In the Bulgarian lands alone, the population doubled between 1800 and 1878.[80] Many people who were looking for work moved from the country to centers of government, commerce, skilled trades, and culture. They brought along rural ways of life, so urban and agrarian cultures mixed.[81] Nevertheless, in the last third of the nineteenth century, only the Romanian capital Bucharest, with its 142,000 residents, corresponded to the dimensions of a large European city. Athens had 41,000 residents, Sofia had 30,000, and Belgrade had 15,000.[82] But even in Bucharest, only about one-tenth of the city enjoyed modern infrastructure. "The main streets are paved, lit with gas and electricity, and there are sewers and running water," a contemporary remarked. But streets in the other neighborhoods were narrow, crooked, and dirty. "Lighting is absent or scarce."[83]

The differentiation of skilled crafts and trades accelerated. Around 1850, for example, there were eighty-six different trades in Ruse, and seventy-three in Plovdiv. New savoir faire came to the central Balkans by way of cities such as Brașov, Bucharest, and Istanbul. Skilled craftsmen produced modern "European" consumer goods including clothing and shoes, and "French" tailoring was especially fashionable. Hungarian and Polish immigrants imported the practice of brewing beer, along with the necessary equipment. Printmaking and photography spread from Vienna to the east and the south by way of Serbia. Hundreds of modern clock towers were built in this era—a clearly visible, and audible, symbol of the new age.[84]

Beginning around 1850, handicrafts and cottage industry evolved into a system of manufacturing that employed tens of thousands. Mills, food production, and breweries formed the nucleus of later industries that were factory-based. A new, profit-oriented class of businessmen gradually emerged. These were often former protoindustrial entrepreneurs or wholesalers who, like the members of the Gümüşgerdan family from Plovdiv, had hundreds of workers under contract and concentrated the purchase of raw materials, production, and distribution under their control.[85]

A new economic bourgeoisie evolved from a particularly market-oriented class of traders, craftsmen, and entrepreneurs. They opposed the privileges of traditional upper classes such as the Croatian nobility, the Romanian boyars, and the Bulgarian-Greek notables, the *čorbadžija*. The new bourgeois sensibility was defined by consumer goods, etiquette, and a particular way of life; its proponents saw themselves as spearheads of a progressive and nationalized social order. The new bourgeoisie—including medical and legal professionals, teachers, and clerics—became the most important advocates of nationalism.

As traditional ways of living dissolved, attitudes and values were transformed. Many people enthusiastically embraced the intrinsic value of education and self-cultivation. One Bulgarian teacher reported that people viewed stepping on a book "as great a sin" as stepping on a piece of bread.[86] The wealthy did not necessarily include churches and monasteries in their wills, as they had done around 1800, but now supported educational institutions of all kinds. Girls' schools, universities, and scholarships were particularly beloved causes.[87]

Antediluvian means of transportation still posed a serious obstacle to the mobility of people and goods. Until the last third of the nineteenth century, residents of the Balkans still traveled frequently by foot. Walking from Sarajevo to Dubrovnik took forty-four hours; from Thessaloniki to Athens, eighty-five and a half hours.[88] These conditions were particularly damaging for trade. Horses, mules, and camels hauled their loads along perilous mountain trails into the interior because drivable roads were few. "Even the most bulky articles of commerce, such as wine and oil in sheepskin bottles, metals, and even timber, were all transported in this manner," one traveler wrote.[89] Such a caravan could travel about three miles per hour, or a maximum of twenty miles per day. Journeys were arduous, risky, and expensive.[90]

Shortly after arriving in Greece, King Otto ordered the prompt expansion of the country's network of roads. By 1840, 850 vehicles were traveling daily between Athens and Piraeus.[91] But with their ungreased wheels, they were "creaking, groaning and screeching in a manner quite inconceivable in civilized countries."[92] Even at the beginning of the twentieth century, transportation costs could be ruinous because of poor road conditions. The Greek consul in Ioannina complained that "millions of litres of wine go to waste every year because transportation is so difficult. People prefer to sell the wine locally for two cents per litre . . . or abandon the vineyards than [to] pay for the costs of transportation."[93] Aside from effects on trade, insufficient transportation infrastructure hindered the integration of regions that were thought to belong together. Until the beginning of the First World War, there was not a single railway connection between Croatia, Dalmatia, and Bosnia-Herzegovina.[94]

The Balkan states nevertheless became more closely integrated within a rapidly expanding system of international trade. Whether they lived in one of the great empires or in an already independent state, all people were affected by the dynamics of European industrialization—growing demand for foodstuffs and raw materials, and the search for new markets. Integration within the world economy was well under way by the last third of the nineteenth century, a process that was driven by foreign credit and the revolution in transportation brought on by steamships and railroads.

The worldwide liberalization of trade systems played a decisive role. The Ottoman-British free trade agreement of Balta Liman opened the Ottoman market in 1838. The sultan entered into similar agreements with France, the United States, and other countries as well. Europe profited most from economic liberalism; while the worldwide volume of trade increased by a factor of sixty-four over the course of the nineteenth century, it increased only ten- to sixteenfold in the Ottoman Empire. The industrial nations' revenues and profits far outstripped those of agrarian states. In this phase of global capitalism, the West profited most.[95]

Free trade did benefit regions that had already made the transition to commercial agriculture, and that were connected to long-distance transportation networks. Hence, grain exports doubled in the Danubian Principalities between 1830 and 1877. Agricultural producers benefited, as did seasonal laborers from less developed regions. Even cattle breeders from the hills and mountain regions, who only farmed seasonally, noticed the difference when they sold their wool in the plains. They too reaped the benefits of rising demand beyond their own region, but they were also affected by fluctuations in the economy and new state regulations.[96]

The lands of southeastern Europe remained overwhelmingly agrarian throughout the entire nineteenth century. Despite an upsurge in trade and commerce, 64 percent of the population in Greece earned a living through agriculture in 1910. In Romania and Bulgaria, it was 75 percent of the population, and in Croatia-Slavonia, Serbia, Montenegro, and Bosnia-Herzegovina, well over 80 percent.[97] Nevertheless, substantial changes were under way in many areas of society. The population grew, and rising foreign demand and liberal trade policies stimulated production, sales, and the expansion of the monetary economy. A new national intelligentsia formed, alongside an entrepreneurial bourgeoisie. By the late nineteenth century, concentrated commercial landscapes provided the necessary start conditions for factory-based industry. Village society changed as well, with the spread of private property and the monetary and market economy. Nearly everyone—even the nonmobile, uneducated majority—encountered new norms and innovations in areas such as education and law that upended their work and living conditions, self-awareness, and everyday routines. These social and economic changes prepared the way for new ideas and movements, improving conditions for social communication within the national collective. As the century progressed, nationalism became a rallying point not only for the middle classes but also for peasants—even if their desire for better living conditions, property, fair taxes, and greater legal security initially outweighed the abstract idea of the nation.

Religion in the Age of Nationalism

The role, function, and symbolism of religion changed in the age of nationalism. Characteristics like language and culture increasingly displaced faith as the key determinant of collective identity. Secular conceptions of the world and the absolutizing of the nation diminished faith communities' dominance in identity formation and social order. Religions became "nationalized." On the other hand, transnational mobilization and globalization gave religious institutions new opportunities to extend their networks and organizational structures into other lands and continents. Modern printing technology allowed religious texts and images to be more easily disseminated, and better travel opportunities for pilgrims and missionaries facilitated closer connections between communities of believers in different parts of the world. Not least, the great powers used the confessions as a resource for the imperial exercise of power. "Deterritorialization" transformed the cultural meaning of religion, and often its political substance as well.[98] This process set the stage for global political movements such as pan-Islamism and Zionism. Religion acquired new meaning in the "long nineteenth century," and its value appreciated on a global scale.[99]

Before the age of nationalism, religion—not language, culture, or place of origin—was the primary source of self-awareness. A Slav who lived alongside Muslims in a multicultural milieu was more likely to identify himself as "Christian" than "Bulgarian" or "Croat." Because the *millet* system sorted the population by religion, Greek Orthodox Bulgarians, Vlachs, Serbs, and Albanians were known collectively as "Greeks." Thus, a trader who lived in the Russian city of Nezhin identified himself in his 1835 will as "the Nezhin Greek *(nezhinskiy grek)* Marko Savov Hartsiz, a Bulgarian from Sofia *(bolgarin iz Sofii)*."[100]

In the nineteenth century, religion was still the primary factor that lent meaning and provided social and moral order in the everyday lives of most people. Piety was both a personal ambition and social obligation. Since a life without faith was a grave sin, the community of Bulgarian Christians kept track of "who entered the church and when, . . . if he stopped by the donation box, how big the candle was that he bought, . . . how many times and in what manner he crossed himself," as one contemporary explained. Fasting was of the utmost importance for Orthodox Christians. An elder in the town of Prilep threatened a teacher: "My dear teacher, I like you very much, but if a see you greasing (i.e., eating meat) on a fast day, I will kill you with my gun."[101]

Despite the *millet* organization and social rules of distinction, there were many common ties between the religions. Nineteenth-century religious elites lived in different spiritual and intellectual worlds because they did not know other religions' languages of education—Arabic, Turkish, and Persian for Muslims, and Greek, Latin, and French for Christians. But in the everyday life of average people, boundaries between the faiths often blurred.[102] Holidays and rites frequently hearkened back to ancient cults that had been officially sanctioned by both religious hierarchies. Muslims in Bosnia and Herzegovina, for example, celebrated Christian festivals like Saint George's Day, the Day of Saint Elijah, and the Assumption of Mary. Catholics, Orthodox Christians, and Muslims celebrated Saint Peter's Day together with a worship service and popular festival at the Herzegovinian monastery in Zavala.[103]

During her eighteenth-century travels, Lady Montagu had already noted that some people were "utterly unable to judge which religion is best. . . . They go to the mosque on Fridays, and to the church on Sundays, saying for their excuse, that at the day of judgment they are sure of protection from the true prophet."[104] Differences in religious teachings were likewise overlooked when Christians collected talismans and holy earth from mosques and dervish monasteries, or when Turks borrowed relics of Saint Nicholas to ward off plagues. In Adrianople, a Muslim *hoja,* followed by a Christian priest and then a Turkish sorcerer, attempted to exorcise the city of vampires.[105] And in Athens, the public supplications of Christians and Muslims proved unsuccessful in ending a drought. Rain came only after residents of "the negro quarter" (most likely, the descendants of black slaves) started to pray. "Why, the negroes have more faith than we have!" the Athenians exclaimed.[106]

Coexistence among the religions was usually peaceful. Members of different faiths helped each other at work and celebrated holidays and festivals together. When the merchant Dimitraki Tsenov married in Vratsa in

1812, the wedding guests included forty-one Muslims (mostly military officers), sixty-three Christian Bulgarians, and one gypsy. Eight guilds and twenty-five villages sent gifts. Depending on the wealth of the givers, presents ranged from a ram or a sack of coffee, to a small amount of sugar or dried fruits.[107] In the 1870s, as nationalist tensions escalated dangerously between nation-states in contested regions, one Bulgarian reported that Turks and Bulgarians were still friends. "We Bulgarians lived our own life, to be sure, we had our own dress, our own customs and stuck to our own faith, while they lived another way, had other customs and other costume, their faith was different too. But all this we took as being in the order of things."[108] Marriage remained an important exception. Muslim Albanians would not marry Christian Albanians, nor would Catholic Bulgarians marry Orthodox Bulgarians. Bulgarian-Greek couples were more common, as long both partners were Orthodox Christian.[109]

With the growing influence of nationalism over the course of the nineteenth century, self-awareness and rules of communal living shifted away from the institutional home of the religious community. The nation began to replace faith as the defining factor of identity formation. With the blessing of priests and religious institutions, national awareness and religious identity entered into a close symbiosis.[110] Religious holidays were repurposed as great national political events—including days honoring Saint Vitus (Vidovdan) in Serbia, the Annunciation of the Virgin Mary in Greece, and Cyril and Methodius in Bulgaria.[111] For the Bulgarians in particular, construction of churches and monasteries became an important national political activity after 1830. As one historian asserted, these religious institutions became "national sanctuaries . . . and centres of the national spirit and consciousness."[112]

In the South Slavic region, where people spoke the same language but practiced different faiths, religion maintained its central role as an identifying characteristic of Orthodox Serbs, Catholic Croats, and Bosnian Muslims. It was, however, redefined in national terms. On one hand, Catholicism solidified its role as a factor of integration for the territorially scattered Croatian nation; on the other, it became an argument for excluding members of other faiths from national participation. Slavic Muslims, by contrast, expressed an ethnic group awareness that still centered around faith, although it increasingly emphasized characteristics like language, customs, and culture.

Priests, scholars of religion, and the religious infrastructure of schools, associations, and the press became architects of nationalization and role models of patriotism. They bound communities of believers closer together and gave shape to confessional milieus where political, social, and ethical questions were negotiated. As long as the nations' areas of settlement were politically and territorially fragmented, religion provided an institutional framework for collective identity formation that transcended borders.[113]

The role and significance of *millets* in the Ottoman Empire changed in the age of nationalism. "Millet" was a multivalent term that previously meant religion, linguistic community, nation, or simply, rite. Through the Tanzimat reforms, which sought to create a secular and efficient centralized state, the meaning of the term shifted toward "nation," particularly since the *millets* acted more and more openly as ethnopolitical interest groups. At the end of the Crimean War, the great powers compelled the sultan to declare general freedom of religion in the Imperial Edict *(Hatt-i Hümayun)* of 1856. All subjects were granted equality under the law, regardless of religion, language, or family background. The traditional system—under which Christians and Jews paid higher taxes and were excluded from serving in the military and from testifying against Muslims—was formally abolished. In practice, religious discrimination continued, but now with quotas in government administration and a differentiated school system. Thus, social structures continued to be upheld by separate confessional pillars.[114] At the beginning of the nineteenth century, only three non-Muslim religious communities were recognized as *millets*—Greek Orthodox, Jewish, and Armenian Apostolic. Because of the reform edict, further *millets* were recognized up until the First World War, including those of the Protestants and Aromanians. In 1914 there were seventeen *millets*—in effect, recognized nations—within the empire.[115]

The proliferation of *millets* was one consequence of the splintering of the universal Greek Orthodox Church into independent national churches, as the nationalists fought to integrate religion within their own ideological systems. Since at least the eighteenth century, Serbs, Bulgarians, and Albanians had been frustrated by Greek dominance within the Orthodox hierarchy. The Ecumenical Patriarch in Constantinople had effectively abolished the autocephaly of the Serbian and Bulgarian Churches in 1766 and 1767. The Greek Orthodox Church still saw itself as a universal church, but its liturgy and rituals favored Greek language and culture, and Greeks dominated the patriarchate and the high clergy. Paisi, the monk from Athos who had highlighted the problem in his *Slavo-Bulgarian History*, was regarded as the founding father of Bulgarian nationalism.

An independent Church of Greece was established in 1833, following Greek political independence. "The eastern church is everywhere joined to the state, never being separated from it, never divided from the sovereigns since Byzantine times, and always subordinated to them," one new church member asserted.[116] In Serbia and Romania, too, the fight for an independent national church ran parallel to the establishment of the nation-state. The two principalities had autonomous church structures even before they were fully independent, but the churches achieved autocephaly only after 1878, when Serbia and Romania became sovereign states. The geographer Vladimir Karić observed that people in Serbia spoke of the "Serbian faith," and so "everyone who is Orthodox, regardless of nationality, is identified as 'Serb.'"[117]

Bulgarians' struggle for their own church drove the founding of their nation-state. Beginning in the 1820s, activists drew attention to the abuses of Greek bishops and demanded a Bulgarian liturgy and priesthood, echoing the monk Paisi's calls decades earlier. After a long, bitter struggle against the patriarchate, the sultan established a Bulgarian exarchate in 1870—or, in his words, a "Bulgarian *millet*." Its jurisdiction included all territories in which two-thirds of the population opted for the new church. From this point on, the Greek and Bulgarian Churches competed doggedly for the favor of the ethnically mixed populations of Macedonia and southern Thrace, whom they each sought to represent. The Bulgarian Church not only threatened Greek religious and cultural identity but also undermined the national "Megali Idea," the unification of all Greek lands in a single state.[118] The population was often perplexed by the tug-of-war between the churches, as a Greek activist in Thessaloniki discovered at the beginning of the twentieth century: "Whenever I asked them, what they were—*Romaioi* [i.e., Greeks] or *Voulgaroi* [Bulgarians] . . . crossing themselves, they would answer me naïvely: 'Well, we're Christians—what do you mean, *Romaioi* or *Voulgaroi?*'"[119]

Albanians likewise pursued their own national church before the establishment of an Albanian state. The writer Sami Frashëri explained that "they should have their Albanian priests and should be able to read the Bible in Albanian, because Christ was neither Greek nor Slavonic."[120]

However, the Albanian Orthodox Church was officially recognized as autocephalous only after the First World War.

In the Habsburg Monarchy, too, faith communities received more rights in the nineteenth century. The Austrian December Constitution of 1867 established freedom of conscience and religion, as well as equality under the law and the autonomy of all confessions. The Catholic Church lost its privileged position in the empire, reducing the influence of the conservative clergy. In Croatia, these changes invigorated a nationally oriented, liberal Catholicism, as espoused by the Bishop of Đakovo, Josip Juraj Strossmayer. He rejected the new dogma of papal infallibility, and he affirmed the church's political role by interpreting religious freedom as national freedom. Together with the historian Franjo Rački, he supported the Cyrillo-Methodian idea of uniting the Croatian Catholic and Serbian Orthodox Churches with a Slavic liturgy, in order to encourage national unity among South Slavs. Strossmayer and Rački were ideologues of Yugoslavism; they understood Croats, Serbs, and possibly Slovenes, despite their historical particularities and different religions, as "branches" of a single primordial nation, united by common descent and shared history. The two men drew inspiration from the famous ninth-century Slavic missionaries and their creation of an "authentic" South Slav Christian script and culture. The project of a Yugoslav national church to unify Serbs and Croats did not succeed, however, due to the opposition of conservative Catholic and Orthodox Church interests. Emperor Francis Joseph even urged the pope to ban the Slavic liturgy.[121]

Because of growing competition between religions, alongside their politicization and loss of social significance, religious hierarchies were compelled to sharpen their profile and authority, thereby promoting confessionalization. They initially concentrated their efforts on improving church administration and the education of priests, since people still upheld all kinds of older faith traditions. The doctor Julije Bajamonti reported that the "most unseemly rites" continued to thrive in Dalmatia at the beginning of the nineteenth century. This included the continuous ringing of church bells to ward off bad weather as well as belief in miracles, fairies, vampires, and demons.[122] The lower Orthodox clergy, in particular, possessed only limited theological knowledge, restricted to the church calendar and familiar ceremonies such as baptisms, weddings, and funerals.[123] Folk customs continued to flourish in western Bosnia at the end of the century. "The celebration of a christening does not last only one day, as is pleasing to God and appropriate for the people," one teacher complained. "Instead, it lasts four to five, and sometimes eight, days, as they always compete over who can drink the most . . . and wherever there is excessive drunkenness, all kinds of evil always occur: They curse, fight, and in the end, they dishonor God, the saints, the people, and everything else."[124]

The churches devoted new attention to highlighting specific confessional characteristics that distinguished themselves from others. In Bosnia and Herzegovina, the celebration, or *slava*, of a family's patron saint was declared to be an old Serbian, and exclusively Orthodox, custom—although it was also upheld by Catholics and Muslims. Marko Popović, a priest from Foča, preached: "We celebrate the baptismal *slava*, we Serbs alone and no one else, and that is how we distinguish ourselves from other people. And whoever celebrates the baptismal *slava* is a Serb."[125] Catholic priests and Franciscans, meanwhile, tried to ban the celebration among their followers, declaring it pagan or Orthodox. But anchoring true faith within the people proved to be a laborious undertaking. Even in the 1930s, not one household in the Belgrade suburb of Rakovica possessed a Bible or a New Testament, although everyone believed in God. "Not only could we not find these books, we also could not find anyone who knew anything about them. . . . Everyone knew only that there are church books, from which the pope reads aloud."[126]

Islamic authorities also worked to standardize and more closely monitor religious tenets, rituals, and practices. The Bektashi order was banned in 1826, because the mystical Sufi brotherhoods were suspected of spreading deviant teachings and undermining the unity of faith. Their monasteries *(tekkes)* had to close, and some were destroyed. In Albania, however, where there were Muslims, Orthodox Christians, and Catholics, the syncretic Bektashi cult was particularly well suited to serve as a spiritual foundation for national integration. Protagonists of the national movement, such as the writers Naim and Sami Frashëri, belonged to the order themselves, and they wanted Sufism to become an integrative Albanian national faith. Sufism did not succeed in displacing the established religions, but the Bektashi brotherhoods, with their decentralized organization, assumed an important function by addressing the people directly and distributing nationalist texts.[127]

As the influence of political ideologies and the sciences expanded in the national age, and the religious and secular spheres grew more distinct, new developments in travel and communications allowed the nationalized

Mecca pilgrims on the Dalmatian coast. Woodcut, 1870, after a drawing by
A. Karinger, *Illustrirte Zeitung* 54, no. 1402 (May 14, 1879), 365. Leipzig.

religions to build organizational structures that crossed political borders.
The great Orthodox monasteries sent monks out into the regions to teach,
collect donations, and serve as missionaries. The Rila monastery alone
had about fifty branches in both urban and rural areas in 1850.[128] Bulgarian traveling monks and priests became important agitators for the
national idea. They used their networks to build larger communities with
common faith and political convictions, and they also mobilized financing for the construction of churches and other national projects.[129] In
this way, nationalism harnessed existing religious infrastructure and the
old missionary idea in service of political goals.

Printing enabled the mass production of religious literature, so many
people could now be reached with Bible and Koran editions, pictures of
the saints, and devotional texts. Thousands of pilgrims undertook long
journeys to experience the community of faith in a new way. The hajj of
Muslims and Christians became a mass phenomenon, in part because
piety brought social prestige. Pilgrimages had once been expensive
and dangerous, affordable only by wealthy merchants, nobles, monks,
and religious scholars. However, by the 1820s there were fewer pirates and
robbers, transportation options improved, and middle-class prosperity

increased. More men and women set out for holy sites by caravan, ship, or on foot. Even so, the trip to Jerusalem took "eight to ten months . . . and several thousand groschens," the trader Mihail Madžarov complained.[130] But the expense allowed him to acquire the honorific title of "haji," thereby improving his chances of obtaining a sought-after public office in the provincial administration. Many well-to-do urban elites now claimed the name "haji" or "haja." The Macedonian trader, entrepreneur, and local leader Gjurčin Kokaleski, who journeyed to the Holy Mountain of Athos, subsequently paid for a church and a mosque in his hometown of Lazaropolje, since charitable donations enhanced social prestige.[131] Moreover, pilgrimages were useful for making social contacts, and they provided a chance to immortalize oneself in a journal or travelogue. In some circles, undertaking a pilgrimage became an early bourgeois status symbol.

The principle of legal equality for all religions, which the sultan affirmed in 1856, allowed foreign churches and private Christian societies to become more active within the Ottoman Empire. Christian missionaries in the age of imperialism not only fanned out across Africa, Asia, and the Pacific; a growing number came to the Balkans as well. English and American Protestant churches actively sought to spread their faith, root out heresies, fight plagues and famines, and establish Christian institutions of education.[132] They were not supposed to recruit other Christians as converts—but by leading these churches back to an understanding of Holy Scripture, one missionary explained, blessings from above would surely follow.[133] Hundreds of young men from the Balkan countries received scholarships to attend the American Protestant Robert College in Istanbul.

The standardization of national languages and the revolution in printing allowed missionaries to adopt a new strategy. They translated the New Testament into Romanian, Bulgarian, Serbian, and Modern Greek, distributing large print runs through local agents. Seventy of the first hundred printed texts in Modern Bulgarian were the products of a mission press. National languages that were still under construction became an important gateway for the globalized religious communities. "It is exactly the right time for planting the seed," a Protestant missionary asserted in 1860. In the next few months, these people [the Bulgarians] will have more about religion to reflect upon than they have had in the past five years."[134]

Albanians came to their written language later than others, so Bible societies assumed an important role in the Albanian national movement;

they were among the only groups to disseminate Albanian literature. In 1900 Redjeb Çudi, an old *hoja* from Tetovo, came to the library of the Protestant Bible society in Monastir in order to obtain Albanian texts. After a missionary gave him gospels, psalms, and other Christian literature, the Muslim scholar returned each day to practice reading Albanian. He later taught others to read.[135] Mission work became an engine for literacy and the development of literary languages in southeastern Europe.

The great powers—particularly Catholic France and Austria as well as Orthodox Russia—used the presence of the faith communities to demarcate spheres of influence in southeastern Europe. Since the eighteenth century, Russia had sought to use its right of intervention on behalf of Orthodox Christians to its political advantage. At the Congress of Vienna, the tsar had portrayed himself as the "natural protector of the Christians of the Greek Oriental rite," but the Treaty of Paris, which concluded the Crimean War in 1856, compelled Russia to share its role as protector of the Ottoman Christians. The Crimean War was preceded by a dispute between the Orthodox and Catholic Churches over access to the Church of the Holy Sepulchre in Jerusalem. Russia had insisted on its right to protect Orthodox Christians in Palestine, and in response, France claimed to protect Latin Christians. In truth, the "monks' quarrel" was a colorful distraction from the underlying political, strategic, and economic interests at stake.

After the Crimean War, Austria, in particular, sought to gain political ground in the Balkans as the protector of Catholics. After the occupation of Bosnia-Herzegovina in 1878, the Archbishop of Sarajevo received a papal mandate to unify Balkan Christians, and to spread Catholicism among Orthodox Christians and Muslims. The number of Catholics, church congregations, and priests multiplied, thanks to generous financial support.[136] Austria's "cultural protectorate" in northern Albanian, Macedonia, and Montenegro was further intended to contain Russian influence, as Austria supported the schools and churches of the Catholic Albanians and subsidized clergy. Emperor Francis Joseph ordered the construction of consulates to enforce his protectorate "always, and in all locations, with the appropriate vigor." Italy, which was likewise Catholic, emerged as a rival and claimed the Mediterranean as its own sphere of influence. It appealed to Albanians through tuition-free schools for girls and boys.[137]

The sultan, too, sought to exert political influence over faith. The Tanzimat period ended in 1876. The great reforms, which sought to create modern state institutions and secularize sovereignty, had unsettled and alienated elites and subjects of the empire. Now the caliphate and Islamic piety were to receive renewed attention. The sultan confirmed his allegiance to the *umma,* the community of all believers, sending his representatives to distant lands to recruit new followers of Islam. Through pan-Islamism, he appealed to the adherents of Salafism, who sought the essence of true faith through the new interpretation of old sources. Instead of the secular state, they looked to the early Muslim forefathers, the *salaf,* and a supranational community of believers.[138] Thanks to modern transportation infrastructure, believers and religious scholars traveled back and forth easily between the Balkans, Anatolia, Egypt, Mecca, and Indonesia, and printed Islamic texts circulated worldwide. These factors helped to create a global Islamic public. Associations, journals, and congresses gave the pan-Islamic movement an institutional framework.[139] Within this context, Bosnian Muslims discussed how believers should respond to progress, technology, and the modern, secular nation-state. Some contemplated the separation between religion and modern society, while others were drawn to the possibility of establishing a supranational, pan-Islamic state.[140] But pan-Islamism became politically virulent among the Balkan Muslims only after the First World War and the collapse of the Ottoman Empire.

Among the Jews, on the other hand, national and religious identities began to develop in different directions. Early proponents of Jewish nationalism, in the form of Zionism, came from southeastern Europe. As early as the 1850s, the rabbi Yehuda Alkalai, who was born in Sarajevo, called for a Jewish state in Palestine. After Alkalai, the rabbi Judah Bibas (in Corfu) and Marco Baruch (in Sofia and Plovdiv) became key protagonists and conduits of a "transnational Jewish nationalism."[141] After the First Zionist Congress in 1897, Zionist publications and associations were established throughout southeastern Europe. They disseminated news about plans for colonization, maintained contacts with sister organizations around the world, and also taught Hebrew. Adherents of the Jewish Enlightenment *(Haskalah)* and the Alliance Israélite Universelle, founded in Paris in 1860, became even more influential. They believed in a universal modern civilization that was characterized by education, secularization, and assimilation. Their network of Jewish elementary schools was financed by wealthy families of traders and bankers, including the Allatinis, Modianis, and Fernandezes.[142]

Islam and Judaism were the apparent losers of a nationalism that subsumed the Christian confessions within its conception of identity. Muslims and Jews became inferior minorities wherever nation-states shaped by Christianity emerged. No wonder, then, that southeastern European Muslims and Jews oriented themselves toward their respective transnational communities. Pan-Islamism and Zionism dramatically expanded their reach as globalized, religiously grounded and politicized ideologies and movements in the second half of the nineteenth century. Pan-Islamism and Zionism overcame the particularism of different linguistic and faith communities or political orientations by emphasizing the sociopolitical unity and solidarity of all believers worldwide. Both movements offered comprehensive models of identity and explanations of the world that merged religious message and practice, social order, and political organization. In addition, they both mobilized followers through local networks—including the construction of mosques and synagogues, charitable institutions and hospitals, journals and associations, and above all, constant reminders of one's belonging within the transterritorial "imagined community" of all believers.[143] Only in the twentieth century, however, did these movements assume broader historical significance.

Thus, religions generally did not lose their relevance in the secular and nationalist era of the "long nineteenth century." Instead, the religious and secular spheres redefined their relationship to one another, and faith became both an indicator and an engine of national identification and integration. Nationalist ideologies and religious institutions invoked the unifying force of religion to mobilize support for national unification. After the first wave of confessionalization in the sixteenth and seventeenth centuries, a second wave adopted similar strategies under the transformed conditions of secular modernity. Religious institutions reformed their internal structures, standardized faith doctrines and practices, won over converts, and rooted out syncretic cults. Nationalization could mean either separating faith communities according to ethnic and linguistic criteria (as with the Greeks and Bulgarians) or redefining a religious community as a national one (as with the Slavic Muslims).

Religious identity and community did not simply disappear in the transcendent global arena. Instead, group identity was reinforced by ties to a worldwide Jewish, Islamic, or Christian public. The religions acquired new significance by functioning across borders as a cultural and political system, which did not necessarily refer to questions of faith. This resulted in an important distinction. On one hand, churches' authority was increasingly subordinate to that of the emerging nation-states, but on the other, faith communities joined together to form transnational and deterritorialized religious "super states."

Republican Nationalism and the International Community

The organic connection between nationalism and political liberalism solidified after the Europe-wide revolutions of 1830/31. The spirit of republicanism was fed by resistance against the Holy Alliance, which had renewed its antirevolutionary pact of intervention and defeated the democratic movements with military force and secret police. Self-declared democrats—for example, the Croats Janko Drašković and Ivan Mažuranić, the Romanians Mihail Kogălniceanu and Ion C. Brătianu, the Serbs Svetozar Miletić and Vladimir Jovanović, and the Bulgarians Georgi Rakovski and Lyuben Karavelov—called for a society of free and equal citizens, based on the emancipation of the individual from state and feudal obligations, politically guaranteed through inalienable human rights and constitutional government, and economically grounded in the free market economy. General education would ensure that achievement, not social background, determined one's position within society. Liberalism, which was not yet a fully formed ideology, was seen as a catalyst for the formation and further development of the national community. The ideals of freedom, progress, and mass education seemed attainable only within an independent, unified nation-state. Internal and external freedom were indivisible, according to this way of understanding the world. Liberals likewise believed that nations would become the building blocks of a democratic world order.[144]

Republican nationalism matured in a historical and political context that was very similar in the different European lands; the movements' protagonists knew each other and exchanged information. The Italian and Polish national movements were particularly influential in southeastern Europe. Giuseppe Mazzini, prominent representative of the Risorgimento and early champion of a united Italy, and Adam Czartoryski, leader of the failed Polish uprising, both spent the 1830s in exile, and they set their sights on the Ottoman and Habsburg Empires. After founding Young Italy, the movement for Italian independence and unity, in 1843 Mazzini organized the Young Europe association in Geneva to coordinate with other national movements. Czartoryski, who had settled in Paris, likewise sought allies in the Balkans. He sent an emissary to Serbia, seeking to convince the prince to help liberate the South Slavs in the Habsburg Monarchy with military force.[145] Mazzini and Czartoryski understood that coordinated action was more likely to topple the autocrats of the Holy Alliance than isolated national uprisings. "What we need," wrote Mazzini, "[is] . . . a single union of all the European peoples who are striving toward the same goal. . . . When we will rise up simultaneously in every country where our movement is currently active, we will win."[146]

Revolutionary nationalist organizations emerged throughout Europe at different times, including Young Germany, Young Poland, United Serbian Youth, Young Bulgaria, and—significantly later—Young Croatia and Young Bosnia. All across the continent, there was hope for a "spring of nations." Its engine was the revolutionary wave of 1848. Beginning in France, the movement reached the Italian states, the German Confederation, the Habsburg Monarchy, and the edges of the Ottoman Empire. Events in the multinational empires of the Habsburgs, Ottomans, and Romanovs were directly tied to one another through the South Slav and Romanian national questions. The interplay of socioeconomic crises, loss of faith in the old regimes, bourgeois political expectations, and nationalist hopes of the national movements gave rise to similar republican demands all over Europe. The events, supporters, and goals of the 1848 revolutions were nationally unique, but their causes and effects were transnational and European.[147]

The events of March 1848 in Paris and Vienna spilled over into Italy, Bohemia, and Hungary, creating a domino effect. The future of the entire Habsburg state was suddenly in question.[148] Since 1847, liberal party delegates in the Hungarian Diet had unsuccessfully called on Austria to introduce greater rights of political participation and democratic reforms, and to resolve the agrarian question by freeing the peasants. Under the leadership of Lajos Kossuth in Pressburg (Bratislava) in 1848, the Hungarian Diet passed the April Laws, which essentially established Hungarian independence. Serfdom and censorship were abolished, and Hungarian was declared the only official state language. Lajos Batthyány became the first prime minister of a liberal government.[149]

Given a jolt by Hungarian nationalism, Slovaks, Croats, Serbs, Slovenes, Romanians, and Ruthenians also made political, democratic, and social demands. Throughout the Habsburg Monarchy, the voice of the national liberal bourgeois opposition could no longer be contained. Associations, clubs, and nationalist parties sprang up overnight, and national symbols like flags, cockades, and traditional costumes flooded the public sphere. The number of newspapers, posters, and pamphlets skyrocketed when censorship was temporarily lifted.[150]

The Croats formed a National Assembly in March 1848. Under the leadership of Ban Josip Jelačić, they declared their independence from Hungary. Liberals called for the union of all Croatian lands in an independent *banate,* with Croatian as its official language. Other demands included a representative constitution, the introduction of human and civil rights, and the abolition of feudalism.[151] Federalist reform of the Habsburg Monarchy beyond the crown lands appeared to be on the horizon, as participants of a Slavic Congress in Prague called for a "federation of nations with equal rights" in May 1848. In addition, a Slovenian national movement coalesced under the leadership of Fran Miklošić. His association sought a united Slovenia (Zedinjena Slovenija) within the Habsburg Monarchy, and the recognition of Slovenian as an official state language.

The fact that the national movements of 1848 cooperated across empires was particularly explosive. The liberal Svetozar Miletić became a spokesman for the Habsburg Serbs in Vojvodina, maintaining contact with like-minded compatriots in the Principality of Serbia. In March 1848, the Austrian consul in Belgrade reported with consternation on the founding of a liberal club that called all South Slavs to establish a Yugoslav kingdom, bringing together Habsburg and Ottoman territories.[152]

The Croats hoped that Austria would support the national political demands that they presented to Hungary. Thus, Ban Jelačić marched into Hungary on the order of the Austrian emperor in September 1848. As a "holy ally," Russia likewise sent in troops to prevent the collapse of the Habsburg Monarchy. In April 1849 Hungarian revolutionaries unsuccessfully attempted to dethrone Emperor Francis Joseph as King of Hungary. That summer, they were forced to surrender after heavy losses in battle. Lajos Kossuth fled with thousands of officers and soldiers to the Ottoman Empire, settling in Bulgarian Shumen. Count Lajos Batthyány and other leaders of the revolution were executed; many of their supporters were sentenced to years of forced labor.[153]

The hopes of the Croats for greater autonomy remained unfulfilled. In 1849 Emperor Francis Joseph imposed a new constitution, which he revoked at the end of 1851. He established a neo-absolutist regime and reordered the empire according to centralist principles, without a parliament or constitution. Hungary was divided into different administrative districts.

Croatia-Slavonia, Transylvania, and Vojvodina were separated and placed under the direct supervision of Vienna. The emperor rescinded the autonomy of the crown lands and declared German the official state language. Neither a "united Slovenia" nor a Croatian "triune kingdom" came to pass within the empire. But the peasants were freed, and modern systems of administration, education, and taxation were introduced, alongside equality under the law and the protection of private property.[154]

Although the counterrevolution prevailed, the liberal demands of the nationalities did not disappear. The events of 1848 mobilized the masses, polarized the public, and strengthened the role of intellectuals and the bourgeoisie, who continued to call for a free press and free expression. More groups within society sympathized with democratic values such as individual freedom, responsible government, general education, and emancipation from ruling dynasties and the feudal nobility. Revolutionary activists traveled throughout Europe, corresponded with one another, and translated each other's texts, giving rise to a pan-European sphere of communication and action where political ideas circulated and demands and forms of activism converged.[155]

The spirit of 1848 also brought together Romanians who lived in different regions—in Moldavia, Wallachia, Bukovina, Banat, and Transylvania. Early national liberal movements had coalesced in these regions during the *Vormärz* era. Their supporters came overwhelmingly from the free academic professions, and were in particular journalists, doctors, and lawyers. They were joined by teachers, clerics, and boyars of middling or lesser wealth. Many belonged to the younger generation and had studied in Vienna, Rome, Leipzig, or Paris. An Austrian consular report expressed frustration at France's outsized intellectual influence in the Romanian lands. "Everyone here speaks French. Books and newspapers are read only in this language. . . . No surprise that the Wallachians see the world only through French glasses, and through the grimiest ones, at that!"[156] Protagonists of the national movement made up only about 0.005 percent of the population, but their demands reached many parts of society. A uniform liberal program did not exist, but a basic consensus centered around the rule of law, a representative constitution, and general education. Some activists denounced clericalism and social and legal injustice, but others advocated more modestly for cultural progress.[157]

A typical liberal and Romanian patriot was Mihail Kogălniceanu, son of a Moldavian boyar. He was an engaged politician with diverse intellectual talents. He studied Montesquieu, Voltaire, and Balzac in France, and he attended the lectures of Fichte and Savigny at the University of Berlin. "One year abroad expanded my horizons more than seventeen in Moldavia," he wrote his sisters. But the longer he lived abroad, the more nostalgic he grew for his Moldavian homeland, which was completely unknown to outsiders. "Love your country and serve it," he wrote to one of his correspondents, "no matter how small or how poor!"[158]

Kogălniceanu began his career as a historian. Leopold Ranke taught him about interpreting historical sources and the goal of scholarly objectivity. These principles informed his two-volume *History of Wallachia, Moldavia, and the Transdanubian Vlachs,* a milestone of modern Romanian historiography.[159] Kogălniceanu believed that history held important lessons for the future, but he rejected the obsession with the past that preoccupied many Romanian nationalists. He scorned the fanaticism with ancient Rome that led some of his contemporaries to boast about the deeds of Romulus and Augustus or to declare Romanians the first Christians. Instead, he asserted that respect was earned through the deeds of the present, not the myths of the past: "Only bankrupt nations refer constantly to their ancestors."[160]

Kogălniceanu got to know Alexander von Humboldt in the salons of Berlin, as well as the jurist Eduard Gans, whose enthusiasm for liberty was infectious. Liberalism transformed the boyar's son into a passionate advocate for the bourgeoisie. "Merit is the true distinction. Birth is nothing," he warned the privileged classes.[161] He wrote more than fifty books on religious, political, social, and literary themes, including his well-regarded sociological-anthropological *Sketch of the History, Customs, and Language of the Gypsies,* in which he took a stand against slavery. He was also the editor of prominent journals. Barely thirty years old when he returned to his homeland on the eve of the 1848 revolution, he was well known, admired, and seemed predestined for a political career. Kogălniceanu, who identified himself "as a man of this nineteenth century," was a confirmed republican—but he was a reformer, not a revolutionary. "The work of this world is accomplished slowly; each passing generation leaves behind just one stone for building the structure that passionate spirits dream about."[162] In 1848 he became the most important political voice of the revolution in Moldavia. He spoke passionately about the "spirit of the century," which demanded the elimination of privileges and corruption, the emancipation of peasants and gypsies, a parliament and an independent judiciary, a modern school system, and an activist state policy to promote the economy. In his mind, "fatherland" and "nation" were one, and "patrie" meant the "fatherland of all Romanians," no longer a single principality. According to Mihail Kogălniceanu, it was "that entire area, where Romanian is spoken."[163] "Romania"—meaning a nation forged by language, national literature, and a sense of community—began to replace "Wallachia" and "Moldavia" in this historical era.[164]

For Mihail Kogălniceanu and his compatriots, the revolution of 1848 provided the decisive push for establishing a united Romanian state. Thousands of demonstrators marched through the streets of Moldavia and Wallachia with printing presses, distributing pamphlets against censorship. They protested against Russian influence and Turkish suzerainty, and they demanded that Romanians in Transylvania be granted equal legal status with Hungarians, Saxons, and Szeklers. They additionally sought the unification of all Romanian-occupied territories and the liberation of the peasants. A revolutionary government in Bucharest lasted only briefly, before Russian and Ottoman troops put down the uprising. Many liberal boyars went into exile. Romanian liberals drew the lesson that there could be no internal freedom without a sovereign, unified nation-state. They started a media offensive for their political goal—uniting Moldavia and Wallachia in a free Romania.[165]

The right conditions were provided by the Crimean War, between 1853 and 1856. It began like this: France and Russia fought over the responsibility to protect Christians in Palestine, although the real issue was spheres of influence in the Ottoman Empire. Tsar Nicholas I seized the opportunity to secure Russian control over the straits, as well as long-desired access to the Mediterranean Sea. He abandoned negotiations for an amicable settlement of the supposed religious conflict and sent eighty thousand soldiers to the Danubian Principalities. After multiple failed rounds of negotiation, the Ottoman Empire declared war. The conflict ended in fiasco for the tsar. According to the terms of the Treaty of Paris of 1856, he had to give up all occupied territories, as well as the protectorate over Moldavia and Wallachia. He lost Bessarabia and the mouth of the Danube, and he had to accept the demilitarization of the Black Sea and the internationalization of the Danube. Moreover, he was forced to share his role as protector of Christians in the Ottoman Empire with the other powers.

The signatories of the Treaty of Paris—Russia, France, Great Britain, Sardinia-Piedmont, the Ottoman Empire, Austria, and Prussia—agreed on a territorial status quo that they would collectively guarantee. Moldavia, Wallachia, and Serbia were to remain autonomous principalities under Ottoman suzerainty, although the other powers wanted to oversee the independence of the principalities' administration, judiciary, trade, and legislation, and the free exercise of religion. France was the only supporter of the Romanian national program, which sought to unify Moldavia and Wallachia in a Romanian state, so the principalities initially remained separate, with two different leaders.[166]

But nationalist Romanian elites circumvented the dictated arrangement. In 1859 both the Moldavian and Wallachian assemblies elected the boyar Alexandru Ioan Cuza as their respective head of state. The principalities were effectively unified through personal union, although they remained under Ottoman suzerainty. Cuza proclaimed the Romanian state in 1861, a reality that the great powers ultimately had to accept. With his liberal prime minister Mihail Kogălniceanu, Cuza pursued a comprehensive program of reform. Milestones included the Romanian constitution, universal male suffrage, adoption of the Napoleonic Code, and liberation of the peasants.[167]

Despite the opposition of the boyars, Kogălniceanu and his compatriots had already initiated a campaign to abolish slavery in the 1830s. The struggle took on a new dynamic after 1861, when civil war erupted in the United States. Events across the Atlantic became a catalyst for an array of domestic reforms. Boyars, soldiers, priests, intellectuals, and educated ladies read the translation of *Uncle Tom's Cabin*, and the press reported extensively on President Lincoln's Emancipation Proclamation.[168] Much of the Romanian press took the side of the states in the North in supporting the abolition of slavery. The *Concordia*, a newspaper printed in Pest, could not "believe that there are people in a modern republic who champion slavery." Parallels were immediately drawn between debates in the United States and Romania. The impending secession of the American South recalled the relationship of the Danubian Principalities to the Romanian state, the independence of the American colonies from Great Britain provided a model for the struggle for liberation from the Ottoman Empire, and the war over slavery pointed toward unfinished, antifeudal reforms at home.[169] Mobilization for the cause was so widespread that Romanian volunteers, such as Gheorghe Pomuţ, traveled to America to fight with the Union. Captain Nicolae Dunca, who lost his life in Virginia at only twenty-two years old, became an icon of the American and Romanian struggle for national unity.[170]

The last remnants of slavery were abolished in Romania in 1864. But these and other unsettling changes went too far for conservatives, wealthy boyars, and the church. Kogălniceanu had to resign first, and then a military coup forced Prince Cuza to step down. In 1866, the great powers installed Charles of Hohenzollern-Sigmaringen on the Romanian throne.[171]

In the meantime, national movements in the Habsburg Monarchy attempted to regroup, heartened by Italian and German movements of unification. Giuseppe Mazzini continued to serve as a transnational agitator against the monarchy, founding the Central European Democratic Committee in 1850. "The revolution may have been defeated, but the revolutionary idea has never been stronger, livelier, or more universal," he insisted.[172] Leading minds of the democratic and national movements from Russia, Poland, Hungary, and Italy remained in close contact. Serbian and Bulgarian liberals consulted with colleagues in London, for example, while a Piedmontese agent operated in Belgrade. Influential groups of supporters could even be found on the other side of the Atlantic, particularly among Hungarian émigrés. They publicized their own experiences, and they watched carefully to see if and when democracy might gain the upper hand in Europe.[173]

Solidarity in the fight for liberty and its aftermath united national liberals within and outside Europe. This solidarity even became a supporting pillar of a progressive humanist vision for the future. The cosmopolitan patriotism of the Enlightenment evolved into liberal, republican nationalism. Working together to organize revolution grew into the broader ambition of constructing a democratic world community of independent nation-states. International cooperation under the auspices of nationalism could mean establishing republican federations according to the model of the United States or Switzerland. In this spirit, Mazzini had already proposed a Balkan union of Serbia, Bosnia, and Bulgaria in 1833, and later a "free confederation" of Italians, Slavs, and Hungarians. Mazzini's four Slavic Letters outlined the establishment of a South Slav federal state in 1857. Later, he also proposed a Slavic-Greek federation.[174] Adam Czartoryski promoted reconciliation and cooperation among the small nationalities between the Baltic and Mediterranean Seas so that larger multiethnic regions might later join together as a confederation. Like many eastern and southeastern Europeans, he was strongly inspired by the French political theorist Alexis de Tocqueville's *Democracy in America*. Countless other projects for liberal Danubian or Balkan federations had been proposed by activists such as the Greeks Theodoros Afendulis and Leonidas Voulgaris, the Romanians Ion Ghica and Nicolae Bălcescu, the Bulgarians Vasil Levski and Lyuben Karavelov, and the Serb Svetozar Marković.[175] They also looked to the United States as a model. The former British colonies were the first to have fought successfully for independence, human rights, and a republican constitution. Republican government had endured in the United States, while restoration gained the upper hand in Europe. Couldn't a union of federal states also be a model for southeastern Europe? None of the southeastern European national movements were one-dimensionally oriented toward establishing their own nation-state. Events in the different lands were seen as interrelated steps toward the realization of a peaceful world order. The Serbian liberal Vladimir Jovanović praised the nation as "a stage in the approaching of international brotherhood"; for the Romanian Ion Brătianu, it was a necessary precondition for the further development of humankind.[176] The goal was not communist internationalism, but a community of democratic nation-states.

When the Italian war of unification broke out in 1859, legions of Hungarian, Greek, Serbian, Bulgarian, and Albanian volunteers rushed to the aid of Garibaldi. This wartime experience figured prominently when Bulgarians and Serbs mustered their own units of irregular fighters in the 1860s, seeking to hasten the collapse of Ottoman foreign rule. The ideas and biographies of intellectuals intertwined with those of paramilitary fighters, resulting in a kind of "cosmopolitan nationalism." Their common goals transcended ethnic and political boundaries, creating a community of experience shaped by émigrés and guerrillas, and informed by similar ideas, thought patterns, practices, discourses, and values.

After Austria was defeated in Italy in 1859, and the Kingdom of Italy was established under Piedmontese leadership in 1861, Emperor Francis Joseph suffered yet another serious military defeat, this time against Prussia in 1866. Forced to stabilize his wobbling empire, he arranged a constitutional compromise *(Ausgleich)* with Hungary. In 1867, the Habsburg Empire became the Dual Monarchy of Austria-Hungary. From this point forward, the empire was composed of two halves with equal legal status, each governed largely independently of the other. The head of the state was Francis Joseph, who served simultaneously as Emperor of Austria and King of Hungary. Foreign policy, defense, and finance were the only remaining areas of common policy. This resolution was particularly disappointing for the South Slavs, whose areas of settlement now fell within the borders of different regimes. Slovenia, Istria, and Dalmatia became part of the western, Austrian half of the empire, and Croatia-Slavonia joined the eastern, Hungarian half.[177]

Hungary conceived of itself as a nation-state, rather than a multinational empire, and it exerted increasing pressure to "Magyarize" other nationalities. In 1868 Hungary reached its own compromise *(Nagodba)* with the Croats. The Kingdom of Croatia-Slavonia was granted autonomy within Hungary—including its own administration, judiciary, and authority over cultural affairs, but not an independent government. Instead, a Hungarian governor presided over an absolutist regime. Politicians and protestors faced government repression, and there was no universal right to suffrage or a free press. The union of Dalmatia with Croatia and Slavonia was never realized.[178] The Nationalities Law of 1868 established Hungarian as the official language of government and school instruction. In the second half of the century, Hungary's aggressive assimilationist policies led two million Germans, Slavs, and Jews to change their names, or to declare themselves as Magyars in state censuses.[179]

In light of this situation, Yugoslavism—the idea of establishing a unified South Slav state, as proposed earlier by the Illyrianists—gained strength throughout the 1860s. The movement was led by the Croat bishop of Đakovo, Josip Juraj Strossmayer, and the historian and theologian Franjo Rački, author of the programmatic text, "Jugoslovjenstvo." The basic idea was that Croats and Serbs, despite certain individual historical characteristics, constituted two "tribes" within a single nation. Slovenes were considered part of this nation as well. The movement's core demand was the consolidation and self-government of the Croatian lands within a "Triune Kingdom of Dalmatia, Croatia, and Slavonia," inside—and perhaps later outside—the Habsburg Monarchy. Yugoslavism developed a steadily growing base of supporters among enlightened, progressive elites, the liberal bourgeoisie, the intelligentsia, and the Catholic clergy. Serbian and Croatian politicians began to work together.[180]

In Serbia, by contrast, nationalism developed in a different direction. The principality had built state institutions and a strong national self-awareness, although it had not achieved full sovereignty. Up to two million Serbs lived beyond its borders—particularly in Bosnia-Herzegovina, southern Hungary, the former military frontier, and Dalmatia. Disappointed by Habsburg centralism, many hoped for support from Serbia. Inspired by the successes of Mazzini and Garibaldi, Serbian students, traders, and craftsmen founded the United Serbian Youth in Habsburg-occupied Novi Sad in the 1860s. They did not have a clearly formulated program, but—like their Italian role models—they supported human rights and a republican constitution as well as national unification on the basis of language, territory, and ethnicity.[181]

Within this context, Prince Mihailo Obrenović officially embraced the greater Serbian program that had been formulated by Ilija Garašanin in his 1844 draft. He hoped that Serbia would be able to assume the role of a South Slav Piedmont.[182] His ambitions were supported by Polish émigrés, who hoped for coordinated action against the Habsburgs.[183] In addition, Serbian leaders embraced a plan to establish a Danubian federation with their neighbors Hungary and Romania, and perhaps Greece as well. Between 1866 and 1868, Serbia entered into secret agreements with Montenegro, Greece, and Romania about a Balkan alliance. The principality likewise arranged to cooperate with Bulgarian émigrés, and later with the pro-Yugoslav Croatian People's Party. These negotiations foreshadowed the later political and military alliance that formed on the eve the First Balkan War in 1912.[184]

An uprising against Ottoman rule broke out in Crete in 1866, and the following year Prince Obrenović succeeded in driving the Ottoman military from its last garrisons in Belgrade—an important step in breaking free of the empire's hated suzerainty. Obrenović was murdered in 1868, ending cooperation in the Balkans for the time being. But the idea of rallying behind a greater Serbia still thrived. Baron Benjámin von Kállay, consul in Belgrade at this time, observed in 1873 that the idea was so deeply rooted in public opinion "that the Serbs no longer can understand that the Slavs of the different Turkish frontiers should seek aid and protection from any state except Serbia."[185]

Bulgarian intellectuals and social revolutionaries were meanwhile planning an anti-Ottoman uprising. Its leaders were émigrés in Belgrade, Odessa, and Bucharest. In Belgrade in 1862, Georgi Rakovski assembled a band of volunteer fighters on the model of the Italian *difesa nazionale*, declaring his intent to "heroically smash the Turkish yoke." In 1866/67, he formed the Bulgarian Secret Central Committee in Bucharest, using the city as a base for staging guerrilla attacks on Ottoman territory. The climate for subversive action was more favorable in Romania than in autocratic Serbia, particularly during Kogălniceanu's years as prime minister. Romania was home to fifty-seven publications in the Bulgarian language, eighteen revolutionary committees, and numerous humanitarian organizations and cultural societies.[186] They even received support from the Romanian government, which had its eye on a "Holy Alliance" between Romania and Bulgaria, promising the Bulgarian revolutionaries "everything that is needed, including money, weapons, munitions, clothing, and sustenance, as well as . . . help in winning the support of the European press."[187] Rakovski, a poet and journalist who wrote obsessively, published his appeal for freedom in many languages, but he died before his great dream, a general anti-Ottoman uprising, was realized.[188] After his death, Lyuben Karavelov, Hristo Botev, Vasil Levski, and others continued his work in the Bulgarian Revolutionary Central Committee. With the help of Romania and Serbia, the Bulgarian struggle against the Ottomans became a pan-European endeavor.

Thus, in many respects the revolutionary era in southeastern Europe can be interpreted through a global historical lens. The revolutions of 1776, 1789, 1830, and 1848 established the ideas of nationalism and liberalism—liberty, democracy, and progress—as dominant patterns of thought and action among the bourgeois intellectual elites of southeastern Europe.[189] These elites shared political goals and forms of action with leading revolutionary actors in the transatlantic world, and there were close ideological and biographical connections between the two groups. Their projects were related in substance and depended on one another for their successful execution.[190] The uprisings and revolutions in southeastern Europe were *transnational* because they occurred in a supraregional sphere of experience, communication, and action. Their influence was *international* because they affected the political order and the great power system. The Eastern Question was one of the central themes of nineteenth-century foreign policy, and liberal revolutionaries believed that nation-states would become the building blocks of a future international, democratic order. Finally, the revolutions were *global,* in that demands for independence, sovereignty, and liberty within the modern nation-state eventually spread all over the world. Conversely, southeastern Europe was drawn into emerging global regimes, from the abolition of slavery to economic liberalism. A developing global public sphere also came to play a significant role. The American Civil War provided Romanians with a discursive model for abolishing the remnants of slavery, and for translating their national concerns into a universal language. And Bulgarian revolutionaries turned to the United States as their model for a federation of free Balkan states. The uprisings and revolutions of southeastern Europe were not only national, transnational, and European but also global in nature.

Plovdiv, Sredna Gora, and the Rhodopes, 1876

On April 14, 1876, seventy-three delegates of the Internal Revolutionary Organization assembled in the Bulgarian mountains of Sredna Gora. They had come from all over Bulgaria to discuss the timing and logistics of an uprising. For years, the "apostles of freedom"—following in the footsteps of Mazzini and Garibaldi—had radicalized innkeepers, craftsmen, teachers, traders, priests, and peasants in Bulgarian villages and hamlets. Their underground infrastructure was particularly extensive in the Sredna Gora. "Police regulations, tax collection, jurisdiction, town orders, etc., had fully passed under the direction of the revolutionary committee," Zahari Stoianov recalled. "At that time a man could more easily travel throughout the region . . . with a pass, delivered by a preparatory commission [for the uprising], than if he had been the bearer of a *turalia teskere* [travel pass] issued on behalf of H. M. the Sultan."[191]

After violence had erupted in Bosnia and Herzegovina in the summer of 1875, the moment appeared right for revolution in Bulgaria, too. Ottoman troops were already committed, and the Bulgarians could count on support from Serbia, which had stored weapons along the border. Preparations for the uprising accelerated at the beginning of 1876. The revolutionaries founded new secret committees, stockpiled weapons and gunpowder in the villages, and built cherrywood cannons. Fighters had to swear an oath, wear a uniform, and bring their own weapon—a pistol, or at least a knife. For inspiration, they carried booklets of verses by the national poets Hristo Botev and Stefan Stambolov. The teacher Raina Futekova contributed a revolutionary flag out of red and green velvet; it was embroidered with a lion and the words "freedom or death."[192]

The center of the uprising, the Sredna Gora, was one of four "revolutionary regions." The largest city in the area was Plovdiv, but because of its massive concentration of Ottoman troops—and growing population of spies—conspirators established their headquarters in the small mountain town of Panagyurishte, about forty-five miles to the northwest. Under the leadership of Georgi Benkovski, the delegates elected a provisional government and appointed commanders. Bridges, telegraph stations, and railroad lines were to be destroyed, and villages burned to the ground, if required.[193] But the "execution of innocent Turks, the incineration of their homes, and the plundering of their possessions" were forbidden. Rape, robbery, and murder were punishable by death. The precise date of the uprising was supposed to be a secret, but everyone sensed it would be May 1.[194]

The rebels' plans began to unravel after Ottoman spies caught wind of the conspiracy, and the gendarmerie and infamous *bashi-bazouk* militias moved north to Koprivshtitsa. The first shot was fired on April 20, ten days ahead of schedule. The local revolutionary committee declared an early start to the uprising and formed a provisional government. A messenger on horseback delivered a letter to rebel headquarters in Panagyurishte, announcing that the fighting had begun. It was signed with the blood of a slain Turkish policeman. Messengers with additional "blood-signed letters" galloped off to spread the word throughout the regions.[195]

As revolts spread into the mountains of Sredna Gora and the Rhodopes, and the revolutionaries captured important mountain passes and fortresses, the Ottomans mobilized thousands of soldiers, militiamen, and gendarmes, who were armed with heavy weapons. Torrential rains gave the well-supplied special units an immense advantage; moreover, they could telegraph for additional support as needed. On April 30, troops led by the commander Abdul Kerim stormed Panagyurishte. Town by town fell to the *bashi-bazouks,* who plundered, massacred, and set fire to their surroundings. Thousands of civilians fled or lost their lives. The uprising's gifted organizer, Georgi Benkovski, was felled by a bullet. His head was sent to Sofia as a sign of Ottoman victory.[196]

Two men had largely prepared the way for revolution in Bulgaria: Vasil Levski, the "Lion," a former monk who had begun to build up the Internal Revolutionary Organization's underground infrastructure at the end of the 1860s, and the émigré Lyuben Karavelov, who gave the uprising its ideological inspiration. Together the two men had directed the Bulgarian Revolutionary Central Committee in Bucharest. Levski was ultimately betrayed, captured, and executed, leaving a devastated Karavelov to share the reins of leadership with other conspirators.

Lyuben Karavelov, son of a notable *čorbadžija* from Koprivshtitsa, had attended a Greek school in Plovdiv and then received a Russian scholarship to study in Moscow. There he discovered the ideas of Alexander Herzen and Nikolay Chernyshevsky, and he became a confirmed opponent of tsarism, aristocracy, and the church.[197] He also came to mistrust the hegemonial nationalism that was painted as pan-Slav, but directed by Russia. "If Russia comes to liberate, she will be received with great sympathy," he wrote in 1870, "but if she comes to rule, she will find many enemies."[198]

Like Levski, Karavelov was a proponent of human and civil rights, a democratic order, and popular education. He was particularly dedicated to the cause of women's rights. His credo was a free Bulgarian republic in a peaceful world community of democratic nation-states. He believed this community should be built on the principles of liberal democracy, not communist internationalism, as proposed by Karl Marx.

As a correspondent for the Russian *Voice* and *Moscow Register,* in 1867 the thirty-four-year-old Karavelov made his way to Belgrade, where the journalist Georgi Rakovski had already put together a band of irregulars to fight for a free Bulgaria. A contemporary described the unusual Bulgarian as "an original man, full of temperament, with a visage of a Tamerlane, . . . a thick black beard and curly black hair." The tall intellectual "would work untiringly, and then for several nights in a row he would celebrate with friends." He joined the United Serbian Youth, engaging in secret discussions of constitutionalism and democracy with liberal-minded students. His idealism soon made him the "political messiah" of an entire generation.[199]

"Sound reason," Karavelov argued, led him to the "logical and unbiased solution" of a Balkan federal republic.[200] Instead of seeking to overpower their neighbors, he warned, the South Slav "tribes"—Serbs and Bulgarians— would be better off joining forces. "Bulgaria is suffering under Turkish rule, and Serbia is dying of hunger; what does it matter whether King Marko [the hero of South Slav folk legends] was a Bulgarian or a Serb?" What is more, he wrote elsewhere, "Romania is duty bound to help Bulgaria; Bulgaria, to help Serbia; Serbia, to help Romania." If we want to be free ourselves, Karavelov argued, we must also want "that same freedom for our friends and neighbors."[201]

He wrote numerous articles praising the constitution and liberal political system of the United States, its superior system of education, and the freedom of American women. The motto on the country's Great Seal— "E pluribus unum," or "Out of many, one"—became his driving ambition. He believed that Bulgarians, Serbs, Romanians, and Albanians should form a "liberal union" like the United States or republican Switzerland: "Let us

Bulgarian students in Belgrade, 1870. Bulgarian State Archive, Sofia.

unite like . . . the Americans . . . and live and free and independent in a confederation."[202]

Karavelov's project was malleable enough that he could envision a Slavic union, a Danubian federation with Romania, or even an expanded Balkan league with Greece and Albania. The specifics of the federation were secondary to its members' status as free, independent, and sovereign nations, coexisting peacefully and enjoying equal rights. In principle, the liberal youth in Serbia were sympathetic to such a project. They loved Karavelov like a brother, Todor Marković confirmed. Readers copied and passed along his poems, and "his songs were sung in the streets."[203] Karavelov landed in a Serbian prison after denouncing the country's "harsh tyranny"—its autocracy and censorship of the press. Without individual freedom, he scolded, there could be no national freedom; otherwise, national despotism merely replaced foreign despotism. Once he was released, he made his way to Bucharest, where the liberal government gave the Bulgarian Revolutionary Central Committee safe harbor and financial support.

Karavelov, who had excellent foreign contacts and had even met Mazzini in person, understood that the new mass press was a powerful revolutionary medium. In addition to his many novels and collections of Bulgarian folkways, he also wrote countless articles and essays for Bulgarian, Russian, Serbian, and Romanian journals.[204] Karavelov was a typical representative of the new, patriotic generation of journalists, which also included Petko Slaveykov, Georgi Rakovski, and Hristo Botev.[205] He was the editor of *Freedom (Svoboda), Independence (Nezavisimost),* and the cultural journal *Knowledge (Znanie),* among other publications.

Mobilizing for the rebellion was more difficult in Plovdiv than in Koprivshtitsa, Panagyurishte, or the villages of the Rhodopes. The city was the seat of the Ottoman governor, or *mutasarrif,* for the entire *sancak.* Aside from the deterrent presence of troops, Plovdiv was too prosperous and bourgeois to back a revolt that had little chance of success.

Plovdiv, known as "Filibe" to the Turks and "Philippopolis" in the West, was one of the Balkans' oldest urban settlements. The city was built on three hills, along the shores of the Maritsa River and the important land route between Istanbul and Belgrade. Its setting was picturesque, as depicted by the Slavicist and historian Konstantin Jireček, "light gray cliffs above green fields, white houses at the top, the sun reflecting in their windows, surrounded by a vast plain and tall mountains everywhere on the horizon."[206] The medieval city boasted typical Ottoman infrastructure—mosques, hostels, caravansaries, baths, markets, and a cobbled bazaar street, the *čaršija,* as a central axis. The city lost its Muslim majority and some of its Eastern flavor in the nineteenth century, as villagers from the Sredna Gora, Balkan Mountains, and Rhodopes moved to Plovdiv in great numbers, seeking work.

Many thousands of people lived in Plovdiv in the mid-1870s; Karavelov cited the Ottoman administration's estimate of 91,300 people.[207] Because of mass migration, about two-thirds of the population were non-Muslims, with Bulgarians probably composing a relative majority. Greeks, Roma, Armenians, Pomaks, Aromanians, Albanians, Arabs, and Jews lived here as well.[208] In accordance with old tradition, residents lived in the separate neighborhoods called *mahalles,* although the borders increasingly blurred. Muslims lived in houses plastered with brown mud on the eastern side of the city, while Greeks, Bulgarians, and Armenians resided in the west. People wore Turkish-style clothing that was typical of the region. Different national groups could be distinguished by the type and color of their head coverings. Every neighborhood and every village had their own distinctive styles. Religious life was colorful, too; there were six Greek and five Bulgarian Orthodox churches, a Paulician and an Armenian church, as well as thirty-one mosques and one synagogue.[209]

Plovdiv's numerous towers, domes, and minarets, and the great Maritsa River, provided an impressive silhouette for distant observers. Up close, however, one visitor groused about the city's "twisting, clumsily paved, hilly, badly drained, narrow streets, and its frail, tightly packed houses." Karavelov, too, complained about the mud and the nauseating filth.[210] In line with the reformist spirit of the era, city planners did straighten and pave streets, put down water and sewage lines, build hospitals, barracks, and schools, and install gas lamps here and there. The new neighborhoods seemed significantly brighter, cleaner, and more open. The city also received modern telegraph and railway connections.[211]

As a result of the Tanzimat reforms, Orthodox, Jewish, and Armenian representatives were allowed to participate in communal administration. By law, Muslims held the majority in the city government and the position of mayor. They also dominated other key positions as governors, judges, civil servants, military officers, gendarmes, and tax collectors. "If one observes the Turkish administration dispassionately," Lyuben Karavelov commented, "it is nothing more than a public system of theft."[212] At every level of the hierarchy, Ottoman governors, kadis, and tax collectors extorted traders, peasants, and moneylenders, in order to enrich themselves or maintain their networks of clients. The Greeks likewise sought only to further their own interests, the newspaper *Makedonija* complained. And "if a Bulgarian says something critical, he is immediately suspected of being a Russian secret agent."[213]

At a lower administrative (neighborhood) level, a body called the *obshtina* had only recently begun to oversee church affairs, charitable organizations, schools, and cultural institutions. It was also responsible for certain taxes and donations, for providing loans and scholarships, and for acts of philanthropy such as caring for the poor. In contrast to the earlier *millet* system, which had exclusively handled civil affairs, the new local administrations had some political responsibilities and allowed Christians to participate more fully. Now the *obshtina* presented itself openly and self-confidently as a national and political institution.[214]

The traditional separation between business and residential districts, the *mahalles,* began to dissolve. Public life assumed a greater role—on the central Majdan square, around the clock tower, in coffeehouses, and of course at the bazaar, where men purchased goods, chatted with sellers, met acquaintances, and exchanged news. Here rumors spread like wildfire.[215]

Proximity to the imperial center of Istanbul made Plovdiv an important economic center for multiple regions. Migration from surrounding areas, commercial development, and a growing market in the nineteenth century facilitated economic growth and accelerated social differentiation. The city became a central hub of transportation and trade, which was no longer overwhelmingly in the hands of the Greeks. There were wealthy Bulgarian long-distance traders like Christo Georgiev, who even maintained their own trading houses in Istanbul, as well as a broad group of middle-class traders and store owners, and—at the lower end of the spectrum—numerous small dealers and peddlers. There was lively trade in wheat, corn, rye, barley, oats, animal hides, wool, and silk, as well as tobacco, cattle, and sheep. Processed goods like rose water, leather items, woolen clothing, braid, lumber, wine, and schnapps were also bought and sold.[216]

Crafts and manufacturing flourished alongside trade in Plovdiv. Almost every other family made a living this way. An important economic sector was the production of coarse and fine cloth (*aba* and *šajak*) and braid (*gajtan*), which urban dealers sometimes acquired from producers in outlying areas. Silk, cotton, woolen, and felt fabrics were produced here, too. Textile producers built far-reaching systems of sales and distribution. The Bulgarian Gümüşgerdan family, for example, established the first factory in Plovdiv, with fourteen mechanical looms. The brothers established agencies in Istanbul, Bucharest, Vienna, and London, and they traded with partners in the Ottoman Empire, Austria-Hungary, France, and Spain. The entrepreneurs produced a large quantity of uniforms for the state, which rewarded them with various honorary titles and privileges.[217]

Each ethnic group specialized in particular trades—the Turks as tobacco makers, weapon makers, and barbers; the Bulgarians and Greeks as tailors, coppersmiths, and millers; the Armenians as tailors; the Jews as moneylenders; and the Roma as musicians and blacksmiths. Each guild was overseen by a group of masters, which regulated training and levied taxes. The ethos of the craftsman—including professionalism, thrift, and hard work—became the moral capital of millers, furriers, cabinetmakers, potters, and practitioners of seventy other trades.[218] Crafts and trade were the

306

basis of a growing economic bourgeoisie, which increasingly supported the national cause and financed institutions like churches and schools. The priest's son Moma Vasiljev, for example, attended a secondary school in Plovdiv thanks to a scholarship from the shoemakers' guild.[219] Well-to-do merchants established a "Cyril and Methodius" school, which the scholar and educator Nayden Gerov turned into a prestigious institution of learning and an incubator of Bulgarian nationalism. In addition to Bulgarian, the school taught French, Russian, Turkish, and Greek, and arithmetic, physics, geography, history, geometry, and religion.[220] The national idea was bolstered by a new and ambitious intelligentsia. The number of priests grew after the founding of the exarchate, the independent Bulgarian Church, and an expanded school system increased the number of teachers.[221]

Plovdiv's prosperity was evident in the representative villas that were built during the era of national "revival" on the picturesque slopes of the Nebet, Djambaz, and Taksim hills. The typical house in Plovdiv was half-timbered, with more than one floor, and also decorative balconies, oriel windows, and pavilions. Wood carvings and frescos adorned the internal walls and ceilings, in the style of the "Bulgarian Baroque."[222] Prosperous homeowners purchased armchairs, cabinets, and secretaries, silverware and works of art. Table-and-chair sets replaced the Turkish *sofra,* the low round table designed for eating meals while sitting on the floor. The school director and national activist Nayden Gerov even owned a harmonium, the crowning emblem of bourgeois culture.[223]

The lifestyle of Plovdiv's "well-mannered and respectable" bourgeoisie reminded Konstantin Jireček "of the residents of small Italian and Greek cities."[224] Gentlemen wore their suits *à la franga,* in the French style, and women removed their scarves and shawls and showed their heads. Women no longer lived their lives exclusively in the private sphere, as when they had relied on small gates, or *komšiluk,* to visit neighbors' gardens without setting foot on the street. Now that there were girls' schools, associations for women, and female authors and teachers, unmarried women were allowed to walk with men, and many women owned or inherited property. On the other hand, the newspaper *Progress (Napredak)* still chided that "our ladies and mistresses are squawking only about fashions, *tournures,* makeups, trinkets, they walk around disguised like monkeys."[225]

The new middle classes upheld bourgeois etiquette, amusing themselves at soirées, balls, and banquets, just as in Vienna and Paris.[226] But this life existed entirely within the private sphere. At night, Plovdiv's streets were deserted. There were no theaters or concerts, and "the only observable places of public recreation are the dingy-looking billiard-rooms and cafés, where smoking the narghilé or 'hubble-bubble,' card-playing, dominoes, and drinking raki and coffee, are the chief amusements."[227]

Plovdiv became a center of the Bulgarian "national revival" through its central location and economic prosperity. An indication of the movement's secular character was that its important meetings were held in schools, not churches. Cafés and reading rooms provided additional sites for discussion. Hristo Danov and Yoakim Gruev founded a publishing house in 1857; they acquired manuscripts, negotiated with foreign publishers, and printed translations of Russian and French books. Hristo Gandev's widely known bookstore was likewise located in Plovdiv.[228] By 1878, 199 Bulgarian titles had been printed in Plovdiv—including 109 primers, 24 religious texts, 21 scientific books, and 12 books on art. Hundreds of thousands of printed calendars and notebooks circulated among the people, along with 32 different newspapers and journals.[229] Plovdiv was the first city to celebrate Bulgarian written culture, beginning in 1858, with a holiday honoring the brothers Cyril and Methodius.

The most important leaders of the Bulgarian national movement and the April Uprising were members of the new bourgeois classes. Most, like Lyuben Karavelov, came from growing medium-sized cities such as Karlovo, Kotel, Gabrovo, and Koprivshtitsa. About half were born into families of merchants, and another quarter from families of priests and teachers; sons of peasants and wage earners were in the minority.[230] Many had traveled abroad because there were no Bulgarian universities. About 40 percent studied in Odessa, Kiev, Saint Petersburg, or Moscow; another 30 percent, in France. Others attended universities in Germany, Austria, England, Greece, or Robert College in Istanbul, which was founded by American Protestant missionaries.[231] Biographies and political undertakings were mutually reinforcing; common themes included the experience of discrimination and emigration, disappointed dreams and ambitions, European role models and cosmopolitan connections, and in the end, alienation from average countrymen, for whom many revolutionaries nevertheless risked their lives.

In the 1860s, the traveler Heinrich Barth reported that "the character of the population of Philippopolis seemed . . . splendid and worthy of praise," while the Christians appeared "to get on well with the Moslems and be respected by them."[232] At the beginning of 1876, however, Muslims had become unsettled by the Bulgarians' apparent preparations for a revolt. On March 4, the Russian vice-consul reported that the Turks were gathering continuously in the mosques, bracing themselves for expected attack by the "infidels." "The tensions on both sides are so great that there will be an enormous spilling of blood when hostilities erupt."[233]

The Bulgarians and Greeks also mistrusted one another. The Greeks had traditionally dominated religious and commercial affairs, treating the Bulgarians like "slaves" or "domesticated animals," according to Karavelov.[234] In particular, the conflict between the Greek and Bulgarian Churches had poisoned the air after students had thrown stones and stormed the residence of the Greek Orthodox bishop.[235] A priest at the Church of Sveta Bogorodica conducted the Christmas Mass in Bulgarian for the first time in 1859, and the following year Metropolitan Paisi officially announced the break with the Greek patriarchate. Since 1870, the Bulgarian Church had been formally independent. Other institutions of Christian society likewise broke into ethnic constituencies. The large guild of *aba* tailors, for example, splintered into Greek and Bulgarian factions. The Bulgarians pejoratively called the Greeks "garčolja," and "Bulgarian" was, in any case, an insult for the Greeks.[236]

But the separation of Christians into ethnic constituencies was not yet complete. Konstantin Morenov, who memorialized the Christians of Plovdiv by creating a street-by-street record of every family, frowned upon the "gudili," or "Graecomans"—meaning the "Graecized" Bulgarians who had embraced Greek language and culture to improve their social standing. He also documented ethnically mixed marriages, so there were many families in which one brother saw himself as Bulgarian, and another as Greek. Still other residents, Morenov reported, "don't know what they are."[237]

The middle classes—the economic bourgeoisie and intelligentsia—not only fought against Muslim dominance and the power of the Ottoman state; they also challenged the status of old native elites. The small oligarchy of the Greek-Bulgarian *čorbadžija* collected taxes for the Ottomans, so they were seen as representatives of a fossilized, despotic order. Rewarded with privileges and status symbols, the *čorbadžija* were considered elitist, arrogant, overbearing, corrupt, greedy, and generally despicable. Lyuben Karavelov himself stated that "Bulgaria will only be saved when the Turk, the *chorbadjiya* [*čorbadžija*], and the bishop are hung from the same tree."[238]

Plovdiv was the capital of the *sancak* that bore the same name. Its 985 villages were populated by Bulgarians and other Christians, who constituted a narrow majority, and also by Turks and Pomaks (descendants of Islamized Slavs who spoke Bulgarian). Some Circassians, who had been driven from the Caucasus by the Russians, lived in the Plovdiv *sancak* as well. The Ottomans had resettled the Circassians within the empire, allowing them to serve as irregular auxiliary troops.[239] The Sredna Gora lay to the north; to the south, on the border with Greece, the Rhodopes stretched for more than 130 miles, with peaks rising close to 7,000 feet. Ami Boué had raved about the impressive mountain amphitheater, where "proud forests" spread below "naked spires of rock," offering a spectacular view over brilliant green plains.[240]

As it was nearly everywhere in the Bulgarian lands, small farms were the dominant economic structure outside of the city. The size of the average farm was just over 8.5 acres. Grain, rice, sesame, anise, tobacco, cotton, silk, wine, and rose oil were among the commodities produced.[241] In the Rhodopes, where fertile soil was scarce, peasants felled trees and produced lumber and charcoal. Many Muslim families combined agriculture with migratory sheep herding, whereas Bulgarian peasants were more likely to engage in home-based industry, spinning and weaving for entrepreneurs in Plovdiv. In about 60 percent of all households, men roamed from place to place as seasonal laborers.[242]

The villages governed themselves, with the faith communities each electing two mayors. In addition, each religious group had a council of elders that was overseen by the local religious leader. Christians and Muslims maintained an orderly coexistence, even in the remote mountain village of Batak. Easter and Bajram were celebrated communally, and villagers helped each other during the harvest, while washing laundry, preparing dowries, or building a home.[243] Bulgarians and Pomaks did, however, sometimes come into conflict over the use of communal fields and forest. The situation was tense, since both Bulgarian nationalist agitation and Ottoman propaganda had stoked fears about the other group's potential misdeeds.[244]

When news about the outbreak of the uprising reached Batak in mid-April, the local revolutionary committee called the residents to arms. As in other Bulgarian villages, they celebrated the beginning of their liberation with a parade. Lacking uniforms, the women sewed "pants in a traditional folk style" out of colorful sacks—an "obligatory symbol of entering a new life," as the writer Ivan Vazov reported. The men took their places "dappled like salamanders, with kalpaks—caps made from an entire sheep or goat—atop their heads." These caps were emblazoned with the typical insignia of a lion.[245]

A few days later, the commander Ahmed Aga approached with a *bashi-bazouk* troop of several thousand men, mustered from neighboring Muslim villages. The Batak revolutionaries managed to fire a few shots from a cherrywood cannon, but the next day they were forced to surrender and give up their weapons. The irregulars took gruesome revenge. One after another, men, women, and children were decapitated indiscriminately, massacred with sabers, or burned alive. None of the villagers who barricaded themselves in the Cyril and Methodius School or the Sveta Nedelya Church were spared.[246] "Atrocities like those in Batak cannot be materially conveyed," Ivan Vazov explained later. "They bring shame to humanity . . . in our civilized nineteenth century."[247]

The uprising in the Rhodopes and other regions came to an end with the horrifying mass crimes in Batak and its neighboring villages. Foreign consuls reported that 50 villages were burned to the ground, and 15,000 people were killed in the Plovdiv and Tatar Bazardjik districts alone.[248] In all of Bulgaria, up to 12,000 men and women had taken up arms, and more than 30,000 were killed during the April Uprising. Eighty settlements were devastated, and 200 were thoroughly ransacked.[249]

Rumors of the "Bulgarian atrocities" so alarmed the Western public that *Daily News* correspondent Januarius MacGahan, accompanied by American consul general Eugene Schuyler, made their way to the Rhodopes to investigate at the end of July. After a strenuous climb of 3,500 feet, the small delegation made a grisly discovery: the decapitated remains of women and children. "It was a heap of skulls, intermingled with bones from all parts of the human body, skeletons, nearly entire, rotting, clothing, human hair, and putrid flesh." The village lay farther below, but "there was not a roof left, not a whole wall standing." Corpses lay everywhere, and the stench of decay hung in the air. For three long months, the dead had not been buried.[250]

The Albanian Ismail Qemali, who had been assigned by the sultan to complete an investigative report, was also shocked. Years later, the eventual founder of the Albanian state recalled: "I never saw or imagined anything so horrible, and the thought of this nightmare affects me even to-day."[251]

Public opinion turned against the sultan after the foreign media reported on the "Bulgarian atrocities." The Bulgarians succeeded the Greeks as the new symbol of the European fight for freedom. Giuseppe Garibaldi, Fyodor Dostoyevsky, and Victor Hugo sang their praises. Although the exact unfolding of events and the number of victims are still disputed, Batak and the April Uprising have become central sites of remembrance in Bulgarians' national memory and historiography. The "Bulgarian Missolonghi" came to symbolize the suffering, will to freedom, and courageous sacrifice of the Bulgarian nation, and the "apostles of freedom," especially the "martyr" Vasil Levski, are still honored as heroes today.[252]

6

Imperialism and Crisis

IN THE PERIOD between 1870 and 1945, the world grew together at an unprecedented speed. The invention of electricity, the telegraph, steamships, and railroads, along with the spread of mass media, accelerated the exchange of goods and ideas and increased mobility across continents. Distances shrank, markets grew together, and communication between regions intensified. For the first time, globalization came to involve interdependence and worldwide economic integration. Globalization ushered in the mutually dependent relationship between nation-states and international markets, brought societies closer together culturally, and promoted a more uniform understanding of time and space.[1] The darker side of the "great acceleration" (Christopher Bayly) included imperialist competition over spheres of influence and world markets, colonialism, and war.

Industrialization, cultural liberalization, and nation-state formation increased social complexity and transformed the intellectual climate in southeastern Europe. Mass society gave the lower social classes a political voice and spawned competing grand ideologies—an exclusionary, ethnic nationalism on one hand, and socialist internationalism on the other.[2] As the processes of global networking accelerated, a sharper awareness of regional, cultural, and social differences emerged, and prejudices and uncertainty grew. The result was an explosive mixture of fear and hope, passion and violence, which accompanied the downfall of the old empires, the era of world wars, and global economic crises.[3]

Imperialism, 1870 to 1912 / 1913

Competition over colonies and global economic and political spheres of influence intensified during the "age of imperialism," the three decades before the First World War. The "compulsion of nations and power holders to acquire a growing share of world sovereignty" became "a directive for action," the Austrian historian Heinrich Friedjung explained.[4] National power interests and solo political maneuvers constantly provoked new crises and conflicts, and being "the best in the world" became the decisive factor of political prestige.

Imperialism focused more aggressively on the Ottoman Empire in the second half of the century. A power vacuum loomed as the rule of the sultan grew increasingly precarious in Serbia, Greece, and Bulgaria, and also in Syria, Palestine, and Egypt. Uprisings in Crete (1866), Bosnia and Herzegovina (1875), Bulgaria (1876), and Macedonia (1887 and 1903) provoked a chain of international interventions. Nationalism that crossed state borders became a source of instability. With every uprising, tens of thousands of civilians and insurgents fled to neighboring empires, leading to deplorable humanitarian conditions. The future of "Turkey in Europe"—the Eastern Question—remained unresolved.[5]

Unlike crisis zones in Ireland, Spain, Portugal, or southern Italy, unrest in the Balkans directly affected the relationships of the great powers to one another because the geopolitical, strategic, and economic interests of the Habsburg, Ottoman, and Romanov Empires intersected in southeastern Europe. The question of the straits and control over the eastern Mediterranean affected rights of passage for warships and access to markets and raw materials, which had been a central concern since industrialization. Southeastern Europe became a laboratory for testing alliances and other instruments of security, for defining foreign policy roles, and for dueling over imperialist rivalries. The region increasingly revealed itself to be the "center of particularly grave, course-altering crises" within the European system.[6]

Eastern Crises

The basic constellation of the Eastern Question had taken shape after the Russo-Ottoman War and Peace of Küçük Kaynarca in 1774, when the Ottoman Empire was forced to give up important territories in southeastern

Europe. Subsequent crises included uprisings in Serbia and Greece and, most recently, the Crimean War, which had divided the concert of powers into hostile camps after an extended period of peace. Even so, the signatory states of the Treaty of Paris still agreed that collective approval was necessary for changing borders or creating new states. But in the age of imperialism, increasingly egoistic and aggressive power politics displaced the international system that had once been grounded in the balance of interests and acceptance of rules.

Once Russia had failed to gain control over the Dardanelles and the Bosporus in the Crimean War, additionally losing its right to protect the Balkan Christians, its most important aim was to revise the Treaty of Paris. The economically vital export of grain from the ports of the Black Sea to the Mediterranean, and the protection of Russian transport routes to Asia, depended on control of the straits. The tsarist empire also wanted to block England's warships from traveling between the Mediterranean and Black Seas. Russia believed that the Balkan states should serve as a cordon sanitaire against the other empires—while allowing Russian access through the straits to the Mediterranean (and thus to world markets). Russia's path to the Suez Canal likewise led through the Dardanelles. For the tsar, there were three possible answers to the Eastern Question: preservation of the Ottoman Empire, with Russian influence over its domestic affairs; division of the empire, to include Russia's acquisition of strategically important territories; or (as seemed increasingly likely) establishment of independent Balkan states under Russian direction.[7]

Russia's main rival in the Balkans and the rest of the world was Great Britain, which competed with Russia over spheres of influence from the Baltic Sea to the Pacific Ocean, particularly in Afghanistan and China. Britain's most important military and trade routes to the Levant and overseas colonies led through the Mediterranean and the Ottoman Empire. The British feared nothing more than these land routes being cut off by the other powers.

After the beginnings of steamship travel and the opening of the Suez Canal in 1869, unhindered access to transport routes became an even more sensitive issue. The Britons saw the eastern Mediterranean, including the outposts of Malta and Cyprus, as their natural zone of influence and security. Beyond these considerations, the market of southeastern Europe and the entire Ottoman Empire was favorable for British industrial products and financial investments. Great Britain had increased its exports to the empire eight times over in the three decades before the Crimean War. Conversely, it imported large quantities of Ottoman raw materials and foodstuffs. Into the 1870s, the axiom of British policy in the Near East was to maintain the integrity and independence of the Ottoman Empire, rather than to create small independent states that could potentially fall under Russian control. Carrying out internal reform, opening the empire to Europe, and holding off liberation movements were the preferred means of encouraging stability. Under no circumstances were the straits to be left to the Russians.[8]

France's interests in the Ottoman Empire were also primarily economic, although France was less interested in the Balkans than in Egypt, Tunisia, Arabia, Syria, Lebanon, and Mesopotamia. Its foremost ambition was a great French colonial empire in Africa. Since Napoleon's defeat, France had played only a subordinate role in the Near East. Thus, the Grande Nation preferred maintaining the Ottoman Empire as a buffer, rather than allowing it to fall under the influence of Russia or England.

The Habsburg Monarchy, too, feared the dissolution of the Ottoman Empire. Every uprising there threatened to spill across its own borders; the revolutions of 1848 had already shown how dangerous this could be. These concerns aside, Emperor Francis Joseph—as did the British—wanted to block Russia's growing influence in the region. He sought to expand toward the southeast, in order to compensate for his empire's lack of colonies outside Europe. Taking possession of Bosnia and Herzegovina was central to this plan—on one hand, to better protect Habsburg naval outposts in Dalmatia, and on the other, to hinder the establishment of a greater Slavic state in the Balkans, which could exacerbate centrifugal forces within the Habsburg Empire by acting as a South Slav Piedmont. Economic interests also played a role. The Balkans were an important market, and the Adriatic served as a springboard for international maritime trade.[9]

The German Empire, founded in 1870/71, became a new actor in the Balkan political drama. Chancellor Bismarck saw the Eastern Question as a lever for enhancing Germany's role in international relations. In a speech before Germany's parliament in 1876, he demonstratively announced that he saw no interest in the Balkans worth "the healthy bones of a single Pomeranian grenadier." But he also believed that a masterstroke of German diplomacy would be "to keep the Oriental ulcer open and so to undermine the unity of the other great powers and ensure peace for ourselves."[10] At the 1878 Congress of Berlin, which will be discussed more in pages to come,

The Treaty of Berlin—and subsequent secret bilateral treaties—had secured Austria-Hungary's political and economic influence over Serbia and Romania, and Russia set the tone in Bulgaria. In 1881 Vienna was guaranteed a controlling influence over Serbian foreign policy and trade.[31] There was, however, long-standing resistance in Serbia to Austrian authority. In 1903 a group of army conspirators led by Dragutin Dimitrijević staged a coup and murdered the autocratic King Alexander Obrenović and his wife. His successor, Peter I Karadjordjević, changed the course of Serbia's domestic and foreign policy. He started a customs war to free Serbia from its dependency on Austria-Hungary, and he brought his country closer to France and Russia.[32] A new "era of democracy" commenced, with the introduction of a constitution and the development of parliamentarism and freedom of the press. But Serbia—with Russian encouragement—also began to style itself as an unabashed benefactor of South Slav nationalism in the Habsburg Monarchy. The Orthodox Church, in particular, reinforced pan-Slav ties with Russia. As early as 1888, a "Catechism for the Serbian People" had declared "the great and powerful Russia" to be the "only steadfast and reliable friend of the Serbs." The strongest opponent, by contrast, was Austria. "What should we do? Hate Austria, as our greatest enemy."[33]

The instability in Macedonia and change of dynasty in Serbia were all the more volatile because they directly affected nationality problems in both halves of the Habsburg Monarchy. The Austro-Hungarian compromise of 1867 had swept aside all proposals for federalist imperial reform, including suggestions by Karl Renner and Aurel Constantin Popovici. Dualism cemented the supremacy of German Austrians in the western half of the empire, and Hungarians in the east.[34]

While the Austrian half of the empire developed more in the direction of a federal multinational state, asymmetry between its ruling and subject peoples persisted. As enshrined in the December Constitution, the nationalities *(Volksstämme)* enjoyed equal rights, and the "customary" languages in each land were to be recognized by the government, in schools, and in public life. In practice, however, Poles, Czechs, Italians, Slovenes, and Croats faced discrimination in the imperial and state diets and were excluded from actual power.[35]

The situation was worse in Hungary, which saw itself as a single, indivisible political nation, with the Magyars by definition exercising dominion over all others. Befitting the adage that "the nation lives in its language," the Hungarian government declared Hungarian the official language of government and education in the Nationalities Law of 1868. Transylvanian self-government was abolished as well. The unification of the crown lands Croatia, Slavonia, and Dalmatia as an autonomous "triune kingdom," promised that same year, existed only on paper. The Croatian-Hungarian compromise allowed the Croatian Diet *(Sabor)* certain authority over its internal affairs, culture, education, and justice, but the most important competencies remained in Budapest. Of all tax revenue, 55 percent went back to Budapest as well. Because of a strict census, only 2 percent of the population had the right to vote, and the Croatian viceroy, or *ban,* had to be approved by the Hungarian government.[36]

The nationalities lobbied relentlessly for an organization of the provinces based on ethnic and federal principles, for recognition of their local languages as official languages, and for proportional representation in the executive and legislative branches. In 1895 representatives of the Serbs, Slovaks, and Romanians assembled one last time at a nationalities congress in Budapest, seeking greater rights within Hungary. The government ignored their proposals. Representatives of the small nations felt increasingly marginalized and disrespected. Romanians and Serbs decided that they had no choice but to turn to their "mother countries."[37] The Croats had not participated in the first place; they were already determined to exit the monarchy.[38]

While there were rumblings among all the nationalities, the "South Slav question" became the linchpin, involving both halves of the empire as well as the sovereign states of Serbia and Montenegro.[39] In Hungarian Croatia-Slavonia and Austrian Istria and Dalmatia, resistance against the "unbearable parliamentary and political conditions" (as one declaration stated) continued to grow. Mass protests erupted in Croatia-Slavonia in 1903, compelling the resignation of Ban Khuen-Héderváry, who had been in office for twenty years. Dalmatia and Istria were also rocked by demonstrations.[40] In 1905, Frano Supilo and Ante Trumbić, leaders of the Croatian Party of Rights in Dalmatia, proposed a "New Course"—a broad coalition of Serb and Croat parties. Some Slovene politicians joined the South Slav program as well. In 1906 and 1908, members of the coalition achieved a majority in regional elections by supporting a South Slav state within—and later, outside—the monarchy.[41] Worried authorities used trumped-up evidence to try leading politicians of the coalition for high treason in two great trials, sparking great public outrage.[42] The writer Hermann Bahr, who traveled to Dalmatia in the spring of 1909, was incensed that the Austrian administration acted as if it were in "enemy territory," following the principle: "Misery is easiest to govern; a person can get insolent when he is no longer hungry."[43]

Tensions escalated in Bosnia-Herzegovina when the longtime governor Benjamin Kállay died in 1903. He had unsuccessfully attempted to foster the concept of *bošnjaštvo,* a shared regional identity that was supposed to transcend religious orientation and serve as an antidote to Serb, Croat, and Muslim nationalism.[44] Serbs and Muslims had been unsuccessful in their demands for religious self-administration and more schools, as well as for territorial autonomy. Kállay had, moreover, promoted a "Bosnian" language, banned any local political organizations, and recruited Catholic colonists from Austria. By 1908, about 150,000 Muslims felt they had no choice but to emigrate. For the time being, Emperor Francis Joseph would not tolerate a constitution, parliament, or voting rights in Bosnia-Herzegovina, while Serbia presented itself as a model democracy with its press freedoms and parliamentarism.[45]

Austria-Hungary presented its occupation of the Balkan provinces as a mission to bring stability and civilization to a troubled region. The administrative expert Ferdinand Schmid emphasized that South Slavs had to be held to a strict disciplinary regime and prodded into the diligent execution of their duties. "Left to itself, the South Slav race [*Stamm*] tends towards a certain indolence and excessive politicizing."[46] Colonial attitudes were evident in many areas. Railroad and mine construction served the foremost goal of delivering raw materials to the Habsburgs' core territory. Other urgently needed investments, by contrast, were rarely made because Austria and Hungary fought over the spoils.[47] Even so, the ossified feudal order remained largely in place. As late as 1910, 91.1 percent of landowners were Muslim, but only 6 percent Orthodox and 2.5 percent Catholic. The unfree *kmets,* by contrast, were about 95 percent Christian.[48] Even a former Austrian minister of trade criticized the distressing "backwardness of agriculture and education."[49] Among the population, 87 percent were illiterate, and for two million residents there were only five secondary schools and no universities because the Austrians feared that higher education was an incubator of nationalism. Finally, the tax burden exploded because the occupied land had to bear the costs of its own occupation. Thus, social tensions mounted alongside national ones.[50]

When the Young Turk Revolution broke out in 1908, Emperor Francis Joseph seized the opportunity to annex Bosnia-Herzegovina. Ferdinand of Bulgaria also recognized an opportune moment. Encouraged by Austria-Hungary, he renounced Ottoman suzerainty and named himself tsar. And a Cretan national assembly promptly proclaimed union with Greece.

The annexation of Bosnia-Herzegovina unleashed violent protests and a grave international crisis. The Treaty of Berlin was essentially nullified, and neither Serbs nor Muslims wanted to become subjects of the Catholic Habsburg Monarchy. Serbia and Austria-Hungary mobilized their armies. Prominent intellectuals and other Serbian citizens founded the paramilitary organization Narodna Odbrana (National Defense), so they could send volunteers across the border. The Habsburg administration took months to bring the situation militarily under control. Germany placed diplomatic pressure on Russia, and Austria-Hungary sent an ultimatum to Serbia.[51] War with Russia and Serbia was averted once again, but the price was a dramatic worsening of international relations.

Austria-Hungary managed to turn the annexation crisis in its own favor, thereby humiliating Russia. Emperor Francis Joseph had broken the Treaty of Berlin and unilaterally created a strategic advantage for himself. Since this also unsettled Great Britain and France, the three great powers moved closer together, cementing their opposition to the Austro-German Dual Alliance of 1879.[52] At the same time, the mood within the Dual Monarchy worsened. Poles, Czechs, Slovaks, Italians, and other nationalities reacted with outrage. Croatian politicians protested against their denied parliamentary rights.[53]

Instead of thwarting South Slav plans for unification, the annexation of Bosnia and Herzegovina further inflamed nationalist sentiments. More than two million Slovenes, Serbs, and Croats already lived in the Austrian half of the empire (7.8 percent of the population), plus another three million in Hungary (15 percent). Now, they were joined by just under two million more Orthodox, Muslim, and Catholic South Slavs.[54] Since Kállay's effort to dispel nationalist sentiments had evidently failed, his successor István Burian recognized political parties in 1906. In 1910 Bosnia-Herzegovina received its own Diet, although its membership was determined by census suffrage, in which only richer people had the right to vote, and it served only an advisory, not a legislative, function. The Diet was also subject to the veto power of Austro-Hungarian institutions.[55]

Wasn't it high time to federalize the empire and create a Slavic entity with equal rights, as a third pillar next to Austria and Hungary? This was the demand of the progressive, revolutionary youth movements Young Croatia and Young Bosnia that joined forces in 1913. Associations with "Yugoslav"—which is to say, South Slav—goals arose in Vienna, Prague, Zagreb, Split, Sarajevo, Belgrade, and numerous other locations.[56]

Emperor Francis Joseph and his heir, Francis Ferdinand, considered different imperial reforms but always returned to the conclusion that more rights for the nationalities would also bring greater instability. Francis Ferdinand eventually excised the project of "trialism" from the official documents of succession because, as written in the internal instructions, "the Slav state unit would be often on the side of Hungary, where surely the interests of the Crown were never to be sought."[57] He also wanted to trim back Hungary's rights. He was a confirmed antiliberal and opponent of universal suffrage, a militant Catholic and open anti-Semite. For all these reasons, he was hated ardently by more than a few Hungarians, Poles, Czechs, Slovaks, and South Slavs.[58]

In 1912 there were demonstrations and street battles with the police and army in many Croatian cities; even schoolchildren went on strike.[59] The Habsburg governor, Slavko Cuvaj, had already dissolved the Diet; now he suspended the constitution and governed by emergency decree. In Sarajevo, too, there were mass demonstrations.[60] A shrinking number of people believed that reform was possible within the Habsburg Monarchy. In March an Austrian informant reported: "The South Slav idea, or the idea of Serbo-Croatian brotherhood . . . has now attained utmost supremacy and . . . [become] the parole for all social classes, not only with respect to politics, but also culture and the economy. This is not only true for Croatia and Slavonia, but also for Bosnia and Herzegovina, and most especially for Dalmatia, where a revolutionary, antimonarchical spirit has directly taken hold."[61]

Nationalism and Internationalism in an Ideological Age

In the history of nationalism, too, a new phase began around 1870. Modern mass nationalism developed out of the patriotism that had been a hallmark of bourgeois, overwhelmingly liberal, core groups. Once the lowest common denominator of the various nationalist movements—an independent nation-state—had been achieved, broad ideologies with more clearly defined agendas began to emerge. Growth, industrialization, and global networks fundamentally transformed economic and social relations, expressions of culture, ways of thinking, and everyday life. These enormous upheavals had to be explained and processed psychologically. New worldviews, ideologies, and political movements proliferated in response to the growing need for comprehensible explanations. Social and geographic mobility, the formation of new middle and lower classes, and improved opportunities for communication and education reinforced national awareness among a broader public. The worsening political, social, and moral crises of the Habsburg and Ottoman Empires sowed dissatisfaction and politicized even the lower social classes. Under a new generation of politicians, the parties splintered into different factions. Issues of economic development and social policy began to receive greater emphasis in party programs, alongside national and civil-democratic rights. Moreover, a world that was primarily ordered by nation-states called for a reassessment of regional and international relations. In response to an increasingly radical, chauvinist nationalism, internationalism began to present itself as a kind of countermovement. Political parties founded "internationals," legal experts formulated international law, and curators and scholars organized world exhibitions and congresses.

Parallel to processes of state and institution building, the political systems and party landscapes of the 1870s assumed more differentiated profiles. Southeastern Europe's formerly autocratic principalities developed into constitutional, parliamentary monarchies. Greece accepted its constitution in 1864, Romania in 1866, Serbia in 1869, and Montenegro in 1905. One after another, the principalities became kingdoms: Romania in 1881, Serbia in 1882, Bulgaria in 1908, and Montenegro in 1910.

In an increasingly complex world, political parties became advocates for different ideologies: conservatism, liberalism, socialism, and agrarianism. Many of the impulses for these developments came from western and central Europe, or from Russia, although the individual Balkan lands embraced and adapted them in very different ways. The interaction of local traditions, national idiosyncrasies, and the economic and intellectual challenges of globalization brought forth an array of outlooks, sometimes regionally specific.

Ideologies are closed systems of ideas, convictions, and values; they seek to explain the world and determine social order. They offer simplified explanations for complex conditions, conveying meaning and orientation. As new social milieus coalesced and religious explanatory models retreated, ideologies provided expressions of collective identity that corresponded to the interests of modern mass society. Popular movements used new forms of political expression and action—elections, demonstrations, and strikes—to convey their political goals. Mobilization strategies, increasingly aimed at the middle and lower classes, were often emotional and demagogic.[62]

Of the large political camps that formed in the last third of the century, it was the bourgeois nationalists who were responsible for governance in the Balkans until the outbreak of the First World War. But competing strains had been evident within this group since the 1860s, as "liberals" and "conservatives" began to develop separate profiles.[63] The two groups had initially worked together on behalf of the sovereign nation-state, but they soon parted ways over the specifics of domestic and foreign affairs. In Serbia, for example, the liberals around Vladimir Jovanović clashed with conservatives around Ilija Garašanin. The worldview of the latter included a strong nation-state dominated by the monarchy, military, and other informal elites, with parliamentary power kept in check; this approach corresponded to the authoritarian system of Prince Obrenović. National conservatives believed in a metahistorical, natural, and organically conceived nation, and they sought to protect and uphold its traditional social order and patriarchal values. They wanted to defend premodern, rural ways of life and religion against Western rationalism.[64] Liberals, on the other hand, called for greater citizens' and parliamentary rights, a modern constitutional state, efficient bureaucracies, compulsory schooling, and targeted state intervention in the economy through monopolies, taxes, and tariffs. The literary critic Jovan Skerlić, for example, asserted that "everything good, beautiful and great that humanity knows comes from the thinking, free, active, and energetic West." As he saw it, the choice was "either to accept Western culture and live, as the Japanese have done, or to oppose it, and be overrun, as has happened to the American Indians and Australian Aborigines."[65]

The symbolic terrain of this ideological confrontation throughout the Balkans was the big, modern city—the seat of state bureaucracy and the economic bourgeoisie, and the point of departure for a modern Western way of life. To conservatives, the metropolis embodied everything that was foreign to the nation—Westernized, exploitative elites; secularism; and the loss of national identity and culture.[66] "The blind striving to imitate the foreigners and to become exactly as they are," the Bulgarian Petko Slaveikov complained, "has made us dislike everything ours."[67] Milan Lazarević, a member of the Serbian National Assembly, also worried about national identity: "Whoever comes to Serbia in order to see her culture, will not find it in Belgrade . . . for Belgrade readily adopts the foreign culture . . . Serbian customs are neglected."[68] In Romania, the Junimea cultural movement led by Titu Maiorescu criticized "form without substance"—that is, superficial modernization and the cult of rationalism. The movement sought to uphold traditional spiritual and religious values, instead of what it saw as a specious imitation of Western "pseudo-culture."[69]

Since the 1860s, socialists and communists had positioned themselves against conservatives and liberals. At first, their ideas lacked structure and were constantly reformulated. Then Karl Marx provided an explanatory model that, for the first time, placed capitalism under comprehensive theoretical scrutiny. He used historical laws of class struggle to explain exploitation and oppression, which meant that the bourgeois-capitalist present was subject to change. Southeastern Europeans were generally receptive to the utopia of a just, classless society with new moral standards. The goal of socialism was to abolish the bourgeois-capitalist order and private ownership of the means of production, and to replace them with a just, united society in the form of a proletarian dictatorship.

However, industrial capitalism in southeastern Europe was in its early stages; most people still earned their living through agriculture. The early socialist movements in Serbia, Bulgaria, and Romania were strongly influenced by Russian Slavophile populism (narodnichestvo).[70] Social revolutionary populists (narodniki) developed socialist doctrine that applied to the conditions of agrarian society, and thus to the Balkan countries, too. They believed that traditional, self-governed Russian village communities could bring progress toward socialism, thereby forgoing the developmental stage of capitalism with its deleterious social effects. Narodniki from Russia, and social democrats from western and southeastern Europe, exchanged ideas as they corresponded and met in person in émigré circles.[71]

The Serb Svetozar Marković became an influential advocate of this kind of socialist ideology; under his leadership, a socialist wing broke away from Serbia's liberal party at the end of the 1860s. His agrarian socialism was grounded in the social order of the village and encouraged traditional extended families and local communities to govern themselves. Since the industrial class state and proletariat that Marx described was hardly present within Serbia, Marković hoped simply to bypass the capitalist phase along the way to socialism.[72] Marković—who was inspired by Nikolay Chernyshevsky, Alexander Herzen, Karl Marx, Friedrich Engels, Ferdinand Lassalle, and Pierre-Joseph Proudhon—founded the first socialist associations in Belgrade, translated the *Communist Manifesto,* and also published the journal *The Worker* and his most famous work, *Serbia in the East.* His goal was an egalitarian people's democracy.[73]

Classical Marxism made inroads into southeastern Europe only in the 1880s and particularly the 1890s, influenced by the writings of Georgi Plekhanov and the German workers' movement. Social democratic parties were established in Bulgaria in 1891, in Romania in 1893, in Croatia-Slavonia in 1894, and in Serbia in 1903—but not until 1918 in authoritarian Greece. Their specific demands included universal and equal suffrage, social reforms, and the eight-hour workday.

If and how socialism could be attained in a peasant society remained the subject of many ideological debates. In contrast to Marković, the Romanian Marxist Constantin Dobrogeanu-Gherea rejected the ideology of Russian populists. He developed a "law of development for backward societies" and predicted that the Western model of capitalist development would prevail in Romania, which already had a significant population of wage earners, in contrast to Serbia and Bulgaria. In his study *Neo-Serfdom (Neoiobăgia),* Dobrogeanu-Gherea described Romania as "semi-capitalist" and called for its complete defeudalization, industrialization, and modernization. He believed that political transformation would occur through elections, not revolutions.[74]

By contrast, in Bulgaria, Dimitar Blagoev believed that class struggle would allow communism to succeed, even in a pure peasant society. His rival Yanko Sakazov instead advocated for a path of reform. In 1903, the socialist party divided into separate "narrow" (revolutionary) and "broad" (reformist) factions.[75] But neither the revolutionaries nor the reformists or revisionists, attracted a substantial following before the First World War. In Bulgaria and the other southeastern European countries, agrarianism became the strongest oppositional force to the liberal capitalist system.

Beginning in the 1890s, populist peasants' parties formed in all Balkan countries. Responding to the great world agricultural crises, the parties oriented themselves against two challenges: capitalism and communism. In Bulgaria, Dimitar Dragiev and Alexander Stamboliyski founded the

Bulgarian Agrarian National Union; in Croatia, the brothers Stjepan and Antun Radić introduced the Croatian People's Peasant Party. In Romania, the agrarian movement of Poporanism gained influence under Constantin Stere.[76] The agrarian ideologies did not develop their own theoretical approach or independent worldview; rather, they held some positions in common with liberalism (pertaining to private property and democracy), and some with communism (a socially just, cooperative order). They were influenced in varying degrees by the Russian *narodniki,* Western agrarianism, and the cooperativism of political thinkers such as Jules Méline, Émile Vandervelde, and Charles Gide.[77]

Although the agrarian ideologies and peasants' parties were constituted differently throughout the lands of southeastern Europe, they put forth similar demands. They saw the peasantry as the backbone of the nation—its authentic social source, its economic foundation, as well as its moral scaffolding. In Croatia, the nationalist undertone of the peasant movement was particularly pronounced. Unlike Bulgaria and Romania, a Croatian nation-state did not yet exist. For Stjepan Radić, Croatian sovereignty was the essential precondition for solving the social problems of the village. Enfranchisement of the third estate could only be realized in a unified, democratic peasants' state. This utopia bundled together all the yearnings of the crisis-ridden rural population. Radić and the other agrarians in southeastern Europe believed that agriculture could and should assert itself over industry as the leading economic sector—one of the aspects of their ideology that distinguished them from socialists. They were antimonarchical and anticlerical, and they embraced the achievements of modernity; they believed that agricultural reforms, cooperatives, technology, professional knowledge, and financial institutions could empower the peasants to better withstand the upheavals of modern industrial capitalism. "Then our villages would have houses with two, even three rooms," the literary critic Garabet Ibrăileanu dreamed. "The people would be well dressed, practically German. The farmer's daughter would play piano or work through Sadoveanu's novellas, and the father would read telegrams about what was happening in the world."[78]

A new Radical Party largely absorbed the voices of agrarianism within Serbia. After its founding in 1881, the party quickly became a defining political force. The Radical Party built on Svetozar Marković's socialist-populist appeal, but replaced its social revolutionary elements with a heightened nationalism. In contrast to the bourgeois Liberal and Progressive (national conservative) Parties, the Radicals idealized village traditions and local self-government. Above all, they stoked resentment against the modern state and the taxes it imposed.[79]

A sharp line of conflict between the political ideologies became apparent in foreign policy. For all the political differences between the bourgeois (that is, conservative and liberal) parties, in the sphere of foreign policy they shared a common goal: a strong, self-confident nation-state that was as homogeneous as possible. Since 1870, all Europe—and thus southeastern Europe, too—had fallen under the sway of aggressive nationalism. The intellectual climate of the era was characterized by a particularist ethno-nationalism and cultural essentialism that fueled imperialism, in tandem with the competition for raw materials. Great power rivalries erupted in wars and local armed conflicts both within and outside Europe. Military conflicts, in turn, further intensified nationalist ideologies. As trade, migration, conquest, and colonialism brought distant peoples into closer contact, identity-based worldviews that emphasized hierarchical differences between cultures and "races" likewise gained strength. In the nineteenth century, most states in Europe—and thus southeastern Europe, too—identified themselves in primarily cultural terms.[80]

Since the beginning of the nineteenth century, ethnic homogenization and expulsions had been part of the tool box of nation-state building in southeastern Europe. Every regime change and territorial acquisition unleashed mass waves of "ethnic cleansing."[81] The first occurred amid the Serbian and Greek uprisings in the early nineteenth century. A second followed in the mid-1860s, as the Turks withdrew from Belgrade and the Cretans revolted. The Great Eastern Crisis of the 1870s uprooted hundreds of thousands of southeastern Europeans, and violent policies of homogenization continued thereafter. Of the estimated 45,000 Muslims who lived in Thessaly in 1881, only 3,000 remained in 1911. On Crete, the Muslim population shrank by two-thirds in the same time period.[82] Between the beginning of the Serbian uprising in 1804 and the events that followed the Paris Peace Conference until 1920 / 21, about 935,000 Muslims were expelled from the Balkan Peninsula, and 1.735 million were killed or lost their lives while fleeing.[83]

Recent historical research has depicted expulsions in Europe and in the colonies as two sides of an interrelated global phenomenon. Great Britain, France, Germany, Russia, and the United States carried out deportations, "ethnic cleansing," and acts of mass murder during the colonization of

Africa, Oceania, and the Americas. In 1830 the democratic United States initiated the forced resettlement of native American peoples, and soon thereafter French colonial troops handled the Arab population similarly in Algeria. The plan to "repatriate" African Americans to Liberia en masse was part of the same phenomenon. Millions lost their lives in this era, as Belgians under Leopold II exploited the Congo for its wealth of natural resources, and Germans in Southwest Africa put down the uprisings of the Herero and Nama. Mass deportations and colonization went hand in hand with new settlements. What was not foreseen, however, was that "civilized" Christian peoples could also fall victim to such proceedings, as occurred in the Balkans.[84]

In the last third of the nineteenth century, ethnic homogeneity became the mantra of a strong and effective nation-state in Europe. Instead of language and culture, ethnicity and ancestry became essential criteria for defining the nation. If liberals in the first half of the nineteenth century had seen themselves as part of a progressive, cosmopolitan community that promoted civil rights, now they were willing to sacrifice individual rights and cooperation across borders for the sake of national freedom and unity. Ethnic nationalism implied hierarchical distinctions between peoples and religions. These distinctions could result in the exclusion of minorities and all who were considered foreign or unwanted. Thus, the Romanian constitution of 1866 contained an article that granted citizenship only to Christians. Romanian politicians—including the liberal Mihail Kogălniceanu, who had fought for emancipation of the gypsies—used the high proportion of Jews in key economic sectors to justify the restrictive citizenship rules.[85]

Jews were strongly represented in the cities, in bourgeois professions and among the educated elite; anti-Semitism became an outlet for social envy and growing criticisms of modernity. Even Jews who were longtime residents of Romania became stateless, thus losing civil and political rights. At the Congress of Berlin, the great powers did compel the revision of this constitutional article, but anyone who wanted to become a Romanian citizen still had to overcome significant bureaucratic obstacles. By 1899, only 4,272 of 266,719 Jews had been "naturalized" as Romanian citizens. The others were barred from working for the state or owning property, and they faced discrimination. Many decided to emigrate.[86] In Greece, Serbia, and Bulgaria—unlike in Romania—there was no comparable state-sanctioned anti-Semitism. Jews in these countries were well assimilated and not stigmatized to the same degree over competitive concerns.

A corollary of ethnically determined nationalism in this era was irredentism. All Balkan states now forged plans of annexation to "liberate" the members of their nations (or those whom they believed to be members), incorporating them within the national community. In Serbia, Slobodan Jovanović warned that "we have to turn a former Turkish *pashalik* into a modern European state with its own civil service and military, its own courts and schools, its own banks and railroads." Logically, this state would be joined by "the other Serbian lands still under foreign rule."[87]

Influential forces in politics and society strove to achieve a "greater Serbia," "greater Romania," "greater Bulgaria," or "greater Greece," thereby transforming the anti-Ottoman struggle for freedom into a struggle between states. Hungary and Romania fought over Transylvania, for example, while Romania and Bulgaria fought over Dobruja, and Greece and Bulgaria fought over Thrace. Macedonia even became an apple of discord for three states: Serbia, Greece, and Bulgaria. Because ethnic majorities were unclear, or because people sometimes did not know which nation to choose, the "imperative of authenticity" (Holm Sundhaussen) prevailed; each side claimed to know the supposedly original identity of the groups of people being fought over and used this knowledge to support territorial claims. Greek nationalists treated Bulgarians and Albanians in the ethnically mixed regions that they claimed for themselves as "Bulgarophone" or "Albanophone" Greeks. Serbia invented the "Arnaut" people, who were supposedly Albanized Serbs, not Albanians. And in Croatia, the Party of Rights asserted that Serbs and Muslims were merely Croats who had been converted to foreign religions; Slovenes, likewise, were actually "mountain Croats." Such ethnic essentialism could override linguistic or religious criteria, if these did not align with territorial claims that were being made in the name of "national unity."

The idea of a Hellenic ecumene and civilizing mission, inclusive of all Orthodox Balkan peoples, disappeared in Greece. Instead, private organizations like the National Defense and the Brotherhood attempted to organize the Greek irredenta for political union during the Eastern Crisis of the late 1870s. In the 1890s the Greek National Society began to provide organizational support for the various irredentist committees. All the committees were brought underneath the umbrella of the state Panhellenic Organization in 1908.[88] In Serbia, politics had been dominated by the Radical Party, led by Nikola Pašić, since the 1890s. According to its national program of 1894, there was "no difference between the interests of the Serbian state and the interests of other Serbs. . . . Cut off from other Serbian lands, Serbia alone is nothing and has no raison d'être."[89] That same year, the Serbian paramilitary organization National Defense (Narodna Odbrana) was established to provide military and cultural support to Serbs in Bosnia-Herzegovina.[90] And the Bulgarian Veliko Jordanov asserted that "all of our efforts" are "oriented towards the fulfillment of our centuries-old ideal: the liberation and unification of the Bulgarian people."[91]

Nationalist associations, committees, cultural societies, and religious activities sprung up in all the Balkan states; their goal was to support co-nationals abroad and reinforce their connection to the nation wherever possible. The idea of a Yugoslav federation, so popular in Croatia, aroused the skepticism of the Serbian Radicals. Since Serbs and Croats were divided by religion and historical and political traditions, the Radicals asked whether "we are actually one people at all." Yugoslavism could, however, potentially offer a broader platform for Serbian plans for national unification.[92]

As state nationalisms became more insistent and aggressive in their territorial rivalries, their relationships with one another were increasingly irreconcilable. In the aftermath of the Great Eastern Crisis, Greeks and Bulgarians constructed a historic Greek-Bulgarian enmity. Greek nationalists spoke of a "Slavic flood," and historians depicted the "worthlessness of this tribe" and its "lack of history." The Bulgarians were said to be "the only people of the Orient without their own language, without a written history or chronicle, without any kind of relic or piece of memory from ancient times."[93] As the rivalry over Macedonia intensified, the thesis about the non-Slavic origins of the Bulgarians gained a wider following. In Romania, meanwhile, the national poet Mihai Eminescu derided "bull-necked Bulgarians" and "pointy-nosed little Greeks" in 1876. Phanariots, liberals, and supposedly parasitic Jews were further targets of his scorn.[94]

As in Germany, France, Great Britain, and Austria-Hungary, the population of southeastern Europe underwent a broad politicization beginning in the 1890s. Patriotic associations and news media spread rapidly. The public discovered national flags, symbols, holidays, cuisine, and other expressions of collective identity and communal belonging. Newspapers received titles like *New Century, New Era,* and *New World,* or even—with a nod toward patriotic ambitions—*Struggle, Victory,* and *Defense.*[95] Anyone who could not read (including the majority of peasants) might still be reached by a printed calendar, or by an illustration with symbolic national and historical themes. Studying the press and discussing politics became part of many people's politicized daily routines. Wherever there was a diet or a parliament, national politics were constantly discussed. And with every new international crisis, such as the annexation crisis, nationalist tunnel vision grew more pronounced. Nationalism and militarism enjoyed popular support. In Serbia, for example, patriotic songs like "The Serb Happily Joins the Army" were heard all the time, and popular plays included *The Kosovo Battle* and *Stanoje Glavaš,* about a heroic *haiduk.* The Turks were inevitably portrayed as cowards, and the Serbs as heroes. According to one contemporary, "national pride and the intense longing . . . to liberate all Serbian regions" unified different political camps and social classes.[96] And in Bulgaria, one activist preached that the "legacy of 'San Stefano'" could no longer remain a "national dream"; it had to become "political religion." In 1910, Pencho Slaveykov stated: "The poet says war."[97]

For the prominent historian Slobodan Jovanović, this all went too far. "Our nationalism," he critically noted, resembles "the fanaticism of a persecuted sect."[98] In Bulgaria, the agrarian politician Alexander Stamboliyski came to believe that his entire nation had lost its mind.[99] It was incomprehensible how nationalist programs could be realized in the ethnically mixed regions of eastern and southeastern Europe without inciting a fratricidal war. State nationalism had become increasingly belligerent, with little regard for its neighbors.[100]

Socialists and agrarians positioned themselves more decisively against the rising tide of bourgeois nationalism. Karl Marx himself had stated that nationalist republicanism "represented nothing better than the old idea of a middle-class republic."[101] The opposition, which saw itself as the voice of workers and peasants, accused the bourgeoisie of an aggressive chauvinism that stirred up hatred between nations. Bourgeois politicians seemed not to know how to help the impoverished lower classes, peasants or workers, in a capitalist age. Wherever liberals or conservatives were in power, they promoted an aggressive nationalism and an escalating arms race.

The two oppositional movements—socialists and agrarians—turned to proposals for a democratic Balkan league as an opportunity to root out nationalism and imperialism. Svetozar Marković had already warned that "the people would come out of the fight for greater Serbia even poorer."[102] Only the ruling class would profit from the politics of annexation, while the threat of a military state loomed at home. Marković, as did socialists elsewhere in southeastern Europe, called for a federation of Balkan states with equal membership rights. The Bulgarian Dimitar Blagoev believed that such a federation could solve the Macedonian problem, and the Serb Dimitrije Tucović thought it might also provide a suitable framework for a free Albania. "The national liberation of the Balkan peoples is impossible without uniting all of the Balkans in a [political and economic] community," Tucović wrote. This necessarily excluded all solutions that proceeded from a federalized Habsburg Monarchy. Only Constantin Dobrogeanu-Gherea promoted a socialist cosmopolitanism, or internationalism, because he believed that the nation could also exist without the nation-state.[103]

Socialists propagated international class struggle and predicted the proletariat would ultimately claim victory over the bourgeoisie. Inspired by the Marxist parole "Workers of the world, unite!" the first Socialist International was established in 1864. At the behest of Dimitrije Tucović, the Balkan socialists organized a Balkan Socialist Conference in Belgrade in 1910; its delegates endorsed the goal of establishing a federative, social, and democratic Balkan republic. Within this framework, the Albanians were also to receive their own state. World revolution would follow in time. In 1915 the Balkan socialists met again in Bucharest.[104] Leading politicians of the peasants' parties in Croatia and Bulgaria also placed their faith in internationalism. After the First World War, they founded a Green International.

In the evolution of worldviews, the decades before and after the First World War were closely related. The central conflict between ideological extremes was already in place before 1914—with communism, internationalism, and universal ideas of a just world order on one side, and cultural essentialism, nationalism, and chauvinism on the other. Embedded within this conflict were challenges of modernity that would continue to intensify after 1918: political and ideological divisions, ethnic and religious strife, uncertainty in the face of epochal social change, longing for simple truths, and quasi-religious structures of meaning. The great ideologies answered these challenges by offering identity and self-assurance as compensation for loss of orientation and fears about the future. From here, we can see the point of departure for the defining conflicts of the twentieth century—including the contest between bourgeois nationalists and communist internationalists over the leadership of the world.

Communication, Technology, and Transnational Mobilization

While the great powers were striving to divide up the world, the continents continued to grow closer together through links forged by science and technology. The steamship and locomotive reduced the time and cost of transporting people and goods, connecting markets and labor markets and also compressing the experience of space and time. New electric-powered technologies enabled the rapid transmission of news throughout the world, and millions of migrants boarded steamships to centers of industry in the New World. More frequent and closer contacts informed the spirit of the era. Congresses, world exhibitions, and international movements provided new, institutionalized forums for a public that transcended state borders. Globalization facilitated connections between local, regional, and transnational communities.[105]

The development of transportation and communications infrastructure clearly illustrates how rapidly the world had changed. Particularly after 1870, new steamship connections, railway networks, and paved roads made traveling faster, cheaper, and more common. In 1883, the luxurious Orient Express shortened travel time between Paris and Istanbul (through Zagreb, Belgrade, and Sofia) by three and a half days, to only fifty-three hours.[106] On the eve of the First World War, about 617,000 passengers were traveling each year on the railway's four lines.[107] However, southeastern Europeans rode the rails much less often than their counterparts in western and central Europe. In 1911 a resident of Romania made an average of 1.6 trips by train each year; a resident of Serbia, only 0.3.[108]

Modern transportation immensely accelerated the spread of news. When letters were still carried on foot or by pack horses and ships, news from Jassy or Belgrade took about two weeks to reach Athens. By railroad, mail from Vienna or Thessaloniki arrived in the Greek capital after only one or two days. The volume of mail multiplied, too. The Bulgarian postal service alone delivered more than twenty-seven million letters each year.[109]

Collectors' card: Mail carrier in Bulgaria fighting
back thieves, around 1890. Private collection.

The first telegraph line in the Ottoman Empire was built during the
Crimean War, in 1855. The first transmission announced the arrival of
Allied troops in Sevastopol. From Shumen, the news traveled to Edirne
and then Istanbul, and from there to the western European capitals.[110] A
half century later, the Ottoman capital already had lines to Belgrade, Bucharest, Thessaloniki, and Athens. After 1880, one could wire from Istanbul
to all the continents. In the Balkans, too, the volume of transmissions increased exponentially after the turn of the century. In tiny Montenegro,
nearly 170,000 telegrams were sent in 1909, more than one-third to other
countries.[111] "Today, practically the entire world lives the same life," the
journalist—and later, Serbian prime minister—Nikola Pašić marveled.
"From Paris to Constantinople, the telegraph cable brings everyone the
same thing, and then the same response is sent back. The whole world lives
together in one house."[112]

News agencies and the international press supplied the southeastern European public with information from all over the world. Contemporaries could now experience the present as an interconnected chain of worldwide events, no longer a primarily local or national occurrence. They encountered entirely new realms of empirical knowledge. As early as the 1850s, 138 different foreign newspaper titles in French, German, Russian, Turkish, Hungarian, and numerous other languages circulated in Serbia.[113] And in Thessaloniki, twenty-nine newspapers from western Europe alone were displayed at kiosks in 1905, including *Le Matin, Il Corriere della Sera,* and *Die Neue Freie Presse.* They were joined by countless titles in Turkish, Greek, and other languages.[114]

Professional war correspondents got their start during the Crimean War. Press reports and photos became indispensable instruments of information and disinformation.[115] Even so, most news continued to come from eyewitnesses, the reports of government emissaries, or through hearsay. The Romanian government learned about the events of the American Civil War, for example, by sending one of its own captains to participate in the general staff of the Northern states. Volunteer fighters also wrote reports for the Romanian press.[116] During the Eastern Crisis of the 1870s, many large newspapers from the Balkan countries were already sending their own reporters and correspondents to the battlefields. Nikola Pašić, for example, reported for the *Narodno Oslobođenje (National Liberation)* from Bosnia and Herzegovina in 1875. Newspapers no longer overwhelmingly relayed Western press and agency reports, but instead sent their own journalists abroad.[117] Around the turn of the century, the Balkan state governments established professional news agencies to disseminate information from their capitals by telegraph.[118]

As the printing press, telegraph, steamship, and locomotive revolutionized news reporting, travel, and the transport of goods, the natural sciences transformed existing conceptions of the world in previously inconceivable ways. Next to biology, chemistry, pharmaceutics, and medicine, physics assumed a prominent role in toppling old certainties through the discovery of invisible forces, magnetic fields, electricity, and radioactivity. In this era, scientific specialists and technical inventors replaced an older generation of natural philosophers who—like Ruđer Bošković—had still been searching for a universal theory to explain the world.

One of the era's most original natural scientists was the physicist Nikola Tesla, son of a Serbian Orthodox priest from Croatia. After living in Prague

The first automobile in Banja Luka, 1908 (owned by the Muslim landlord Smail Džinic Bey). National Museum of Bosnia and Herzegovina, Sarajevo.

and Budapest, the twenty-seven-year-old Tesla headed to New York City in 1884, a bundle of calculations and plans for a self-built flying machine under his arm. After a short period of collaboration with Thomas Edison, the two men parted ways, and Tesla founded his own company. At first, the New World disappointed him: "What I had left was beautiful, artistic and fascinating in every way; what I saw here was machined, rough and unattractive." But after five years, he became convinced that America was "more than one hundred years AHEAD of Europe."[119]

Tesla, who strove for "the complete mastery of mind over the material world," made groundbreaking discoveries in the fields of electricity and electrical engineering. He experimented with high-frequency and polyphase electrical currents, discovered radio transmission, AC motors, and electrical remote controls, and he lent his name to coils, transformers, and turbines. Tesla's vision was the wireless transmission of energy and information, which he hoped would unleash a "second electrical revolution."[120] He worked feverishly to send information and energy wirelessly across the Atlantic with the help of magnifying transmitters and radio systems. In

Timetable for the Austrian
steamship company.

the end, he believed that he had found a comprehensive "world system"
that would allow all telegraph and telephone stations around the globe to
communicate with one another and to wirelessly transmit signals, texts,
and photos. "Within a few years a simple and inexpensive device . . . will
enable one to receive on land or sea the principal news, to hear a speech, a
lecture, a song or play of a musical instrument, conveyed from any other
region of the globe."[121]

Tesla was considered an outsider and an eccentric, both within and outside his profession.[122] After meeting the famous Bengali yogi Swami Vive-
kananda at the World's Parliament of Religions in Chicago in 1893, he
developed an enthusiasm for Hinduism, which he believed could contribute
to a better understanding of the modern sciences and the universe. He saw
the transmission of information, transportation of passengers, and transfer
of energy as contributions to universal peace. "What we now want most is
closer contact and better understanding between individuals and communities all over the earth," he wrote in 1898.[123] Seventeen years later, in the
middle of the First World War, he envisioned a "wonder world to be

created by electricity." He fantasized about electrotherapy and talking computers, illumination of the oceans and the global control of precipitation. "Distance, which is the chief impediment to human progress, will be completely annihilated in thought, word and action. Humanity will be united, wars will be made impossible and peace will reign supreme."[124]

Today, the idea of wirelessly transmitting information is taken for granted, while wirelessly transmitting power is still a utopia. During Tesla's lifetime, sponsors and investors rejected nearly all of the visionary inventor's proposals as impracticable. The scientific unit of magnetic flux density was, however, later named the "tesla" in his honor. Not least, his legacy now includes the current generation of electric automobiles from Tesla Motors.[125]

Tesla's biography was "global" in many ways, and not only because he began a new life on another continent. In contrast to many world travelers of earlier eras, he was aware of the global significance of his actions; he did his best to accelerate the pace at which the world was growing together. He was determined to present his system of wirelessly transmitting information and power across the Atlantic at the Paris world exhibition of 1900. He theorized about universal knowledge and sought solutions for global problems and world peace, aiming to make a positive contribution with his inventions.

The masses of migrants who left their homelands over the course of the nineteenth century to look for work in the New World also possessed global biographies. Their most common destination was the United States, but many also headed to Canada, Latin America, South Africa, New Zealand, and Australia. The Atlantic migration from all of Europe reached its peak between 1880 and 1914; from southeastern Europe, only after 1900. The dramatic population growth brought on by demographic transition occurred first in western and central Europe. Political restrictions also curbed migration from southeastern Europe; emigration from Austria-Hungary was permitted only after 1867, and from the Ottoman Empire, only after 1892. Between 1900 and the outbreak of the First World War, 738,500 southeastern Europeans set out for America—including 250,000 Greeks, 80,000 Bulgarians, 83,000 Romanians, but only 1,500 Serbs. More than 200,000 departed from Croatia and Slavonia, and another 124,000 from European Turkey.[126]

Unlike Nikola Tesla, most people emigrated for reasons of bitter economic distress. There was not enough work, and the social bonds of the traditional extended family were fraying. Meanwhile, booming industrial economies overseas lured workers with the promise of secure wages. Modern forms of transportation had finally given people the practical means to flee a seemingly hopeless economic situation. Agencies and steamship lines began to recruit unskilled southeastern European workers for mining and factory jobs, even coordinating their overseas passage. Migrants from Hungary, Croatia, and Dalmatia rode by train to the port of Fiume, or to Hamburg, Bremerhaven, or Cherbourg, and then continued their journey by steamship.[127] Recruiting agencies distributed posters and flyers, and the letters of emigrants likewise contributed to the highly romanticized image of a land of boundless opportunity. Even so, the magazine *Slovenec (The Slovene)* warned in 1909: "The idea that America is a gold mine, from which one can dig up golden dollars and return to one's homeland as a rich man, should be forgotten. Here, work is hard to find, and one must work hard for one's pay."[128]

Motives for migration were both political and economic. Many members of the nationalities, for example, wanted to escape military service in the Habsburg Empire. Between 1881 and 1914, anti-Semitic repression compelled about 125,000 Jews to emigrate from Romania to England, America, Australia, or Palestine. Among them were the pitiful *fusgeyers* who set out from Jassy, Brăila, or Galați, determined to make their way out of the country on foot. Jewish organizations assisted them with the rest of their journey.[129]

The great majority of emigrants were male, young, unskilled, penniless, and single, but a disproportionate number could read and write.[130] Many came from classic areas of migration in the southern Balkans. "They once went primarily to Romania . . . and worked as masons or carpenters," one expert wrote in 1914. "But now they go more frequently to North America, where they work as wage earners in factories, slaughterhouses, or with the railroads."[131] The more unpleasant and dangerous the working conditions were on assembly lines and automatic looms, in coal mines and steel mills, the more likely southeastern Europeans were to be hired. Permanent skilled positions were typically reserved for natives.

In many regions, labor migration alleviated the problem of rural underemployment; the demographic surplus shrank noticeably. But because it was primarily younger and better-educated residents who left, their homelands lost human capital.[132] The American Emily Balch, who researched "our Slavic fellow citizens" after the turn of the century, reported on vast stretches of land that had been depopulated by emigration. Some state authorities felt compelled to intervene. "Our newspapers write so much what a bad thing it is for whole families to go," one teacher from Croatia reported. "But it is no use. People must eat. . . . There is too little land."[133] At the end of the nineteenth century, state authorities in Hungary and Croatia-Slavonia banned the recruiting of guest workers. But efforts to contain the flows of migration did not succeed.[134]

Most guest workers planned to return home at some point. In fact, half did come back, bringing along new attitudes and expectations. Hungarian politicians complained about the newly self-confident Slavs who were suddenly concerned about individual liberties and a more efficient bureaucracy. They seemed to have lost respect for authority and were even openly disseminating pan-Slav ideas. The liberal Ferenc Kossuth, by contrast, approvingly noted that "the emigrants return with higher ideals and a better idea of the world."[135] People said that anyone who had been to America was immediately recognizable. Returnees were more independent, better workers, and more interested in education—but they no longer fit in with the old ways of life.[136]

Transatlantic migrants—about three-quarters of a million people in all—were just a small fraction of all labor migrants before 1914. Even at the height of the emigration wave, the majority of those who moved to find work did so within Europe. Of all migrants from Austria-Hungary, 95 percent moved internally within the empire; the metropolises of Prague and Vienna exerted the greatest pull. In the Ottoman Empire, too, many migrated to the capital, or labored in the great grain fields of Romania and Bulgaria.[137] Globalization played an important role. The demand for foodstuffs and raw materials in Western industrial countries spurred on agricultural production, and thus the demand for labor. The international division of labor influenced migration flows in quite different ways.

Multilayered contacts developed between emigrants and their home society. Migrants sent relatives tickets for travel, and they helped newcomers find work, encouraging more to follow. Of Europeans who arrived in the United States at the beginning of the twentieth century, 94 percent headed toward a location where they already had friends or kin. Pennsylvania, Ohio, and Illinois became centers of migration, particularly Pittsburgh, Cleveland, and Chicago, respectively.[138] Associations, coffeehouses, cooperatives, and churches sprang up with names such as the Serbian Benevolent Society, First Croatian Benefit Society, and Bulgarian People's Union. Between 1884 and 1920, about 3,500 newspapers and journals were published in the United States in immigrant languages. They provided not only information about the host country but also a forum for political debate. Croatian critics of the Habsburg Monarchy read the *Hrvatski Svijet (Croatian World),* while supporters of the Austrian Emperor preferred the *Domovina (Homeland).*[139]

Globalization also allowed national identity to be experienced in different ways. Living in a socioculturally foreign milieu heightened awareness of difference and otherness, raising questions about who migrants were, where they came from, and who they wanted to be. A new, still amorphous "Yugoslav" identity began to gain ground. Traditional forms of social and family organization broke down in industrial society, and the American "melting pot" became a practical example of transnational community building.[140]

Many guest workers sent savings to their families, so the home countries profited from mass emigration as well. In the first quarter of the twentieth century, about 400,000 Greeks sent 50 to 80 million U.S. dollars back to their homeland.[141] Expanded opportunities for consumption, and also the reports of those who returned home, opened up new horizons for people in even the most remote regions of the old homelands. Many families had members who lived abroad, so in a sense the New World became a part of the Old. Nevertheless, differences in wealth and income between the sending and receiving countries did not diminish, but actually intensified, because the wealth of the industrial countries was growing so much faster.[142]

Fan Noli was another interesting emigrant in the years before the First World War. In his mid-twenties when he came to America, he represented the political dimensions of the transnational space. Noli came from an Albanian family in the Turkish part of Thrace. His father, a cantor in the Orthodox Church, sent the talented boy to a Greek secondary school, and then to Edirne to train as a priest. But Noli, who was an enthusiast of Shakespeare, became an actor in a traveling theater company and toured across the Balkans. In Alexandria, where he worked as a teacher and cantor, he immersed himself in the library of his Albanian colleague, the writer Spiro Dine. He studied philosophy and all subjects related to the precarious situation of his people. Consumed with the idea of establishing an Albanian state, after three years in Egypt he left for Boston in 1906, seeking to win over his countrymen in the United States for the Albanian national cause. He was greeted with a certain skepticism, as were thousands of other young emigrants. "This proved to be not the New World but the Dirty World," he complained to his Egyptian friends.[143]

Fan Noli saw himself as an "Albanian revolutionary." He was an outstanding intellectual and a free spirit, artistically inclined, eloquent, and deeply moved by the patriotic cause. He was ordained as a deacon by a Russian archbishop in Brooklyn, New York, and he simultaneously received the right to celebrate the liturgy in Albanian (instead of Greek). He studied at Harvard, and in the following years he established an independent Albanian Orthodox Church. After the First World War, the church was formally recognized by the new Albanian state, and Fan Noli became its first archbishop. In 1937, the patriarch of Constantinople affirmed the autocephaly of the national church, which was itself a product of globalization.[144]

Fan Noli developed his passion for the liberation of the Albanian people at a time when their neighbors already had nation-states, and were eyeing areas of Albanian settlement. At Harvard he immersed himself in the history of the folk hero Skanderbeg, who—as we have seen—rose up against the Ottomans in the fifteenth century. Noli later wrote his dissertation on Skanderbeg.[145] Similar to Kosovo for the Serbs, for Albanians the history of Skanderbeg offered an inexhaustible source of symbols and allegories that could reinforce feelings of community, create historical meaning, and provide orientation for the future. Noli translated Molière, Stendhal, Shakespeare, and Poe, and he was an enthusiast for the works of Nietzsche and Wagner. He also created a series of books that made world literature accessible to readers of the Albanian language. His biography recalled the cosmopolitanism of eighteenth-century Enlightenment thinkers, but it ultimately took another turn in the era of the nation-state and industrial modernity.

While still in the United States, the indefatigable Albanian published the émigré newspaper *Dielli (Sun),* and he headed the pan-Albanian organization Vatra (Hearth), which worked toward the founding of an Albanian nation-state. At Vatra's behest he traveled to Albanian communities in Kishinev, Odessa, Bucharest, and Sofia, becoming one of the most influential protagonists of a sovereign Albania. His dramatic training made him an engaging speaker, able to draw in listeners with his perspicacity and wit. He knew how to weave in an anecdote or famous quote so it would bring on gales of laughter. Noli's example shows how opportunities for travel, printing, and new communication technologies facilitated connections across long distances between émigré communities on different continents, creating transnational bonds. Modern technology amplified the snowball effect, as audience members' relatives and acquaintances became part of the network, too.

Political émigrés like Noli used the new means of mass communications and transportation to spread nationalist literature in locations where it was banned. In the Ottoman Empire, no Albanian-language texts were allowed to be printed and distributed before 1908. So grammar and reading books, as well as books in history, geography, and arithmetic, were produced abroad—particularly in Italy, Bulgaria, Romania, and Greece, but also in Egypt and the United States. The works were sent by mail or smuggled into the country by consuls, traders, and migrant workers. Caravan drivers stashed them in their saddle bags on the two-week-long journey from Bucharest to Korçë, by way of Sofia and Monastir. The books and newspapers were then distributed through informal networks of local politicians, religious leaders, teachers, civil servants, traders, and craftsmen, or sold at the market. Many books were copied by hand, and newspapers passed from person to person. Reading lessons were held in secret—in madrasas and *tekkes,* in shops at the bazaar, in hostels, private homes, and stables, and even in prison. The French consul in Ioannina reported that "the Albanian script is being learned feverishly by the Albanian soldiers, officers, and civil servants who are posted in the city." And in Vlorë in 1897, "on many a winter evening the young read Albanian books aloud to their elders."[146] The sale of Albanian books was permitted officially (and the question of the alphabet resolved) only after 1908, in the aftermath of the Young Turk Revolution. Only then could commercial presses and a more modern system of sales and distribution develop.[147]

Transatlantic connections also played an important role in Croatia-Slavonia, where Habsburg press censorship sought to stem a rising tide of patriotic publications. Political associations were forbidden, so the public formed around reading associations and reading rooms, where all kinds of news media were available. Not only the rich and educated exchanged information in this way.[148] "In every village there is a library bought by peasants alone," Emily Balch discovered in Croatia, "and in winter they often come together to have someone read to them, not only newspapers but more solid literature, such as translations of Tolstoy, Turgenieff, and Dostoyevsky." Here, too, influences from the New World were evident.[149]

The political dimensions of the connection between nationalization and globalization were apparent in yet another phenomenon. Political agitation abroad assumed such significance for Albanians, Serbs, Slovenes, and

Croats because it was strictly forbidden in the great empires that ruled their homelands. But in American factory halls and workers' residences, Albanian and South Slav activists could speak out comparatively freely on behalf of autonomy, and later independent statehood, with newspapers, flyers, and speeches. In addition, lobby groups mobilized the U.S. public on behalf of an Albanian and a Yugoslav nation-state. Not least, emigrants became an important resource in the nationalist struggle at home. They provided financial support and volunteered to serve on the battlefield in the Balkan Wars and the First World War.[150]

Fan Noli's biography embodies the new era of "globalized nationalism," as well as the processes of internationalization and transnationalization. He maintained connections to Albania during his time in Egypt and the United States, and he was politically active in his new and old homes at the same time. He mediated between cultures, practices, and worldviews with his own writings and translations. He worked to bring the Albanian diasporas together as political actors with a common agenda, mobilizing them across state borders on behalf of nationalism and the nation-state. Noli assumed a prominent role on the international stage when Albanian independence became a topic of negotiation for the first time in 1912, during the First Balkan War. He rushed to the Conference of the Ambassadors in London to drum up support for the new state. Albania was occupied by foreign troops during the First World War, and at the Paris peace negotiations he convinced U.S. president Woodrow Wilson to recognize Albania, at last, as a sovereign nation-state. Fan Noli subsequently moved to Tirana to become a member of parliament. We will meet him again in the 1920s as the foreign minister and prime minister of Albania.[151]

Established nation-states worked to uphold and promote transnational relations. The Kingdom of Greece established and financed schools for the Greek Orthodox population of the Ottoman Empire, particularly in Epirus, Macedonia, and Thrace, as well as Anatolia. It also maintained ties with the approximately quarter million Greeks who had emigrated to America before the First World War.[152] Especially in the interwar era, the other Balkan states similarly created ministries and agencies to forge a bond between émigré communities and the nation-state, seeking to bring together, control, and guide the "deterritorialized" nation. Not least, the sending countries recognized the economic importance of the guest workers' remittances.[153]

The state did not always have an easy time asserting its influence, however. Wealthy Greek merchants, shipowners, and internationally recognized intellectuals did not see themselves as subject to the demands of the Greek bureaucracy. They had been used to acting on their own, sometimes even as a stand-in for the state, since the early modern era—by investing their capital, for example, in Greek schools, publishing houses, banks, and companies.[154] The state had an interest in promoting their businesses and in offering them lucrative government posts. But the émigrés themselves did not necessarily seek a closer relationship with the state, particularly if it might involve responsibilities of citizenship like paying taxes.[155]

Despite the numerous connections between nationalities around the globe, a "transnational society" or a great "transnational village" did not coalesce. The country of origin and the diaspora did not form a coherent sociocultural space, despite the diverse "flows" between them. Many emigrants upheld their native language, customs, and cultural practices, but unconsciously adopted new ideas and behaviors at the same time. In 1920, American authorities estimated that one-third of Slovenes and one-quarter of Croats had already been integrated within the American melting pot. By the end of the 1920s, 60 percent of Yugoslav immigrants had taken American citizenship.[156] Migrant groups did not simply reflect their society of origin, but instead developed a new understanding of community through socialization and acculturation. At some point, many groups assimilated completely within the new culture. A family name was often the only indicator that remained of one's ancestry.[157] National traditions were supplemented by new social identities and interests in the receiving country, such as those represented by workers' associations and socialist organizations.

Many dimensions of nationalization and globalization were closely intertwined; one was unimaginable without the other. A dramatic increase in geographic mobility brought not just a small elite, but large cross-sections of the population, into contact with foreign worlds—especially through labor migration. In a foreign location, differences between the "self" and the "other" were readily evident and possibly assumed greater psychological importance. National identity took on new meaning in a global context. This became politically significant as transnational actors like Fan Noli capitalized on the historical moment by thinking nationally and acting globally. They acted as agents of "glocalization," establishing ties between a local, regional, and global public—between Harvard and the traditional hostels known as *hans*. Globally connected actors like Noli could now use foreign locations as their stage for publicizing and garnering national support across borders and continents. Decades earlier, the revolutions of 1848 had already highlighted the transnational dimension of nationalism. And now, for the first time, telecommunications and the steam engine provided a practical means for thinking about and activating the deterritorialized national community within a global context. The diaspora could, for example, set the nationalist agenda and attract ideological, political, and financial support. Transnational media and voluntary associations emerged as new global actors, upholding the connection between emigrants and their homelands. For nationalism and national movements (and this is a general observation, applicable to other phenomena as well), synchronic occurrences within an expanded global context were nearly as important as long-term diachronic processes within a single country. Exchange between continents played an increasingly important role in the emergence of new ideas, forms of awareness, and groups of historical actors.

The Effects of Globalization

Beginning in the 1870s, the world economy underwent a fundamental transformation. Unparalleled growth in productivity, trade, and investments, along with improved channels of transportation and communication, multiplied the quantity of goods that were moved from place to place. More states (including those in southeastern Europe) participated in world trade, and new technological advances increased mobility. An integrated, global economic system emerged. The concentration of capital and enterprises accelerated, while international agreements and monetary standards encouraged the growth of multinational companies that expanded across continents. Foreign capital investments grew much faster than production, as did the proportion of world income derived from trade. In the decades before 1914, economic integration reached a level that was not reached again until the late twentieth century, following the two world wars and a longer phase of deglobalization.[158]

How did the expansion and consolidation of international systems of finance and trade specifically affect southeastern Europe? Did globalization encourage industrial development and rising prosperity, or did it instead entrench poverty and economic dependency? Through integration, could the Balkan lands succeed in catching up to the industrial states' level of development?

In 1878, although Serbia, Montenegro, Romania, and Bulgaria had become independent states that for the first time were able to develop their own trade and economic policies, their scope of action remained limited. The Austro-Hungarian government did not disguise its economic interests while negotiating the terms of the new Balkan order at the Congress of Berlin. These included favorable trade treaties, the construction of railway networks, and a strong voice in oversight of the Danube, which was declared neutral from its mouth to the Iron Gates by a European commission. Habsburg entrepreneurs, traders, and businesspeople saw the Balkans and the Near East as their "natural market." In response to the world economic crisis, states had given up free trade in favor of rigid protectionism after 1873. Vienna pursued two goals. First, it sought to protect its own economy from cheap agricultural imports, and second, it sought new markets for industrial products. In the spirit of informal imperialism, the Viennese diplomats ensured that the Treaty of Berlin set low import and transit duties for the Balkan states.[159]

Significant parts of the treaty dealt with railway construction, which had already begun in the 1850s. In the 1860s, international investors backed the construction of an Oriental railway that led from Vienna to Budapest, Belgrade, Sofia, Edirne, and Istanbul, connecting the Balkan markets with western and central Europe. The significance of southeastern Europe as a transit area for goods headed toward the Mediterranean only increased after the opening of the Suez Canal in 1869. At the Congress of Berlin in 1878, Austria-Hungary obligated Serbia, Bulgaria, and the Ottoman Empire to complete the railway network at their own expense. Vienna saw this network as essential to its economic and military penetration of southeastern Europe and the Near East. Serbia and Bulgaria founded state railroads, which granted Austria-Hungary preferential rates. Turkey was obliged to construct a railway line in Macedonia to the port of Thessaloniki, and to connect it with the railways of the other Balkan lands. Thus, the pace of railway construction picked up speed at the end of the 1870s. By 1914, there were 2,175 miles of railroad in Romania, 1,300 in Bulgaria, and 620 in Serbia. Even so, these countries' rail networks remained comparatively sparse. In Bulgaria and Serbia, there was about one mile of railroad for every 31.5 square miles of land. In Germany and England, by contrast, there was one mile of railroad for just 5.6 square miles of land.[160]

Nevertheless, railway construction gave work to many people; it stimulated mining, industry, and engineering, and it significantly increased mobility and invigorated foreign trade. As the transport of goods accelerated and multiplied, traditional trade fairs and caravan routes lost their earlier significance.[161]

Thessaloniki was among the cities that experienced an economic boom. The city was home to the third most important port in the Ottoman Empire. Between 1880 and 1912, the volume of goods traded in Thessaloniki doubled from one to two million tons. There were railway connections to Vienna and Istanbul. New local factories produced flannel, woolen, and cotton products, as well as cigarettes. Important exports included leather, silkworms, raw materials for textiles, and especially tobacco, the production of which took off around the turn of the century. Thirty-eight of fifty large companies in the city were owned by Jewish families (whom we got to know in Chapter 4). The majority of these families specialized in the import-export business.[162] Conversely, more English cotton and linen fabrics, Prussian iron and steel products, Austrian shoes and clothing, and other manufactured goods began to appear at local markets and trade fairs.

Given the antiquated state of transportation, railway construction was an urgent necessity on one hand, but a great financial burden on the other. The Balkan states had to keep assuming new debt in order to meet their obligations from the Treaty of Berlin. In 1914, together with Russia, they were the largest borrowers within Europe, with the majority of foreign capital coming from France and Germany.[163] Debt and interest payments grew steadily. Serbia, for example, spent almost one-third of its budget on servicing its debt after the turn of the century.[164] Foreign loans came with political conditions, and many people within the borrowing countries sharply criticized their governments' dependence on lenders. The newspaper *Macedonia* warned that "it won't be long before we find ourselves, much to our regret, empty-handed and as naked and starving on dry hills as the Africans in their deserts."[165] Members of the Serbian parliament asked whether railway construction was leading them to the same fate "as the Indians after the discovery of America." They thought of Columbus, who "brought European culture to America, but also the chains of slavery."[166]

Railway construction contributed significantly to the constant financial distress of the southeastern European states. Worldwide foreign investment surged from six billion pounds sterling in 1870, to forty-three billion in 1914.[167] But foreign capital reached southeastern Europe (with

"Money or Life": Creditors threaten Greece. Honoré Daumier, *Le Charivari* 46 (February 15, 1850), 75. Paris.

the exception of Greece) relatively late, not until the 1890s—and even then, it came mostly in the form of government loans, not investments. Only Romanian oil production attracted a sizable number of international investors, who held 80 percent of all industry shares and 75 percent of bank capital. The Romanian government diverted half of its foreign credit to railway construction, and another one-fifth to the military, and the other Balkan states did the same. The Greek, Serbian, and Bulgarian states went bankrupt in the 1890s, after they could no longer cover their budget deficits or obtain foreign loans. Like the Ottoman Empire, which had already become insolvent in 1876, they were placed under international financial supervision.[168]

The transportation revolution consolidated the global system of trade and brought far-flung regions into closer contact, opening up new economic opportunities for the Balkan lands. Railroads accelerated economic penetration into the hinterlands, and steamships created faster connections to supraregional markets in the Ottoman Empire, central and western Europe, and around the Mediterranean basin. In the 1840s, the Austrian Steamship Company introduced the first regular ferry service between Thessaloniki and Istanbul. Additional companies—including Austrian Lloyd, the Ottoman Steamship Company, the French Messageries Maritimes, and the Italian Trinacria—took up operations and added direct connections to Istanbul, Galaţi, Beirut, and Alexandria. By 1900, 95 percent of maritime trade in the eastern Mediterranean was conducted by steamships.[169]

The transportation revolution renewed the great powers' interest in transcontinental connections, several of which passed through southeastern Europe. This called for new international regulations. The Treaty of Paris, which ended the Crimean War in 1856, declared the Danube an international river. A European Commission of the Danube was tasked with clearing the mouth of the river to facilitate trade. In 1869 the Suez Canal became an international hub, providing a direct, 102-mile-long connection between the Mediterranean Sea and the Indian Ocean. The canal realized a dream that had been harbored by the grand vizier Mehmed Sokollu back in the sixteenth century. The great project attracted merchants, engineers, soldiers, colonial officers, workers, and tourists from many countries, and it enhanced the strategic importance of southeastern Europe.[170]

The growth of foreign demand stimulated production, earnings, and sales in southeastern Europe. Residents began to cultivate more land, and they oriented their production toward commodities that were in high demand. Long-distance trade expanded because of falling transportation costs, and states took in more taxes and duties. Greater export profits could be invested in other economic sectors, like industry. But imperialist competition for markets and investment opportunities intensified at the same time, with a growing focus on the Balkans. As the "second" Industrial Revolution began around 1870, the dramatic expansion of western Europe's mechanical and electrical industries created new interest in minerals that were present in southeastern Europe: copper, aluminum, zinc, nickel, silver, and lead. Romanian and Albanian crude oil, which was used as fuel for ships, automobiles, and airplanes, later became a focus of private and state investors.

The consequences of globalization were immediately apparent in the agricultural sector. After 1870 Romania and Bulgaria sought to profit from a "wheat boom" by increasing production and exports. Export revenues in Romania increased by a factor of thirty-two between 1832 and 1913, and more than three-quarters of these exports were grain. By 1910 Romania had become the world's fourth-largest exporter of wheat, surpassing even the United States. Wheat and corn were now cultivated on 86 percent of all fields.[171] The tendency toward monoculture increased southeastern Europeans' dependence on the world market. By telegraph, merchants conducted business all over the globe, taking just one day for transactions that had once required months. There was growing competition from abroad, where inexpensive land, cheap labor, and technological and scientific progress increased productivity and lowered prices. Closer integration meant that global fluctuations in demand, production, and prices had an immediate effect on producers and consumers in southeastern Europe. Cotton exports from Macedonia, for example, could not keep pace with the supply from America, India, and Russia.[172] Southeastern Europe's deepening integration within the world market brought profitable sales opportunities on one hand, but dangerous dependence on the fluctuations of the global economy on the other.

The consequences were painfully apparent during the Great Depression of 1873–1896, as massive quantities of wheat flooded the European market from Russia and overseas because of global overproduction. After prices plummeted in 1873, the industrial states erected customs barriers to protect against cheap agricultural imports. Three-quarters of all exports from Bulgaria and Romania were grain, so these two countries were particularly devastated by the contraction of the markets and their commodities' loss in value. Greek and Serbian producers of dried fruit felt the crisis as well. In 1889, the British vice-consul in Macedonian Kavala remarked that "it was pitiful to see men weep while they were selling their crops" because prices had sunk so low.[173] Foreign trade picked up again only after the recovery of the world economy in the 1890s. There was an actual boom after 1900, and the per capita value of exports from Romania, Serbia, and Greece about doubled by 1913.[174]

Between 1850 and 1913, the value of exports from Serbia increased by a factor of five, and from Romania by a factor of fourteen. Yet exports had little effect on overall economic growth and industrialization, primarily because of high population growth (more than 1.0 to 1.5 percent each year) that also increased internal consumption.[175] In addition, low agricultural productivity limited the growth of exports.[176] The volume of trade increased in absolute numbers, but the export rate remained low. In 1910 Romania, it was 20 percent—and in Serbia, 8.8 percent, in Bulgaria, 6.5 percent, and in Greece, just 5.6 percent.[177] Thus, external trade did not encourage large-scale capital formation.

Unfavorable terms of trade placed the agricultural countries at a further disadvantage. Raw materials and agricultural products were inexpensive on the world markets, while industrial goods cost more. The price gap became an increasingly ominous problem for southeastern Europeans. Because newly created wealth tended to move toward the manufacturing sectors, Western industrial countries continuously widened their competitive advantage over the agricultural countries of southeastern Europe. Between 1860 and 1914, Great Britain improved its global terms of trade by one-fifth. This meant that if British exports remained constant, on the eve of the First World War the empire could import 20 percent more raw materials than it had fifty years earlier.[178]

In the 1890s, nearly all developed European states and Japan followed the United States in placing new tariffs on industrial products.[179] The industrial states' neomercantilist protectionism and unfavorable terms of trade brought policy changes to the Balkan states and the Ottoman Empire as well. They, too, placed import duties on finished goods and adopted more assertive trade policies. Romania waged a customs war against Austria-Hungary between 1885 and 1891, seeking to assert economic independence. Serbia—which sent 88 percent of its exports, mostly cattle, to the Habsburg Monarchy—followed suit in 1906. When the Serbian government refused to accept an unfavorable trade agreement, Austria-Hungary closed its borders to Serbian goods. The customs war lasted until 1911, allowing Serbia finally to break free of its trade dependency.[180]

Integration in the world economy had very different effects on all kinds of manufacturing and trades, depending on region, economic sector, and type of production. Between 1830 and the outbreak of the First World War, clothing and thread imports in the Ottoman Empire increased more than one hundred times over. Textile manufacturers fell onto hard times across

Tobacco caravan, Plovdiv, 1914. Regional State Archive, Plovdiv.

the whole Ottoman Empire. Before the empire's free trade agreement with Great Britain in 1838, 97 percent of its demand for textiles was met by domestic production. By 1870, 75 percent of consumer textile purchases were foreign imports.[181]

Western competition devastated not only the Turkish textile industry but also its counterparts in Bulgaria, Macedonia, and Greece—spinning mills were affected first, followed by weaving mills after 1870. More than two-thirds of textile jobs in the Ottoman Empire were lost. By the eve of the First World War, the production of hand-spun thread had shrunk by 93 percent.[182]

Globalization did not, however, threaten all branches of the industry. The production of cotton goods almost completely fell victim to competition from Western imports, but the protoindustrial processing of sheep's wool in the mountainous regions of Bulgaria, Greece, and Macedonia held on. Traditional woolen cloth and braid (*aba, šajak,* and *gajtan*) in the Ottoman Empire and the Balkan states remained cheaper and more popular than English fabrics for some time. Silk production even expanded because of strong European demand.[183]

Integration within the world market did not automatically result in deindustrialization. In fact, some traditional trades and sectors of manufacturing in the Balkans successfully made the leap to industrial production.

The decisive factor was whether the products found markets beyond their own region—and thus, whether substantial quantities could be sold by long-distance traders. In 1870, the Bulgarian town of Koprivshtitsa sent about three hundred tons of semifinished textile goods by caravan to Istanbul, accompanied by a troop of tailors and apprentices. From the Ottoman capital, Bulgarian woolen cloth, braid, and other products made their way to Egypt, the Anatolian coast, and the Aegean Islands.[184] The town of Samokov sold its wares in Bosnia and Albania; Kotel found customers in Greece. In the 1870s, wares from Plovdiv, especially silk, were sent to England, France, Germany, Russia, and the Ottoman capital. The cultivation and sales of tobacco likewise grew exponentially.[185]

The industrialization of southeastern Europe differed from that of the rest of the continent in a variety of ways: it took off later, more slowly, and in other branches of industry. Only after the mid-nineteenth century did certain trades mechanize production at all. Iron machinery replaced wooden spinning wheels and looms; water, steam, and coal power reduced the work of human hands. New, regional industries developed—including the production of glass and ceramics, electrical devices, and agricultural machines, as well as the mining of coal, copper, lead, and zinc. But industrialization progressed slowly until the First World War, especially in Serbia, Bulgaria, and Greece. Small farmers could hardly turn a profit, so there was a shortage of capital for any investment. An efficient system of banking and loans did not yet exist. Moreover, widespread poverty kept demand for finished goods low, so the domestic market provided little stimulus for production. Industrialization progressed faster only in regions with a more prosperous peasantry, or where large estates brought higher profits, as in Romania and Croatia.

Since the 1880s the state had assumed a more active role in promoting industrialization.[186] Legislation passed in Romania in 1887, in Bulgaria in 1894, and in Serbia in 1898 made importing machinery easier, and offered tax breaks and other incentives to lower production and transportation costs. The states also guaranteed the purchase of domestic industrial products. In addition, Romania took steps to nationalize its economy with legislation that denied citizenship to Jews, forcing them out of industry and banking, and that ensured Romanians would hold an equal management role in foreign subsidiaries. State commissions were given only to companies that were majority Romanian-owned.[187]

Thanks to state intervention—but also an improving economy—industrialization advanced more rapidly after 1900, although there were differences between regions and sectors. Serbia, Bulgaria, and Romania succeeded in increasing industrial production by 7 to 10 percent each year.[188] In 1896, only 13 percent of finished goods sold in Bulgaria were locally produced, but this proportion had increased to 43 percent by 1911. The number of factory employees increased sixfold; capital investments rose by a factor of eight.[189] But the gap with developed European countries remained wide. In 1900 per capita industrial production in Greece was just 48 percent of the European average; in Serbia, it was 39 percent, and in Bulgaria and Romania, 33 percent.[190] Compared to the most highly developed countries, the discrepancy was even wider. In 1913, per capita industrial output in southeastern Europe was only 4 to 6 percent of that in the United States and Great Britain.[191]

In contrast to the societies that pioneered the Industrial Revolution, industry in southeastern Europe tended to develop out of traditional handicrafts, rather than workshops or cottage industry. This had significant consequences for economic development. Whereas the leading industrial sector in England was textiles—and in Germany, coal, iron, and steel—mills, breweries, food production, and timber led the way in southeastern Europe. This distinctive pattern of development derived in part from the available raw materials and technologies, but also from specific export demands and competition on the world markets. In 1910 food processing constituted 55 percent of the total value of Serbian industrial production; textiles, only 8 percent. Timber was initially dominant in Croatia, where industrial production diversified more broadly only after 1900.[192] In Bosnia-Herzegovina, the Austro-Hungarian administration promoted the development of heavy industry.[193]

Depending on the leading sector of industrialization, it may or may not have a spin-off effect on other economic sectors. Because the processing of foodstuffs and wood did not require extensive start-up costs or high technical competence, there was little incentive to invest in the metal industry, machinery, or engineering. The main export commodities, such as Greek raisins and Serbian prunes, also did not promote industrialization. Even Romania did not foster an industrial spin-off. After 1900, crude oil made up about 10 percent of Romanian exports, but all of the processing took place elsewhere.[194]

The experience of southeastern Europe contradicts the thesis that late-comers generally benefit from the "privilege of backwardness" (Alexander Gerschenkron) because they can bypass certain phases of development through the import of modern technologies and international capital.[195] Despite state intervention, the industrialization gap between the Balkan countries and those of more developed societies continued to widen. Before 1914, only 14 percent of Serbia's national income came from industrial production; in Romania, it was 20 percent. All of the other southeastern European countries lay somewhere in between.[196] The state could provide some assistance through loans, tax reductions, and tariff policy, and also by supporting education. But it was an illusion to think that the chasm was easily bridged. For one thing, a much higher level of investment and specialized knowledge was needed to build a competitive factory at the end of the century than it had been one hundred years earlier, when the western and central European countries had begun to industrialize. And even with duty-free imports, contemporary technologies were so expensive that the southeastern Europeans often had to buy used or outmoded equipment. Moreover, qualified workers who knew how to use the latest technologies were in short supply. Thus, the potential to save on expensive development costs through imports existed only in theory. In practice, the necessary conditions were lacking.[197]

All in all, the southeastern European countries profited from their growing integration within the world economy. The national economies grew, industrialization took off, and incomes increased. Calculations and estimates vary, but it is plausible that per capita gross domestic product rose by as much as 1 percent per year in all southeastern European countries between 1870 and 1913.[198] While the rate of growth was low compared to other states, the cumulative effect was great. On the eve of the First World War, the Balkan states' per capita production had increased by half since 1870. Consumption expanded, and many new professions and fields of specialization emerged.[199] But because the economies of the industrial countries grew faster than the agrarian ones, the prosperity gap widened. Before the beginning of the First World War, Greece had attained 39.3 percent of the European standard of living; Bulgaria, 36.6 percent, and Serbia, just 31.2 percent.[200]

In contrast to earlier historical studies, which looked for causes of backwardness, today's global history tends to ask why the industrial states expanded so dynamically—an unprecedented occurrence at that time. This had to do with technical ingenuity, modern institutions, a favorable climate, and a religious worldview that was compatible with capitalism—but above all, with the availability of raw materials and labor in the colonies. The Western economic boom was grounded in "a global network of land, labor, transport, manufacturing, and sale"—a transcontinental system of production and distribution that had no rival.[201]

In summarizing the problems that the rise of the industrialized states and global competition brought to southeastern Europe, three bundles of issues emerge. First, the Balkan lands struggled with structural problems that made it difficult for them to meet the demands of the capitalist world economy. National historiographies tend to assign blame for persistent poverty and backwardness to centuries of exploitation under the "Ottoman yoke." This may seem to be an exaggeration to Western and Turkish historians, but—at least for the eighteenth and nineteenth centuries—it should not be dismissed out of hand. The Ottoman state skimmed off a significant portion of revenues, and the Balkan lands inherited social and economic structures that initially hindered the mobility of labor, property, capital, and goods. The historical legacies of Ottoman rule included high demographic growth, low agricultural productivity, chronic shortages of domestic capital, and high dependence on foreign credit. There were also negative foreign trade balances and weak domestic demand, lagging efforts to build up industry and infrastructure, and insufficient education and health care. All this meant that in the nineteenth century (and to a certain extent, in the twentieth), production in southeastern Europe cost more, but lagged behind the developed West in quantity and quality.

A second set of problems had to do with external economic and political conditions. Dependencies, low export quotas, unequal trading relationships, and imperialist competition reinforced the region's peripheral status. For Germany, southeastern Europe became a supplementary zone of economic activity *(Ergänzungsraum),* whereas Austria-Hungary treated the region more as an ersatz colony. Quasi-hegemonic structures and foreign competition slowed growth, innovation, and investment in the less developed countries of Romania, Bulgaria, Montenegro, and Serbia. These countries could only partially realize a development strategy that relied on using profits from foreign trade to invest in domestic industry.

Third, contingent factors—the particular timing of the late take-off— also played a role. The later a country began to industrialize, the greater problems it had catching up.[202] The young Balkan states entered the global markets just as an unfavorable world economy sent agricultural prices plunging, and most states had moved toward economic nationalism. They reduced the competitive pressure by instituting their own protectionist policies, and—as the world economy turned around—they began to experience industrial "mini-spurts."

All in all, the countries of southeastern Europe joined the process of globalization under structural and economic conditions that were less favorable than their industrial forerunners. The interplay of internal, external, and cyclical economic factors made it difficult to break the vicious cycle of poverty. Both an export-oriented development strategy (increasing the amount of exports) and import substitution (building up national industries) were difficult to implement. Globalization accelerated the overall socioeconomic transformation of southeastern Europe, but it also widened the gap between poor and wealthy countries.

The Colonialization of Perceptions

As the Eastern Question intensified, the Balkans moved to the forefront of European attentions. Within the mental map of Europe—shaped by Crusades, Ottoman wars, and the Renaissance—the region had once been considered part of "the Orient." But since the Serbian and Greek uprisings of the early nineteenth century, "the Balkans" was increasingly perceived as its own distinct entity. In Germany, Johann Wolfgang von Goethe, the Brothers Grimm, the historian Leopold von Ranke, the geographer Felix Kanitz, and the philhellenes contributed to a romanticized image of Christian peoples who were fighting heroically against Ottoman despotism. The Great Eastern Crisis and the Congress of Berlin, when the great powers competed openly over the division of former Ottoman possessions, marked a shift toward perceptions that were more strongly colored by imperialist interests. Oriental clichés and stereotypes were transferred to "the Balkans," so that the region began to appear overwhelmingly anarchic, violent, and backward—thereby compelling the powers to reinstate order and civilize its inhabitants.

In contrast to "Orientalism," "Balkanism" did not imagine the object of its fantasy as a polar opposite to the European self, but rather as a zone of transition between East and West, largely because of its majority Christian population. Similar to the Orient, the Balkans exuded an exotic mysticism—including the romanticism of simple peasant life, the eroticism of the harem, the adventures of fierce, noble warriors, and the horrors of archaic violence. Countless ethnographic portraits steeped in colorful folklore made the rounds. All this provided a wistful, romantic contrast to the uncertainties brought forth by the technical advances of the modern era. The Balkans became a space of projection for repressed fantasies and escapism.[203]

The rapidly developing mass press and new medium of photography encouraged the spread of the Balkanist discourse. The first illustrated war reportage came from the Crimean War. The *Illustrated London News,* the German *Illustrirte Zeitung,* and other newspapers covered the Great Eastern Crisis with pictures as well as words. The news, commentary, and readers' letters pages teemed with emotional depictions of politically sensitive events, and new visual media such as photography and lithography conveyed (or sometimes feigned) authenticity. The London *Daily News* reports of journalists Januarius MacGahan and Eugene Schuyler on the "Bulgarian horrors" helped to stir up popular opinion.[204] Because of censorship, however, war correspondents' reports on frontline events were generally secondhand accounts. The London *Daily Chronicle* wryly noted that many reporters wrote about battles "which have only been fought in the heated imagination of the author." The press nevertheless outdid itself with spectacular embellishments about carved-out eyes, severed tongues, and other grisly details. In 1876 the *Kölnische Zeitung* complained that such reports were based largely on the "tangles of lies" that were spun by the official dispatches of the warring capitals.[205] These stories fed the voyeurism of a sensation-seeking public.

These events coincided with burgeoning scholarly, literary, and artistic interest in foreign cultures, including the "wild Balkans." Balkan themes were a familiar staple of nineteenth-century bourgeois culture, which was fascinated by things foreign. In the 1890s, German author Karl May wrote about the "land of the Skipetars" and the "ravines of the Balkans," which he had never seen. Bram Stoker, who had likewise never set foot in the region, invented his fictional protagonist Count Dracula, a Transylvanian vampire, around the same time. The character's inspiration was the fifteenth-century Wallachian prince Vlad, who had fought bravely against the Turks and impaled his political opponents en masse. The bloodthirsty figure united exoticism and barbarism and confirmed the darkest stereotypes of Eastern atrocities, in line with the zeitgeist of a Western public that was unsettled by Balkan upheavals and technological change.

Nothing symbolizes the relationship between Balkanism and modernity as tangibly as the Orient Express. The bestselling author Bram Stoker even had his title character take the famous train to his terrifying adventures. In the twentieth century, too, it became the backdrop for detective and mystery stories by Eric Ambler, Agatha Christie, Graham Greene, and Alfred Hitchcock. The Orient Express was a parable of technical progress, cosmopolitan lifestyles, and a modernized mobility that pointed southeast. It symbolized repressed anxieties about the unforeseeable upheavals of modernity, and it became a metaphor for the journey into an unknown, dangerous future.[206]

The Balkans claimed the space of an Orientalized, semi-European region on the mental map of Western observers, unsettling progressive Europe with its wars, barbarism, and infighting among many small states. The image of "Balkanization" was reinforced by reports of atrocities and mass expulsions during the crises in Bulgaria and Bosnia, the ongoing guerrilla war in Macedonia, the assassinations of the royal family in Serbia, and later the Balkan Wars of 1912 / 13.[207]

The powers' imperialist interests were cloaked in the metaphors of a barbaric Balkan Peninsula that needed to be civilized and tamed. For Austria-Hungary, which possessed no territories outside of Europe, the Balkans became a kind of ersatz colony. At the Congress of Berlin, when the great powers divided up northern Africa and parts of southeastern Europe from the possessions of the Ottoman Empire, the Habsburg emperor secured his country's occupation of Bosnia-Herzegovina. This did not amount to world power, but the *Bosnische Post* agreed with Bismarck: "That little slice of Herzegovina could well be worth more than the whole of East Africa."[208]

Even as Western nationalism, imperialism, and racism unleashed unimaginable outbreaks of violence in the colonies, the topos of endemic violence was projected only onto the Balkans within public awareness. This repression occurred on both sides. Southeastern Europeans blamed Western racism and western Europeans for the barbarism of the Balkans, thereby externalizing feelings of guilt and relieving their own consciences.[209]

Growing South Slav nationalism in the provinces of the empire contradicted the self-image of a good and just Habsburg civilizing mission. But the extreme measures taken in Africa and Asia were not possible among European possessions. The Balkan lands were nearby, and many people from the provinces migrated to the Habsburg core territories, particularly Vienna, looking for work. Vienna's population quintupled in the fifty years before the First World War, not least because of the influx of members of the nationalities who were seeking employment. The imperial center and periphery were thus much more closely connected than Western capitals and colonies outside Europe could ever be. This promoted a "frontier Orientalism" that was directed toward the empire's own territory. The southeastern European lands were merely "semi-foreign," unlike the altogether religiously and culturally exotic lands beyond Europe's boundaries.[210]

The colonialism of perceptions was supported by an underlying hegemonial understanding. The metaphor of the "family of nations," led by Emperor Francis Joseph as the benevolent father, signaled that cultural differences could be reconciled through Habsburg imperial culture.[211] Vienna worked to build unity by promoting its imperial ideology. In Bosnia-Herzegovina, the Austrian emperor commissioned the excavation of archaeological remains from the Roman era, emphasizing the supposed heritage of the Holy Roman Empire. Ottoman structures like the famous stone bridge in Mostar were summarily declared part of the Roman heritage.[212] New buildings were constructed in the Habsburg "universal style," or in the neo-historic, pseudo-Moorish style of the Islamic School for Theology and Sharia Law and the city hall (Vijećnica) of Sarajevo. "All that was cruel and grasping [in Habsburg rule] was concealed by the dignity and glitter of traditional forms," Ivo Andrić wrote in his famous novel, *The Bridge on the Drina*. "The people still feared the authorities but in much the same way as they feared sickness and death."[213]

Ethnography also contributed to the colonialist discourse. A newly founded regional museum in Sarajevo presented exhibitions on history, geography, and anthropology—an ethnological display that reflected the spirit of its times. Occupation authorities promoted crafts like carpet weaving and saber making, less to support local artisans than to invent a souvenir industry that was oriented toward the Viennese market. Prototypes were made in Vienna that "improved upon the taste of the natives . . . accommodating the traditional style to the needs of our time . . . and ensuring that Bosnian products will be sold and used in homes."[214]

The rest of the world, too, needed to witness the good work of the Habsburg Monarchy in the Balkans. At the Paris world exhibition of 1900, the regime presented a Bosnian pavilion built in the neo-Moorish style with handcrafted, folkloric adornments—and plenty of colonialist and Orientalist stereotypes. Bosnia-Herzegovina appeared as a once-wild land, which had been tamed, explored, developed, and civilized by the monarchy.

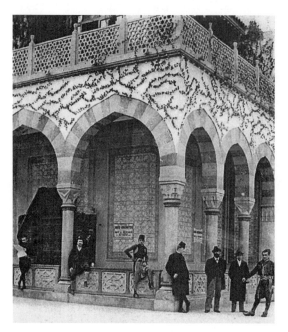

The Bosnian pavilion at the Paris world exhibition,
1900. National Museum of Bosnia and Herzegovina,
Sarajevo.

Ethnographers showed how after the inferior Asiatic rule of the Turks, it
was now the responsibility of Europe to "reclaim" this land. The proud
emperor possessed a model European protectorate, which could serve as an
example to the great powers in Africa and Asia.[215]

Many natives did, however, sympathize with the Austro-Hungarian approach, especially when they benefited personally from it. One of them
was the writer and journalist Milena Mrazović, the daughter of a local government official from Croatian Bjelovar. After the Austrian occupation,
she and her parents moved to Bosnia. She interned with the German-
language *Bosnische Post* in Sarajevo, and she became its editor at the age of
twenty-six. She later acquired the newspaper as well as its print shop. She
said that "good fortune" led her to marry an Austrian eye doctor named
Preindlsberger, who worked in the Koševo hospital. He was among the
burgeoning ranks of the *kuferaši*—civil servants, officers, engineers, and
other specialists who had come to Bosnia from the monarchy and were seen
as "carpetbaggers" (or literally, "suitcase carriers") by the natives. The mother
of two later wrote for the Austrian newspapers *Österreichische Rundschau*

and the *Reichspost* under the male pseudonym "Milan." She became the first female member of the Anthropological Society in Vienna.

The *Wiener Stimme* described Milena Mrazović-Preindlsberger as "one of the most remarkable personalities of Austrian Bosnia." Indeed, she traveled extensively all over the region, by railroad and on horseback, and she was also an amateur composer. An acquaintance said that behind her "delicate form" and "ladylike grace" lay a "bold male spirit . . . with admirable versatility."[216] An Austrian government official, on the other hand, found her to be insufferable, combative, and hysterical. He must have been unsettled by her powers of assertion, which were quite unusual for women of her day.[217] "A female journalist was still unheard of at that time," the *Wiener Stimme* later explained, "and then Europe's first female political editor-in-chief appeared in Bosnia, of all places."[218]

While the *Bosnische Post* was formally independent, in practice it sought to encourage the Austrian business community to invest in the occupied provinces, and also to popularize the Austrian protectorate. Milena Mrazović did this to the best of her ability, leading the Sarajevo historian Vladislav Skarić to scorn her perpetual "hymns to wise government policy." In countless articles and commentaries, she reproduced and adapted the topoi of a colonial discourse that was familiar outside of Europe, too—for example, the "motherland" (in this case, Austria), and "the youngest child entrusted to her care." She further emphasized that Austria and Bosnia-Herzegovina were separated by a "cultural border" that distinguished them from one another like "good and evil, day and night, prose and poetry." On one side, she saw "modern culture"; on the other, the "Middle Ages."[219]

She lauded the railroad as a symbol of modernity and progress, which—thanks to Habsburg rule—connected Sarajevo with Višegrad. Its opposite was a fabled, Oriental Bosnia. In her editions of Bosnian fairy tales, she told of the "noble, delicate sons of the golden Bosna and the brave Herzegovina." She depicted painterly, "heroic" landscapes, melancholy Slavic temperaments, and deeds of exemplary honesty, conscientiousness, and courage. Her stories were embellished with generous doses of Oriental color, Islamized names and customs, and—of course—the presence of the harem.[220] Folklorists doubted the authenticity of her fairy tales, which she presumably revised for effect.

Orientalist and Balkanist lines of division continued to develop in the first quarter of the twentieth century. The "imperialism of the imagination" produced cultural stereotypes and clichés such as the "powder keg," which justified military interventions.[221] In conjunction with a police mission sent to Macedonia in 1903, one Austrian commentator opined about the "spiritually and economically unsophisticated population," which was driven by an "animalistic lust for murder" and "unconscionable hatred."[222] What else could be more urgent than finally taming this barbarism?

The persistent topos of Serbians as the "murderers of kings" emerged after the assassination of King Alexander Obrenović and his wife Draga in 1903. His successor, Peter I, no longer looked to Austria as an informal protector and instead brought his country closer to France and Russia. In Austrian propaganda, Serbia now appeared as an "outpost of Russia," and as the driving force of nationalism and greater Serbian irredentism.[223] The cliché of a notoriously violent and outwardly aggressive Serbia received further embellishment as tensions between Vienna and Belgrade increased, and especially as nationalism within the Habsburg Monarchy continued to grow. During the First World War, these culminated in the battle cry "Serbia must die!" *(Serbien muss sterbien!)* Colonialist discourse joined with other ideologemes as necessary—providing cover, for example, for atrocities against civilians in the First and Second World Wars. An Austrian combatant in 1914 confirmed that the Serbs were not viewed as counterparts worthy of respect, but instead as "characterless, mean, deceitful opponents."[224]

Depending on the situation, these stereotypes could apply to the rest of the Balkans as well. They hardened into a tough essentialism that persisted even after 1918. Rebecca West admitted that "violence was, indeed, all I knew of the Balkans," before she set out for Yugoslavia in the 1920s. Agatha Christie brought the point home by inventing the state of "Herzoslovakia" in one of her mystery stories: "Principal rivers, unknown. Principal mountains, also unknown, but fairly numerous. Capital, Ekarest. Population, chiefly brigands. Hobby, assassinating kings and having revolutions."[225] The negative stereotypes of "greater Serbia" and "royal assassins" that developed before 1914 enjoyed a remarkable comeback in journalistic depictions of the Yugoslav wars of the 1990s, and most recently, in new literature about the First World War.[226]

What images of the Balkans did actors in the region seek to produce and popularize themselves? The world public was an important resource for the national movements. Paintings of murderous deeds and wartime upheaval by the Frenchman Eugène Delacroix, the Czech Jaroslav Čermák,

Abduction by Bashi-Bazouks in a Christian Village in Herzegovina, Jaroslav Čermák, 1861. Dahesh Museum of Art, New York.

and the Russian Vasily Vereshchagin created an independent Balkan iconography that adapted archetypal motifs from European art history. Čermák's depictions of uprisings in Herzegovina—for example, *Spoils of War* and *Abduction by Bashi-Bazouks*—even found their way into the illustrated press.[227] These images can be read as allegories of the ideals of liberty, which were suppressed not only in the Balkans, but throughout much of Europe during the restoration era. The Polish artist Antoni Piotrowski's painting, *The Massacre in Batak,* and photographs of scenes that he staged on site, can still be seen in schoolbooks and museums today.[228]

The national movements, which hoped to attract international support, welcomed the mediatizing of current events through history painting—and especially through telegraphy, photography, and the mass press. The Macedonian Revolutionary Organization understood the importance of staging its assassinations for the media, whether the goal was to encourage loyalty and obedience in its own ranks or to attract international attention. Its ring-leaders gave orders to kill disobedient Christians so that it appeared as if the culprits were Ottoman security forces. Two witnesses had to pledge in court "with full conviction and assurance" that a murder had been com-mitted by tyrannical agents of the state. The Ottoman authorities reacted angrily, responding to terrorist attacks with executions and torture—which incited additional acts of revenge from the guerrillas and new repressive government measures, creating a never-ending spiral of violence.[229] Leon Trotsky observed that "when they prepared to explode a bomb, they first, and very competently, ascertained what echo it would produce in the 'in-fluential' European press."[230] Reports about the abduction of a female American missionary and the bombings of an Ottoman bank and French steamship created a furor in the media after the turn of the century.[231]

In the nationally impassioned nineteenth century, Balkan actors con-tributed to the discourse of Orientalism that remains alive today. This discourse, briefly stated, held the "Ottoman yoke" responsible for back-wardness, despotic oppression, cultural decline, and loss of identity. Even in popular culture, "the Turk" appeared as an uncouth foreigner, as one Greek proverb illustrates: "When the bristles of a pig become silk, then the Turk will accept culture and the just order of things."[232] Folk epics and heroic songs (such as those about Prince Marko or the Kosovo legend) by contrast, romanticized ideals of honor, bravery, martyrdom, and heroic re-sistance against foreign rule.

The governments of the Balkan states used world exhibitions to present their nations to an external audience, since "even educated Americans . . . viewed Bulgaria as one of the lands of Central Africa," as one correspon-dent remarked in Chicago in 1893.[233] Since 1851, expositions had been held in rotating locations; their goal was to curate and present the global diver-sity of countries, cultures, and scientific progress. In addition to amazing inventions such as moving sidewalks and Ferris wheels, the achievements of the European nation-states were placed on display alongside the exoti-cism of the cultures and colonies they ruled.[234] World exhibitions became a tourist attraction for southeastern Europeans of means; visiting a world's fair was a sign of status. In 1867 the Greek banker Andreas Syngros re-placed his planned pilgrimage with a trip to the Paris Expo.[235]

The Romanian principalities began to participate in the world exhibi-tions in 1867; Serbia followed suit in 1889, and Bulgaria in 1893. National committees were tasked with selecting—or in some cases, constructing—identifying characteristics and traditions. The Balkan countries' pavilions showcased the eclectic architecture of newly created national styles, which combined folkloric, religious, as well as modern elements. Presenting a national historical master narrative to the world public helped to solidify conceptions of "the nation." Identities were created, reinforcing feelings of communal belonging.[236] Peasant artifacts and artisanal and folk creations were displayed alongside newer high cultural, scholarly, and technical achievements. The Bulgarian pavilion featured genre paintings of girls in traditional dress, market scenes in Sofia, and depictions of Turkish atrocities. In the same vein, Serbia showed off monumental oil paintings of the Kosovo memorial and the coronation of the medieval tsar Dušan, while the Greeks exhibited ancient artifacts.[237] Serbia further impressed visitors with a calculating machine that could solve differential equations; its inventor, Mihailo Petrović, won multiple awards for his achievement.[238]

Although they did not yet have their own nation-state, Yugoslav-oriented artists and intellectuals used the world exhibition as an opportunity to present a supraregional South Slav culture shared by Serbs, Croats, and Slovenes.[239] In 1910, the Croatian sculptor Ivan Meštrović exhibited the model of a "Vidovdan temple" in the Viennese Secession building. It featured a number of large Caryatides representing figures from the epic Kosovo cycle. The architectural-sculptural ensemble was meant to honor the idea that the South Slav peoples constituted a single Yugoslav nation, which was imagined as a primordial entity, united by common descent, language, and culture.[240] The British historian R. W. Seton-Watson remarked that "the national poetry of the Southern Slavs knows nothing of the artificial frontiers by which alien conquerers have sought to isolate and disunite the race."[241] World exhibitions not only provided a stage for presenting the nation to an international public; they also encouraged new forms of symbolic expression. At the world's fairs, the relationship between a globalized public and national identity formation was close and mutually reinforcing.

Serbian, Romanian, and Bulgarian intellectuals criticized how the political establishment exoticized their countries at the world exhibitions by openly imitating Western cultures and even reproducing their stereotypes. The architect Anton Tornyov made fun of the eclectic new "Bulgarian style" of his homeland's pavilion, which looked like "a European colony that had just torn away the Turkish yoke." And Stefan Bobchev was troubled "when I look at our Bulgaria sitting so abashed, so modest and neatly dressed, as if it were ashamed of its poverty, here at this majestic, splendid, enormous table where the other nations are putting on a great show with their brilliant attire."[242]

It was, in fact, while visiting the 1893 world exhibition in Chicago that the writer Aleko Konstantinov invented one of the best-known figures of Bulgarian literature: the uncultivated rose oil peddler Bay Ganyo "Balkanski," who traveled through Europe and made blundering attempts to mimic Western civilization. His odor of sweat and garlic preceded him, and he wore an elegant Belgian cape with a worn-out Bulgarian sheepskin cap. By playing with the contrast between progress and backwardness, Bay Ganyo was a satire of the Bulgarian and southeastern European self. He became the most popular and most analyzed *Homo balkanicus*.[243]

Aleko Konstantinov did not want to poke fun of the backwardness of Bulgaria or the Balkans as a whole. Rather, his target was a certain type of unscrupulous, primitive parvenu from the liberal era. The figure of Bay Ganyo primarily reflected contemporary social criticism, rather than typical Balkan residents' understanding (or rejection) of their own identity. Similar to Aleko Konstantinov, the Romanian Ion Luca Caragiale and the Serb Branislav Nušić sent up the "semi-cultivated or, at best, falsely cultivated oligarchy" in their works for the theater.[244] In a satirical essay, Aleko Konstantinov even recommended to Bulgarian authorities that, rather than folklore and architectural kitsch, their pavilion should instead showcase electoral fraud and political assassinations.[245]

In later literary accounts, too, the topos of the backward Balkans appeared as a social and political critique against those in power, not as self-exoticization.[246] For the Serbian writer Jovan Dučić, the "Balkan Orient" of the 1920s remained "a true Turkish wasteland."[247] Similarly, in the 1930s the writer Miroslav Krleža sneered at the superficial modernization of the elite Hotel Esplanade in Zagreb: "Hot and cold water, French cuisine, roulette, lifts, uniformed bell-boys, *'on parle français,'* "Europe," good!'" But just a few steps away there were "open cesspits, stench, malaria, typhus . . . All grey, all disgusting, all offensive. All—Balkan, a sorry province."[248]

On the other hand, as the world grew together it became easier for the elites of southeastern Europe to place themselves on the side of the developed West. Since the 1870s, Bulgarian schoolchildren of second-grade age and older learned both Bulgarian history and "world history." Russian lesson plans taught the history of the Slavs alongside that of India and the

Near East.[249] Schoolbooks distinguished between civilized lands, including Bulgaria, and "barbarian" tribal societies. From translations of August Ludwig Schlözer's eighteenth-century *Universal-Historie,* it was understood that in prehistoric times the entire world had been "primitive," subsequently developing to higher stages of civilization. Why wouldn't southeastern Europe continue to advance?[250]

The prolific Romanian historian and politician Nicolae Iorga recognized that the global and the national exerted a mutual influence on one another.[251] In the 1920s, he wrote a four-volume history of human civilization in order to identify the historical location of the Romanian nation. He emphasized the Latin (and thus ancient) origins of the Romanians, as well as their supposed continuities with Eastern Roman civilization, which he brought to the point in his famous book title, *Byzantium after Byzantium.* He ordered his narrative in concentric circles: "First, the history of my country and my race, then the history of the entire Christian East and the Muslim Orient, and finally, last but not least, universal history."[252] By the end, one could recognize that Romania was one of the oldest cultural nations in the world, hardly touched by Ottoman influence. Clearly, the Romanians ought to be trusted with a regional leadership role.

The world was now perceived as a whole. Travel literature, news reports, and scholarly works about the geography, statistics, cartography, and ethnography of distant continents underwent a quantitative leap. Here, too, southeastern Europeans saw themselves on the side of progress. In 1885, the Belgian king Leopold II sent the Serb Kosta Dinić to serve as a doctor and judge in the Congo Free State, which had been created by the colonial powers. Dinić unambiguously saw himself as a representative of developed Europe. In his *Letters from the Congo,* he described the exoticism of the Dark Continent for the Serbian public: superstitions and rites, tattoos and body painting, polygamy and cannibalism. With colonial condescension, he depicted the "natives" as primitive, ungrateful, devious, and fickle, and he praised Leopold's efforts to "plant [the seeds of] civilization within his still untamed subjects."[253] The writer Rastko Petrović, who traveled 2,500 miles through Guinea, Sierra Leone, Sudan, and Senegal in the interwar era, affirmed colonialist discourse by making Africans the object, never the subject, of his narrative. He depicted African physicality, sexual licentiousness, and incest with disgust, while alluding to the foreign culture's erotic temptations. Thus, even from the Balkans, Africa represented mystery, anti-civilization, and the breaking of taboos;

(southeastern) Europeans sought to define themselves in opposition to these qualities.[254]

Images of the self and the foreign other coexisted in a complex reciprocal relationship. As the image of a primitive, anarchic, violent, and vicious Balkan culture and society (associated with the Orient) took shape in the years between the Congress of Berlin and the First World War, "the Balkans" displaced "European Turkey" on the mental map of the West. This shift provided readily comprehensible explanations for complex processes, demarcated friend and foe, and justified political goals and strategies. Depending on the historical context, these stereotypes could join with imperialist and colonialist ideologemes. Southeastern European elites helped to reproduce the Balkanist discourse—whether by drawing attention to themselves, or exercising social criticism. They were also not immune to colonialist arrogance. Establishing distance between themselves and the "archaic cultures" of Africa alleviated their own feelings of inferiority, allowing them to relocate themselves mentally on the side of the advanced West.

Belgrade, 1913

Early in the morning on August 13, 1913, a great crowd assembled on Šumadijska Street before a newly constructed triumphal arch. The people were impatiently awaiting the return of Crown Prince Alexander and his army from the Second Balkan War. Not long after the Bulgarian attack, Serbia had claimed impressive victories on all fronts. Frenetic cheering erupted when the military commander at last appeared with his general staff. In the name of the city, the mayor presented a magnificent saber to "the avenger of Kosovo, the victor of Kumanovo, the hero of Bitola" and his courageous soldiers. Then a memorial to Karadjordje, leader of the First Serbian Uprising, was unveiled on the Kalemegdan plateau.[255]

In the fall of 1912, the allies Serbia, Bulgaria, Greece, and Montenegro had declared war on the sultan, with the aim of taking away his remaining European territories. The moment seemed right, as Italy had already conquered Ottoman Tripolitania, Cyrenaica, and the Dodecanese in 1911/12. On the day of mobilization, enthusiastic demonstrators marched through Belgrade with the tricolor flag, singing patriotic songs, and chanting "Long live King Peter!" and "Long live greater Serbia!"[256] Only the social democrats and trade unions, rallying behind the slogan "war on war," attempted to call for a great antiwar demonstration and a peaceful Balkan federation.[257]

The journalist Leon Trotsky was amazed at how the whole city entered a state of alert resembling a military camp: "Everyone and everything is subordinated to the demands of the mobilization."[258] Nearly thirty thousand fighters boarded trains heading south, nearly one-third of the population of the capital city. "No living person would have dreamed that Belgrade had as many fighters, conscripts, as departed from Belgrade today," one eyewitness marveled.[259] Schools were closed and repurposed as sick bays. Many young people volunteered to provide medical assistance.[260] Switzerland, England, Austria, and Germany sent medical teams, and Russia even sent a "whole railroad train full of supplies: beds, mattresses, . . . stretchers, operating and bandaging tables with all kinds of surgical instruments and medications."[261]

By the spring of 1913, the Serbian army had conquered Vardar Macedonia, Kosovo, and the Sandžak, increasing Serbia's territory by 81 percent. Members of the regiments marched off to the front wearing "khaki uniforms and *opanki*," with "green sprigs stuck in their caps. . . . This is not the conventional, outwardly fleeting impression, but rather a tragic sense of doom," Trotsky observed. "The bark sandals on their feet and those green sprigs in their caps, together with their full set of military equipment, give the soldiers a somehow touching appearance."[262]

In the Treaty of London, signed on May 30, 1913, the sultan had to cede nearly all its European territories to the Balkan League. But Bulgaria did not receive all the territory it had hoped to win, so one month later it attacked its former allies Serbia and Greece, thereby provoking the Second Balkan War. Unlike the year before, the Belgrade residents' reaction was comparatively muted. The Serbian newspaper *Politika* wrote that the people "had not only gotten used to war, but also to victory."[263] Just two days later, though, the first train arrived with injured fighters: "And then a horrible procession would be formed, of stretchers, men with makeshift crutches, . . . young men with broken limbs, with pierced stomachs, shattered heads, with their eyes gouged out," the writer Jovan Skerlić moaned.[264] Each day Bulgarian, Albanian, and Turkish prisoners of wars were brought into the city, along with captured artillery and machine guns. Seeing the prisoners in this conquered, miserable state, the Belgraders began to talk about Austria: "After the Bulgarians, you're next!" That Austria's intentions toward Serbia were hostile, *Politika* explained, now seemed "self-evident and immutable."[265]

On August 10, 1913, the Treaty of Bucharest ended the Second Balkan War. A victorious but exhausted Serbia kept the territories it had conquered; in all, about 14,000 Serbian soldiers and 39,000 civilians had lost their lives in both wars. The costs of maintaining the army, along with weapons and armaments, had brought military expenditures to three times the size of the entire state budget.[266]

The annexation of "South Serbia" was celebrated in September 1913. Only the socialist Dimitrije Tucović criticized Serbian nationalism and expansionism for denying Albanians and Macedonians their rights of self-determination.[267] Guerrillas representing these minorities now took arms against their new rulers, who responded with persecutions and expulsions. The government later settled about 12,000 Serbian colonists in the southern borderlands. King Peter believed that South Serbia had to become a strong pillar of a reinvigorated "Greater Serbia."[268]

"These great historical events have unfolded so rapidly before our eyes that we haven't yet had enough time to assess them calmly and thoroughly," Foreign Minister Nikola Pašić said before the Serbian parliament in October. He emphasized that the Serbian people would now need a longer period of peace to develop the economy, promote education, and otherwise cultivate the acquired territories. He did not forget to thank Russia, France, England, and even Germany, for their support in the Balkan Wars.[269] But an uneasy sense of impending danger remained. The border to Austria-Hungary was over 350 miles long, and Bulgaria and Albania were waiting to exact revenge. The Serbian secret service was convinced that Austria-Hungary was urgently seeking a pretense to attack Serbia, while it was still exhausted from battle.[270]

By 1900, industrialization had begun to visibly change the social structure of Serbia, particularly its capital city. Between 1906 and 1910 alone, machine power and the number of factories quadrupled.[271] Belgrade now had more than fifty factories that produced bricks, textiles, shoes, foodstuffs, chocolate, tobacco, metal products, and chemicals.[272]

Serbia's economic mini-spurt was not nearly as dramatic as industrialization in England. Most people still earned their living through agriculture, and many factories resembled larger workshops. Small companies with just a few employees and not much machine power prevailed. There

Knez Mihailova Street, postcard with postmark from Skopje, 1912. National Museum, Belgrade.

was a shortage of investment capital and qualified workers. One contemporary described industrialization like this: It began with an existing workplace, which gradually hired more workers. "Then, machine by machine, steam-powered devices are replaced by motorized ones, and a growing portion of the labor is mechanized."[273] The food industry dominated this first phase of industrialization, claiming more than half of the value of all factory production, while the textile industry brought in less than one-tenth.

Because poverty had driven thousands to the cities looking for work, the population of Belgrade had quadrupled within a half century. Now about 100,000 people lived in the Serbian capital, and two-thirds were recent arrivals.[274] A new social class formed through migration and industrialization: wage-dependent workers. Many still owned property elsewhere or resided in the city only seasonally. They all lived in poverty, engaging in extremely strenuous work that was dangerous to their health. Women and children, too, toiled up to eighteen hours each day for subsistence wages. The disparity between rich and poor grew.[275]

Beyond the districts of Varoš, Vračar, Dorćol, Palilula, Savamala, and Terazije in the bourgeois city center, slums with a distinct peasant character provided a home for the lower classes—small farmers, factory workers, seasonal laborers, servants, and beggars. There was no municipal infrastructure. The stench of refuse and open sewers was everywhere; children played between garbage and latrines, and chickens and goats roamed freely. People lived in small, one-story farmhouses with a garden, stable, and outhouse. In these overcrowded lodgings, people ate communally from one bowl, bathed rarely, and slept on the floor.[276] Tenements in the city center were just as overcrowded, unhygienic, squalid, and overpriced. The authors of a 1906 survey came to the conclusion "that there is a close causal relationship between life in such dwellings and the three greatest enemies of public health—tuberculosis, alcoholism, and venereal disease."[277] As we shall see, the environment was also hospitable to political radicalism.

The workers did not yet form a proletarian class, as in England, Germany, or France. They had different sensibilities, lifestyles, and forms of consciousness, but not (yet) shared traditions. The first workers' associations coalesced in the 1890s; a central federation of trade unions and the socialist party were founded in 1903. But only an estimated one out of ten wage earners was organized in a union. Labor conflicts nevertheless shut down production frequently. Between 1907 and 1912, there were 275 strikes in Serbia over issues like the ten-hour workday, but in 1913 the workers' movement effectively came to a standstill with the mass mobilization for the Balkan Wars.[278]

Belgrade in 1913 was a society in transition. The city was full of contradictions, a local newspaper noted, embodying both "the old, Balkan, semi-wild Serbia . . . and the new, reborn, cultivated, patriotic Serbia."[279] In the late nineteenth century, Serbia's capital had transformed into a bourgeois metropolis with a Western appearance. It gained representative boulevards like the broad Knez Mihailova Street, modern residential and government buildings, the Terazije central business district, as well as schools, theaters, libraries, museums, and a public park adjacent to the old fortress. In the city center, the government paved streets, laid water and sewage lines, installed electric lighting, and built streetcar tracks.[280]

Urbanization ushered in a new metropolitan lifestyle that departed fundamentally from traditional life in agrarian society. Changed forms of sociability and associational life, as well as new educational ideals and conceptions of morality, were part of the new bourgeois culture. The prosperous middle classes maintained private salons, with a designated day of the week for receiving guests ("jour de réception," or "žur").[281] On the weekends, they met others at tennis tournaments and horse races. They attended balls, theatrical and circus performances, and even the movies—Belgrade's first cinema opened in 1908. The well-to-do spent holidays at baths in Austria-Hungary, or splurged on long-distance travel. One contemporary marveled at the materialism and hedonism of the young men and women who lived freely and promoted free love. In peacetime, "no strong wind, mud, or ice could stop young and old from hurrying from one diversion to the next. . . . Everyone was entertained!"[282]

European standards, styles, and status symbols dominated the world of fashion. Bourgeois convention demanded proper clothes for every occasion; Vienna and Paris set the tone. Belgrade gentlemen wore straw hats, spats, and cuffed shirts with stiff collars, and they also carried walking sticks. Veiled, wide-brimmed hats with floral decorations were fashionable for women, along with corsets and high lace-up shoes.[283] In 1913, an extensive article in the *Mali žurnal (Little Journal)* informed readers about the trends of the great European fashion salons; elegant ladies were supposed to tie silk sashes, bows "à la propeller," and floral garlands around the bodices of their evening dresses.[284] The bobbed hairstyle was introduced that same year. Only peasants still donned traditional clothing in the capital: "In the winter, they wore robes; in the summer, white pants with long shirts, belted with a colorful sash. They all had *opanki* with laced stockings, and fur caps atop their heads."[285]

Important institutions including theaters, publishing houses, museums, and academies were located in Belgrade. The essayist Milan Lazarević recalled "an enviable cultural life. . . . Foreign books . . . reached our intellectuals within just a few days. . . . One traveled and spoke foreign languages."[286] This international orientation was reflected in the repertoire of the National Theater, four-fifths of which was composed of foreign (mostly German and French) works in 1913.[287] Many members of the educated bourgeoisie had studied in Germany, Austria, or France, which is why most felt closer to the West than to Russia.

The small group of the "haute bourgeoisie," high state officials and military officers, occupied the top of the social pyramid. The most affluent and well-respected independent professionals—for example, entrepreneurs, lawyers, doctors, and writers—also belonged to this group. Clientelism, political ties, and informal relationships determined who received prestigious government posts or lucrative public commissions. The journalist Milan Jovanović Stoimirović remarked that "almost all Belgrade was somehow related by blood or by marriage, somehow connected through business or friendship."[288] Next came the broad mass of the middle- and lower-middle classes. The academic professions in law, medicine, and education had grown significantly. Civil servants and their families alone now made up one-fifth of the population of Belgrade. The older middle classes—shopkeepers, artisans, and other tradesmen—were less uniform in appearance, but they, too, exerted a formative influence on urban life.[289]

Politically speaking, the bourgeoisie was represented by three broad movements: the western European-oriented Liberals, the national conservative Progressives, and the national social Radicals. The latter was the defining political force in 1913.[290] Followers of each party gathered in their own establishments for eating and drinking; indeed, a significant part of public life transpired in cafés, taverns, and clubs. "This is where men met to finalize contracts, where they held business meetings, even where attorneys met with clients . . . and where all official documents, except for wills, were composed," the writer Branislav Nušić observed. Men of all classes frequented establishments with others who shared their worldview. "The old traders of the *čaršija* [bazaar], Serbs and Tsintsars, . . . who have stayed true to the Oriental art of doing business, living, and thinking, did not want to mix with the 'new' gentlemen who wore top hats instead of fezes."[291] Politicians and legislators met at the "London," near the parliament, while the Belgrade *bohème*—writers, artists, painters, actors, and intellectuals—frequented the Theater Café or one of the famed taverns on the Skadarlija, the romantic cobbled street in the Old Town.

Freedom of the press encouraged the publication of eighty-nine different print media, including fifteen daily newspapers of various political leanings, fifteen cultural and literary journals, and forty-four publications that represented associations or particular fields of interest. Popular newspapers such as *Večernje novosti (Evening Newspaper)*, *Mali žurnal (Little Journal)*, and *Beogradske novine (Belgrade News)* reached the middle and lower classes, too. Twenty-five thousand domestic and foreign newspapers and journals were sold in Belgrade each day.[292] When street vendors brought out the evening editions, one Belgrader recalled, the city's numerous taverns and cafés were soon full of patrons. "Now voracious newspaper reading begins, especially in impassioned times, which is, unfortunately, a permanent condition in Belgrade. Even the most modest peddler has joined a political party and reads his . . . favorite paper from start to finish."[293] Since 1912, the issue that dominated all else was "agitation for war—never mind with whom: Austria, Bulgaria, Turkey, even the whole Concert of Europe," Leon Trotsky summed up.[294]

In 1913, the Belgrade public was in a permanent state of nationalistic frenzy, spurred on by gymnastic, singing, and charitable associations as well as by professional organizations, youth groups, and women's leagues. Alongside the performance of patriotic songs, a history competition was introduced in Belgrade in 1912. "Who is the greatest Serb of all time? (Saint Sava). Of all the Slavic languages, which is the most beautiful? (Serbian)." Sokol, the pan-Slav sport movement, warned its members: "The hour of reckoning is drawing near! Take arms!"[295]

In Serbia's "golden age of democracy," women assumed a greater public role. According to the Civil Code, they were still not considered legally competent, nor were they allowed to vote or pursue higher professions. But unlike in the Habsburg Monarchy, women in Serbia could attend university; one out of every ten students was female. A critical mass of women doctors, teachers, writers, artists, and journalists soon began to address the "woman question" head on. The first women's associations and social institutions were established in the last third of the nineteenth century, and feminist publications such as *Domaćica (Housewife), Ženski svet (Women's World),* and *Jednakost (Equality)* advocated for better education, equal rights, and a modern image of women. In 1913, for example, *Srpkinja (Serbian Woman)* spoke out against the prejudice "that women who write and work outside the home are crazy, and . . . lose their feminine charm through intellectual labor."[296] The Serbian Women's League maintained contact with the International Women's League, a kind of feminist International. In Serbia, too, women fought for political and civil rights and for equal wages. Working women in Belgrade petitioned the Serbian parliament, or Skupština, for the right to vote because "this part of the nation also possesses reason, works, and pays taxes."[297]

One of the era's most prominent emancipated women was Isidora Sekulić—the first well-known female author and literary critic within an otherwise completely male-dominated Serbian literary scene. The daughter of an attorney, Sekulić was orphaned at a young age. She left her home village in the Hungarian Vojvodina to train as a teacher, the only academic profession allowed for women in the Habsburg Monarchy. In 1909 she moved to Serbia and earned her living as a mathematics and physics teacher before gradually becoming more involved in the literary community.

Her first short story collection, *Fellow Travelers (Saputnici),* received glowing reviews in 1913, and the writer Jovan Dučić declared it "one of the ten best poetic books in our entire literature."[298] Only Jovan Skerlić, literary giant and supporter of the patriotic National Defense, criticized her text as too "personal," "exotic," and "not national enough." One year later, in the same vein, he accused her *Letters from Norway (Pisma iz Norveške)* of "cosmopolitanism at the worst possible moment"; he was devastated by the bloody battles on the Balkan fronts. "In an age of so many national responsibilities," Skerlić wrote, "she just had to travel to Norway."[299]

Isidora Sekulić was not a classical feminist. She wanted to assert herself in a man's world without constantly addressing her identity as a woman. But she was convinced that "a time will come when there will also be brilliant women, first-class philosophers. However, there is still a long way to go."[300] Widowed after a brief marriage in 1913, she never married again.

Traveling did not inoculate Sekulić against the national euphoria of the Balkan Wars. "What a lovely idea, to transform the day of Saint Vitus

(Vidovdan) . . . into a great and vivid day of remembrance, into a day of deliberate reckoning and active enthusiasm," she commented.[301] At the same time, she opposed "a narrow chauvinism, filled with epic poems and songs of mourning," and the preaching of "naked, brute violence" in the run-up to war. Instead, she called for a "cultural nationalism" that was superior in form as well as content, adopting a cosmopolitan and humanist-universalist tone: "Morality, humanism, ethics, integrity. Not only . . . first-rate Serbian virtues, but human ones as well."[302] She was deeply affected by Skerlić's criticism. In an interview years later, after the Second World War, she said that the famous literary critic had not understood "that there can be no true nationalism without internationalism."[303]

In 1913 Isidora Sekulić belonged to the circle of intellectuals, artists, scholars, and authors around the organization and journal *Slovenski jug (Slavic South),* which advocated for the Yugoslav idea of a unified Serbian-Croatian-Slovenian state—an enthusiasm she shared even with her critic, Jovan Skerlić. In 1913, he proposed a linguistic compromise between Serbs and Croats: "Religious and national proselytizing are not possible, nor are cultural or political hegemony."[304]

For decades, intellectuals and artists had imagined and mentally constructed a Yugoslav nation that transcended state borders. Theater companies from Belgrade and Zagreb had made mutual guest appearances since the 1840s. Even during the times of harshest confrontation between Serbia and the Habsburg Monarchy, works by Croatian writers were still performed in Belgrade; there were exhibitions and stagings of operas from "over there." The Croatian singing club Mladost (Youth) and the Zagreb Opera received enthusiastic applause and critical laurels.[305]

An Academy of Sciences was established in Belgrade in 1892, and a university in 1905. The city became a magnet for "progressive" intellectuals and artists from the entire South Slav region. Serbian scholars worked with the Yugoslav Academy in Zagreb on its initiative for a Yugoslav encyclopedia. Activists in the South Slav network included the sculptor Ivan Meštrović, the playwright Ivo Vojnović, and the author Antun Gustav Matoš (all from Croatia); the ethnologist Niko Županič and the poet Ivan Cankar (Slovenia); and the writer Ivo Andrić (Bosnia-Herzegovina). In his "anthropogeography" of the Balkan Peninsula, the geographer Jovan Cvijić declared the Serbs, Croats, Bulgarians, Slovenes, and Macedonians to be a single "Yugoslav" people.[306]

Political cooperation between Serbs, Croats, and Slovenes became more concrete. In Dalmatia, the Serb-Croat coalition won the Diet elections for a fifth time in 1913. The coalition's "new course" aimed to establish a South Slav federal state that was independent of Hungary, or perhaps even an independent Yugoslavia.[307] Proponents of the South Slav idea looked hopefully toward Belgrade. It was even written in the newspaper of the Catholic Croatian movement in Rijeka during the Balkan Wars that "the victories of the Balkan peoples are our victories, too."[308]

Stojan Novaković, historian and president of the Serbian Academy of Sciences, presented the utopia of a unified, prosperous, and progressive South Slav state in his essay, "After One Hundred Years." Imagining the year 2011, he looked back in amazement at the particularism, provincialism, and religious antagonism of an earlier time. In Novaković's (fictional) 2011, all these troubles were in the past. "Our cultural and literary unity is so strong that political powers are compelled to respect it. Each defends the other: the one from Timok in the East defends his compatriot at the Adriatic coast, and the one from Fruška Gora defends the other in Prizren." But this was not yet enough. "We Yugoslavs, having achieved the agreement and community of Serbs, Croats, and Slovenes, want the Bulgarians to join us." Closer political ties with the Romanians and Greeks might even be considered in the future. "How backward and barbaric those [earlier] times must have been!"[309]

In the spring of 1912, the devoted South Slav nationalist Gavrilo Princip set off for Belgrade on foot to complete his studies there. Princip was the nineteen-year-old son of a Serb peasant from Bosnia's Grahovo Polje. The young bookworm had attended school in Sarajevo, and then Tuzla, where he joined the secret society Young Bosnia. Like similar militant groups in other European countries, Young Bosnia wanted to overturn Austro-Hungarian rule through revolutionary action and assassinations. Its young male members—including the later Nobel Prize winner in literature, Ivo Andrić—were Yugoslav nationalists who fought for the political union of Serbs, Croats, Muslims, and Slovenes.[310] They read Plato, Aristotle, Rousseau, Nietzsche, Jaurès, Le Bon, Ibsen, and Marinetti, and they devoured the writings of the Czech Tomáš Masaryk and Russian political philosophers and anarchists—particularly Nikolay Chernyshevsky, Alexander Herzen, and Mikhail Bakunin. They were also inspired by the Kosovo myth and the epic tale *The Mountain Wreath* by Prince-Bishop Petar II Petrović Njegoš.[311]

In May 1913, following the First Balkan War, the military governor of Bosnia-Herzegovina declared a state of emergency, imposed martial law, dissolved the Diet, and banned Serb associations. There were more than two hundred trials for high treason in the first half of the year.[312] Many more South Slav nationalists left for Belgrade. Like Princip, they settled in "Little Bosnia" near the Zeleni Venac marketplace (where a street is named after him today). The neighborhood was infamous for its miserable accommodations and high rates of crime and tuberculosis. "These were hard times—no money, no food," his roommate later recalled. "Sometimes we were obliged to sell even our books to procure money for bread, but Princip refused to part with his favorite books."[313]

Many young men from Bosnia-Herzegovina had resettled in Belgrade, whether motivated by nationalism or economic need. The Serbs from the other side of the Drina were treated like social outcasts; Belgraders looked down on the miserable refugees from "over there" with contempt. The migrant slums, where hopeful expectations met bitter reality, became an incubator of political radicalism.[314] Princip wanted to fight as a volunteer with the patriotic National Defense in the Balkan Wars. He dreamed of liberating sacred Kosovo, decked out with a bandolier and fur cap bearing the characteristic symbol of the skull and crossbones. But the militia turned down the diminutive, weakly Bosnian, who subsequently decided to accomplish another great deed in his lifetime.

Princip met up with other Bosnian emigrants and volunteers in taverns like the Acorn Wreath *(Žirovni venac),* Green Wreath *(Zeleni venac),* and Goldfish *(Zlatna ribica).* He already knew the revolutionary and anarchist Nedeljko Čabrinović from Sarajevo. Like many others, he had been banned from his homeland by the Austro-Hungarian authorities. Princip later testified that he had been determined to assassinate a prominent Austrian since 1912. "I am not a criminal because I eliminated an evildoer," he stated on October 12, 1914. "I hated the way the Austrian press wrote," Čabrinović explained, "and if until this point I had been against all nationalism, now I understood the need for it."[315] Both men sought to free Bosnia from the Habsburg Monarchy and unify all South Slavs in one state, so the Yugoslavs would view themselves as one nation. Princip envisioned a monarchy, while Čabrinović favored a republic.

In 1914 they and their countryman Trifko Grabež received weapons from agents of the Black Hand to assassinate the Austrian crown prince. Members of this officers' clique had already murdered the King of Serbia,

Alexander Obrenović, and his wife in 1903, forcing a change of dynasty. Six of the assassins were sent into retirement, but conspirators in the army continued to influence Serbian politics. They founded the secret Black Hand society, led by Colonel Dragutin Dimitrijević, who was known as Apis ("Holy Bull"), in 1911. Because the officers wanted to institute an authoritarian regime, they clashed with the government under Nikola Pašić. They also supported anarchist and revolutionary activities abroad, as a means toward uniting all Serbs, or all South Slavs, in a common state. Serbia had tried to suppress these activities after the Bosnian annexation crisis. Rivalries over hegemony in the territories that Serbia had acquired in the Balkan Wars caused a serious government crisis in 1913.[316]

After the assassination, Princip and the other defendants testified in court that they had thought the plot up themselves and had merely received the weapons in Serbia. They all provided different motives, both political and private. Princip said that he "had had the idea of killing any high person in Austria who represented its power" for nationalist reasons since 1912.[317] Nedeljko Čabrinović likewise sought vengeance "because of the oppression suffered by the Serbs in Bosnia and Herzegovina, particularly under the state of emergency." He was furious "that a foreigner who didn't belong here was driving me out of my country."[318] Trifko Grabež called the assassination "the greatest revolutionary act in history, asserting that "Austria 'and Francis Ferdinand in particular' should pay for everything that was going on in Bosnia and Hercegovina and for 'all evil things there.'"[319] Anarchism was a political force all over Europe at this time. A Croatian student had attempted to murder Austria-Hungary's hated governor in Croatia, Slavko Cuvaj, in June 1912. Other victims of assassination included the French president Carnot (1894), the Austrian empress Elisabeth (1898), the U.S. president McKinley (1901), the Serbian king Alexander (1903), and the Greek king George I (1913).

On October 28, 1914, the Austrian court sentenced the three main conspirators to twenty years of hard labor, including a day of fasting once a month and confinement in a dark cell each year on June 28. All three died from the inhumane conditions of their imprisonment, in Theresienstadt in Bohemia.

7

From the Balkan Wars to the Second World War

THE BALKAN WARS of 1912/13—followed by the First World War and conflicts over the legacy of the Ottoman Empire that persisted until 1923—brought southeastern Europeans a decade of nearly uninterrupted violence, "ethnic cleansing," and social misery. For the first time, the region was at the brink of "total war," fought by technologically advanced armies with vast destructive capabilities and enabled by an unprecedented mass mobilization of manpower. A hitherto unknown level of violence transformed the experience of warfare for ordinary soldiers and entire societies.[1] From a regional perspective, the Great War of 1914–1918 was just one of several way stations on the road to the nation-state. The "three Balkan wars" fundamentally rearranged the international order, but also bred endemic conflicts over borders and minorities, ideologies and political systems, which ultimately erupted in the violence of the Second World War.

From the Balkan Wars to the Treaty of Lausanne, 1912/1913 to 1923

In the Balkan Wars of 1912/13, the young nation-states first fought side-by-side to free their countrymen from the "Ottoman yoke," before turning against one another to fight over the division of the spoils. The goal of both Balkan Wars was the political and ethnic reorganization of vast stretches of land. The European public watched the advances of the Balkan armies and subsequent mass expulsions with dismay. The Bulgarian army conquered Adrianople, and Serbian troops took Skopje, Prilep, Bitola, and eventually all of Macedonia and Kosovo, pushing toward the Adriatic Sea. While Greece occupied Thessaloniki, Ioannina, and the Aegean Islands, Montenegro marched into Scutari (Shkodër). Military leaders methodically expelled, persecuted, and in some cases, eliminated entire groups of undesired peoples. The journalist Leon Trotsky reported that the Serbs in Kosovo and Macedonia "are engaged quite simply in systematic extermination of the Muslim population."[2] Experts from the Carnegie Endowment for International Peace noted: "Houses and whole villages reduced to ashes, unarmed and innocent populations massacred . . . with a view to the entire transformation of the ethnic character of regions." Hundreds of thousands of southeastern Europeans uprooted themselves out of fear: "The Turks are fleeing before the Christians, the Bulgarians before the Greeks and the Turks, the Greeks and the Turks before the Bulgarians, the Albanians before the Servians."[3] A journalist depicted the horrifying scene as thousands stormed the Skopje train station in 1912, trying to escape: "The hundreds of abandoned freight cars were full of people; women and children squeezed into one car by the hundreds, and the miserable beings were also perched on the roofs . . . tangles of people, refugees, knowing only that they had to call out, ask, beg for one thing: Away, escape, help!"[4]

The "ethnic cleansing" of the Balkan Wars was the climax of an extended series of expulsions that accompanied the founding of nation-states throughout the "long nineteenth century." As we have seen, there were ideological and pragmatic reasons for the waves of expulsions. On one hand, the ideal nation-state was supposed to incorporate all members of the nation; on the other, it excluded outsiders to create as uniform a national culture as possible. In a nationalist age, the makeup of a population became grounds for legitimating one group's territorial claims over those of another. Homogenization clarified power relations and neutralized resistance, particularly in times of war.[5] The arrogance toward others was palpable, as when the Serbian journalist Jaša Tomić reported with disgust on the wretched houses, neglected fields, and miserable cattle in Prishtina. There was plenty of land, but "the Arnauts [Albanians] . . . don't even tolerate Muslims, let alone Christians. They kill anyone else who wants to settle there."[6] Strategic and economic interests, such as attaining access to the Adriatic Sea, also figured prominently. In contrast to

Ismail Qemali (wearing the black cap) and the Albanian delegation on the way to the London Conference of the Ambassadors in 1912. National Museum of Albania, Tirana.

earlier centuries, the homogenizers could now use new communications technologies such as the telegraph and aerial reconnaissance.[7]

These developments were particularly alarming to Albanians, who feared that the Balkan states would divide up all the territory for themselves. In November 1912 Ismail Qemali proclaimed the independent state of Albania at the National Congress in Valona (Vlorë). Beginning in December, he negotiated for the establishment of an independent state at the London Conference of the Ambassadors. When the Treaty of London ended the First Balkan War on May 30, 1913, Albania was recognized as an independent principality under Ottoman suzerainty. The sultan's only remaining European territory was a small part of eastern Thrace. The great powers decided to install Prince William of Wied, a cousin of the German emperor, as the prince and governor of the youngest Balkan state.[8]

The Albanians now had their own state, but substantial areas of Albanian settlement in Kosovo and western Macedonia had become part of Serbia—a situation that would foster discontent throughout the entire twentieth century. Nationally minded Bulgarians were especially outraged by the humiliating terms of peace that had concluded the Balkan Wars, which assigned Macedonia to Serbia and Greece, and Southern Dobruja to Romania. The new borders, which largely remained in place even after the First World War, sowed seeds of unrest that later grew into violent conflicts.[9] For the Ottoman Empire, the Balkan Wars became a watershed moment. Deep national trauma after military fiasco and the loss of remaining European territories gave rise to a "culture of defeat" that was characterized by a search for consolation and revenge in the run-up to the First World War.[10]

The consequences of the Balkan Wars were far-reaching, both nationally and internationally. Aggressive nationalism was rewarded, although the winners paid a steep price. The states of the Balkan League lost more than 100,000 soldiers; the Ottoman Empire, about 125,000. Up to 200,000 civilians, overwhelmingly Muslims, died from violence, hunger, and disease. Up to 400,000 people fled or were purposefully expelled during the fighting. Entire regions were devastated, their populations depleted, state coffers emptied. Regime changes, nationalization, and colonization unleashed further waves of flight and expulsion; another half million people were uprooted after the peace settlement. All in all, 890,000 men, women, and children lost their homes because of the Balkan Wars. The "ethnic cleansing" nevertheless left behind many gaps. At least half of the prewar Muslim population remained in their homelands. For this reason (as in the case of Bulgaria and the Ottoman Empire), mutual agreements safeguarded the rights of minorities with respect to religious freedom, education, and citizenship.[11]

The Balkan Wars also represented an international turning point, since they heightened the stakes of the Eastern Question to an even more dangerous level. The risk of a war between Russia and Austria-Hungary or Germany grew, and the opposing systems of alliances became more entrenched. On one side, Russia and France moved closer together, and on the other, Austria-Hungary and Imperial Germany. Serbia's power and self-assurance grew dramatically, and Habsburg leaders became convinced that peaceful means would no longer be enough to stabilize the region.[12]

Militarists in Austria impatiently pushed for war against Serbia, which continued to undermine the stability of the Habsburg Empire by stoking South Slav nationalism.[13] Even worse, Serbia and Montenegro were negotiating a union that would give Belgrade access to the Mediterranean Sea—precisely what the founding of Albania was supposed to have prevented.

Viennese diplomats were dismayed by Serbia's irredentism in Bosnia-Herzegovina and the expansion of Russian influence. In December 1912, Emperor William II was already convinced that "Austria must deal energetically with the foreign Slavs (the Serbs), otherwise she will lose control of the Slavs in the Austro-Hungarian monarchy. If Russia supports the Serbs . . . then war would be unavoidable for us too."[14] By the spring of 1914 at the latest, the hawks in Vienna successfully asserted their position that the "Serbian swine" would have to be militarily "eliminated."[15] Thus, alongside long-term causes of the First World War—the system of international alliances, the arms race and imperialist competition in Asia, Africa, and Latin America, as well as growing social and domestic political crises—there were concrete Austrian plans to attack Serbia.[16] In a memorandum to Emperor William of Germany dated June 24, 1914, the Viennese foreign office recommended the adoption of a more aggressive foreign policy, with German assistance. The assassination of Crown Prince Francis Ferdinand in Sarajevo on June 28, 1914, provided an opening.[17]

Gavrilo Princip and the other supporters of Young Bosnia were upset by the announcement that the heir to the Austrian throne planned to visit the occupied provinces of Bosnia and Herzegovina for military exercises on the anniversary of the symbolic Battle of Kosovo. They received weapons from agents of the Black Hand, the Serbian secret society, and posted themselves along the route of the royal convoy on the morning of June 28. Austrian diplomats and security forces ignored warnings from the Serbian government, which had heard about the machinations of the Bosnian Serbs—and the nineteen-year-old assassin thus succeeded in gunning down the crown prince and his wife.[18] In the trial that followed, Austrian prosecutors attempted to prove that the Serbian government was behind the assassination. But neither they nor subsequent historical scholars could conclusively substantiate Serbia's role.[19]

After Viennese officials intentionally formulated an ultimatum with terms that would have been "completely impossible for Serbia to accept," Austria-Hungary declared war on Serbia on July 28, 1914. Emperor Francis Joseph was firmly in favor of taking up arms.[20] His military leaders counted on defeating their opponent quickly, and keeping the intervention local. But after Russia mobilized its forces, the conflict escalated into world war. Germany and Bulgaria took the side of Vienna, while France and Great Britain joined with Russia on Serbia's behalf. Among southeastern European neighbors, only Montenegro supported its brother state; Greece

Mobilization in Belgrade, July 1914.

and Romania initially remained neutral. Only later, as the Central Powers seemed to be losing, did they enter the war in the hope of realizing their own territorial goals. Thus, the world conflict also possessed dimensions of a third Balkan war.

On the western front, German, British, and French armies engaged in trench warfare and enormous battles of attrition, but the war proceeded quite differently in eastern and southeastern Europe and Anatolia. Here, enemy territory was conquered and occupied for years. Because the occupiers practiced a scorched-earth strategy and shamelessly exploited local resources, the number of victims and the extent of economic damages in the southeast was much larger than in the west. One-third of Serbian and Romanian soldiers died, more than double the rate of casualties in the German or French army.[21]

In August 1914, Austro-Hungarian troops advanced across the Bosnian border into Serbia and Montenegro. Strategic errors, logistical problems, and the highly motivated (if exhausted) Serbian army put the troops from Austria-Hungary in a bind. The Austrians, who feared a bloody guerrilla war, invoked the army's right to defense in wartime emergency and per-

394

petrated terrible mass crimes.[22] They took civilians as hostages, killed thousands of men, women, and children in retaliation for partisan attacks, burned down villages, and plundered all they could carry. This occurred in Serbia as well as on the other side of the Drina in Bosnia-Herzegovina. "Our troops," one soldier reported, "have struck out terribly in all directions, like the Swedes in the Thirty Years War."[23] In 1914 Rudolph Archibald Reiss, professor of criminology and forensic science in Lausanne, visited the Serbian fronts and documented indescribable atrocities. Men were viciously slain, women raped, and entire localities ravaged past the point of recognition.[24] While Austria-Hungary was forced to retreat in December 1914, Serbia suffered intensely from hunger and a typhus epidemic during the first winter of the war.[25]

After the Central Powers had succeeded in attracting Bulgaria to their side, German, Austro-Hungarian, and Bulgarian troops marched back into Serbia in October 1915. The slaughter was over in a month, but the Balkan state did not surrender. Instead, King Peter's army and government, followed by hundreds of thousands of civilians, retreated over the mountains to the Mediterranean coast, in a long march that cost many human lives. Some 140,000 soldiers evacuated to Corfu.[26]

The Austro-Hungarian, German, and Bulgarian victors decided to eliminate Serbia from the political map. The Austrian military government banned political organizations, monitored schools, and ruthlessly eradicated all signs of resistance. The occupation authorities were determined "to bring this land all of the suffering that it deserved for willfully provoking this war."[27] Because the occupiers laid claim to agricultural and industrial production, thousands died from hunger in the winter of 1916.[28] In eastern Serbia, Macedonia, and parts of Kosovo, the Bulgarian military government initiated policies of Bulgarization and economic exploitation that were no less punishing.[29]

Over the course of 1916, the Central Powers occupied more southeastern European lands. They first took Montenegro, and part of the "friendly occupied country" Albania; Prince William had hastily taken flight soon after the outbreak of the war, leaving Albania to the occupation of Serbian, Montenegrin, Greek, and Italian troops. Romania entered the war on the side of the Entente in August 1916, but it was quickly overwhelmed; much of the country fell under German military administration by the end of 1916.[30] Only in Macedonia did the Entente manage to establish a solid foothold, after the landing of a French-British expeditionary force

Austrian soldiers shoot prisoners in Serbia during the First World War.

in October 1915. Near Thessaloniki, the troops of the Allied and Central Powers became ensnarled in a bloody war of attrition along a more than thirty-mile front. When Bulgaria (which had already annexed Romanian Southern Dobruja) marched into Greek eastern Macedonia in June 1917, Greece gave up its neutrality and entered the war on the side of the Entente. The Allies finally broke through the Thessaloniki front in mid-September 1918, marching on toward Istanbul and the Danube River.

The Ottoman Empire entered the war on the side of Germany and Austria-Hungary in 1914, hoping to recoup its losses on the Balkan Peninsula, but instead it drew closer to its final military defeat. An offensive against Russia ended in disaster during the first winter of the war. In the spring of 1915, Armenians revolted in Van, in eastern Anatolia. After the Russian army marched into the region, supported by a legion of Armenian volunteers, the Ottoman government (with the assistance of German military advisers) deported hundreds of thousands of Greeks and Armenians away from areas near the front. For years, Armenian nationalists had demanded their own state, disrupting eastern Anatolia with assassinations, abductions, and terrorist attacks. Now Turkish troops drove almost the entire Armenian population, by foot or by railroad, across the Anatolian highlands to the Syrian coast. Death marches and targeted mass killings—as well as hunger, sickness, and epidemics—caused the deaths of at least 40 percent of all Armenians. The Turkish government today still refuses to identify this as genocide, asserting that the Armenians suffered no worse a fate than the hundreds of thousands of Muslims who were expelled from the Balkan Peninsula.[31]

The great empires of the Romanovs, Ottomans, and Habsburgs broke down at the end of the First World War, fulfilling dreams that had long been harbored by national politicians in eastern and southeastern Europe. From their exile in London and Paris, Tomáš Masaryk and Edvard Beneš, leaders of the Czech National Council, called for a "New Europe" of "constitutional, democratic, and republican states." Czechs, Poles, and South Slavs cooperated closely, founding national committees that the Allies accepted as legitimate representational bodies.[32] Representatives of Italians, Czechs, Slovaks, Poles, Romanians, and South Slavs gathered in Rome in April 1918, calling for the right of every people to establish their own nation-state. The nationalities repeated these demands in May at a congress in Pittsburgh, where they fought to win over American public opinion.[33] In October, the Austrian Emperor Charles undertook a fruitless attempt to save the monarchy through federal reform.

The philosopher Masaryk, an icon for politicians representing the nationalities of the Habsburg Empire, was amazed by the dedication of the exiled South Slav politicians, who had founded a Yugoslav Committee in London in November 1914. Under the leadership of the Croat Ante Trumbić, the committee proposed a unitary "South Slav Programme," which declared Serbs, Croats, and Slovenes "one and the same people . . . with three different names" and called for a common state.[34] Trumbić's colleague Frano Supilo, according to the former British prime minister Herbert Asquith, was like a "force of nature" in rallying the Western powers to the South Slav cause.[35] Within southeastern Europe, too, a growing number of people came to believe in a future Yugoslav state. Years of traumatic wartime experiences had created common bonds. Tens of thousands of people had died; each day millions faced the threat of annihilation or expulsion, and they suffered from hunger, sickness, and epidemics. All this forged a deeper sense of community and solidarity. Linguistic and cultural similarities and common areas of settlement, shared socioeconomic challenges and fear of imperialist rule, and—not least—the political, military, and moral bankruptcy of the Habsburg Monarchy, all seemed to recommend a South Slav state.[36]

Soon the empires had become so weak that a new national politics was practically a fait accompli. Politicians from the Habsburg Monarchy and Serbia called for the establishment of a Yugoslav kingdom in the Corfu Declaration of July 1917. Czechs and Slovaks decided in favor of a Czechoslovak state in May 1918, while the Romanians in Transylvania announced their union with Romania. When the armistice between the Entente and the Central Powers took effect in November 1918, the new map of states was already a reality.[37] The Kingdom of Serbs, Croats, and Slovenes (SHS) was formally established on December 1, 1918, and the union of Transylvania with Romania was realized as well.

Between 1919 and 1923, a completely changed political landscape emerged in eastern-central and southeastern Europe, as codified in the peace treaties of St. Germain, Neuilly, Trianon, Sèvres, and Lausanne. The new order was based on the right of national self-determination, which had been delineated by U.S. president Woodrow Wilson in his Fourteen Points of January 1918. All European peoples were to have the right to establish their own nation-state and freely determine their own form of government. Only later did it become clear that Wilson had touched off calls for independence all over the world, threatening Western colonialism as well.[38] In southeastern Europe, disorderly patterns of settlement meant that the principle of self-determination immediately led to a thicket of incompatible claims. Criteria like language, ancestry, and religion were not always helpful in determining which groups should or should not be recognized as a nation. Economic, historic, and strategic arguments also had to be considered when drawing new borders. The high-minded principle of self-determination clashed with victors' rights. During the war, the western powers had entered into secret treaties that promised to Italy the territories of South Tyrol, Trieste, Istria, and Dalmatia—and to Romania, the Bukovina, Transylvania, and Banat—in return for these countries' entrance into the war.[39]

The Kingdom of Serbs, Croats, and Slovenes—the first Yugoslavia—united Serbia and Montenegro with lands that had previously belonged to the Habsburg Monarchy and the Ottoman Empire. Romania received Bessarabia, Bukovina, Transylvania, Southern Dobruja, Banat, Crişana, and Maramureş, just about doubling its territory and population. Greece also grew substantially, acquiring western Thrace and other new territories.

As one of the war's losers, Bulgaria got off relatively easily, with only small territorial losses, but it had to accept a drastic reduction in its army and reparations totaling one-quarter of its national assets. The Albanians were in a particularly difficult position, fearful that Italy and Greece would completely divide up their occupied land. After difficult negotiations, Albania was finally recognized as a sovereign and independent state, with the borders of 1913, at an international conference of ambassadors in 1921. In practice, however, it became a quasi-protectorate of Italy.[40]

With respect to state borders, the new order in eastern and southeastern Europe was often inconsistent and unsatisfying to those who lived in ethnically mixed regions. Only in exceptional circumstances did the peacemakers allow plebiscites to determine state boundaries—as in 1920, when a majority of southern Carinthians voted to remain in Austria instead of joining the SHS state. Because of complicated settlement patterns, the redrawn borders in eastern and southeastern Europe meant that millions of people were now living as minorities in one of the successor states. With the partition of Hungarian Banat, 75,000 Romanians came under the jurisdiction of the SHS state, and 65,000 South Slavs found themselves in Romania.[41] Thus, the victorious powers obliged the SHS, Poland, Czechoslovakia, Romania, and Greece to protect "linguistic, racial, and religious minorities" by outlawing discrimination, upholding religious and organizational freedom, and securing the right to school instruction in the minorities' native languages. Other eastern European states had to accept similar conditions in their peace treaties, or make declarations to this effect. The League of Nations, founded in 1919, became the guarantor of the new system for protecting minorities.[42]

The protection of minorities sparked conflicts and dissatisfaction. The system lacked credibility because it applied only to the eastern European states, not to the Western powers—a point of contention especially for representatives of Yugoslavia and Romania. They had difficulty accepting that Hungarian and German minorities in their own states were entitled to collective rights, but not (for example) Slovenes and Croats in Italy. The Western powers hoped that "nations of citizens" would develop over time, and that assimilation would preclude the need for special ethnic rights. In 1926, the British foreign secretary stated that the goal of the treaties was "to secure for minorities that measure of protection and justice which would gradually prepare them to be merged in the national community to which they belonged."[43]

Disarmament and the prosecution of war crimes through international law were supposed to undercut future aggression. The losers of the war—Germany, Austria, Hungary, Bulgaria, and Turkey—were also required to reduce the size of their armies. The Ottoman Empire, moreover, was obliged to extradite those who were responsible for the massacre of Armenians—although this never transpired because of the revolution set into motion by Mustafa Kemal.[44]

Both the victors and the vanquished were dissatisfied with the new state order. Border conflicts became endemic. According to the terms of the Treaty of Trianon (1920), Hungary lost more than 70 percent of its territory and 63 percent of its population to Czechoslovakia, Yugoslavia, and Romania. More than 3.2 million Hungarians became minorities in neighboring states. In the superheated political climate of the interwar era, "Trianon" became shorthand for a humiliating victors' peace. The Hungarian governments of this period obsessively pursued a revisionist agenda with respect to the Burgenland, Vojvodina, southern Slovakia, and territories ceded to Romania. Bulgaria was no less insistent in demanding Southern Dobruja, Macedonia, and Thrace from its neighbors. Yugoslavs were also dissatisfied with the borders, having been compelled to give up Trieste, Istria, southern Carinthia, and parts of Carniola. Finally, the Soviet Union coveted Bessarabia, and Italy wanted the Dalmatian coast and Albania.[45]

New outbreaks of violence and expulsions occurred alongside the Paris peace negotiations. In May 1919, Greek troops landed in Smyrna, on the western coast of Asia Minor, seeking to realize the Megali Idea at the expense of the Turks; they sought a greater Greece on both sides of the Aegean, including the former Constantinople. Here, the politics of the fait accompli succeeded only in part. To the outrage of the Turks, the Treaty of Sèvres awarded Greece most of Thrace, as well as Smyrna and surrounding areas (if not Istanbul). As Greek troops pushed farther east in 1921, the Turkish army under Mustafa Kemal responded with a devastating counterattack. Hundreds of thousands fled to Smyrna. Turkish irregulars penetrated the city, murdering Greeks and Armenians, plundering their houses, and finally setting Smyrna aflame. One of the greatest refugee crises of the twentieth century ensued. Up to 700,000 desperate people attempted to make their way across the sea on completely overcrowded boats; up to 100,000 perished in the turmoil.[46] "The conditions of these people upon their arrival in Greece was pitiable beyond description," the American

Henry Morgenthau wrote. During the crossing "there was neither food to eat nor water to drink, and in numerous cases the ships were buffeted about for several days at sea before their wretched human cargo could be brought to land. Typhoid and smallpox spread through the ship."[47]

Following the Greek defeat, parts of the Treaty of Sèvres were revised. The 1923 Treaty of Lausanne divided the Ottoman Empire into mandates and spheres of influence in the Near East and Asia Minor. An organized population exchange was arranged at the suggestion of Lord Curzon, the British foreign secretary. Up to one million Greeks had to leave Turkey, which in turn received about a half million Muslims from Greece—with grave humanitarian, socioeconomic, and political consequences on both sides.[48] In the Treaty of Neuilly, Greece and Bulgaria had already agreed to the "mutual emigration" of their nationals in Thrace and Macedonia. The phase of expansionist foreign policy, or "national completion," in Greece thereby came to an end.[49]

The events of the First World War accelerated changes within the Ottoman Empire, where nation-state formation and homogenization were closely connected. After Ottoman military power collapsed on all fronts in the fall of 1918, the Turkish Grand National Assembly in Ankara drew up a constitution that was based on popular sovereignty. The last sultan fled Istanbul in November 1922. Mustafa Kemal Pasha, leader of the Anatolian resistance, proclaimed the republic in 1923. The caliph was expelled, and the capital moved to Ankara. Under the leadership of Kemal, who later adopted the surname Atatürk, the multireligious Ottoman Empire transformed itself into a Western-oriented, secular, Turkish nation-state.

An entire decade of nearly uninterrupted warfare and "ethnic cleansing" in the Balkans did not end until the Treaty of Lausanne in 1923. As the multiethnic great powers of Austria-Hungary and the Russian and Ottoman Empires collapsed in the First World War, and nation-states prevailed throughout the region, at least 2.8 million people were forced from their homes.[50] Thus concluded a process that had begun with the rise of national movements more than one century previous, setting into motion groundbreaking intellectual, social, and economic changes. In this sense, the Great War was a catalyst, but not the cause. In earlier centuries, imperial loyalties had created a bond that held together the sultans' and emperors' expansive domains. Later, these loyalties unraveled to the degree that dynasties neglected the central demands of up-and-coming educated and economic elites: political and economic participation and equal cultural rights. In the end, the collapse of the empires following the Great War marked the greatest political reordering since the French Revolution. Contemporaries hoped that this would at last create the conditions for building liberal democratic polities that protected citizens' welfare.

From Democracy to Dictatorship

In the aftermath of the First World War, a new system of successor states with parliamentary systems arose from the ruins of the great empires of the Habsburgs and Ottomans. Small nations were now recognized as full members of the international community. The successor states aligned themselves with liberal systems of governance, the capitalist economy, and bourgeois culture as well as educational, technical, and scholarly progress. But the young democracies faced enormous pressures from the very beginning. Institutions, bureaucracies, and armies had to be built from the ground up, national elites—especially doctors, engineers, civil servants, and lawyers—trained, and disparate regions welded into a functioning body politic. Far-reaching structural reforms like land redistribution and the introduction of social welfare policies and compulsory education brought additional challenges.

As in most other European states, the political situation remained chronically unstable. Wherever monarchies remained—as in Romania, Bulgaria, and the Kingdom of Serbs, Croats, and Slovenes—the king was responsible for forming a government that respected the parliamentary majority. Elections now reflected the right of universal suffrage for men. Because of proportional representation, the party landscape splintered into many small factions, and lasting government majorities were rare. Intense ideological disputes and nationality conflicts added to this volatile mix. As in numerous other states, the parliamentary systems of the southeastern European countries moved toward authoritarianism and dictatorship at the end of the 1920s, in some cases even before the harsh effects of the worldwide economic crisis were fully apparent.

After 1918, no country fully embodied the nationalist ideal that had become the organizing principle of politics: a polity based on a single, organically conceived nation that was as homogeneous as possible. Around 1930, the titular nation was 92 percent of the total population in Albania, 87 percent in Bulgaria, 85 percent in Greece, 83 percent in Yugoslavia, and less than 73 percent in Romania.[51]

New forms of centralism and unitarism were supposed to encourage greater national cohesion. In the Kingdom of Serbs, Croats, and Slovenes (after 1929, Yugoslavia), Slovenes and "Serbo-Croatians" became the titular nation, which was also home to Montenegrins, Bosnian Muslims, and Macedonians. According to prevailing opinion, there was a single South Slav people that was composed of three tribes and had three names. By then, however, most of the peoples already had a clearly defined sense of a separate national identity as Croats, Serbs, or Macedonians, which resisted absorption into a single South Slav nation. The "Croatian Question," which led to the claim for autonomy, was particularly explosive.[52]

The situation was also confusing in Romania, where dramatic territorial expansion increased the proportion of minorities from 8 percent to nearly 28 percent of the country's population. Nationally minded Romanians felt as if they had become a minority within their own state. "Walking through Romanian cities," the intellectual Mircea Vulcănescu complained, "one might hear just two or three Romanian voices, in all classes of society."[53] That was a great exaggeration, but the annexed territories were in fact ethnically mixed, and minorities dominated in many cities. Because these territories were also more urban and industrially developed than the older Romanian core, minorities—especially the Jews—became the focus of anti-urban, xenophobic, and anti-Semitic resentment.[54] The "nationalization" of education, government administration, and the economy was widely accepted as a foundation for progress and stability in the interwar era, not only in Romania. Ethnic and religious minorities in the other successor states also faced pressure to assimilate or emigrate.[55]

A key part of the structural crisis of east-central and southeastern Europe was chronic revisionism and irredentism, which triggered diverse bilateral territorial conflicts. The governments were concerned not only about the amount of land they controlled but also about the protection of conationals—whether labor migrants or minorities—who were living in other states, and they sought to uphold these peoples' connection to the nation. Nationally minded Greeks and Albanians were dismayed that up to half of their people lived in neighboring or other foreign states. Thus, the Greek prime minister Venizelos lobbied for a population exchange with Bulgaria because—in the words of one colonel—Greeks who lived there would otherwise be "Bulgarized or annihilated." Instead, he argued, they could become colonists in Greece's newly acquired territories and serve as "the nucleus for the Hellenization of all Bulgarian villages."[56] "Greece cannot be understood without its children in the diaspora," was a widespread sentiment in the 1930s.[57]

All the successor states suffered greatly from the consequences of the war. Serbia lost more than 16 percent of its population; Romania, more than 9 percent; Bulgaria and Greece, between 3 percent and 4 percent.[58] Industry, mining, agriculture, and hundreds of miles of railway tracks had been destroyed in the war. All this, plus dismantling and requisitioning, meant that industrial production in 1919 was less than half the level of 1913.[59] Moreover, Romania and Yugoslavia had to contend with serious integration problems because economic areas that had grown together over time were now split apart. Yugoslavia inherited seven different currency, taxation, infrastructure, and legal systems. Refugees were yet another burden. Bulgaria had to accept a quarter-million displaced persons—and Greece, more than one million—into a population of less than five million.[60] Talk of revolution was everywhere since the last months of the war. Strikes, uprisings, and coup attempts marked the transition from war to peace at the end of the decade, and in some cases, well into the 1920s.

The nearly unchallenged preeminence of the conservative and liberal parties and coalitions before 1914 now began to falter. Leading politicians like Ion Brătianu in Romania, Eleftherios Venizelos in Greece, and Nikola Pašić in Serbia provided personal continuities with the prewar era. But the disastrous consequences of the war had strengthened the communists and agrarians, and now universal suffrage turned the mass of the population—peasants and workers—into a decisive political factor.[61]

In Bulgaria, the bourgeois parties paid for their country's humiliating military defeat with an electoral one. In 1919 the Bulgarian Agrarian National Union claimed an unambiguous victory with 31 percent of the vote. The agrarian party presided over hundreds of local groups (known as *druzhbi*), cooperatives, and reading circles, and it used parades, banners, flags, and music to bring the peasants to the polls.[62] Its forceful leader, Alexander Stamboliyski, pushed for an egalitarian, peasant-led society and the "rule of the people" *(narodovlastie)*. Stamboliyski, who was a notorious womanizer and came from peasant stock himself, had already played a formative role in the party before the war. He developed his political program after spending time as a student in the German town of Halle. Influenced by Russian populism as well as the German idea of workers' cooperatives, he proposed a middle way between capitalism and Bolshevism.[63]

During the war, Stamboliyski had spent three years in jail because of his pacifist and antimonarchical leanings. This exceptional politician stood out with his thick dark hair, his artfully curled moustache, and the combative gleam in his eyes. After a failed rebellion in 1918, he worked to achieve systemic change through the ballot box instead. He believed that women should have the right to vote and to participate in Bulgaria's political life.[64]

As head of the government, Stamboliyski initiated a seemingly utopian project in 1920. This included comprehensive land, taxation, judicial, and educational reform; he also outlawed large estates. He was no lofty intellectual, but instead resembled "a boar, forced by the whims of fate to sit at a desk."[65] From here, he redistributed land to refugees and peasants, built up cooperative and educational institutions, introduced a national labor service, constructed streets and bridges, and laid railway and telephone lines. With his "massive build, broad shoulders, unrefined movements, and intense manner of speaking," one acquaintance recalled, he impressed "everyone with his energy, his earnestness, and his fearlessness."[66] Thanks to the successes of his great modernization program, the Agrarian Union captured 53 percent of the vote in the parliamentary elections in 1923.[67]

But Stamboliyski offended the Bulgarian tsar, the church, and the bourgeois establishment. He restricted the middle classes' freedom to choose their professions, and he introduced a "committee for peasant dictatorship" to circumvent the parliamentary system and push through initiatives. He was authoritarian and quick-tempered. He oversaw the liquidation of his political opponents by the paramilitary Orange Guard. "Our rule is not a rule, but a war," he asserted, "a true internal and external war."[68]

In 1920 Stamboliyski arranged for Bulgaria to join the League of Nations. One year later, in Prague, he founded the Green International to unite peasants' parties across Europe. And he had long dreamed of a democratic federation of Balkan states, even before the First World War. "If the small nations want to stay independent, they must unite with neighboring small nations to form an area that will have all of the same rights as large countries," he explained at the time. "We small nations have already been oppressed and tormented enough, forced into all kinds of adventures."[69] Thus, under his administration schoolchildren were supposed to learn Esperanto, a newly invented universal language.

Stamboliyski sought a compromise with the SHS state over the Macedonian question, recognizing that "everywhere in the world, peace depends on good neighborly relations."[70] In 1923 he entered into an agreement with Belgrade to dissolve the armed bands of the Macedonian underground organization, which had built a state within a state in the Pirin Mountains. In response, Macedonian nationalists and his opponents in the Bulgarian military undertook a putsch. They captured Stamboliyski, cut off his hand, which had signed the antirevisionist pact with Yugoslavia, and tortured him to death. A right-wing, authoritarian government known as the Democratic Concord subsequently took power. That same year, the regime responded to an uprising and failed assassination attempt on Tsar Boris III with a "blood orgy" against members of the Communist and Agrarian Parties.[71] The potential of a leftist government in Bulgaria was thus shut down for the foreseeable future. Rancor and revanchism now drove Bulgarian foreign policy.[72]

An experiment with radical reform failed in Albania as well. The country was devastated by the war, financially depleted, and overwhelmed by refugees. Italian, Yugoslav, and Greek troops remained on Albanian soil years after the war's end, and anarchic conditions prevailed. Two different interest groups fought bitterly—on one hand, large landowners and tribal leaders who wanted to hold on to their privileges, and on the other, representatives of the liberal democratic bourgeoisie in the cities and diaspora. They disagreed on everything—reforms, foreign policy, and the type of government.[73]

The Orthodox cleric Fan Noli, who had advocated so strongly for the founding of Albania while living in the United States, returned to Europe in 1920 as an envoy for the National Assembly. His months of lobbying in the capitals for Albania's acceptance in the League of Nations was ultimately a success. Representing his Vatra organization, he became a member of parliament in 1921. Amid ongoing domestic turmoil and political violence, Noli placed himself at the forefront of a "Democratic Revolution" in 1924. His government program sought to abolish feudalism, improve conditions for the peasants, introduce a fair system of taxation and justice, and modernize health care and education. But implementation was slow, and the resistance of large landowners grew. The international community refused to support the "red bishop." Six months after taking office, Noli was forced out by the right-wing authoritarian Ahmet Zogu. Noli fled the country, and Zogu was elected president with unlimited powers.[74]

Since the last months of the war, revolutionary sentiments had been brewing in other countries, too. In the SHS state, the Croatian Peasant

Party, under the leadership of the charismatic Stjepan Radić, established itself as the third-largest political force in 1920. In Romania, the National Peasant Party even won three-quarters of all parliamentary seats in 1928.[75] Workers, small farmers, and the impoverished rural and urban underclasses were also drawn to communism, with its promise of social justice and national equality. Communists won 12.5 percent of the vote in the first elections in the SHS state; in Bulgaria, they even won 18 percent.[76] Because of hostilities between the peasants' parties and communists, a broad antibourgeois coalition did not materialize. Only once, in Romania, did the parties form an electoral alliance.[77] Communist parties were banned in Yugoslavia and Romania in 1921, in Bulgaria in 1923, and in Greece in 1936; their supporters were brutally persecuted or forced into exile. But the communist danger did not disappear. Illegal, Soviet-style cadre parties remained active underground.[78]

From the very beginning, all the successor states harbored serious doubts about the legitimacy and functionality of the democratic order. The Romanian constitution was approved by a majority of only one vote because of criticisms of centralism and the "national, unitary character of the Romanian state."[79] In the multiethnic SHS state, there was even less enthusiasm for the strict centralist constitution, which served the interests of the Serbian dynasty and secured Serbian hegemony. Slovenes and Croats made their opposition known while Yugoslavia was still in the early stages of its founding.[80] The Peasant Party politician Stjepan Radić repeatedly called for a federal solution, ensuring that the "Croatian question" remained on the domestic agenda. Radić, the most prominent opponent of Serbian centralism, fell victim to an assassin's bullet while in parliament in 1928.[81]

The murder of the opposition leader dramatically demonstrated the weaknesses of parliamentarism and the broader political culture in this era. There was no tradition of resolving conflicts of interest through compromise, nor a will to begin. Boycotts of governments and elections occurred daily; the instability was chronic. In Greece, the government changed twenty-one times between 1924 and 1936; in Yugoslavia, it changed thirty-nine times between 1918 and 1941.[82]

The prestige of parliamentarism was largely dependent on economic success, but the Great Depression sent the world economy reeling in 1929. Falling prices, slumps in production, mass unemployment, and poverty confounded national governments and international crisis management, and the parliamentary systems lost credibility at breakneck speed.[83]

Most southeastern European countries were already on the path to authoritarianism even before the world economic crisis unfurled its full destructive power. Conservative national interests had never wholly accepted the fundamental decision for parliamentarism, democracy, and the bourgeois order after 1918. The disastrous effects of liberalization and market globalization strengthened the desire for a strong state. Even liberal bourgeois politicians began to look for alternatives to representative, elected government.[84] Liberal political institutions had been on the retreat worldwide since Mussolini's rise to power in 1922. One after another, the southeastern European states abandoned their parliamentary systems. The number of democracies around the world decreased by half between 1920 and 1938. Of the twenty-eight democracies in Europe, only eleven remained. Growing international tensions reinforced a global context that was decidedly hostile to democracy.[85]

The democratic experiment ended first in Albania, where the authoritarian president Ahmet Zogu was declared king in 1928. Following the Italian example, he built up mass organizations and introduced an unprecedented leadership and personality cult, styling himself as the successor of Skanderbeg or Alexander the Great. In Belgrade, King Alexander used the assassination of Stjepan Radić as a pretext for dissolving the parliament in 1929, reorganizing his state as the "Kingdom of Yugoslavia" according to the model of French *départements,* and forcibly asserting an integral Yugoslav national identity.[86] Bulgaria and Romania likewise became royal dictatorships in the 1930s. Tsar Boris suspended parliamentarism after the military coup of the right-wing Zveno organization in Sofia in 1935. Carol II of Romania followed suit in 1938, writing in his diary that he would now be free "to adopt harsher measures . . . to free both the country and myself from the often unpatriotic tyranny of petty party interests."[87] Only in Greece, where General Ioannis Metaxas seized power in 1936, did dictatorship come in military guise, rather than under the auspices of the monarchy, which had been restored one year earlier. Metaxas's party claimed just 4 percent of the popular vote, but was eager to emulate German and Italian fascism and Turkish Kemalism, and it promoted a racially based nationalism.[88]

The royal dictatorships and authoritarian regimes pursued the ideal of an ethnically, socially, and politically unified nation, which they sought to realize through dictatorial means, and by eliminating the multiparty system. Powerholders suspended the constitution, censored the press,

Southeastern Europe in 1930

Baltic Sea

Klaipėda •
LITHUANIA
Kaunas •
• Vilna
Smolensk •

Danzig • Königsberg •
• Minsk
Byelorussian SSR

East Prussia
SOVIET UNION

Pomerania
• Stettin
• Toruń
• Białystok

Elbe

• Berlin
GERMANY
• Poznań
Warsaw •
POLAND
• Brest-Litovsk

• Łódź

Kiev •
Dnieper

Dresden •
Breslau •
Oder
• Oppeln
• Lublin
• Łuck

Prague •
• Kraków
Lviv •
• Tarnopol
Ukrainian SSR

Bohemia
CZECHO-
• Brno
SLOVAKIA
• Košice
• Stanisławów
Bug

Vienna •
• Bratislava
Chernivtsi •
Prut
Dniester

• Salzburg
Tisza
• Debrecen
Iaşi •

AUSTRIA
• Budapest
HUNGARY
• Chişinău

Klagenfurt • Graz
Drava
• Cluj
ROMANIA

Ljubljana •
Mureş

Venice •
Zagreb •
• Timişoara
Sibiu •
Brăila •

Rijeka (Fiume) •
Sava

SAN MARINO
• Banja Luka
Belgrade •
• Bucharest

Zara (Ital.) •
YUGOSLAVIA
Danube
Varna •

• Ancona
Split •
• Sarajevo
Niš •
BULGARIA
• Burgas

ITALY
• Mostar
• Sofia

Lagosta (Ital.)
• Cetinje
Skopje •
• Plovdiv

• Rome
Adriatic
Tirana •
Edirne •
Istanbul •

Benevento •
• Foggia
• Ohrid

Naples •
• Bari
ALBANIA
• Thessaloniki
TURKEY

Taranto •
• Brindisi
Pergamon •

Corfu
Ioannina •
• Larissa
Lesbos
İzmir •

GREECE
Aegean
Chios

Palermo •
Messina •
• Reggio
• Athens

Sicily

• Syracuse
Dodecanese (Ital.)
Rhodes

Mediterranean Sea
Crete

• Malta
Heraklion •

0   100   200   300 km

disenfranchised parliaments, parties, and unions, and "cleansed" the administration of political opponents. In contrast to the fascist and National Socialist regimes, the royal dictatorships did not seek revolutionary social change. They did not represent totalitarian ideologies, but rather, paternalistic notions of governance. They emphasized conservative values and traditional culture, without entirely losing sight of the goal of modernization "from above" through technological progress.[89]

The authoritarian systems and royal dictatorships were grounded in an alliance of the old elites, the royal bureaucracy, the military, and the wealthy bourgeoisie.[90] But people with lesser means also longed for security and clarity, for traditions and values that conveyed stability and trust. Conservatives saw the village as the original, purest form of communal life and experience—the idealized antithesis of individualism, liberalism, and capitalism. The retreat into tradition and religion originally had less to do with ideology than with an emotional reaction and outlook on life, but as the century progressed, mistrust in democracy and human rights increasingly took the shape of radical, exclusive nationalism. The younger generation, in particular, longed for new solutions—as with the Neo-Albanians, the Young Bulgarians, and the Young Generation and Legionnaires in Romania. They sought progress, moral renewal, a unifying national awareness grounded in religion, and a totalitarian state.[91] Their criticisms targeted not only capitalism and the industrialized world but also parliamentarism and multiparty democracy, which they saw as a threat to the survival of the nation and the nation-state. They linked fears of modernization with antiliberal, anti-Semitic, and anticapitalist resentment, adding pessimism for the future and a critique of civilization.[92]

An eloquent champion of this mindset was the philosophy professor and columnist Nae Ionescu, one of Romania's most distinguished intellectuals. He was born in Brăila and studied philosophy in Munich, writing his dissertation on "Logic as an Attempt at a New Foundation of Mathematics." He taught logic, the history of logic, and metaphysics at the University of Bucharest, and he edited the intellectual journal *Cuvântul (Word)*. Ionescu was the intellectual forefather of the Young Generation, which sought to revolutionize Romanian culture amid the upheavals of the 1920s. His students included diverse figures such as Mircea Eliade (later a renowned religious scholar), philosopher Emil Cioran, playwright Eugène Ionesco, and writer Mihail Sebastian, all of whom participated in the Criterion group after 1932.[93] The young men and women revered the young professor who challenged them to question all values, proclaiming a radical antirationalism and anti-individualism from his crowded lecture halls. His philosophy of *trăirism* proceeded from collective experience and faith, not deified reason.[94]

Ionescu was "brown-haired, pale, with thick, Mephistophelian eyebrows and large, unusually bright eyes of dusky, metallic blue," as Mircea Eliade recalled. He dressed with a casual elegance, and he captivated his audience because he did not speak in the style of a typical professor. "One felt that what Nae Ionescu said could not be found in any book. It was something new, his thoughts taking shape right there in our presence."[95] In fact, Ionescu's worldview was hardly original, and it was even plagiarized in part. His inaugural lecture paraphrased an essay by Max Scheler, and long stretches of his other lectures borrowed the words of Oswald Spengler.[96] Other sources of inspiration included the interpretive psychology of Wilhelm Dilthey, sociologist Ferdinand Tönnies's theory of community, and Nikolai Berdyaev's work on religion. He was particularly influenced by Ludwig Klages, a member of the Cosmic Circle in Munich, who proposed that Judaism was responsible for the apocalyptic decline of modern civilization.[97] Ionescu combined fears of economic collapse, loss of status, and the effects of urban civilization with racist nationalism, antirationalism, cultural pessimism, and an aversion to progress.[98] "Democracy and constitutionalism are obsolete," the magician of the new nationalism proclaimed to his fascinated audience.[99] He saw national identity as an inalterable state of nature. A non-Orthodox Christian, let alone a Jew, could never be a "good Romanian."[100]

Although Nae Ionescu himself was not a member of the fascist Iron Guard, he served as its most important ideologue and intellectual forefather and called Hitler a "great politician."[101] The founder and charismatic leader of the Iron Guard was Corneliu Zelea Codreanu, a protagonist of the anti-Semitic student movement in the 1920s. The organization was inspired by the parties of Mussolini and Hitler. Like other fascist movements, it was characterized by radical antiliberalism and anticommunism. But its quasi-religious rituals, parades, and cult of heroic sacrifice also possessed culturally specific features, such as the glorification of the peasantry and the Orthodox Church. King Carol fought back brutally against the Legionnaires, imprisoning their leaders and ordering their deaths without trial. Nae Ionescu, too, was imprisoned for months as a sympathizer. Once entirely a student movement, the Iron Guard—despite persecution—steadily gained followers and became a sizable parliamentary force, earning 16 percent of the vote in 1937.[102]

Aside from Romania, Croatia was the only other place in southeastern Europe where fascism made notable strides. Here, the extreme right took the form of the separatist Croatian Party of Rights, which called for an independent, ethnically homogeneous Croatian nation-state and therefore ran afoul of the Yugoslav king. While in Italian exile in 1929, the attorney Ante Pavelić founded the underground organization Ustasha (Rebels), which was militantly anti-Yugoslav, anti-Serb, antiliberal, and anticommunist. The Ustasha engaged in acts of terrorism to compel the establishment of an independent greater Croatian state, which was to include Bosnia-Herzegovina, Sandžak, Montenegro, and part of Vojvodina. Like the Iron Guard, the Ustasha promoted the cult of a strong leader, glorified violence, and maintained paramilitary units. Its other role model was the Internal Macedonian Revolutionary Organization, a partner in many endeavors. In 1934 a collaborator of these groups murdered King Alexander and the French foreign minister Louis Barthou during a state visit in Marseille.[103]

Unlike their Romanian counterparts, the Croatian fascists did not attract a substantial base of voters before the outbreak of the Second World War. Extreme right-wing and fascist groups were even weaker in Bulgaria, Serbia, and Albania. In the agrarian societies of southeastern Europe, fascism gained a foothold only where disoriented, economically threatened middle classes provided the appropriate ideological and social milieus, as in Croatia and Romania. Most southeastern Europeans still lived within firmly grounded confessional, familial, and social relationships; a revolutionary transformation of existing conditions, as propagated by the fascists, had little appeal. Moreover—in contrast to Italy, Germany, and Spain—old elites were not prepared to share power with the radical right. Without the support of Hitler, neither the Iron Guard nor the Ustasha would have acquired historical significance during the Second World War.[104]

The 1930s became a decade of steadily intensifying ideological extremes and internal conflicts. Ideological conflicts combined with social, ethnic, and religious ones, leading to growing street violence and, at times, even conditions resembling civil war. The media and political events like demonstrations, parades, and strikes mobilized the masses and stirred up supposed opponents. As doubts in the legitimacy of the political and social order grew, radical political action began to look more attractive.[105] Parties founded paramilitary organizations and militias that brought political violence into the streets, and this in turn reinforced the inclination to expand executive authority to restore law and order.[106] As compromise between political camps and interest groups became less likely, and the international situation grew increasingly grim, acceptance of the parliamentary system—and the entire state order—sunk to new lows.

Internationalism and Multilateralism on the World Stage

In the Balkans, it was readily apparent that the old conference diplomacy of the great powers had outlived its usefulness. War and the politics of violence, economic and humanitarian crises that brought hunger and political unrest—these challenges called for collective action and strategies that transcended state borders.[107] The League of Nations, founded in 1919, provided the forum for the new diplomacy. As a pillar of the new international system, the league was to help solve transnational problems and interstate conflicts with the participation of all involved member states. Of course, exclusive meetings among the ambassadors of the great powers continued to play a role in international relations. But now smaller states could also participate in the collective decisions of the league's Assembly, Council, and Secretariat, as well as its numerous committees and suborganizations.[108] Economic and cultural cooperation expanded and was gradually accepted as an instrument of international peacekeeping. Multilateralism and internationalism—the counterpoint to nationalism—developed into a significant feature of the twentieth century.[109]

The League of Nations became an important reference point for government representatives, interest groups, and experts from small, newly established countries—even if the United States did not participate in the organization at all, and the Soviet Union, Germany, and Japan only did so inconsistently. The league provided a welcome platform for bringing concerns and complaints before the world community, for exchanging information, and for implementing decisions about problems that transcended state borders.[110] The successor states of the great empires took this international dimension quite seriously and dispatched their best ministers to Geneva. Czechoslovakia sent Edvard Beneš, Romania sent Nicolae Titulescu, and Greece sent Nicolas Politis—outstanding statesmen who represented their countries' interests with professionalism and made an impression on the world.

The League of Nations was vitally important to the successor states for multiple reasons. To begin with, their sovereignty and territorial integrity depended on recognition from the international community. Thus, on December 17, 1920, the Albanian Fan Noli stood before the delegates of the world organization in Geneva with "eyes dimmed by tears and a lump rising in my throat." After heated debate, his country had been admitted into the league with thirty-five votes in favor and seven abstentions.[111] Albania's sovereignty and borders had been secured, and financial support was possible as well. The *Manchester Guardian* wrote that Noli would have been considered just as remarkable in any other country: "An accomplished diplomat, an expert in international affairs, a skillful debater, from the outset he made a deep impression in Geneva."[112]

Bulgaria, one of the war's losers, also fought to become a member of the world organization. Bulgaria was most interested in repairing its damaged reputation and attracting political support.[113] By contrast, Romania and Greece, whose territory had grown dramatically after the war, and also the newly founded SHS state, hoped that the system of collective security would protect them from the revisionism of their neighbors, particularly Bulgaria. After all, the League of Nations was committed to the renunciation of violence, peaceful conflict resolution, and collective problem-solving. Negotiators in Geneva did, in fact, achieve a notable success in 1925, when they used diplomatic channels to contain a dangerous crisis between Greece and Bulgaria. And the world organization had already chased Greek and Serbian troops out of Albania with the threat of sanctions, thereby upholding standards of international law.

In addition to its referee function in the resolution of interstate conflicts, as a corporate actor, the League of Nations addressed issues such as migration, disarmament, terrorism, and the combat of disease, which were not contained by state borders.[114] The refugee problem, which had taken on unprecedented dimensions during and after the war, was particularly urgent for southeastern Europeans. Through 1926, about 9.5 million people within Europe were compelled to emigrate or resettle. They had lost homes and citizenship after taking flight or being forcibly expelled.[115] The first high commissioner for refugees, the Norwegian explorer Fridtjof Nansen, had to contend with one to two million Russian and Armenian refugees, many of whom had made their way to southeastern Europe and the Near East. The Greek-Bulgarian treaty of 1920 introduced a voluntary population exchange, and three years later the Treaty of Lausanne instituted a mandatory one between Greece and Turkey. The first instance resulted in the resettlement of 280,000 people; the second, 1.5 million. Greece, which took in a total of 1.2 million refugees, threatened to collapse under the humanitarian burden. Athens and Thessaloniki alone sheltered as many refugees as they had residents. "Save in China," wrote one observer, "I have never been in a place where the sense of crowding is more acute."[116] In Greece, the High Commission eventually set up camps for the impoverished new arrivals; it also distributed humanitarian aid and gave loans to migrant entrepreneurs. Given the extent of the social challenges, this was hardly more than a drop in the bucket. But without Nansen's courageous efforts, Greece and the other states would have directed even fewer resources toward unpopular refugee assistance.[117]

Through specialized programs, the League of Nations encouraged the development of modern economic and social systems in southeastern Europe. In 1920 balanced budgets, measures to control inflation, and the establishment of central banks and internationally compatible systems of credit became the preconditions for member states to receive international assistance.[118] The southeastern European states implemented the corresponding reforms under the direction of foreign financial, economic, and legal advisers. Bulgaria and Greece received millions in loans. The world organization made a significant contribution to the restoration of shattered economic systems. Only Albania failed to implement the recommended measures and compensate its experts.[119]

Through the activities of the International Labor Organization (ILO), the establishment of the social welfare state in southeastern Europe became a genuinely transnational undertaking. In response to the international workers' movement and the growing lure of communism, the community of states resolved to move forward with social reform.[120] The southeastern European governments sent delegations of diplomats, employers, and trade unionists to Geneva. Progressive conventions on the eight-hour workday, protections for workers and mothers, and social security were quickly adopted, but ratification and implementation at home moved forward much more slowly. A socialist delegate from Yugoslavia scolded that the delay hurt not only the working class but also Yugoslavia's reputation in the world.[121] Nevertheless, the international conferences strengthened universalist discourse about social rights, and changed cultural attitudes toward approaching and solving problems. At the height of the world economic crisis, the ILO planned a European infrastructure program to create a half million jobs—an idea that many national governments, including Yugo-slavia, affirmed.[122] In addition to unemployment, many other problems began to be addressed within a global framework, including overpopula-tion, birth control, and migration policy. The immigration restrictions of many industrialized countries, which were hard on the economies of south-eastern Europe, became a topic of critical discussion at the World Popula-tion Conference of 1927.[123]

A further international problem was the situation of ethnic and linguistic minorities, whom the League of Nations had committed to protect. The peacemakers had failed to construct a universal regime for protecting mi-norities, along with effective mechanisms for implementation; these short-falls endangered the legitimacy of the world organization. The league received hundreds of petitions protesting the infringement of religious and organizational freedom, and the right to school instruction in minority lan-guages.[124] Structural discrimination against nationalities (for example, with land reform) became a contentious political issue, as states seeking to revise their borders instrumentalized the problem politically. With the sup-port of Sofia and Tirana, Macedonian and Albanian rebels in southern Yugoslavia fought to join the states of Bulgaria or Albania instead. Berlin and Budapest, meanwhile, encouraged Germans and Hungarians in Tran-sylvania and Vojvodina to launch demagogic attacks against the League of Nations and the treaties of Versailles and Trianon. And the Bulgarian government missed no opportunity to clamor for the revision of state bor-ders, pointing to the supposedly desperate conditions of the Bulgarian mi-norities.[125]

The League of Nations provided a forum for measures against interna-tional terrorism to be negotiated for the first time within a multilateral framework.[126] The immediate motivation was the murder of the Yugoslav king Alexander and the French foreign minister Louis Barthou by Mace-donian and Croatian assassins in Marseille in 1934. The Internal Macedo-nian Revolutionary Organization had established branches in Vienna, Geneva, Paris, Berlin, Rome, and other cities, acquiring access to illegal networks that procured money, automobiles, telephones, weapons, and mu-nitions. Other sources of income included the tobacco, poppy, and heroin trade, which brought the well-connected organization into the world market for drugs.[127] Although the League of Nations considered terrorism a top transnational threat, and French investigators could trace the assas-sins' connections in Italy and Hungary, the member states ultimately declined to pursue international sentencing for the conspirators. The discussion focused on conventions for preventing and prosecuting terrorism, and the proposal for an international criminal court.[128]

The Romanian Nicolae Titulescu was a committed proponent of the League of Nations idea, despite its practical weaknesses. The son of an attorney from Craiova, Titulescu received an international education in Switzerland and France before becoming a legal scholar, university professor, and delegate in the Romanian parliament. He represented Romania at international conferences and served in various government posts, including as finance minister and foreign minister. He also served his country at the League of Nations, where Romania was a founding member. Born in 1882, Titulescu was considered an exceptional political talent, distinguished by his sharp intellect, gift for public speaking, and captivating presence.[129] "Titulescu was an impressive appearance," a former official in the Romanian foreign office recalled. "Tall, with his slightly Mongoloid features, exquisitely dressed in a sober way, he radiated charm, sympathy, warmth, and youthfulness. He was an outstanding *causeur*, able to animate a whole evening with peerless liveliness, abundant humour and fascinating verve."[130]

Nicolae Titulescu was an equally enthusiastic and prominent spokesman for multilateralism—a Mr. League of Nations, so to speak. He successively served as Romania's permanent representative to the league, as a member of the commission for intellectual cooperation (the predecessor of UNESCO), and as chair of the finance committee. He was the only person to be elected as Assembly president twice in row, in 1930 and 1931. The indefatigable politician presented his arguments for expanding the international system in countless lectures, speeches, and books. In a highly regarded speech at the Berlin Reichstag in 1929, Titulescu depicted the new world order as a system of independent, sovereign nation-states whose rights and responsibilities were regulated by international law, as foreseen by Immanuel Kant in his 1795 essay, *Perpetual Peace*. Global connections had long influenced the fields of culture, economics, and social institutions. Now, Titulescu argued, international law needed to expand to include the principle of nonintervention, the effective protection of territorial integrity, condemnation of war, and mechanisms of conflict resolution.[131] Under his leadership, the Romanian delegation in Geneva promoted initiatives for disarmament, peaceful conflict regulation, and the expansion of international law.[132] "Maybe the so-called smaller countries have a better knowledge of the demands of peace," Titulescu proposed, "because they are more afraid of war, and they are more exposed to it."[133]

"Titus" was a favored guest in elite political circles. Winston Churchill, Aristide Briand, and Gustav Stresemann (who affectionately scolded him as "a devil") appreciated his knowledgeability and analytical talents. To the writer Paul Valéry, Titulescu was the most unusual and idiosyncratic person he had ever met.[134] The impassioned protagonist of the League of Nations promoted his cause with all available rhetorical means—sometimes temperamentally and with theatrical flair, sometimes by employing every convention of diplomatic finesse. The Austrian envoy complained that at home he behaved like "a hysterical prima donna from the movies, playing the spoiled child or almighty tsar." He traveled "with a nearly royal entourage, in a salon car" through Europe, gladly receiving visitors at the train when he reached his destination.[135]

Titulescu's efforts earned Romania a nonpermanent seat on the League of Nations Council in 1935. The *Echo de Paris* remarked that "the Assembly intended to express its exceptional appreciation . . . to the Romanian statesman who represents the struggle of the small nations against imperialism with the greatest intelligence, eloquence, and power of persuasion."[136] Titulescu continued to advocate for the League of Nations even after it lost much of its relevance and credibility in the 1930s. Only through the league's continued existence, he argued, could a state that had been wronged alert the world community and bring about sanctions.[137] Titulescu normalized Romanian relations with the Soviet Union in order to reach a compromise in the Bessarabian question, which he identified as one of the "most important acts" of his entire political career. He lobbied no less enthusiastically to gain the support of the Latin American states for his security initiatives in the league. He was passionate in organizing majorities against the aggressive foreign policy of Italy and Nazi Germany, and he pushed for economic sanctions against Mussolini, who occupied Abyssinia in 1935. He was hated by the Italian and Romanian fascists, who put him on their hit list and set his library on fire. Through all of this, the sovereignty and territorial integrity of his homeland remained especially close to his heart. As late as 1937, Titulescu still declared that there could be "no political life without the League of Nations," elsewhere adding this qualification: "I, who am deeply human, have the courage to state publicly that mankind does not concern me unless Romania finds her place within it."[138]

The symbiotic relationship between love of homeland and multilateralism could hardly be expressed more succinctly.

Titulescu believed that regional cooperation was a central building block of the new, post–First World War architecture of security, and this, too, was a thorn in the eye of the war's losers. In 1920 and 1921, Yugoslavia, Romania, and Czechoslovakia formed the Little Entente with a system of bilateral treaties to protect against Hungarian, Bulgarian, and Austrian revisionism. France, which had encouraged this "little League of Nations" within the larger organization, signed friendship treaties with Prague, Bucharest, and Belgrade. The Czechoslovakian foreign minister Edvard Beneš stated that the Little Entente "is against territorial revision; it is against the Anschluss [German annexation of Austria]; it is against the restoration of the Habsburgs, in whichever form." The alliance would support these goals "without wavering, without compromise, and without giving in."[139] Despite various overtures, the Little Entente was not able to expand its membership in the following years. Albania showed interest, but Italy's veto stopped it from joining. Instead, Albania was compelled to enter into separate friendship and defense pacts with Italy in 1926 and 1927. After the murder of Stamboliyski, who had been a great proponent of a Balkan federation, Bulgaria's government turned toward revisionism.[140]

Independent of foreign policy alliances and orientations, Romania, Bulgaria, Albania, Yugoslavia, Greece, and Turkey sought to encourage closer cultural ties by rallying broad segments of the population on behalf of peace. Beginning in 1929, they organized Balkan Games (modeled after the Olympics) to encourage friendship and cooperation in southeastern Europe.[141]

In the 1930s, amid growing international tensions and the danger of war, the southeastern European states stepped up their efforts to create more effective regional security structures.[142] In the spirit of the motto "The Balkans for the Balkan Peoples," plans for a federation were taken up at four Balkan Conferences. The Greeks' proposal went furthest, suggesting a political union of sovereign states without internal barriers to travel or trade. They also supported shared school curricula and scholarship programs, and uniform social legislation.[143] But the international climate, influenced by Hitler's rise to power, dashed hopes for establishing a common front of the Great War's winners and losers. Greece, Turkey, Romania, and Yugoslavia were the only signatories of the Balkan Pact on February 9, 1934; their aim was to protect their borders against military aggressors—in other words, Bulgaria and Italy. The Balkan Pact countries formed a standing council of foreign ministers to coordinate their cooperative efforts, but their work was undermined by the growing influence of the revisionist states as well as bilateralism. The Balkan Pact never became an effective instrument of foreign policy.[144]

Meanwhile, other internationalist proposals—Count Coudenhove-Kalergi's pan-European movement, French foreign minister Aristide Briand's suggestion for a European union, and French prime minister André Tardieu's project for a Danubian-Balkan federation with a common market—also attracted prominent supporters in southeastern Europe. The Greek prime minister Venizelos, like Titulescu, lobbied for an architecture of security arranged in concentric circles. He envisioned a Balkan federation as part of a larger European union, which would necessarily include Turkey as well.[145]

Internationalism continued to develop outside the realm of official government policy. In 1919, one year before the founding of the League of Nations, the Bolsheviks established the Communist International to coordinate socialist movements and spread the workers' revolution. One of its leading functionaries at the end of the 1930s was the Bulgarian Georgi Dimitrov. From the communist perspective, the liberal internationalism of the League of Nations was nothing but a masquerade that allowed a "Holy Alliance of the capitalists to suppress the workers' revolution."[146] In 1920, communists in Romania, Yugoslavia, Bulgaria, and Greece proclaimed their plan to establish a "Communist Balkan Federation" on the Soviet model once the current governments were successfully overthrown. In Vienna, the editors of a journal called *Balkan Federation* took up the cause in French, Greek, Turkish, Serbian, Croatian, Romanian, Bulgarian, and Albanian.[147]

The Spanish Civil War became a symbol of international solidarity in 1936. The war was a high-water mark in the existential battle between fascism and democracy, and a proxy conflict between the Axis powers and the Soviet Union. Less than one century after hundreds of Europeans had supported Garibaldi's freedom fighters in Italy, thousands of leftists and communists from more than fifty countries joined International Brigades to fight alongside the Republican army—including about 1,500 Yugoslavians, Albanians, and Bulgarians, and 400 Romanians. Comparatively few volunteers fought for Franco.[148] The antifascists lost the war, but the events in Spain were important for the socialization and training

Nicolae Titulescu (third from the left) signing the Balkan Pact in Athens, February 9, 1934.

of European leftists. The Spanish Civil War turned internationalism into lived experience, strengthened communist networks across state borders, and prepared activists for partisan battles in their home countries (which were not yet foreseeable at the time). The communist parties' conspiratorial efforts ultimately allowed the volunteers, men and women alike, to cross multiple borders illegally; once they reached France, they completed their journey on foot, crossing the Pyrenees into Spain. In many ways, the era provided a template for the cooperation of the communist countries after 1945.[149] Manès Sperber drew from this material in his famous novel, *Like a Tear in the Ocean,* which followed the protagonist Donjo Faber and his comrades through the communist underground in Germany, Russia, Yugoslavia, Poland, France, and Italy.[150]

Analogous to the socialists, the European peasants' parties founded the Green International, an initiative of the Bulgarian Alexander Stamboliyski, in Prague in 1921. The Green International did not seek to create a new world order, but rather a framework for coordinating and representing the interests of the agrarian parties.[151] In 1923 Moscow responded with the Red Peasant International (Krestintern), which was supposed to win over the peasantry to the cause of workers' revolution.[152] Communists, socialists, and agrarians made the idea of international cooperation in general, and a

Balkan federation in particular, part of their political program for the masses—something promoted only by isolated idealists and revolutionaries before 1914.[153]

International contacts, conferences, and meetings had been part of scholarly networks and civil society since the end of the nineteenth century. Now there were genuine "transnational" nongovernmental organizations dedicated to universal values and humanitarian concerns, such as the League for Human Rights. Activists in the feminist movement fought against the global problem of discrimination against women.[154] Women's groups from southeastern Europe joined international women's associations and founded regional bodies such as the Little Entente of Women, the Slavic Women's Committee, and the Balkan Women's Conferences for Peace.[155]

Nicolae Titulescu and the advocates of internationalism lost the battle for a new, peaceful world order. The League of Nations was powerless against Japanese aggression in China, Italian aggression in Abyssinia, and Germany's annexation of Austria and dismemberment of Czechoslovakia. The protests of Jewish organizations against the anti-Semitic Nuremberg Laws in Germany, and the expulsion of thousands of Jews from Romania, came to nothing under the pressure of the authoritarian member states.[156] By 1938, the Geneva system of collective security, minority protection, and the entire League of Nations was effectively dead. Work continued only in subsidiary bodies such as the international labor and health organizations. Nevertheless, important actors in politics and civil society still believed that internationalism was the only way to prevent another great war. Nicolae Titulescu believed that even an imperfect instrument of peace was better than war.[157] King Carol II, who disapproved of Titulescu's treaty negotiations with the Soviet Union, dismissed the impertinent internationalist from the Romanian government in 1936. He died in French exile in 1941.

At the end of the 1930s, the League of Nations at last collapsed under the weight of its unmistakable weaknesses—a lack of authority, the nonparticipation of important powers, and the inability to take political or military action. It was unable to provide effective solutions for the world economic crisis or rising fascist aggression. From the standpoint of internationalism, however, it was an important innovation. The league provided southeastern Europeans with a forum to affirm their national statehood, to propose international solutions for problems that were not contained by state borders, and to participate in an emerging system of global governance. Southeastern Europeans were active participants in international associations, specialized societies, and world organizations of all kinds, which continued to grow in number and institutionalize cooperation despite—or precisely because of—ascendant nationalist aggression. Political realism and international idealism were not necessarily at odds; rather, the two outlooks coexisted and complemented one another.[158] And even though the Geneva system broke down miserably in the 1930s, multilateralism could no longer be wished away.

Deglobalization and Great Depression

The First World War interrupted transcontinental flows of labor, capital, and goods, and the world economy ground to a halt. This process of deglobalization was reinforced by the Paris peace treaties. In Europe, nine new national economies, thirteen additional currencies, and more than twelve thousand miles of international borders and customs barriers impeded international trade and the flow of capital in the interwar era. The world economic crisis encouraged economic nationalism and accelerated the dismantling of relationships of exchange. Currency devaluation, restrictions on foreign trade, protectionism, and bilateralism shrunk the value of international trade and capital flows. Only in the 1970s did the world economy once again reach the same degree of integration that it had before 1913.[159]

The southeastern European successor states suffered heavily from the consequences of war—physical destruction, requisitioning, and the flood of refugees. To alleviate socioeconomic misery in the countryside and quell revolutionary sentiment, the governments made agricultural reform an early priority, abolishing latifundia and feudal obligations. In Yugoslavia, more than six million acres—and in Romania, about fifteen million acres—were redistributed to small farmers, veterans, refugees, and other landless persons. The agricultural reforms had not only social but also national political motivations. Instead of "foreign" Hungarian, Turkish, and Russian estate owners, now Romanians, Serbs, or Croats could take possession of the land that they worked. Colonists were encouraged to settle in newly acquired territories and border regions, so these areas could be "nationalized." There was land reform in Bulgaria, too, where large estates had already been broken up in the years before the war. Only in Albania did the feudal class remain.[160]

Around 1930, 70 to 80 percent of the population in Romania, Yugoslavia, and Bulgaria still made their living through agriculture; in Greece, it was less than 50 percent.[161] Despite—and in part, because of—agricultural reform, the majority of southeastern European peasants remained poor. High demographic surpluses and low economic growth exacerbated the chronic underemployment that had existed since the second half of the nineteenth century. Improved medical care and persistently high birthrates accelerated population growth. The population in Albania, Bulgaria, and Yugoslavia grew by nearly one-third between 1920 and 1939; the growth rate was slightly less in Romania. More and more people relied on unprofitable farms for their sustenance. There was a lack of credit, machinery, and specialized knowledge for improving productivity. The mass of the rural population owned too little land even to support themselves. In Romania and Yugoslavia, three-quarters of the peasants farmed less than thirteen acres of land; in Bulgaria, it was about two-thirds.[162] About half of all peasant households in Albania owned no land at all, but instead rented farmland from the owners of large estates.[163]

In the 1930s the productivity of each agricultural laborer in the Balkan countries was less than half the European average.[164] Peasants in Bulgaria and Albania still used mostly wooden plows and hardly any agricultural machinery. Sowing, harvesting, and threshing was done by hand; artificial fertilizers were too expensive for many farmers. Yields were correspondingly low. According to League of Nations calculations for 1930, Albania had a "surplus" agricultural population of up to 70 to 80 percent; this group was unable to sustain itself from the land. The surplus agricultural population was 62 percent in Yugoslavia, and up to 53 percent in Bulgaria, Romania, and Greece.[165] An expert commission from the League of Nations found severe malnourishment and insufficient consumption of meat and dairy products, and a dramatically elevated rate of child mortality, in many parts of southeastern Europe.[166]

A significant consequence of the war with consequences for the world economy was the United States overtaking Europe as the leading economic power and creditor nation. But this did little to change southeastern Europe's asymmetric foreign trade structure, which had been established in the nineteenth century. Southeastern European exports continued to be mostly foodstuffs and raw materials; each country often had only one or two dominant products. Tobacco made up 55 percent of Greek exports in the 1920s, and dried fruits and wine, another 25 percent. Up to 77 percent of Romanian exports were grain and crude oil. Imports, by contrast, were primarily industrial consumer and intermediate goods.[167] Before and after the war, foreign trade balances in southeastern Europe were beset by low export volumes, low levels of diversification, and unfavorable terms of trade.

The United States, Canada, and Latin America took the lead in global agricultural production with their immense expanses of cultivated land, mechanized farming techniques, and the use of artificial fertilizers. Falling transportation costs secured their competitive advantage. After the mid-1920s, oversupply on the world markets led to a dramatic decline in prices.[168] Global wages and earnings, domestic demand, and industrial production fell sharply after the New York stock market crash in October 1929. The volume of trade plummeted, until the world trade system effectively collapsed with the gold standard in 1931.[169]

The world economic crisis hit the southeastern European agrarian states in mid-1930—later than in the industrial countries, but with longer and more serious consequences. Because the industrial countries erected barriers to keep out cheap imports, the successor states lost access to important markets. By 1933, Albania's exports had shrunk to just 40 percent of their precrisis level; Romania was at 51 percent, and Yugoslavia, 67 percent.[170] Because world market prices had plummeted, agricultural earnings dwindled to a dangerous low. Between 1929 and 1933, overall agricultural prices shrank by about 60 percent; the decline was even steeper for grain.[171]

The world economic crisis hurt all sectors of the southeastern European economies, but the peasants were hit hardest. In Yugoslavia, for example, the average income of a peasant family sank by two-thirds between 1925 and 1933.[172] Many farmers fell deep into debt or had to find work elsewhere. Unemployment shot upward. The number of people who were registered as looking for work rose from 150,000 to 651,000 between 1930 and 1939. Hunger, homelessness, poverty, and desperation defined the daily experience of an entire generation.[173]

Labor migration was no longer a reliable escape. Classic receiving countries like the United States and Australia introduced rigid immigration quotas and residency restrictions, heightening the pressure within southeastern European labor markets. While up to 50,000 men and women emigrated overseas annually in the first decade of the twentieth century, this number fell to less than 7,000 in the 1930s.[174] The ranks of the unemployed rose exponentially, which in turn caused wages, prices, and national income to spiral downward. State expenditures had to be financed by borrowing, so the debt burden grew. As governments cut expenditures, deflation—the general decline of prices and wages—increased.[175]

Since agricultural prices fell faster than those of industrial goods, the Balkan countries' terms of trade worsened. As more and more European banks demanded repayment of their loans, insolvency loomed. Many contemporaries lost faith in supporters of free-market liberalism, who had trusted in the ability of the economy to right itself. Old strategies could not keep up with the new challenges of mass unemployment and poverty. Many states around the world turned to protectionism. In 1930, the United States raised tariffs to as much as 60 percent of the value of inbound goods. Nationalist economic policies hollowed out the formerly liberal system of world trade.[176]

Governments in southeastern Europe introduced exchange controls and payment moratoriums, and they curtailed foreign trade. They abolished the gold standard, reduced state expenditures, and formed monopolies and state agencies for regulating agricultural exports and loans, with the aim of protecting the impoverished peasantry from ruin. Interventionism spread to a growing number of economic sectors.[177] By 1934 the worst of the crisis had passed and world production began to recover. But governments held fast to economic nationalism, especially since international tensions raised concerns about a new war. Thus, the growth of world trade—and globalization—remained sluggish.[178]

Since the 1920s, the governments of the successor states had promoted import substitution, spurring on industrialization so that expensive imports could be replaced by national production. Romania, Bulgaria, Yugoslavia, and Greece eliminated tariffs on the import of machinery and raw materials, particularly in sectors relevant to military armament—including iron and steel production, mechanical engineering, and the chemical and textile industries. States offered discounted freight tariffs and tax rates, while erecting customs barriers for goods that could be produced at home. The goal was to attract domestic and foreign investors, and to increase production at the same time. The traumatic collapse of agricultural prices and the withdrawal of foreign capital during the Great Depression lent additional urgency to state interventionism. Governments in the 1930s imposed monopolies for tobacco, salt, explosives, and other products. They also established state-owned companies and financed large-scale public works. Their policies were driven by the dislocations of world trade and by corporatism and the buildup of arms. Unlike in Italy and Germany, the idea of autarky did not figure prominently in southeastern Europe.[179] In 1930s Bulgaria, one out of every three industrial companies was subsidized by the state. In

Romania, the state purchased 70 percent of all coal and 80 percent of all metals at the end of the 1930s.[180]

Mihail Manoilescu, a professor from Bucharest and later state minister of public works, was a prominent theoretician of economic nationalism. He published his *Theory of Protectionism* in Paris in 1929, arguing that national economies needed to minimize exchange with the world market in order to prosper. He hailed "the century of corporatism" and one-party rule in 1934.[181] His thinking was not only emblematic of the European spirit of the times; it also influenced economic and political theory worldwide. The Latin American states, in particular, embraced Romania's example. The Argentinean Raúl Prebisch, whose ideas informed dependency theory, was a notable disciple; we will encounter him again in Chapter 8.[182]

The southeastern Europeans' economic nationalism—protectionism and state intervention—accelerated industrialization. Industry began at a very low level, but it grew faster than all other sectors throughout the entire interwar era. The per capita annual growth rate was 2.1 percent in Yugoslavia, 2.4 percent in Romania, 3.4 percent in Greece, and 7.1 percent in Bulgaria. Even by the end of the 1930s, however, the volume and value of industrial production in southeastern Europe still lagged far behind highly developed industrial countries; per capita production in Bulgaria reached only 3.7 percent, and in Yugoslavia, 6.3 percent, of the level in Britain. In Hungary, it was more than 20 percent, and Czechoslovakia, more than 40 percent.[183] But compared to the situation before the First World War, the transformation was striking. Industrial production in Romania and Yugoslavia doubled between 1913 and the eve of the Second World War; industrial growth was even stronger in Bulgaria. Only Albanian industry—with the exception of crude oil production—lagged far behind.[184] Albania had not emerged as a nation-state until shortly before the Great War, and it was decades behind the other Balkan states in developing an independent economic and development policy. Its semicolonial status, high population growth, extremely low levels of education, remainders of feudalism, and indifferent decision makers continued to hinder socioeconomic change in the interwar era. At the end of the 1930s, per capita income in this land of just one million people was only half that in Yugoslavia or Romania.[185] Growth rates were highest in Greece, but it also had a higher level of debt; Greece did not succeed in reforming its one-sided export structure.[186]

Protected by tariffs, the textile, leather, and garment industry became the strongest economic sector—replacing food production, mills, and breweries.

On the eve of the Second World War, it represented about one-quarter of all industrial production. The other consumer goods industries caught up as well. By the end of the 1930s, Bulgaria and Romania had reduced their consumer imports by half, while Yugoslavia's consumer imports had shrunk by one-quarter. These countries improved their foreign trade balance, which had been a significant motivation behind state interventionism.[187] But import substitution in the consumer sector had serious disadvantages, too. The Balkan countries missed the global structural transformation toward capital- and technology-intensive sectors such as mechanical engineering and the electrical, chemical, and automotive industries, which dueled for primacy on the world markets. In the meantime, the textile sector amounted to less than 10 percent of all industrial production in western Europe.[188]

Industrialization transformed the structure of employment, although this was less apparent in the Balkan lands than in other states of the European periphery. At the end of the 1930s, about 11 percent of Yugoslav workers, and about 8 percent of Bulgarian and Romanian workers, were employed in the industrial sector. The proportion of industrial workers in Albania was less than 1 percent.[189] In Spain, Portugal, Hungary, and Finland, by contrast, every other worker was now employed in the industrial or service sector. Only after the Second World War did the agrarian population of southeastern Europe begin to shrink in absolute numbers—a transition that had already happened in England in 1820, in Germany in 1850, and in Italy in 1920.[190]

Reasons for the slow pace of industrialization were well known. There was a shortage of electrical power, investments, technology, and specialized knowledge, and domestic markets were weak. Agricultural earnings and wages continued to fall after the mid-1920s. The overall level of education was low, and specialized professionals were few. At the beginning of the 1930s, more than 40 percent of seven- to ten-year-olds in Romania and Yugoslavia could not read or write; in Albania, it was 80 percent.[191]

Before and after 1914, lack of capital was one of the most pressing problems that affected the pace of industrialization in southeastern Europe. Struggling with high budget deficits at the beginning of the 1920s, the countries of the region turned to foreign government loans. State-owned companies provided foreign investors with incentives to purchase stock to attract direct investment. Foreign loans were paid back at high rates of interest. Entrepreneurs and bankers from Europe and the United States, who had lost their investments in the Soviet Union following the Bolshevik

Revolution, now looked toward east-central and southeastern Europe instead. Foreign capital soon dominated the region's joint-stock corporations, banks, and insurance companies; dependency on foreign capital was greatest in Romania and lowest in Bulgaria. Some 90 percent of Romanian crude oil production and more than 80 percent of Yugoslav mining were in the hands of foreign owners. Foreign capital concentrated in sectors that promised foreign investors the greatest profits, such as the extraction of raw materials—not in sectors that would most benefit the national economy or have the greatest spin-off effects.[192]

The export of capital to east-central and southeastern Europe was an integral part of the global business and financial flows that came from the creditor states of Great Britain, France, and the United States. On one hand, investments allowed the creditor nations to gain a foothold in the markets of southeastern Europe; on the other, investments facilitated closer political ties. Eastern and southeastern Europe became the third most important site for global business and financial investments, behind the British Empire and Latin America. Foreign banks that called in their capital after the stock market crash of 1929 unleashed a chain reaction of bankruptcies worldwide—including in southeastern Europe.[193]

In the 1930s, the problem of government debt became practically unmanageable. Romania owed more than 1 billion gold dollars in 1931; Yugoslavia owed 634 million, and Bulgaria, 139 million. In 1937, 89 percent of the national debt in Romania was held abroad; in Yugoslavia, the proportion was 82 percent, and in Bulgaria, 72 percent. A growing share of export earnings had to be used to service the debt—about 36 percent in Yugoslavia and Romania, and as much as 44 percent in Greece, in 1931/32.[194] Since the beginning of the 1930s, the sum of payments on interest and principal had exceeded the sum of capital imports. Governments responded to the economic crisis by introducing strict import-export controls to service their debt more easily.[195]

The Great Depression marked not only an economic turning point but also one in foreign policy. Berlin became more involved in the region in the early 1930s, seeking to gain political influence through economic ties. Germany filled the void that the withdrawal of British and French creditors left behind. In a memorandum of March 1933, the state secretary of Germany's foreign ministry, Bernhard Wilhelm von Bülow, underscored that the direction of Yugoslav and Romanian foreign policy could "be significantly influenced in this way."[196]

As Germany prepared for war, its interest in southeastern Europe grew. The region was a useful source of raw materials and agricultural commodities that were important for waging war, and also an attractive market for German industrial goods.[197] The Balkan Peninsula was key to the National Socialist concept of a "greater economic space," intended to secure the greatest possible autarky for Hitler's Germany. Thus, Germany and the southeastern European states entered into a series of economic agreements that, in contrast to earlier treaties, allowed Berlin to exercise influence over its partners' production. As one authoritative source put it, the Balkan countries were largely expected to "adjust to the needs and demands of German consumption and production."[198]

To this end, Germany's most important instrument was the "clearing system" it offered to Yugoslavia, Romania, and Bulgaria in a series of bilateral treaties. Germany bought its partners' agricultural products at prices above the world market level, obliging them to accept German consumer goods in return.[199] Over time, Germany became the Balkan states' most important economic partner. Between 1929 and 1938, Germany's share of all imports rose from 22 percent to 52 percent in Bulgaria, from 24 percent to 40 percent in Romania, and from 16 percent to 39 percent in Yugoslavia. Dependency on Germany grew with respect to exports as well. Exports to Germany rose from 23 percent to 59 percent in Bulgaria, and from 8.5 percent to 52 percent in Yugoslavia.[200] Only Albania, which had effectively become an Italian protectorate with the Tirana Pact in 1926/27, sent 78 percent of its exports to Italy at the end of the 1930s. Rome had already secured concessions for exploiting Albanian oil fields.[201]

Scholars continue to debate which side reaped greater benefits from the clearing agreements, which encompassed more than four-fifths of the foreign trade of the participating southeastern European countries at the end of the 1930s. Germany profited by acquiring foodstuffs and raw materials that were important for waging war, and even by reexporting southeastern European products that it obtained through the clearing system. It penetrated the region's markets and acquired substantial political influence. But this also helped the Balkan states, which found a reliable buyer for their agricultural commodities in difficult economic times. By 1935 at the latest, however, the clearing system revealed itself to be a losing venture for southeastern Europe. With the revival of the global economy, the Balkan states could have obtained higher prices and currency earnings by selling their goods on the world markets—a particular source of frustration for

Romanian crude oil producers. Moreover, Germany steadily raised the prices of its consumer products, which the southeastern European states were contractually bound to purchase. The economic agreements cemented an asymmetrical system of exchange that discouraged development and hindered the countries' efforts to build up their own national industry.[202]

At the end of the interwar era, the states of southeastern Europe had a mixed economic balance. Industry and consumption had grown despite the Great Depression, though not at the same pace as before the war. Standards of living at the end of the 1930s were just 15 to 20 percent higher than in 1913.[203] Although gross national product estimates for the individual countries are inconsistent, there is consensus that the gap in prosperity between western and southeastern Europe continued to grow. Between 1913 and 1929, per capita income in the region grew about 0.3 percent annually, compared to 0.64 percent in northern and western Europe and 1.03 percent in the United States.[204] At the end of this period, Bulgaria and Romania had reached about 20 percent of British per capita income; Yugoslavia had reached 25 percent; and Greece, 42 percent.[205]

If one considers the phase between 1870 and 1939 as a whole, it is evident that globalization played a central role in invigorating the southeastern European national economies—by increasing demand, and by simultaneously motivating the governments to adopt a more proactive economic policy. Growing worldwide interdependence made the state an increasingly important actor in economic life. Before the First World War, the southeastern European governments had already pursued strategies of import substitution, as well as partial economic dissociation from the world market through protectionism and promotion of industry. The shock of the world economic crisis reinforced support for these policies, since the debt-ridden lands of southeastern Europe were particularly hard hit by falling prices and the withdrawal of capital. Competitive pressure and global crises heightened demands to shelter the markets from external risks, as more and more people came to believe that the state should provide not only military protection but also social security against world economic threats. Authoritarianism and royal dictatorship—and a heightened economic nationalism—were logical alternatives for many southeastern Europeans. Globalization did not weaken the nation-state or render it irrelevant, but rather reinforced its institutions worldwide. By subjecting international capital flows, migration, and foreign trade to tighter regulation, a dynamic of deglobalization in the name of national interests began to take hold.[206]

Protectionism, promotion of industry, and import substitution—the core elements of economic nationalism in the interwar era—did encourage development in southeastern Europe, although internal preconditions ultimately determined each country's degree of success. On the brink of insolvency, the southeastern European countries found themselves compelled to enter into a dubious political alliance with Hitler's Germany.

Dimensions of Cultural Globalization

On July 8, 1930, in the middle of the world economic crisis, the Yugoslav national soccer team disembarked in Montevideo after a three-week ocean crossing. The year before, the world soccer organization FIFA had decided to hold a world championship every four years—and to the Europeans' disappointment, Uruguay was chosen as the host country after extended deliberations. Only four European states agreed to send their best players to the opposite side of the globe: France, Belgium, Yugoslavia, and Romania.[207] Taking part in the championship was not just about sports, according to the vice president of the Yugoslav soccer league, Kosta Hadži, but also about strengthening ties with guest workers and promoting Yugoslavia. Masses of flag-waving fans gave the team a rousing welcome.[208] Romania was eliminated in the preliminary round, but the Yugoslav team beat Brazil and Bolivia to advance to the semifinals, ultimately losing 6:1 to Uruguay, the eventual World Cup champion. The team's strong showing inspired pride back in Yugoslavia, where "the final was the only topic of conversation in every café and every home." It was even more meaningful, the daily newspaper *Politika* reported, that "in the deciding matches Yugoslavia was granted the honor of defending the reputation of the Old World against the New."[209]

No other phenomenon illustrates the cultural changes of the postwar era as colorfully as soccer—an urban, popular, mass sport that could entice tens of thousands of enthusiastic fans into stadiums worldwide. With its associational structures and championships, world soccer served as a force of globalization—and nationalization, too.[210] On one hand, the sport introduced uniform competitions, rules of play, and fan cultures worldwide. British clubs signed Croatian players, and the Yugoslav national team hired an English coach. On the other hand, the world championships brought state-supported national teams into competition with one another, and this at once strengthened identities and promoted diversity.

The footballers represented their sending nation in a global arena. Thousands of fans cheered on "their" team, as when the Czechoslovak Union Žižkov, or the British Oxford Club, played in Belgrade. When the teams traveled to other countries, their supporters followed along in special trains.[211] Fan-club networks even reached overseas guest workers, providing an emotional connection across continents to the "imagined" national community.

The game of soccer also illustrates how the state became a driver of transcontinental nationalism.[212] The diaspora, representing a global extension of the national self, figured prominently in successor states' policy decisions. The 760,000 or so Yugoslav immigrants in the United States were sometimes called Yugoslavia's "Tenth Banovina," while Pittsburgh laid claim to the status of the fourth-largest Yugoslav city. Guest workers were an important economic factor. Before the world economic crisis, they transferred up to 20 million U.S. dollars each year back to their families in their old homelands. Because the United States—like other industrial nations—had introduced new limits on immigration after the First World War, sending countries now had to assume a more activist role. They passed migration laws, founded emigration offices, and distributed passports. To improve efficiency, the Yugoslav Central Organization (Jugoslovenska Centralna Organizacija) was established in the United States in 1932. Yugoslavia thus sought to "reterritorialize" a nation that had been "deterritorialized" through mass labor migration before the First World War. Yugoslav guest workers were not only to become part of a culturally imagined community, but one that actually existed in legal, political, social, and economic terms. When Yugoslavia ceased to exist during the Second World War, the émigré community carried on as a kind of ersatz nation.[213]

While the globalization of the world economy was slowed and partially reversed by economic nationalism, the Balkan societies could not escape Westernized modern culture—as the Croatian scholar Vladimir Dvorniković observed in the 1920s.[214] Big cities, in particular, encouraged the homogenization of fashion, lifestyles, habits, and values. Beyond the conveniences of urban infrastructure, such as electricity and streetcars, cultural changes were evident in consumer goods, science, technology, and art. Radio and the proliferation of print media played a role, as did cultural institutions, voluntary associations, and bilateral friendship societies.[215]

After the nationalistic excesses of wartime, cosmopolitanism was back in style. The "mad longing" for travel gripped an entire generation of intellectuals. For Isidora Sekulić, it was "an innate instinct," even "a question of existence," as she titled one of her books. "One travels, not to stave off boredom or kill time, but rather . . . to grow beyond oneself and cast a brief glance into the riddle and oppressive illusion of time."[216]

Other artists considered themselves part of a worldwide avant-garde, representing the "classical" modern styles of expressionism, cubism, dadaism, and surrealism in Belgrade, Sofia, and Bucharest.[217] The Romanian Tristan Tzara was a cofounder of dadaism in Zurich and a participant in the Cabaret Voltaire. He worked closely with Hans Arp, André Breton, and Louis Aragon. The Yugoslav journal *Nova Literatura (New Literature)* had a thirty-five-person masthead, including Albert Einstein, Maxim Gorky, George Grosz, Sergei Eisenstein, Hugo Kersten, and Upton Sinclair.[218] And the philosopher Miloš Djurić invented "pan-humanism" in 1922. He believed that a universal, pan-human culture could transcend nationalism and patriotism, which were responsible for war.[219]

Urban life encouraged a new mobility. Automobiles were imported from the United States and Germany, or produced—as in Bucharest—in Ford company plants. Leisure activities became more "American," too; soccer, handball, swimming, and boxing became mass sports. Big-city residents attended movies, jazz concerts, nightclubs, cabarets, and bars. In addition to polkas and waltzes, they now danced the Charleston, fox-trot, and tango, and they read comic books featuring characters like Mickey Mouse and Donald Duck. Yugoslavia alone imported about five hundred American films in 1939.[220]

Distant cultural influences found their way even to rural villages. In Bulgarian Dragalevtsi—where peasants still lived conservatively, according to traditional social norms—the school, newspaper, army, and compulsory labor service introduced new ideas. Rural workers regularly made their way to the city to sell goods and produce. They read newspapers and discussed world events at the local tavern. In 1934, there were two radios and one telephone for the 279 families in the village. Forty different newspapers and magazines were sold every day. And tourists and summer visitors began to pass through more often.[221]

Global trends manifested themselves in gender roles, too. More women worked outside the home, gaining self-confidence and greater visibility in public.[222] The image of the "modern girl" spread to New York, London and Berlin, Beijing and Bombay, Belgrade and Bucharest. All over the world, "new women" broke with the traditional roles of wives and mothers. The insignia of their emancipation and attributes of physical attractiveness—

cosmetics, cigarettes, and fashion—came from the world of consumerism that was popularized through advertising and film.[223]

The biography of Johann "Johnny" Weissmuller—a Banat Swabian from the Romanian town of Freidorf, who emigrated with his parents to Pennsylvania before the war—encapsulates many of the era's important cultural trends. A gifted swimmer, Weissmuller won five gold medals for the United States in the 1924 Olympics before pursuing an acting career. Beginning in the 1930s, he made film history by portraying Tarzan in twelve Hollywood productions. As the courageous, well-muscled man from the jungle, he embodied the "noble savage" of the modern era, living far removed from urban civilization, with its mania for technology and capitalist greed. The story of the white boy who was raised by apes can be read as an allegory of the search for identity in a globalized world. The adventures of the athletic, white jungle hero entertained millions and shaped ideals of masculinity—possibly in reaction to women's emancipation, which was unsettling for some. Tarzan also reproduced colonialist and racist stereotypes, as dark-skinned "natives" appeared in his adventures exclusively as savages or slaves.[224] His figure made the white, male body a symbol of American modernity.[225]

As cultural globalization pushed relentlessly into the everyday life of southeastern Europeans, it became a source of anxiety for nations that had only recently achieved statehood and were still building their own national culture. War, dislocation, and colonialism shattered the idealized view of "Europe" as a model for the future, so critiques of rationalism and modernity by thinkers like Friedrich Nietzsche and Oswald Spengler now found fertile ground in southeastern Europe as well. "The myth of endless progress, belief in the formative role of science and industry on the way to world peace and social justice, the primacy of rationalism, and the prestige of agnosticism—all this broke down on the field of war," the religious scholar Mircea Eliade recalled.[226] Nationally minded intellectuals came to see the Balkans as a vibrant, morally superior synthesis of spirituality and vitality—a counterpoint to the misguided cult of Western rationality. The avant-gardist Ljubomir Micić even heralded the "Balkanization of Europe" in the program of his Zenitist movement. His utopian "Barbarogenius" embodied the Balkan "anti-Europe," the opposite of the old, decadent, superficial continent that had overrun the world with its unrestrained violence.[227]

For the many southeastern Europeans and others who sought an alternative to Western rationalism in the aftermath of the war, Asia presented itself as an alluring stronghold of deep spirituality. The young Eliade sought spiritual refuge and new religious experiences in India.[228] The twenty-one-year-old studied theology and philosophy in Calcutta for three years and later wrote influential works such as *The Sacred and the Profane, Shamanism: Archaic Techniques of Ecstasy, Yoga,* and *A History of Religious Ideas.* The Yugoslavs looked to India, too. A translation of *Nationalism,* written by the Bengali philosopher and Nobel Prize winner in literature Rabindranath Tagore, was published in Zagreb in 1922. Tagore confronted the rational West with the spiritual East, writing that "neither the colourless vagueness of cosmopolitanism, nor the fierce self-idolatry of nation-worship is the goal of human history." Despite the caste system and the persistence of walls between the races, India had developed "the spiritual recognition of unity."[229] Tagore's thought appeared to offer an ideal model for coexistence in a multinational state.

India represented more than a hazy longing for spirituality; it also provided a test case for critiques of civilization and colonialism. The contradictions of the European model of progress were immediately evident in India's colonial reality. Mircea Eliade was shocked by the brutality of the British police who violently beat back Indian demonstrators: "cracked skulls and broken limbs . . . children trampled by horses, bleeding from blows with hooves and sticks." The prestige "of the white man" was lost. "Indian boys spit before the 'Europeans' in streetcars."[230] In 1931, the Romanian writer Mihail Sebastian visited the International Colonial Exhibition in Paris, where guests could observe "natives" from Asia, Africa, and Polynesia engaged in typical handicrafts. He was appalled by the display: "In God's name, do not talk about the 'civilizing mission' of Europe." The frightened people had "the same confused stare of caged beasts at the zoo." Unlike other intellectuals who embraced the colonialist discourse, his judgment of the scene was unequivocal: "It is immoral."[231]

As the secular nation-state continued to gain acceptance as the model political order, its religious opponents became more vocal. After Mustafa Kemal Pasha proclaimed the secular republic in 1923, abolishing the caliphate the year thereafter, the Balkan Muslims no longer had a political and religious center. Even in Turkey, religion and the state were henceforth treated as separate spheres. Religious clothing and the veil were forbidden, and only civil marriage was valid under the law. On one hand, these changes encouraged nationalistic pan-Turkism, which was embraced by emigrants from Russia, central Asia, and Crimea. Voluntary associations devoted to

"Turanism," which emphasized the common origins and unity of all Turkic peoples, arose in the Balkans.[232] On the other hand, religious Muslims began to seek new ways of organizing the Islamic community across state borders. In 1926, however, the attempt to establish a new caliphate in Egypt failed when opposing Islamic strains were unable to find common ground.

Islamic scholars from all over the world, including those in Bosnia and Albania, began to orient themselves toward Al-Azhar University in Cairo. The missionary, Islamic reformist Ahmadiyya sect in India and Pakistan—and the Egyptian Muslim Brotherhood founded in 1928—gained influence among critics of the secular nation-state who favored a distinctively Islamic society and form of government, or possibly even a pan-Islamic state based on the *umma*.[233] These ideas also found support among the Turkic peoples of the Soviet Union, in the Indian Khilafat movement, and the Islamic national movement in Indonesia. A global, pan-Islamic public began to emerge; its goal was to create a religious "super state" through world congresses, publications, foundations, mosques, and scholarships.[234] Balkan Muslims, too, participated in these efforts. The Albanian Hafiz Abdullah Zëmblaku from Bilisht, one of the most prolific translators of Islamic literature, illustrates the scope of these contacts. He communicated with partners in Greece, Kosovo, Bosnia, Turkey, Egypt, Australia, America, France, Italy, and India, even traveling personally to these sites.[235]

Before 1914, pan-Islamism had found an intellectual home in Bosnia-Herzegovina with the journal *Behar (Blossom)*. The movement gained strength in the 1930s, when representatives of the Islamic Community (Islamska vjerska zajednica) traveled to the world congresses in Geneva and Jerusalem. Reformers and traditionalists in Bosnia fought over the correct interpretation of Islam—a question that lay at the heart of Slavic Muslims' national identity. Under the influence of the Egyptian Muslim Brotherhood, groups of intellectuals (not Islamic scholars) began to create networks of young Muslims in Zagreb, Sarajevo, and Mostar in 1939. The Young Muslim association was officially founded in Sarajevo in 1941. It was grounded in old traditions, like Islamic rules of dress and the sharia. Although the communists banned the pan-Islamic organizations after the Second World War, their networks continued to exist underground, eventually resurfacing in the 1970s.[236]

The First World War also transformed the system of coordinates for approximately one million southeastern European Jews. The establishment of nation-states and the politics of assimilation, discrimination, and "national-

Sarajevo in the 1930s.

ization" shined new light on the fundamental questions of Jewish identity. Should Judaism be treated as a religion or a nationality? Should Jews speak Ladino, Yiddish, or Hebrew, or the majority language of their society? Should Jews assimilate, become part of a national diaspora, or emigrate to Palestine? Jewish nationalists and socialists, integrationists, Zionists, autonomists, and Sephardim had very different answers to these questions.[237] Zionism gained momentum in the Balkans after the Balfour Declaration promised British support for the establishment of a Jewish state in 1917. In 1922, the League of Nations received the mandate to create a "national homeland for the Jewish people" in Palestine, and to encourage Jewish settlement. Associations like Bar Giora in Vienna, Betar in Thessaloniki, Judeja in Zagreb, Bnei Zion in Sarajevo, and the organization of Sephardic Jews in Belgrade promoted the cause.[238] Zionists founded emigration offices, joined the World Zionist Organization, and traveled to its congresses. About 100,000 Sephardic Jews emigrated to Israel between 1919 and 1949.[239]

The Orthodox clergy also pondered how to promote their faith in the age of nation-states. The understanding of an organic connection between the nation and religion, and between church and state, precluded the establishment of a central Orthodox world organization. The autocephalous churches that were founded in Serbia in 1920, in Romania in 1925, and in

Albania in 1937 tended to mistrust the Ecumenical Patriarchate's supra-national claims to leadership.[240] But the traditionalist clerics were of one mind when it came to critiquing the Enlightenment, modernity, and Western values. In 1917 the Serb theologian Nikolaj Velimirović denounced the "repulsive nakedness" and "inner poverty" of Europe. "Everything has turned out to be a lie: culture, civilization, progress, modernization."[241] In the 1930s he became an influential proponent of Svetosavlje, the mystical and anti-modernist ideology that was centered around Saint Sava. Other Serb theologians had been introduced to the Slavophile, messianic theology at the theological academies in Petersburg, Moscow, Kiev, and Kazan. After the Russian Revolution, they came to believe that Serbia had been called to carry on the universal idea of Christianity through Orthodox mission.[242] Connections to Russia were reinforced by the tens of thousands of Russian emigrants who fled to seminaries in Serbia and Bulgaria.[243] The national Orthodox Churches were further united in their efforts to drive out religious competitors—particularly Catholic orders such as the Jesuits, Lazarists, and Ursulines, and sects like the Jehovah's Witnesses, who reached out to millions of refugees with humanitarian aid.[244]

Culture, alongside politics and economics, became an influential force of globalization in the interwar era. The different strands of globalization proceeded asynchronously. The deglobalization of the economy had no parallel in the spheres of culture and science. Even in times of the most intense nationalism, Europeanization and Americanization brought the world's cultures closer together. Homogenization and heterogenization were two sides of the same coin; part of globalization was the characteristic interplay between the local and the global, between particularism and universalism. On one hand, Americanization, mediatization, and international exchange encouraged greater uniformity in cultural life, consumption, and external appearances. On the other hand, cultural globalization created a backlash, inspiring ideological retreat into national and local identities, as well as a variety of local adaptations. Far from rendering the nation-state obsolete, the globalization of culture made it stronger. By reinforcing ties between diaspora and homeland, globalization became an agent of national "reterritorialization." A more closely networked world created an apparent paradox: the internationalization of nationalism. More than ever before, the postwar nation-states sought to present their achievements in the best possible light, asserting themselves within the context of global action and communication.

Bucharest, 1939

As it was every New Year's Eve, speeches by the Romanian king and his prime minister were broadcast on the radio at midnight. This year, listeners heard that a more resolute approach in policy toward the Jews would be an important task for the months ahead.[245] In 1938 the government had already begun to review Jews' citizenship and pushed tens of thousands to emigrate; by the end of 1939, it would be more than 600,000. The goal was to "Romanianize" schools, railways, and private business.[246] "The government's expressed stand on the Jewish question has warped the love Jews felt for Romania," the Jewish doctor Emil Dorian confided in his diary on January 2, 1939. "Discord is creeping into the relationship of Christians and Jews. It is much like a crumbling marriage, in which the spouses still share the same roof but no longer feel anything for one another."[247]

Anti-Semitic laws and polemics created an uncomfortable situation for the author Mihail Sebastian (who was born Iosif Hechter). Sebastian had become a well-known figure in the cultural life of Bucharest through his novels, plays, essays, and critical reviews, and he had recently edited a Romanian edition of the correspondence of Marcel Proust. But he noted with apprehension how his plays were being turned down for production, and how friends who were formerly close had begun to keep their distance. His 1934 roman à clef, *For Two Thousand Years,* grappled with growing anti-Semitism and the Jewish search for identity. "The state is free to declare me a ship, a polar bear or a camera. Despite all this, I will not stop being a Jew, a Romanian and a man from the banks of the Danube."[248] He had astounded his teacher, Nae Ionescu, by asking Ionescu to write the book's preface. In return, the "most interesting and the most complex person I know" gave him a treatise drenched in anti-Semitism.[249] "Are you, Iosef Hechter, a man of the Danube? No. You are a Jew." Nothing about this could change: "Iosef Hechter, you are sick . . . substantially sick."[250] By printing Ionescu's preface, Sebastian unleashed a torrent of outrage upon himself. Only Mircea Eliade, whom he knew from their student days, came to his defense. But Eliade, too, was moving farther and farther to the right, at a time when many intellectuals—as Sebastian put it—were suffering from "a case of syphilis with anti-Semitic symptoms." Sebastian wrote: "When we are alone together we understand each other reasonably well. In public, however, his right-wing position becomes extreme and categorical. He said one simply shocking thing to me, with a kind of direct

aggressiveness: 'All great creators are on the right.'" As Eliade drew closer
to the Legionnaires, even expressing outrage at theatrical productions
with a "Jewish spirit," their friendship was in crisis. In September 1939, as
countless Polish Jews fled to Romania to escape the German army, Eliade
stated: "Only a pro-German policy can save us. . . . Rather than a Romania again invaded by kikes, it would be better to have a German protectorate."[251]

After Bucharest became the capital of an independent Romania, its size,
appearance, social makeup, and power structure changed. The city's population doubled between 1918 and 1939, to about 870,000. According to a
1930 census, about 77 percent of its residents were Romanians, and another 10 percent were Jews. The remainder were Hungarians, Germans,
Roma, and members of countless other nationalities.[252]

The rise of big industry acted as a magnet for migration and a motor of
change. Social differentiation accelerated within "Little Paris," with its great
representative structures like the Palace of Justice, National Bank, Parliament, and Royal Palace, as well as magnificent hotels like the Grand Hotel
de France and the Athénée Palace, banks, and elegant mansions.[253]

A growing divide between rich and poor was evident in the city's outward
appearance. Upscale neighborhoods for the civil servants, academics, and
businesspeople in the new middle class formed on the city's west side—such
as Parcul Bonaparte and Parcul Filipescu, home to luxurious villas, parks,
and sporting grounds. These wedge-shaped neighborhoods grew from
outlying recreational areas, pushing inward to create islands of prosperity
within the city center.[254] Public transportation boomed with the expansion
of tram and bus lines; there was more electrical lighting and an updated
telephone network. Rising prosperity was evident in stately thoroughfares
like the Boulevard Brătianu and the Calea Victoriei, with their banks and
temples of consumption like the Galeries Lafayette. It also brought more
automobile traffic. Of the barely 26,000 automobiles registered in Romania
in 1939, 41 percent were on the road in Bucharest.[255]

Long-established merchants and craftsmen, meanwhile, upheld traditional ways of life in the alleys of the old town. They displayed their wares
on the street, as their forefathers had done for centuries: copper kettles,
woven baskets, sausages, peppers, leather vests, horse tack, and twine. Itinerant merchants and water carriers, the *precupeți* and *sacagiu,* had been a

Boulevard Brătianu, September 1939. Photograph by
Willy Pragher. Provincial Archives Baden-Württemberg.

familiar presence in the city since premodern times. "Wearing clean, white,
traditional costumes . . . underneath a wooden yoke hung with large, white
baskets, the sellers offered golden carp from the Danube delta, lamb's heads
soaked with black blood, great vats of yogurt, and live chickens (seven
francs a pair)." Their loud market cries carried into the well-to-do neighborhoods.[256]

Lower- to middle-class workers and members of the military settled in
the Floreasca, Balta Albă, and Progresul city districts. Veterans and civil
servants received land from the state to build new neighborhoods with colorful names like "Volunteer Fortress" and "Defenders of the Fatherland."[257]

Those who could not afford the city center remained in the *mahalles* on the periphery. Sprawling slums like the Câmpul Veseliei arose as migrants built makeshift lodgings from clay, wood, cardboard, and straw.[258] The shantytowns spread out like tentacles from the main roads. Bucharest "is expanding like an oil stain," the authors of the city's general plan complained in 1934. But all countermeasures failed: "No guards, no boundary markers, no trenches, no laws, no peripheral zones—nothing can restrain the expansion of urban development."[259]

Streets were straightened and paved as part of a municipal reform in 1925; significant improvements were made to the water and sewage systems, and the city received new parks and recreational areas. But despite the work of urban planners, architects at the end of the 1930s despaired at the city's disjointed, even neglected and shoddy, appearance. The signs of uneven development were readily apparent: "On one and the same street, one can find a commercial building with shops, a small one-story house, a workshop, and a warehouse next to a wealthy family residence with multiple floors."[260] Above all, Bucharest suffered from a dramatic housing shortage. Half of the population lived in one- or two-room apartments. In 1930, there were seven thousand households with more than ten people living in a single room. Some 60 percent of residences had access to only the most basic toilets without running water, and 82 percent had no bathroom at all. Half of all residences were lit with kerosene lamps. Infectious disease and tuberculosis were rampant.[261] Even so, dynamic industrial development reinforced the sense of living in an age of progress and modern sophistication. At the end of the 1930s, more than 17 percent of all Romanian industrial production was concentrated in Bucharest, providing a livelihood for more than forty thousand workers.[262] Government subsidies for arms production and other industries brought large, modern factories into the city. These facilities processed aluminum and manufactured pipe, electrical cable, electrical devices, locomotives, motors, and airplanes. Malaxa, Wolf, Grivița, and Metaglobus were among the city's important employers, in addition to the Chemical Works and a Romanian Ford plant.[263]

The new workplaces adopted modernist industrial design that earned Romanian architects an international reputation. Instead of wood and bricks, new factories were built from glass, iron, and steel, with clear, functional aesthetics.[264] The Malaxa factories, for example, had washrooms with warm and cold running water, cloakrooms, and a medical clinic—evidence of "workplace beauty and worker safety," the *Bukarester Tageblatt* praised.[265]

Cultural institutions, voluntary associations, and friendship societies acted like a cultural transmission belt. Media, including newspapers, radio, and film, opened up new worlds for a mass audience. Wealthy consumers could purchase foreign products such as aspirin, Olympia typewriters, Franck coffee, Pschorr beer, or Osram lights—or they could even visit a plastic surgeon to work on their "face wrinkles, crow's feet, saddle and aquiline noses, protruding ears."[266]

Gender roles shifted alongside changing tastes, fashions, values, and consumer desires. Now 30 percent of students were women. The sexes interacted more freely with one another, not just on university campuses, and strict codes of sexual morality eased. After a hard-fought battle, women gained national voting rights in 1939. Previously, they could only vote in local elections. All voters, however, were required to be over thirty years of age and able to read.[267]

A lively cultural and intellectual scene responded to the far-reaching social changes in a provocative way. Scholars, authors, critics, and journalists wrote and translated literary works, debated new ideas, and commented on current events. Their ranks included the "Young Generation" of the Criterion group and contributors to the *Cuvântul (Word)*. In 1939, thirty daily newspapers and nineteen magazines appeared in Bucharest alone. In addition to numerous publishing houses, the city was home to forty-three well-attended lecture halls, which provided a forum for the literary and political public.[268]

In the summer of 1939, the city was looking forward to the Fourteenth International Congress of Sociology, with the theme "Village and Town." The event was to be hosted by Dimitrie Gusti, one of Romania's most influential scholars and intellectuals, but it was canceled because of the outbreak of a new world war.[269] An innovator in the use of statistical and empirical methods in research on villages, Gusti had been responsible for the Romanian pavilion at the 1939 World's Fair in New York (and the previous world exhibition in Paris). Alongside frescos depicting historical events and traditional costumes and music, Gusti showcased the latest technical achievements in aeronautics, industry, and crude oil production. Romania presented itself as a nation that was vital, dynamic, and spiritually profound; the autocratic King Carol was lauded for his country's achievements.[270]

The social changes of the interwar era affected attitudes and daily routines. High-rise buildings like the ARA, Scala, Lido, and Mica transformed the city's physiognomy, while its internal character was influenced by a growing mass culture and entertainment industry with countless cinemas, musical theaters, dance clubs, and sporting events. Cinemas showed not only Romanian films, but American, French, and English ones, too—including *Sherlock Holmes, Señorita,* and *The Last Gangster,* as well as German box-office hits with the actor Harry Piel. What was exciting and liberating to some, was threatening or alarming to others: "Tantalizing jazz beats set the rhythm of the night; red and green neon lights scream the language of advertising," the *Bukarester Tageblatt* wrote on May 1, 1939. "And lustful vice slinks around dark street corners, looking for prey."[271]

"A capital city is no average city," the architect George M. Cantacuzino instructed his readers. It "is the symbol of state authority."[272] Master plans underscored the city's representative role as the seat of government for this country of just under twenty million residents. Long boulevards like Aviatorilor and Bălcescu directed the eye toward the city center, with its representative squares and monumental structures.[273] A British visitor recognized "the personality of King Carol everywhere in the new developments of Bucharest. It is almost as if the great city . . . is a symbol of his reign."[274]

Despite Carol II's authoritarian "new regime," elections were to be held in early June 1939 and organized according to corporatist principles. There were no parties on the ballot, only groups of professions participating in the National Renaissance Front. This arrangement ensured that parliament would be unconditionally loyal to the king. His other governing strategies included declaring emergency powers as needed, and using censorship and repression to suppress criticism from both the left and the right.[275]

Important positions in the king's camarilla and the state and government bureaucracy went to members of the new haute bourgeoisie, industrialists and financial oligarchs who clustered around the Liberal Party. King Carol II's entourage of advisers and favorites included his mistress Elena Lupescu, as well as the politician Constantin Argetoianu and the industrialist Nicolae Malaxa.[276] The boyars—the old landed nobility—had lost their earlier dominance because of agricultural reforms and other changes, but they still held significant influence.[277] The wealthy bourgeoisie and moneyed nobility enjoyed a social life à la française. The *haute volée* gathered at formal dinners, balls, hunts, and horse races, rubbing shoulders at the aristocratic Jockey Club.[278] These elite circles resembled "the social life of New York," the English author Derek Patmore remarked, noting that most Romanians "have studied or were brought up in Paris. . . . They are beautifully mannered." The Romanian people resented "being stigmatised as Balkan," a British secret agent emphasized. "They regard their country as the Eastern outpost of Western civilisation."[279]

Since Bucharest was the showpiece and emblem of the new greater Romania, its emerging urban landscapes were supposed to reflect a uniquely Romanian national culture. Architecture was tasked with invoking traditions that were rooted as far back in the past as possible, presenting greater Romania as a natural entity—not a mere political construct—and serving as a unifying factor for its disparate regions. Since the last third of the nineteenth century, architects had promoted an autochthonous national style that was specifically "Romanian," whatever that meant. They drew from a repertoire that included secular Phanariot buildings of the seventeenth and eighteenth centuries, sacred Orthodox architecture, and the wooden structures of peasants. Pediments, balustrades, and a wealth of ornamental touches adorned many of the public buildings that were built after 1918.[280] Technical modernism and architectural historicism sometimes joined together in an original way, as in the hybrid blocks of buildings on the Magheru-Bălcescu and Tache Ionescu-Ion C. Brătianu boulevards.[281]

Such a young nation-state, which had emerged only in the nineteenth century, increasingly looked to the past for reassurance in an uncertain present.[282] The heritage of the Roman Empire received new attention, as statues of the Lupa Romana, the she-wolf with Romulus and Remus, were erected in Bucharest, Klausenburg, Timișoara, and other cities—an act of symbolic appropriation in territories that had not been part of Romania until after the First World War. A fresco in the concert hall of the Romanian Athenaeum showed the victorious Roman emperor Trajan after the conquest of Dacia, while the mausoleum for the fallen soldiers of the First World War and the tomb of the unknown soldier in Bucharest recalled the Roman victory monument in Adamclisi. A copy of Trajan's Column in Rome was planned for Victory Square, near the new foreign ministry.[283]

The cultural avant-garde had no patience for idealized folklore and fantasies of the past. A younger generation of writers and artists maintained contacts in Paris, Berlin, and Zurich, bringing dadaism, cubism, surrealism, and other modernist styles to Bucharest in the 1920s.[284] Artists like Max Herman Maxy, Marcel Janco, and Ion Vinea—and the journals *Contimporanul, 75 HP, Integral,* and *Punct*—sought to revolutionize tired forms and transform musty bourgeois aesthetics into a radically modern art that was connected to everyday life through sober, functional design. Artists founded the Academy of Decorative Arts in Bucharest, inspired by the example of the Bauhaus in Weimar Germany. The avant-garde wanted to be modern, as the journal *Integral* declared in a manifesto: "We live, irrevocably, in the era of the city. Intelligence-filter, clarity-surprise, rhythm-speed . . . (old) classes descend, new economies develop. The proletarians set the form."[285]

The metropolis provided the terrain for social utopias of modern urbanity, and also for scenarios of civilizational decline. In his manifesto "Bucharest's Utopia," Marcel Janco envisioned a comprehensive modernist reconstruction of the capital city.[286] Other architects suggested creating an all-new capital called "Românesti," or moving the city of Bucharest to the Carpathian Mountains. "A new spirit needs a new home. . . . We have to move the capital city. . . . Nothing that once was, should continue to exist."[287]

Proponents of the Romanian national style responded with a fundamentalist critique of modernism, accusing the avant-garde of "aesthetic charlatanry" and the dilution of Romanian culture with foreign influences.[288] They railed against the "collectivist," "capitalist," "American," "internationalist," and "democratic" tendencies of modernism—"the exact opposite of what should distinguish Romanian style," as expressed by the writer and theologian Nichifor Crainic.[289] Thus, Bucharest attracted an array of aesthetic programs and visions, which were associated with modernism and antimodernism alike.

Officials at the foreign ministry in the Palatul Sturdza watched the international situation worsen with growing concern. After the *Anschluss* with Austria, the Germans marched into Czechoslovakia in March 1939, bringing the Third Reich closer to Romania's borders. Hungarian troops occupied Carpatho-Ukraine, and Slovakia became a German vassal state. The Romanians apprehensively noted that the Western powers were not willing to defend the postwar political order that they themselves had created. Prime Minister Armand Călinescu worried that the next stage "could be the subjugation of Romania."[290] Mihail Sebastian experienced "the obliteration of Czechoslovakia . . . as a personal drama" that brought him to tears. "It's possible that there will be war this spring, and possible that I'll die this spring in a trench somewhere."[291]

Romania's foreign policy options grew narrower with each passing month. The dilemma was how to maintain close relations with the Western powers without unduly provoking Hitler's Germany. The growing appetite of revisionist neighboring states also had to be held in check; their minorities—Hungarians, Ukrainians, Russians, and Bulgarians—made up more than 15 percent of Romania's population.[292] In March, the king decided to maintain a policy of equilibrium and not join a pact of mutual assistance directed against Germany. But the country would defend itself militarily in case of an attack.

For months, Berlin had exerted growing pressure on Romania so that it would align more closely with the Axis powers, Germany and Italy. In an internal strategy paper dated January 23, 1939, foreign minister Grigore Gafencu emphasized that Germany's interests were Romanian oil and control over the mouth of Danube. It was essential that Romania remain steadfast in "all matters that could endanger our independence and sovereignty."[293] Yet King Carol continued to steer his country more deeply into German waters. Already in January 1939, the Romanian minister of the interior had approved an independent organization with "cultural, economic, and social goals" that would "comprehensively represent Romanian Germans" under National Socialist leadership, to be financed by the Reich's Liaison Office for Ethnic Germans (Volksdeutsche). The "German Ethnic Community in Romania" (later, the "German Ethnic Group in Romania" (Deutsche Volksgruppe in Rumänien) was organized according to the National Socialist model. In October, the SS began to recruit about one thousand Romanian Germans.[294]

Hitler pushed for a bilateral economic treaty that would guarantee the Reich a privileged position in foreign trade and additional political influence. German diplomats spread rumors in Bucharest that the Führer would march into Romania if his political advances were spurned.[295] The Romanian government gave in, hoping to turn down the heat of the diplomatic cauldron before it boiled over.[296] The treaty of March 23, 1939, foresaw a joint German-Romanian company that would exploit oil reserves and implement a program of drilling and processing. In return, Romania would receive weapons and military equipment. Although the treaty was

Bucharest–Berlin soccer match (1:0), November 19, 1939. Photograph by Willy Pragher. Provincial Archives Baden-Württemberg.

implemented only gradually, by August the Reich had secured more than 38 percent of Romanian oil exports.[297]

The radical left, meanwhile, mobilized its supporters against the growing influence of National Socialist Germany. On May 1, twenty thousand demonstrators in Bucharest called for the abrogation of the German-Romanian economic treaty and resistance against fascism. To defend Romanian territorial integrity and sovereignty against Hitler's Germany, the communists proposed joining with the bourgeois parties in a patriotic front. But the influence of the Communist Party was limited, and the political class tended to see Bolshevism as a greater danger than National Socialism.[298]

Uncertainty grew after Mussolini decided to expand his sphere of interest in southeastern Europe. On April 7, Italian troops marched into Albania, and King Zog fled to Greece. The Italian king Victor Emmanuel II accepted the Albanian crown, joining the two countries in personal union. The Italians unambiguously asserted their claim to hegemony in the Mediterranean. The possibility that they might attack Greece, Yugoslavia, or Romania alarmed the countries in the region and the great powers alike.[299] After promising to come to the aid of Poland, the British and French extended a similar guarantee to Romania and Greece on April 13. Above all, these countries were being rewarded for their strategic location, as they were expected to help contain Germany's desire for expansion into eastern Europe. From the perspective of diplomats in Bucharest, however, the declaration had a serious flaw; it upheld a state's independence in the case of "unprovoked aggression," but it did not guarantee existing borders—a concession to the Soviet Union, which had its eye on Bessarabia. Great Britain and France signed several economic and credit agreements with Romania, followed by a mutual assistance pact with Turkey in October.[300]

With the dismemberment of Czechoslovakia, the Little Entente—a pillar of Romanian security policy since the 1920s—effectively ceased to exist. The tug-of-war between the Western powers and Nazi Germany for the favor of the southeastern European states grew increasingly fierce.[301] The Romanian government undertook intensive shuttle diplomacy to forge a neutral bloc of states that could include Romania, Poland, Greece, Turkey, Yugoslavia, and possibly Bulgaria, too. Romania's foremost goal was to protect Bessarabia against Soviet claims. Conciliation between Romania and Bulgaria would also have allowed the Western powers to establish an unbroken line of defense.[302] But the explosive international situation, Italian and German objections, and Bulgaria's ongoing revisionist demands made negotiations difficult. In the end, little more was achieved than general declarations in favor of peace and economic cooperation.[303]

With Germany's expansion into central Europe and the Italian occupation of Albania in April 1939, Yugoslavia was surrounded by revisionist powers. Like Romania, it also feared a Hungarian or Bulgarian attack. Disappointment over French and British policies of appeasement was great. To take the wind out of the sails of Croatian separatists—who could now point to the precedent of an independent Slovakia—the government agreed to recognize an autonomous Croatian *banovina* (region) on August 26, 1939.[304] Foreign policy remained a balancing act; Prince Paul promised the Germans "benevolent neutrality" and negotiated with all sides for shipments of arms. The Romanians did the same—as foreign minister Gafencu remarked, his country was "guaranteed by Britain and armed by Germany."[305]

Bulgaria, which was friendly with the Germans, and Anglophile Greece faced a similar dilemma. Berlin already controlled a large portion of Bulgarian foreign trade; it supplied weapons and credit and was urging Sofia to join the Axis. Tsar Boris informed his diplomats in April that his country "would continue to conduct, as long as it is possible, an independent foreign policy without committing herself to anyone."[306] Greece's economy and military capabilities were closely linked to Great Britain, but here, too,

Germany had gained substantial ground. London's promises of assistance remained vague. Greece's king was afraid of being drawn into a war between Germany and the Western powers—a losing proposition for his poorly armed country. Like Bucharest and Belgrade, therefore, Athens was compelled to give up its policy of equilibrium in favor of neutrality toward German aggression.[307]

The German-Soviet Nonaggression Pact of August 23, 1939, thwarted all efforts for a stable Balkan entente. It likewise foiled the British-French strategy of bringing the Soviet Union into a "grand alliance" against Germany. In a secret protocol, Hitler and Stalin agreed to divide eastern Europe into spheres of influence, partitioning Poland between them. The Soviets emphasized their "interest in Bessarabia," while Germany affirmed its "disinterest." Thus, Moscow renounced the principle of collective security in favor of classic hegemonial politics. As long as the countries of southeastern Europe continued to supply the German war economy with the necessary raw materials, Hitler made no territorial demands in the region. "I can't remember having ever spent a worse night than when I received the news of Ribbentrop's travel to Moscow," Foreign minister Gafencu despaired. The Romanians did not initially know about the secret protocol, but they felt cornered into a position of neutrality, should Germany attack Poland. "I think the situation is very serious," Prime Minister Armand Călinescu affirmed. "Have they agreed to divide up Poland and Romania amongst themselves?"[308]

After German troops invaded Poland on September 1, and France and Great Britain declared war on Hitler, Romania, Bulgaria, and Yugoslavia hurried to declare their neutrality—just as Hitler intended.[309] On September 2, the Yugoslav ambassador Jovan Dučić reported to Belgrade: "With good reason and in all honesty, Romania would like to remain neutral. But it is aware that a great war . . . might also draw Romania into the conflict."[310] When Soviet troops moved into eastern Poland shortly after the German attack, the overall strategic situation changed. Prime minister Călinescu commented on September 19: "The German danger is retreating. Now the Russian threat is front and center."[311]

On September 21, a Romanian radio broadcast was interrupted by an unexpected announcement at 2:05 P.M. Assassins from the Iron Guard reported that they had shot the prime minister to avenge the killing of Codreanu and his compatriots (they had been shot in prison one year earlier, "while attempting to flee").[312] But the Swiss ambassador René de Weck and many others were convinced that Germany was in fact behind Călinescu's assassination, as it sought to change the prime minister's policy of neutrality and bring him closer to the Tripartite Pact. "If the calculus is correct . . . it will lead to the total subjugation of Romania by Germany," Weck surmised.[313] The Iron Guard's new commander, Horia Sima, and some of his followers escaped to Germany, but the Romanian government struck back by executing 253 Legionnaires all over the country. "With unrestrained curiosity, the shaken population of Bucharest filed by the seven corpses on the spot where the prime minister had been assassinated," the doctor Emil Dorian reported.[314] Many observers understood that the fascist threat had not passed. "End of year, almost all hearts stand still," Dorian wrote in his diary on December 31, 1939. "Not so much because of what was as because of the fearful days ahead. . . . For the first time, truly, the worn-out question 'What next?' reverberates with real meaning. What next? What next?"[315]

Southeastern Europe in the Second World War

After the German invasion of Poland in September 1939, Hitler continued to push for the revision of the Paris peace treaties in central and southeastern Europe. National Socialist Germany had already annexed Austria and the Sudetenland in 1938, and with the two Vienna Awards it also sought to satisfy the territorial claims of its Hungarian ally. The First Vienna Award compelled Czechoslovakia to give up parts of southern Slovakia and Carpatho-Ukraine in November 1938; the Second Vienna Award took northern Transylvania from Romania in August 1940. Romania lost additional territory as the "New Order" took shape. After Stalin presented Romania with an ultimatum in June 1940, Bessarabia and Northern Bukovina became part of the Soviet Union. Three months later, Romania ceded Southern Dobruja to Bulgaria in the Treaty of Craiova.[316]

These foreign policy defeats led to the abdication of Romania's King Carol II on September 6, 1940. The defense minister, General Ioan Antonescu, became *Conducător* (Leader) with full dictatorial powers, and he moved his country toward an economic and political alliance with Hitler's Germany. Already in October 1940, German advisers and a half million training forces *(Lehrtruppen)* moved into Romania to secure its oilfields for the German army. In addition, Romania was expected to supply the Reich with food and grain, and also to contribute militarily to the invasion of the Soviet Union. At the instigation of the German authorities,

Romania suspended the civil rights of Jews and, in some cases, seized their property. Like many other Jews, the writer Mihail Sebastian was no longer allowed to practice his profession.[317]

After Germany attacked the Soviet Union in June 1941, Antonescu declared "holy war" against Bolshevism. Romanian troops crossed the Prut River together with the Wehrmacht, conquering back Bessarabia and Northern Bukovina and occupying Odessa. Additional Romanian units fought in the Crimea, Caucasus, and southern Soviet Union. The Romanian leaders hoped that their loyalty would be rewarded with a revision of the Vienna Awards, and with the restitution of lost territory, particularly Transylvania, in a future peace settlement.[318] Unlike Romania, Bulgaria declined to send troops to the Soviet Union. But Tsar Boris speculated about invading southeastern Macedonia and western Thrace in the upcoming war to create a greater Bulgaria with Hitler's support.[319]

The economic and strategic significance of southeastern Europe grew after the beginning of the Second World War in September 1939. The region provided the German Reich with 17 percent of its food supply, and also with raw materials that were essential for waging war—including crude oil, bauxite, zinc, manganese, and chromium.[320] To secure access to these resources and hinder a Balkan alliance against the Axis (an ambition of the western powers), Hitler worked to integrate the countries of the region within the fascist Tripartite Pact between Germany, Italy, and Japan. The Wehrmacht saw southeastern Europe as a launching, transit, and resupply area for its planned invasion of the Soviet Union. In response to massive pressure from the Axis, Hungary, Romania, and Slovakia were compelled to join the Tripartite Pact in November 1940. Bulgaria and Yugoslavia followed in March 1941.[321]

Mussolini had long sought to expand Italy's sphere of influence in the Adriatic region. He occupied Albania in April 1939, then marched his troops into Greece in October 1940.[322] His Greek campaign soon faltered. Although Hitler had not originally planned to wage war in southeastern Europe, hoping to deter British and Soviet intervention, he subsequently altered course. He decided to occupy part of Greece not only to secure his armies' southern flank for their impending invasion of the Soviet Union but also to hinder a British landing on the Greek mainland and to safeguard Germany's access to raw materials, particularly the Romanian oilfields. Greece could then become a launching pad for further operations in Egypt or the Middle East.[323]

Antonescu's emergency declaration (Comunicat) Bucharest, January 1941.
Photograph by Willy Pragher. Provincial Archives Baden-Württemberg.

Serbian generals opposed the Yugoslav government's decision to join the Tripartite Pact and staged a coup that deposed the king on March 27, 1941. That same evening, Hitler ordered that the multinational state be crushed "as quickly as possible."[324] The German air force began its attack on Yugoslavia and Greece on the morning of April 6, 1941. The armies of both states surrendered the same month; the monarchs and their governments fled into exile. Their states were dismembered and divided into occupied territories. All southeastern Europe became part of the "New Order" planned by Hitler and Mussolini, consisting of annexed territories (Slovenia), occupied countries (Serbia, Montenegro, Albania, and Greece), vassal states (Croatia and Slovakia), and allies (Romania, Bulgaria, and Hungary).

Yugoslavia disappeared entirely from the political map. The Independent State of Croatia, led by the fascist Ustasha, arose on the territory of Croatia and Bosnia-Herzegovina. It was divided into German and Italian zones of occupation. The state's new leader *(Poglavnik)* Ante Pavelić, who returned from Italian exile, established a National Socialist–style dictatorship and a regime of violence enforced by militias, the army and secret police, special courts, and concentration camps.[325] The remainder of Yugoslavia was divided between the revisionist powers. Germany annexed northern Slovenia outright, also occupying Serbia and the Banat. Italy received southern Slovenia, Dalmatia, and Montenegro. Kosovo and western Macedonia went to Albania, and Bulgaria occupied eastern Macedonia. Hungary occupied the territory between the Tisza, Danube, and Mur Rivers. Greece, too, was dismembered. Bulgaria received southeastern Macedonia and western Thrace, and Germany took possession of southern Macedonia, along with Thessaloniki, Athens, and much of Crete. Italian troops occupied most of the Greek mainland and the Ionian Islands. They did not establish their own military government, but instead placed their occupied lands under the administration of the Germans, who thus retained access to the region's chromium, nickel, and bauxite deposits.[326]

Beginning in June 1941, the highest occupation authority in Yugoslavia and Greece was the Wehrmacht Commander Southeast. Alongside the Wehrmacht, SS units and special commandos of the Security Police and Security Service (SD) were active in the fight against "leading emigrants, saboteurs, terrorists, etc." Numerous other civilian and military authorities with frequently shifting competencies participated in the occupation.[327] In both countries, Hitler installed collaboration regimes that were subordinate to the German occupiers, similar to France under Henri Philippe Pétain. The ultraconservative Serbian general Milan Nedić and his Government of National Salvation—along with his Greek colleague, General Georgios Tsolakoglou and Tsolakoglou's successors—became "willing executioners" of the Nazi regime so that they could implement their own ethnonationalist, anti-Yugoslav, antiliberal, antimodern, and anticommunist agendas. Both men saw the occupation as an opportunity for national regeneration.[328]

Ethnic Germans *(Volksdeutsche)* assumed a key role in Hitler's "New Order." Throughout eastern Europe—and so, too, in Hungary, Yugoslavia, and Romania—they were seen as a vanguard who would advance the new racial order, contribute to a greater economic area under Nazi leadership, and fight loyally on the eastern front and in SS special units against partisans in their own homeland. In Romania, Croatia, and the Serbian

Banat, ethnic Germans enjoyed an autonomous legal status that placed them directly under the National Socialist apparatus of the Reich.[329]

Hitler ordered the various parts of Yugoslavia and Greece to grant the Reich economic privileges and a certain percentage of all exports. The entire economy—including infrastructure, mines, and defense-related industries—was oriented toward the Four Year Plan. The Serbian Banat, which was controlled by ethnic Germans, sent about 900,000 tons of food and 305,000 pigs to the Reich in the first three years of the war.[330] Germany's allies were also expected to pay a high price; the Bulgarians gave up ore and chromium mines, and the Hungarians ceded their oilfields. Even Italy was compelled to provide bauxite from Dalmatia, iron ore from Bosnia-Herzegovina, and lead and zinc from Kosovo.[331] Tens of thousands of people in the occupied lands were forced to work in factories and mines. Between 1939 and 1945, 16,300 Bulgarians, 15,700 Greeks, 60,200 Croats, and 37,600 Serbs were compelled to labor within the Reich.[332]

In addition, these countries were expected to finance the Wehrmacht and the costs of their own occupation. Serbia contributed well over 1.5 billion reichsmarks, and Croatia, more than 1 billion.[333] Three tons of gold coins were taken from Albania.[334] The result was horrendous inflation and widespread impoverishment. By 1944, prices in Croatia had climbed to between 2,500 and 3,000 percent of prewar levels—and on the black market, to more than 9,000 percent. In Serbia, the cost of living rose more than 2,700 percent between mid-1941 and the end of 1943. At the same time, real wages sank by more than half. By the end of the war, Yugoslavs had lost about four-fifths of their income.[335] In Greece, too, the value of looted goods was in the billions. In 1942 alone, Greece had to pay more than 2,551 million reichsmarks for its own occupation, although national income was only 756 million reichsmarks. Food prices at the end of 1942 were 23,467 percent higher than in 1940.[336] Mussolini remarked that "the Germans have taken from the Greeks even their shoelaces."[337] Athens suffered from a catastrophic famine in the winter of 1941/42, leading the American diplomat Burton Berry to ask "how a prosperous and industrious city . . . without physical change, has become the abode of hordes of destitute, starving people. . . . Of course the answer is the German army of occupation."[338] According to the Red Cross, up to 250,000 Greeks died of hunger between 1941 and 1943.[339]

Throughout eastern and southeastern Europe, German occupation authorities began to implement the "ethnic cleansing" (völkische Flurb-

ereinigung) that Hitler had first announced on October 6, 1939. The "Germanization" of annexed territories and the resettlement of millions of ethnic Germans would enable the creation of a Greater German Reich. Slovenes in the annexed territories of Styria, southern Carinthia, and Upper Carniola were to be racially evaluated and then "Germanized." Tens of thousands were expelled or sent to camps. Tens of thousands of ethnic Germans were brought to the Reich from Bosnia, Syrmia, and Slavonia, so they could later resettle in Poland and Galicia. In Italian-occupied Albania, strategic colonization and "Albanianization" policies had been directed against the Serbs since 1939. Mussolini subsequently initiated mass deportations of the "inferior, barbaric Slavic race" from Istria and Dalmatia.[340] Hungarians and Bulgarians also undertook "ethnic cleansing" in their occupied territories.

Immediately after the invasion of Yugoslavia and Greece, Jews and Roma became the target of National Socialist racial policy. They were stigmatized, disenfranchised, persecuted, herded into camps, and systematically murdered.[341] All over southeastern Europe, Jews lost their jobs, property, and civil rights; they had to be registered and identified. They were subject to police raids, hostage shootings, mass executions, and—by October 1941 at the latest—systematic annihilation. There were, however, vast differences between the individual countries. There was little original anti-Semitism in Albania, Bulgaria, Greece, and Serbia, but natives of Romania and Croatia persecuted Jews on their own ideological initiative. Even here, however, the Holocaust was primarily planned, directed, and systematically implemented by German authorities.[342]

National Socialist plans for a new racial order gave local power holders the cover to remove undesirable minorities—both Jews and non-Jews—through assimilation, resettlement, or partial annihilation. In the Independent State of Croatia (Nezavisna Država Hrvatska, or NDH), the Ustasha began to pursue its ideological agenda: the creation of an ethnically homogeneous Greater Croatia. The NDH's population of just under 6.3 million was extremely heterogeneous; Croats made up a narrow majority of just 3.3 million. They were joined by about 2 million Serbs, 700,000 Muslims, 150,000 ethnic Germans, and other minorities.[343] The Croatian fascists took coordinated action against their supposed archenemy, the Serbian Orthodox population. Muslims were not granted recognition or special status in the centralized order of Greater Croatia; they were proclaimed "Croats of Islamic faith."[344] Ethnification challenged long-standing traditions of religious coexistence, cosmopolitan culture, and civic consciousness in multiethnic communities such as Sarajevo. Muslim elites in the city also speculated about the realization of nationalist goals. In November 1942, Mayor Mustafa Softić sent a personal letter to Hitler to request an ethnically homogeneous Muslim state on Bosnian soil. Hitler promptly rejected the appeal.[345]

The Ustasha was driven by a mélange of anti-Serb resentment and fascist ideology, old vengeances and new demons, as well as by military, political, and economic interests in removing Serbs from territory governed by Croats. Of the up to 330,000 Serbs who were killed in the four years of the war, 217,000 were victims of fascist terror.[346] As in Spain and Italy, fascism and the Catholic Church entered into an unholy alliance.[347] The clergy promoted assimilation by performing mass baptisms. As the *Katolički tjednik (Catholic Weekly)* asserted, "It is our desire that this Croatian state be a Catholic state."[348]

The Serb nationalist Chetniks led by Dragoljub-Draža Mihailović, meanwhile, sought a greater Serbian monarchy. They initially fought against the Wehrmacht, but also pursued the goal of creating a "homogeneous Serbia" in much of the former Yugoslavia. More than four million people were to be expelled or resettled, according to a memorandum of June 1941.[349] On December 20, 1941, the Chetnik leader Mihailović ordered that the disputed territory be "cleansed of all national minorities and non-national elements."[350] In the following months, the Chetniks depopulated large stretches of land in Bosnia and Herzegovina. "All Muslim villages . . . were totally burned. . . . All property was destroyed," the responsible commander reported on February 13, 1943. "During the operation the total destruction of the Muslim inhabitants was carried out regardless of sex or age."[351]

In neighboring Romania, General Antonescu enacted his own program of "ethnic cleansing" *(purificarea etnică)* by resettling and deporting minorities. Romania and Bulgaria implemented a population exchange in November and December 1940, resettling about 61,000 Bulgarians from Romanian Northern Dobruja, and about 100,000 Romanians and members of other ethnic groups from Bulgaria.[352]

Jews and Roma were the largest group of victims in the Romanian "ethnic cleansing." After Germany invaded the Soviet Union in the summer of 1941, the Romanian government and army initiated a large-scale program of persecution and annihilation in the occupied areas of Bessarabia

Jews engaged in compulsory labor in Chernivtsi, July 1941. Photograph by Willy Pragher. Provincial Archives Baden-Württemberg.

and Northern Bukovina, continuing down an ideological path that had been prepared by right-wing intellectuals in the 1930s. The occupied territories became a testing ground for much more comprehensive plans to "ethnically cleanse" all of Romania. Anti-Semitic pogroms took place in Bucharest, Jassy, and other cities in 1941, before Antonescu decided to follow Germany's lead in registering, disenfranchising, and deporting all Jews. In a first step, they were to be taken to Transnistria from Bukovina and Bessarabia—and then from Moldavia and the rest of Romania.[353] By the fall of 1941, 70 to 80 thousand Jews had already been moved to camps or ghettos; tens of thousands were subsequently deported.[354] In the "old" Reich, where Jews were compelled to labor involuntarily and pay special taxes, plans for systematic murder were put off until the Wannsee Conference of January 1942.[355] All Romanian Jews were then incorporated into the "Final Solution." Antonescu did not stop the deportations until the military advance came to a standstill in the fall of 1942. In all, more than 200,000 Jews met their deaths in Romanian-controlled territory.[356] In May 1942, a decision was made to deport all "gypsies" from Romania to lands on the other side of the Dniester River. Up to 25,000 were seized and "evacuated," more than half of whom lost their lives.[357]

The National Socialists' plan of annihilation was fully implemented in the occupied territories, including the Croatian Ustasha state. In fascist Croatia, Jews were driven into camps and deported through April 1944, when the German police attaché reported to Berlin that "the Jewish question could largely be seen as resolved."[358] In occupied Serbia and Greece, the Wehrmacht High Command had branded Jews as "bandits" and enemies of the state, shooting them to death in "atonement campaigns" (*Sühneaktionen*), since the beginning of the war. In Serbia, the SS began to use a mobile gas van in the spring of 1942. By August, the SS group leader Harald Turner reported that "the Jewish question and the gypsy question" had been "settled."[359] In all, up to 60,000 of about 72,000 Jews in the territory of Yugoslavia were killed; about one-third perished in German extermination camps.[360]

More than 60,000 Jews (more than 90 percent of the Jewish population) were taken from the different regions of Greece and brought to German extermination camps, where they were murdered. In Bulgaria, where there had been anti-Semitic laws since 1940, about 11,000 Jews were deported from the occupied territories. In mid-1942, a "Commissariat for Jewish Affairs" was established to coordinate the confiscation of property and deportations from the core Bulgarian lands as well, although the government was slow to implement its plans. Many Bulgarian Jews were thus saved from annihilation. In Italian-controlled Albania, where only a few thousand Jews resided, persecution remained comparatively limited. The same was true in the Italian-occupied Croatia, where many Jews fled from their country's interior.[361]

Already in the summer of 1941, resistance groups of different ideological persuasions coalesced in the occupied lands of Yugoslavia, Greece, and Albania. Broadly stated, there were two main groups of resisters: monarchist national conservatives on one hand, and communist partisans on the other. At first, both groups fought together against the occupiers, but civil-war-like conditions soon developed between the ideological camps. Special forces, militias, and paramilitary bands terrorized the civilian population to intimidate rebellious, or simply undesired, groups and force them to flee. This occurred not only in the spring of 1941, when the new Ustasha leaders "cleansed" Herzegovina, but also in early 1942, when Serb Chetniks overran eastern Bosnia.[362]

The attacks and mass crimes set into motion a dangerous social dynamic in many multiethnic regions, resulting in an extremely brutal civil war.

Fear, insecurity, lived injustice, and killings fostered paranoia and the desire for revenge, compelling ordinary people to participate in collective violence. Economic and interpersonal conflicts, or simply greed, drove some neighbors to attack each other on an ethnic axis. Contingent events or specific instances of violence could crystallize or transform people's sense of collective identity and spark ethnic conflict.[363] On the other hand, many people also defended the victims and publicly criticized the deportation of Jews.[364]

The Wehrmacht and the mobile killing squads of the SS proceeded mercilessly against resistance groups, communists, nationalists, and apolitical civilians. Already on April 28, 1941, Field Marshal von Weichs, commander of the Second Army, ordered the shooting of one hundred civilians from all classes of the population as "atonement" for every German soldier who was hurt or killed in an attack. The bodies were publicly displayed.[365] More than twenty-five thousand Serbs fell victim to the Wehrmacht's punitive actions between October and December 1941 alone.[366] The Wehrmacht also committed mass crimes in Greece, as with the taking of Crete in May 1941. General Kurt Student ordered mass shootings, the burning of villages, and the "extermination" of all men in entire regions. In Greece and Yugoslavia, the Wehrmacht took doctors, teachers, priests, and other respected persons hostage. They were then shot "as a deterrent," or as retribution for Partisan attacks.[367] The Italians also used the utmost brutality to quell resistance in their occupied territories. Villages were bombarded and burned to the ground, and masses of civilians were interned in concentration camps or shot in reprisals.[368]

The occupation forces had to deal with Partisan groups in all of the southeastern European countries, but no resistance fighter created a greater headache for Hitler than Josip Broz Tito. The Croat mechanic and trade unionist had spent six years in Yugoslav prisons for his communist activities. In 1934, the Communist Party of Yugoslavia (CPY) called him to serve on its Central Committee and sent him to Russia for training. In early 1939, the Comintern appointed him general secretary of the illegal CPY.[369] Underground, he and other leading comrades—including the Montenegrin Milovan Djilas, the Serb Aleksandar Ranković, the Jew Moša Pijade, and the Slovene Edvard Kardelj—transformed the CPY into a tightly organized, Leninist cadre party. Many of the communist leaders had volunteered to fight in the Spanish Civil War.[370]

In early July 1941, after the German invasion of the Soviet Union, Tito called for a general uprising to "liberate the peoples of Yugoslavia."[371] His recipe for success was the motto "brotherhood and unity"; solidarity and friendship between nations would bring an end to religious and racial hatreds. He promised equality for all national groups, and also social revolution. "The words *national liberation struggle* would be nothing but words, and even deception . . . if they did not mean, together with the liberation of Yugoslavia, the liberation at the same time, too, of Croats, Slovenes, Serbs, Macedonians, Arnauts [Albanians], Moslems and the rest."[372] At first, Tito found support for the multinational Partisan units especially within Serbia and among the persecuted Serbs in the Ustasha state. But soon other groups joined as well—first, Muslims who were persecuted by the nationalist Serb Chetniks, followed by Croats, Slovenes, and members of other nationalities.

By the end of 1941, Tito had locked horns with Draža Mihailović, who enjoyed the support of the British and the Yugoslav government in exile until the middle of 1943.[373] Stalin, too, failed to provide urgently requested support. At the beginning of 1943, Tito telegraphed to Moscow: "Am I obliged once again to ask you if it is really quite impossible to send us some sort of assistance? Hundreds of thousands of refugees are menaced by death from starvation."[374] But Stalin himself needed the Allies to open up a second front, so that the Germans would have to divert more divisions away from the east. He held back in order to allay Western fears that he was seeking to Sovietize southeastern Europe—and herein lie the roots of the later Yugoslav-Soviet split. Only after the defeat of Hitler's Germany grew imminent, and Mihailović had been irreparably tainted as an Axis collaborator, did the Allies recognize the Partisans as wartime partners in November 1943.

Tito's Partisans had already succeeded in winning multiple, bloody battles, liberating larger areas and placing the Wehrmacht on the defensive. Tito's reputation grew at home and abroad. The German general Rudolf Lüters admitted in July 1943: "The view that the German Wehrmacht serves in a friendly country [Croatia] is long obsolete. The majority of the population support the insurgents."[375]

The charismatic Tito, who was reverently called "Stari" (old man, or father) by his companions, exuded self-confidence, determination, and natural authority. "He gave an impression of great strength held in reserve, the impression of a tiger ready to spring," the British liaison officer Fitzroy Maclean reported from the Partisan leader's headquarters in 1943. "He was unusually ready to discuss any question on its merits and to take a decision there and then, without reference to a higher authority. He seemed perfectly sure of himself; he was a principal, not a subordinate."[376] Many people projected their hopes onto him.

The stronger the Partisans became, the more brutally the Wehrmacht worked to crush the resistance and capture Tito. In the winter of 1942 / 43, German and Romanian troops experienced a military disaster at Stalingrad. The British undertook an offensive in northern Africa; the threat of a large-scale Allied invasion of the Balkans loomed. The Waffen-SS redoubled its efforts to crush the enemy. In 1943 / 44, about 50,000 ethnic Germans from Croatia, Serbia, and the Banat were serving in the military; another 18,500 came from territories occupied by Hungary.[377] The ethnic German division "Prinz Eugen" was particularly notorious for its perpetration of serious war crimes.[378]

Around the end of 1942, the recruiting of Muslim volunteers picked up with assistance provided by the Grand Mufti of Jerusalem, Mohammed Amin al-Husayni, who had lived in exile in Berlin since 1941. He announced that National Socialism and Islam shared similar values, as well as the same enemies. The Bosnian Muslim volunteer SS division "Handžar" (Saber) formed in Croatia in March 1943, followed by the Kosovo Albanian "Skanderbeg" in May 1944. These divisions also incorporated Muhamed Hadžiefendić's volunteer regiment *(Domobranska dobrovoljačka pukovnija)*.[379] They liquidated rebels and other suspects alongside the German troops, burning down villages and depopulating vast stretches of land in order to "drain the swamp."[380]

As the occupiers and their collaborators transformed their surroundings into "bloodlands," the appeal of the Partisans grew. In a total war—which simultaneously possessed dimensions of a race war, a civil war, and a war of economic exploitation—hundreds of thousands underwent existential, borderline experiences every day. Merely belonging to the "wrong" nationality could result in death. Thus, the Partisans' ambition to replace pervasive ethnic hatred with social reconciliation had a liberating and mobilizing effect on much of the population. The People's Liberation Army epitomized the ideal of "brotherhood and unity" in a pure form. This multinational force consisted of 53 percent Serbs, 18.6 percent Croats, 9.2 percent Slovenes, 5.5 percent Montenegrins, 3.5 percent Bosnian Muslims, and 2.7 percent Macedonians; the rest were Albanians, Hungarians, "Yugoslavs," and members of other ethnic groups.[381] The People's Liberation Struggle *(Narodna oslobodilačka borba)* brought far-reaching social change that narrowed the old chasms between city and countryside, elites and lower classes, men and women, and mobilized many people on behalf of the resistance. The communists advocated explicitly for women's causes, granting women in liberated territories active and passive voting rights for the first time in the fall of 1942. The approximately 100,000 women fighters gained social recognition and greater rights through military service.[382] Finally, the communists remained politically uncompromised, unlike the former governing and opposition parties. The king, his government, and influential representatives of the other parties had all fled the country. Tito and his tightly led People's Liberation Army proved that resistance was possible and could succeed. Every victorious battle brought new fighters to their side. The communists succeeded in bundling very different ideological, social, and ethnic milieus under the motto of "people's liberation." A new, supraethnic Yugoslav Partisan culture acquired legitimacy with rituals, songs, dances, poems, and typical symbols that adapted the heroic imagery of Balkan folklore to the revolutionary patriotic cause. By May 1945, the People's Liberation Army had grown to 800,000 fighters, both men and women. Yugoslavia became the second country in Europe (after the Soviet Union) where communism prevailed through its own volition.

Italy exited the war in September 1943, after the Allied troops landed in Sicily. Germany took over the occupation in Albania and Montenegro, but large stores of weapons and munitions fell into Partisan hands.[383] During the night of November 29–30, 1943, Tito called together the second session of the Anti-Fascist Council for the People's Liberation of Yugoslavia (AVNOJ) in the central Bosnian town of Jajce. Delegates from all parts of the country agreed to rebuild the postwar Yugoslav state as a socialist federation of equal peoples and republics. In May 1944, as the Allies were already preparing for the landing at Normandy, Tito narrowly escaped the Germans' final "Rösselsprung" offensive. The British brought Tito and his staff to the Adriatic island of Vis, paving the way for his later rise to power.

In Greece, as in Yugoslavia, the communist resistance—the National Liberation Front and its People's Liberation Army—competed with monarchists in the National Republican Greek League. Here, too, the German occupiers engaged in brutal acts of retribution against the civilian population. They destroyed entire villages, including Kalavryta, Komeno, and Distomo.[384] After the end of 1943, the rival resistance groups in Greece were locked in a bloody civil war. Patriotism and ideology—but also notions of honor, masculinity, and solidarity—motivated men to fight; many of them changed sides more than once during the war. Violence against civilians—enemies, traitors, and average peasants—loomed large in the guerrilla and civil war. The violence was sometimes dictated from above, but it was also informed by regional social structures and cultural traditions and used to settle older intercommunal conflicts.[385] A similar constellation emerged in Albania, where Enver Hoxha's communist National Liberation Army fought against not only the occupiers but also the Balli Kombëtar, a nationalist movement.[386]

The civil wars in Albania, Yugoslavia, and Greece (and also in Spain) were distinguished by similar origins and parallel political constellations. Furthermore, these conflicts were directly related to one another through their actors, leading fighters, and the communist parties. These revolutionary transnational connections helped to shape the new postwar political order—as when Yugoslavia, Bulgaria, and Albania supported the Greek communists, or when the postwar governments worked for a communist Balkan federation.[387]

But first, the revolutionary upheavals at the end of the Second World War cleared the way for communist rule. Terror against civilians, large-scale "ethnic cleansing," persecution, and mass murder not only demonstrated the illegitimacy of the occupation regimes but also discredited those who had not resisted energetically enough. The total collapse and irrevocable loss of respect for the old regime, the radical transformation of social relationships, deep ideological divides, and a specific international constellation set the tone for a new beginning after 1945.

8

Globalization and Fragmentation

The incredible, almost comical melting-pot of peoples and nationalities sizzling dangerously in the very heart of Europe" (Tadeusz Borowski) met its end in the Second World War.[1] War, occupation, expulsion, and genocide created a map of states that was more clearly oriented toward ethnic principles than ever before. By 1944, at least 6.5 million people had been displaced by "ethnic cleansing" throughout eastern and southeastern Europe, a figure that does not include forced laborers or victims of the Holocaust.[2] The Europeans themselves had not determined the outlines of their future borders; this was done by the "Big Three"—the leaders of the United States, Great Britain, and the Soviet Union—at conferences in Teheran (November / December 1943), Yalta (February 1945), and Potsdam (July 1945). Winston Churchill and Joseph Stalin had already agreed to divide Europe into spheres of influence at the Moscow Conference in October 1944. The Western powers' priority was Hitler's unconditional surrender; with the exception of Greece, they did not consider the Balkans a critical theater of war. They ceded to Stalin those countries that he effectively already controlled. A total 90 percent of Romania and 75 percent of Bulgaria were to become part of the Soviet sphere of influence, while the British claimed 90 percent of Greece. Yugoslavia and Hungary were to be divided equally between the two great powers. Albania was the only country in the region that was not mentioned in the plan.[3] Southeastern Europe lay precisely at the interface of the future bipolar world order, making the countries in the region dependent on the great powers' decisions. Years later, global changes such as decolonization and the Sino-Soviet conflict eventually gave the governments of southeastern Europe expanded room for maneuver. The region became a microcosm of different ideologies, systems, and independent approaches in foreign policy.

Building Communism

The war in southeastern Europe was mostly over by the fall of 1944, and the communists prepared to take power. During the war, Partisans in Yugoslavia, Albania, and Greece had already established the first state-like structures in the territories they controlled. Numerous British attempts to reconcile opposing forces, with the intent of thwarting the communists' rise to power, did not succeed.[4] In August 1944, a successful Red Army offensive had forced the surrender of Romania and Bulgaria, compelling them to change sides. King Michael of Romania ordered Antonescu's arrest. Communists as well as liberals mobilized national interests by seeking the restitution of Transylvania, where thousands had been murdered, expelled, and subjected to Magyarization during the Hungarian occupation.[5] Antonescu was sentenced to death by a special tribunal and executed in May 1946. In Bulgaria, meanwhile, the communist-led Fatherland Front gained strength and prepared to take over the government, maneuvering it toward the Soviet sphere of influence.[6]

The German army had already begun to vacate Albania, Greece, and Yugoslavia in August 1944, seizing important economic assets and leaving a wake of massive destruction. Since the fall of 1943, the Liaison Office for Ethnic Germans had evacuated hundreds of thousands of Germans—particularly from the territory of the Soviet Union, Transnistria, Transylvania, Croatia, and Banat. Damages from the war were vast throughout southeastern Europe. In Greece, about 1,600 villages and small towns had been razed to the ground, and 1 million people were homeless. Some 91,000 men and women had been shot as hostages, and another 30,000 civilians were murdered in "punitive actions" meant to deter further Partisan activity. The small Balkan country lost more than a half million people, or 7.2 percent of its prewar population. In Albania, about 1,850 villages were completely destroyed and 28,000 people killed—about 2.5 percent of the population.[7] Yugoslavia fared the worst, with up to 1.7 million official casualties—a population loss of 10.8 percent, 3.3 million people were homeless, and the value of the economy had been reduced by 46.9 billion dollars.[8] Decades later, researchers from the different Yugoslav republics found that the country lost about two million inhabitants because of the Second World War—one million war dead, and another million through emigration, abduction, dislocation, and a decrease in births.[9]

The changeover to communism followed a similar pattern in all of the countries of central and southeastern Europe. Once the occupiers were driven out of the capitals, communists, social democrats, and representatives of other "antifascist" parties established coalition governments with names like the People's Front (Yugoslavia), National Democratic Front (Romania), and Fatherland Front (Bulgaria). Communists simultaneously settled the score with political rivals and former collaborators. By the end of the war, tens of thousands of their opponents had disappeared or been executed.[10] In the months before and after the war's end, Yugoslav Partisans systematically murdered their political opponents. Tens of thousands were killed in rearguard fighting in Bleiburg, on death marches, in court-martials, and in prison camps. There were massacres in Slovenian Kočevski Rog, Tezno, and Huda Jama.[11] In Bulgaria, one-third of the Presidium and nearly half of the delegates of the Agrarian Union were imprisoned by the summer of 1946. The party leader Nikola Petkov was executed in 1947.[12] In Romania, show trials were held to punish the peasant party leader Iuliu Maniu and the liberal Constantin Dinu Brătianu. They died as inmates in Sighet prison. The Chetnik leader Draža Mihailović was executed after his sentencing in Yugoslavia.

The communists may well have prevailed in Greece, as in Yugoslavia and Albania, had British troops not intervened on behalf of the royalist government in exile in October 1944. After King George II returned in 1946, a bloody civil war erupted between communists and supporters of the old order. By 1949, about 108,000 people had lost their lives in this new round of fighting, reprisals, and mass executions. Seventeen hundred villages were destroyed, and hundreds of thousands of people were uprooted and persecuted. In the end, the communists were defeated, and anticommunism became the foundational doctrine of the postwar Greek state.[13]

In the following years, the communist regimes secured power by orienting themselves toward the model of the Soviet Union. They established state security services with networks of agents that targeted not only foreign enemies but also their own citizens: the Romanian Securitate, the Bulgarian DS, the Albanian Sigurimi, and the Yugoslav UDBA. In the first

Arrival of the Red Army in Bulgaria, fall 1944. Photograph by Yevgeny Khaldei.

postwar years, tens of thousands of Romanians landed in labor camps for the "reeducation of enemies of the republic." The Romanian government deported about 40,000 people from a fifteen-mile-long stretch of land along the Yugoslav border after they were deemed a security risk.[14] The country maintained about 230 political prisons, labor camps, and deportation centers, 15 psychiatric institutions, and 90 execution sites.[15] The communist terror came to an end everywhere in the 1950s, but purges remained a frequent, unpredictable occurrence in Albania long after the war's end. Enver Hoxha was the only member of the Albanian communist party's founding generation to survive all the waves of persecution.[16]

Ethnic Germans who had not already been resettled or evacuated during the war by the Liaison Office for Ethnic Germans also faced persecution. In Yugoslavia, they were accused of collaboration, dispossessed, prosecuted as war criminals, or interned in camps. Many fell victim to acts of Partisan revenge. After the notorious detention camps were dissolved in 1948, most internees were sent to Hungary or Austria.[17] In Romania, by contrast, ethnic Germans were not persecuted or expelled, but they were subject to attack by Soviet troops and (as in Yugoslavia) deportation.[18]

Parliamentary elections took place in an atmosphere of widespread insecurity and violence, and the communist parties secured overwhelming majorities. One after another, they proclaimed "people's republics"—Yugoslavia at the end of 1945, Albania and Bulgaria in 1946, and Romania in 1947. They received constitutions that closely resembled the Soviet model, but with a centralized government structure. Only Yugoslavia was established as a federation with six republics and two autonomous regions. Slovenes, Croats, Serbs, Macedonians, and Montenegrins—and in the 1960s, Bosnian Muslims—were recognized as constituent peoples. A unitary Yugoslav nation was no longer promoted by the state, as in the interwar era.

In February 1947, the Paris Peace Treaties with Italy, Romania, Hungary, and Bulgaria largely restored the territorial order before the outbreak of the war. The Vienna Awards were revoked. Bucharest had to give up Dobruja, Bessarabia, and northern Bukovina, but retained Transylvania.[19] In contrast to earlier eras, the minorities question was now to be resolved according to Marxist-Leninist principles. Yugoslavia and Romania created autonomous provinces where Albanians and Hungarians could maintain their own language and culture and administer themselves, in cooperation with other nationalities. Other national groups also enjoyed comparatively liberal linguistic, cultural, and educational policies.

The socialist revolution comprehensively reshaped all areas of life. The communists promised a just, classless, modern, and humane society. Their model was the Soviet Union, where leading communists from southeastern Europe, such as Josip Broz Tito and Georgi Dimitrov, had spent years in exile. As in the Soviet Union, rigidly hierarchical one-party states adhered to a system of "democratic centralism," as it was known in communist jargon. All power was concentrated within the party's Central Committee and its executive organ, the Politburo. Every person had to participate in one of the new mass organizations, although only a minority joined the communist party. Rates of membership ranged between 3.4 percent (Romania) and 6.1 percent (Bulgaria) in the mid-1950s.[20]

The core goal of communist ideology was to move beyond capitalism, and to promote social justice through industrial progress. The communist social model included collectivization of agriculture, state ownership of the means of production, emphasis on heavy industry, and central economic planning. The societies were to be thoroughly modernized so that better education, health care, and social benefits could create culturally sophisticated "new humans." A mixture of optimism, euphoric planning, and modernization backed by terror was supposed to transform traditional peasant societies into modern industrial nations in just a short period of time.[21]

A key element of economic reconstruction and patriotism was work—the right and duty of every citizen. In the first postwar years, 1.3 million young men and women in Yugoslavia, and a half million in Bulgaria, participated in "voluntary" work brigades to rebuild railroads, streets, and factories.[22] In the words of Georgi Dimitrov, "The new Bulgarian man and the new Bulgarian woman were brought up and steeled" by the brigade movement.[23]

Agriculture was collectivized in all communist states. Millions of acres of land from banks, companies, churches, large landowners, and ethnic Germans were redistributed to veterans and other landless individuals. The rural population was gathered into cooperatives.[24] Yugoslavia reversed its collectivization policy amid growing supply problems and its pivot toward the West in 1952, but the practice continued in Bulgaria, Albania, and Romania into the 1960s. Soviet kolkhozes provided the model for the new agricultural order; peasants received a small amount of land for sustaining themselves, but otherwise were compelled to labor within giant agro-industrial complexes.[25]

The most important instrument of economic policy was the five-year plan. The communists believed that political regulation could overcome the crises of overproduction and social injustice that were inherent in an anarchic, irrational capitalism. They devoted all their resources to forced industrialization, which was supposed to create jobs, satisfy demand for consumer goods, and kick-start sustainable economic growth. Industrialization was considered the motor of prosperity and a new, modern society. In the first postwar years, enormous sums were taken from the agricultural sector and invested in industry, iron and steel works, coal power plants, and arms production. This fostered resentment in rural areas, sparking regional protests and isolated uprisings. Only Albania, with its still rudimentary industrial sector, did not adopt the same emphasis.[26]

The massive investments in industry, which were bolstered by a favorable global economy, brought unprecedented economic growth. Gross national product (GNP), industrial production, productivity, and real wages climbed upward at an astonishing rate in the twenty years following the war's end. The socialist countries of southeastern Europe, like the entire continent, experienced an "economic miracle." Growth rates even exceeded those in the West. Yugoslavia in the 1950s led the world in industrial growth, surpassing even Japan with a growth rate of 13.83 percent. Earnings rose about 5.9 percent each year between 1953 and 1959.[27] Between 1950 and 1977, per capita GNP in constant prices grew 8.3 percent annually in Romania, 7.4 percent in Bulgaria, 6.1 percent in Yugoslavia, and 4.7 percent in Albania.[28] Noncommunist Greece boasted annual economic growth of 5.2 percent, surpassing Spain and Portugal.[29] Real earnings in Yugoslavia, Romania, and Bulgaria increased by more than 150 percent between 1950 and 1970, much more than in Poland, Hungary, and Czechoslovakia. In Albania, per capita income for white-collar workers increased nearly 40 percent between 1960 and 1981; for agricultural workers, nearly 57 percent.[30]

The agricultural societies of southeastern Europe underwent fundamental transformation in the two decades after 1945. Before the Second World War, agriculture constituted about three-quarters of the region's total economic output; in Greece, it was about a half.[31] Whereas the great majority of the population had previously worked on farms, after the 1960s fewer workers in the region—with the exception of Albania—were employed in agriculture than in the industrial and service sectors. By the end of the 1980s, the agricultural sector only made up 10 to 16 percent of GNP in Yugoslavia, Bulgaria, and Romania. Only in Albania was it still more than one-third.[32]

After the end of the war, millions of people left the countryside and resettled permanently in the city. Many became commuters and part-time industrial workers.[33] Urbanization was considered a pillar of modern society and a symbol of progress. The cities of southeastern Europe acquired functional, monotone apartment blocks, magnificent Stalinist structures and futuristic skyscrapers, modern hospitals, universities, libraries, hotels, radio stations, and sports stadiums. Industrialization and urbanization occurred side by side in all-new socialist cities like Bulgarian Dimitrovgrad. The communists were convinced that "as the great factory and thermal electric power plant [in Dimitrovgrad] grew, hundreds of superb new people, confident builders of a new life, would grow alongside them."[34] By the 1980s, more people in Yugoslavia, Bulgaria, and Romania lived in cities than in rural areas.[35] This was true in capitalist Greece as well.

Another supporting pillar in the house of socialism was the revolution in education and culture—including political awareness campaigns, agitation and propaganda, and marginalization of religion. Public events,

Reading lesson at the Gračanica company in Kosovo. Kosovo Archive, Prishtina.

night courses, schoolbooks, and the media spread socialist—which is to say, "cultivated"—ways of life among the people. Kindergartens, schools, mass organizations, companies, communist parties, media, and cultural institutions all played a role. The state promoted its cultural ideals by supporting theater, opera, museums, book publishing, and sports.[36]

Between the end of the war and the beginning of the 1980s, an unparalleled educational offensive shrunk the rate of illiteracy in Yugoslavia from 50 percent to just 10 percent of the population. Illiteracy in Albania fell from 80 percent to 30 percent in the same time period. Universities expanded as well. In 1945 there were just three universities and two colleges in all Yugoslavia; Albania had none. Three decades later, Yugoslavia had become one of the European states with the most students of higher education per capita, behind only Sweden, the Netherlands, and the Soviet Union. Albania was catching up, with six newly founded universities. Social mobility grew alongside the new educational opportunities. Many students came from families of peasants, workers, and craftsmen.[37]

According to official ideology, a socialist had to be raised in the "spirit of proletarian internationalism and socialist patriotism," which included "national pride, awareness of duty, and a sense of responsibility to one's homeland."[38] "The nation and the State will continue to be the basis of the development of socialist society," one Romanian functionary explained. "Not only does this not run counter to the interests of socialist internationalism, but on the contrary, it fully corresponds to these interests, to the international solidarity of the working people."[39] Socialist cultural policy also included the support of historical research institutes and the publication of voluminous, multivolume national histories. Earlier periods of history became a particular focus of national pride. Bulgarians observed the holiday for Cyril and Methodius, incorporated medieval khans into the pantheon of national heroes, and discovered the Bulgarian Empire as a subject of historical film. Without the old rulers, the Bulgarian party leader Todor Zhivkov asserted, "there would be no Bulgarian state and no Bulgarian nation."[40] In Romania and Albania, too, historians emphasized important milestones of national history and highlighted continuities with ancient times.[41] The Illyrians, Skanderbeg, and nineteenth-century nationalists were presented as the forefathers of a free Albania. Socialist promotion of tradition and folklore necessarily included ensembles like choirs and folk dance groups, and the declaration of entire towns as living museums.[42]

The goal of socialist enlightenment was to eradicate all traces of backwardness, and the communists identified religion as a foremost offender. Cultural institutions spread atheistic propaganda, and clerics faced harassment. Church leaders spent years in prison or under house arrest. Religious communities and practices were tolerated, however, as long as they did not challenge the regime. Yugoslavia abolished the sharia, closed religious foundations and schools, and forbade women—as in Turkey— to wear the veil.[43] State-sanctioned socialist rituals and ceremonies replaced religious ones such as baptism, the veneration of icons, and church marriage. Bulgaria, for example, celebrated September 9 as the Day of Revolution. In Yugoslavia, May 1 was the Day of Youth, and August 23 was Romania's Anniversary of Liberation. Albania went furthest, imposing a Chinese-style cultural revolution and declaring itself an atheistic state in 1967. Christmas and New Year's Day were merged into one holiday so that Christmas trees became New Year's trees, and Santa Claus became a New Year's grandfather.[44]

Women in Sarajevo, 1947. Museum of Sarajevo.

Similar to Stalin, state and party leaders in southeastern Europe promoted an extensive personality cult.[45] They were honored as "heroes of the people" or "heroes of socialist labor" and immortalized in paintings, statues, and busts. Josip Broz Tito was celebrated by cheering, flag-waving crowds in demonstrations and parades; the masses called out "We belong to Tito! Tito belongs to us!" and choirs sang "Comrade Tito, we pledge ourselves to you."[46] Yugoslavia celebrated his birthday as the Day of Youth, with a countrywide relay race.[47] Nicolae Ceaușescu liked to be called "Son of the Sun" or "Genius of the Carpathians," and he appeared in portraits as the *Conducător* (Leader) with a scepter and imperial orb.[48] In the 1980s, an entire neighborhood in Bucharest's old town gave way to his monstrous palace of government, the largest building in all of Europe.

The extent of socialism's cultural changes was most evident in the countryside. "I could not even imagine that there were places so far removed from the world," Rajka Borojević wrote in her diary, after arriving in the Serbian mountain village of Donji Dubac in 1951.[49] The schoolteacher and entrepreneur from Herzegovina had returned to the village for the first time since the war. She and her husband Vukašin, who was injured as a Partisan, had taken refuge in Donji Dubac to evade the Ustasha, and they had gratefully promised one day to return the villagers' kindness. Immediately after the war, the couple moved to Banja Luka in Bosnia, where they developed a plan to build a medicinal herb factory in remote Donji Dubac.[50]

Conditions in Donji Dubac, as in many rural areas, at the beginning of the 1950s were antediluvian. "Here backwardness reigns unbowed," Rajka noted in her diary. The villagers still believed in the evil eye, and in spirits and miracles. Even the most rudimentary knowledge about hygiene was lacking. In the neighboring house, for example, there was only one washtub. "This is used for everything. For bathing, too. They soften leather for tanning . . . and when the children have to go at night, they use the same tub."[51]

Although the socialist constitutions now granted women full legal, social, and economic equality, in rural areas a woman still had to ask permission from her husband or mother-in-law for nearly everything. "The less women know, the better," a village elder remarked, summing up prevailing gender roles.[52] Over the objections of the village's older residents, the communist district secretary nevertheless supported Rajka's plan to organize courses for women in subjects like nutrition, cooking, sewing, household management, hygiene, childrearing, and etiquette. The party provided funding, the Red Cross built a pharmacy, and various publishers donated brochures and magazines. "It's such a pleasure to work with the women in the village," Rajka recalled. "They're so eager to learn."[53]

But as long as the town had no streets or means of transportation, it was impossible for women to secure paid work. Many never left the village, producing cloth and carpets from hemp and linen on ancient looms. "Then it struck me," Rajka recalled, "the tradition of weaving—working at home!"[54] In the mid-1950s, she established Yugoslavia's first cooperative for female weavers in Donji Dubac. "If they had the opportunity to use their skills . . . to produce and sell their products . . . women could improve their and their family's living standard. And even more importantly—

they would create a better position for themselves, build their esteem in the family and in society. They would become autonomous."[55] And this is just what happened. The collective gave women in the village the opportunity to earn their own money for the first time; they traveled to other cities in Yugoslavia, and eventually to other countries. They turned their traditional home work into a business model that was not only successful in Yugoslavia, but "in demand around the world," the party newspaper *Borba* reported. In 1968 the women weavers were particularly pleased to receive a commission from Coco Chanel.[56]

In no other era did relations between the sexes change as rapidly as the postwar period. The state made enormous investments in women's education, employment, and social policy (such as child care). In less than two decades, the educational opportunities for women and men had become nearly equal.[57] Nearly one-third of all paid workers were women in 1960— and by 1988, half were. Women also made inroads into typically "male" professions. At the same time, however, they were expected to keep birth rates high. In Yugoslavia, family planning was seen as a private matter, and abortion was considered a human right. But beginning in the late 1960s, leaders in Greece, Albania, Bulgaria, and Romania sought to encourage motherhood by limiting the right to abortion, raising taxes for workers without children, and paying childbirth bonuses. But these measures could not reverse the trend for fewer children that was evident everywhere. Natural population growth in the 1980s was about as low in southeastern Europe as elsewhere on the continent; the exceptions were Albania and Kosovo, where demographic transition had been delayed. The gap in overall life expectancy narrowed as well.[58]

Communists everywhere initially imitated the Soviet-Stalinist model, but the first cracks began to show in the communist bloc not long after the war's end. Josip Broz Tito was behind the rupture, declaring as early as May 1945 that Yugoslavia did "not wish to be petty cash used in bribes; we do not wish to be involved in a policy of spheres of interest."[59] In 1947 he entered into agreements with Bulgaria and Albania that were supposed to lead to a Balkan federation, which might eventually expand to include Greece as well. The undertaking corresponded to plans for a regional federation that the socialists had harbored since the nineteenth century.[60] Stalin, who saw his sphere of influence in southeastern Europe receding, lost his patience and expelled the Yugoslav Communist Party from the Communist Information Bureau (Cominform) on June 28, 1948, the historically momentous day of Saint Vitus. In early 1949, Yugoslavia was shut out of the newly founded Council for Mutual Economic Assistance (Comecon).[61]

The U.S. president Harry S. Truman saw Yugoslavia's isolation as a useful opportunity to drive a wedge in the socialist camp. He offered generous military economic assistance to "keep Tito afloat."[62] Belgrade began to orient its trade relationships toward the West in order to break free of Soviet dependency.[63] Between 1948 and 1960, more than 1.5 billion dollars of American loans flowed into Belgrade's coffers.[64] In return, Tito withdrew his support for the Greek communists. Their insurgency collapsed in 1949, ending the Greek Civil War.[65] In his own country, Tito forced communists loyal to Moscow—the Cominformists—into emigration by the thousands; others were interned in the infamous camp on Goli Otok (Naked Island). The anti-Stalinist purges continued until the end of the 1950s.[66]

Since the Yugoslav leadership did not want to renounce communism, a model had to be found that distinguished itself sufficiently from the Soviet system. Under the direction of Edvard Kardelj, the Yugoslavs invented socialist "self-management." Instead of the state, democratic workers' councils assumed a leading role in all enterprises and social organizations. Market economic principles and private companies were also permitted. Unlike the Eastern bloc, the Yugoslav system tolerated a certain pluralism in literature and the arts, and soon, in scholarship and political theory.

Yugoslavia's expulsion from the communist bloc encouraged Albania's head of state, Enver Hoxha, to free himself from Tito's patronage. Since the end of the 1930s, the Yugoslavs had helped to build Albania's communist party and exerted a dominant influence ever since. Between 1945 and 1948, Albania received about 33 million dollars in economic aid from Belgrade, signing multiple agreements on economic cooperation, trade, and a customs union, and also a treaty of friendship and mutual assistance, in order to advance Tito's plan for a communist Balkan federation.

Enver Hoxha, who was the best educated and most bourgeois of all the southeastern European communist leaders, eventually became Stalin's most loyal supporter. He came from a Muslim family of traders and large landowners; he attended the French-language school in Korçë and then studied in France. In 1930s Paris, the charismatic young intellectual led the life of a Bohemian and wrote for publications such as *L'Humanité*, *Le Monde*, and the *International Herald Tribune*.[67] In 1946, he followed Stalin's

Socialist agitprop painting of Enver Hoxha.

lead and consolidated all key functions in his person. He served not only as the head of state and of the communist party, but also as the minister of defense and foreign affairs. He began to complain about Tito's "fascist" and "revisionist" clique, and he renounced all treaties with Yugoslavia in 1948. The Soviet Union subsequently assumed the role of Albania's protector and financier. By 1961 it had loaned Albania about 156 million U.S. dollars, most of which it did not expect to be repaid. About 3,000 military and economic advisers and 100 million dollars in technical assistance flowed from the Soviet Union into Albania. For Hoxha, Stalin was the undisputed savior of Albanian independence. This attitude persisted even after the Soviet dictator's death in 1953, and the beginning of the Soviet "thaw" in 1956.[68]

Communism did not take hold in Greece, and the monarchy was restored after the end of the civil war. Nevertheless, democracy faltered in the southernmost Balkan country. In April 1967 Georgios Papadopoulos led officers of the Greek army in a coup d'état and established a military dictatorship. They suspended civil liberties and "cleansed" the armed forces and state bureaucracy. Thousands of political opponents disappeared into camps; they were murdered by the junta or driven into exile. Challenged by growing economic problems, student protests, and the Turkish invasion of Cyprus, the extreme nationalist military regime fell apart by the middle of 1974. Democracy was restored and the monarchy abolished.[69]

Southeastern Europe and the Cold War

The great powers staked their claims in southeastern Europe even before the end of the Second World War, turning the region into an object of negotiation in an emerging confrontation between East and West. The Trieste crisis heralded the onset of the Cold War in 1945. The port city, which lay precisely on the border between the spheres of interest that the great powers had painstakingly negotiated in Yalta, was contested between Italy and Yugoslavia.[70] As the Second World War drew to a close, Yugoslav and British army units faced off here. Tito's Partisans had already united Istria and Dalmatia with Yugoslavia, but the Western powers—later joined by Stalin—believed that Italy should receive Trieste as a reward for having changed sides during the war.[71] Military threats ended in compromise in June 1945. The Yugoslav troops pulled out of Trieste, and the surrounding area was divided into Allied and Yugoslav zones of occupation.[72] According to a 1947 peace treaty, Yugoslavia retained Dalmatia and Istria, while Trieste and northern Istria became a neutral Free Territory under United Nations supervision. Zone A (the city of Trieste) fell under British and American military administration, and Zone B (the surrounding lands) was administered by the Yugoslavs. The arrangement remained in place until 1954.

Differences between the four victorious powers over the peace settlement for Germany and Austria intensified following the foreign ministers' conference in Moscow in the spring of 1947. Observing the communists' seizure of power in the eastern and southeastern European countries, the U.S. deputy chief of mission in Moscow, George F. Kennan, called for a policy of containment in February 1946. In March 1947, U.S. president Harry S. Truman proclaimed his doctrine to "support free peoples," protecting all democracies from Soviet expansion. One year later, the U.S. Congress authorized the 12.4-billion-dollar Marshall Plan for the rebuilding of Europe. In southeastern Europe, only Turkey and Greece participated in the plan, while the communist states turned down Western assistance by order of Moscow.

In response to Truman's speech, the Soviet Union founded the Communist Information Bureau (Cominform) to coordinate communist movements worldwide in September 1947. At its founding meeting, the Soviet delegate Andrei Zhdanov delivered his famous speech depicting the division of the world into two camps—an American-dominated, imperialist, antidemocratic camp on one hand, and a Soviet-led, anti-imperialist, democratic camp on the other. When the Soviet Union cut off all land and water routes between western Germany and Berlin in the spring of 1948, the Cold War was on.[73]

From this point forward, tensions between the United States and the Soviet Union continuously grew. The Cold War took place in all possible arenas: the arms race, espionage, economics, society, and politics. Its front lines ran through the middle of southeastern Europe. In 1949, ten western European states joined the United States and Canada to form NATO; Turkey and Greece became members in 1952. In 1955, the Soviet Union established the Warsaw Pact with several eastern European states, including Romania, Bulgaria, and Albania (until 1968). Only Yugoslavia maintained a special role outside of the alliances. As North Korea, China, and Vietnam installed communist regimes, the focus of the Cold War increasingly shifted toward East Asia. The countries of Latin America and Africa also found themselves caught between the fronts as a result of decolonization.

The death of Stalin in 1953 signaled the beginning of a "thaw" in the Soviet Union. In his famous speech at the Twentieth Party Congress in 1956, Nikita Khrushchev denounced the personality cult surrounding Stalin and the dictator's political purges. The Soviet Union subsequently embraced a system of collective leadership and the principle of "peaceful coexistence" with the capitalist world. That same year, Khrushchev and Tito jointly declared that "the paths of socialist development vary." Yugoslavia was effectively rehabilitated, and it resumed relations with the Soviet Union.[74] Equidistance between the capitalist West and the communist East gave Tito freedom to maneuver. In 1957 he formally recognized the German Democratic Republic (East Germany). The (western) Federal Republic of Germany responded by imposing sanctions, as its state policy—expressed in the 1955 Hallstein Doctrine—was not to negotiate with any country that recognized its eastern rival. Relations between West Germany and Yugoslavia were eventually normalized in 1968.[75]

In Bulgaria, where Todor Zhivkov worked his way to the top of the Communist Party in the early 1950s, a process of de-Stalinization likewise commenced.[76] The terror came to an end, and thousands of political prisoners were released. Beginning in 1965, the Bulgarian leadership undertook various economic reforms that allowed enterprises greater autonomy. Cultural life was liberalized as well. In foreign policy, however, Bulgaria remained loyal to Moscow across the decades. In 1973 Todor Zhivkov remarked that the Soviet Union and Bulgaria acted as a "single body, breathing with the same lungs and nourished by the same bloodstream."[77] He twice suggested that his country should join the Soviet Union.

Romania, like Bulgaria, began the process of de-Stalinization in the second half of the 1950s. But its leader, Gheorghe Gheorghiu-Dej, had never unreservedly accepted the Soviet Union's patronage. Over time he became more assertive in objecting to Romania's economic dependency within Comecon, and in challenging the Soviet party line in foreign relations. At the beginning of the 1960s, the Sino-Soviet conflict over communist world leadership became a lever for opening up greater freedom of action within the Soviet orbit. In March 1964 a Romanian delegation traveled to Beijing and Moscow to serve as a diplomatic intermediary. When the mission failed, the Romanian Workers' Party famously announced its independence from Soviet foreign policy in April 1964.[78] Bucharest subsequently worked to maintain good relations with China and opened up trade relations with both Western and Third World countries.[79] After 1965, Gheorghiu-Dej's successor, Nicolae Ceaușescu, repeatedly snubbed the Soviet Union, as when he initiated diplomatic relations with West Germany. In contrast to other Eastern bloc states, Romania also maintained relations with Israel after the Six-Day War in 1967. In 1968 Romania—like Yugoslavia, Albania, and China—condemned Soviet intervention in Czechoslovakia.[80] The reason for Soviet intervention was the Czechoslovak program of reform and democratization, which aimed to create "socialism with a human face." A key article on the Brezhnev Doctrine in *Pravda,* the central organ of the Soviet communist party, unambiguously stated that "the sovereignty of each socialist country cannot be opposed to the interests of the world of socialism."[81] Bulgaria was the only state in southeastern Europe that sent troops to support Moscow's invasion.

Albania also used the Sino-Soviet conflict to free itself from the grip of the Soviet Union. Hoxha, like the Chinese leaders, still believed in the inevitability of a world war between communism and imperialism. Because he rejected the policy of peaceful coexistence, he refused to follow the Soviets' lead in condemning the Chinese Communist Party. The Soviets attempted to bring Albania in line by reducing their economic assistance and threatening to expel the country from the Warsaw Pact. But in 1960, Hoxha traveled to Moscow and provocatively accused Khrushchev of betraying Marxism-Leninism in front of the delegations of eighty-one different communist and workers' parties. He also took the side of China. The Soviet Union and other Eastern bloc states (except for Romania) stopped their development aid to Albania and cut off diplomatic relations. China became Albania's only international partner, providing 838 million dollars in loans through 1975 and sending experts and technical assistance to support its program of industrialization.[82] Once China, too, began to open to the West, Albania drifted into deeper isolation. In 1976 a new constitution forbade the stationing of foreign troops, the acceptance of licenses from foreign companies, and international loans. When China cut off its assistance to Albania (primarily for economic reasons) in 1978, Hoxha began to work toward autarky. Fearing an invasion by enemy powers, he constructed hundreds of thousands of small cement bunkers, which even today provide a physical reminder of his paranoid system of rule.[83]

The socialist states' independent approaches to foreign policy were also evident at the level of international organizations. Communists had long promoted the idea of "socialist" or "proletarian" internationalism. This was ideally grounded in the complete equality and right to self-determination of all nations, the close cooperation of communist parties, and the cooperation and mutual solidarity of all socialist countries. In the short term, they believed, "peaceful coexistence" with the capitalist world was possible and even necessary. Thus, they advocated for strong international organizations, particularly the United Nations.

The UN became an important sphere of action for the socialist Balkan states, for reasons that were practical and political as well as ideological. Yugoslavia was a founding member of the UN, but Albania, Bulgaria, and Romania did not join until 1955. Tito, whose state became a nonpermanent member of the Security Council in 1949, asserted: "The small nations can play an outstanding role in preventing the outbreak of a new world war, if they strive, unitedly and together, for equitable relations between large and small."[84] Albania and Romania likewise saw the UN as a protective umbrella against the overwhelming hegemony of the great powers, and also as an arena of independent foreign policy. In 1956 Romanian delegates to the General Assembly always voted together with the Soviet Union, but by 1977, they shared Moscow's position in less than two-thirds of all votes.[85] The southeastern European countries played an active role in the various suborganizations—especially the UN Economic Commission for Europe (UNECE), UN Conference on Trade and Development (UNCTAD), UN Industrial Development Organization (UNIDO), International Labor Organization (ILO), and the UN Educational, Scientific and Cultural Organization (UNESCO).

With varying emphases, the socialist states' favored themes included peace and disarmament, the further development of international law, the democratization of the UN, decolonization, and—beginning in the 1970s—a New International Economic Order and a New World Information and Communication Order. Romania explicitly sought to build on the legacy of its renowned foreign minister from the 1930s, Nicolae Titulescu, by encouraging the formation of regional security systems. During the Cold War, southeastern Europe risked becoming the site of a nuclear showdown, as American nuclear weapons were stationed in Greece and Turkey, and Soviet launch systems were stationed in eastern (although not southeastern) Europe. In 1957 Romania proposed to its neighbors (Albania, Bulgaria, Greece, Yugoslavia, and Turkey) that the Balkans ought to become a nuclear weapon-free zone.[86] The project was supported by the Soviet Union but immediately rejected by the Western nuclear powers; it was raised again from time to time, with little success. In 1981 Bucharest sought to make the Balkans a "peace zone" and a model for détente in all of Europe, lobbying for the withdrawal of Soviet missiles and against the stationing of Western Pershing and cruise missiles. Greece also joined the initiative.[87]

Yugoslavia, meanwhile, sought a new foreign policy identity, having been shut out of the Cominform in 1948 and Comecon in 1949. An opportunity arose with the collapse of the European empires in Africa and Asia, where the colonial powers had responded to independence movements with emergency measures and brute force, arbitrary shootings, the use of gas and torture, and deportations.[88] But the process of decolonization could not be stopped after British India gained its independence in 1947. This was followed by Dutch Indonesia, French Indochina and Algeria, and the founding of Israel from the British mandate in Palestine.[89]

Southeastern Europe shared common ties with two other world regions that likewise became important Cold War arenas: the Near East and Asia.

Since the beginning of the 1950s, the young states of Asia had found themselves under growing pressure to take sides in the global Cold War. After the United States launched the Southeast Asia Treaty Organization in 1954, India and Indonesia, in particular, feared for their ability to remain neutral. In 1955 presidents Sukarno and Jawaharlal Nehru invited representatives from twenty-nine Asian and African countries to a conference in Bandung, in order to assert the right of self-determination for all peoples. Other points in their declaration concerned respecting human rights and abstaining from intervention in other countries' internal affairs. The states further warned against a nuclear war of annihilation.

The "Global South" now firmly advocated for decolonization within the framework of the United Nations, which had not yet clearly asserted the right of self-determination in its own charter. Through the initiative of the Bandung states, the General Assembly passed a Declaration on the Granting of Independence to Colonial Countries and Peoples in 1960. The United States, United Kingdom, and other European colonial powers abstained from the voting. The British scholar Martin Wight called the "Bandung powers" a "Mazzinian revolutionary league" and warned of the dangers of "Balkanization," or a *Kleinstaaterei* of weak States, fiercely divided among themselves by nationalistic feuds . . . a battle-ground for the surrounding Great Powers."[90] But the movement of decolonization could not be stopped. Between 1945 and 1970, sixty-four states claimed independence.

As an outgrowth of the Bandung Conference, where Yugoslavia was not even a participant, Josip Broz Tito developed his signature project: the Non-Aligned Movement. In 1954 Tito traveled through Asia for two months on the state yacht *Galeb*. During his visit to India, he and prime minister Jawaharlal Nehru, who had led his country to independence in 1947, jointly announced a policy of "active neutrality." In 1949 both states had become nonpermanent members of the UN Security Council, and they had maintained good relations ever since. The young Egyptian prime minister, and later president, Gamal Abdel Nasser joined their advocacy for a "third way." He needed allies in order to free Egypt from its dependency on the West. "Egypt is trying to become another Yugoslavia," a high-ranking Egyptian diplomat explained to the Yugoslav foreign minister. "Our situation is somewhat similar. While you are working to preserve your independence, we are trying to win ours." The still-inexperienced Nasser described Tito as an outstanding role model, not least because Tito showed him "how to get help from both sides without joining."[91] In

Nasser, Tito, and Nehru (left to right) initiate the Non-Aligned Movement in
Brioni, July 20, 1956.

July 1956, on the Croatian island of Brioni, Tito, Nasser, and Nehru affirmed the principles of nonalignment and peaceful coexistence. They saw
the new politics as an act of mediation between the blocs, in the spirit of
the UN Charter.[92]

In September 1961 Tito hosted a "second Bandung" in Belgrade, which
resulted in the formal constitution of the movement of nonaligned states.
Delegates from twenty-five countries denounced the imperialist and neo-
colonial politics of the great powers. They called for further decolonization and rejection of the arms race, and in later years they also advocated
for a just world economic order.[93] In subsequent conferences, the movement committed itself to strict neutrality and peaceful coexistence, military neutrality, and the support of national liberation movements. It
grew to 102 members. The Non-Aligned Movement represented a counterweight to Cold War politics and, in some cases, successfully undermined the bipolar order. But its appeals for peace were often wasted paper.
With the wars against Israel—from the Six-Day War in 1967 to the Yom
Kippur War in 1973—the Arab states found themselves in the middle of
a Cold War hot zone. Pakistan and India were likewise embroiled in a
decades-long military conflict over Kashmir.[94]

Nevertheless, in the 1960s and 1970s Tito transformed the nonaligned states into allies and rallied them behind his "third way," simultaneously gaining international prestige for himself and his state. The struggle against colonial rule was also part of Yugoslav history, as the Slovenes, Croats, and Serbs had freed themselves from imperial rule in an earlier era. Tito impressed his foreign colleagues with his natural charisma and authority as a victorious Partisan marshal. He received state guests warmly at his residence on Brioni, and he led them on tours of important sites in the Partisan struggle.[95] From 1944 until 1980, he made 169 official visits to 92 countries, spending almost 1,000 days abroad. In addition, he hosted 175 heads of state and 110 prime ministers, as well as hundreds of other ministers and political leaders.[96]

In the 1960s and 1970s, he was an untiring ambassador of "active peaceful coexistence" and a mediator between the blocs.[97] In the midst of the Cold War and the Berlin and Cuba crises, he castigated the bipolar division of the world as a fundamental evil of the international system. Upon Yugoslav initiative, the UN General Assembly passed its declaration of principles on "peaceful coexistence" in 1970. In 1973, Tito was even suggested as a nominee for the Nobel Peace Prize.[98]

The Non-Aligned Movement brought Yugoslavia untold contacts all over the world. Exports from the Yugoslav weapons, shipbuilding, and construction industries to the Third World brought in 1.5 billion dollars annually, and thousands of young people from developing countries came to study in Yugoslavia each year.[99] Conversely, good relations with the Islamic world allowed Yugoslav Muslims to receive scholarships for study in Egypt, Iraq, Libya, Morocco, Syria, and Sudan. Nasser, Muammar Gaddafi, and the Shah of Iran gave the Yugoslav mosques valuable carpets, built student dormitories, and donated animals to the Belgrade zoo. Nonalignment became a key element of Yugoslavia's identity and stability. "Active neutrality" reconciled rival foreign policy orientations—toward the West, the Soviet Union, and the Islamic world—within the multinational state. This compensated for some of the frustrations with the darker side of the socialist system.

The United States and other Western industrial countries dominated the United Nations and its General Assembly, and the UN suborganizations and advisory boards, in the 1950s. Smaller members, for example, the countries of eastern Europe or the Third World, had little influence.[100] But this asymmetry weakened after 1960, as decolonization brought more and more new members to the world organization. Developing countries gained more authority—as did Yugoslavia. In 1976 Romania joined the Group of seventy-seven developing countries and received guest status in the Non-Aligned Movement. By the 1980s, the Third World outnumbered other member states within the UN system.[101] For the Balkan states, this not only meant that they supported the concerns of the Third World but also that they could count on more advocates for their own causes within the UN.

Yugoslavia took special care to maintain good relations with the Arab world; in several Arab states, secular military elites had come to power, not unlike the Young Turks in the Ottoman Empire decades before. These relations were important to the just under 1.5 million Bosnian Muslims, and to the 1.9 million Albanians, Slavs, Turks, and Roma in Yugoslavia who were also followers of Islam.[102] The Yugoslav state maintained a relatively liberal religious policy toward Muslims, who were organized in the Islamic Religious Community. The state supported the construction of mosques, and also allowed the publication of Islamic periodicals like *Preporod (Rebirth)* and *Islamska misao (Islamic Thought)* and the dissemination of the Koran. An Oriental Institute was established in Sarajevo, with professorships in Oriental studies and Islamic theology. The religious leadership under the *reis-ul-ulema* was consequently pro-Yugoslav.[103]

But Yugoslavia also harbored supporters of a political Islam, who likewise looked toward the Arab world. In Egypt, Nasser—a self-declared protagonist of Egyptian nationalism and secular pan-Arabism—was fighting the pan-Islamic Muslim Brotherhood. After an attempt on Nasser's life, the organization was dissolved, but subsequently moved its activities to Syria, Yemen, and Palestine. One of its chief ideologues, Sayyid Qutb, was executed in 1966, after calling for the overthrow of Nasser's regime and introduction of the sharia.[104] The Muslim Brotherhood was not rehabilitated in Egypt until 1970.

Saudi Arabia, meanwhile, promoted the pan-Islamic movement. At the height of its conflict with Egypt, it supported the founding of the Muslim World League in 1962. The organization styled itself as "a state above the state," sponsoring religious institutions, media, schools, and charitable institutions throughout the world in order to strengthen the *umma,* the global Islamic public.[105] Islamists gained influence wherever—as in Egypt, Pakistan, and Malaysia—there was widespread social dissatisfaction among the urban poor, anxiety about the loss of identity through Westernization and modernization, and a desire for spiritual fulfillment and religious community among middle-class believers.[106] Hearkening back to the early Muslim forefathers (the *salaf*) and a supposedly original Islam served as an instrument of differentiation and identity politics, while also creating an oppositional discourse against ossified political regimes.

As supporters of secular nationalism competed for hegemony with the various strains of politicized Islam throughout the Islamic world, the Yugoslav communists decided to elevate the status of Bosnian Muslims. One of the strongest advocates for this approach was the communist Džemal Bijedić. The son of a wealthy trader from Mostar, Bijedić had joined the communist youth organization in 1939 and was imprisoned multiple times for his political activism. His home region, Herzegovina, was one of the poorest in Yugoslavia. Relations between Muslims, Catholics, and Orthodox Christians were severely damaged during the war, and the consequences of mass crimes reverberated well beyond 1945. During the short lifespan of the Independent State of Croatia, the tall, lanky comrade with the "long, gaunt face and beautiful head of dark curls" had organized illegal party activity in Sarajevo and distributed flyers calling for national unity. He survived the bloody battle on the Sutjeska River in June 1943, and went on to establish the first Partisan administration in liberated eastern Bosnia. After the war, he held several government offices in Bosnia-Herzegovina and became known as a political pragmatist. "We have to recognize that we will not be able to eradicate religious practice in our lifetime. Our task should be winning the hearts and minds of believers, so that they become loyal helpers in building socialism."[107]

For Bijedić, communist nationalities policy was the only humane and practicable approach for his homeland. Bijedić asserted that Muslims "are one of the peoples of Bosnia-Herzegovina, with a distinct national character, just like Serbs and Croats."[108] Immediately after 1945, Muslims were identified as "nationally unspecified," or as "Muslim Serbs" or "Muslim Croats," but in 1968 they were recognized as Yugoslavia's sixth constituent nation.[109] This reflected the fact that many Slavic Muslims (or Bosniaks) saw themselves as members of a distinct nation, not merely members of a religious community. Their identity was no longer primarily defined by religious membership, as had been typical up to the beginning of the twentieth century. Modernization and secularization decreased the significance of religion, although it still provided a framework for traditions, rituals, everyday habits, symbols, and values that colored communal identity, regardless of whether one was a believer or not. Ancient customs, songs, traditional foods—and even attending a mosque—had sociocultural functions, and even communists gave their children Muslim names. Muslim intellectuals worked to emphasize nonreligious national characteristics such as language, literature, and history, in order to substantiate a purely ethnic identity.[110] Bijedić decisively opposed the "glorification" of Muslims since he saw all three peoples (Serbs, Croats, and Muslims) as inseparably linked. "I think everyone who wants to make Bosnia-Herzegovina a purely Muslim republic is on the wrong track," he warned. "That is pure nationalism and chauvinism."[111] In 1971 he became the first Muslim prime minister of Yugoslavia.

The communists supported a uniform, secularized understanding of the Muslim nation, known as *muslimanstvo*. This did not, however, discourage supporters of political Islam, including students of the theological academy (Gazi Husrev-beg medresa) and the Islamic Theological Faculty of the University of Sarajevo. They continued to read the works of Sayyid Qutb and Muhammad Iqbal, and like these authors, they called for the return to a supposedly original Islam. They opposed marriage to Christians and the consumption of alcohol and called upon women to wear the veil.[112] In 1970—the year that Tito's ally and friend, the Egyptian president Gamal Abdel Nasser died, and the Ayatollah Khomeini wrote *Islamic Government*—Alija Izetbegović wrote his *Islamic Declaration*. After 1945, he was imprisoned for his participation in the anticommunist secret society Young Muslims, which called for the "unification of the Islamic world in one great state" and demanded "doggedness and fanaticism" from its members. Although many of his compatriots went into exile, Izetbegović stayed in Yugoslavia and practiced law after his release in 1949.[113] He kept in touch with Muslim brothers in Syria, Sudan, and Jordan, and also with Bosnian Muslim political exiles in Turkey, Austria, the United States, and Switzerland.[114] Two decades later, he still espoused the unity of religion, state, and social order and called for a unified, centrally governed pan-Islamic state "from Morocco to Indonesia, from Africa to Central Asia." "Islamic order and ways of living" would prevail, and the Pakistani model could serve as guide for Islamization. "Our goal: the Islamization of Muslims. Our motto: believe and struggle."[115] He rejected Western culture and its conceptions of order, arguing that the public and the media ought to be controlled.

Thus, southeastern Europe not only became an arena of East-West confrontation; it was also linked, in different ways, with two other flashpoint regions in the Cold War: Asia and the Near East. The rise of communist

China was one of the developments that drove a wedge in the Eastern bloc, giving countries like Albania and Romania greater room for maneuver. The interests of Yugoslavia and the countries of the Third World came together in the Non-Aligned Movement. Their cooperation was mutually advantageous. Orientation toward the Arab world and (as we will see) world trade and international financial markets encouraged a variety of global connections. While the decline of the European colonial empires and decolonization tended to disrupt connections between western Europe and the wider world, the effect was exactly the opposite in southeastern Europe.

Cultural Exchange and Global Civil Society

Although Western politicians spoke of an "Iron Curtain" that supposedly sealed off the communist part of Europe from its noncommunist neighbors, many different cultural and social relationships existed across the East-West divide. The 1950s, in particular, were still strongly informed by propaganda from the United States and the Soviet Union; the Cold War encompassed not only political, military, and economic affairs but also cultural policy. In 1938, U.S. president Franklin D. Roosevelt had already established a Division of Cultural Relations within the State Department, seeking to promote the spread of American ideals like freedom and democracy abroad. Additional sources of propaganda came later, including the radio broadcaster Voice of America, which focused its programming on eastern and southeastern Europe, and the U.S. Information Agency, which worked to spread the "American Dream" and fight communism throughout the world.[116] Soviet propaganda, by contrast, emphasized themes of anti-imperialism, the fight against colonialism and racism, and international solidarity. A central message was the close connection between internationalism and world peace. Moscow organized world youth and world women's gatherings, and also founded a World Peace Council that attracted Western intellectuals. The Council's Stockholm Appeal, which condemned nuclear weapons, received millions of signatures in both the East and the West. As in the United States, specialized news agencies like Novosti worked to spread Soviet propaganda around the world.[117]

Through the Truman Doctrine, the United States became a protecting power for Greece and Turkey, which also shaped cultural policy. During the civil war, Greek communists received significant backing from the Cominform, Yugoslavia, Albania, and Bulgaria. Once the war ended, the hunt for communists began, and anticommunism effectively became the state ideology of Greece in 1949. The Cominform continued its propaganda in Bucharest with the radio broadcaster Free Greece, but within Greece, communist organizations were declared unpatriotic and banned, and communist sympathizers were removed from state service. The U.S. Embassy in Athens financed the Central Information Agency, a Greek intelligence organization modeled after the American CIA.[118]

Soviet culture provided the model for the socialist countries of southeastern Europe in the immediate postwar era. Socialist realism predominated in architecture, literature, painting, and the visual arts. Novels, poems, pictures, sculptures, and plays were supposed to be educational and optimistic, reinforcing traditional folk culture as well as party politics. Typical themes included the everyday experience of workers and peasants, and the celebration of technical innovations such as dams, tractors, electrification, or the Sputnik satellite. Praise for the Communist Party and heads of state and depictions of the antifascist struggle in the Second World War were other common features. In Yugoslavia, there was a special emphasis on "brotherhood and unity"—the celebration of different but related peoples living together in one society. The foremost message of agitprop culture was the promotion of socialist values: the Marxist worldview, humanism, openness, solidarity, equal rights for men and women, and the "correct" approach to morality and family life.[119]

In the 1950s, Yugoslavia's rejection of Stalinism was already accompanied by a turn toward modern, abstract art. The National Museum in Belgrade mounted an exhibition with works by Van Gogh, Picasso, and other artists who had once been considered decadent and been held in contempt. The Museum of Contemporary Art, inspired by the example of the Museum of Modern Art in New York, opened in 1965. It displayed Yugoslav "junk" and conceptual art, and works that reflected the Neo-Dada, Fluxus, and Arte Povera movements. The Belgrade International Theater Festival brought avant-garde productions to the stages of the capital.[120] By the end of the 1950s, Romania had likewise begun to loosen Soviet cultural constraints in favor of a new "socialist humanism." Intellectuals once criticized as nationalists—including the writer Mihai Eminescu, the philosopher Constantin Noica, and the historian Nicolae Iorga—were rehabilitated. Even in Stalinist Albania, privileged artists enjoyed certain freedoms. The writer Ismail Kadare made his name with novels such as *The General of the Dead Army* and *The Siege*, which depicted Skanderbeg's battle against the Turks.

The Romanian poet Ana Blandiana recalled the years after 1964, when she published her first book of poetry, as by far "the most liberal time in the history of Romanian communism." Blandiana was the daughter of an Orthodox priest and theologian from Timişoara who had been jailed by the communists for illegally owning a weapon, and she thus faced discrimination in her youth. In order to attend university as the child of an "enemy of the people," she first had to work as an apprentice in construction. "The communists believed that hard physical labor could purge 'unhealthy origins.' I handed bricks to masons, mixed cement, and even learned how to plaster."[121] Blandiana received numerous Romanian and international literary awards for her poetry, and she was invited to travel abroad. But each Romanian who left the country was permitted to exchange only ten dollars per trip. "That's how we got to know Italy in 1969. We left home with twenty dollars and a suitcase with sixty-five kilograms of powdered milk, cocoa, sugar, salami from Sibiu, soft cheese, zwieback—in short, our sustenance for the next month in Italy." The intellectual climate shifted again in the 1970s, and several of her poems were banned. "Some periods were awful; others bordered on tolerable. There was a constant, fiendish battle of nerves, a constant tightening and loosening of the screw."[122]

Despite the Cold War, people on either side of the Iron Curtain still communicated with one another. As early as the mid-1950s, new transnational economic discussion between the socialist East and capitalist West stimulated fresh thinking about competitive markets and central planning alike.[123] New institutions and academic exchange programs brought professional economists together with southeastern European reformers and émigrés to discuss the nature and prospects of socialism. International conferences, UNESCO associations, and professional journals promoted transnational scholarly dialogue, expanding liminal spaces that were critical of both Soviet state socialism and American free-market capitalism. Scholars and reformers developed new, innovative ways of thinking about social and economic organization, particularly with respect to Yugoslav socialist self-management and Hungarian market socialism.

The U.S. government believed that it could best transmit Western thinking—and, in the long run, change Eastern bloc countries' foreign and domestic policies—by educating Eastern scholars in the social sciences and humanities. As the Ford Foundation explained, "It would seem important to help increase their [Eastern European countries'] contacts with the West and thereby penetrate these East European areas with Western democratic influences."[124] Yugoslavia and the United States concluded a formal academic exchange agreement as early as 1951; it formally took effect in 1955.

Yugoslavs were permitted to travel abroad after the early 1960s, and more than 300,000 people did so each year.[125] Belgrade signed guest worker agreements with Germany, France, Austria, Sweden, and other countries. In 1971, more than 773,000 Yugoslavs were temporary residents of another country—about 3.8 percent of their country's population.[126] The socialist Yugoslav state built on prewar nationalism to stay in touch with migrant communities. The state brokered jobs, supported Yugoslav associations, and financed language classes in foreign schools. Anticommunist political émigrés, meanwhile, kept less welcome connections alive. Croat and Serb nationalists, especially supporters of the Ustasha, spread anti-Yugoslav propaganda and even assassinated representatives of the Yugoslav state who were traveling abroad. In response, the Yugoslav secret service arranged for the murder of foreign "terrorists" and "enemies of the state."[127]

An even higher proportion of guest workers came from Greece, on the opposite side of the Iron Curtain. By 1981 more than two million Greeks, or about 12.2 percent of the total population, were temporarily living and working abroad. Through the diaspora in Europe, the United States, Latin America, the Near East, Egypt, Turkey, and Lebanon, there were networks of Greeks practically everywhere in the world.[128] Just as did Yugoslavia, the Greek state supported language classes, radio and television programs, and other cultural activities for its nationals abroad.[129]

In the 1970s, after various industrial states stopped recruiting guest workers, Belgrade began to pursue a national remigration strategy.[130] Belgrade used the new situation to present itself as an active partner to the Organization for Economic Cooperation and Development (OECD) (which sought to promote market economies and democracy in Europe), and it signed an agreement of cooperation with the European Community in 1971. Belgrade was able to trade upon the industrial countries' interest in sending guest workers home to acquire access to financial aid for European returnees.[131]

Ethnic Germans and their descendants created yet another bridge with southeastern Europe. This group included Germans who had been expelled from southeastern Europe in the immediate postwar era as well as "late" resettlers (Spätaussiedler). The Federal Republic of Germany made secret arrangements with Romania to pay several thousand West German marks for every Romanian German who was allowed to exit the country.

By 1989, about 200,000 members of the German minority had emigrated to West Germany, a lucrative deal that earned Romania millions.[132] The country adopted a similar strategy to encourage Romanian Jews to emigrate to Israel.[133]

Tourism became an important driver of international exchange. In the 1980s, Yugoslavia's highly subsidized tourist industry brought millions of visitors to the Adriatic. Bulgarian and Romanian spas, ski resorts, and coastal areas welcomed millions of vacationers from other socialist countries.[134] In Greece, tourism became the second-largest employer; 4.3 million visitors entered the country each year in the mid-1970s.[135] The vacation industry promoted modernization, employment, and social transformation throughout southeastern Europe. Hotel and street construction, holiday rentals, shops, restaurants, and cafés provided jobs for many people. Average levels of education, employment, and income rose significantly in coastal regions and on islands that were once very poor.[136]

Even at the height of the Cold War, there were border areas of cultural interaction between the capitalist and socialist countries. Both sides showcased their outstanding achievements at world exhibitions, which had long served not only as belts of transmission for technology and knowledge transfer but also as sites of national image and identity construction.[137] At the 1958 Brussels Expo, Yugoslavia emphasized four themes: State and Social Organization, Contemporary Art (including the naive paintings of Ivan Generalić), Economy, and Tourism. The Yugoslav pavilion, designed by Croatian architect Vjenceslav Richter, was internationally celebrated as a modernist *Gesamtkunstwerk,* similar to Mies van der Rohe's exemplary German pavilion from 1929.[138] The socialist countries also sponsored international trade fairs. At the Plovdiv Fair, Bulgarians admired Western consumer goods, typewriters, and communications technology from companies like Philips.[139]

UNESCO—which sought to promote peace and security through cooperation in education, science, and culture—provided another important forum for cross-cultural exchange.[140] The Balkan states invigorated UNESCO's motto of "one world" in a bipolar age with the International Association for Southeast European Studies, located in Bucharest. The association organized congresses and published the work of Balkanologists, historians, and linguists who were from, and wrote about, southeastern Europe. The region became a focus of scholarly research that transcended borders and political alliances. Also within UNESCO, the Romanian

Gheorghe Gheorghiu-Dej and the Bulgarian Todor Zhivkov put forth a resolution on "good neighborly relations among European states belonging to different socio-political systems." The new Balkanism presented itself as a positive counter-model to a world that was divided and threatened by East-West confrontation.[141]

People also experienced other countries, cultures, and political systems on an individual level. The full breadth of the communications revolution reached southeastern Europe in the postwar era. The telephone, radio, and television brought news, different kinds of music, and even consumer advertising to the most remote regions. Between 1960 and 1975, sales of TVs in Romania rose from 25,000 to 395,000 per year.[142] In Yugoslavia, the number of households with a radio rose from 1.4 million in 1960 to 4.6 million in 1978. The number of broadcasters multiplied by a factor of ten, from 19 to 190. The proliferation of televisions was even more dramatic. In 1958, the entire country had only 6,000 TVs; twenty years later, it had more than 3.95 million.[143] Albania, the least developed country, had postal delivery in every village by 1965; by the 1970s, it also had telephone service.[144] In 1980, 90 percent of Albanian families owned a radio, and 25 percent (89 percent in Tirana) owned a TV.[145]

Television and radio were the most important transmitters of a global youth culture that was centered around rock and pop music. After jazz bands were allowed to perform for the first time at the 1957 World Festival of Youth and Students in Moscow, the ban on "decadent" capitalist music styles eased. Romania experienced a jazz revival in the 1960s, building on the musical culture of the interwar era. Stars like Louis Armstrong and Duke Ellington were allowed to perform in concert, and their music could be heard on the radio along with songs by the Beatles and Rolling Stones.[146] There was less freedom for American cultural imports in Bulgaria, where official propaganda and censorship were more rigid. But even in Sofia, rock bands from around the world performed before an enthusiastic audience of 20,000 in 1968. The suppression of the Prague Spring that same year ended a short-lived phase of cultural liberalism within the Eastern bloc. The Romanian pop broadcaster Metronom had to move to Radio Free Europe in Munich. Bulgaria and Romania, however, still had homegrown rock bands like the Crickets (Shturtsíte) and Diana Express in Sofia, as well as Phoenix and Sphinx in Bucharest.[147] And Western popular music was still performed in the Eastern bloc by Yugoslav artists. The singer Ivo Robić turned "Morgen" by the German composer Peter Moesser into an international hit, and familiar Western songs like Gilbert Bécaud's "Nathalie" or Chubby Checker's "Let's Twist Again" were performed in translation.[148]

In the 1960s, Yugoslavia became a magnet for Western leftists who were attracted by Praxis philosophy, which represented a nondogmatic Marxism similar to that of Critical Theory in West Germany. Many of the inspirations for this philosophy came from outside Yugoslavia—including Critical Theory, existentialism, and the New Left in western Europe, Latin America, and the United States.[149] The concept of "praxis" emphasized humans' freedom of action as a starting point for critically examining socialist reality. Sociologists, philosophers, and political scientists from all over Europe made pilgrimages to the summer school on the Adriatic island of Korčula. Supporters of the Praxis movement included Herbert Marcuse, Erich Fromm and Jürgen Habermas, Leszek Kołakowski and Ágnes Heller, Henri Lefebvre and Georg Lukács.[150] Yugoslavia also became known for subversive genres in literature, theater, and film. Želimir Žilnik and the other Black Wave directors made critical films; Bora Ćosić's novel *My Family's Role in the World Revolution* was an award-winning send-up of socialism.[151]

Young people were the driving force of the new interconnectivity. International protests against the American war in Vietnam reached a peak in 1968. The United States dropped 2.5 million tons of bombs—more than in the entire Second World War—and sprayed herbicides with dioxin to defoliate Vietnamese forests. The governments of Hungary, Poland, and Yugoslavia began to organize demonstrations against the Vietnam War in 1965. Hundreds of thousands of protesters took to the streets. Tito initiated an appeal among the nonaligned states against the American intervention, and more than a million workers in Yugoslavia donated to a solidarity fund.[152]

In the context of the worldwide student protests of 1968, demonstrations against the Vietnam War in the socialist countries sometimes took off in another direction.[153] As in the West, a large "baby boom" generation had by now reached the age of young adulthood. This generation's biographical experience, unlike that of their parents, was not defined by war and economic distress. Instead, their formative experiences included rising prosperity, greater security, and rapid social change—giving them hope that plannable changes would bring about a better future. Greater liberalization and openness allowed alternative movements such as feminism, environmentalism, and the New Left to take root in southeastern Europe. Youth in East and West alike were disappointed by politics. The antinuclear movement played a leading role in West Germany, England, and Scandinavia, while youth in the United States focused on the Vietnam War and the civil rights movement, and in France, on the unresolved colonial war in Algeria. The dissatisfaction of east-central and southeastern European youth was increasingly directed against authoritarian rule and Stalinist social structures. For these young people, "Vietnam" became a metaphor, a means of translating criticism of the communist system into a globally comprehensible language.[154]

Youth dissatisfaction remained at a low rumble in Romania, Bulgaria, and Albania. But a wave of demonstrations hit Belgrade, Ljubljana, Zagreb, and Sarajevo in June 1968; these protests were directed less against imperialism than internal grievances, particularly the conditions at Yugoslav universities.[155] After Tito acknowledged the students' calls for reform and promised speedy improvement, the demonstrators pulled back.[156] Student protests also erupted in Greece, where a military junta had held power since 1967. The Greek protests primarily took aim against the military dictatorship supported by Washington. Demonstrators were punished harshly, but there was a consequential epilogue to their story. In 1973, after Augusto Pinochet established a military dictatorship in Chile with American assistance, students occupied a university building in Athens. They protested against U.S. imperialism worldwide, including the military junta in Greece. Government authorities stormed the university and threw the instigators in prison—but the junta's days were numbered.

The motivations of the demonstrators varied from place to place, but they shared a worldwide bond. They were united in the struggle against American imperialism, colonial exploitation, and the threat of nuclear annihilation, and they were inspired by the New Left's conception of democratic socialism.[157] International events like the 1968 World Youth Festival in Sofia helped to build institutional connections. A global culture of specific types of political action emerged—including teach-ins, demonstrations, strikes, and provocations against the establishment. Protestors all over the world embraced an alternative lifestyle that was symbolized by long hair for men, unconventional clothing, and freer attitudes toward sexuality.[158] Even if the students' demands from Berkeley to Berlin, Prague to Buenos Aires, and Belgrade to Tokyo remained unfulfilled in the end, the protest movements were an important milestone. They exposed gaps in the credibility and legitimacy of "American imperialism" and "Soviet dictatorship" alike, directly challenging the Cold War order that had been created in Yalta. Mass mobilization became a familiar instrument of political engagement.

In the 1970s, the politics of détente nudged East and West closer together. Representatives of the nuclear powers held Strategic Arms Limitation Talks, while multilateral negotiations of the Commission on Security and Cooperation in Europe (CSCE) commenced around the same time.[159] In 1975, representatives of the blocs affirmed the Helsinki Final Act, which was composed of three parts, or "baskets": confidence-building measures, economic and scientific cooperation, and freedom of movement and human rights. Since the eastern European states had abstained from the UN General Assembly's vote on the Universal Declaration of Human Rights in 1948, the "third basket" of the Helsinki Accords provided—for the first time—a legal basis for the demands of civil rights activists. Subsequent CSCE meetings in Belgrade, Madrid, and Vienna provided the West with a forum for exerting pressure on the communist regimes to respect human rights.

Decolonization, the Vietnam War, and famine in Biafra raised new, worldwide awareness for universal human concerns. Human rights began to be seen as a global problem, becoming the focus of civil rights movements in Latin America, the United States, South Africa, and the Eastern bloc.[160] Countless international nongovernmental organizations such as Helsinki Watch and Amnesty International kept the issue in the public eye.[161] "The world is so small and so much more interdependent today than it used to be," an activist remarked in the early 1970s, "that it is morally right . . . to feel responsible for possible political injustice anywhere on the globe."[162] Transnational discourses and institutional relationships developed in this context. Activists from Brazil, Chile, Argentina, the eastern and southeastern European countries, and representatives of transnational nongovernmental organizations regularly engaged with one another at congresses and seminars.[163] Their interactions loosened and disrupted rigid communist systems long before the Internet revolutionized global communication.[164]

Oppositional movements formed in southeastern Europe, but they were never as strong as their counterparts in the central European countries. Neither the church and the unions (as in Poland), nor intellectuals (as in Hungary and Czechoslovakia) became powerful voices of opposition. Critics of the southeastern European regimes were more likely to be national extremists. This was especially true in Yugoslavia, where the expression "brotherhood and unity" was the all-encompassing state ideology. The egalitarianism of socialist doctrine also alienated certain elites and average citizens. In 1967 intellectuals and cultural organizations in Croatia called for a distinct Croatian literary language, sparking debates about national identity in the other republics as well. The dissatisfaction culminated in the Croatian Spring and *Maspok* (mass movement) of 1971. Party leaders, students, the media, and the cultural organization Matica Hrvatska called for greater Croatian autonomy, a separate army and foreign policy, and new "greater Croatian" borders.[165] The historian Franjo Tudjman emerged as one of the movement's leading figures. In Serbia, an economically liberal wing with unorthodox demands emerged around the same time. Tito abruptly dismissed the party leaders in Zagreb and Belgrade, and instigators of the Croatian Spring were brought to trial. Nationalism was brewing in Kosovo, too, where Albanian demonstrators called for their own republic and the consolidation of all Albanian territories in 1968. The protests turned violent and were put down with force, but the rallying cry "Kosova Republika" could no longer be suppressed.[166]

In contrast to multinational Yugoslavia, where nationalism threatened the cohesion of complex state institutions, communist leaders in Albania, Romania, and Bulgaria saw nationalism as a useful tool for bolstering their regimes vis-à-vis intellectuals and nonconforming thinkers. In Romania, Ceaușescu announced his July Theses in 1971. His "mini cultural revolution" sought to weaken cosmopolitanism and promote amateur participation in the arts. Here, nationalist attitudes and communist rhetoric went hand in hand—potentially enhancing support among critical intellectuals, many of whom tended toward national conservatism. There was a complex mutual relationship between communist and nationalist ideology. On one hand, communists embraced nationalist ideas; on the other, nationalist thinkers proved willing to adopt conformist, Marxist rhetoric as long as it furthered their own agenda.[167]

The career of Lyudmila Zhivkova, the Bulgarian minister of culture (and daughter of party leader Todor Zhivkov), provides an illustrative example. Zhivkova became a member of the Politburo and Central Committee, and she led the Committee for Art and Culture from 1975 to 1981. She wrote a well-received dissertation on English-Turkish relations in the 1930s, and afterward spent time in Oxford and Moscow to conduct historical research. She idolized art, which she saw as a means of liberation from "the prejudices of the past and the limitations of the petty, drab, egocentric consciousness." Art was also, in her view, the antidote to slanderous, imperialist radio broadcasters and Western consumer capitalism, which encouraged "meanness" and "eroticism" and pandered to people's worst instincts.[168]

Zhivkova's years in office occurred in an era of national homogenization. A new 1971 constitution no longer mentioned ethnic minorities, but instead referred to citizens of "non-Bulgarian heritage." Turkish schools closed and publishing was restricted. An unprecedented campaign for assimilation compelled Turks, Pomaks, and Roma to Bulgarize their names. More than 350,000 Turks emigrated as a consequence of the euphemistically named "rebirth" of Bulgaria in the 1970s and 1980s.[169] Despite protests from Turkey and human rights organizations, Zhivkova saw the emergence of a "new national consciousness" as a triumph of socialism.

Zhivkova wanted to show that the Bulgarians "could also give something to the world." "Every country, every nation, and every people has made a contribution to the universal historical and cultural process."[170] She arranged for Bulgaria's collection of Thracian gold treasures to tour the United States, Europe, and Japan. Other international exhibitions were dedicated to historic Bulgarian icons, medieval manuscripts, and the achievements of the Slavic apostles Cyril and Methodius. In 1981 she organized the great festivities honoring the thirteen hundredth anniversary of the first Bulgarian Empire, emphasizing the organic unity of the past, the present, and the future.[171]

Zhivkova left her mark on the city center of Sofia with a monumental palace of culture, and she also built cultural centers in New Delhi and Vienna. She was careful to foster good relations with the West. In 1977 she was the only member of the party establishment to be received by U.S. president Jimmy Carter for the signing of a bilateral cultural agreement. As the need arose, she also spoke out on "hard" political issues, such as when she advocated for disarmament and Third World liberation movements at the UN General Assembly in 1979.[172]

As did the representatives of other Balkan countries, Zhivkova sought the stage of international organizations. She lobbied for the rights of women and children through UNESCO and the children's aid organization UNICEF.[173] The UNESCO International Children's Assembly was established on her initiative. The entire world looked to Sofia in 1979, when the city hosted the Banner of Peace children's festival as part of the UN's International Year of the Child.[174] Bulgaria's opening to the West did create friction with the Soviet Union, where party leaders had had enough Balkan autonomy after the rift with Ceauşescu. Conservative communist functionaries in Bulgaria kept their distance from Zhivkova as well. Politically isolated, lonely, and depressed, she died suddenly from a brain hemorrhage at the age of thirty-nine.[175]

By the 1970s, southeastern Europeans were full participants in modern industrial society. Social policy, the revolution in education, the spread of technology and media, and changed aesthetic standards in art, literature, architecture, and films had transformed nearly every aspect of human experience. Of course, powerful regional discrepancies remained, and in many places people continued to live in traditional circumstances. Nevertheless, a new set of values that revolved around personal happiness and self-realization was increasingly apparent. The individualization of lifestyles and a certain acceptance of consumerism threatened the legitimacy of the socialist system, as ideology began to lose significance in everyday life. Southeastern European countries deliberately instrumentalized nationalism, emphasizing national political and cultural traditions over socialist internationalism.

Global Consumption, Global Crises

Even before the end of the Second World War, the United States and Great Britain agreed on a new, multilateral world economic order at Bretton Woods in 1944. It was based on a global system of fixed exchange rates, which were anchored to the value of the U.S. dollar in gold. The protectionism of the interwar era was abandoned in favor of established rules to govern international economic relations. Beginning in 1945–1947, the International Monetary Fund (IMF), the International Bank for Reconstruction and Development (later part of the World Bank), and the General Agreement on Tariffs and Trade (GATT) established the framework for an economic order based on multilateralism and free competition.[176]

The United States, with a GNP that had doubled over the course of the war, now led the world economy. By the war's end, it was responsible for half of global industrial production and possessed nearly all of the world's financial reserves.[177] The United States and the countries participating in the European Recovery Program, or Marshall Plan, imposed an embargo against the communist states in 1947. In response, the Soviet Union, Poland, Bulgaria, Romania, Czechoslovakia, and Hungary established the Council for Mutual Economic Assistance in order to promote trade and economic cooperation among themselves in 1949. Comecon became the Eastern bloc's economic pillar, alongside the political organization of the Cominform and the military alliance of the Warsaw Pact. Albania joined Comecon in 1949, and East Germany joined in 1950. More states (including China, Cuba, and Vietnam) participated as observers or cooperated with Comecon in other ways (such as Finland, Mozambique, and Iraq).[178]

Moscow envisioned Comecon as a closed economic system for the communist world. At the beginning of the 1960s, the Soviet state and party leader Nikita Khrushchev attempted to introduce a supranational "socialist division of labor," to the benefit of the more industrialized states such as Hungary, Czechoslovakia, and East Germany. But Romania, Bulgaria, and Albania unambiguously opposed these plans, which would have limited their role to providing foodstuffs and raw materials. Enver Hoxha accused Khrushchev of wanting "Albania to be turned into a fruit-growing colony which would serve the revisionist Soviet Union," and Nicolae Ceaușescu protested as well.[179] The plan for creating an integrated socialist economic system was shelved in 1962, although the Comecon states did agree to more closely coordinate their national economic plans.[180]

In the 1960s, U.S. enterprises began to invest more aggressively in companies and subsidiaries in Europe and other parts of the world. A revolution in transportation, communication, and information technology took place at the same time. Shipping costs sank dramatically as telex, telephone, and satellite connections transcended borders and brought faraway locations closer together. The integration of the world economy accelerated. In the mid-1960s, international trade in manufactured goods grew twice as fast as global production.[181]

The dynamic expansion and concentration of international trade relations encouraged closer relations between the socialist and capitalist worlds. In the 1960s, the communist states of southeastern Europe—like their nineteenth-century predecessors—worked to expand trade relations with the Western industrial states. Yugoslavia and Romania, in particular, focused on import-oriented strategies for growth. Foreign trade grew even faster than national income in the socialist countries, with the greatest increases coming from trade with the capitalist world.[182] There was new talk of "internationalization" and (later) "globalization"—growing economic, political, cultural, and ecological interconnectivity and mutual dependence.

In the aftermath of the anticommunist uprisings in East Germany (1953) and Poland and Hungary (1956), the southeastern European governments decided to shift the emphasis of economic planning from heavy industry to the production of consumer goods. Industrialization, urbanization, and the dramatic growth of real wages brought rising expectations and new consumer desires. By the 1960s, all socialist countries were to produce more electric toothbrushes and shavers, electric stoves, mixers, sewing machines, telephones, televisions, and stereos. Instead of fetishistic Western consumerism that was driven by greed, the communists hoped to develop a democratic consumer culture that could provide people with modest, useful, beautiful things. Consumption of "modern goods" was even thought to be essential for a modern socialist consumer.[183] But an unintended consequence of socialist advertising was that it hastened the trend toward individualism—and eventually Westernization, too, since the desire for Western items constantly grew.[184]

The "economic miracle" that dramatically increased real earnings created conditions for a new socialist consumer culture. This happened so quickly that mass consumption spread earlier and faster than in the poorest countries of capitalist Europe: Greece and (especially) Portugal.[185] In Romania, sales of refrigerators alone rose from 7,000 to 260,000 per year between 1960 and 1975.[186] By 1975, 76 percent of Bulgarian households owned a radio, 66 percent owned a television, and 59 percent owned a washing machine and a refrigerator. Nearly every Bulgarian family owned these useful devices by 1988.[187] In Yugoslavia, abundance was even seen as a cultural model for the country as a whole. In a sense, consumption served as an identity marker and unifying force in this highly diverse country.[188]

Growing consumption and more leisure time created new demands and aspirations for a higher quality of life. As in the West, consumer goods were presented as symbols of the success of the economic system that produced them. New gender roles followed. "Fashion is no longer considered to be a frivolous matter," the Romanian magazine *Moda* declared, but instead has "become a mandatory preoccupation for every woman." Women were encouraged to look beautiful and attractive, and the modern man was supposed to participate in caring for domestic responsibilities. The rigid Puritanism of the immediate postwar period gave way to more permissive and open attitudes toward the body and sexuality.[189]

Liberalization and a growing orientation toward consumerism opened the door to Americanization. According to Western Cold War ideology, consumerism and democracy were inextricably intertwined. Decades ear-

Tobacco factory in Plovdiv, 1969.

lier, U.S. president Woodrow Wilson had asserted that the "democracy of business" would lead "the struggle for the peaceful conquest of the world" and expand the preeminence of the market economy. In 1947 assistant secretary of state William Clayton emphasized that the goal of the Marshall Plan was not only to contain communism but also to satisfy the "needs and interests of the people of the United States. We need markets—big markets—around the world in which to buy and sell."[190]

The profit-seeking interest of corporations—and global business networks, advertising, and brand-name fetishism—placed America at the forefront of a worldwide consumer culture that was defined by jazz, pop, and Hollywood films as well as by goods like nylon stockings, Coca-Cola, and blue jeans.[191] The new culture particularly appealed to young people, who developed a taste for certain music, clothing, and lifestyles. They were the most important target group for "Coca-colonization," which did not hesitate in its advance toward the Eastern bloc. Bulgaria was the first of the communist countries to produce the sugary soda, adopting the ad line "Everything is better with Coca-Cola" in 1965. Yugoslavia and Romania became licensed producers of Pepsi-Cola soon thereafter.[192]

Americanization was most pronounced in Yugoslavia. In 1969 the party newspaper *Borba* reported that drugstores, blue jeans, popcorn, chewing gum, Coca-Cola, and hot dogs had become part of everyday life in

Belgrade.[193] The party establishments in Yugoslavia and the Eastern bloc countries nevertheless resisted the "terror" of Western consumerism. One Bulgarian functionary complained that "every stocking, every tape recorder, every record player, every refrigerator, every perfume, every lipstick, all shoes and clothes, and especially every car are sent to our country as ideological diversion."[194] It was possible to integrate Western styles in music and clothes into everyday socialist life without necessarily raising ideological contradictions. But consumerism created expectations of continued economic growth that could not be satisfied indefinitely, as would soon become clear.[195]

To build up valuable industrial sectors such as chemicals, automobile manufacturing, and aeronautics, Nicolae Ceauşescu (who succeeded Gheorghiu-Dej as head of state in 1965) pursued cooperation and licensing agreements with Western firms.[196] The first Romanian "people's car," the Dacia 1100—built under license from Renault—rolled off the assembly line in Piteşti in 1967. By 1980, about 90,000 new automobiles were manufactured here each year.[197] Yugoslavia, meanwhile, began its successful production of the Fiat 600, affectionately nicknamed "fićo."[198] Individual car ownership gradually became more common in southeastern Europe. By the 1980s, Albania was the only country in the region with few private automobiles on the road.[199]

The first signs of economic problems in the communist countries became apparent in the 1960s. Industrial growth shrank, necessitating reforms. Strict planning targets and price controls were lifted, trade restrictions loosened, and profitability became more important. In 1965, Yugoslavia completed its transition to a "socialist market economy" by abolishing state control over production, prices, and wages, and also the state fund for subsidies and investments. Private companies with up to five employees were now allowed.[200] Romania and Bulgaria likewise introduced reforms to increase productivity, although these were not as far-reaching as in Yugoslavia. Only Albania remained faithful to the centrally planned economy, right up to the death of Enver Hoxha in 1985.

As superpower rivalry extended into the Third World, the ideological struggle between (American) capitalism and (Soviet) communism played out on the new terrain of development policy. Each bloc wanted the former colonies to adopt its own social model, and to this end generously plied them with financial resources, experts, capital, and consumer goods. Students in developing countries received scholarships to attend European,

American, and Soviet universities. Southeastern Europeans also provided development assistance. Yugoslavia signed agreements for scientific and technical cooperation with sixty-three different countries, and it sent experts to twenty-five African, Asian, and Latin American states. In 1976, for example, 450 Yugoslav doctors were working in three Libyan hospitals.[201] Bulgaria sent 2,000 doctors to Libya in 1981 alone. Students from the Third World received scholarships, and engineers, doctors, and teachers provided their services to developing countries.[202]

Development policy created new global connections, but also a new layer of competition between capitalist and socialist Europe. Western modernization theory—explicitly conceived as a counternarrative to Marx—postulated that the advances made by Western industrial countries could be repeated in "underdeveloped" regions. Western development aid could foster an incremental process of growth and democratization in the developing world. The Third World needed to create social structures that followed the Western model and to uphold the existing liberal world economic order.[203] By contrast, economists in Latin America (where the export of agricultural products had collapsed) identified market liberalism as the root cause of the relations of economic dependency and exploitation between industrial countries and the Third World. The Argentinean Raúl Prebisch recommended import substitution and industrialization—a prescription that Romanian economists (including the prophet of corporatism, Mihail Manoilescu) had developed back in the 1930s. Thus, the "correct" path of development was fiercely disputed between the blocs. Would a new economic nationalism, or rather more efficient social structures and an open world economy, better help developing countries rise out of poverty?

Although the extent of the continuities in the world economy between the colonial and post–Second World War eras is a matter of dispute, the developing countries' dependency on the industrial nations in both eras is undeniable. Third World countries overwhelmingly exported raw materials and agricultural products, and imported manufactured goods and capital in return. The exchange was disadvantageous for the former colonies because their products were much cheaper on world markets than European and American finished goods. Between 1953 and 1963, world trade grew by 94 percent. By 1979, it had grown another 200 percent, much faster than world economic output. In this second phase, trade in manufactured goods rose by 282 percent—as opposed to 96 percent for agricultural products, and 101 percent for raw materials. The Western industrial countries profited most from the accelerated globalization in trade, especially since many of them adopted tariffs to protect their own agricultural products against cheap competition. Between 1953 and 1995, they were responsible for two-thirds of all exports.[204]

Politicians and economists in eastern and southeastern Europe, Latin America, and India developed different theories to explain underdevelopment, but they made similar political recommendations.[205] The "Global South" had begun to advocate for a more just world economic order in the aftermath of the Bandung Conference of 1955. On the initiative of Yugoslavia and other nonaligned states, the United Nations Conference on Trade and Development (UNCTAD) was established over U.S. and European opposition in 1964. Its first general secretary was Raúl Prebisch, and within its framework the developing countries of Asia, Africa, and Latin America formed the Group of 77.[206] These and other nonaligned states initiated the Declaration for the Establishment of a New International Economic Order, which was adopted by the UN General Assembly in 1974. The Yugoslav prime minister Džemal Bijedić complained that in only one year the developing countries' trade deficit had doubled from 10 billion to 20 billion U.S. dollars. The industrial countries had to see "that it is in their own interest to recognize, at last, the right of developing countries to have sovereign command over their natural treasures."[207]

At the beginning of the 1970s, American hegemony in trade and industry received its first serious challenge after twenty-five years of sustained growth. The western European economies had made a strong recovery, but the exorbitant costs of the Vietnam War compelled the United States to give up the gold standard. The international monetary system moved to floating exchange rates in 1973; Bretton Woods was dead. That same year, the Yom Kippur War between Israel and its Arab neighbors touched off the first oil crisis, as OPEC reduced production and doubled prices. The economic miracle of the postwar decades came to a halt; undervalued currencies and cheap oil were now a thing of the past. The world economy skidded into a deep recession. Unemployment rose quickly, as it had during the Great Depression of the 1930s. A brief recovery was followed by a second oil crisis in 1979, as the Islamic revolutionary regime that toppled the shah in Iran stopped delivering oil to the West, sending prices skyward once more. Inflation, interest rates, and unemployment climbed to record levels, and GNP sank worldwide. The world economic crisis was eventually overcome in 1985, but the "trente glorieuses," the thirty years of the postwar economic boom, were now over.[208]

As in the 1930s, the global depression struck eastern and southeastern Europe particularly hard. The leading sectors of the socialist economies, mining and heavy industry, suffered from the dramatic decline in prices on world markets. Poor planning, mismanagement, insufficient investment, and a technology gap contributed to the socialist states' worsening terms of trade. Imports became more expensive and trade deficits grew, as the Eastern bloc felt the effects of worldwide inflation.[209] The Western countries found their way out of the crisis with the help of technical innovations like microelectronics and computers, which led to a "third industrial revolution," while the socialist states clung to large, energy-intensive industrial systems that were no longer competitive. They did not have the flexibility or specialized knowledge to shift their production and exports to the new, high-demand sectors. Between 1973 and 1989, the planned economies' average annual per capita growth rate was only 1.2 percent, compared to 3.9 percent in the twenty years previous.[210] Greece, too, suffered from the effects of the depression. There had been progress in industrialization since the end of the civil war, but it was overwhelmingly concentrated in the production of food, tobacco, and textiles, and also in shipbuilding and the highly speculative construction industry.[211]

The states of eastern and southeastern Europe—like those in the Third World—turned to financing by credit, massive state investments, and wage increases to alleviate the effects of the world economic crisis.[212] The high price of oil allowed OPEC and the international oil cartels to rake in great profits, so there was more money circulating in the financial markets of the 1970s than ever before. After the United States eased controls on capital exports, enormous quantities of petrodollars landed in the international credit markets. The debt of the central European states rose from 6 billion to 110 billion U.S. dollars between 1970 and 1990.[213] Yugoslavia owed 19 billion U.S. dollars, and Romania owed 10.2 billion, in 1981. Bulgaria's liabilities totaled 3.1 billion U.S. dollars.[214] The Greek government, too, initiated a dangerous cycle of military spending, borrowing, inflation, and public hiring—thereby institutionalizing a system of state subsidies and patronage.[215] At the end of the 1970s, state spending made up 30 percent of domestic production; one decade later, this proportion had climbed to 51 percent.[216]

The United States, Japan, the states of western Europe and East Asia, and even the Third World competed over technological advances, production sites, markets, and profits as never before. The IMF and World Bank pushed for the continued liberalization of capital markets, the dismantling of trade barriers, and free markets—policies now associated with the term "neoliberalism."[217] In response to the instability of exchange rates and the global financial system, the IMF began to link aid to certain conditions, insisting upon liberalization, privatization, and deregulation. The new policies accelerated globalization, the interdependence of banks and capital markets around the world, and the growth of foreign debt. The value of world trade surged to new heights, rising from 57 billion to 6 trillion U.S. dollars between 1947 and the end of the 1990s.[218] Critics in the late 1970s and 1980s were already accusing the United States and its allies of "market fundamentalism" and postcolonial hegemonial politics. They predicted that the strict austerity of Reaganomics and Thatcherism would escalate economic crises and social inequality, thereby increasing poverty and political instability.[219]

The global shockwave made the socialist states painfully aware that there could be no more closed economic systems. In the 1980s, the Eastern bloc countries conducted up to 40 percent of their foreign trade with the Soviet Union, and up to 23 percent with one another. The Asian Tiger states (Hong Kong, Singapore, South Korea, and Taiwan) had, in the meantime, successfully penetrated world markets with their manufactured goods, leaving eastern and southeastern Europe far behind.[220] Growing economic problems, failed reforms, and continued Soviet domination eroded Comecon and turned southeastern Europeans' attention toward the steadily strengthening European Common Market. The Americans introduced a new economic boycott of the Eastern bloc in response to the Soviet invasion of Afghanistan in 1979. President Ronald Reagan was determined to drive the communist enemy to economic and moral ruin.[221]

After the IMF gave up its policy of supporting the international monetary system by providing additional credit to debtor states and rescheduling loans for developing countries, private banks retreated in the 1980s. The U.S. Federal Reserve pursued a sharply deflationary policy that massively increased the interest rate on the U.S. dollar, thereby increasing the debt burden of borrowing countries. The economic growth of the socialist countries collapsed; as in Mexico, growth had largely been financed on credit. Reminiscent of the years before the Second World War, dependency caused by foreign debt had devastating consequences.

The effects were particularly dramatic in Yugoslavia, the country most integrated within the world economy. Its debt burden quadrupled between 1973 and 1981. Credit became more expensive; between 1975 and 1981 interest rates tripled from 5.8 percent to 16.8 percent. Yugoslavia's terms of trade worsened, as prices for imports climbed significantly higher than those for exports, costing the country 6 percent of its national income. Because the republics refused to cut back their spending, the Yugoslav central government in Belgrade had little recourse beyond constantly printing new money and driving up inflation.[222]

The far-reaching crisis brought smoldering conflicts of interest between Yugoslavia's constituent republics to a full burn in the second half of the 1980s. The constitution of 1974 had transferred significant competencies to the republics and autonomous provinces. Only the execution of federal law, regulation of the economy, and national defense remained the responsibility of the federal government, which had to abide by complicated rules that divided power proportionally among the different ethnic groups. In the tug-of-war over the appropriate course of action for macroeconomic stabilization, the republics blocked each other and effectively paralyzed the political system. The Yugoslav parliament passed only eight of twenty-five important laws in 1983; the rest had to be tabled because of deep differences of opinion between the republics.[223]

In the early 1980s, the Yugoslav government responded to IMF pressure by adopting a course of strict austerity to address its shortage of capital. Food subsidies were halted in order to save funds, and imports were limited to only the most essential items. Two currency reforms devalued the dinar by 90 percent between 1979 and 1985. State and private firms curbed production and laid off employees, driving unemployment upward. Real earnings shrank, and savings melted away. At the beginning of 1987, the dire financial situation compelled Yugoslavia to renew negotiations with the IMF and to implement a radical program of market economic reform—including reductions in wages and public expenditures as well as contraction of the money supply and devaluation of the dinar.[224] Socialist property law and socialist self-management were abolished at the end of 1988. In the meantime, inflation reached a record high of 2,700 percent. "Shock therapy" did not succeed. Production collapsed in mid-1990, and inflation and unemployment resumed their climb to staggering heights.[225]

The crisis also had devastating consequences in Romania, where the rate of growth fell from 10 percent at the beginning of the 1970s, to just 3 percent in the 1980s. Production and sales of consumer goods fell sharply, creating serious problems in supply.[226] Nicolae Ceaușescu adopted a rigid savings plan to repay his state's debts, which totaled about 10 billion U.S. dollars. Food and fuel were rationed, and electrical power was cut off for hours at night. There were frequent shortages of dietary staples, even bread. Mismanagement, poor investments, bureaucratization, and the black market exacerbated the crisis. The debts had been nearly repaid by the end of the 1980s, but the Romanian people were hungry, cold, and increasingly frustrated with the regime.[227]

The government's fear of criticism heightened repression. Ana Blandiana, who had previously been allowed to travel abroad, now faced closer scrutiny. The regime was displeased by her satirical poems that appeared in the student journal *Amfiteatru* in 1984, and several of her poems were banned. "I was isolated and received no mail. My house was watched by the Securitate. The libraries were no longer allowed to lend out my books; I disappeared from the catalogs. It was forbidden even to mention me."[228] Even so, she did not want to emigrate. "To me, it seemed that by going I would legitimate Ceaușescu, leaving him my country, so that he, by staying, could prove that he represented the Romanian people more than I, who left."[229]

Greece joined the European Community in 1981, but it, too, suffered from foreign debt, inflation, and a growing budget deficit. The country did benefit from the assistance of European regional policy, which aimed to alleviate socioeconomic disparities by transferring funds to the poorer member states. Nevertheless, growth and employment remained low.[230] In the 1980s, per capita gross domestic product (GDP) fell to less than half of the western European average.[231]

Socioeconomic data reveal a mixed balance sheet for the communist era. Economic growth was stronger than in any other historical period. Between 1937 and 1989, GNP in Yugoslavia grew nearly 640 percent; in Romania, 516 percent; and in Bulgaria, 547 percent.[232] Industry and cities grew rapidly. In 1989, only 50.5 percent of the population in Albania was still employed in agriculture; in Bulgaria, 18.7 percent; in Yugoslavia, 25 percent; in Romania, 27.9 percent; and in Greece, 27 percent.[233] Illiteracy had been conquered, and in some places the proportion of university students exceeded that of the capitalist world. In East and West, birthrates and life expectancy, consumer behavior, and values grew closer together.[234]

On the other hand, the communist countries of southeastern Europe were unable to close the prosperity gap with the capitalist market economies in an enduring way, even if a few—like Bulgaria and Yugoslavia—made great strides in catching up. In the 1980s, the average per capita standard of living was still about one-third of western Europe's, and one-quarter of the United States'. There were considerable disparities with southeastern Europe. In 1989, per capita GDP in Albania was 2,477 U.S. dollars (adjusted for purchasing power parity); in Romania, 3,941 dollars; in Bulgaria, 6,216 dollars; and in Yugoslavia, 6,250 dollars.[235] Overall, they fared better than Third World countries, which had grown poorer by comparison. But the promise of catching up to the West had not been realized. Instead, acute supply problems raised ever greater doubts in the efficacy and credibility of the communist system.[236]

The Soviet Union, too, found itself in a deep crisis in the 1980s. Economic problems, persistent state paternalism, war in Afghanistan, and the arms race with the United States brought the state to the edge of ruin. In 1985, the new general secretary of the Soviet Communist Party, Mikhail Gorbachev, announced the new policies of glasnost and perestroika (literally, "transparency" and "restructuring," meaning openness and reforms), and entered into a comprehensive process of disarmament with the United States. In 1988, he renounced the Brezhnev Doctrine, which had justified the Soviet intervention in Czechoslovakia in 1968, and in Afghanistan in 1979. By establishing that every country could freely determine its own form of government, he gave the Eastern bloc countries permission to hold democratic elections.

In the 1980s, more voices of opposition sounded in all of the socialist countries, although not always to the same degree or with the same emphasis as in central Europe. In Yugoslavia, critics of the regime organized petitions and open letters against professional restrictions at universities. As in Poland and Czechoslovakia, they founded "flying universities," held critical meetings and assemblies, and published oppositional journals. The Committee for the Defense of Freedom of Thought and Expression, founded by Dobrica Ćosić and others in Belgrade in 1984, issued a "Proposal for Establishing the Rule of Law," which called for abolition of the one-party system, free elections and media, and an independent judiciary.[237]

Intellectuals in Bulgaria criticized the violation of human rights, particularly the forced assimilation of the Turkish minority. But only at the end of the 1980s did groups like the Club for Glasnost and Democracy, the independent trade union Podkrepa (Support), and the environmental organization Eco-Glasnost begin to coordinate protests. Only in Romania, where the workers demonstrated, did the critical intellectuals remain largely silent. Opponents of the regime gathered around the journal *România literară,* while philosophers were drawn to Constantin Noica—a pupil of the Criterion group in the 1920s and a proponent of "neo"-*trăirism,* in the intellectual tradition of Nae Ionescu.[238] Ana Blandiana later admitted feeling guilty because "in 1987, I did nothing when the workers from Brașov took to the streets. . . . Why were the Polish intellectuals in Gdańsk, but we weren't in Brașov?"[239]

By the second half of the 1980s, the collapse of socialism was only a matter of time. The rigidity of the planned economy, overbureaucratization, and mismanagement resulted in qualitatively inferior, insufficient production. Unfavorable terms of trade, Western agricultural protectionism, and the high cost of borrowing created additional burdens for less developed countries. The temporary crisis of the capitalist world economy turned lethal for the communist systems. Political as well as economic factors contributed to their demise. The new intellectual middle classes—forming a socialist bourgeoisie—were no longer willing to be squeezed into the ideological corset of a "workers' and peasants' state," and they called for freedom of expression, democracy, and civil rights. Individualistic lifestyles and plans for the future, and the relativizing of traditional values and customs— including less restrictive sexual morals as well as the spread of hedonism, consumerism, and entertainment culture—undermined the legitimacy of the socialist system. As the regimes struggled to acquire legitimacy by offering their citizens greater prosperity, leisure time, and opportunities for consumption, Marxist ideology lost more and more practical relevance in everyday life. Expanding transnational connections heightened this trend. Economic prosperity became a fundamental, shared European experience. Consumer and cultural ties between East and West brought ways of thinking and living, and conceptions of democracy, much closer together. A globally connected civil society demanded human and civil rights, and many people longed for a higher standard of living and prosperity that seemed unattainable within the existing structures of their society.

Sarajevo, 1984

On February 8, 50,000 people gathered in the newly renovated Koševo Stadium to watch the opening ceremonies of the XIV Olympic Winter Games. Just under 1,500 athletes from forty-nine countries and more than

3,000 journalists joined the spectacle on the Jahorina, Bjelašnica, Trebević, and Igman Mountains. For a Yugoslavia that was deeply in debt and crippled by internal conflicts, the Winter Games were a grandly staged feat of public relations. For twelve days, the friendly wolf mascot Vučko greeted millions of television viewers all over the world with the singsong call of a muezzin: "Sa-ra-jee-voo-oo-oo!"

At the Winter Games, Sarajevo presented itself as a symbol of "brotherhood and unity," and its country, Yugoslavia, as a supporter of international understanding. The head of the Olympic Committee and later Yugoslav prime minister, Branko Mikulić, affirmed that the ideals of the Olympics were "identical with the peaceful policy of Tito's non-aligned Yugoslavia."[240] The Winter Games were, moreover, a powerful agent of economic development; the renovations and building began shortly after Sarajevo was selected as host. In addition to the Zetra sports complex and Olympic village, there were freshly built bobsled runs, ice rinks, ski jumps, and cross-country ski trails, as well as the Hotel Igman, Hotel Vučko, and the bright yellow cube of the Holiday Inn. The Butmir Airport received a new terminal; the postal and telegraph service, water and sewage system, and gas and coal heating supply were all modernized. More than 2,600 new apartments and 9,500 jobs were created.[241]

The residents of Sarajevo, who had bested the other Olympic applicants in Sapporo and Göteborg, were proud to be "the center of the world" for two weeks. "What will Olympic dining look like?" the magazine *Svijet (World)* asked. "Do we want to serve Wiener schnitzel and hamburgers to our guests from all over the world . . . or mostly Yugoslav specialties?"[242] Naysayers from Slovenia suspected that the Bosnians' efforts would end in organizational chaos, but they were proved wrong; snow-clearing brigades, soldiers, and volunteers shoveled out the streets and event sites with impressive zeal after days of massive snowfall and ice storms.

In the end, East Germany distinguished itself as the competition's most successful team, earning twenty-four medals. The East German gold medalists included skier Jens Weissflog, speed skater Karin Enke, and the eighteen-year-old figure skater Katarina Witt. By contrast, West Germany brought home only four medals despite its large national team. International Olympic Committee president Juan Antonio Samaranch lauded the best Winter Games in history, and the West German team coordinator Walter Tröger confirmed: "It couldn't have been done any better!"[243] In the end, the organizers could congratulate themselves on bringing in a net profit of 10 million U.S. dollars.[244] The Olympics positively impacted tourism, the leading sector of the Yugoslav economy. Sarajevo welcomed 385,000 visitors in 1984, a number that successively increased in the years thereafter.[245] The earnings of the Yugoslavia tourist industry doubled between 1982 and 1987, reaching 1.7 billion U.S. dollars.[246]

Sarajevo has two faces, according to the writer Ivo Andrić—"one dark and severe, the other bright and gentle." The city was founded by the Ottomans in the mid-fifteenth century. More than 1,600 feet above sea level, it is surrounded by mountains and hills on three sides, with an open view to the south. "Only a few houses, public buildings and streets are clustered in the lowlands; most climb up the hillsides."[247] The Ottoman old town and its bazaar, the Baščaršija, lay in the historic heart of Sarajevo. After the war, the Baščaršija had been reconstructed with the same appearance as before. The wooden stands of the furriers and *opanak* makers were nestled into the narrow streets of the Ćurčiluk, the workshops of the goldsmiths in the Kujundžiluk, and those of the tailors in the Abadžiluk. Natives and tourists alike raved over the best *ćevapčići* in Yugoslavia: small, crispy, and grilled over a charcoal fire. Other local specialties included mocha brewed in a long-necked *džezva,* and the sticky-sweet baklava that were sold in countless small bakeries.[248]

About one hundred mosques and many more *hamams* (public baths), Koran schools, dervish monasteries, caravansaries, churches, fountains, cisterns, and also a synagogue pointed to the city's former wealth, which arose from its strategic location at the crossroads of important trade routes between the Orient and Occident.[249] The Gazi Husrev-beg mosque, among the most distinguished examples of Islamic architecture, had stood proudly for four and a half centuries; close by, the old clock tower displayed the time in Mecca. Next to the Turkish old town was the Austro-Hungarian quarter, with the courthouse and other government buildings, theater, regional museum *(Landesmuseum),* and main post office. During the occupation, Emperor Francis Joseph made sure that the Oriental city adopted the Habsburg "universal style," which left its mark on the Turkish caravansaries, dervish monasteries, and the old marketplace for swords and sabers. Other representative structures—such as the old city hall, now the National Library—were subsequently constructed in a pseudo-Moorish style.[250] Bauhaus-inspired modernist architecture came to Sarajevo, as elsewhere in Europe, in the 1920s and 1930s.[251]

Not far from the Baščaršija, an old Ottoman stone bridge crossed the Miljacka River. At its northern end, the Bosnian Serb Gavrilo Princip shot the Habsburg crown prince Francis Ferdinand on June 28, 1914. The assassin, whose lethal shots had led to the First World War, was honored by the city with a memorial plaque. At the site where he had fired his Browning pistol, his footprints were molded into the surface of the sidewalk. Nearby, the Museum of Young Bosnia and Gavrilo Princip displayed the conspirators' personal belongings and other objects from that time. The young men were seen as early fighters for a free Yugoslavia. In 1939 the assassins' bodily remains had been brought from Theresienstadt in Czechoslovakia to a memorial chapel in the city's Koševo district.

As a socialist realist and modernist counterpoint to the Ottoman old town, the Marindvor neighborhood arose in the western city center after 1945. The great Vojvoda Putnik street and a streetcar line led to the park in Ilidža with its renowned thermal springs.[252] Architects from Sarajevo, Zagreb, Belgrade, and Ljubljana designed the main train station, modern faculty buildings for the University of Sarajevo, and the Museum of the Revolution. The republic's Executive Council Building, a futurist construction of steel and glass, arose here as well. Zlatko Ugljen, Ivan Štraus, Boris Magaš, and others designed some of Yugoslavia's best-known and impressive modern structures in this part of the city: high-rise buildings, banks, sport arenas, hospitals, colleges, libraries, hotels, radio stations, and freeways.

As the state attempted to meet the demand for more living quarters with the gray, functional prefabricated building blocks that cropped up everywhere, very different settlements arose in Grbavica, Hrasno, and Koševsko brdo, and later in Alipašino polje and Drobinja. Tens of thousands of migrants simply laid claim to open land in the city and its outlying areas. These sprawling illegal settlements initially had no water or sewage lines, no electricity or trash removal. In a sense, they resembled living conditions in the prewar era. These neighborhoods were finally renovated in the 1970s with the help of international loans, and urgent problems with the gas and water supply and transportation infrastructure were also addressed.[253]

Like all large cities in Yugoslavia, Sarajevo had grown rapidly after 1945; its population climbed from about 70,000 to 477,000 in 1984.[254] The city's residents formed a colorful ethnic and religious mosaic. In 1981, about 42 percent of the population were Bosnian Muslims, 29.5 percent Serbs, 8 percent Croats, and 16 percent "Yugoslavs"—that is, people who did not identify with one particular nationality. Some 22 percent of marriages were ethnically mixed.[255]

On a map, Bosnia-Herzegovina appeared to be the heart of Yugoslavia, and it was the only republic where three constituent nations—Serbs, Croats, and Muslims—shared power. The communists emphasized "together-ness" *(zajedništvo),* while a mechanism called the "national key" was sup-posed to ensure that the different groups were proportionally represented in state and social institutions. The Cyrillic and Latin alphabets were, for example, taught equally in the schools.[256]

After the communists had recognized the Muslims as a constituent na-tion in the 1960s, the peoples' representatives began to renegotiate the sharing of power. Because the approximately 1.63 million Muslims formed a relative majority in Bosnia-Herzegovina, Muslim politicians and intel-lectuals called for greater influence in the republic's institutions. They also wanted an independent Bosnian language, script, and literature, and in-dependent national cultural institutions.[257] Serb and Croat nationalists complained that Tito had created an artificial nation as means of neutral-izing their influence.[258]

In May 1984, Yugoslav historians met at a congress in Sarajevo to seek resolution in a bitter conflict over the *Encyclopedia of Yugoslavia.* The au-thors of the planned entry on "Socialist Republic of Bosnia-Herzegovina" had to defend themselves against accusations that they were promoting a nonhistoric theory of continuity, an invented regional identity, and Muslim nationalism in general.[259] That same month, language scholars gathered to discuss the standard literary language of Croats, Serbs, Montenegrins, and Muslims, which experts at the time considered to be divided into a western-Croatian and an eastern-Serbian variant. Bosnia-Herzegovina, however, had only one regional "standard linguistic form of expression"— in effect, a mixture of the two variants, namely, "Serbo-Croatian" or "Croato-Serbian."[260] Bosnian linguists were concerned that "Serbian" and "Croatian" would gradually evolve into separate languages, leaving the (not officially recognized) Bosnian variant by the wayside. Nevertheless, there was still an overall desire for compromise.[261]

As politicians and intellectuals fought over nationalities policy, most Bosnians perceived ethnic relations in their neighborhood, republic, and the whole Yugoslav state as satisfactory or good.[262] They thought of themselves primarily as Yugoslav citizens, and only secondarily as members of a certain national group.[263] They were also receptive to the wider world; 44 percent saw themselves as world citizens, and 53 percent as Europeans.[264] Many were, however, concerned about increasing nationalist propaganda and political chauvinism. At the same time, more people—about one-third—now expressed reservations about entering into friendships or marriages with members of other ethnicities.[265] Prejudices, nationalism, myths, and hatred were gaining ground, particularly among the younger generation.[266]

As one of the poorest and least developed areas in Europe, Bosnia-Herzegovina transformed rapidly thanks to state investments after 1945. Per capita economic output quadrupled between 1947 and 1983. The proportion of workers in the agricultural sector fell from 62.2 percent in 1953, to 17.3 percent in 1981; illiteracy declined in the same period from 40.2 percent to 14.5 percent.[267]

Bosnians' overall standard of living was one-third lower than the Yugoslav average, although their access to everyday necessities—food and shelter—was just as good. The republic lagged behind in consumer goods, but even so, about 79 percent of Bosnians owned a refrigerator, 77 percent owned a television, and 26 percent owned an automobile.[268] The capital city of Sarajevo offered numerous cultural opportunities—including twenty-seven public libraries, five adult education centers, six cultural centers, eighteen cinemas, five theaters, and multiple orchestras. In Bosnia-Herzegovina 461 newspapers and magazines were published; statistics counted 2.6 million moviegoers each year. Some 728,000 families received radio broadcasts, and 601,000 had television reception, too. As it was everywhere in Yugoslavia, foreign films and TV shows were part of everyday life—from Alfred Hitchcock and the Smurfs, to *Dallas* and *Dynasty*.[269]

On the surface, Sarajevo was a young, diverse, and dynamic city. In 1984, 15 percent of Bosnian industry was concentrated here, along with 20 percent of the republic's workforce and 60 percent of its university students. The most important economic sectors were metalworking and mechanical engineering, as well as the transportation, textile, graphics, chemical, and electronics industries. Large companies like Energoinvest, ŠIPAD, UNIS, and Graming provided an income for many families.[270] But the city was hurt by the grave economic crisis, which threatened to erase the achievements of recent decades. To bring dramatically overextended public budgets into line, the republic's leaders cut expenditures at the beginning of the 1980s, causing investments to shrink. Inflation raced upward, while economic growth slowed to just 0.8 percent per year.[271] Almost daily, the press reported on new negative records. In January 1984, 70 percent of industrial capacity was not being used; in September, 59 percent of all investments were financed on credit.[272] The contraction of the economy brought a large leap in unemployment, affecting the younger generation in particular. In 1952, only 4,000 people in the republic had been looking for work, but in 1984, it was 220,000. An additional 134,000 people lived abroad as guest workers.[273] The cost of living rose by 60 percent in 1983— and this was only the beginning of accelerating impoverishment. In September, retiree Ahmed Lemeš walked around the Sarajevo marketplace but could not afford provisions for the winter. "Right now, everything is too expensive . . . I'm waiting until prices go down."[274]

As the crisis intensified, so too did chronic conflicts over the allocation of resources between the richer and poorer parts of the country. Bosnia-Herzegovina was—along with Macedonia, Montenegro, and Kosovo—a recipient of federal aid; in the 1980s, it received about 16.5 percent of redistributions. More than half of the money now went to Kosovo, leaving less and less for Bosnia-Herzegovina. The standard of living in the small multinational republic declined in comparison to Slovenia and Croatia—and even in comparison to Yugoslavia as a whole. The low agricultural and raw materials prices that were dictated by socialist industrialization policy benefited the industries of the northern republics. Even though they sent 6 to 10 percent of their GDP to the federal government to support the less developed regions, their economies were still the fastest-growing. The prosperity gap continued to widen. In 1947, per capita income in Bosnia-Herzegovina was at 86 percent of the level for all Yugoslavia; by 1980, it had fallen to just 66 percent.[275] By the end of the decade, the Slovenes were almost four times wealthier than the Bosnians, and almost nine times wealthier than the Kosovars.[276]

Nevertheless, the wealthier republics of Slovenia and Croatia were frustrated by federal aid for the less developed republics, which they saw as a bottomless pit. Financing for the Olympics became a point of contention, with Slovene leaders expressing concern about an already high public debt.

Bosnia-Herzegovina subsequently assumed responsibility for 85 percent of the costs, or 4.7 billion dinars.[277] Citizens of the republic had to pay an extra Olympic tax. A 1987 finance scandal involving the food company Agrokomerc, located in the western Bosnian town of Velika Kladuša, showed that doubts about good economic management were not entirely misplaced. The head of the company, Fikret Abdić, had issued uncovered bills of exchange for years, investing the borrowed capital in local infrastructure and his corporate empire. As he expanded his political power, banks were left with debts totaling hundreds of millions of U.S. dollars. Leading Bosnian politicians were forced to resign.

In January 1984, the director Emir Kusturica began to shoot his new film, *When Father Was Away on Business,* on the streets of Sarajevo. Kusturica, the son of a Muslim atheist and Partisan who later became a communist functionary, studied at the respected television and film academy in Prague. He worked for Bosnian radio and then made his first films. After *Do You Remember Dolly Bell?* a highly successful coming-of-age film, he decided to tell the story of the low-level functionary Meša, who was sent to the island prison camp of Goli Otok after a romantic affair in 1948. The director wanted to depict the era of the persecution of Cominformists "through the eyes of a [six-year-old] boy who lives through all of the consequences of his father being arrested."[278]

The party bigwigs in the Bosnian production company Sutjeska Film thought the plot was too vulgar and socially critical; in addition to the politically sensitive topic of government persecution, it depicted the clash between traditional Muslim values and communist norms. The responsible commission relented only after Kusturica threatened to move to Belgrade, where he could make his film with fewer creative constraints. The renowned writer Meša Selimović had already resettled in Belgrade. "Belgrade was a political Sodom and Gomorrah for the figures who were supposed to make decisions in Sarajevo," Kusturica recalled. But "for me, the city was the window to freedom."[279]

Kusturica, the first Yugoslav winner of the Palme d'Or at Cannes in 1985, was among a younger generation of directors who were emerging from the shadow of the popular and highly subsidized Yugoslav and Bosnian film industry. Its more than two hundred Partisan films, made in a style resembling Hollywood Westerns, were particularly beloved. Movies such as *Kozara, Battle on the Neretva,* and *Walter Defends Sarajevo* became box-office hits. They featured international stars including Richard Burton and Curd Jürgens (Curt Jurgens), promoting patriotic virtues through tales of heroism, exciting battle sequences, and wartime romances. Yugoslav productions that gained a worldwide audience included the Winnetou films (based on the stories of German author Karl May), as well as *The Day That Shook the World,* starring Maximilian Schell. In response, critical avant-garde directors like Emir Kusturica, Vesna Ljubić, Miroslav Mandić, and Bahrudin Čengić depicted the contradictions of socialist reality and set new aesthetic standards.[280]

Rock, punk, heavy metal, and techno groups brought subversive energy to the music scene, too.[281] In May 1984, the Bosnian rock group Zabranjeno Pušenje (No Smoking) brought out their first album in Sarajevo. They were part of the New Primitivism, a subculture that mixed Bosnian folklore and *sevdah* ballads with Roma music and techno rock. In contrast to the nationalist sounds in Ljubljana, the youth and rock scene in Sarajevo had an intentionally Yugoslav orientation.[282] With their hit album *Das ist Walter,* an ironic reference to the 1972 Partisan spy thriller *Walter Defends Sarajevo,* Zabranjeno Pušenje was named Yugoslav Band of the Year in 1984.[283] New music trends appeared in the other regions, too. In Bulgaria, there was Chalga, and in Serbia, turbo-folk, a new pop-folk style.[284]

Other bands riding Sarajevo's subversive wave included Elvis J. Kurtović & His Meteors, Crvena Jabuka (Red Apple), and Bijelo Dugme (White Button) featuring Goran Bregović, who later worked with Kusturica and enjoyed success in the West. The satirical radio and TV show *Top List of Surrealists* earned cult status by sending up Yugoslav politics in an anarchic, Monty Python–like style. Radio Sarajevo and an increasingly self-assured youth press provided a forum for alternative protest culture throughout Yugoslavia.[285] As in other republics, a new political generation wanted to rethink Yugoslav socialist federalism, in order to bring about greater freedoms and a new sense of civic identity and Europeanness.[286]

Sarajevo was also a center of high culture, with its prominent festivals for literature, drama, music, and folklore. From Neoromanticism to minimalism, installation art to post-conceptualism, all kinds of visual art flourished in the city, as represented by the work of Vojo Dimitrijević, Ismet Mujezinović, Mica Todorović, and Behaudin Selmanović. Braco

Dimitrijević and Jusuf Hadžifejzović, who established the Yugoslav Documenta and the Sarajevo Biennial, also found international fame.[287]

On May 4, 1984, sirens in Sarajevo wailed at 3:00 P.M. As happened every year, people all over Yugoslavia paused for a minute of silence. In Bosnia-Herzegovina, where the consequences of nationalism had been especially brutal during the Second World War, the founder of Yugoslavia was extraordinarily revered. Tito was admired, honored, and loved; on his birthdays, he had received baskets upon baskets full of greeting cards and presents. "After Tito—Tito!" became the party motto. The father of Yugoslavia lived on even after his death; his portrait adorned public buildings, stores, restaurants, and private homes.[288] But the icon of "brotherhood and unity" was no longer unchallenged. Since the publication of Vladimir Dedijer's *New Contributions to the Biography of Josip Broz Tito* in 1980, a wave of disparaging literature about Yugoslavia's founder had swept across the country, depicting him as a power-hungry, conceited, and politically misguided dictator.[289] Intellectuals, the middle classes, representatives of civil society, and the media began to criticize socialist self-management and call for greater democracy and freedom of expression.[290]

New revisionist historical debates focused on the numbers of people killed, tortured, and expelled during the Second World War. The topic was ideal for challenging the central dogma of "brotherhood and unity." Serb and Croat historians outdid themselves in over- and underestimating the number of victims in the Croatian concentration camp Jasenovac, or the number of Partisans murdered by the Ustasha.[291] The arithmetic of victimhood also came to Sarajevo, where the Vraca Memorial Park opened in 1981 to honor more than eleven thousand named victims of the Second World War. Unresolved traumatic experiences provided fertile soil for national mobilization, which had long provided a sense of purpose and orientation in times of growing uncertainty and anxiety about the future.

In the meantime, extreme right-wing nationalists unabashedly expressed their opposition to the communist regime. In 1984 the daily newspaper *Oslobođenje* reported regularly on "intensified enemy activity" against "brotherhood and unity." The "fascist emigration," in particular, had escalated its propaganda and terrorist activities abroad.[292]

A new, restrictive law that cracked down on hostile and counterrevolutionary activity was passed in 1975, providing a basis for legal proceedings all over the country. In July 1984, a court in Sarajevo sentenced the Bosnian Serb sociologist Vojislav Šešelj to years in prison for his "counter-revolutionary threat to the social order of Yugoslavia," according to Article 114. In his article "What Is to Be Done?" he called for eliminating the republics of Bosnia-Herzegovina and Montenegro and the autonomous provinces; Yugoslavia would comprise only Slovenia, Croatia, Serbia, and Macedonia, and Bosnia-Herzegovina would lose its right to existence.[293] Oppositional voices in the neighboring republics sided with the self-declared Serb nationalist, blaming "Islamic nationalists" in Bosnia-Herzegovina for Šešelj's sentence. Branko Mikulić, president of the Bosnian republic, immediately rejected this "monstrous" accusation.[294] Like many political prisoners, Šešelj did not end up serving his full sentence. In the 1990s, he founded the Serbian Radical Party, whose volunteer paramilitary forces participated in the Yugoslav wars of succession. In 2018, the International Criminal Tribunal for the Former Yugoslavia in The Hague found him guilty of "ethnic cleansing" on appeal.

Political trials also took place in the other republics. In Zagreb, a group of Croatian nationalists close to the historian Franjo Tudjman found themselves in court. The later president of Croatia was accused of undercounting the number of Serb victims in the Ustasha concentration camp Jasenovac.[295] And in Kosovo, Adem Demaçi, cofounder of the Revolutionary Movement for Albanian Unity, and other Albanian activists were accused of nationalist machinations.[296]

In the meantime, the lawyer Alija Izetbegović and twelve other followers of the anticommunist Young Muslims had been jailed for propaganda on behalf of a pan-Islamic state and for their contacts to the regime of the Iranian ayatollah. In 1983 a court had decided that calls for the sharia, requiring women to wear the veil and banning mixed marriages, represented an attack on the principle of "brotherhood and unity." Izetbegović's *Islamic Declaration,* which called for a centrally governed pan-Islamic state, had just been republished.[297] Also in 1983, five Muslim intellectuals traveled to Teheran to participate in a world congress of imams. They admired the Iranian revolution and supported Iran's touted reconciliation between Shiites and Sunnis (including the Bosnian Muslims).[298]

The long prison sentences for the Islamists touched off international protests. High-ranking representatives of the Yugoslav Islamic Community responded with multiple articles in the *Oslobođenje* in January 1984, seeking to correct the "fraudulent" reports of emigrants about the trial and situation of Muslims in Yugoslavia. They pointed out that the communists had built 406 new mosques and 317 houses of prayer since 1945. Appearing regularly were twenty-five Islamic periodicals, and hundreds of copies of the Arabic Koran were distributed.[299]

Even as the Islamic Community pursued a constructive relationship with the communist state, greater numbers of clerics began to seek a more prominent role for religion. They invoked Muslim tradition in order to reactivate religious commandments, rites, and customs such as the fasting period of Ramadan, reading of the Koran, undertaking of pilgrimages, and, for women, the wearing of veils. They also emphasized religious names and instruction for children, as well as a strict ban on mixed marriages and the consumption of alcohol. In Sarajevo, one journalist observed young men with the "vitality, elan, confidence, and faith in the future" to bring about a "renaissance of Islam in all Yugoslavia."[300] Even so, in 1990 only 37 percent of Bosnian Muslims considered themselves religious, in contrast to 60 percent of Slovenes and 53 percent of Croats. More than 60 percent never attended a mosque.[301]

1989 and After

The year 1989 was one of the central peripeteia in the history of Europe and the world in the twentieth century. Communist regimes collapsed throughout central and southeastern Europe—including Bulgaria and Romania in 1989, Yugoslavia in 1990, and Albania in 1991. The prehistory of these events and how they unfolded were different in each country. In Bulgaria, the Politburo forced Todor Zhivkov's resignation in November 1989, engaging in round-table negotiations with the opposition over the transition to multiparty democracy. The longest-serving party and state leader in the Eastern bloc was sentenced to years of house arrest. In Romania, there were violent protests, strikes, and clashes with the military and Securitate in December 1989. The army arrested Nicolae Ceaușescu and his wife Elena, and they were executed after a speedy trial on December 25, 1989. Albanian leader Ramiz Alia attempted reform, but in 1990 a great wave of protests rolled across the country and brought the system literally to the point of collapse. The head of state was imprisoned. In Yugoslavia, the transition to multiparty democracy tore apart the state and initiated a bloody war of succession.[302]

The transition to democracy fundamentally transformed southeastern Europe. The former communist states became democracies, and the republics of Yugoslavia won independence, as did those in Czechoslovakia and the Soviet Union. These events also affected the western half of the continent. Communist parties lost influence in Italy, France, Spain, and Portugal, and the political identity of the neutral states of Austria, Sweden, Finland, and Switzerland changed with the end of the Cold War. The fall of the Berlin Wall became a symbol of the reunification of Europe. In the following years, the European Community evolved into a more integrated European Union (EU), engaging with southeastern Europe and also serving as an aspirational model. At the same time, the United States encouraged closer Western and transatlantic ties with the east-central European states, and later those of southeastern Europe, through the institution of NATO.[303]

The upheavals of 1989 occurred within a broader global context, which was influenced not only by the world economic crisis of the 1970s but also by a "third wave of democratization."[304] Greece, Spain, and Portugal overcame authoritarianism; Argentina and Chile ended their military dictatorships. Elections were held in the Philippines, South Korea, and Taiwan in the 1980s, before the fall of socialism in eastern and southeastern Europe. And in the 1990s, most African countries finally introduced multiparty systems.[305] The processes of democratization in the different parts of the world functioned like communicating vessels. Popular movements against the communist regimes in eastern and southeastern Europe, against military dictatorship in southern Europe and Latin America, against racial discrimination in the United States, and against apartheid in South Africa communicated with and mutually influenced one another. They followed similar patterns of criticizing authority, social mobilization, and nonviolent protest. In this respect, 1989—like 1968—was a transnational event. Moreover, influential actors in the democratic transition had been politically socialized during the student movements twenty years earlier, providing yet another connection between the two historical turning points.[306]

On one hand, the dissolution of Yugoslavia was the result of globalization; on the other, it accelerated the globalization process. Since its founding, the multinational state had suffered from grave structural problems—including unresolved historical conflicts and ethnosocial disparities as well as regional development gaps and related conflicts over the allocation of resources. The postwar economic miracle, the ideology of "brotherhood and unity," and Tito's international prestige had only papered over the deep political rifts. Because the socioeconomic and ethnopolitical dimensions

Street fighting in Bucharest, December 1989.

of the problems were mutually reinforcing, a highly explosive situation emerged in the crisis-ridden 1980s. The asymmetries of the global economy between developed and poorer countries existed in miniature within Yugoslavia itself, and the opening to the world market only exacerbated these regional disparities. In 1945 per capita income in Slovenia was about three times higher than in Kosovo, but in 1989 it was nine times higher.[307] In the West, the nation-state was seen as a relic from an earlier time, unable to handle the increasingly complex problems of a globalized world. But in southeastern Europe, growing world economic integration actually encouraged renationalization. The belief was that only a strong state—or in the case of Yugoslavia, an independent republic—could handle crises effectively, particularly with respect to economic concerns. Once the collapse of communism and the end of the Cold War unraveled the remaining ties between the constituent republics, disintegrative tendencies gained the upper hand. Only a few years after Tito's death in 1980, Yugoslavia's "third way" of socialist self-management and foreign political nonalignment was already obsolete.

At the height of a far-reaching economic and political crisis, the Yugoslav republics were no longer willing or able to agree on a common approach for handling the debt, inflation, and unemployment, or for instituting federal constitutional reform. While Slovenia and Croatia pleaded for (even) more rights for the constituent republics, Serbia sought greater centralism. In 1989, Belgrade limited the autonomy of its provinces Kosovo and Vojvodina—a consequential step that dangerously heightened fears about plans to institutionalize Serbian dominance at the federal level. The Albanian majority in Kosovo subsequently created a shadow state and planned for independence.[308]

As in many ethnically plural states, democratization fanned the flames of unrest. In difficult times, many people trusted only those leaders who prioritized the interests of their own national group.[309] At the beginning of 1990, the League of Communists of Yugoslavia, the single ruling party, fell apart at its extraordinary fourteenth congress. Federal institutions, the media, and the state security apparatus underwent an unprecedented process of disintegration, as the republics continued to grow farther apart. In the first multiparty elections in 1990, national conservative parties triumphed in Slovenia and Croatia. Milan Kučan became president of Slovenia, and Franjo Tudjman, one of the protagonists of the Croatian Spring, assumed the presidency in Croatia. In Bosnia-Herzegovina, three ethnopolitical parties achieved a majority and formed a coalition under president Alija Izetbegović. In Serbia, the former communist Slobodan Milošević, who had become president of Serbia in 1989, consolidated his power. He used nationalist slogans to rally support for a strong Serbia at mass events such as the six hundredth anniversary of the Battle of Kosovo.

The new nationalist governments were reluctant to seek compromise in handling all kinds of problems. The Slovenian and Croatian governments wanted independence at all costs, seeking to promote democratization, a market economy, and closer relations with the European Community. But this threatened the national unity of the Serbs, more than one-quarter of whom lived outside their mother republic. Belgrade's priority was to preserve Yugoslavia, the first state ever to have unified the Serbs. If this were not possible, then the minimum goal was to hold together all the areas occupied by Serbs—a plan that the Yugoslav People's Army generals also supported. Once again, the diaspora played a significant role; Slovenia, Croatia, and Kosovo collected millions of dollars in foreign donations for the purchase of weapons, mobilizing guest workers and exiled nationals in support of independence.[310]

The Yugoslav crisis received little attention in the West. German reunification, the Iraq War, the coup in Moscow, and the Maastricht Treaty all took precedence. Nevertheless, in the spring of 1991 the German foreign minister signaled the potential recognition of Slovenia and Croatia as independent states, even though the UN, the United States, and the western European governments supported keeping Yugoslavia intact, afraid of touching off an uncontrollable domino effect. Encouraged by Germany, Slovenia and Croatia declared independence on June 25, 1991. While the ten-day "little war" in Slovenia between the republic's territorial defense and the Yugoslav People's Army unfolded relatively painlessly, much larger combat operations commenced in Croatia. The Croatian and Bosnian Serbs staked out autonomous territories, building them into para-states and declaring allegiance to Yugoslavia. In the fall of 1991, the Yugoslav People's Army began a great offensive, shelling Dubrovnik and largely destroying Vukovar. Serb forces brought one-third of Croatia under their control and expelled about a half-million people. In December 1991, they proclaimed the Serb Republic of Krajina.[311]

Despite voices of warning at home and abroad, in the face of escalating combat operations and a growing refugee crisis, Germany decided unilaterally to recognize Slovenia and Croatia before Christmas 1991. By internationalizing the crisis, the intent was to deter the Yugoslav People's Army from carrying out further attacks. But Germany's Basic Law tied its own hands militarily, and no other state was prepared to undertake a humanitarian intervention. To maintain political unity, the European Community had no alternative but to recognize Slovenia and Croatia on January 15, 1992. As UN peacekeeping troops moved into Croatia, the conflict expanded to other regions, spilling into Bosnia-Herzegovina (1992–1995), Kosovo (1998–1999), and Macedonia (2001).

Now that only a "rump" Yugoslavia dominated by Serbia remained after the secession of Slovenia and Croatia, representatives of the Bosnian Croats and Muslims declared the independence of their republic over the opposition of the Bosnian Serbs in October 1991. The governing coalition fell apart, and all other state institutions, including the security apparatus, subsequently splintered into ethnic components. A referendum ordered by the European Community indicated that a clear majority of those in Bosnia-Herzegovina favored independence, although the referendum was boycotted by the Serbs. Bosnia-Herzegovina was internationally recognized on April 6, 1992, the anniversary of the German attack on Yugoslavia in 1941, and the liberation of Sarajevo in 1945. Bosnian Serbs, meanwhile, founded the Republika Srpska. Supported by the Yugoslav People's Army,

War damage at the Musala Bridge in Mostar. Sputnik.

their forces overtook large swathes of Bosnian territory in a kind of blitz-krieg within just a few weeks. They besieged Sarajevo and numerous other cities and villages. The international community was confounded by the dissolution of the original military alliance between the Bosnian Muslims and Croats in early 1993; the latter group wanted to create a Bosnian Croat state, Herzeg-Bosna. In the ensuing battles between the (now) three warring parties and numerous warlords, hundreds of thousands were driven from their homes. Mostar and its historic Old Bridge were almost completely destroyed. Only in March 1994 did international mediators succeed in setting aside the "war within a war" in favor of a Bosniak-Croat federation. But the fighting continued in many regions.

The escalation of the war brought a form of mass crime once thought to have been overcome back in the public eye: "ethnic cleansing." As had occurred during the nineteenth century, the Balkan Wars, and the Second World War, unwanted population groups were deported, expelled, and sometimes murdered en masse. Entire villages and important cultural landmarks fell victim to planned destruction. By the summer of 1992, more than 2.2 million people, half of the Bosnian population, had been displaced. Bosnian Serb forces "homogenized" territories under their control with the utmost brutality and resolve. But Croatian and Bosniak armies also perpetrated "ethnic cleansing" when they conquered new areas, although these were fewer in number.[312]

The unimaginable atrocities turned the first armed conflict on European soil after the Second World War into a global media event. Recent technical advances played an important role. Thanks to satellite technology and digital recording, editing, and transmission capabilities, international news channels—especially CNN, BBC, and later Al Jazeera—brought images of the war directly from the crisis regions to the rest of the world. Correspondents and investigative journalists sent photos of detention camps and mass graves all over the globe. The media were also influenced by government propaganda and professional PR agencies, which systematically disseminated false information in order to win the sympathies of the domestic and global public.[313]

The shocking news reports mobilized global civil society, which had grown substantially since the bloody events in Mozambique, Afghanistan, and Rwanda in the 1980s. The number of international nongovernmental organizations advocating for human rights, refugees, and wartime humanitarian assistance had multiplied. In 1951, there were only 832 registered international nongovernmental organizations; in 1972, there were just under 2,200, and in the 1980s, about 4,500. Countless activists streamed into Yugoslavia's crisis areas to provide humanitarian aid or initiate peace projects.[314]

Political scientists identified Yugoslavia as an archetype for the "new war"; the term described informal, privatized conflicts that were financed by warlords and diasporas and that particularly targeted civilian populations. Comparable forms of fighting could be found all over the world since the end of the Cold War—including in Burundi, Sierra Leone, Somalia, Liberia, Congo, Angola, Chechnya, and Afghanistan.[315] In Yugoslavia, however, as in other countries, it was not the form of war that was new, but rather the way in which it was perceived and presented by a globalized public and media. The legal proceedings at the International Criminal Tribunal for the Former Yugoslavia in The Hague (which was established in 1993) made clear that "ethnic cleansing" was not, in fact, primarily initiated and executed by private actors, but was instead planned by local authorities and then implemented by regular armies with the help of warlords. In October 1991, half a year before the outbreak of war, Bosnian Serb leaders had begun to plan for separating non-Serbs from Serbs in case of conflict.

Mass crimes were overwhelmingly ordered by higher authorities; they were not driven primarily by the ethnic hatred of neighbors against neighbors. Self-reinforcing processes and revenge certainly played a role, but they were in no way decisive. This was also true of countless other "new wars" in the postcolonial world, as in Angola, Mozambique, Congo, Sudan, Sri Lanka, Indonesia, and also the Middle East.[316]

As horrific images from Yugoslavia appeared nightly on the world's TV screens, and some public voices began to call for military intervention, the war became one of the most pressing international problems of the 1990s. Actors such as the United States, Russia, the European Community, the UN, and NATO tried in vain to negotiate ceasefires and peace agreements, or at least to alleviate the worst humanitarian suffering. At first, it seemed as if the historical alliances that had formed around the Eastern Question in the nineteenth and early twentieth centuries would rise again. Russia, Great Britain, and France favored the Serbian side, while Germany and Austria openly supported Croatia and Slovenia. But as the war progressed, these opposing positions began to dissolve. The United States, Russia, Germany, France, Great Britain, and later Italy adopted a common political line through the Bosnia Contact Group. Even so, the warring parties rejected one international peace plan after another, dealing a serious blow to the stature of the international community.[317]

Another international dimension of the war was the role of the Islamic world, which stepped up its political and humanitarian engagement in the region. Saudi Arabia, Egypt, Sudan, Iran, Yemen, Malaysia, and a variety of Islamic aid organizations provided financial and military support for the Muslims, who now officially called themselves Bosniaks. Up to five thousand Iranian, Afghani, and Saudi mujahideen fought on their side.[318] Although conflicts between Saudi Arabia and Iran, between the Sunnis and Shiites, stood in the way of a unified Islamic policy, pan-Islamic solidarity did strengthen the worldwide network of the "imagined" community of believers, the Islamic *umma*. This encouraged the re-Islamization of Bosnian Muslims, who felt abandoned by the West.[319]

The Western states, in the meantime, focused on a strategy of humanitarian damage control. They imposed an arms embargo and tasked the UN with distributing food and medicine in Sarajevo. Serbia and Montenegro, which together formed the Federal Republic of Yugoslavia, were hit with comprehensive economic and diplomatic sanctions in May 1992.[320] In the spring of 1993, the UN Security Council declared Srebrenica, Sarajevo,

Tuzla, Žepa, Goražde, and Bihać "safe areas." Under the cover of NATO war planes, lightly armed Blue Helmet peacekeepers were to provide humanitarian relief for the growing tide of refugees. Their rules of engagement were to remain impartial, using force only in self-defense. The Blue Helmets lacked the mandate and human and military resources for a combat mission. Instead of the 34,000 soldiers that UN headquarters had requested for the six protected areas, the member states sent just 7,500.[321] On the morning of July 11, 1995, Bosnian Serb army and police units stormed the Srebrenica safe area after days of siege. More than 8,200 men were systematically executed. The tragedy brought the wholly insufficient response of the international community to the attention of the entire world.[322]

The massacre in Srebrenica became a turning point in Balkan policy. NATO began the massive bombardment of Serbian positions in Bosnia-Herzegovina. With the help of American weapons and military advisers, previously outgunned Croat and Bosniak forces gained new strength.[323] The Croatian government likewise received American support, allowing it to overtake the Serb Republic of Krajina in its Operation Oluja (Storm) of August 1995, and to expel about 150,000 to 200,000 Serbs.

By the end of the summer of 1995, there was a military stalemate in Bosnia-Herzegovina. The Bosnian Serbs and the reluctant Croat-Bosniak allies each held about half of the state's territory. Neither side could count on further territorial gains. In light of this situation, U.S. special envoy Richard Holbrooke presented a peace plan that reduced the fundamentally incompatible goals of the warring parties to a common denominator. After difficult negotiations, the war ended with the Dayton Agreement on November 21, 1995. Bosnia-Herzegovina remained a unified state with its prewar borders, but was now divided into two largely independent federal entities. The Federation of Bosnia-Herzegovina, governed by Croats and Muslims, received 51 percent of the state's territory, and the Republika Srpska received 49 percent. All refugees and internally displaced persons were to be allowed to return to their home regions. A high representative with quasi-dictatorial powers, supported by a sixty-thousand-head NATO peacekeeping force, was responsible for implementing the highly complex constitution and all other rulings.[324]

Although the Dayton Agreement ended the fighting and allowed reconstruction of the war-torn land to begin, hopes for a self-sustaining peace process were ultimately disappointed. About 100,000 people had been killed in the war, more than two million displaced, and the wounds of the past were deep. The political elites of 1995 had in no way given up their original war aims, but only temporarily set them aside. The country remained ethnically, politically, institutionally, and mentally divided. Nearly twenty-five years later, a shared understanding of the state has yet to develop. Today, neither the political elites nor the different ethnic groups have come to accept the profoundly dysfunctional state structure.[325]

The international community assumed that the Yugoslav war of succession had ended in Dayton, but they quickly learned otherwise. Amid grave violations of human rights and an intensifying socioeconomic crisis, the Albanian Kosovo Liberation Army appeared on the scene in 1996, after Serbia and the West had continued to ignore the calls for independence by the "forgotten of Dayton." After Serbian security forces severely cracked down on the rebels, the conflict escalated into war in March 1998. Once again, thousands took flight. Attempts at international mediation, leading to negotiations at the Château de Rambouillet, were unsuccessful. Without a UN Security Council resolution, NATO began airstrikes against Serbian military installations, infrastructure, and industrial sites in March 1999. One of the largest refugee movements in postwar European history took place parallel to the war, as some 800,000 people fled or were expelled from Kosovo. Three months after the beginning of the military intervention, in June 1999, Belgrade accepted a UN resolution to turn Kosovo into an international protectorate.[326]

Because the NATO mission took place without a UN mandate—and thus, in the opinion of many experts, in violation of international law—it had a legitimacy problem. But NATO developed a clever propaganda strategy. In the words of Wesley Clark, NATO's supreme allied commander in Europe, the world media became "part of the battlefield."[327] NATO spokesman Jamie Shea later proudly explained the global media strategy that was coordinated by Washington, Brussels, and Berlin: "Our credo at NATO was just to be on the air the whole time, crowd out the opposition, give every interview, do every briefing."[328] NATO always held its press conference at 3:00 P.M., when the greatest number of people around the world were watching TV. In the United States, it was 9:00 A.M.; in Asia, early evening, and in Australia, late evening. The core NATO message was that the goal of military intervention was to prevent a "humanitarian catastrophe" or "another Auschwitz."[329] The supporting evidence was the Yugoslav army's supposed "horseshoe plan" for the expulsion of the Albanians, which had been presented by the German government as grounds for a "just war." It was later shown that such a plan had never existed.[330] But the NATO strategy was a success. The Atlantic alliance served as a source for 61 percent of all CNN reports on the Kosovo War.[331]

Not only the war itself but also the transition to peace became transnational events. After the NATO victory in Kosovo, the democratic opposition in Serbia successfully drove Slobodan Milošević from office in October 2000. The opposition received support from the United States and the EU through programs like Energy for Democracy. After a lost election, mass demonstrations, and a march on Belgrade, Milošević stepped down. He was extradited to the International Criminal Tribunal for the Former Yugoslavia in 2001. In contrast to the state-organized marches ten years before, the new protests in Serbia were led by groups like Otpor (Resistance), with professional media and mobilization strategies that addressed an international public. The cell phone and Internet became the main media of mobilization. These strategies later provided a model for the "color revolutions" around the world. Serbian activists advised opposition movements in Georgia, Belarus, Ukraine, Kyrgyzstan, and Egypt.

With the end of the war in Kosovo in 1999, the Kosovo Liberation Army sought a new field of action in neighboring Macedonia. In 2001 conflict was escalating between Albanian rebels and Macedonian security forces over the union of all Albanian-occupied areas. More than 200 people were killed, and about 100,000 fled or were expelled. In August 2001, the EU and the United States brokered a peace agreement that gave the Albanians more rights and the country at least temporary hope for greater stability.[332]

As Yugoslavia experienced harrowing mass crimes, expulsions, and acts of destruction, the international community's inability to take action ultimately led to substantial innovations in the system of global governance. Over the course of the war, the instrument of "humanitarian intervention" gradually gained political and legal acceptance.[333] In 1992 the Security Council for the first time allowed the use of military force under chapter VII of the UN Charter, as a means of reducing the humanitarian toll of the civil war in Somalia. In 2001, this led to the UN-endorsed principle of "responsibility to protect," which established the obligation of every state to protect its citizens from genocide, war crimes, crimes against humanity, and "ethnic cleansing." Should a state be unable to meet this obligation, the international community had the responsibility to adopt nonmilitary or military countermeasures. In 2011 the UN Security Council invoked this principle to approve military intervention in Libya.

Not least, the common foreign, security, and defense policy of the EU was shaped by the formative experience of the Yugoslav wars. In the 1990s, the region became a laboratory and testing ground for new instruments of conflict prevention and conflict management. In postwar Bosnia-Herzegovina, for example, the EU introduced European-led police and peacekeeping forces for the first time in its history. New special representatives and envoys were sent to conflict regions such as Bosnia-Herzegovina and Macedonia with a mandate to mediate between conflicting parties or monitor peace implementation. And in Kosovo, the EU introduced its largest rule of law mission to date, helping to build up the judiciary and the police.

International law continued to develop with the establishment of the International Criminal Tribunal for the Former Yugoslavia in The Hague in 1993. Initially derided as a toothless tiger, the tribunal and its proceedings came to earn worldwide respect and introduce new approaches in criminal justice. This ad hoc UN tribunal, and a similar institution for Rwanda, laid the groundwork for a permanent International Criminal Court. By December 2017, the tribunal had concluded all 161 of its cases and was closed down; no suspects were still at large, including the Bosnian Serb general Ratko Mladić and Bosnian Serb president Radovan Karadžić.

Thus, at the end of the twentieth century, the Yugoslav wars brought on a new kind of "Balkanization": the breakdown of a state into ethnically defined political components. The sweeping processes of imperial disintegration that had begun at the end of the eighteenth century, accelerating and radicalizing over the course of the nineteenth century, came to a close for the time being. The multinational Yugoslav state broke into seven successor states: Slovenia, Croatia, Bosnia-Herzegovina, Serbia, Montenegro, Macedonia, and Kosovo (which became independent in 2008). More than four million people were displaced. The Bosnian Muslims' centuries-long process of nation-building—their transition from a religious community to a secular nation of Bosniaks—moved forward, as did the seemingly contradictory process of re-Islamization. Today state- and nation-building in the former Yugoslavia is not yet finished, and numerous questions of identity, borders, and status remain unresolved.

The breakdown of Yugoslavia points to further lines of historical continuity. The different national movements had interacted with one another since the nineteenth century, as the Ottoman Empire fell apart piece by piece. They counted on the support of outside actors such as exiles and volunteer fighters, and they vied for the attention of the media and the global public. Even in the nineteenth century, transnational nongovernmental organizations were on site in southeastern Europe. Of course, the opportunities for outside involvement increased exponentially over the course of the twentieth century, with respect to both the number of actors and their geographical reach. Today the European Union, the United States, Russia, Turkey and the Islamic world, and China with its New Silk Road strategy all exercise a prominent influence in the region.

International conflict management, which began with the Eastern Question, has since gone global. Yugoslavia became a playing field where international actors negotiated their roles and tested new instruments of conflict management. For West Germany, the disintegration of Yugoslavia was the catalyst for giving up decades of foreign policy reticence in order to participate in NATO military missions "out of area"—and if necessary, anywhere in the world. Multilateralism found new expression as the European Union tested its common foreign, security, and defense policy in the Balkans, and the United Nations continued to develop its tools of peacekeeping and peacebuilding. The grave violations of human rights in the former Yugoslavia encouraged the formation of global governance regimes: international criminal justice and a new doctrine of humanitarian intervention, the "responsibility to protect." Finally, the Yugoslav wars bolstered the process of transnationalization, as the worldwide civil society that advocated for universal human rights forged new connections in the global arena. After the wars' end, however, many activists moved on to other areas of crisis.

Southeastern Europe in the Global Present

Europeanization and globalization took on a new dynamic after the end of the Cold War. European integration and rising prosperity—but also European values such as freedom, democracy, solidarity, human rights, and state commitment to social welfare—turned western Europe into a magnet for the Balkan states. After completing their transition from communism, they hoped to be accepted into the European Community (later EU) as quickly as possible. Bulgaria, Romania, and Slovenia obtained Association Agreements and a path to accession in 1993, but for the other Yugoslav successor states and Albania (the so-called Western Balkan countries), this became possible only after the end of the Kosovo War in

1999. Slovenia was the first to join the EU as part of the union's eastern enlargement in 2004. Bulgaria and Romania followed in 2007, and Croatia—the first of the Western Balkan countries—in 2013. In mid-2018, the European Union reaffirmed the "European perspective" for candidates and potential candidates from the region.

All Western Balkan states see accession to the EU as their highest political priority, overriding any national caveats. As full members, they hope finally to be recognized as equal partners in the European family of nations, able to participate actively in collective decision making, and to benefit from freedom of movement and economic advantages. The experience of east-central Europe has shown that even candidate status significantly brightens a country's economic outlook. Aside from access to EU financial assistance and structural funds, improvements in governance and business climate that are associated with EU candidacy build the trust of foreign investors.[334]

Conditions for EU integration include the establishment of democratic systems, transformation to a market economy, and structural adjustments to enable acceptance of the European *acquis communautaire*. Despite wide regional disparities, the Western Balkan states have made good progress overall and edged closer toward the European Union. Regional cooperation, another condition for accession, has continued to improve. The countries of southeastern Europe work together in refugee and migration policy, combating organized crime and corruption, and also in matters concerning connectivity—namely, trade, investment, energy, and infrastructure. But they do not see regional cooperation as a substitute for EU accession.[335]

Since 1989, global governance, international financial institutions, and transnational enterprises have played a larger role in the region than ever before. All southeastern Europe is now closely involved in the process of worldwide economic integration as well as in global communications and mobility, the expanding presence of international organizations and transnational networks, and global ways of life and consumption. The first steps were taken in the 1950s and 1960s, with the activity of the UN, OECD, and World Bank, the globality of the Cold War and the monetary system of Bretton Woods, and the worldwide expansion of trade, transportation, and media. The Balkan countries were affected by all these phenomena to differing degrees. The Eastern bloc states and especially Albania had fewer connections than Greece and Yugoslavia to the world market.

The liberalization of trade and capital flows accelerated the globalization of the economy and investments beginning in the 1980s, and especially after 1989. In 1998 worldwide exports represented 17 percent of all global economic output—more than double the proportion (8 percent) in 1913. Integration within the world economy accelerated in southeastern Europe, although not as rapidly as in western Europe. In eastern Europe, exports represented just 13 percent of GNP, compared to 28 percent in western Europe.[336] The globalization process, which had been so dynamic and innovative in the years before 1914, once again expanded in scope and intensity after the interruption of the two world wars. Globalization took on a new look.[337]

After the fall of communism, the socialist systems transformed themselves by embracing global principles of liberalization, deregulation, and privatization that had been affirmed by the IMF, the World Bank, and the United States. The goal was to fight economic crises and unemployment, and also to enable structural adjustments so that debtor nations could manage their economies more efficiently and pay back their debts faster. Ten specific measures were encouraged: establishing rigid fiscal discipline, cutting state expenditures, reducing budget deficits, reforming taxes, deregulating markets and prices, completely liberalizing trade policy, privatizing public enterprises and limiting employee rights, devaluating currencies, supporting foreign direct investments, and protecting private property.[338]

There were considerable differences in the implementation of reforms. Starting conditions varied widely; the post-Yugoslav states had the system of self-management, Romania and Bulgaria, reformed state socialism, and Albania, Stalinist autarky. Unlike Poland and the Czech Republic, not all southeastern European states adopted the economic "shock therapy" recommended by World Bank adviser Jeffrey Sachs.[339] Romania kept strategic industries in the hands of the state, while Slovenia only partially privatized its enterprises. Some 40 percent of shares were sold; the remainder went to employees or were transferred to investment, compensation, and pension funds. In Bulgaria and the post-Yugoslav lands, privatization was sometimes delayed and proceeded haphazardly.[340] The pressure to privatize state-owned companies created a glut in supply and pushed down prices. There were inside deals, and a thin stratum of domestic and foreign entrepreneurs and oligarchs frequently acquired former state assets well below their market values.[341]

Because the southeastern European states began their reforms later than Poland, Hungary, the Czech Republic, and Slovakia, they hoped to attract investors with their lower tax rates and social security contributions. Wages and salaries in the privatized companies plummeted. Social inequality grew, as did the disparities between urban and rural areas.[342] In Bulgaria and Romania, the reprivatization of agriculture led to a complete collapse in production and a rural unemployment rate of more than 50 percent.[343]

In the 1990s, all of southeastern Europe's postsocialist countries experienced a deep economic slump. Production contracted, while trade deficits and budget deficits grew.[344] Decades of mismanagement, bad investments, and technological deficiencies had created economic structures that were largely unprofitable and not competitive internationally. After state subsidies dried up, many enterprises collapsed under the new conditions of the market economy. On average, the unemployment rate climbed to 20 percent—from 11.5 percent in Romania, to 39 percent in Bosnia-Herzegovina. In 1997 the Albanian state nearly fell apart because of a fraudulent investment scheme; thousands fled across the Adriatic. The Italian-led UN Operation Alba helped to restore order amid civil-war-like conditions.[345]

The Balkan countries' economic output shrank significantly in the 1990s, widening the prosperity gap with western Europe by up to two-thirds. In 1998 per capita income in the southeastern European countries ranged between 72 percent (Macedonia) and 86 percent (Albania) of 1989 levels. Only in Slovenia did per capita income increase by just a few percentage points.[346] After 2000, the national economies expanded again, although without fulfilling the (neo-)liberal expectation that the gains in prosperity would trickle down to broader segments of society.[347] High unemployment persisted, averaging more than 20 percent even at the height of the boom. Sought-after foreign direct investments remained at a modest level. Western firms moved operations to the region to take advantage of the low wages and well-qualified workers. But in many cases, these firms merely worked with local subcontractors to assemble components on site that had been manufactured elsewhere. There was more international cooperation, but little investment in productive sectors, higher wages, or more hiring, and only limited growth. The Balkan states relied principally on labor-intensive sectors and the export of raw materials, falling back into disadvantageous relationships of exchange.[348]

On the other hand, the southeastern European states also received substantial financial and technical support. The European Bank for

Reconstruction and Development was established in 1990; its mission was to ease the eastern and southeastern European states' transition to market economies, thereby strengthening democracy. In 2002 alone, the EU, World Bank, and bilateral donors provided about 6.8 billion euros in aid through the Stability Pact for South Eastern Europe, which was intended for the reconstruction and expansion of infrastructure after the end of the Kosovo War. After this peak year, the level of support contracted sharply, and the majority of funds have since been made up overwhelmingly of loans. The most important donor today is the EU, with aid programs that support its pre-accession and integration policy.[349]

In the fall of 2008, the global economic, banking, and financial crisis interrupted the Balkan countries' economic recovery. The crisis was the result of an artificial boom, brought on by deregulation, speculation, and a policy of cheap money in the United States.[350] Once the American real estate bubble burst and numerous international commercial banks fell into distress, southeastern Europe was also affected. Three-quarters of the region's banking capital belonged to foreign financial institutions; in some countries, it was more than 90 percent. With the exception of Albania, all southeastern European countries, including Greece, fell into recession in 2009 and 2010, with industrial production decreasing more sharply than overall economic output. Foreign trade deficits and debt burdens grew in all southeastern European countries. In Montenegro, Slovenia, Bulgaria, and Croatia, foreign liabilities were about equal to GDP.[351]

The situation was exacerbated by the financial crisis and threat of state bankruptcy in Greece, which had adopted the euro in 2001. The state had obtained a large amount of credit on favorable terms on international capital markets. After many of its government bonds expired in 2008, Greece was no longer able to refinance its debts. After the international rescue efforts of the EU and IMF and substantial attempts at reform, a meaningful recovery may have begun in 2017.[352] Instead, interconnected capital flows, the decline in foreign trade, and rising unemployment allowed Greece to infect its neighbors.[353]

By 2014, the countries of the region had regained macroeconomic stability, but their standards of living remained well below the EU average. Per capita income in Bulgaria was just 45 percent of the EU average; Romania was at 54 percent; Croatia, 59 percent; and Slovenia, 83 percent. Greece fell back to 72 percent because of the financial and economic crisis. The countries lagging farthest behind were Bosnia-Herzegovina and Albania (about 29 percent) and Serbia, Macedonia, and Montenegro (35 to 39 percent). According to EU statistics, between 35 percent (Romania) and around 40 percent of the population in Bulgaria, Serbia, and the other Western Balkan countries were still at risk of poverty in 2017.[354] A significant reason for this is persistently high unemployment. On average, the employment rate is about 40 to 45 percent of the adult population— significantly lower than in the EU's poorest states. Strict monetary and fiscal policy, the decline in public investments, and rising taxes have discouraged new investments and hiring.[355] The European Commission and international financial institutions have consistently emphasized that greater flexibility in the labor market, stable institutions, rule of law, and a more aggressive approach toward corruption will create a better business climate.[356] But the IMF predicts that the prosperity gap is unlikely to close in the coming decades because of low economic growth.[357]

The large gap in prosperity has encouraged millions of people to emigrate from southeastern Europe since 1989, about one-quarter of the entire population. Hundreds of thousands of Albanians, Romanians, "Yugoslavs," and Greeks now live abroad. The region's poorest economies rely on the remittances of guest workers, which make up nearly 14 percent of GDP in Albania, and more than 11 percent in Bosnia-Herzegovina.[358] Young, well-qualified workers are most likely to emigrate. According to IMF estimates, the "brain drain" has drawn away one-quarter of all qualified workers in Macedonia and Bosnia-Herzegovina, and about one-fifth in the other countries.[359]

Surveys conducted in 2015 indicate that a quarter of Croatians, half of Bosnians, and a third of Albanians expressed a desire to emigrate.[360] That same year, about 120,000 migrants from the Western Balkan countries made their way just to Germany; most came from Kosovo and Albania, followed by Serbia.[361] Most of these migrants were sent back to their "safe countries of origin" within a year. At the same time, hundreds of thousands of refugees from Syria, Iraq, and Afghanistan traveled through the Balkans to seek asylum in certain EU countries. In the summer of 2015, and especially the spring of 2016, dramatic scenes unfolded along the Greek-Macedonian and Serbian-Hungarian borders. Because most of the refugees came through Turkey, it also became involved in the search for a "European solution."

The European Union has become the most important political and economic partner of the southeastern European countries, although the

United States also possesses great influence in the region. Membership in NATO is the first step toward integration with the West. The United States has become an important political actor through its embassies, military bases, and participation in international missions, and sometimes competes with the Europeans for regional influence. Russia's long-standing cultural ties with the Balkan Slavs, by contrast, have assumed a more symbolic significance, aside from Russian support for Serbia's Kosovo policy. In addition to Serbia and Russia, five EU states (Spain, Slovakia, Cyprus, Romania, and Greece) have not recognized Kosovo as Europe's newest independent state. Regional hopes for Russian investment have been fulfilled only in part. Commercial ties declined after Moscow abandoned construction of the South Stream gas pipeline at the end of 2014.[362]

In the 1990s, conservative and Islam-friendly politicians and intellectuals in Turkey promoted the ideology of Neo-Ottomanism as a counternarrative to EU integration in southeastern Europe. The underlying idea is that Turkey should assert a protective influence over former Ottoman territories in the Caucasus, Near East, and Balkan Peninsula. The university professor and later prime minister Ahmet Davutoğlu developed his doctrine of "strategic depth" to describe Turkey's "geopolitical and geocultural lifeline"—specifically, "the axis from Bihać, through central and eastern Bosnia, across the Sandžak, Kosovo, Albania, Macedonia . . . toward eastern Thrace."[363] Neo-Ottomanism has imperial and Islamic variations. After 1992, Turkey not only provided humanitarian aid, reconstruction assistance, and support for cultural initiatives and academic exchange in Bosnia-Herzegovina; it also played a role in re-Islamization. Turkey has an explicit interest in containing the influence of the Arab world and Iran. However, Turkey lags far behind the EU, and even behind Russia, in trade and investment in southeastern Europe.[364]

Alongside Turkey, the Islamic states also strove for regional influence. They financed the restoration and construction of numerous mosques, and hundreds of southeastern European students received scholarships in Saudi Arabia, Kuwait, Egypt, Iran, and other countries. The influence of pietist Salafism has grown through the work of the charitable Al-Haramain Foundation, the Saudi High Commission, and countless other Islamic charities and foundations. The Ahmadiyya community, which first established contacts among the Balkan Muslims at the beginning of the twentieth century, used humanitarian aid as a means for reinvigorating the religious rules of Islam in Bosnia-Herzegovina.[365] Through these activities, a once-homogeneous Bosnian Islam divided into differing strains—including groups that had not been present in the region until after 1989. Sufi missionaries, Wahhabis, and independent preachers of a "New Age" Islam became newly active.[366] The globalization of terrorist jihad also came to the Balkan Peninsula. Volunteer fighters for Syria and Iraq were recruited in Bosnia-Herzegovina, Macedonia, Albania, and Kosovo. The transit route for volunteers from western Europe who were headed to the war zones ran through the Balkans.[367]

Representatives of other religions, including Orthodox Christianity, sought to emancipate themselves from the nation-state and promote a transnational religious identity. To this point, the only significant pan-Orthodox movement had been associated with immigrants in the United States.[368] In the Balkan states, the Orthodox churches still largely understood themselves as protagonists of national identity. Thus, an independent Montenegrin Orthodox church formed after the dissolution of Yugoslavia. The Macedonian Orthodox church had already declared its autocephaly from the Serbian patriarchate in 1967.

China, a newcomer to the region, is pursuing its New Silk Road project, a southeastern European transport corridor that will serve as a gateway to all of Europe. By the end of 2017, Beijing had invested more than 10 billion dollars in industries and power plants—and in port, rail, and road infrastructure—to create transport connections and open access to cheap Chinese consumer goods. China continues to expand its financial institutions, loans, and trading networks with an eye to creating strategic partnerships, but also new dependencies.[369]

Global civil society has a greater presence in southeastern Europe today than ever before. The Yugoslav wars and subsequent era of reconstruction once drew so many organizations that cynics spoke of a "humanitarian invasion." Since the hundreds of bilateral and international donors and transnational nongovernmental organizations all support partners on site, an artificially inflated civil society "scene" has emerged.[370] German, European, and American political foundations continue to play an active role, along with private citizens such as the financial investor George Soros, who has directed billions of his earnings into the ex-communist countries to promote democracy through his Open Society Institute (today's Open Society Foundations).[371] Local civil society has become part of a greater transnational civil society. Many southeastern Europeans now advocate in a global arena for humanitarian causes such as the fight against poverty, environmental destruction, and war. They seek to influence global actors, including the United Nations, World Bank, and European Union. In this respect, the trend toward transnationalism has continued even after the end of the Yugoslav wars.[372]

Today, nowhere in southeastern Europe has been left untouched by globalization. In contrast to earlier eras, the "flows" of globalization are now direct, no longer mediated by metropolises and elites, as before the Second World War. Transnational corporations, labor migration, and the Internet are part of everyday life, even in rural areas.[373] A prototype of one such "global village" is, for example, the museum town of Koprivshtitsa, which we encountered in Chapter 5. Because of its remote location, the Bulgarian revolutionaries organized their April Uprising in the village about 150 years ago. Today an international folklore festival takes place here every year; its dance groups, choirs, and reenactments attract visitors and journalists from all over the world.[374]

Southeastern Europe's big cities have become home to migrants from distant continents. These newcomers have "globalized" the region's culture with their restaurants, grocery stores, and voluntary associations. Americanized and Europeanized styles of consumption are now accompanied by products from East Asia, especially electronics, clothing, and toys. But American advertising, business chains, movies, and television programming still predominate; an "Asianization" of southeastern Europe is out of the question. In this respect, too, the societies of western, eastern, and southeastern Europe have become remarkably similar. The same is true of demographic trends, industrialization, de-agrarianization, consumption patterns, lifestyles, social and professional structures, family models, gender roles, social inequality, attitudes, and values. Southeastern Europe today is part of the global information society.[375]

The darker sides of globalization have also become more prominent since 1989. As a crossroads between continents, southeastern Europe is a chief transit area toward the lucrative markets of western Europe for international organized crime.[376] Each year, sixty to sixty-five tons of heroin from Afghanistan travel through Turkey into Bulgaria. From there, the narcotics are transported along land routes to Romania or Macedonia, or by ship across the Black and Adriatic Seas. Tons of cannabis are cultivated in Albania and then sold in Germany, the Netherlands, and Italy. Cocaine from Latin America is likewise smuggled through southeastern Europe.[377] Yet the rates of crime for burglary, robbery, and assaults are no higher—and

Alexander memorial in Skopje, photographed by Dominic Dudley.

in some cases, significantly lower—than in western Europe. More private citizens own a firearm, legally or illegally, in Switzerland and Finland than in Bosnia-Herzegovina or Kosovo, relative to the total population.[378]

As the world grows together, the impulse to grapple with one's own past has also grown stronger. Projects investigating guilt and responsibility in the communist era are now under way, even if popular attitudes often fluctuate "between amnesia and nostalgia."[379] The former heads of state have been toppled from their pedestals and, in some cases, even prosecuted. The Dimitrov mausoleum was torn down in Bulgaria, and Ceaușescu's enormous presidential palace has been repurposed as the seat of Romania's parliament. Citizens' movements have called for lustration and a critical assessment of the communist past. In Romania, for example, the writer Ana Blandiana helped to establish the Sighet Memorial, a memorial and research center dedicated to the victims of Romanian communism and the anticommunist resistance, and a public authority responsible for the Securitate files.

Facing deep social instability and uncertain prospects for the future, many people prefer to seek refuge in an idealized past and a nostalgic reimagining of the communist era. "Yugo-nostalgia" and "Titostalgia" also represent a reaction against the new nationalism, which does not appeal to everyone in the successor states. Coming to terms with crimes of the Yugoslav wars remains a sensitive topic. Notable progress has been made in the arena of criminal justice, with the extradition of high-ranking defendants to The Hague, including the Serbian head of state Slobodan Milošević. But processes of collective repression have not yet been overcome. More than two decades after the war's end, many people remain unwilling to acknowledge that there were perpetrators as well as victims within their own nation.

Unresolved questions of identity continue to disrupt the relations of neighboring states. Since 1991, Macedonia and Greece have fought over ancient names and symbols, including the Vergina Sun from the era of Philip II, a stylized version of which adorns the Macedonian state flag today. The Greek government has accused Macedonia of irredentism and the usurping of national identity, and it long refused to recognize the name "Macedonia," thereby blocking the admission of its small neighbor into the EU and NATO. The Macedonian government escalated the conflict with its project Skopje 2014, spending millions of euros to enhance the appearance of the capital city with representative neoclassical structures and historical statues before a new government stopped the venture in early 2018.[380] The object of greatest contention was the seventy-two-foot-tall equestrian statue in Skopje's main square, facing toward Greece. The statue apparently depicts Alexander the Great, but is officially titled "Warrior on Horseback." Countless international attempts at mediation failed until the opposing parties finally agreed upon the name "Republic of North Macedonia." Although the compromise met with fierce resistance from nationalist parties in both countries, Macedonia's parliament voted to commence the renaming process in October 2018. In both states, the ancient era continues to provide the touchstone for a constructed identity that hearkens back to a distant, glorious past, with the storied Macedonian commander Alexander as its ideal embodiment.

Conclusion

Southeastern Europe and the World

THE BALKAN PENINSULA has been a crossroads for different empires, civilizations, and transcontinental networks of production and exchange since ancient times. People from the region forged connections with others wherever there was something to be experienced, discovered, or earned—around the Mediterranean and the Arabian Peninsula, in central and western Europe, Russia, and Scandinavia, as well as along the Silk Road and into central Asia, China, and Japan. In the modern era, the countries of Latin America, Africa, and Asia also became important partners. For more than two thousand years, political, social, economic, and cultural entanglements—both within southeastern Europe and with the rest of the world—have played a far greater role than is often depicted in national histories.

Over the centuries, the region's diverse cultural ties have given rise to a colorful—and constantly changing—mixture of peoples, languages, and civilizations. Mass migrations and expulsions brought together very different groups of people; names of ethnic communities adapted or disappeared, and religious and cultural contacts influenced identity formation. Foreign rule by Rome, Byzantium, and Venice—followed by the Ottoman, Habsburg, and Russian Empires—brought variegated and far-reaching imperial cultural influences to the region. Last but not least, in the modern era, the nation-state and its politics of identity, assimilation, and colonization emerged as a powerful and defining political force. Upon closer observation, theories about ethnogenesis and essentialist assumptions about the innate, timeless, and intrinsic character of individual peoples can be exposed either as myths or as historical and political constructions. Even so, today's nations in southeastern Europe emerged as the result of a long and complicated process of historical development that built on certain objective conditions, which first drew the attention of intellectuals and politicians, and later the masses. Scholars and politicians shaped and fostered their nations, but they did not freely invent them by their own imaginative force.

The cultural landscape of southeastern Europe encompasses an impressive diversity of faiths and religions. The division of the universal Roman Empire and world Christianity meant that Rome and Byzantium, the Latin and Greek Churches, competed for hegemony on the Balkan Peninsula. Even in the Middle Ages, their rivalry left some room for independent churches and "heretical" faith practices to develop. The Ottoman period brought conversions to Islam and, over time, the formation of new Muslim identities and national groups. Neither Islam nor Catholic or Orthodox Christianity were homogeneous, and the religions never formed distinct geopolitical units that were bound to states. Although the great empires and respective religious hierarchies fought each other as they strove for universal dominion in the era of the Ottoman conquests, there was no "clash of civilizations" that transcended historical eras. On the contrary, southeastern Europe was and still is characterized by many multicultural and multireligious contact zones and borderlands that challenge monolithic visions of identity, culture, and civilization. The protagonists of the modern nation-state were the first to be concerned with building communities that were as ethnically and culturally homogeneous as possible, with clearly defined territorial boundaries.

Because the Balkan peoples lived in a region that was economically and strategically important to the empires and great powers, it was their centuries-long fate to live under foreign rule. Most of the peoples were divided across multiple empires; they were at home in the Ottoman Empire, the Habsburg Monarchy, and Venice, and they possessed sizable diasporas in central Europe and throughout the Mediterranean. The identity of these peoples was not initially a matter of much concern for the multiethnic and multireligious empires of the Habsburgs and the Ottomans. These empires built legitimacy by granting local elites a certain degree of participation, in different ways. Their dominion remained relatively stable for centuries because dynastic rule and the ideology of empire were largely accepted by the subject peoples, and thus even had an integrative effect. Not least, the empires also protected economically useful groups such as long-distance traders, regardless of their religion.

Each of the empires stood under the hegemony of a single people and its culture—the German Austrians in the Habsburg Monarchy, the Italians in Venice, and the Turks in the Ottoman Empire. Other nationalities enjoyed only local administrative authority or religious autonomy, but they were excluded from effective participation in political, social, and economic life until the First World War. Under foreign rule, the Balkan provinces served first and foremost as colonies that provided the imperial core with taxes, raw materials, labor, and food. By the late eighteenth century, and particularly the nineteenth century, the vision of a political order in which nationalities could govern themselves had become increasingly prevalent. Intellectuals as well as political and economic elites began to question the imperial model of governance, which was ultimately deemed unacceptable by a majority of the population.

The Balkan peoples of the Middle Ages had been part of the Christian Occident and considered themselves its bulwark. The deep and long-lasting influence of Ottoman rule was a beneficial legacy as well as a curse for the Balkan peoples, in several different respects. First, their national identities and ideas of political order formed in dialogue with, and in opposition to, foreign despotic rule. Second, as the result of Ottoman conquest, the old Balkan nobility and non-Muslim landowning class eventually disappeared or became part of the Ottoman elite. This transformed local societies and delayed the development of an urban bourgeoisie. Third, a significant part of all wealth generated in the Balkan provinces ended up in Istanbul; the majority of Ottoman revenues derived from the peasantry. Fourth, Ottoman imperial culture profoundly influenced local architecture and everyday life, as well as local cuisine, music, languages, and literature. A final notable Ottoman legacy, and a significant departure from the Latin West, was the largely peaceful coexistence of religions. This saved the lives of many European Jews, from the Reconquista to the Holocaust.

Both the Ottomans and the Habsburgs sought universal dominion under a single dynasty and religion, leading to the collision of their empires in the Balkans and Mediterranean, in the Crusades and Ottoman Wars. In the age of exploration, beginning in the late fifteenth century, they became more interested in the world beyond Europe; the Habsburgs reached all the way to America, and the Ottomans pushed into Asia and

Africa. By the sixteenth century, voyages of discovery and advances in geography and astronomy allowed both cultures to develop not only a common understanding of the continents, the earth, and the universe but also shared perceptions and interpretations of their global context.

This global context was not an abstract force, but was shaped by people. The earliest cultural brokers and protagonists of cross-border networks were people with transcultural, or even global, biographies—for example, the Orthodox Herzegovinian merchant Sava Vladislavich (the emissary of Peter the Great who negotiated the border between Russia and China), or the Greek slave boy who made his career as the grand vizier Ibrahim Edhem in the nineteenth-century Ottoman Empire. Others, identified by scholars as "transimperial" or "transcultural" subjects, were already at home in multiple cultures because of their social background; they included dragomans, Phanariots, long-distance traders, and political émigrés.

Eastern and Western intellectual influences had commingled in southeastern Europe since ancient times. Scholars and clerics from the Balkans were involved in the production of geographic, astronomical, medical, and natural philosophical knowledge—for example, the monks in Dubrovnik who developed new medicines; the Serb, Romanian, and Bulgarian scribes who copied and added to philosophical texts; and distinguished scholars such as the Albanian astronomer Johannes Gazulus and the Croatian natural philosopher Ruđer Bošković, who invented new theories and devices to explain and survey the universe. Many were already aware of the global significance of their actions. In the midst of the great battles of the First World War, Nikola Tesla dreamed that his inventions would help to build a progressive and peaceful "wonder world."

The different positionality of groups like city-dwellers and peasants, scholars and priests, men and women, and Catholics and Muslims influenced their interpretations of the world well into the modern era. The Greek revolutionary Rhigas Velestinlis was already thinking in categories of enlightened cosmopolitanism around the year 1800, while a half century later the Bosnian kadi Mustafa Muhibbi still viewed the world exclusively through the lens of Islamic scholarship. Historical actors adopted very different strategies for coming to terms with the world. On the cusp of the modern era, the noblewoman Marija Giorgi Bona brought the world to Dubrovnik with the books in her salon, and the Romanian boyar Dinicu Golescu traveled through Europe and reported back to his countrymen about his amazing experiences. Although many people did not knowingly experience the world in this way, few were left untouched as it grew closer together. Even nomadic shepherds who lived apart from civilization felt certain price fluctuations when they occasionally visited regional markets to buy or sell goods.

Points of view differ as to when globalization—the closer economic, political, and cultural integration of the world—began. Since ancient and medieval times, southeastern Europe had participated in the transcontinental economic networks of the Mediterranean Sea, the Black Sea, and the Silk Road. After the northern Atlantic became the center of the world economy around 1600, the lands of southeastern Europe began to reorient themselves toward northwestern Europe. Demand in northwestern Europe stimulated production and exports in specific regions, encouraging a transition to the cultivation of global raw materials such as cotton.

After the mid-seventeenth century, southeastern Europe was drawn more closely into the emerging division of labor between capitalist core regions and those still defined by feudal relations and agriculture—between centers, peripheries, and semiperipheries. Southeastern Europe's role, which persisted into the modern era, was to supply foodstuffs and raw materials. A dangerous dependency on world markets and price fluctuations became apparent in many parts of southeastern Europe. The division of labor grew even more pronounced as England shifted to industrial mass production in the eighteenth century. Traditional trades such as spinning and weaving faced great competitive pressure in the rest of Europe and the Ottoman Empire, including the Balkans. Only a few specialized branches—such as *aba* and silk production—were able to keep pace or even expand, as long as they found long-distance markets. Growing integration within the world market brought the potential of greater sales and profits on one hand, but a dangerous dependency on the fluctuations of the global economy on the other. This had dramatic consequences in the nineteenth and particularly the twentieth centuries.

Globalization in the narrower sense was fully under way by the 1890s, but the process was inconsistent and contradictory. The rise of the industrialized states meant that the countries of southeastern Europe lagged further behind their global competitors. Most Balkan countries did not industrialize significantly until around 1900. They inherited social and economic structures that only gradually connected labor, property, capital, and goods with new methods of production. In addition, unequal trading relationships hindered innovation, investment, and growth in the peasant societies. Timing also played a role because the later a country began to industrialize, the more difficult it was to catch up. The Balkan states achieved independence just as an unfavorable world economy depressed agricultural prices, and as most states were moving toward economic nationalism and erecting new tariff barriers. Under these conditions, an export-oriented development strategy (increasing exports) and import substitution (building up national industries to avoid expensive imports) were difficult to implement. Thus, the Balkans remained—together with southern and eastern Europe and Ireland—the underdeveloped periphery of Europe.

Changes in the world economy and its inherent asymmetries altered perceptions of southeastern Europe. As the center of the world economy moved from the Mediterranean toward the Atlantic, the focal point of culture likewise moved north. The temporal coincidence of changes in the world economy with the "Ottoman threat" reinforced shifting perceptions. During the age of Enlightenment, the southeast moved to the margins of the western European mental map, becoming a peripheral, backward, and culturally inferior alter ego. As the Ottoman Empire violently dissolved over the course of the nineteenth century, the image of the Balkans underwent further transformation. Stereotypes of a cruel, despotic, but also beguiling and erotic Orient carried over to "the Balkans" and combined with imperialist ideologemes. The Balkanist discourse underscored the great powers' pretended obligation to civilize and restore order to such an apparently anarchic and violent region. The West is not entirely free of these attitudes today. During the Yugoslav wars of the 1990s, commentators revived the "powder keg" cliché that had emerged before the First World War. It could be used as justification for all kinds of actions: military interventions, protectorates, and the export of particular political systems. Then and now, certain actors in southeastern Europe have encouraged this discourse themselves, whether to mobilize world opinion or criticize their political opponents.

Although globalization and nationalization are often considered opposite phenomena, each has strongly influenced the other, from the late eighteenth century to the present day, in a variety of ways. The social basis of traditional agrarian societies faltered as a result of rising incomes and expanding global economic interconnectivity. At the end of the eighteenth century, new intellectual trends and ways of thinking emerged—including the Enlightenment, although this is sometimes purported not to have occurred in the region. New, upwardly mobile social groups including traders, shipowners, and manufacturers competed with old local elites, and cosmopolitan intellectuals began to see themselves as part of a pan-European and transatlantic enlightened public, who were rethinking politics and taking action within the context of global changes. As the world grew together over the course of the nineteenth century, new national forms of solidarity coalesced in the Balkans and elsewhere. The "polygenesis of nationalism" (Christopher Bayly) took place in an era of global revolution, even if the nationalisms in southeastern Europe had primarily local motivations: political, socioeconomic, and intellectual. But even at the beginning of the nineteenth century, rebels in Serbia and Greece communicated with leading politicians in neighboring countries, in Europe, and even in the United States. These kinds of relationships influenced not only political thought but also the national movements, revolutions, and newly established nation-states of the nineteenth and twentieth centuries.

As in other parts of the continent, nationalism in southeastern Europe joined with political liberalism around 1830. The motto "one nation—one state" specifically meant "one nation—one republic." The revolutionaries of 1848 from Croatia, Serbia, Romania, and Bulgaria maintained relations with each other and with compatriots from Italy, Poland, and Hungary. They read the same texts, formulated like-minded political goals, and chose similar forms of political action. Since then, political movements have no longer been limited to one national framework. All the great ideologies that formed over the course of the nineteenth and twentieth centuries were by nature European, or even global. Members of the liberal, socialist, and agrarian movements of the nineteenth century—and of course, communism, fascism, and pan-Islamism in the twentieth and twenty-first centuries—interacted on many levels, across countries and continents. Historical scholarship has insufficiently emphasized how important not only the European countries, including Russia, but also the United States were for southeastern Europe. Many revolutionaries saw the United States as a role model; the American colonies had successfully liberated themselves, adopted a republican constitution, and established a federation that offered a positive example to southeastern Europeans. The United States further showed how lingering restrictions on freedom, like slavery in Romania, might finally be abolished.

Subsequent historical developments—from national movements to the nation-state—also receive fresh emphasis in a transnational and global context. Global constellations and synchronic events played a significant role in advancing historical transformations. The Albanian example demonstrates how revolutionary changes in transportation and communication brought together groups that lived far apart, allowing politicians and intellectuals as well as migrant workers and political émigrés to act as agents of transterritorial national awareness and mobilization. They used far-flung locations as a political stage for promoting the nation-state, and for winning the support of co-nationals and the great powers. Voluntary associations and news media on both sides of the Atlantic became agents of nationalism and "glocalization" as intellectuals, politicians, liberation movements, and terrorists discovered an emerging world public as their key audience. In sum, interactions that transcended borders and continents were as important for nation-building as long-term diachronic processes in a single country.

Nineteenth-century nationalism inspired reflections about the political world order of the future. The cosmopolitan patriotism of the Enlightenment eventually merged into liberal republican nationalism; the solidarity of the world's peoples in the fight for freedom and unity—as paradigmatically invoked by Giuseppe Mazzini—became one of the movement's core principles. The liberal revolutionaries of southeastern Europe recognized that it would take concerted action at the European level (by Italians, Poles, Czechs, South Slavs, and other peoples) to topple the great empires. They did not merely seek to create nation-states, but a democratic community of nations and a democratic international order. Since then, both internationalism and nationalism have been important characteristics of southeastern European history in the nineteenth, twentieth, and twenty-first centuries.

As the world grew together on many different levels, the nation-state continued to gain importance in southeastern Europe. Already in the nineteenth century, it appeared to be the best means of protecting communities from globalized competition and encouraging further development. Governments were no longer responsible only for foreign relations and international agreements; growing economic interdependence gave the state an increasingly important role as the regulator of economic life. Competitive pressure and global economic crises reinforced the belief that it was the responsibility of the state to protect markets, stimulate production, provide social security, and promote the well-being of its citizens through authoritarian and protectionist measures. In fact, the southeastern European economies did make faster—if not always enduring—progress when the state intervened, and this proved to be true under quite different political systems. In the late nineteenth century, protective tariffs and state promotion of industry increased economic growth. State interventionism and public investment programs were a hallmark of the authoritarian regimes of the 1930s, and the socialist industrialization and modernization policy that followed after 1945.

Regardless of who governed them, nation-states saw themselves as cross-border advocates for members of their national group. The nineteenth-century nation-states thus continued a tradition that had begun with nationally minded intellectuals, revolutionaries, and irregular fighters. State agencies, authorities, and associations supported irredentism, financed voluntary fighters, and spread nationalist propaganda abroad. After the First World War, the minorities question became an important field of activity. Before and after 1945, there were ministries and offices that attended to guest workers and the overseas diaspora, which both the bourgeois and communist regimes viewed as an economic and political resource.

The formation of nation-states created new kinds of fragmentation, but communication and travel provided new opportunities for ideas and beliefs to overcome political borders. The religions began to understand and organize themselves as transcontinental, global communities. Worldwide Jewish, Islamic, and Christian confessional publics and political movements (such as pan-Islamism and Zionism) that transcended the nation-state first emerged in the nineteenth century. At the same time, supraregional networking and deterritorialization accelerated differentiation within the faith communities. Thus, certain religious groups—Protestant sects in the nineteenth century, and Islamic movements such as the Muslim Brotherhood and the Wahhabis in the twentieth century—gained a foothold in southeastern Europe for the very first time. Neither nationalism nor globalization condemned the religions to irrelevance, even if their position in world society was henceforth subject to constant negotiation. In a secularized world, the religions developed from primarily spiritual communities into broader cultural and political systems that lent meaning and order.

The Eastern Question, the decline of the Ottoman Empire, had been one of the most important foreign policy challenges for the European system of states since the eighteenth century. It became particularly explosive in the nineteenth century, as the Habsburg and Romanov Empires pushed toward the Balkans. Germany, France, and Great Britain also sought to assert their political, military, strategic, and economic interests in the region. The Balkan Peninsula was a small but central element in the global arena where the great powers competed for influence. It also played an indirect role in broader imperialist rivalries—as a zone of military deployment, as a transit area to overseas colonies, or even as their substitute. This created both advantages and disadvantages for the countries in the region. On one hand, they were able to find powerful supporters for their own goals (like independence); on the other, they were at the mercy of external interests.

In all eras, competition, isolationism, and hostility have been part of globalization. As trade, migration, conquests, and colonialism brought more and more groups into closer contact, those who felt threatened by globalization more emphatically articulated discourses of isolationism and ethnically exclusive ideologies. In the last third of the nineteenth century, liberal patriotism evolved into modern mass nationalism, adopting increasingly aggressive and ethnically exclusive features. The retreat into tradition, religiosity, and feelings of national superiority was part ideology, part emotional reaction to transformative social and political changes; this connection was later evident in the twentieth century, too. Ethnic nationalism bundled together fears of economic decline and loss of status—outgrowths of urban civilization and cultural modernity that were widespread among the middle classes and the educated bourgeoisie. Thinkers of this stripe saw ethnic homogenization as a means of uniting the nation and strengthening its defenses against external threats. Mistrust of bourgeois democracy grew as the twentieth century progressed, and extreme ideologies on the left and right became more appealing. However, even in eras of heightened nationalism, a strong countermovement and dedicated supporters of internationalism continued to thrive. Since the late nineteenth century, men and women have been active in a growing number of different international organizations, specialized societies, and world associations.

Aggressive nationalism, chauvinism, and militarism drove the governments into the Balkan Wars in 1912/13, leading to massive "ethnic cleansing" that became paradigmatic for the twentieth century. These stood in continuity with past centuries, although the expulsions of earlier eras tended to have religious rather than ethnic motivations. Then and now, these acts of violence have occurred whenever conquests brought regime change, or empires and states fell apart, opening the door for rival groups to fight over state boundaries and the political order. Most recently, the dissolution of Yugoslavia in the 1990s unleashed a series of wars, newly founded nation-states, and "ethnic cleansings." This process has not yet ended, as diverse conflicts about nation-states, territories, and identities remain unresolved at the beginning of the twenty-first century—including, for example, the Serbian and Albanian questions, which involve multiple countries. It should not be forgotten that "ethnic cleansing" in the Balkans resembled the actions of the colonial powers outside Europe; in each case, unwanted population groups were expelled and harassed as the result of new territorial acquisitions. Both proceedings had the same ideological roots. But the colonial states did not want "civilized" Christian peoples in the middle of Europe to fall victim to this kind of politics, especially when these states' own strategic or economic interests were involved.

Since the early modern era, the Balkans have served as a testing ground for new forms of crisis management and instruments of diplomacy and international law. Beginning in the fifteenth century, the Christian and Islamic world adopted regular procedures for trade and maritime travel around the Mediterranean, and other arrangements for coexistence, diplomacy, and international law. The Greek war of independence at the beginning of the nineteenth century introduced the "humanitarian intervention," and a few decades later the powers tested out their first international police mission in Crete and Macedonia. The first organized population transfers in Europe also took place in the Balkans. The resettlement of undesired ethnic and religious groups became a model of interstate conflict management—first, when the Muslim population was forcibly moved from "European Turkey" to Anatolia, then in formally arranged population exchanges (as outlined in the Treaty of Lausanne in 1923), and finally in the Potsdam Agreement, which sanctioned the mass resettlement of the German population from eastern (but not southeastern) Europe in 1945. In addition, the first attempts to fight international terrorism at the level of the League of Nations got their start in the Balkans, after the Yugoslav king and French foreign minister were assassinated in 1934. Finally, the Yugoslav wars of succession triggered an array of innovations, such as the establishment of a permanent International Criminal Court and the UN-endorsed principle of "responsibility to protect"—the right, but not the obligation, of the international community to intervene militarily on behalf of persecuted populations in other states, also known as "humanitarian intervention."

The small, young, and relatively poor nation-states of southeastern Europe were more interested than the great powers in a world order shaped by international law and multilateralism, since their existence depended on it. The most important forum after the First World War was the League of Nations, where the successor states of the multinational empires exchanged information, presented political concerns, implemented decisions about cross-border problems, and helped to create global regimes. Efforts to showcase national achievements in the best possible light resulted in an "internationalization of nationalism," whether at world exhibitions or soccer world championships. After 1945, Albania, Romania, Yugoslavia, and sometimes Bulgaria presented themselves as independent, freethinking actors within the United Nations system. They pursued an agenda oriented toward national interests, dressed up in the discourse of international friendship and solidarity. They advocated for the democratization of the world organization and greater rights of participation, the decolonization of the Third World, the expansion of global governance and international law, and a just order for communications and the world economy—all concerns that fit within the ideological system of socialist internationalism, but that were also oriented toward protecting the smaller, poorer, and dependent states and their national interests from great power dominance.

In the twentieth century, too, the Balkans remained an object of great power rivalry, even if attention shifted to regions outside of Europe, especially after 1945. Southeastern Europe was linked to other regional theaters of the Cold War—namely, the Middle East and Asia. Yugoslavia embraced India's policy of active neutrality to create its doctrine of active coexistence, and Arab national politicians such as Gamal Abdel Nasser and Muammar Gaddafi looked to Tito as a role model. Following the Yugoslav example, they sought to modernize and emancipate Egypt and Libya from superpower hegemony. These and other countries worked together in the Non-Aligned Movement, which created a new dynamic within the bipolar international system.

Within the world economic order after 1945, the states of southeastern Europe assumed a role similar to that of the Third World. Once again, they were primarily producers of raw materials for the industrial nations. Even before the Second World War, Argentinean and Brazilian economists had adapted and developed Romanian economic theories, seeking a path of autocentric development and an escape from dependency. After the Second World War, the Group of 77 formed within the United Nations to fight for a New International Economic Order. Through the Non-Aligned Movement, Yugoslavia became a spokesperson for the Third World on several issues. Tito understood how to rally the non-European developing countries behind him, so that he was able to represent his own country's interests more effectively.

From the nineteenth century until the present day, regional cooperation has helped to structure the international order of nation-states. Liberals and socialists, and later agrarians and communists, believed that a Balkan federation could become an instrument for securing peace and prosperity. They envisioned a confederation of nations, along the lines of the United States or Switzerland. The more aggressive nationalism and chauvinism became in the last third of the nineteenth century, the greater the appeal of a Balkan federation as a project for the future. Communists, socialists, and agrarians adopted it in their party programs after the First World War, and millions cast votes in favor of the proposal during the interwar era. After 1945, Tito took up the idea by suggesting that Yugoslavia, Albania, Bulgaria, and Greece could join together in a regional confederation. But Stalin put his foot down and stopped the project, even ousting Yugoslavia from the Eastern bloc. In the 1950s, Romania proposed a nuclear-free zone for the Balkan Peninsula, but this undertaking was foiled by American opposition.

Even in times of heightened nationalism, protectionism, and political isolationism—before and after 1945—global culture has continued to act as a force of convergence and harmonization, including Europeanization and Americanization. Southeastern Europe experienced a burst of cultural globalization in the 1920s and then again in the 1960s, due to an import-oriented strategy of growth, greater travel freedoms, and an orientation toward consumerism and Western culture. Independent of political differences, the societies in Europe (including southeastern Europe) unintentionally became more similar—with respect to social stratification, demography, education, the spread of media and technology, as well as patterns of consumption, lifestyles, and values. These societies simultaneously became more complex, and social inequality grew, particularly after 1989.

Events and historical turning points with a transnational character multiplied as the modern era progressed. The year 1789 united Europe's enlightened thinkers, and 1848 brought together national liberal revolutionaries. The First and Second World Wars were global by nature; despite far-reaching differences, they created common experiences. Apart from these conflicts, the Spanish Civil War became a key moment for the communists in 1936;

it made internationalism a lived experience, strengthened communist net-works across state borders, and—although not foreseen at the time—prepared activists for the partisan battles of the Second World War. The student move-ments of 1968 similarly united Eastern and Western youth protesters—creating not only an intellectual, biographical, and organizational bond across continents but also an opportunity to translate local concerns into a universal language. The student movements made "Vietnam" a metaphor for anti-imperialism, and in eastern and southeastern Europe they became a stand-in for the critique of Soviet dominance and the lack of freedom in the socialist systems. The student movements became the nucleus of a transnational civil society that prepared the way for broader democratic change. The upheavals of 1989—and unfortunately, the Yugoslav wars as well—ultimately became transnational and global events.

The collapse of communism created the conditions for a new beginning, although this was overshadowed by the bloody dissolution of Yugoslavia. At the time, there was much talk about the "return of history" after the end of the East-West conflict. In fact, multiple experiences felt like déjà vu: hyperbolic nationalism, "ethnic cleansing," and mass crimes seemed to be revenants from the distant past, while alliances and enmities from the two world wars appeared to rise again. But much had also changed since these past historical eras. The different international actors arrived at a common Balkan policy, and the states of southeastern Europe ultimately built democratic systems and largely normalized their relations with one another. Today, the great majority of the governments and populations share a pro-European orientation. After the downturn of the 1990s, Slo-venia, Croatia, Bulgaria, and Romania have come closer to the average per capita income of Europe as a whole—not only as a consequence of EU membership but also as a condition for accession. This suggests that the Balkan countries are in no way fated to remain in the poorhouse of Eu-rope, but that they themselves have the resources to change their difficult situations. And it further shows that interests and political constellations can transform fundamentally as part of the historical process.

What can be gained for the future by studying the past ultimately de-pends on one's perspective and the kinds of questions one poses. And these questions must always be formulated anew, since the present itself is rap-idly changing. In this spirit, I conclude with words attributed to Mark Twain, a good friend of Nikola Tesla: "History does not repeat itself, but it rhymes."

Chronology

1054	"Great Schism" between the Eastern and Western Churches
1071	Battle of Manzikert: Byzantium is defeated by the Seljuks
1102	*Pacta Conventa:* Hungarian royal house accepts Croatian crown
Mid-12th century	Migration of Saxons to Transylvania
From 1166	Founding of the Serbian kingdom under Stefan Nemanja
1180–1204	Bosnian kingdom under Ban Kulin
1185–1393	Second Bulgarian Empire
1204	Constantinople falls to Crusaders
1204–1261	Latin kingdom (and patriarchate)
1217	Serbian kingdom under Stefan Nemanjić
1219	Serbian church under Sava
13th century	Osman establishes his emirate
Mid-14th century	Emergence of the principalities of Wallachia and Moldavia
1346	Stefan Dušan is crowned tsar (emperor) of Serbia
1354	Ottoman conquest of Gallipoli
1371	Serbian defeat in the Battle of Maritsa
1389	Battle of Kosovo
1392/93	Ottoman conquest of Bulgaria
1417	Ottoman conquest of southern Albania
1443–1468	Skanderbeg's uprising in central Albania
1444	Battle at Varna
1448	Second Battle of Kosovo
1453	Fall of Constantinople (end of the Byzantine Empire)
1459	Ottoman conquest of the Serbian despotate
1460	Ottoman conquest of the Peloponnese
1463	Ottoman conquest of Bosnia
1479	Ottoman conquest of Albania
1492	Columbus's first voyage to America
1497/98	First recorded voyage from Europe to India via the Atlantic Ocean
1516/17	Ottoman conquest of Syria and Egypt
1517	Ottoman sultan assumes the caliphate
1522	Ottoman conquest of Rhodes
1526	Hungarians defeated by the Ottomans at the Battle of Mohács
1529	Ottomans' first siege of Vienna
1541	Autonomous principality of Transylvania under Ottoman sovereignty
1566	Beginning of the Habsburgs' second Turkish War

1568	Peace of Adrianople (recognition of Ottoman sovereignty over the Danubian Principalities and Transylvania)
1571	Ottoman defeat in the sea battle near Lepanto
1630	*Statuta Valachorum*
1683	Second siege of Vienna; beginning of the Great Turkish War
1690	Great migration of the Serbs
1691	Transylvania joins the Habsburg Empire; *Diploma Leopoldinum*
1699	Peace of Karlowitz (Hungary and Slavonia join the Habsburg Empire)
1711	Beginning of Phanariot rule in Moldavia (1715 in Wallachia)
1718	Peace of Passarowitz
1739	Peace of Belgrade
1774	Peace of Küçük Kaynarca
1791	*Supplex Libellus Valachorum* in Transylvania
1804–1813	First Serbian Uprising under Djordje Petrović Karadjordje
1814	Founding of the Filiki Eteria
1815	Second Serbian Uprising under Miloš Obrenović
1821	Uprisings in Wallachia and Moldavia; end of Phanariot rule
1826	Disbanding of the janissary corps in the Ottoman Empire
1827	London convention on the founding of a Greek state; Battle of Navarino
1828 / 29	Russo-Ottoman War
1828	Danubian Principalities become protectorate of Russia
1829	Peace of Adrianople
1830	London Conference (recognition of an independent Greece; Miloš Obrenović becomes the hereditary prince of Serbia; Organic Statute for the Danubian Principalities)
1832	Otto of Wittelsbach becomes King of Greece
1839	Hatt-i Sharif of Gülhane (Tanzimat)
1848 / 49	Revolutions in the Habsburg Empire and the Danubian Principalities
1852	Montenegro becomes a hereditary principality
1853–1856	Crimean War
1856	Treaty of Paris; Hatt-i Hümayun (Christians receive equal legal status in the Ottoman Empire)
1859	Alexandru Ioan Cuza is elected prince of Moldavia and Wallachia

1861	Unification of the Danubian Principalities
1862	King Otto of Greece is deposed
1866	Alexandru Ioan Cuza is deposed; Charles of Hohenzollern-Sigmaringen becomes Carol I, prince of Romania
1867	Austro-Hungarian compromise establishing the Dual Monarchy
1868	Hungarian-Croatian compromise (Nagodba)
1870	Bulgarian exarchate
1876	April Uprising in Bulgaria
1877	Russo-Ottoman War; Romania declares independence
1878	Treaty of San Stefano; Albanian League of Prizren; Congress of Berlin (independence for Montenegro, Romania, and Serbia; autonomy for Bulgaria and eastern Rumelia)
1881	Kingdom of Romania
1882	Kingdom of Serbia
1885	Autocephaly of the Romanian Orthodox church; unification of eastern Rumelia and the Bulgarian Principality; Serbo-Bulgarian War
1887	Ferdinand of Saxe-Coburg becomes prince of Bulgaria
1893	Founding of Internal Macedonian Revolutionary Organization
1896/97	Anti-Ottoman uprising on Crete
1903	Assassination of King Alexander Obrenović in Serbia; Ilinden Uprising in Macedonia; Mürzsteg Agreement
1908	Young Turk revolution; Albanian National Congress; annexation of Bosnia-Herzegovina; Kingdom of Bulgaria
1910	Prince Nicholas of Montenegro takes the title of king
1912/13	First Balkan War; Albania declares independence
1913	Second Balkan War; Assassination of King George I of Greece; London Ambassadors' Conference (independence of Albania); Peace of Bucharest
1914	William of Wied becomes prince of Albania; assassination of Archduke Francis Ferdinand of Austria, heir presumptive to the Austro-Hungarian throne, in Sarajevo
1914–1918	First World War
1915	Yugoslav Committee
1917	Corfu Declaration for the unification of the South Slavs
1918	Kingdom of Serbs, Croats, and Slovenes (SHS) is founded
1919–1922	Greco-Turkish War

1919/20	Paris peace treaties
1920–1938	Little Entente
1921	Vidovdan Constitution in the SHS state
1923	Treaty of Lausanne; proclamation of the Turkish republic; Ferdinand I is crowned King of Romania
1924	Greek Republic
1925	Albanian Republic
1926/27	First and second Tirana Pacts between Italy and Albania
1928	Albanian monarchy under King Zog I
1929	Yugoslav royal dictatorship and Kingdom of Yugoslavia
1930	First Balkan Conference in Athens
1934	Balkan Pact; Bulgarian coup; King Alexander is assassinated in Marseille
1938	Royal dictatorship of Carol II in Romania; first Vienna Award
1939	Italian occupation of Albania; German-Soviet Nonaggression Pact; Germany invades Poland; beginning of Second World War
1940	Second Vienna Award; Soviet occupation of Bessarabia; Italy invades Greece
1941	Romania, Bulgaria, and Yugoslavia join the Tripartite Pact; coup in Belgrade; Germany invades Yugoslavia and Greece
1941–1945	Second World War in Southeastern Europe
1942	United States declares war on Bulgaria and Romania; founding of the Albanian National Liberation Front and the Anti-Fascist Council for the National Liberation of Yugoslavia (AVNOJ)
1943	Second AVNOJ session in Jajce; Italy surrenders
1944	Antonescu arrested in Romania; Red Army invades Romania and Bulgaria; Belgrade and Tirana are liberated
1945	End of the Second World War
1946–1949	Greek Civil War
1947	Paris peace treaties between the Allies and Bulgaria, Italy, Romania, and Hungary; founding of the Cominform
1948	Yugoslavia is excluded from the Cominform
1949	Founding of Comecon and NATO
1954	London memorandum on the administration of Trieste
1955	Founding of the Warsaw Pact; Albania, Bulgaria, and Romania join the UN; Bandung Conference

1956	Uprising in Hungary; Todor Zhivkov assumes power in Bulgaria
1958	Soviet troops leave Romania
1960	Independence of Cyprus
1961	Founding of the Non-Aligned Movement in Belgrade
1964	Founding of the Group of 77
1965	Nicolae Ceaușescu becomes party leader in Romania
1967–1974	Military dictatorship in Greece
1968	Suppression of the Prague Spring; Albania leaves the Warsaw Pact
1971	Croatian Spring
1974	Greek monarchy is abolished; Turkish military intervention in Cyprus
1975	Final Act of the Commission on Security and Cooperation in Europe, in Helsinki; Treaty of Osimo (resolution of the Trieste question)
1980	Death of Tito
1981	Greece joins the European Community (EC)
1983	Turkish Republic of Northern Cyprus
1985	Death of Enver Hoxha
1989	Collapse of the communist regimes in Bulgaria, Romania, Czechoslovakia, and Hungary
1990	Multiparty elections in Bulgaria, Romania, and the Yugoslav republics; regime change in Albania
1991	Slovenia, Croatia, and Macedonia declare independence; beginning of the Yugoslav wars of succession in Slovenia and Croatia
1992	Recognition of Slovenia and Croatia by the EC; declaration of independence and beginning of war in Bosnia-Herzegovina
1993	Macedonia accepted into the UN as "The Former Yugoslav Republic of Macedonia" (FYROM); establishment of the International Criminal Tribunal for the former Yugoslavia (ICTY) in The Hague
1995	Croatian military offensives Bljesak and Oluja; Dayton Agreement
1997	Rebellion and state crisis in Albania
from 1997	Guerrilla war in Kosovo

1999	NATO intervention in the Kosovo War; Stability Pact for Southeastern Europe
2001	Conflict in Macedonia; Ohrid Framework Agreement
2003	EU Thessaloniki Summit offers "European perspective" to the Western Balkans
2004	Slovenia joins the EU
2007	Romania and Bulgaria join the EU
2008	Kosovo gains independence
2013	Croatia joins the EU

Glossary

aba: Woolen cloth

aga *(ağa):* "Older brother," lord, village leader, estate owner, janissary officer

ahdname: Capitulations

akçe: Small silver coin (and later unit of account); replaced by the kurus

akinji (akıncı): "Stormers," irregular light cavalry

askeri: "Soldiers"; Ottoman elites who were exempt from paying taxes

ayan: Muslim notable, local elite

ban (banus): Slavic title for a ruler or viceroy

bashi-bazouk (başıbozok): Literally, "crazy heads"; Muslim irregular troops

bektashi (bektaşi): Dervish order (see *dervish*) founded by Haji Bektash

berat: Diploma (patent) of appointment from the sultan, which affirmed certain powers and privileges

bey *(beğ):* Lord, prince, commander

beylerbey (beğlerbeğ): Provincial governor

beylik (beğlik): Principality, province

boza: Drink of fermented millet

čaršija: Bazaar, shopping street

Chetniks *(četnici):* Serbian irregular fighters

çiftlik: Originating in the late Roman Empire, a small parcel of farmland that could be worked with a team of oxen; beginning in the eighteenth century, also the large estate of an *ayan*

colonatus: Tenant farming

čorbadžija (çorbacı): Bulgarian notables or representatives in local government

dahije: Renegade janissary leaders

dervish *(derviş):* "Member of a brotherhood," member of a Muslim order

Glossary

devshirme (devşirme): Child levy

dhimmi: "Protected persons" (Christians and Jews in the Ottoman Empire)

dimotiki: Demotic Greek; the modern vernacular form of the Greek language

dragoman: Interpreter, translator

eyalet: Large province overseen by a bey until 1884, then called "vilayet"

falaka: Foot whipping, or bastinado

firman: Decree (from the sultan)

gajtan: Piping or braid

gazi: Warrior for Islam

giaour: Infidel, nonbeliever

gurbetçi: Migrant laborers or guest workers

haiduks: Hungarian border soldiers in the Turkish wars; Slavic irregular fighters

hamam: Public bath

han: Older title for a Turkish ruler; commercial building; hostel for caravans

haraç: Ottoman land or head tax

harem: The part of a house occupied only by women and children

Hatt-i Sharif: Decree from the sultan

herem: Jewish excommunication

hoja: Muslim schoolmaster; religious teacher; imam

hospodar: Romanian title for a ruler

janissary: Member of the elite infantry that answered directly to the sultan

kadi *(kadı):* Muslim judge, head of a judicial district

kanun: Ottoman secular / imperial law

klephts: Literally, "thieves"; Greek armed bands of robbers; freedom fighters

kmets: Tenant farmers

knez: Serbian village leader, prince

kocabaşi: Greek representatives in local government; Greek notables

komitadji: "Committee members"; rebel bands or irregular fighters against
    Ottoman rule

komšiluk: Small gates, can also mean "neighborhood"

kul: Military slave, member of a caste that answered directly to the sultan

kurus *(kuruş):* Small silver coin

madrasa: Islamic school

malikane: Ottoman tax farming system with lifetime contracts, introduced in the
    late seventeenth century

mahalle (mahale): City district

martolos (armotoloi): Auxiliary military troops that were recruited from the
    Christian population of the Ottoman Empire

millet: Name for non-Muslim religious communities; later, nation

molla: Judge of an important city, high-ranking *kadi,* scholar

Glossary

Morlachs (Maurovlachs): Community of people in the Adriatic coastal areas

mutasarrif (mutasarrıf): Governor of a *sancak*

mütesellim: Deputy governor, financial administrator in a *sancak*

opanki: Traditional leather shoes

örf: Ottoman customary law

pasha *(paşa):* High-ranking Ottoman titleholder; later, general

pashalik (paşalık): Territory administered by a pasha

pečalbari: Seasonal itinerant laborers (from Serbia and Macedonia)

Phanariots: The Greeks of Istanbul, named after the city's Fener (Phanar) district; group of influential Greek families who also held political office

reaya: Tax-paying lower classes; later, only Christian lower classes

reis-ul-ulema: Highest-ranking Islamic official in Bosnia-Herzegovina; grand mufti

Sabor: Croatian assembly (Diet), parliament

šajak: Cloth

salaf / Salafism: Literally, "ancestors, forefathers"; ultra-conservative Islamist movement

sancak: Military district or province

seraglio: Palace of the sultan

serhad: Border area

sharia *(şaria / şeriat):* Canonical law that also governs relations between people and God, draws no distinction between religious and secular spheres

sipahi (spahi): Cavalryman granted a fief *(timar)*

Skupština: Serbian and Yugoslav parliament

Sufi: Islamic mystic (see also *dervish*)

sultan: Islamic sovereign

Tanzimat: "Reordering"; describes the era of Ottoman reforms between 1839 and 1876

tekke: Monastery (see also *dervish*)

timar: Fief for a cavalryman *(sipahi)*

türbe: Mausoleum

ulema: Islamic religious scholars

umma: Islamic community of all believers

Uskoks: Orthodox Balkan refugees

Ustasha: Croatian fascists ("rebels")

Vidovdan: Feast day of Saint Vitus (June 28)

vilayet: Administrative division; large province overseen by a bey, composed of multiple *sancaks* (called *eyalet* until 1864)

vizier *(wezir):* "Friend and helper"; leader or minister of a central administration

voivode (voyvode / voyvoda): Title of regents in Christian principalities; administrator of land granted by the state

voynuks: Christian auxiliary soldiers

waqf (vakf/ vakıf): "Pious foundation"; it supported mosques, madrasas, and other religious causes, in addition to caring for the poor and the sick

zadruga: Literally, "house communion"; extended peasant family that functioned as an economic collective, found throughout the central regions of southeastern Europe

Notes

Introduction

1. Todorova, *Imagining;* Said, *Orientalism.*
2. For Balkan history, see Mazower, *Balkans;* Wachtel, *Balkans in World History.*
3. Geyer and Bright, "World History."
4. Bayly, *Birth,* 2.
5. Drace-Francis, "Südosteuropakonzept"; Drace-Francis, "Prehistory."
6. As defined by Kenneth Pomeranz in *Great Divergence.*
7. Hausberger, *Globale Lebensläufe.*
8. Bayly, "Globalization."
9. Reinhard, Introduction, 9; Abu-Lughod, *Before European Hegemony.*
10. Iriye, *Cultural Internationalism.*
11. *Translator's note:* Because there have been many different names and spellings for cities, regions, and people over the centuries, some inconsistencies are unavoidable. In the interest of readability, the book generally uses the most familiar English forms, even if sites are officially identified otherwise today (for example, Bucharest is used here instead of Bucureşti, and Kosovo instead of Kosova).

1. Southeastern Europe before 1500

1. Demandt, *Alexander der Große,* 405ff.; Veloudis, *Alexander der Große,* 44ff.
2. An exception is Hösch, *Balkanländer.*
3. Boué, *La Turquie d'Europe,* 1.
4. Seidl and Ende, *Ami Boué,* 199.

5. *Rumeli und Bosna,* xii.

6. Mazower, *Balkans,* xxvff.

7. Cvijić, *Balkansko poluostrvo,* 13ff.

8. Mazower, *Balkans,* xxviii–xxix.

9. Klaniczay, Werner, and Gecser, *Multiple Antiquities.*

10. Sanader, *Dalmatia,* 19ff.

11. Demandt, *Alexander der Große,* 56ff.; Bengtson, *Philipp und Alexander,* 9–10.

12. Proeva, *Studii;* Kotsakis, "The Past Is Ours."

13. Bengtson, *Philipp und Alexander,* 9–10.

14. Wilkes, *Illyrians,* 87ff.

15. Budak, *Hrvatska povijest,* 417.

16. Fine, *Early Medieval Balkans,* 10.

17. Gudea and Lobüscher, *Dacia.*

18. Gabucci, *Rom,* 145ff.

19. Gudea and Lobüscher, *Dacia,* 89ff.

20. Sanader, *Dalmatia,* 95ff.

21. Mirković, *Moesia Superior,* 64ff.

22. Ibid., 82ff.

23. Gudea and Lobüscher, *Dacia,* 4ff., 58ff.

24. Georgescu, *Romanians,* 8ff.; Pop, *Romanians and Romania,* 19ff.

25. A summary of the different theories can be found in Schramm, *Donau-grenze,* 275ff.

26. Schmitt, *Die Albaner.*

27. Bartl, *Albanien,* 18ff.; Schmitt, *Die Albaner,* 16ff.

28. Malcolm, *Bosnia,* 5.

29. Pohl, *Awaren,* 121.

30. Ibid., 96.

31. Ziemann, *Wandervolk,* 106.

32. Gimbutas, *Slavs,* 58ff.

33. Fine, *Early Medieval Balkans,* 26.

34. Ibid., 49ff.

35. Curta, *Making of the Slavs;* Dzino, *Becoming Slav.*

36. Seidl, *Bayern in Griechenland,* 44.

37. Jireček, *Geschichte,* 1:113ff.

38. Gimbutas, *Slavs,* 133ff.

39. Budak, *Etnogeneza Hrvata;* Fine, *When Ethnicity Did Not Matter.*

40. Aladžov, "Religion."

41. Ziemann, *Wandervolk.*

42. Hösch, *Balkanländer,* 21.

43. Noble, *Roman Provinces,* 3ff.; Kaiser, "Archaeology and Ideology."

44. Elbern, *Rom,* 114.

45. Lilie, *Byzanz,* 7.

46. Ibid., 24.

47. Papadakis, "Historical Tradition."

48. Oeldemann, *Kirchen des Christlichen Ostens,* 34ff.

49. Obolensky, *Byzantine Commonwealth,* 272ff.

50. Mirković, *Moesia Superior,* 98ff.

51. Bajić, *Bogovi starih slovena,* 16ff.

52. Belaj, *Hod kroz godinu.*

53. Gimbutas, *Slavs,* 151ff.

54. Aladžov, "Religion."

55. Čajkanović, *Stara srpska religija,* 161ff.

56. Kreuter, *Vampirglaube.*

57. Boué, *Europäische Türkei,* 413.

58. Pitz, *Ökumene,* 67ff.

59. Budak, *Hrvatska povijest,* 59ff.

60. Belaj, "Postati kršćaninom," 11.

61. Bajić, *Slovenski bogovi.*

62. Jireček, *Geschichte,* 1:175–76.

63. Hannick, "Byzantinische Missionen," 354ff.

64. Budak, *Hrvatska povijest,* 82ff.

65. Fine, *Ancient Greeks,* 113ff.

66. Oeldemann, *Kirchen des Christlichen Ostens,* 133ff.

67. Schachner, "Kirche."

68. Jireček, *Geschichte,* 2–1:53.

69. Oeldemann, *Kirchen des Christlichen Ostens,* 171.

70. Hristov, "Athos," 39ff.

71. Obolensky, *Byzantine Commonwealth,* 288.

72. Klaić, *Povijest Hrvata,* 82–83.

73. Steindorff, *Kroatien,* 35; Schmitt, *Das venezianische Albanien,* 187–88.

74. Kočev, *Christijanstvoto,* 46ff.

75. *Krunisanje,* 6ff.

76. Hösch, *Geschichte des Balkans,* 39.

77. Jarnut and Wemhoff, *Umbruch zur Erneuerung.*

78. Borst, *Katharer,* 75.

79. Čajkanović, *Stara srpska religija,* 226ff; Dragojlović, *Istorija filozofske misli,* 8ff.

80. Lambert, *Cathars,* 29ff.

81. Lambert, *Medieval Heresy,* 16.

82. Borst, *Welten des Mittelalters,* 203–4, 241.

83. Ibid., 208.

84. Runciman, *Medieval Manichee*, 94ff; Borst, *Katharer*, 104ff.

85. Lambert, *Medieval Heresy*, 161.

86. Malcolm, *Bosnia*, 11.

87. Hösch, "Bemerkungen."

88. Džaja, *Bosnische Kirche*, 45–46.

89. Fine, *Bosnian Church*, 12.

90. Džambo, *Franziskaner*, 53; Fine, *Bosnian Church*, 289ff.

91. Džambo, *Franziskaner*, 48–49, 139.

92. Džaja, *Konfessionalität*.

93. Ostrogorsky, *Byzantinische Geschichte*, 156–57; Ostrogorski, "Vizantija i južni sloveni."

94. Ferluga, *Byzantium*, 300.

95. Stephenson, *Balkan Frontier*, 319–20.

96. Jireček, *Geschichte*, 1:113ff.

97. Budak, *Hrvatska povijest*, 146ff.

98. Ziemann, *Wandervolk*, 413ff; Slatarski, *Geschichte der Bulgaren*.

99. Obolensky, *Byzantine Commonwealth*, 272ff.

100. Ostrogorsky, *Byzantinische Geschichte*, 150.

101. Klaić, *Povijest Hrvata*, 71ff.

102. Fine, *Early Medieval Balkans*, 248ff.

103. Budak, *Hrvatska povijest*, 159ff; Ostrogorski, "Vizantija i južni sloveni."

104. Hösch, *Balkanländer*, 35.

105. Bojović, *Kraljevstvo i svetost*, 351ff.

106. Fine, *Late Medieval Balkans*, 7ff.

107. *Krunisanje*, 6ff.

108. Buchenau, *Orthodoxie und Katholizismus*, 42.

109. Obolensky, *Byzantine Commonwealth*, 347.

110. *Krunisanje*, 6ff.

111. Budak, *Hrvatska povijest*, 407ff.

112. Reinhard, *Staatsgewalt*, 80ff.

113. Jireček, *Geschichte*, 2–1:11–12, 85.

114. Lešić, *Istorija*, 19ff.

115. Obolensky, *Byzantine Commonwealth*, 351ff.

116. Onasch, *Einführung*, 85ff.

117. Ćurčić, *Architecture*.

118. Tihon, *Science*.

119. Kočev, *Filosofskata misăl*, 140; Borgolte, *Vielfalt*, 288ff.

120. Obolensky, *Byzantine Commonwealth*, 325ff.

121. Dragojlović, *Istorija filozofske misli*, 77ff; Jireček, *Geschichte*, 2–1:92.

122. Dragojlović, *Istorija filozofske misli*, 19ff; Kočev, *Filosofskata misăl*, 159–60.

123. Novak, *Slaveni u renesansi.*

124. Dadić, "Natural Sciences."

125. Ibid.; Novak, *Slaveni u renesansi.*

126. Borgolte, *Vielfalt,* 281–82.

127. Ibid.

128. Siraisi, *Medicine,* 1ff.

129. Grmek, "Medicine in Croatia."

130. Eckart, "Raum—Antike."

131. Fuhrmann, *Einladung,* 18–19.

132. Rautman, *Daily Life,* 2.

133. Dragojlović, *Istorija filozofske misli,* 24ff.

134. Faroqhi, *Geschichte,* 11; Kreiser, *Osmanischer Staat,* 4ff.

135. Ćirković, *Kosovska bitka;* Zirojević, "Kosovo."

136. Hösch, *Balkanländer,* 79–80.

137. Cardini, *Europa und Islam,* 13.

138. Polo, *Book of Ser Marco Polo,* 119.

139. Larner, *Marco Polo.*

140. Münkler, *Marco Polo,* 108.

141. Orlić, "Curious Case"; Paveškovic, "Marco Polo."

142. Islam, *Ethics of Travel,* 118ff.

143. Münkler, Marco Polo, 109–10; Dinzelbacher, *Mentalitätsgeschichte,* 485.

144. Braudel, *Civilization and Capitalism,* 3:96–97.

145. Fleming, *Faithful Sea;* Horden and Purcell, *Corrupting Sea,* 429ff.

146. Goitein, "Mediterranean Trade"; Goitein, "Mediterranean to India."

147. Ascherson, *Black Sea,* 92–93.

148. Bratianu, *Mer Noire,* 47–48, 225; King, *Black Sea,* 115.

149. King, *Black Sea,* 116.

150. Borgolte, *Vielfalt,* 233.

151. Braudel, *Civilization and Capitalism,* 124–25.

152. Larner, *Marco Polo,* 32, 116ff.

153. Maddison, *Weltwirtschaft,* 19.

154. Abu-Lughod, *Before European Hegemony,* 353ff.

155. Abulafia, *Great Sea,* 355–56; Abu-Lughod, *Before European Hegemony,* 34.

156. Höllmann, *Seidenstraße,* 65–66.

157. Ibid., 70–71.

158. Maddison, *Weltwirtschaft,* 59.

159. Nicol, *Byzantium and Venice,* 283ff.

160. Kocka, *Geschichte des Kapitalismus,* 36–37.

161. Bayly, "Globalization."

162. Parker, *Global Interactions,* 72ff.

163. Bayly, *Birth*, 41ff.; Wallerstein, *World-System I*, 15ff.; Hopkins, *Globalization*, 11ff.

164. Parker, *Global Interactions*, 83.

165. Krekić, "Cultural Symbiosis"; Grubiša, "Forms of Government."

166. Kovačević, *Trgovina*, 65ff.

167. Fabijanec, "Hygiene and Commerce."

168. Krekić, "Italian Creditors."

169. Quoted in Stipetić, "Scientific Economic Thought," 820.

170. Ibid.

171. Cotrugli, *O trgovini*.

172. Šoljić, "O ranoj renesansi."

173. Boué, *La Turquie d'Europe*, 107.

174. Jireček, *Geschichte*, 1:5.

175. Jireček, *Geschichte*, 2–1:55ff.

176. Niedermaier, *Städte*, 319–20.

177. Moldt, *Deutsche Stadtrechte*, 144.

178. Gündisch, "'Saxones' im Bergbau."

179. Krekić, "Italian Creditors."

180. Kovačević-Kojić, *Srednjovjekovna Srebrenica*, 153ff.

181. Budak, *Hrvatska povijest*, 345.

182. Weithmann, *Donau*, 71.

183. Obolensky, *Byzantine Commonwealth*, 20.

184. Sugar, *Southeastern Europe*, 73.

185. Popović, "Srednjovekovna epoha," 121ff.

186. Ibid.

187. Goitein, "Unity."

188. Varlik, "Conquest."

189. Panzac, *La peste*, 597.

190. Çelebi, Dankoff, and Kim, *Ottoman Traveller*, 199ff.

191. Fabijanec, "Hygiene and Commerce."

192. Kadaré, *Siege*, 7.

193. Schmitt, *Skanderbeg*, 169.

194. Barleti, *Scanderbeg*, 217ff.

195. Noli, *George Castrioti*, 60.

196. Schmitt, *Skanderbeg*, 72ff.

197. Rogers, *Medieval Warfare*, 363.

198. Noli, *George Castrioti*, 28ff; Hösch, *Balkanländer*, 85–86.

199. Schmidt-Neke, "Skanderbegs Gefangene"; Schmitt, *Skanderbeg*.

200. Noli, *George Castrioti*, 36.

201. Ibid., 47ff., 118ff.; Schmitt, *Südosteuropa*.

202. Schmitt, *Das venezianische Albanien*, 47ff.

203. Bartl, *Albanien,* 39.
204. Schmitt, *Das venezianische Albanien,* 576.
205. Ibid., 98 ff.
206. Ibid., 184ff.
207. Noli, *George Castrioti,* 37; Schmitt, *Skanderbeg,* 89ff.
208. Schmitt, *Skanderbeg,* 108ff.
209. Braudel, *Mediterranean,* 1:85ff.
210. Kaser, *Hirten,* 36ff.
211. Atsiz, "Albanerbild der Türken," 18.
212. Nicol, *Last Centuries,* 253ff.
213. Tanović, *Historija Bosne,* 69ff.
214. Fine, *Late Medieval Balkans,* 558ff.
215. Heer, *Territorialentwicklung,* 1ff.
216. Pop, Bolovan, and Andea, *History of Romania,* 189ff.
217. Haumann, *Dracula,* 8–9.
218. Ibid., 30ff.
219. Noli, *George Castrioti,* 120; Radonić, *Skenderbeg i Arbanija,* 20.
220. Krekić, "Contributions."
221. Tadić, "Johannes Gazulus"; Šoljić, "O ranoj renesansi."
222. Dadić, "Natural Sciences."
223. Grant, "Cosmology"; North, *Astronomy.*
224. Grmek and Dadić, "O astronomiji."
225. Cited in ibid., 59.
226. Krekić, "Cultural Symbiosis," 330; Jurić, "Prilozi," 457.
227. Quoted in Schmitt, *Das venezianische Albanien,* 554.
228. Quoted in ibid., 561.
229. Ibid., 560ff.
230. Bartl, *Albanien,* 46ff.

2. Rise of the Ottoman Empire

1. Osterhammel, "Europamodelle"; Burbank and Cooper, *Empires,* 1ff.
2. Darwin, *After Tamerlane,* 74.
3. Cf. Reinhard, Introduction; Conrad, *Globalgeschichte,* 224–25.
4. Cited in Lewis, *Muslim Discovery,* 30.
5. Crowley, *Empires,* 2.
6. Kreiser, *Istanbul,* 30–31; Kia, *Daily Life,* 77–78.
7. Inalcik and Quataert, *Economic and Social History,* 1:26.
8. Lewis, *Muslim Discovery,* 29; Crowley, *Empires,* 2.
9. Lewis, *Muslim Discovery,* 174; Lewis, "Der Westen."
10. Lewis, *Muslim Discovery,* 59–60; Faroqhi, *Ottoman Empire,* 2ff.

11. Kieser, "Djihad."

12. Brummett, "Ottoman Expansion," 68.

13. Sugar, *Southeastern Europe,* 15–16.

14. Lowry, *Ottoman Balkans,* 7.

15. Lowry, *Ottoman Realities,* 174; Lowry, *Ottoman Balkans,* 11.

16. Inalcik, "Methods."

17. Faroqhi, *Geschichte,* 22–23.

18. Braudel, *Mediterranean,* 2:668.

19. Burbank and Cooper, *Empires,* 159ff.

20. Boom, *Süleyman,* 141–42.

21. Fodor, *Quest,* 51ff.; Teply, *Türkische Sagen,* 34ff.

22. Kreiser and Neumann, *Geschichte,* 115.

23. Katsiardi-Hering, "Migrationen."

24. Rozen, *Homelands;* Tziovas, *Greek Diaspora.*

25. Hegyi and Zimányi, *Muslime und Christen,* 71.

26. Cited in Burbank and Cooper, *Empires,* 119.

27. Özyurt, *Türkenlieder.*

28. Pippidi, *Visions;* Schwoebel, *Shadow of the Crescent.*

29. Barkey, *Empire of Difference,* 1.

30. Reinkowski, "Antikoloniales Imperium," 44.

31. Koller and Kreuter, "Südosteuropa."

32. Brummett, "Ottoman Expansion."

33. Sugar, *Southeastern Europe,* 93.

34. Ibid., 122–23.

35. Faroqhi, "Ottoman Empire," 236.

36. Sugar, *Southeastern Europe,* 31ff.

37. Mihailović, *Memoirs,* 79.

38. Papulia, *Ursprung,* 113.

39. Koller, "Geschichte."

40. Lewis, *Muslim Discovery,* 191.

41. Toledano, *Ottoman Slave Trade,* 5ff.

42. Inalcik and Quataert, *Economic and Social History,* 1:307; Erdem, *Slavery,* 29.

43. Burbank and Cooper, *Empires,* 138ff.

44. Schilling, "Das konfessionelle Europa."

45. Todorova, "Historische Vermächtnisse."

46. Inalcik and Quataert, *Economic and Social History,* 1:26.

47. Inalcik, "Methods."

48. Kiel, "Incorporation, 148ff.

49. Inalcik, "Methods."

50. Donia, *Sarajevo,* 8ff.

51. Minkov, *Conversion,* 30.

52. Koller and Karpat, *Ottoman Bosnia,* 85.

53. Minkov, *Conversion,* 40ff.

54. Lewis, *Muslim Discovery,* 63; Vaporis, *Witnesses.*

55. Handžić, "Origins."

56. Krstić, "Light of Islam."

57. Clayer, "Netzwerke."

58. Adanir, "Formation."

59. Džaja, *Konfessionalität.*

60. Braude and Lewis, *Christians and Jews.*

61. Sugar, *Southeastern Europe,* 75ff.

62. Adanir, "Religious Communities."

63. Levy, *Sephardim,* 19.

64. Mazower, *Salonica,* 49.

65. Runciman, *Great Church,* 167ff.

66. Turczynski, *Kulturbeziehungen,* 162.

67. Runciman, *Great Church,* 186ff.

68. Cited in Podskalsky, *Griechische Theologie,* 47.

69. Ibid., 18–19.

70. Fine, *Bosnian Church,* 29.

71. Strauss, "Ottoman Rule."

72. Buchenau, *Orthodoxie und Katholizismus,* 45–46; Frazee, *Catholics.*

73. Fichtner, *Habsburg Monarchy,* 168.

74. Ibid., 26.

75. Greene, *Catholic Pirates,* 101; Frazee, *Catholics,* 88.

76. Faroqhi, *Ottoman Empire,* 34ff.; Greene, *Catholic Pirates,* 103.

77. Prelog, *Povijest Bosne,* 156.

78. Korade, Aleksić, and Matoš, *Jesuits,* 93.

79. Budak, "Gegenreformation."

80. Valentić and Čoralić, *Povijest Hrvata,* 183–84.

81. Jakelic, *Collectivistic Religions,* 104ff.

82. Budak, "Gegenreformation"; Sunajko, "Juraj Križanić."

83. Buchenau, *Orthodoxe Antiwestler,* 68.

84. Hitchins, *History of Romania,* 48.

85. Runciman, *Great Church,* 338ff.

86. Hering, *Ökumenisches Patriarchat,* 13–14, 323ff.

87. Dialetis, Gavroglu, and Patiniotis, "Sciences."

88. Candea, "Les intellectuels," 201ff.

89. Nikolaidis, *Science,* 130ff.

90. Kreiser and Neumann, *Geschichte,* 233ff.; Scholem, *Sabbatai Sevi.*

91. Zilfi, "Kadizadelis."

92. Krstić, *Contested Conversions;* Hagen, "Ottoman Understandings," 244ff.

93. Krstić, "Light of Islam."

94. Schilling, "Das konfessionelle Europa."

95. Hinrichs, *Handbuch.*

96. Cf. Schilling, "Nationale Identität."

97. Casale, *Ottoman Age,* 6–7.

98. Beckert, *Empire of Cotton,* 31–32.

99. Casale, *Ottoman Age,* 200.

100. Ibid., 11.

101. Faroqhi, "Ottoman Empire," 287.

102. Darwin, *After Tamerlane,* 76.

103. Samardžić, *Mehmed Sokolović,* 16.

104. Ibid., 33.

105. Veinstein, "Sokollu Mehmed Pasha."

106. Quoted in Samardžić, *Mehmed Sokolović,* 113.

107. Ibid., 270.

108. Ziroyevic, "Mehmed Pascha Sokolli," 64.

109. Rolf, "Imperiale Biographien."

110. Casale, "Sokollu Mehmed."

111. Casale, *Ottoman Age,* 119ff., 148, 234.

112. Ibid., 135ff.

113. Kuran, *Sinan.*

114. Krstić, "Translation."

115. Crowley, *Empires,* 199ff.

116. Quoted in Samardžić, *Mehmed Sokolović,* 544.

117. Veinstein, "Sokollu Mehmed Pasha"; Ziroyevic, "Mehmed Pascha Sokolli."

118. Lewis, *Cultures,* 68–69.

119. Emiralioğlu, *Geographical Knowledge,* 13ff., 91ff.

120. Braudel, *Mediterranean,* 2:759ff.

121. Hegyi and Zimányi, *Muslime und Christen,* 94; Faroqhi, *Ottoman Empire,* 194ff.

122. Casale, *Ottoman Age,* 185–86.

123. Faroqhi, *Ottoman Empire,* 183–84.

124. Kafadar, *Between Two Worlds;* Şahin, *Empire and Power.*

125. Fleischer, *Bureaucrat,* 243; Faroqhi, *Kultur und Alltag,* 91–92.

126. Lewis, *Muslim Discovery,* 60.

127. Koller and Karpat, *Ottoman Bosnia,* 86–87.

128. Emiralioğlu, *Geographical Knowledge,* 80–81.

129. Hagen, "Fremde im Eigenen"; Lewis, *Muslim Discovery,* 159.

130. Heinen, *Islamic Cosmology,* 7ff.

131. Ragep, "Islamic Culture"; Grant, "Cosmology."

132. Hagen, "Ottoman Understandings," 220ff.

133. Reis, *Baḥrīje.*

134. Goodrich, *Ottoman Turks,* 9, 73ff.

135. Ibid., 15ff.

136. Braudel, *Mediterranean,* 2:762ff.

137. Elliott, *Old World,* 6.

138. Gruzinski, *Quelle heure,* 196ff.

139. Bayly, "Globalization."

140. Darwin, *After Tamerlane,* 50ff.

141. Braudel, *Civilization and Capitalism,* 167ff.

142. Beckert, *Empire of Cotton,* 31–32; Wallerstein, *World-System II,* 37ff.

143. Kocka, *Geschichte des Kapitalismus,* 48–49; Landes, *Wealth and Poverty,* 121.

144. Bayly, *Birth,* 60ff.; Wallerstein, *World-System II,* 50ff.

145. Wallerstein, *World-System I,* 86.

146. Ibid.

147. Beckert, *Empire of Cotton,* 31–32; Pomeranz, *Great Divergence.*

148. Kocka, *Geschichte des Kapitalismus,* 47.

149. Darwin, *After Tamerlane,* 104ff.

150. Ibid., 39; Braudel, *Civilization and Capitalism,* 469–70.

151. Braudel, *Civilization and Capitalism,* 18.

152. Pach, "Levantine Trade"; Faroqhi, *Kultur und Alltag,* 58.

153. King, *Black Sea,* 121ff.

154. Inalcik and Quataert, *Economic and Social History,* 1:156ff.

155. Pach, "Colony"; Braudel, *Mediterranean,* 1:583–84.

156. Lewis, *Muslim Discovery,* 190.

157. King, *Black Sea,* 116.

158. Lewis, *Muslim Discovery,* 188–89.

159. Inalcik and Quataert, *Economic and Social History,* 1:192ff.

160. Burbank and Cooper, *Empires,* 183.

161. Eldem, "Capitulations"; Kaiser, "Politik und Geschäft."

162. Greene, *Catholic Pirates,* 52ff.

163. Inalcik and Quataert, *Economic and Social History,* 1:265.

164. Braudel, *Mediterranean,* 1:287.

165. Inalcik and Quataert, *Economic and Social History,* 1:285ff.; Chirot, *Social Change,* 38ff.

166. Gestrin, "Trgovina."

167. Greene, *Catholic Pirates,* 133–34.

168. Braudel, *Mediterranean,* 1:363.

169. Bono, *Piraten,* 151.

170. Bracewell, *Uskoks.*

171. Pach, "Diminishing Share."

172. Adamček, *Bune i otpori;* Chirot, *Origins,* 71; Pach, *Hungary,* 75ff.

173. Sundhaussen, "Wandel."

174. Wallerstein, *World-System II,* 134ff.; Gestrin, "Trgovina."

175. Murgescu, *România,* 42ff.; Pach, *Agrarentwicklung.*

176. Koller and Kreuter, "Südosteuropa," 241ff.; Fleet, "Ottomans."

177. Pach, "Levantine Trade."

178. McGowan, *Economic Life,* 58ff.

179. Gestrin, "Trgovina."

180. Inalcik and Quataert, *Economic and Social History,* 2:474ff.; Braudel, *Civilization and Capitalism,* 467ff.

181. Chirot, *Social Change,* 40–41; Murgescu: *România,* 37–38.

182. Stoye, *Siege of Vienna,* 20.

183. Ibid., 18ff.

184. Ibid., 152.

185. Kreutel, *Kara Mustafa,* 58.

186. Ibid., 81, 86, 124.

187. Kreiser, *Istanbul,* 36.

188. Faroqhi, *Kultur und Alltag,* 167, 304.

189. Coller, "East of Enlightenment."

190. Kreiser, *Geschichte Istanbuls,* 73.

191. Mantran, *Istanbul,* 44ff.

192. Lewis, *Istanbul,* 127.

193. Kreiser, *Istanbul,* 46.

194. Faroqhi, *Kultur und Alltag,* 166ff.

195. Inalcik and Quataert, *Economic and Social History,* 1:179ff.; Boyar and Fleet, *Social History,* 158ff.

196. Kreiser, *Geschichte Istanbuls,* 78; Boyar and Fleet, *Social History,* 249ff.

197. Eldem, Goffman, and Masters, *Ottoman City,* 137.

198. Lee, *Guild Dynamics,* 22–23; Kreiser, *Istanbul,* 123–24.

199. Lee, *Guild Dynamics,* 27.

200. Kreiser, *Istanbul,* 126ff.

201. Agoston, "Habsburg Rivalry."

202. Faroqhi, *Ottoman Empire,* 179ff.

203. Ghobrial, *Whispers,* 65ff.

204. Ibid., 95.

205. Braudel, *Mediterranean,* 1:359ff.

206. Faroqhi, *Kultur und Alltag,* 74ff.

207. Wurm, *Hezārfenn,* 9.

208. Faroqhi, *Kultur und Alltag,* 88–89.

209. Samardžić, *Mehmed Sokolović,* 100.

210. Rothman, *Brokering Empire;* Krstić, "Translation."

211. Quoted in Ghobrial, *Whispers,* 104.

212. Podskalsky, *Griechische Theologie,* 49ff.

213. Camariano, *Alexandre Mavrocordato,* 42ff.

214. Philliou, "Communities"; Philliou, *Biography.*

215. Hagen, "Order of Knowledge," 410.

216. Ghobrial, *Whispers,* 65ff.; Candea, "Les intellectuels," 198.

217. Candea, "Les intellectuels," 197.

218. Wurm, *Hezârfenn,* 12ff.

219. Hagen, "Order of Knowledge," 415ff.

220. Lewis, *Istanbul,* 145ff.

221. Radtke, *Weltgeschichte.*

222. Wurm, *Hezârfenn,* 78ff.

223. Küçük, "Early Enlightenment," 104ff.

224. Emiralioğlu, *Geographical Knowledge,* 147.

225. *Rumeli und Bosna,* 78.

226. Hagen, "Ottoman Understandings," 231.

227. Lewis, *Muslim Discovery,* 153.

228. Dankoff, *Ottoman Mentality.*

229. Çelebi, *Im Reiche des Goldenen Apfels,* 38–39, 105ff.; Dankoff, *Ottoman Mentality,* 66.

230. Dankoff, *Ottoman Mentality,* 49.

231. Hagen, "Ottoman Understandings," 227; Faroqhi, *Ottoman Empire,* 207.

232. Hagen, "Ottoman Understandings," 235ff.; Hagen, "Order of Knowledge," 449ff.

233. Faroqhi, "Istanbuler Derwisch."

3. Challenges of the Ancien Régime

1. Barkey, *Empire of Difference;* Tezcan, *Second Ottoman Empire.*

2. Parvev, *Habsburgs.*

3. Samardžić, *Kosovo i Metohija,* 133.

4. Malcolm, *Kosovo,* 158.

5. Sundhaussen, *Sarajevo,* 106–7.

6. Sundhaussen, "Migrationsgeschichte."

7. Parvev, *Habsburgs,* 132.

8. Seewann, *Geschichte,* 1:214; cf. Rothenberg, *Military Border.*

9. Kaser, *Freier Bauer.*

10. Roksandić, *Triplex confinium,* 14ff.; Kaser, *Freier Bauer,* 133ff.

11. Helmedach and Koller, "Gewaltgemeinschaften."

12. Ingrao, Samardžić, and Pesalj, *Peace of Passarowitz,* 6.

13. Hroch, *National Interest,* 44.

14. Duchhardt, *Barock,* 102.

15. Kessler, *Politik,* 9–10.

16. Turczynski, *Konfession und Nation.*

17. Hösch, *Balkanländer,* 149–50; Turczynski, *Konfession und Nation;* Maner, "Rumänische Nation."

18. Kappeler, *Russland,* 25ff.; Darwin, *After Tamerlane,* 121.

19. Hildermeier, *Geschichte Russlands,* 405ff.

20. Kostić, "Kult Petra Velikog."

21. Dučić, *Sava Vladislavić,* 90ff.; Kosanović, *Sava Vladislavić-Raguzinski,* 10ff.

22. Cited in Kostić, "Kult Petra Velikog," 91.

23. Kosanović, *Sava Vladislavić-Raguzinski,* 20–21.

24. Leezenberg, "Oriental Origins."

25. Bochmann, *Dimitrie Cantemir.*

26. Lemny, *Les Cantemir,* 47.

27. Cernovodeanu, "Cantemir," 646.

28. Grasshoff, *Kantemir,* 20.

29. Lemny, *Les Cantemir,* 265; Grasshoff, *Kantemir,* 215.

30. Bîrsan, *Dimitrie Cantemir.*

31. Lemny, *Les Cantemir,* 143ff.

32. Philliou, *Biography,* 7ff.

33. Bošković, *Reise,* 88.

34. Candea, "Les intellectuels," 198ff.

35. Lozovan, "Cantemir," 98.

36. Pušić, *Kapija od žada,* 18–19.

37. Dučić, *Sava Vladislavić,* 350ff.

38. Kosanović, *Sava Vladislavić-Raguzinski,* 10ff.

39. Kitromilides, "Athos and the Enlightenment."

40. Zaimova, "Moine Paissij."

41. Paisy, *Slavo-Bulgarian History,* 156.

42. Hristov, "Athos."

43. Kitromilides, "Athos and the Enlightenment," 271.

44. Turczynski, "Gestaltwandel."

45. Pocock, *Barbarism;* Porter, *Enlightenment.*

46. Turczynski, "Gestaltwandel."

47. Brnardic, "Exchange and Commerce," 83.

48. Herzog, "Aufklärung"; Küçük, "Early Enlightenment."

49. Dimaras, *La Grèce,* 63.

50. Daskalov, *Bulgarian Revival,* 32ff.

51. Lemny, "Rumänische Aufklärung."

52. Argyropoulos, "Les Lumières."

53. Lemny, *Les Cantemir,* 265; Kostić, "Volter kod Srba."

54. Kostić, "Volter kod Srba."

55. Dimaras, *La Grèce,* 61.

56. Cited in Kostić, "Volter kod Srba," 67.

57. Hoško, *Biskup Vrhovac;* Lemny, "Rumänische Aufklärung."

58. Casanova, *History,* 205ff.

59. Krasić, *Ivan Dominik Stratiko,* 50ff.

60. Supek, *Ruđer Bošković,* 403ff.

61. Kitromilides, *Enlightenment, Nationalisms, Orthodoxy.*

62. Duțu, *Intellectual Movements,* 133ff.

63. Trencsényi and Kopeček, *Discourses,* 1:77ff.

64. Paisy, *Slavo-Bulgarian History,* 241.

65. Cited in Fischer, *Dositej Obradović,* 130–31.

66. Turczynski, *Sozial- und Kulturgeschichte,* 43ff.

67. Brnardic, "Exchange and Commerce."

68. Fischer, *Dositej Obradović,* 121–22.

69. Duțu, Hösch, and Oellers, *Briefwechsel.*

70. Turczynski, "Entwicklung der Aufklärung."

71. Turczynski, "Role," 426.

72. Israel, *Enlightenment Contested,* 19.

73. Golescu, *Aufzeichnung,* 91.

74. Quoted in Kessler, "Buchproduktion," 474.

75. Goody, *Interface.*

76. Duțu, *Humanisme,* 94–95.

77. Velculescu, "Kopisten," 304–5.

78. Quoted in Duțu, *Intellectual Movements,* 81.

79. Ibid., 82.

80. Kessler, "Buchproduktion."

81. Dimaras, *La Grèce,* 105.

82. Duțu, *Intellectual Movements,* 151; Duțu, *Humanisme,* 89.

83. Velculescu, "Kopisten," 306.

84. Israel, *Enlightenment Contested,* 15ff.

85. Stollberg-Rilinger, *Aufklärung,* 114ff.

86. Supek, *Ruđer Bošković,* 42.

87. Kutleša, "Ima li mjesta."

88. Supek, *Ruđer Bošković,* 104.

89. Kadum, "Ruđer Bošković," 23.

90. Kitromilides, *Enlightenment as Social Criticism,* 144ff.

91. Makrides, *Religiöse Kritik,* 36ff., 92ff.

92. Pippidi, *Byzantins,* 298.

93. Makrides, *Religiöse Kritik,* 115.

94. Dimaras, *La Grèce,* 75ff.

95. Zelepos, *Orthodoxe Eiferer.*

96. Makrides, *Religiöse Kritik,* 473.

97. Koselleck, "Theoriebedürftigkeit," 15.

98. Stassinopulou, *Weltgeschichte.*

99. Tóth, *Literacy,* 89.

100. Helmedach, *Verkehrssystem,* 210–11.

101. Bošković, *Reise,* 88.

102. Ibid., 25, 38, 88.

103. Golescu, *Aufzeichnung,* 56.

104. Ibid., 54ff., 109, 216.

105. Ibid., 7, 93.

106. Trencsényi and Kopeček, *Discourses,* 1:71.

107. Fischer, *Dositej Obradović,* 83.

108. Paić-Vukić, *Svijet Mustafe Muhibbija.*

109. Zeman, *Reise,* 73ff.

110. Fortis, *Sitten der Morlacken.*

111. Zeman, *Reise,* 63ff.

112. Trencsényi and Kopeček, *Discourses,* 1:57ff.

113. Krasić, *Ivan Dominik Stratiko,* 60.

114. Cited in Perinić Lewis and Rudan, "Došlo je doba svjetlosti," 90.

115. Quoted in Krasić, *Ivan Dominik Stratiko,* 336.

116. Lemberg, "Entstehung des Osteuropabegriffs."

117. Pippidi, *Visions;* Schwoebel, *Shadow of the Crescent.*

118. Said, *Orientalism.* For a critical review of related literature, see Wiedemann, "Orientalismus."

119. Quoted in Lemny, "Rumänische Aufklärung," 41.

120. Gibbon, *History,* 23.

121. Wolff, *Inventing Eastern Europe.*

122. Braudel, *Civilization and Capitalism,* 469–70.

123. Frangakis-Syrett, "Market Networks."

124. Stoianovich, "Orthodox Merchant," 275.

125. Özveren, "Framework."

126. Eldem, "Capitulations."

127. Boogert, *Capitulations,* 7–8.

128. Kreiser and Neumann, *Geschichte,* 304.

129. Beckert, *Empire of Cotton,* xv–xvi.

130. Eldem, "Capitulations."

131. Kasaba, *Ottoman Empire,* 19; Beckert, *Empire of Cotton,* 41.

132. Stoianovich, "Orthodox Merchant," 260.

133. Beaujour, *Commerce of Greece,* 43.

134. Beckert, *Empire of Cotton,* 200; Kurmuş, "Cotton Famine."

135. Inalcik and Quataert, *Economic and Social History,* 2:525–26, 646, 729ff.

136. Stoianovich, "Orthodox Merchant," 269.

137. Koller, "The Penjez."

138. Stoianovich, "Orthodox Merchant."

139. Katsiardi-Hering and Stassinopoulou, "Greek Commerce."

140. Millo, "Creation," 222.

141. Stoianovich, "Orthodox Merchant," 289.

142. Beckert, *Empire of Cotton,* 232; Genchev, *Vŭzrozhdenskĭiat Plovdiv,* 38.

143. Davidova, *Balkan Transitions,* 24.

144. Ianeva, "Commercial Practices."

145. Davidova, *Balkan Transitions,* 157–58, 198.

146. Ianeva, "Commercial Practices."

147. Davidova, *Balkan Transitions,* 24ff.; Todorov, *Balkan City,* 233.

148. Matkovski, *Gjurčin Kokaleski.*

149. Samuelsson, *Religion.* For a contrasting view, see Landes, *Wealth and Poverty,* 174ff.

150. Beaujour, *Commerce of Greece,* 188–89.

151. Turczynski, *Sozial- und Kulturgeschichte,* 115.

152. Beaujour, *Commerce of Greece,* 188ff.; Katsiardi-Hering, "Migrant Groups."

153. Stoianovich, "Orthodox Merchant," 308.

154. Gârleanu, *Volksaufstand,* 8; Berend and Ránki, *Economic Development,* 35ff.

155. Gandev, "L'apparition."

156. Barkey, *Empire of Difference,* 229ff.

157. Vlachopoulou, "Lokale Auslöser," 113.

158. Barkey, *Empire of Difference,* 229ff.

159. Inalcik and Quataert, *Economic and Social History,* 2:658ff.

160. Sadat, "Rumeli Ayanlari."

161. Turczynski, *Sozial- und Kulturgeschichte,* 104.

162. Vlachopoulou, "Lokale Auslöser," 113.

163. Kadić, "Ruđe Bošković."

164. Varićak, "Ulomak Boškovićeve korespondencije," 167.

165. Špoljarić, *Rudjer Bošković,* 65.

166. Foretić, *Povijest Dubrovnika,* 298ff.

167. Berković, "Vanjska politika Dubrovačke republike," 217.

168. Luetić, *O pomorstvu,* 28ff., 46.

169. Quoted in ibid., 16.

170. Luetić, *Brodari i pomorci,* 136.

171. Luetić, *Pomorci i jedrenjaci,* 44.

172. Novak, *Dubrovnik Revisited,* 6.

173. Miović, *Dubrovačka diplomacija,* 128ff.

174. Mitić, *Dubrovačka država,* 149.

175. Berković, "Vanjska politika Dubrovačke republike," 206.

176. Ljubić, "Izvještaj," 66.

177. Foretić, *Povijest Dubrovnika,* 282ff.

178. Novak, *Dubrovnik Revisited,* 159, 161.

179. Ljubić, "Izvještaj," 100.

180. Božić-Bužančić, *Privatni i društveni život,* 64–65.

181. Novak, *Dubrovnik Revisited,* 110.

182. Stojan, *Vjerenice i nevjernice,* 163.

183. Ljubić, "Izvještaj," 107.

184. Novak, *Dubrovnik Revisited,* 78.

185. Mitić, *Dubrovačka država,* 56–57.

186. Ljubić, "Izvještaj," 66.

187. Valentić and Čoralić, *Povijest Hrvata,* 306–7.

188. Novak, *Dubrovnik Revisited,* 54ff.

189. Vojnović, "Crkva i država" (1894), 36–37.

190. Vojnović, "Crkva i država" (1895).

191. Vanino, *Isusovci i hrvatski narod,* 3.

192. Ljubić, "Izvještaj," 71.

193. Novak, *Dubrovnik Revisited,* 65; Krasić, "Apothecary Activity."

194. Grdinić, *Ljekarništvo,* 10.

195. Krasić, "Apothecary Activity."

196. Budak, "Gegenreformation."

197. Deanović, "Đuro Matijašević," 152.

198. Marković, *Pjesnikinje starog Dubrovnika,* 355.

199. Ibid., 375ff.

200. Deanović, "Đuro Matijašević," 154.

201. Vojnović, "Crkva i država" (1894), 28.

202. Novak, *Dubrovnik Revisited,* 162–63.

203. Foretić, *Povijest Dubrovnika,* 260–61.

204. Stulli, *Židovi u Dubrovniku,* 41.

205. Miović, *Jewish Ghetto,* 65, 78.

206. Stulli, *Židovi u Dubrovniku,* 48.

207. Stojan, *Vjerenice i nevjernice,* 243–44.

208. Körbler, "Istraga protiv mladića."

209. Foretić, *Povijest Dubrovnika,* 159.

210. Miović, *Dubrovačka Republika,* 195.

211. Ibid., 50–51.

212. Miović, *Dubrovačka diplomacija,* 202, 207.

213. Foretić, *Povijest Dubrovnika,* 257–58, 260–61, 265–66.

214. Novak, "Kultura u Dubrovniku."

215. Foretić, *Povijest Dubrovnika,* 290ff.

216. Ibid., 273.

217. Špoljarić, *Rudjer Bošković*, 63.

218. Kostić, "Volter kod Srba."

219. Foretić, *Povijest Dubrovnika*, 413.

220. Božić-Bužančić, *Južna Hrvatska*, 252.

221. Stojan, *Marije Giorgi Bona*, appendix.

222. Ljubić, "Izvještaj," 103.

223. Božić-Bužančić, *Privatni i društveni život*, 155; Novak, *Dubrovnik Revisited*, 77.

4. The Age of Global Revolutions

1. Hobsbawm, *Age of Revolution*.

2. Osterhammel, *Transformation of the World*, 514ff.

3. Thamer, *Französische Revolution*, 7.

4. Osterhammel, *Transformation of the World*, 406, 526ff.

5. Woodhouse, *Rhigas Velestinlis*, 112.

6. Ibid., 278.

7. Outram, *Enlightenment*, 126ff.

8. Woodhouse, *Rhigas Velestinlis*, 67ff.

9. Karaberopoulos, *Revolutionsschriften*, 89.

10. Fahrmeir, *Revolutionen und Reformen*, 23ff.

11. Prodan, *Supplex Libellus Valachorum*.

12. Rumpler, *Chance für Mitteleuropa*, 38ff.

13. Legrand, *Documents*, 6ff., 164ff.

14. Kitromilides, *Adamantios Korais*, 9ff.

15. Chaconas, *Adamantios Korais*, 123ff.

16. Kaltchas, *Constitutional History*, 16.

17. Fischer, *Dositej Obradović*, 85.

18. Stojković, *Životni put Dositeja Obradovića*, 97ff.

19. Venturi and Woolf, *Italy and the Enlightenment*, 18ff.

20. Trencsényi and Kopeček, *Discourses*, 1:178–79.

21. Berindei, "Revolutionäre Ereignisse," 156.

22. Kitromilides, *Enlightenment as Social Criticism*, 62.

23. Prodan, *Supplex Libellus Valachorum*, 364–65.

24. Stavrianos, *Balkans since 1453*, 211–12.

25. Ibid., 199ff.

26. Ćosić, *Dubrovnik*, 70.

27. Ibid., 99ff.

28. Fleming, *Muslim Bonaparte*.

29. Davenport, *Ali Pasha*, 307.

30. Bartl, *Albanien*, 77ff.

31. Fleming, *Muslim Bonaparte,* 25ff., 44ff.

32. Matuz, *Das Osmanische Reich,* 209ff.

33. Gradeva, "Osman Pazvantoglu."

34. Wraza, *Leben,* 24.

35. Ibid.

36. Quoted in in Mazower, *Balkans,* 22.

37. Koliopoulos, *Brigands with a Cause,* 20ff.; Hobsbawm, *Bandits,* 77ff.

38. Quoted in Sundhaussen, *Geschichte Serbiens,* 54–55.

39. Quoted in Fleming, *Muslim Bonaparte,* 40.

40. Adanir, "Haiduckentum."

41. Anscombe, "Revolutionary Age."

42. Osterhammel, *Transformation of the World,* 58ff.; Outram, *Enlightenment,* 197.

43. As defined in Osterhammel, *Transformation of the World,* 515.

44. Pavlowitch, "Society in Serbia"; Stoianovich, "Orthodox Merchant," 282.

45. Sundhaussen, *Geschichte Serbiens,* 65ff.

46. Quoted in Pantelić, *Beogradski pašaluk,* 224–25.

47. Sundhaussen, *Geschichte Serbiens,* 66.

48. Gavrilović, *Istorija srpskog naroda,* 25ff.

49. Ranke, *Serbische Revolution,* 116–17.

50. Nenadović, *Memoirs,* 157.

51. Quoted in Bataković, *Nova istorija,* 140.

52. Stojković, *Životni put Dositeja Obradovića,* 97ff.

53. Nenadović, *Memoirs,* 114.

54. Stojančević, "Prvi srpski ustanak"; Dojnov, "Srăbsko văstanie."

55. Sundhaussen, *Geschichte Serbiens,* 65ff.

56. Todorov, "La participation des Bulgares."

57. My thanks to Ioannis Zelepos for this reference.

58. Stavrianos, *Balkans since 1453,* 275.

59. Ibid., 280.

60. Hering, *Die politischen Parteien,* 55–56.

61. Ibid., 61.

62. Brewer, *Flame of Freedom,* 26ff.

63. Todorov, *Balkanski izmerenija,* 51; Papadrianos, *Hellēnikē palingenesia,* 28ff.

64. Todorov, *Balkanski izmerenija,* 56ff.

65. Hitchins, *History of Romania,* 74–75.

66. Berindei, *L'année révolutionnaire.*

67. Turczynski, *Sozial- und Kulturgeschichte,* 117.

68. Pop, Bolovan, and Andea, *History of Romania,* 457ff.

69. Turczynski, *Sozial- und Kulturgeschichte,* 118.

70. Hitchins, *History of Romania,* 80.

71. Turczynski, *Sozial- und Kulturgeschichte,* 126.

72. Ibid., 136.

73. Papadrianos, *Hellēnikē palingenesia.*

74. Todorov, *Balkanski izmerenija,* 66ff.; *Hellēnikē palingenesia,* 45.

75. Vasdravellis, "Fototypisis."

76. Turczynski, *Sozial- und Kulturgeschichte,* 119.

77. Kaelble, *Wege zur Demokratie,* 24ff.

78. Despot, *Amerikas Weg,* 62–63.

79. Quoted in Papazoglou, "Thessaloniki," 421.

80. Mazower, *Salonica,* 15–16.

81. Papazoglou, "Thessaloniki," 426.

82. Ibid., 427–28.

83. Beaujour, *Commerce of Greece,* 31; Svoronos, *Commerce de Salonique,* 7.

84. Levy, *Sephardim,* 92–93; Benbassa, *Geschichte,* 81.

85. Quoted in Mazower, *Salonica,* 164.

86. Baer, "Globalization."

87. Vakalopoulos, *History of Thessaloniki,* 101.

88. Ginio, "Musulmans."

89. Nicolaidy, *Les Turcs,* 1:45.

90. Prokesch von Osten, *Denkwürdigkeiten,* 645.

91. Bauer, *Thessaloniki,* 9.

92. Ginio, "Aspects of Muslim Culture."

93. Trivellato, *Familiarity of Strangers.*

94. Mazower, *Salonica,* 94–95.

95. Nicolaidy, *Les Turcs,* 1:32.

96. Beaujour, *Commerce of Greece,* 13.

97. Anastassiadou, *Salonique,* 82.

98. Prokesch von Osten, *Denkwürdigkeiten,* 637.

99. Quoted in Anastassiadou, *Salonique,* 78.

100. Anastassiadou, "Profil demographique."

101. Beaujour, *Commerce of Greece,* 2, 27.

102. Ibid., 27–28.

103. Ibid., 28–29.

104. Dumont, "Social Structure," 50.

105. Benbassa, *Geschichte,* 75.

106. Beaujour, *Commerce of Greece,* 29.

107. a-Levi, *Jewish Voice,* xiv.

108. Ibid., 3, 27ff.

109. Anastassiadou, *Salonique,* 64ff.

110. Vakalopoulos, *History of Thessaloniki,* 101.

111. Papazoglou, "Thessaloniki," 423.

112. Ibid., 424.

113. Vasdravellis, *Greek Struggle,* 32ff.

114. Ginio, "Coffee."

115. Inalcik and Quataert, *Economic and Social History,* 2:738.

116. Vakalopoulos, *History of Thessaloniki,* 98.

117. McGowan, *Economic Life,* 150.

118. Holland, *Travels,* 324ff.

119. Ginio, "Migrants and Workers," 128ff.

120. Mazower, *Salonica,* 52.

121. Anastassiadou, "Profil demographique," 90.

122. Beaujour, *Commerce of Greece,* 33.

123. Hassiotis, "Thessaloniki," 144.

124. Vasdravellis, *Greek Struggle,* 74–75.

125. Müller, *Athos,* 61–62.

126. Vasdravellis, *Piracy,* 38–39.

127. Pyrros, *Periigisis,* 101.

128. Kantakuzenos, *Briefe eines Augenzeugen,* 74.

129. Vasdravellis, *Greek Struggle,* 81.

130. Müller, *Athos,* 67.

131. Soulis, "Thessaloniki," 586.

132. Lascaris, "Révolution grecque," 150.

133. Baumgart, "Orientalische Frage."

134. Anderson, *Eastern Question,* 1ff.

135. Hösch, "Griechisches Projekt."

136. Schwartz, *Ethnische "Säuberungen,"* 244.

137. Anderson, *Eastern Question,* 28ff.

138. Rodogno, *Against Massacre,* 19ff.; Schroeder, "International System."

139. Gruner, *Wiener Kongress,* 8–9; Duchhardt, *Wiener Kongress.*

140. Osterhammel, *Transformation of the World,* 473.

141. Quoted in Schwartz, *Ethnische "Säuberungen,"* 242.

142. Rodogno, *Against Massacre,* 68–69.

143. Schwartz, *Ethnische "Säuberungen,"* 243.

144. Turczynski, *Sozial- und Kulturgeschichte,* 144.

145. Rodogno, *Against Massacre,* 66.

146. Konstantinou, *Ausdrucksformen.*

147. Athanassoglou-Kallmyer, *French Images.*

148. Rodogno, *Against Massacre,* 80.

149. "Asien und Europa," 489.

150. Rumpler, *Chance für Mitteleuropa,* 133ff.

151. Treaty between Great Britain, France, and Russia for the Pacification of Greece, accessed February 12, 2018, https://sourcebooks.fordham.edu/mod/1827 gktreaty.asp.

152. Turczynski, *Sozial- und Kulturgeschichte,* 154ff.

153. Zelepos, *Geschichte,* 50–51.

154. Rodogno, *Against Massacre,* 88.

155. Krug, *Gesammelte Schriften,* 277.

156. Rodogno, *Against Massacre,* 24–25.

157. Schwartz, *Ethnische "Säuberungen,"* 247.

158. Rodogno, *Against Massacre,* 85.

159. Schwartz, *Ethnische "Säuberungen,"* 235.

160. Clogg, *Movement.*

161. Jelavich and Jelavich, *Establishment,* 90ff.

162. Schulz, *Intervention,* 395ff.

163. Zelepos, *Geschichte,* 55.

164. Treaty between Great Britain, France, and Russia for the Pacification of Greece.

165. Panzac, *La peste,* 198.

166. Ibid., 59, 66, 358.

167. Quoted in ibid., 65.

168. Boué, *Europäische Türkei,* 342.

169. Panzac, *La peste.*

170. Schraud, *Geschichte der Pest.*

171. Müller, "Darstellung," 191ff.

172. Panzac, "Plague and Seafaring," 59.

173. Bajamonti, *Storia della peste,* 64ff.

174. Ibid., 180.

175. Perinić Lewis and Rudan, "Spectemur Agendo" and "Došlo je doba svjetlosti."

176. Skenderović, "Kuga u Požegi."

177. Panzac, *La peste,* 297.

178. a-Levi, *Jewish Voice,* 39.

179. Müller, "Darstellung," 42.

180. Buda, "Black Death."

181. Skenderović, "Kuga u Požegi."

182. Bulmuş, *Plague,* 97ff.

183. Osterhammel, *Transformation of the World,* 190.

184. Bono, *Piraten,* 109ff.

185. Vasdravellis, *Piracy,* 22ff.

186. Quoted in Panzac, *Barbary Corsairs,* 271.

187. Bono, *Piraten,* 63.

188. Williams, *Capitalism and Slavery,* 108ff.

189. Quoted in ibid., 124.

190. Stauber, *Wiener Kongress,* 243ff.

191. Toledano, *Ottoman Slave Trade,* 5ff.

192. On the slave trade before 1800, Fontenay, "Routes et modalités" and Davis, "Geography of Slaving."

193. Toledano, "Ottoman Concepts."

194. Frank, "Children of the Desert," 421.

195. White, *Three Years in Constantinople,* 2:282.

196. Erdem, *Slavery,* 293.

197. Ibid., 26.

198. Kolev, "Krajat na 'turskoto robstvo.'"

199. Koken, Constant, and Canoutas, *Greeks in the Americas,* 44ff.

200. Toledano, *Ottoman Slave Trade,* 9ff.

201. Frank, "Children of the Desert," 424.

202. Kurtynova-D'Herlugnan, *Tsar's Abolitionists,* 25ff.

203. Kolev, "Krajat na 'turskoto robstvo.'"

204. Kurtynova-D'Herlugnan, *Tsar's Abolitionists,* 166; Erdem, *Slavery,* 103–4.

205. White, *Three Years in Constantinople,* 2:290.

206. Pinson, "Ottoman Colonization."

207. Toledano, *Ottoman Slave Trade,* 18.

5. Toward the Nation-State

1. Quoted in Ekmečić, *Stvaranje Jugoslavije,* 475.

2. Opfer, *Im Schatten des Krieges,* 41.

3. An overview of different definitions, theories, and stages of development can be found in Hroch, *Europa der Nationen.* See also Trencsenyi, *History,* 67ff.

4. Hroch, *Europa der Nationen,* 20.

5. Fischer, *Dositej Obradović,* 140.

6. Quoted in Meininger, *Formation,* 143.

7. Langewiesche, *Nation,* 16–17.

8. Sundhaussen, "Nation und Nationalstaat."

9. Hroch, "National Movement to the Fully-Formed Nation."

10. Trencsényi and Kopeček, *Discourses,* 1:142–43.

11. Georgescu, *Mémoires et projets,* xix.

12. Mazower, *Governing the World,* 49.

13. Hroch, "National Movements."

14. Gross, *Izvorno pravaštvo.*

15. Hroch, *Europa der Nationen,* 191ff.

16. Trencsényi and Kopeček, *Discourses,* 2:343.

17. Golescu, *Aufzeichnung,* 96.

18. Hopf, *Sprachnationalismus.*

19. Trencsényi and Kopeček, *Discourses,* 1:260.

20. Karanovich, *Development of Education,* 45.

21. Drace-Francis, *Modern Romanian Culture,* 40.

22. Ibid., 114ff.

23. Rumpler and Urbanitsch, *Habsburgermonarchie,* 503ff.

24. Turczynski, *Politische Trägergruppen,* 236ff.

25. Hroch, *Europa der Nationen,* 20.

26. Sundhaussen, *Einfluss,* 52ff.

27. Čolović, *Smrt.*

28. Weber, *Suche,* 46ff.

29. Hroch, *Europa der Nationen,* 145.

30. Maner, "Rumänische Nation," 80.

31. For example, in Riedel, *Erfindung der Balkanvölker.*

32. Quoted in Georgescu, *Romanians,* 117.

33. Ibid.

34. Trencsényi and Kopeček, *Discourses,* 2:234.

35. Magaš, *Croatia,* 202.

36. Zelepos, *Ethnisierung,* 264.

37. Ibid., 266; Skopetea, *"Uzor-kraljevina,"* 195ff.

38. Protić, *Uspon i pad srpske ideje,* 49; Trencsényi and Kopeček, *Discourses,* 2:241.

39. Čubrilović, *Istorija političke misli,* 160ff.

40. Ljušić, *Knjiga o Načertaniju,* 144.

41. Rumpler and Urbanitsch, *Habsburgermonarchie,* 7.

42. Quoted in Sundhaussen, *Geschichte Serbiens,* 75.

43. Sundhaussen, "Eliten"; Daskalov, *Bulgarian Revival,* 110.

44. Barkey, *Empire of Difference,* 264ff.

45. Gross, *Anfänge.*

46. Gounaris, *Steam over Macedonia,* 17.

47. Jakir, *Dalmatien,* 145–46.

48. Achim, *Roma,* 27.

49. Kogălniceanu, *Esquisse sur l'histoire,* 11ff.

50. Džambo, *Buchwesen,* 39, 41.

51. Karanovich, *Development of Education,* 13.

52. Crampton, *Bulgaria,* 51ff.; Drace-Francis, *Modern Romanian Culture,* 143ff.

53. Trencsényi and Kopeček, *Discourses,* 1:260.

54. Hannes Grandits, "'Europäisierung' im spätosmanischen Südosteuropa im 19. Jahrhundert: Von einer romantischen Idee zu rücksichtsloser Realpolitik," accessed February 12, 2018, http://www.europa.clio-online.de/essay/id/artikel-3569.

55. Mishkova, "Literacy."

56. Turczynski, *Politische Trägergruppen,* 49ff.

57. Mazower, *Balkans,* 150–51.

58. Reinkowski, *Dinge der Ordnung,* 156.

59. Ibid., 77–78.

60. Kaser, *Familie,* 229.

61. Berend and Ránki, *European Periphery,* 46; Lampe and Jackson, *Balkan Economic History,* 281.

62. Calic, *Sozialgeschichte Serbiens,* 59.

63. Erlich, *Family in Transition,* 32ff.

64. Kaser, "Household"; Novaković, *Selo,* 144ff.

65. Todorova, "Situating the Family."

66. Lampe and Jackson, *Balkan Economic History,* 289; Berend and Ránki, *Economic Development,* 37ff.

67. Thiersch, *L'état actuel,* 1:294.

68. Palairet, *Balkan Economies,* 47–48.

69. Chirot, *Social Change,* 140–41; Berend and Ránki, *Economic Development,* 35ff.

70. Quoted in Mazower, *Balkans,* 27.

71. Calic, *Sozialgeschichte Serbiens,* 75.

72. Ibid., 77.

73. Peričić, "Oskudica i glad u Dalmaciji."

74. Calic, *Sozialgeschichte Serbiens,* 103ff.

75. Palairet, *Balkan Economies,* 66.

76. Ibid., 66–67.

77. Calic, *Sozialgeschichte Serbiens,* 186.

78. Brown, *Loyal unto Death,* 56.

79. Calic, *Sozialgeschichte Serbiens,* 184.

80. Meininger, "Social Stratification."

81. Iosa, *Bucarest,* 34.

82. Sundhaussen, "Südosteuropäische Gesellschaft," 401.

83. Höpken, "Schrittmacher," 83.

84. Ianeva, "Main Characteristics."

85. Todorov, *Balkan City,* 240ff.

86. Daskalova, *Gramotnost,* 140.

87. Davidova, *Balkan Transitions,* 141.

88. Papakonstantinou, "Transport."

89. Strong, *Greece as a Kingdom,* 33–34.

90. Papakonstantinou, "Transport."

91. Strong, *Greece as a Kingdom,* 35.

92. Quoted in Gounaris, *Steam over Macedonia,* 35.

93. Quoted in Papakonstantinou, "Transport," 375.

94. Karaman, *Hrvatska,* 216.

95. Quataert, *Ottoman Empire,* 126.

96. Karakasidou, *Fields of Wheat,* 46–47; Berend and Ránki, *Economic Development,* 36.

97. Berend and Ránki, *European Periphery,* 159.

98. Casanova, "Religion in Modernity."

99. Bayly, *Birth,* 325ff.

100. Detrez, "Pre-National Identities," 37.

101. Gavrilova, *Bulgarian Urban Culture,* 100, 102.

102. Paić-Vukić, *Svijet Mustafe Muhibbija,* 189–90.

103. Grunert, *Glauben im Hinterland,* 94.

104. Montagu, *Letters,* 113.

105. Mazower, *Balkans,* 56ff.

106. Hasluck, *Christianity and Islam,* 1:64.

107. Davidova, *Balkan Transitions,* 40.

108. Mazower, *Balkans,* 66.

109. Detrez, "Pre-National Identities."

110. Langewiesche, *Nation,* 3.

111. Roudometof and Robertson, *Nationalism,* 101ff.

112. Crampton, *Bulgaria,* 46.

113. Fejzić, "Political Thought."

114. Karpat, *Social Foundations.*

115. Abu Jaber, "Millet System."

116. Mazower, *Balkans,* 75.

117. Karić, *Srbija,* 226.

118. Daskalov, "Bulgarian-Greek Dis / Entanglements."

119. Mazower, *Balkans,* 39.

120. Trencsényi and Kopeček, *Discourses,* 2:304.

121. Gross, *Anfänge,* 227ff.

122. Perinić Lewis and Rudan, "Spectemur Agendo," 59–60.

123. Buchenau, *Orthodoxe Antiwestler,* 29ff.

124. Grunert, *Glauben im Hinterland,* 79.

125. Ibid., 83.

126. Petrović, *Rakovica,* 2:57.

127. Clayer, *Religion et nation,* 39.

128. Gavrilova, *Bulgarian Urban Culture,* 213.

129. Rogel, "Wandering Monk."

130. Giūrova and Danova, *Kniga za bŭlgarskite khadzi,* 32.

131. Matkovski, *Gjurčin Kokaleski,* 154ff.

132. Despot, *Amerikas Weg,* 144.

133. Heyer, *Orientalische Frage,* S. 9.

134. Ibid., 93.

135. Clayer, *Religion et nation,* 35.

136. Aleksov, "Habsburg Confessionalism."

137. Deusch, *Kultusprotektorat,* 51.

138. Rosenberg, *World Connecting,* 875; Bayly, *Birth,* 338.

139. Schulze, *Islamischer Internationalismus,* 49ff.

140. Filandra, *Bošnjaci i moderna.*

141. Benbassa, "Relais nationalistes"; Brenner, *Geschichte des Zionismus,* 10–11.

142. Benbassa, *Geschichte,* 144, 207.

143. Casanova, "Religion."

144. Wallerstein, *World-System IV,* 1ff.

145. Čubrilović, *Istorija političke misli,* 240ff.

146. Mazower, *Governing the World,* 49–50; cf. Siemann, "Asyl."

147. Kaelble, *Wege zur Demokratie,* 33ff.; Fahrmeir, *Revolutionen und Reformen,* 251ff.

148. Rumpler, *Chance für Mitteleuropa,* 287ff.

149. Fahrmeir, *Revolutionen und Reformen,* 277ff.

150. Rumpler and Urbanitsch, *Habsburgermonarchie,* 2151.

151. Valentić and Čoralić, *Povijest Hrvata,* 394.

152. Stavrianos, *Balkans since 1453,* 255.

153. Osterhammel, *Transformation of the World,* 545.

154. Gross, *Anfänge,* 263ff.

155. Kaelble, *Wege zur Demokratie,* 33ff.; Osterhammel, *Transformation of the World,* 544.

156. Turczynski, *Politische Trägergruppen,* 252.

157. Ibid., 248.

158. Zub, *Mihail Kogălniceanu 1817–1891,* 13, 22.

159. Zub, *Mihail Kogălniceanu: Istoric,* 265ff.

160. Trencsényi and Kopeček, *Discourses,* 2:49.

161. Zub, *Mihail Kogălniceanu 1817–1891,* 22.

162. Ibid., 96–97.

163. Dumbrava, *Geschichte,* 49.

164. Drace-Francis, *Modern Romanian Culture,* 129ff.

165. Ibid., 137–38.

166. Jelavich and Jelavich, *Establishment,* 114ff.

167. Zub, *Mihail Kogălniceanu 1817–1891,* 71.

168. Achim, *Roma,* 98.

169. Suciu, "Echo in Romania," 752.

170. Cernovodeanu and Stanciu, "Romanians."

171. Jelavich and Jelavich, *Establishment,* 114ff.

172. Quoted in Toth, "Biographien," 150.

173. Ibid.

174. Stavrianos, *Balkan Federation,* 81–82.

175. Djordjević, "Projects."

176. Mishkova, "Balkan Liberalisms," 143.

177. Clewing, "Staatensystem," 496ff.

178. Feichtinger, Prutsch, and Csáky, *Habsburg postcolonial.*

179. Katus, "Magyaren."

180. Schödl, *Kroatische Nationalpolitik,* 51ff.

181. Čubrilović, *Istorija političke misli,* 240ff.

182. Protić, *Uspon i pad srpske ideje,* 47.

183. Čubrilović, *Istorija političke misli,* 160ff.

184. McClellan, *Svetozar Marković,* 36; Čubrilović, *Istorija političke misli,* 230.

185. Stavrianos, *Balkans since 1453,* 397.

186. Siupiur and Cain, "La culture."

187. Velichi, "Romanian-Bulgarian Relations"; Velichi, *La Roumanie,* 126ff.

188. Jelavich and Jelavich, *Establishment,* 135–36.

189. Osterhammel, *Transformation of the World,* 516ff.

190. Armitage and Subrahmanyam, *Age of Revolutions.*

191. Kosev, "Uprising," 153.

192. Ibid.

193. Kosev, *Istoriia na aprilskoto vŭstanie.*

194. Kolarov, *Plovdiv,* 55.

195. Kosev, "Uprising"; Kosev, *Istoriia na aprilskoto vŭstanie.*

196. Jelavich and Jelavich, *Establishment,* 143ff.

197. Zaharia, "Liuben Karavelov," 57–58.

198. Jelavich, *Balkan Entanglements,* 270.

199. Quoted in Zaharia, "Liuben Karavelov," 80–81.

200. Quoted in ibid., 136.

201. Karavelov, *Amerika,* 145; Zaharia, "Liuben Karavelov," 284ff.

202. Kavalski, "Balkan America?" 138–39.

203. Marković, "Ljuben Karavelov."

204. Karavelov, *Zapiski za Bŭlgariia.*

205. Meininger, "Journalists."

206. Jireček, *Fürstenthum Bulgarien,* 383.

207. Karavelov, *Zapiski za Bŭlgariia,* 62.

208. More, *Under the Balkans,* 16–17.

209. Karavelov, *Zapiski za Bŭlgariia,* 62.

210. More, Under the Balkans, 9–10; Karavelov, *Zapiski za Bŭlgariia,* 61.

211. Harbova, "L'espace culturel."

212. Karavelov, *Zapiski za Bŭlgariia*, 76.

213. Jančeva, *Etnologija*, 75.

214. Crampton, *Bulgaria, 1878–1918*, 48.

215. Gavrilova, *Bulgarian Urban Culture*, 127ff.

216. Palairet, *Balkan Economies*, 61–62; More, *Under the Balkans*, 18–19.

217. Ersoy-Hacısalihoğlu, "Textile Trade."

218. Jančeva, *Etnologija*, 38ff.

219. Gavrilova, *Bulgarian Urban Culture*, 163.

220. Kolarov, *Plovdiv*, 53.

221. Daskalov, *Bulgarian Revival*, 133.

222. Kolarov, *Plovdiv*, 41–42.

223. Gavrilova, *Bulgarian Urban Culture*, 144.

224. Jireček, *Fürstenthum Bulgarien*, 387.

225. Gavrilova, *Bulgarian Urban Culture*, 148.

226. Genchev, *Vŭzrozhdenskiiat Plovdiv*, 447ff.

227. More, *Under the Balkans*, 11.

228. Crampton, *Bulgaria*, 58.

229. Genchev, *Vŭzrozhdenskiiat Plovdiv*, 424ff.

230. Meininger, *Formation*, 123ff.

231. Genchev, "Bulgarian Cultural Revival."

232. Barth, *Reise*, 48.

233. Kosev, *Istoriia na Aprilskoto vŭstanie*, 332.

234. Zaharia, "Liuben Karavelov," 289.

235. Meininger, *Formation*, 168.

236. Gavrilova, *Bulgarian Urban Culture*, 49, 72.

237. Moravenov, *Pametnik za plovdivskoto khristiiansko;* Detrez, "Relations"; Lory, "Immigration."

238. Crampton, *Bulgaria*, 89.

239. Georgieva, "Pomaks."

240. Boué, *Europäische Türkei*, 61.

241. Palairet, *Balkan Economies*, 58.

242. Brunnbauer, "Families."

243. Brunnbauer, *Gebirgsgesellschaften*, 79ff., 345ff.

244. Baleva and Brunnbauer, *Batak*.

245. Wasow, *Rhodopen*, 353.

246. Kosev, *Istoriia na Aprilskoto vŭstanie*, 359ff.

247. Wasow, *Rhodopen*, 364.

248. MacGahan, *Turkish Atrocities*, 11.

249. Kosev, "Uprising."

250. MacGahan, *Turkish Atrocities*, 22–23.

251. Kemal, *Memoirs,* 126.

252. Todorova, *Bones of Contention.*

6. Imperialism and Crisis

1. Conrad, *Globalgeschichte,* 149. See also Snyder and Younger, *Balkans.*

2. Raphael, *Imperiale Gewalt,* 9.

3. Rosenberg, *World Connecting,* 9–10.

4. Schöllgen, *Zeitalter des Imperialismus,* 45.

5. Baumgart, "Orientalische Frage."

6. Gall, "Die europäischen Mächte," 4. See also Zechlin, "Türkische Meerengen."

7. Jelavich, *Balkan Entanglements,* 27ff.

8. Baumgart, *Europäisches Konzert,* 337.

9. Donia, "Bosnia and Herzegovina."

10. Baumgart, *Europäisches Konzert,* 417.

11. Schöllgen, *Zeitalter des Imperialismus,* 66.

12. Schöllgen, *Imperialismus und Gleichgewicht,* 80.

13. Keisinger, *Unzivilisierte Kriege.*

14. Rodogno, *Against Massacre,* 154ff.

15. Jelavich and Jelavich, *Establishment,* 141ff.

16. Schwartz, *Ethnische "Säuberungen,"* 263.

17. Baumgart, *Europäisches Konzert,* 423.

18. Ibid., 425.

19. Ballantyne and Burton, "Empires."

20. Schöllgen, *Zeitalter des Imperialismus,* 52f.

21. Schwartz, *Ethnische "Säuberungen,"* 254.

22. Ibid., 245ff.

23. Rodogno, *Against Massacre,* 118ff.

24. Schwartz, *Ethnische "Säuberungen,"* 279ff.

25. Brown, *Loyal unto Death,* 97; Troebst, *Mussolini,* 97ff.

26. Adanir, *Makedonische Frage,* 106ff.; Karakasidou, *Fields of Wheat,* 77ff.

27. Brown, *Loyal unto Death,* 4–5.

28. Rodogno, *Against Massacre,* 238ff.; Sowards, *Austria's Policy.*

29. Rodogno, *Against Massacre,* 244.

30. Matuz, *Das Osmanische Reich,* 249ff.

31. Hösch, *Balkanländer,* 177.

32. Popović-Obradović, *Parlamentarizam.*

33. Quoted in Buchenau, *Orthodoxe Antiwestler,* 67.

34. Seewann, *Geschichte,* 2:9.

35. For a thorough description of the state constitutions, see Heuberger, "Politische Institutionen."

36. Steindorff, *Kroatien,* 113–14.

37. Seewann, *Geschichte,* 2:8ff.

38. Rumpler, *Chance für Mitteleuropa,* 521.

39. Seton-Watson, *Southern Slav Question.*

40. Szabo, "Uzroci."

41. Magaš, *Croatia,* 450.

42. Williamson, *Austria-Hungary and the Origins,* 21ff.

43. Stachel, "Halb-kolonial," 169–70.

44. Hajdarpasic, *Whose Bosnia?* 176ff.

45. Aleksov, "Habsburg Confessionalism"; Okey, *Taming Balkan Nationalism,* 92.

46. Quoted in Heuberger, "Politische Institutionen," 2405.

47. Kraljačić, *Kalajev režim;* Okey, *Taming Balkan Nationalism;* Juzbašić, *Politika i privreda;* Donia, "Bosnia and Herzegovina"; Sugar, *Industrialization of Bosnia-Hercegovina.*

48. Purivatra, *Nacionalni i politički razvitak,* 142.

49. Baernreither, *Fragmente,* 68.

50. Dedijer, *Road to Sarajevo,* 175ff.

51. Williamson, *Austria-Hungary and the Origins,* 61ff.

52. Dülffer, Kröger, and Wippich, *Vermiedene Kriege,* 614.

53. Veliz, *Politics of Croatia-Slavonia,* 112.

54. Kann, *Geschichte des Habsburgerreiches,* 581.

55. Macartney, *Habsburg Empire,* 791.

56. Behschnitt, *Nationalismus,* 202; Hajdarpasic, *Whose Bosnia?* 129ff.

57. Dedijer, *Road to Sarajevo,* 135–36.

58. Afflerbach, *Dreibund,* 596; Bled, *François-Ferdinand d'Autriche,* 328ff.

59. Dedijer, *Road to Sarajevo,* 263.

60. Okey, *Taming Balkan Nationalism,* 194ff.

61. Jakir, *Dalmatien,* 13.

62. Wallerstein, *World-System IV,* 11.

63. Stokes, *Politics as Development,* 177ff.

64. Perović, *Između anarhije,* 262.

65. Quoted in Milutinović, *Getting over Europe,* 66, 73–74.

66. Stojanović, "Anti-Urban Discourse," 72–73.

67. Quoted in Daskalov, "Ideas," 144.

68. Stojanović, "Anti-Urban Discourse," 69, 72–73.

69. Heinen, *Legion "Erzengel Michael,"* 72ff.

70. Dimou, *Entangled Paths,* 303.

71. Polexe, *Netzwerke,* 117ff.

72. Perović, *Srpski socijalisti.*

73. Njagulov, "Early Socialism," 205ff.

74. Ibid., 210ff.

75. Dimou, *Entangled Paths,* 301ff.

76. Daskalov, "Agrarian Ideologies," 293ff.; Andreas Moritsch, "Bauernparteien."

77. Daskalov, "Agrarian Ideologies."

78. Quoted in Heinen, *Legion "Erzengel Michael,"* 78.

79. Stokes, *Politics as Development;* Protić, "Ideology."

80. Maier, "Leviathan 2.0."

81. Schwartz, *Ethnische "Säuberungen,"* 244.

82. Mazower, *Balkans,* 116.

83. McCarthy, *Death and Exile,* 339.

84. Schwartz, *Ethnische "Säuberungen,"* 185ff.; Bayly, *Birth,* 439ff.

85. Storfa, *Politische Schriften,* 74ff.; Oldson, *Providential Anti-Semitism,* 106.

86. Benz and Bergmann, *Handbuch des Antisemitismus,* 101–2; Fink, *Defending the Rights,* 5ff.

87. Jovanović, *Vlada Aleksandra Obrenovića,* 390.

88. Zelepos, *Ethnisierung,* 275.

89. Protić, "Ideology," 161–62.

90. Ekmečić, *Stvaranje Jugoslavije,* 494–95; Skopetea, *"Uzor-kraljevina,"* 219ff.

91. Quoted in Weber, *Suche,* 166.

92. Protić, "Ideology," 170–71.

93. Zelepos, *Ethnisierung,* 159, 201.

94. Bochmann, "Patriotismusbegriff," 55.

95. Ekmečić, *Stvaranje Jugoslavije,* 487.

96. *Beograd u sećanjima,* 183.

97. Weber, *Suche,* 166, 169.

98. Jovanović, *Vlada Aleksandra Obrenovića,* 433.

99. Todorova, "Course and Discourses," 78.

100. Mazower, *Governing the World,* 61ff.

101. Quoted in ibid., 60.

102. Quoted in Njagulov, "Early Socialism," 262.

103. Čubrilović, *Istorija političke misli,* 396–97.

104. Ibid., 261ff.

105. Bayly, *Birth.*

106. Turnock, "Railways."

107. Gounaris, *Steam over Macedonia,* 236–37.

108. Berend and Ránki, *European Periphery,* 100.

109. Gounaris, *Ta Valkania,* 541; Rusev, "Poštenski službi."

110. Papakonstantinou, "Transport," 390–91.

111. Cvjetković, "Telegrafska i telefonska služba."

112. Pašić, *Sloga Srbo-Hrvata,* 66–67.

113. Karanovich, *Development of Education,* 181.

114. Gounaris, *Steam over Macedonia,* 281.

115. Daniel, "Krimkrieg."

116. Suciu, "Echo in Romania."

117. Gounaris, *Ta Valkania,* 546ff.

118. Mager, *Historia tou Hellēnikou typou,* 111–12. I am grateful to Anna Vlacho-poulou and Ioannis Zelepos for gathering the information on news reporting.

119. Tesla, *My Inventions,* 71.

120. Ibid., 57.

121. Tesla, "Transmission," 22.

122. Carlson, *Tesla,* 403ff.

123. Tesla, *My Inventions,* 101.

124. Nikola Tesla, "The Wonder World to Be Created by Electricity," *Manufacturer's Record* 9 (September 1915), accessed March 22, 2018, http://www.tfcbooks.com/tesla/1915-09-09.htm.

125. Skala, "Bošković's Fundamental Theory."

126. Lampe and Jackson, *Balkan Economic History,* 196.

127. Brunnbauer, "Labour Emigration."

128. Quoted in Klemenčić, "Images of America," 210.

129. Benz and Bergmann, *Handbuch des Antisemitismus,* 101–2.

130. Despot, *Amerikas Weg,* 209ff.

131. Savić, *Zanati i industrija,* 210.

132. Čizmić, "Emigration from Croatia." For a discussion of numbers, see Brunn-bauer, *Globalizing Southeastern Europe,* 40ff.

133. Balch, *Slavic Fellow Citizens,* 189.

134. Prpic, *South Slavic Immigration,* 84.

135. Puskás, *Hungary,* 84–85.

136. Balch, *Slavic Fellow Citizens,* 181.

137. Hoerder, "Migrations," 498.

138. Ibid., 472.

139. Despot, *Amerikas Weg,* 220ff.

140. Kralj, "Balkan Minds," 209–10.

141. Spiliotis, *Transterritorialität,* 51.

142. Brunnbauer, *Globalizing Southeastern Europe,* 318–19.

143. Smirnova, "Albania's 'Red Bishop,'" 34.

144. Kacza, *Fan Stylian Noli,* 3.

145. Noli, *George Castrioti.*

146. Clayer, *Religion et nation,* 36–37.

147. Hetzer, *Geschichte des Buchhandels,* 78–79.

148. Rumpler and Urbanitsch, *Habsburgermonarchie,* 1295.

149. Balch, *Slavic Fellow Citizens,* 169.

150. Despot, *Amerikas Weg,* 231ff.

151. Pipa, "Fan Noli."

152. Roudometof, "Transnationalism."

153. Brunnbauer, *Globalizing Southeastern Europe,* 207ff.

154. Spiliotis, *Transterritorialität,* 25ff.

155. Ibid., 322ff.

156. Stamenovitch, *L'émigration yougoslave,* 303; Purić, *Naši iseljenici,* 66.

157. Hoerder, "Migrations," 480ff.

158. Graff, Kenwood, and Lougheed, *Growth,* 79; Conrad, *Globalgeschichte,* 158ff.

159. Palotás, "Wirtschaftliche Aspekte."

160. Aldcroft, *Europe's Third World,* 27.

161. Berend and Ránki, *European Periphery,* 98; Plaschka, Drabek, and Zaar, *Eisenbahnbau.*

162. Benbassa, *Geschichte,* 142–43.

163. Graff, Kenwood, and Lougheed, *Growth,* 27–28.

164. Calic, *Sozialgeschichte Serbiens,* 125.

165. Lilova, "Barbarians," 19.

166. Perović, *Između anarhije,* 262.

167. Topik and Wells, "Commodity Chains," 618.

168. Berend and Ránki, *European Periphery,* 83; Tunçer, *Sovereign Debt.*

169. Gounaris, "Salonica."

170. Huber, *Channelling Mobilities;* Paulmann, "Straits."

171. Berend and Ránki, *Economic Development,* 170; Chirot, *Social Change,* 122.

172. Gounaris, *Steam over Macedonia,* 26, 91ff.

173. Ibid., 104.

174. Berend, "Balkan Economic Development," 282.

175. Jackson, "Balkan Demographic Experience."

176. Murgescu, *România,* 119ff.; Bairoch, *Commerce extérieur.*

177. Aldcroft, *Europe's Third World,* 21.

178. Berend and Ránki, *European Periphery,* 117.

179. Bairoch and Kozul-Wright, "Globalization Myths."

180. Calic, *Sozialgeschichte Serbiens,* 170ff.

181. Pamuk and Williamson, "De-Industrialization," 167.

182. Pamuk, "Decline."

183. Palairet, *Balkan Economies,* 54.

184. Ibid., 74–75.

185. More, *Under the Balkans,* 19; Neuburger, *Tobacco,* 54–55.

186. David, *Nationalisme économique,* 97.

187. Berend and Ránki, "Polen," 786; David, *Nationalisme économique,* 120ff.

188. David, *Nationalisme économique,* 146.

189. Ianeva, "Main Characteristics."

190. Berend and Ránki, *European Periphery,* 144.

191. Graff, Kenwood, and Lougheed, *Growth,* 128.

192. Karaman, *Industrijalizacija,* 56ff.

193. Sugar, *Industrialization of Bosnia-Hercegovina.*

194. Berend and Ránki, *European Periphery,* 120ff.; Chirot, *Social Change,* 122.

195. Gerschenkron, *Economic Backwardness;* Landes, *Wealth and Poverty,* 289.

196. Gyimesi, "Motive und Probleme."

197. Calic, *Sozialgeschichte Serbiens,* 446.

198. A comparison of different economic estimates can be found in Pamuk, *Estimating* and Aldcroft, *Europe's Third World.* The methodology of Good, "Economic Lag" is questionable; its data appear inflated.

199. Piketty, *Capital,* 95.

200. Pamuk, *Estimating,* 237.

201. Beckert, *Empire of Cotton,* xx, 94–95; Pomeranz, *Great Divergence.*

202. Berend and Ránki, *European Periphery,* 143–44.

203. Jezernik, *Wild Europe;* Goldsworthy, "Imperialismus der Imagination."

204. Clarke, "Reporting the Bulgarian Massacres."

205. Keisinger, *Unzivilisierte Kriege,* 46.

206. Goldsworthy, *Inventing Ruritania,* 101ff.

207. Todorova, *Imagining,* 116ff.

208. Quoted in Reynolds-Cordileone, "Displaying Bosnia," 31.

209. Schwartz, *Ethnische "Säuberungen,"* 185ff.

210. Gingrich, "Kulturgeschichte"; Feichtinger, "K. u. k. Orientalismus"; Hajdarpasic, *Whose Bosnia?* 186ff.

211. Stachel, "Der koloniale Blick."

212. Donia, "Bosnia and Herzegovina."

213. Andrić, *Bridge,* 174.

214. Reynolds, "Vorstellung Bosniens in Wien," 248; Reynolds-Cordileone, "Displaying Bosnia."

215. Stachel, "Der koloniale Blick"; Donia, "Bosnia and Herzegovina."

216. Džambo, "Milena Preindlsberger-Mrazović."

217. Sparks, "Good Woman of Sarajevo."

218. Džambo, "Milena Preindlsberger-Mrazović," 183.

219. Ibid.

220. Preindlsberger-Mrazović, *Bosnische Volksmärchen,* ix.

221. Goldsworthy, *Inventing Ruritania;* Michail, "Western Attitudes."

222. Hubka, *Österreichisch-ungarische Offiziersmission,* 1.

223. Vidojković, *Helden und Königsmörder,* 537–38.

224. Schanes, *Serbien im Ersten Weltkrieg,* 13, 53.

225. Todorova, *Imagining,* 177.

226. For example, in Clark, *Sleepwalkers;* Bjelić and Savić, *Balkan as Metaphor;* Bakić-Hayden, "Nesting Orientalism."

227. Baleva, *Bulgarien im Bild,* 72.

228. Baleva, "Nationalmythos Batak"; Vezenkov, "Projekt."

229. Brown, *Loyal unto Death,* 172ff.

230. Trotsky, *Balkan Wars,* 234.

231. Troebst, *Mussolini,* 97ff.; Boškovska, "Entführung."

232. Quoted in Hering, "Osmanenzeit," 371.

233. Quoted in Hristov, *Otvăd identičnostta,* 113.

234. Greenhalgh, *Fair World;* Rosenberg, "Transnational Currents."

235. Davidova, *Balkan Transitions,* 132ff.

236. Aronsson and Elgenius, *National Museums;* Hajdu, "Pavilions."

237. Dušković, *Srbija na svetskoj izložbi.*

238. Hristov, *Otvăd identičnostta,* 148; Dušković, *Srbija na svetskoj izložbi.*

239. Trgovčević, "South Slav Intellectuals."

240. Ignjatović, "Images."

241. Ćurčin, *Ivan Meštrović,* 56.

242. Dobreva, "Bulgarien auf der Pariser Weltausstellung," 142, 115–16.

243. Neuburger, "Chicago and Back"; Todorova, *Imagining,* 39ff.

244. Quoted in Todorova, *Imagining,* 42.

245. Neuburger, "Chicago and Back."

246. Mishkova, "Balkan Occidentalism."

247. Milutinović, *Getting over Europe,* 111; Gvozden, *Jovan Dučić putopisac,* 165.

248. Quoted in Bracewell and Drace-Francis, *Balkan Departures,* 15.

249. Meininger, *Formation,* 155.

250. Hecker, *Russische Universalgeschichtsschreibung;* Lilova, "Barbarians."

251. Nagy-Talavera, *Nicolae Iorga,* 93.

252. Iorga, *Essai de synthèse,* ix.

253. Dinić, *Srpska pisma,* 10.

254. Milutinović, "Oh, to Be a European!" 269.

255. Ilić-Agapova, *Istorija Beograda,* 373–74.

256. *Dnevnik pobeda,* 11ff.

257. Dimitrijević, *Socijalistički radnički pokret,* 107ff., 204ff.

258. Trotsky, *Balkan Wars,* 62.

259. *Dnevnik pobeda,* 17–18.

260. *Beograd u sećanjima,* 39.

261. *Dnevnik pobeda,* 274.

262. Trotsky, *Balkan Wars,* 63.

263. *Politika,* June 28, 1913, 1.

264. Quoted in Milutinović, *Getting over Europe,* 40.

265. *Politika,* June 28, 1913, 1.

266. Boeckh, *Von den Balkankriegen,* 122.

267. Tucović, *Srbija i Arbanija.*

268. Živojinović, *Kralj Petar I Karađorđević,* 508.

269. Evropski pokret, *Spoljna politika Srbije,* 106.

270. Bjelajac, "Novi (stari) zapleti," 24.

271. Calic, *Sozialgeschichte Serbiens,* 174.

272. Petrović, *Istorija industrije Beograda,* 72–73.

273. Calic, *Sozialgeschichte Serbiens,* 226.

274. Čubrilović, *Istorija Beograda,* 297.

275. Calic, *Sozialgeschichte Serbiens,* 321ff.; Dimitrijević, *Socijalistički radnički pokret.*

276. Mišković, *Basare und Boulevards,* 307.

277. Quoted in ibid., 306.

278. Njagulov, "Early Socialism," 235, 254–55.

279. Stojanović, *Srbija i demokratija,* 386.

280. Stojanović, *Kaldrma i asfalt.*

281. Mišković, *Basare und Boulevards,* 262.

282. Prošić-Dvornić, *Odevanje u Beogradu,* 215ff., 519ff.

283. *Beograd u sećanjima,* 40.

284. Prošić-Dvornić, *Odevanje u Beogradu,* 473ff.

285. *Beograd u sećanjima,* 47.

286. Lazarević, *Sabrana dela,* 391.

287. Stojanović, *Kaldrma i asfalt,* 201.

288. Prošić-Dvornić, *Odevanje u Beogradu,* 187.

289. Antonić and Tasić, *Istorija Beograda,* 213.

290. Stokes, *Politics as Development.*

291. Prošić-Dvornić, *Odevanje u Beogradu,* 58, 183.

292. Skerlić, *Istorijski pregled,* 72–73.

293. Kanitz, *Königreich Serbien,* 85.

294. Trotsky, *Balkan Wars,* 103.

295. Quoted in Stojanović, *Kaldrma i asfalt,* 351, 353.

296. Prošić-Dvornić, *Odevanje u Beogradu,* 138.

297. Quoted in Peković, "Ženski časopisi," 127.

298. Tasić, *Znamenite srpske žene,* 35–36.

299. Ibid., 12–13.

300. Quoted in Petzer and Richter, *"Isochimenen,"* 154.

301. Quoted in ibid., 33.

302. Ibid., 37–38.

303. Tasić, *Znamenite srpske žene,* 24.

304. Wachtel, *Making a Nation,* 29, 54.

305. Stojanović, *Kaldrma i asfalt,* 230–31.

306. Trgovčević, "South Slav Intellectuals."

307. Bartulović, *Od Revolucionarne Omladine,* 22ff.

308. Matković, "Hrvatska percepcija."

309. Aleksov, "One Hundred Years."

310. Plaschka, *Avantgarde,* 453.

311. Ekmečić, *Stvaranje Jugoslavije,* 532ff; Dedijer, *Road to Sarajevo,* 175ff., 214ff.

312. Sageman, *Political Violence,* 340.

313. Dedijer, *Road to Sarajevo,* 196.

314. Van Hengel, "Gavrilo Princip."

315. "Der Prozeß," 389–90, 406–7; Dedijer, *Road to Sarajevo,* 341.

316. Dušan T. Bataković, "Nikola Pašić, les radicaux et la 'Main noire': Les défis à la démocratie parlementaire serbe 1903–1917," accessed February 18, 2018, http://www .doiserbia.nb.rs/img/doi/0350-7653/2006/0350-76530637143B.pdf.

317. Dedijer, *Road to Sarajevo,* 339.

318. "Der Prozeß," 397.

319. Dedijer, *Road to Sarajevo,* 338.

7. From the Balkan Wars to the Second World War

1. Höpken, "'Modern Wars,'" 19–90.

2. Quoted in Malcolm, *Kosovo,* 253.

3. International Commission, *Other Balkan Wars,* 151, 154–55.

4. Quoted in Schwartz, *Ethnische "Säuberungen,"* 299.

5. Bartov and Weitz, *Shatterzone of Empires,* 6.

6. *Dnevnik pobeda,* 125.

7. Levene, *Genocide;* Weitz, *Century of Genocide;* Biondich, *Balkans.*

8. Vickers, *Albanians,* 53ff.

9. Hall, *Balkan Wars.*

10. Ginio, *Culture of Defeat.*

11. Ther, *Dunkle Seite,* 71ff.; Boeckh, *Balkankriege,* 78ff.

12. Rauchensteiner, *First World War,* 16.

13. Mommsen, *Der Erste Weltkrieg,* 26.

14. Quoted in Röhl, *Kaiser,* 162.

15. Angelow, "Kriegsfall Serbien," 322.

16. Berghahn, *Der Erste Weltkrieg;* Mommsen, *Der Erste Weltkrieg,* 34ff.; Fried, *Austro-Hungarian War Aims.*

17. Williamson, *Austria-Hungary and the Origins.*

18. Cornwall, "Serbia."

19. Krumeich, *Juli 1914,* 128. Clark, *Sleepwalkers,* 96ff. has recently taken up the Austrian argumentation, but he, too, relies on speculation. Cf. Calic, "Kriegstreiber."

20. Rauchensteiner, *First World War,* 30ff.

21. Janz, *14—Der Große Krieg,* 9–10.

22. Gumz, *Resurrection,* 21; cf. Kramer, *Dynamic.*

23. Strachan, *First World War,* 27.

24. Reiss, *Šta sam video,* 65.

25. Mladenović, *Porodica u Srbiji,* 17–18.

26. Ekmečić, *Stvaranje Jugoslavije,* 755; Strachan, *First World War,* 159; Fryer, *Destruction of Serbia,* 97ff.

27. Scheer, "Manifestation," 221.

28. Gumz, *Resurrection,* 62ff.

29. Opfer, *Im Schatten des Krieges;* Mitrović, *Srbija,* 311ff.

30. Mayerhofer, *Zwischen Freund und Feind.*

31. Kreiser and Neumann, *Geschichte,* 371ff.

32. Paulová, *Tajný výbor Maffie.*

33. Hösch, *Balkanländer,* 193.

34. Quoted in Wachtel, *Making a Nation,* 70.

35. Magaš, *Croatia,* 465.

36. Calic, *Geschichte Jugoslawiens,* 79ff.

37. Stavrianos, *Balkans since 1453,* 572ff.

38. Manela, *Wilsonian Moment,* 219ff.

39. Sharp, *Versailles Settlement,* 139–40; Fisch, *Selbstbestimmungsrecht der Völker,* 144ff.

40. MacMillan, *Peacemakers,* 119ff.; Bartl, *Albanien,* 195.

41. Sharp, *Versailles Settlement,* 141.

42. Fisch, *Selbstbestimmungsrecht der Völker,* 182ff.

43. Kessler, "Gescheiterte Integration."

44. Sharp, *Consequences of Peace,* 133ff.

45. Rothschild, *East Central Europe,* 9.

46. Abulafia, *Great Sea,* 587ff.

47. Cited in Marrus, *Unwanted,* 100.

48. Hirschon, *Crossing the Aegean;* Pentzopoulos, *Balkan Exchange.*

49. Zelepos, *Geschichte,* 121ff.

50. Ther, *Dunkle Seite,* 69ff.

51. Teichova, "East-Central and South-East Europe," 894.

52. Calic, *Geschichte Jugoslawiens,* 85ff.

53. Boia, *Rumänische Elite,* S. 46–47.

54. Livezeanu, *Cultural Politics,* 10ff.

55. Pezo, *Zwangsmigration.*

56. Dragostinova, *Between Two Motherlands,* 121, 132.

57. Spiliotis, *Transterritorialität,* 156ff., 216.

58. Innerhofer, "Post-War Economies."

59. Lenger, *Metropolen der Moderne,* 904.

60. Mazower, *Greece,* 19.

61. Gligorijević, *Parlament.*

62. Daskalov, *Debating the Past,* 110.

63. Bell, *Peasants in Power,* 55ff.

64. Schultz, *Europäischer Sozialismus,* 174ff.

65. Nejkow, *Unruhiger Balkan,* 174.

66. Quoted in Schultz, *Europäischer Sozialismus,* 193.

67. Bell, *Peasants in Power,* 154ff.

68. Quoted in Daskalov, *Debating the Past,* 98.

69. Nejkow, *Unruhiger Balkan,* 175.

70. Ibid.

71. Grišina, "Balkany v planach Kominterna"; Bushkoff, "Revolutionary Tradition."

72. Crampton, *Concise History of Bulgaria,* 149ff.; Daskalov, "Agrarian Ideologies."

73. Austin, *Founding a Balkan State.*

74. Bartl, *Albanien,* 204–5; Belegu, "La révolution."

75. Hitchins, *History of Romania,* 168ff.

76. Burks, *Communism,* 76–77.

77. Jackson, *Comintern and Peasant,* 158ff.

78. Djilas, *Contested Country,* 91ff.

79. Maner, *Parlamentarismus in Rumänien,* 44ff.

80. Calic, *Geschichte Jugoslawiens,* 92.

81. Moritsch, "Bauernparteien," 381.

82. Calic, *Geschichte Jugoslawiens,* 93.

83. Polanyi, *Great Transformation.*

84. Raphael, *Imperiale Gewalt,* 98.

85. Mazower, *After the War,* 49; Schulze, *Staat und Nation,* 297; Hobsbawm, *Age of Extremes,* 109ff.

86. Nielsen, *Making Yugoslavs.*

87. Quoted in Maner, *Parlamentarismus in Rumänien,* 255.

88. Spiliotis, "Metaxas-Diktatur."

89. Raphael, *Imperiale Gewalt,* 193.

90. Moore, *Social Origins,* 441.

91. Habibi, "Regime Ahmed Zogus."

92. Herbert, *Geschichte Deutschlands,* 44ff.

93. Calinescu, "1927 Generation."

94. Costantini, *Antiliberalismo nazionalista,* 50ff.

95. Eliade, *Erinnerungen,* 137–38.

96. Laignel-Lavastine, *Cioran, Eliade, Ionesco,* 98–99.

97. Costantini, *Antiliberalismo nazionalista,* 50ff.

98. Laignel-Lavastine, *Cioran, Eliade, Ionesco,* 103ff.

99. Surugiu, "Nae Ionescu," 69.

100. Eliade, *Erinnerungen,* 179.

101. Ornea, *Romanian Extreme Right,* 265ff.; Costantini, *Antiliberalismo nazionalista,* 155–56; Sebastian, *Journal,* 8–9.

102. Heinen, *Legion "Erzengel Michael."*

103. Krizman, *Ante Pavelić;* Jelić-Butić, *Ustaše.*

104. Blinkhorn, *Fascists and Conservatives;* Blinkhorn, *Fascism and the Right.*

105. Raphael, *Imperiale Gewalt,* 12.

106. Höpken, "Strukturkrise."

107. Cabanes, *Great War.*

108. Walters, *History of the League of Nations,* 169ff.

109. Iriye, *Cultural Internationalism,* 27.

110. Rittberger and Zangl, *Internationale Organisationen,* 23–24.

111. Austin, *Founding a Balkan State,* 20.

112. Quoted in Pipa, "Fan Noli, 245."

113. Iacobescu, "Inițiative"; Dimitrov, *La Bulgarie.*

114. Pedersen, "League of Nations."

115. Marrus, *Unwanted,* 51; Skran, *Refugees in Inter-War Europe,* 31ff.

116. Quoted in Marrus, *Unwanted,* 103.

117. Cabanes, *Great War,* 133ff., 173ff.; Marrus, *Unwanted,* 88.

118. Calmès, *Situation économique.*

119. Clavin, *Securing the World Economy,* 25ff.; Clewing, "Völkerbund und Albanien."

120. Daele, *ILO Histories.*

121. Milenković, "Međunarodna organizacija rada."

122. Cabanes, *Great War,* S. 127.

123. Bashford, "Nation."

124. Fink, *Defending the Rights,* 267ff.; Scheuermann, *Minderheitenschutz.*

125. Dimitrov, *La Bulgarie,* 10ff.

126. Walters, *History of the League of Nations,* 311ff., 602ff.

127. Troebst, *Mussolini,* 97ff.

128. Ditrych, "International Terrorism"; Hoptner, *Yugoslavia in Crisis,* 52.

129. *Nicholas Titulescu,* 7ff.

130. Ibid., 30.

131. Ibid., 73ff.

132. Osăceanu, *Pagini de diplomaţie romanească,* 119ff.

133. *Nicholas Titulescu,* 87, 90.

134. Ibid., 31, 66.

135. Matsch, *Internationale Politik,* 264.

136. *Nicholas Titulescu,* 18.

137. Titulescu, Potra, and Turcu, *Romania's Foreign Policy,* 272.

138. Osăceanu, *Pagini de diplomaţie romanească,* 199; *Nicholas Titulescu,* 29.

139. Quoted in Sundhaussen, *Geschichte Serbiens,* xx.

140. Janković, *Balkans in International Relations,* 149ff.; Dimitrov, "Bulgarian Neutrality."

141. Kissoudi, "Sport."

142. Oprea, *Nicolae Titulescu's Diplomatic Activity,* 81ff.

143. Kerner and Howard, *Balkan Conferences,* 21ff.

144. Steiner, *Triumph of the Dark,* 68; Milo, "Albania."

145. Campus, *Ideea federală;* Llewellyn-Smith, "Greece and Europe."

146. Mazower, *Governing the World,* 177.

147. Fišera, "Communisme et integration"; Stavrianos, *Balkan Federation,* 205.

148. Polexe, *Auf engen Pfaden,* 10; Minehan, *Civil War,* 136.

149. Iacob, "New Perspective."

150. Sperber, *Träne.*

151. Gollwitzer, *Europäische Bauernparteien.*

152. Gligorijević, *Kominterna.*

153. Stavrianos, *Balkan Federation,* 223; Case, "Strange Politics."

154. Boli and Thomas, *Constructing World Culture;* Petrescu, "Les liens"; Costa-Foru, *Folterkammern Rumäniens.*

155. Smith, *Women in World History,* 185ff.

156. Fink, *Defending the Rights,* 343ff.

157. *Nicholas Titulescu,* 16ff., 137.

158. Iriye, *Global Community,* 64.

159. James, *End of Globalization,* 105; Feinstein, Temin, and Toniolo, *European Economy,* 8ff.; Raphael, *Imperiale Gewalt,* 24.

160. Teichova, "Bilateral Trade," 39ff.

161. Moore, *Economic Demography,* 26.

162. Berend and Ránki, "Polen," 780.

163. Bartl, *Albanien,* 214.

164. Aldcroft, *Europe's Third World,* 6; Moore, *Economic Demography,* 36.

165. Moore, *Economic Demography,* 63.

166. Political and Economic Planning (PEP), *Economic Development,* 17ff.

167. Aldcroft, *Europe's Third World,* 13.

168. Osterhammel and Petersson, *Geschichte der Globalisierung,* 80–81.

169. James, *End of Globalization.*

170. Teichova, "East-Central and South-East Europe," 940; David, *Nationalisme économique,* 155.

171. Aldcroft, *Europe's Third World,* 56; Berend, *Central and Eastern Europe,* 244–45.

172. Vučo, *Agrarna kriza u Jugoslaviji,* 196.

173. Calic, *Sozialgeschichte Serbiens,* 368ff.

174. Stavrianos, *Balkans since 1453,* 606.

175. James, *End of Globalization,* 186.

176. Ibid., 109ff.

177. David, *Nationalisme économique,* 215ff.

178. James, *End of Globalization,* 105.

179. Kofman, "Economic Nationalism."

180. Teichova, "East-Central and South-East Europe," 910; David, *Nationalisme économique,* 204ff.; Kofman, "Economic Nationalism."

181. Szlajfer, *Economic Nationalism.*

182. Love, *Crafting the Third World,* 59ff.; Love, "Theorizing Underdevelopment."

183. David, *Nationalisme économique,* 238ff.; Raphael, *Imperiale Gewalt,* 170.

184. Berend and Ránki, "Polen," 796.

185. Aldcroft, *Europe's Third World,* 168–69.

186. Mazower, *Greece.*

187. Teichova, "East-Central and South-East Europe," 957.

188. Berend and Ránki, "Polen," 798.

189. David, *Nationalisme économique,* 32.

190. Calic, *Sozialgeschichte Serbiens,* 423.

191. Aldcroft, *Europe's Third World,* 5.

192. Teichova, *Kleinstaaten,* 76ff.

193. Ránki, *Economy,* 7ff.

194. Aldcroft, *Europe's Third World,* 55.

195. Berend and Ránki, "Polen," 810; Teichova, "East-Central and South-East Europe," 933.

196. Quoted in Sundhaussen, *Wirtschaftsgeschichte Kroatiens,* 20.

197. Hehn, *Low Dishonest Decade.*

198. Freytag, *"Drang nach Südosten,"* 60.

199. Schreiber, "Deutschland," 330ff.

200. Steiner, *Triumph of the Dark,* 374.

201. Teichova, "Bilateral Trade."

202. Teichova, "East-Central and South-East Europe," 955–56.

203. Berend and Ránki, "Polen," 803.

204. Bairoch, *Commerce extérieur;* Maddison, *World Economy;* Latham, *Depression,* 153.

205. David, *Nationalisme économique,* 30–31.

206. James, *End of Globalization,* 187ff.

207. Burghardt, "Tango-Duell."

208. *Politika,* July 24, 1930, 8, and August 1, 1930, 7.

209. *Politika,* July 28, 1930, 9.

210. Giulianotti and Robertson, "Recovering the Social."

211. Marković, *Beograd i Evropa,* 7–8.

212. Appadurai, *Modernity,* 21–22; Brubaker, *Grounds for Difference,* 119ff.; Barlas and Köksal, "Turkey's Foreign Policy."

213. Brunnbauer, *Globalizing Southeastern Europe,* 216, 243.

214. Milutinović, *Getting over Europe,* 102–3.

215. Gašić, *Beograd u hodu ka Evropi.*

216. Quoted in Petzer and Richter, *"Isochimenen,"* 107.

217. Krleža et al., *Enciklopedija Jugoslavije,* 517ff.

218. Marković, *Beograd i Evropa,* 172.

219. Milutinović, *Getting over Europe,* 88–89.

220. Marković, *Beograd i Evropa,* 65ff., 139ff.; Vučetić, *Koka-kola socijalizam,* 31ff.

221. Sanders, *Balkan Village,* 238ff.

222. Majuru, *Stadt der Verlockungen,* 84–85.

223. Weinbaum et al., *Modern Girl;* Bogdanović, *Modernism.*

224. Donauschwäbisches Zentralmuseum, *Johnny Weissmüller.*

225. Kasson, *White Male Body,* 19.

226. Eliade, *Erinnerungen,* 176–77.

227. Subotić, *Likovni krog revije "Zenit."*

228. Nayhauss, "Indisches Tagebuch."

229. Tagore, *Nationalism,* 15.

230. Eliade, *Indisches Tagebuch,* 282, 296.

231. Georgescu, "Excursions," 317.

232. Landau, *Pan-Turkism;* Köksal, "Transnational Networks"; Merdjanova, *Rediscovering the Umma,* 14–15.

233. Mitchell, *Society of the Muslim Brothers;* Schulze, *Islamischer Internationalismus,* 47ff., 445ff.

234. Bowen, "Beyond Migration."

235. Clayer, "Transnational Connections."

236. Bougarel, "Emergence"; Bougarel and Clayer, *Le nouvel islam;* Filandra, *Bošnjaci i moderna,* 313ff.; Karčić, *Bosniaks.*

237. Benbassa, *Geschichte,* 15ff.

238. Köbsch, *Juden im Vielvölkerstaat Jugoslawien,* 54ff.; Birri-Tomovska, *Jews of Yugoslavia,* 153ff.

239. Benbassa, *Geschichte,* S. 272.

240. Leuştean, *Orthodox Christianity and Nationalism*.

241. Quoted in Buchenau, *Orthodoxe Antiwestler*, 170–71.

242. Roudometof, Agadjanian, and Pankhurst, *Eastern Orthodoxy*.

243. Buchenau, *Orthodoxe Antiwestler*, 65ff.

244. Roudometof and Makrides, *Orthodox Christianity*.

245. *Bukarester Tageblatt*, January 4, 1939, 1.

246. Heinen, *Logik der Gewalt*, 54–55.

247. Dorian, *Quality of Witness*, 53–54.

248. Roberts, "Romanian," 31.

249. Sebastian, *Journal*, 17–18.

250. Eliade, *Nae Ionescu*, 121, 132.

251. Sebastian, *Journal*, 29, 82, 119, 238.

252. Institutul central de statistică, *Recensământul general*, xliv–xlv.

253. Giurescu, *Geschichte der Stadt Bukarest*, 74ff.; Parusheva, "La vie quotidienne."

254. Vossen, *Bukarest*, 174.

255. Draşovean, "Industria auto interbelică."

256. Morand, *Bucarest*, 137.

257. Giurescu, *Geschichte der Stadt Bukarest*, 93.

258. Vossen, *Bukarest*, 174.

259. Ibid., 162–63.

260. Iosa, *Bucarest*, 47.

261. Vossen, *Bukarest*, 167, 188.

262. Giurescu, *Geschichte der Stadt Bukarest*, 80, 89ff.

263. Georgescu, *Bukarest*, 43.

264. Machedon and Scoffham, *Romanian Modernism*, 286ff.

265. *Bukarester Tageblatt*, May 15, 1939, 8.

266. *Bukarester Tageblatt*, January 1, 1939, 14.

267. Boia, *Rumänische Elite*, 87.

268. Giurescu, *Geschichte der Stadt Bukarest*, 101.

269. Rostás, "Sociological School"; Golopenţia, "Sociological School."

270. Vlad, *Imagini ale identităţii naţionale*, 104.

271. *Bukarester Tageblatt*, May 1, 1939, 5.

272. Iosa, *Bucarest*, 51; Pippidi, *Bucureşti*, 82ff.

273. Georgescu, *Bukarest*, 44; Sonne, "Hauptstadt."

274. Andraş, "Europe," 101.

275. Maner, *Parlamentarismus in Rumänien*, 490ff.

276. Ibid., 103.

277. Stokes, "Social Origins."

278. Rădulescu, "Romanian Aristocracy."

279. Andraş, "Europe," 96, 102.

280. Prügel, *Zeichen der Stadt*, 162.

281. Machedon and Scoffham, *Romanian Modernism*, 33ff.

282. For Germany, see Herbert, *Geschichte Deutschlands*, 48.

283. Born, "Römer."

284. Prügel, *Zeichen der Stadt*, 66ff.

285. Quoted in ibid., 73.

286. Pippidi, *Bucureşti*, 304ff.

287. Iosa, *Bucarest*, 78.

288. Prügel, *Zeichen der Stadt*, 195ff.

289. Iosa, *Bucarest*, 50, 56.

290. Lungu, "European Crisis," 391.

291. Sebastian, *Journal*, 203–4.

292. Heinen, "Hitler-Stalin-Pakt."

293. Moisuc, "Orientation," 329.

294. Milata, *Rumäniendeutsche*, 39–40, 49.

295. Moisuc, "Orientation."

296. Hillgruber, *Hitler*, 42ff.

297. Eichholtz, *Deutsche Politik*, 23ff.; Glass, *Verfolgung der Juden*, 24.

298. Petrişor, "Marea demonstraţie."

299. Steiner, *Triumph of the Dark*, 743.

300. Eichholtz, *Deutsche Politik*, 30ff.

301. Hillgruber, *Hitler*, 31.

302. Iordan, "Relations interbalkaniques."

303. Lungu, *Romania and the Great Powers*, 203ff.

304. Djokić, *Elusive Compromise*, 208; Boban, *Sporazum Cvetković-Maček*; Sojčić, *"Lösung" der kroatischen Frage*, 53ff.

305. Milata, *Rumäniendeutsche*, 44.

306. Dimitrov, "Bulgarian Neutrality," 202.

307. Steiner, *Triumph of the Dark*, 957ff.; Weinberg, *Hitler's Foreign Policy*, 734–35; Koliopoulos, "Greek Foreign Policy."

308. Gafencu, *Vorspiel zum Krieg*, 339.

309. Hillgruber, *Hitler*, 57; Lungu, *Romania and the Great Powers*, 195ff.

310. Dučić, *Rapoarte diplomatice*, 382.

311. Hillgruber, *Hitler*, 59.

312. Dorian, *Quality of Witness*, 71.

313. Weck, *Journal de guerre*, 67–68.

314. Dorian, *Quality of Witness*, 72.

315. Ibid., 81.

316. Balta, *Rumänien*, 71ff. For an overview of these developments, see Overy, *Origins*.

317. Glass, *Verfolgung der Juden;* Benjamin, *Evreii din România;* Ancel, *Holocaust in Romania;* International Commission on the Holocaust in Romania, *Final Report.*

318. Case, *Between States,* 75ff.

319. Hall, *War in the Balkans,* 245–46.

320. Gross, *Export Empire,* 331.

321. Seckendorf, *Okkupationspolitik,* 29–30.

322. Tomasevich, *War and Revolution,* 45–46.

323. Vogel, "Eingreifen Deutschlands."

324. Directive No. 25 from March 27, 1941, in Hubatsch, *Hitlers Weisungen,* 106ff.

325. Kisić Kolanović, *NDH i Italija,* 60ff.; Yeomans, *Utopia.*

326. Hall, *War in the Balkans,* 126–27; Seckendorf, *Okkupationspolitik,* 64.

327. Manoschek, *"Serbien ist judenfrei,"* 29; Shepherd, *Terror in the Balkans.*

328. Prusin, *Serbia,* 158–59; Ramet and Listhaug, *Serbia and the Serbs.*

329. Shimizu, *Deutsche Okkupation;* Zakić, *Ethnic Germans.*

330. Schlarp, *Wirtschaft und Besatzung,* 318, 353.

331. Tomasevich, *War and Revolution,* 622.

332. Spoerer, *Zwangsarbeit,* 211.

333. Schlarp, *Wirtschaft und Besatzung,* 416–17.

334. Seckendorf, *Okkupationspolitik,* 79.

335. Schlarp, *Wirtschaft und Besatzung,* 416–17; Sundhaussen, *Wirtschaftsgeschichte Kroatiens,* 301.

336. Seckendorf, *Okkupationspolitik,* 65–66.

337. Ibid., 65; Mazower, *Inside Hitler's Greece,* 32.

338. Quoted in Mazower, *Inside Hitler's Greece,* 23.

339. Ibid., 41, 68.

340. Glišić, "Albanization"; Malcolm, *Kosovo,* 293ff.

341. Tomasevich, *War and Revolution,* 608ff.

342. Livezeanu, *Cultural Politics,* 11ff.; Korb, *Schatten des Weltkriegs,* 127ff.

343. Jelić-Butić, *Ustaše,* 106.

344. Tomasevich, *War and Revolution,* 366ff.

345. Greble, *Sarajevo,* 157ff.

346. Goldstein and Goldstein, *Holocaust in Croatia,* 158.

347. Tomasevich, *War and Revolution,* 366ff.; Jelić-Butić, *Ustaše,* 106.

348. Greble, *Sarajevo,* 122.

349. Stevan Moljević, "Homogena Srbija," (June 30, 1941), as quoted in Dedijer and Miletić, *Genocid,* 8–16; Yeomans, *Visions.*

350. Komanda četničkih odreda Jugoslovenske Vojske, Gorski štab, Str. Pov. Dj. Br. 370, 20 decembra 1941 god., as quoted in Dedijer and Miletić, *Genocid,* 25–30; Tomasevich, *Chetniks,* 166ff.

351. Dedijer and Miletić, *Genocid,* 330; Hoare, *Bosnian Muslims,* 104.

352. Ther, *Dunkle Seite,* 156; Solonari, *Purifying,* 95ff.

353. Glass, *Verfolgung der Juden,* 11.

354. Solonari, *Purifying,* 202.

355. International Commission on the Holocaust in Romania, *Final Report,* 176ff.

356. Benz, *Dimension des Völkermords,* 16.

357. Solonari, *Purifying,* 264ff.

358. Quoted in Benz, *Dimension des Völkermords,* 13.

359. Friedländer, *Years of Extermination,* 364.

360. Sundhaussen, "Jugoslawien."

361. Ristović, *U potrazi za utočištem;* Benz, *Dimension des Völkermords,* 16.

362. Gobetti, *L'occupazione allegra,* 62ff.; Dulić, *Utopias,* 123ff., 190ff.

363. Bergholz, *Violence,* 312; Korb, "Genocide."

364. Dulić, *Utopias,* 210–11.

365. Hamburger Institut für Sozialforschung, *Verbrechen der Wehrmacht,* 508ff., 550.

366. Manoschek, *"Serbien ist judenfrei,"* 161ff., 41–42.

367. Mazower, *Inside Hitler's Greece,* 173ff.

368. Rodogno, *Il nuovo ordine mediterraneo;* Gobetti, *L'occupazione allegra;* Nenezić, *Jugoslovenske oblasti;* Burgwyn, *Empire on the Adriatic.*

369. For Tito's biography, see Goldstein and Goldstein, *Tito,* and Pirjevec, *Tito.*

370. Djilas, *Contested Country,* 91ff.; Minehan, *Civil War,* 136.

371. Quoted in Jović, "Communist Yugoslavia," 298–99; Vranicki, *Geschichte des Marxismus,* 998.

372. Šuvar, *Nacije i medunacionalni odnosi,* 57.

373. Hoare, *Genocide and Resistance.*

374. Dedijer, *Tito Speaks,* 190.

375. Quoted in Seckendorf, *Okkupationspolitik,* 241.

376. Maclean, "Tito."

377. Tomasevich, *War and Revolution,* 208; Casagrande, *SS-Division.*

378. Redžić, *Muslimansko autonomaštvo.*

379. Bougarel et al., "Muslim SS Units"; Bougarel, "Islam"; Zaugg, *Muslime.*

380. Quoted in Schmider, "Partisanenkrieg," 907ff.

381. Hoare, "The Partisans and the Serbs," 207.

382. Batinić, *Women,* 260.

383. Schmider, *Partisanenkrieg in Jugoslawien,* 535.

384. Zelepos, *Geschichte,* 159–60; Mazower, *Inside Hitler's Greece,* 155ff.

385. Tsoutsoumpis, *History,* 258ff.

386. Fischer, *Albania at War,* 121ff.

387. Minehan, *Civil War.*

8. Globalization and Fragmentation

1. Judt, *Postwar,* 9.
2. Ther, *Dunkle Seite,* 166.
3. Djilas, *Contested Country,* 138ff.
4. Bokovoy, "Separate Road," 17; Mazower, *Inside Hitler's Greece,* 265ff.
5. Case, *Between States,* 94–95.
6. Hall, *War in the Balkans,* 57–58.
7. Seckendorf, *Okkupationspolitik,* 79–78.
8. Ibid., 60, 76.
9. Kočović, *Žrtve;* Žerjavić, *Population Losses.*
10. Tomasevich, *War and Revolution,* 751ff.
11. Vodušek Starič, *Kako su komunisti osvojili vlast.*
12. Judt, *Postwar,* 134.
13. Kalyvas, *Logic of Violence,* 248–49; Stergiou, "Antikommunismus."
14. Deletant, *Romania,* 64ff.
15. Deletant, *Ceauşescu.*
16. Bartl, *Albanien,* 234ff.; Janos, *East Central Europe,* 283–84.
17. Portmann, *Kommunistische Revolution.*
18. Douglas, *Orderly and Humane;* Beer, *Flucht und Vertreibung,* 86ff.
19. Lane, *Britain,* 53ff.
20. Janos, *East Central Europe,* 246.
21. Hoffmann, *Stalinist Values,* 7ff.
22. Obradović, *"Narodna demokratija,"* 158.
23. Brunnbauer, *Sozialistische Lebensweise,* 105, 111.
24. Sjöberg, *Rural Change,* 84ff.
25. Bokovoy, "Separate Road," 38–39.
26. Schnytzer, *Stalinist Economic Strategy,* 22; Janos, *East Central Europe,* 286.
27. Bilandžić and Vukadinović, *Osnovne,* 124; Sekelj, *Process of Disintegration,* 21ff.; Janos, *East Central Europe,* 291.
28. Aldcroft, *European Economy,* 163ff.; Gianaris, *Economies,* 86.
29. Sapelli, *Southern Europe,* 64.
30. Aldcroft, *European Economy,* 171; Sjöberg, *Rural Change,* 126.
31. Brunnbauer, "Gesellschaft," 665.
32. Aldcroft, *European Economy,* 170–71; Brunnbauer, "Gesellschaft," 669.
33. Kamberović, *Prema modernom društvu,* 148ff.
34. Brunnbauer, "Dimitrovgrad," 199.
35. Brunnbauer, *Sozialistische Lebensweise,* 234–35; Sjöberg, *Rural Change,* 53.
36. Brunnbauer, *Sozialistische Lebensweise,* 270ff.
37. Sjöberg, *Rural Change,* 65ff.
38. Hoppe, "Politik," 250.

39. Quoted in Verdery, *National Ideology,* 117.

40. Quoted in Brunnbauer, *Sozialistische Lebensweise,* 345.

41. Petrescu, "Community Building."

42. Lubonja, "Glory."

43. Radelić, *Hrvatska,* 234.

44. Gries, "Dramaturgie."

45. Fischer, *Balkan Strongmen.*

46. Mojić, "Evolucija kulta."

47. Nikolić, *Tito.*

48. Dalos, *Aufruhr,* 72.

49. "Neke nove žene," *Vreme,* April 12, 2007.

50. Herbst, "Women."

51. Borojević, *Iz Dubca,* 11.

52. Ibid., 21.

53. "Neke nove žene," *Vreme,* April 12, 2007.

54. Ibid.

55. Borojević, *Iz Dubca,* 188.

56. "Where Everything Is Yet to Happen, 2nd chapter: Exposures," accessed March 28, 2018, https://www.academia.edu/1317643/Where_Everything_is_Yet_to _Happen_2nd_chapter_Exposures.

57. Brunnbauer, *Sozialistische Lebensweise,* 530–31.

58. Brunnbauer, "Gesellschaft."

59. Djilas, *Jahre der Macht,* 102–3; Banac, *Stalin against Tito,* 17.

60. Petranović, *Balkanska federacija.*

61. Kačavenda and Tripković, *Jugoslovensko-sovjetski sukob;* Clissold, *Yugoslavia.*

62. Lees, *Keeping Tito Afloat.*

63. Vučetić, *Koka-kola socijalizam,* 52–53.

64. Kuljić, *Tito,* 342; Lees, *Keeping Tito Afloat,* 83.

65. Heuser, *"Containment" Policies.*

66. Banac, *Stalin against Tito,* 150, 223; Dedijer, *Novi prilozi,* 3:464.

67. Standish, "Enver Hoxha's Role"; Fevziu, *Enver Hoxha.*

68. Bartl, *Albanien,* 245–46.

69. Zelepos, *Ethnisierung,* 204ff.

70. Jennings, *Flashpoint Trieste.*

71. Magaš, *Croatia,* 581.

72. Radelić, *Hrvatska,* 53.

73. Dülffer, *Europa.*

74. Grottian, *Regierungssystem,* 25.

75. Nećak, *Tito med Zvezno.*

76. Marčeva, *Todor Živkov;* Baeva and Kalinova, *Bălgarskite prechodi;* Crampton, *Bulgaria.*

77. Quoted in Crampton, *Concise History of Bulgaria,* 199.

78. Dragomir, *Cold War Perceptions,* 178ff.; Oşca, *O fereastră.*

79. Liu, *Sino-Romanian Relations,* 33ff.

80. Ionescu, *Communism in Rumania;* Deletant, *Romania;* Tismaneanu, *Stalinism.*

81. Loth, "States," 109; "The Brezhnev Doctrine," accessed March 28, 2018, https://sourcebooks.fordham.edu/mod/1968brezhnev.asp.

82. Bartl, *Albanien,* 251ff.; Schnytzer, *Stalinist Economic Strategy,* 25–26.

83. O'Donnell, *Albania.*

84. Quoted in Mojsov, *Dimensions of Non-Alignment,* 144; Jovanović, *Jugoslavija,* 37.

85. Weiner, *Romanian Foreign Policy,* 5, 185.

86. Ibid., 67–68; Weiner, "Deviance."

87. Klick, "Nuclear Weapon-Free Zone."

88. Klose, *Menschenrechte,* 115ff.

89. Westad, *Global Cold War,* 8ff.

90. Quoted in Mazower, *Governing the World,* 260, 262.

91. Čavoški, "Nasser's Neutralism," 90, 92.

92. Dinkel, *Bewegung.*

93. Zeiler, "Opening Doors," 255ff.

94. Kaser, *Balkan,* 391; Jakovina, *Treća strana.*

95. Vučković, *Nesvrstanost;* Rajak, "No Bargaining Chips"; Petrović, *Titova lična diplomatija.*

96. Petrović, "Summit Diplomacy."

97. Petrović, *Titova lična diplomatija,* 319.

98. Petković, *Nesvrstanost.*

99. Kuljić, *Tito,* 354.

100. Mazower, *Governing the World,* 216, 245ff.

101. Janev, *Odnosi Jugoslavije,* 73ff.

102. Canapa, "L'islam," 149.

103. Hadžijahić, Traljić, and Šukrić, *Islam i Muslimani,* 160ff.

104. Jalal, "Islam's Contemporary Globalization."

105. Schulze, *Islamischer Internationalismus,* 445–46.

106. Bowen, *New Anthropology,* 176–77.

107. Kamberović, *Džemal Bijedić,* 32, 61.

108. Ibid., 167.

109. Purivatra, *Nacionalni i politički razvitak,* 30ff.

110. Pearson, "Muslims' Nation-building Process."

111. Bartolović, *Džemal,* 13.

112. Bougarel, "Islam et politique," 1:137ff.

113. "Kako ćemo se boriti," in Trhulj, *Mladi Muslimani,* 122–23.

114. Omerika, *Islam in Bosnien-Herzegowina,* 298ff.

115. Izetbegović, *Islamic Declaration,* 3.

116. Hixson, *Parting the Curtain.*

117. Kaelble, *Kalter Krieg,* 58; Goedde, "Global Cultures," 549ff.

118. Stergiou, "Antikommunismus"; Zelepos, *Geschichte.*

119. Rosandić and Pešić, *Ratništvo.*

120. Calic, *Geschichte Jugoslawiens,* 224ff.

121. Kilzer, "Interview," 274.

122. Ibid., 276.

123. Bockman, *Markets,* 17ff.

124. Ibid., 62.

125. Velimirović, "Odevanje," 350.

126. Brunnbauer, *Globalizing Southeastern Europe,* 311.

127. Ibid., 257ff.

128. Sapelli, *Southern Europe,* 40.

129. Roudometof, "Transnationalism."

130. Rass, *Institutionalisierungsprozesse,* 158–59, 196ff.

131. Bernard, "Return of the Gastarbeiter," 85ff.; Schierup, *Migration,* 15ff.

132. Deletant, *Romania,* 110.

133. Kolar, *Rumänien,* 368.

134. Becker, Hopfinger, and Steinecke, *Geographie;* Petrescu, "Entrepreneurial Tourism."

135. Brunnbauer, "Gesellschaft," 682.

136. Vuković, *Povijest hrvatskog turizma,* 153ff.; Grandits and Taylor, *Yugoslavia's Sunny Side.*

137. Péteri, "Sites"; Paulmann, "Grenzüberschreitungen."

138. Kulić, "Avant-Garde Architecture."

139. Neuburger, "Consuming."

140. Sluga, *Internationalism,* 104ff.

141. Iacob, "Balkans in UNESCO."

142. Deletant, *Romania,* 113.

143. Majstorović, *Cultural Policy,* 93–94.

144. Sjöberg, *Rural Change,* 158.

145. Ibid., 160.

146. See the contributions in *East Central Europe* 38 (2011); Ramet, *Rock Music.*

147. Trendafilov, "Formation."

148. Janjatović, *Ilustrovana.*

149. Vranicki, *Geschichte des Marxismus.*

150. Stefanov, "Message."

151. Goulding, *Liberated Cinema.*

152. Mark et al., "Transnational Solidarities."

153. Vučetić, "Yugoslavia."

154. Tismaneanu, *Promises.*

155. Kanzleiter and Stojaković, *"1968" in Jugoslawien,* 23.

156. Bilandžić, *Historija,* 337–38.

157. Horn and Kenney, *Transnational Moments.*

158. Klimke and Scharloth, *1968 in Europe.*

159. Zielinski, *Die neutralen und blockfreien Staaten.*

160. Eckel, "Rebirth."

161. Morgan, "The Seventies"; Brier, *Entangled Protest.*

162. Quoted in Eckel, "Rebirth," 256.

163. Kenney, "Opposition Networks."

164. Kaldor, *Global Civil Society.*

165. For the viewpoints of the leading actors, see Tripalo, *Hrvatsko proljeće;* Dabčević-Kučar, *Hrvatski snovi;* Čuvalo, *Croatian National Movement.*

166. Schmitt, *Kosovo,* 234ff.

167. Todorova, "Course and Discourses."

168. Brunnbauer, *Sozialistische Lebensweise,* 328, 330; Zhivkova, *Lyudmila Zhivkova,* 140.

169. Merdjanova, *Rediscovering the Umma,* 18.

170. Zhivkova, *Lyudmila Zhivkova,* 133ff., 248ff.

171. Atanasova, "Lyudmila Zhivkova," 300.

172. Zhivkova, *Lyudmila Zhivkova,* 75ff.

173. Ibid., 13.

174. Gencheva, "Assembly."

175. Atanasova, "Lyudmila Zhivkova"; Aleksandrov, *Kultura,* 71ff.

176. Zeiler, "Opening Doors."

177. Judt, *Postwar,* 105.

178. Zeiler, "Opening Doors," 225ff.

179. Quoted in Vickers, *Albanians,* 184.

180. Graziani, "Dependency Structures"; Țăranu, *România;* Dragomir, *Cold War Perceptions,* 240.

181. Zeiler, "Opening Doors," 278.

182. Aldcroft, *European Economy,* 186–87.

183. Bren and Neuburger, *Communism Unwrapped,* 5ff.

184. Ibroscheva, "Unbearable Lightness."

185. Therborn, *Gesellschaften,* 165ff.

186. Deletant, *Romania,* 113.

187. Brunnbauer, *Sozialistische Lebensweise,* 284.

188. Patterson, *Bought and Sold,* xvii.

189. Massino, "Black Caviar," 231ff.

190. Zeiler, "Opening Doors," 219; De Grazia, *Irresistible Empire,* 1.

191. De Grazia, *Irresistible Empire,* 11.

192. Vučetić, *Koka-kola socijalizam,* 331ff.

193. Ibid., 31ff.

194. Quoted in Brunnbauer, *Sozialistische Lebensweise,* 331.

195. Patterson, *Bought and Sold,* 319.

196. Massino, "Black Caviar."

197. Gatejel, *Auto und Sozialismus,* 75.

198. Žanić, *Smrt crvenog fiće,* 34.

199. Seitz and Müller, *Albanien,* 47.

200. Lydall, *Yugoslav Socialism,* 81; Rusinow, *Yugoslav Experiment,* 172ff.

201. Kamberović, *Džemal Bijedić,* 291.

202. Crampton, *Concise History of Bulgaria,* 199–200.

203. Latham, *Modernization;* Mazower, *Governing the World,* 273ff.

204. Graff, Kenwood, and Lougheed, *Growth,* 276–77.

205. Love, "Theorizing Underdevelopment."

206. Petković, *Nesvrstanost.*

207. Bijedić, *Samoupravljanje,* 230.

208. Maier, "Crisis of Capitalism."

209. Berend, *Central and Eastern Europe,* 222–23.

210. Berend, *Soviet Bloc,* 34.

211. Sapelli, *Southern Europe,* 64ff.

212. Berend, *Soviet Bloc,* 25ff.

213. Berend, *Economic History,* 183ff.

214. Janos, *East Central Europe,* 293.

215. Zelepos, *Ethnisierung,* 217ff.

216. Brunnbauer, "Gesellschaft," 681ff.

217. Zeiler, "Opening Doors," 284ff.; Mazower, *Governing the World,* 343ff.

218. Steger, *Globalization,* 41ff.

219. Ther, *Neue Ordnung,* 22ff.

220. Sjöberg, *Rural Change,* 4.

221. Zeiler, "Opening Doors," 254ff.

222. Calic, *Geschichte Jugoslawiens,* 255ff.

223. Ramet, *Yugoslavia,* 9.

224. Woodward, *Balkan Tragedy,* 50ff.

225. Ibid., 96ff., 127ff.

226. Sjöberg, *Rural Change,* 50ff.

227. Verdery, "Socialism"; Massino, "Black Caviar."

228. Kilzer, "Literarisches Werk," 172.

229. Blandiana, "Heimat DIN A4," 73.

230. Sapelli, *Southern Europe,* 5ff.

231. Bradley et al., *Regional Aid,* 14.

232. Janos, *East Central Europe,* 346.

233. Brunnbauer, "Gesellschaft," 669.

234. Therborn, *Gesellschaften,* 50.

235. Maddison, *World Economy,* 101.

236. Janos, *East Central Europe,* 349.

237. Latić, *Boja povijesti,* 70–71.

238. Mungiu-Pippidi, "Romanian Political Intellectuals."

239. Kilzer, "Interview," 284.

240. Pedrotty, "Yugoslav Unity," 337.

241. *Little Global Cities,* 50; Štraus, *Arhitektura,* 167ff.

242. Organizacioni komitet, *U znaku Sarajeva,* 80.

243. Valérien, *Olympia,* 211.

244. Nauright and Parrish, *Sports,* 406.

245. *Statistički godišnjak Jugoslavije,* 32:714.

246. Pedrotty, "Yugoslav Unity."

247. Isaković and Lovrenović, *Putopisi,* 36.

248. Libal, *Balkan,* 289–90.

249. Ibid., 284–85.

250. *Little Global Cities.*

251. Kurto, *Sarajevo,* 105ff.

252. Donia, *Sarajevo,* 233.

253. *Prilozi historiji Sarajeva,* 386ff.

254. Čelić, *Sarajevo,* 34.

255. Republički zavod za statistiku, *Materijalni i društveni razvoj,* 19; Velikonja, *Religious Separation,* 224.

256. Pearson, "Nationalitätenpolitik."

257. Purivatra, *Nacionalni i politički razvitak,* 30ff.

258. Lucic, "Service."

259. Kamberović, *Džemal Bijedić,* 28–29.

260. Okuka, *Eine Sprache,* 96ff.

261. "Srpskohrvatski optimizam," *NIN* (May 13, 1984), 24ff.

262. *Jugosloveni o društvenoj krizi,* 72ff.

263. Flere, "Nacionalna identifikacija."

264. Baćević, *Jugoslavija,* 236.

265. Mihailović, *Deca krize,* 170; Pantić, "Nacionalna distanca."

266. Trhulj, *Mladi Muslimani.*

267. Republički zavod za statistiku, *Materijalni i društveni razvoj,* 15ff., 234.

268. Ibid., 73–74, 198, 244.

269. *Statistički godišnjak Jugoslavije,* 32:721–22; Republički zavod za statistiku, *Materijalni i društveni razvoj,* 67ff.; Čelić, *Sarajevo,* 38ff.

270. *Prilozi historiji Sarajeva,* 508ff.

271. Republički zavod za statistiku, *Materijalni i društveni razvoj,* 33, 102, 234.

272. *Oslobođenje* (January 18, 1984), 3, and (September 1, 1984), 14.

273. Republički zavod za statistiku, *Materijalni i društveni razvoj,* 74, 230–31.

274. *Oslobođenje* (January 13, and September 3, 1984), 7.

275. Bombelles, "Federal Aid."

276. Pleština, *Regional Development,* 124.

277. Pedrotty, "Yugoslav Unity."

278. Quoted in Goulding, *Liberated Cinema,* 162.

279. Kusturica, *Unbestätigtes Gerücht,* 188.

280. Goulding, *Liberated Cinema,* 146ff.

281. Ramet, *Social Currents.*

282. Jovanovic, "Yugoslavness," 140ff.

283. *Oslobođenje* (May 13, 1984), 17.

284. Trendafilov, "Formation."

285. Jovanovic, "Yugoslavness," 146ff.

286. Spaskovska, *Yugoslav Generation.*

287. *Prilozi historiji Sarajeva,* 451ff.

288. Mojić, "Evolucija kulta."

289. Nikolić, *Tito.*

290. Gagnon, *Myth of Ethnic War,* 26ff.

291. Tomasevich, *War and Revolution,* 726ff.

292. *Oslobođenje* (May 5, 1984), 3.

293. Šešelj, *Šta da se radi,* 34.

294. Filandra, *Bošnjačka politika,* 341–42.

295. Krušelj, *Franjo Tuđman,* 98.

296. Danilović, *Upotreba neprijatelja,* 252–53.

297. Filandra, *Bošnjačka politika,* 325ff.

298. Omerika, *Islam in Bosnien-Herzegowina,* 298ff.; Bougarel, *Islam and Nationhood,* 99.

299. *Oslobođenje* (January 12, 1984), 2, and (January 13, 1984), 2.

300. Libal, *Balkan,* 285.

301. Pantić, "Prostorne," 222.

302. Ramet, *Politics;* Pridham and Gallagher, *Experimenting;* Tismaneanu, *Revolutions.*

303. Kaelble, *Wege zur Demokratie,* 71ff.

304. Huntington, *Third Wave.*

305. Munck, Skalnik, and Leff, "Modes of Transition."

306. Kenney, *1989;* Horn and Kenney, *Transnational Moments.*

307. Pleština, *Regional Development,* 124.

308. On the dissolution of Yugoslavia, see Calic, *History of Yugoslavia.*

309. Mansfield and Snyder, *Electing to Fight.*

310. Hockenos, *Homeland Calling.*

311. Calic, *Geschichte Jugoslawiens,* 308ff.

312. Calic, "Ethnic Cleansing."

313. Gilboa, "Global Communication"; de la Brosse, *Political Propaganda.*

314. Kaldor, *Global Civil Society;* Iriye, *Global Community.*

315. Kaldor, *New and Old Wars;* Münkler, *Neue Kriege,* 9–10.

316. Chojnacki, *Wandel;* Kalyvas, "Civil Wars"; Newman, "New Wars."

317. Calic, *Krieg und Frieden,* 217ff.

318. Attanassoff, "Islamic Revival in the Balkans," 30–31; Benthall and Bellion-Jourdan, *Charitable Crescent,* S. 128ff.

319. Mandaville, "Transnational Muslim Solidarities"; Rucker-Chang, "Turkish Connection."

320. Eisermann, *Weg nach Dayton;* Woodward, *Balkan Tragedy.*

321. "Report of the Secretary-General Pursuant to General Assembly Resolution 53 / 55: The Fall of Srebrenica" (November 15, 1999), accessed November 8, 2018, http://undocs.org/A/54/549.

322. For a thorough reconstruction of events, see Fink, *Srebrenica.*

323. Central Intelligence Agency, *Balkan Battlegrounds,* 1:283ff.

324. See the thorough depiction in Calic, *Krieg und Frieden.*

325. Bose, *Bosnia after Dayton;* Bieber, *Post-War Bosnia;* Džihić, *Ethnopolitik.*

326. Biermann, *Lehrjahre.*

327. Reeb, "Öffentlichkeit," 197.

328. Kutz, *Öffentlichkeitsarbeit,* 192ff; see also Shea, "Kosovo-Krise," 215; Fachot, "Media Dimension," 55.

329. Schwab-Trapp, *Kriegsdiskurse.*

330. Biermann, *Lehrjahre;* Kutz, *Öffentlichkeitsarbeit,* 206ff.

331. Herman and Peterson, "CNN"; De Franco, *Media Power.*

332. Ibid.

333. Wheeler, *Saving Strangers,* 242.

334. Dobrinsky and Havlik, *Economic Convergence.*

335. Calic, "Stabilitätspakt."

336. Kaelble, *Kalter Krieg,* 258–59.

337. Bairoch and Kozul-Wright, "Globalization Myths."

338. Steger, *Globalization,* 53; Zeiler, "Opening Doors," 326ff.

339. Wirsching, *Preis der Freiheit,* 95ff.

340. Ramet, *Politics,* 23; Berend, *Soviet Bloc,* 58.

341. Ther, *Neue Ordnung,* 35, 104ff.

342. World Bank, *Transition,* xiv, xxii.

343. See the introduction in Duijzings, *Global Villages.*

344. Maddison, *Weltwirtschaft,* 176; Berend, *Soviet Bloc,* 74.

345. UNODC, *Crime,* 45.

346. Therborn, *Gesellschaften,* 161–62.

347. Murgasova, *Western Balkans,* 20.

348. Kaser, "Economic Reforms."

349. Office for South East Europe, *Report.*

350. Wirsching, *Preis der Freiheit,* 392ff.

351. Bartlett and Prica, *Variable Impact.*

352. Eurostat, accessed May 25, 2018, http://ec.europa.eu/eurostat/tgm/refresh TableAction.do;jsessionid=lQddzGkXML2mlCavwrgsJ5w1qPOOVUvNkt0trr2So 83lZUhMczy0!1614172686?tab=table&plugin=1&pcode=t2020_50&language=en.

353. Panagiotou and Valvis, *Sovereign Debt Crisis.*

354. Eurostat, accessed May 25, 2018, http://ec.europa.eu/eurostat/web/main /home.

355. Vladimir Gligorov, "Wachstum, Löhne und Beschäftigung auf dem Balkan," *Blickpunkt Kroatien* (August 24, 2015), 9–12.

356. Murgasova, *Western Balkans,* 35.

357. Ibid., 13–14.

358. UNODC, *Crime,* 27, 45.

359. Kovtun, "Boosting Job Growth," 19.

360. *Blickpunkt Kroatien* (August 24, 2015), 1.

361. "Migrationsprofil Westbalkan," accessed May 25, 2018, https://www.bamf .de/SharedDocs/Anlagen/DE/Publikationen/WorkingPapers/wp63-migration sprofil-westbalkan.pdf?__blob=publicationFile.

362. Bechev, *Rival Power.*

363. Quoted in Tanasković, *Neoosmanizam,* 93, 104.

364. Çolak, "Ottomanism"; Populari, *Political Romance;* Mitrović, "Turkish Foreign Policy," 54ff.

365. Benthall and Bellion-Jourdan, *Charitable Crescent,* 128ff.

366. Attanassoff, "Islamic Revival in the Balkans," 39; Karčić, "Islamic Revival"; Attanassoff, "Bosnia and Herzegovina."

367. Makarenko, "Crime"; Makarenko, *Crime-Terror Nexus.*

368. Roudometof, "Transnationalism."

369. Jens Bastian, "China's Balkan Silk Road: Examining Beijing's Push into Southeast Europe," *Reconnecting Asia* (November 20, 2017), accessed November 16, 2018, https://reconnectingasia.csis.org/analysis/entries/chinas-balkan-silk-road/.

370. Akkaya, *Nichtregierungsorganisationen,* 106.

371. "Die Revolutions-GmbH," *Der Spiegel* 46/2005, accessed April 23, 2018, http://www.spiegel.de/spiegel/print/d-43103188.html.

372. Kostovicova and Glasius, *Bottom-Up Politics;* Bojičić-Dželilović et al., *Civil Society.*

373. Duijzings, *Global Villages.*

374. Mellish, "Koprivshtitsa Festival."

375. Therborn, *Gesellschaften,* 367ff.; Eurostat, *Pocketbook,* 184.

376. Benedek et al., *Transnational Terrorism.*

377. UNODC, *Illicit Drug Trade.*

378. UNODC, *Crime,* 23ff.

379. Brunnbauer and Troebst, *Amnesie und Nostalgie.*

380. Ibid.

Works Cited

Abu Jaber, Kamel S. "The Millet System in the 19th Century Ottoman Empire." *Muslim World* 57, no. 3 (1967): 212–23.

Abulafia, David. *Great Sea: A Human History of the Mediterranean.* Oxford University Press, 2011.

Abu-Lughod, Janet L. *Before European Hegemony: The World System A.D. 1250–1350.* Oxford University Press, 1989.

Achim, Viorel. *The Roma in Romanian History.* Budapest: Central European University Press, 2004.

Adamček, Josip. *Bune i otpori: Seljačke bune u Hrvatskoj u XVII stoljeću.* Zagreb: Globus, 1987.

Adanir, Fikret. *Die makedonische Frage: Ihre Entstehung u. Entwicklung bis 1908.* Wiesbaden: Franz Steiner, 1979.

———. "The Formation of a Muslim Nation in Bosnia-Hercegovina: A Historiographic Discussion." In *The Ottomans and the Balkans: A Discussion of Historiography,* edited by Fikret Adanir and Suraiya Faroqhi, 267–304. Leiden: Brill, 2002.

———. "Heiduckentum und osmanische Herrschaft: Sozialgeschichtliche Aspekte der Diskussion um das frühneuzeitliche Räuberwesen in Südosteuropa." *Südost-Forschungen* 41 (1982): 43–116.

———. "Religious Communities and Ethnic Groups under Imperial Sway: Ottoman and Habsburg Lands in Comparison." In *The Historical Practice of Diversity: Transcultural Interactions from the Early Modern Mediterranean to the Postcolonial World,* edited by Dirk Hoerder, 54–86. New York: Berghahn Books, 2003.

Afflerbach, Holger. *Der Dreibund: Europäische Großmacht- und Allianzpolitik vor dem Ersten Weltkrieg.* Vienna: Böhlau, 2002.

Agoston, Gábor. "Information, Ideology, and Limits of Imperial Policy: Habsburg Rivalry." In *The Early Modern Ottomans: Remapping the Empire,* edited by Virginia H. Aksan and Daniel Goffman, 75–103. Cambridge University Press, 2007.

Akkaya, Gülcan. *Nichtregierungsorganisationen als Akteure der Zivilgesellschaft: eine Fallstudie über die Nachkriegsgesellschaft im Kosovo.* Wiesbaden: Springer VS, 2012.

Aladžov, Živko T. "Die Religion der heidnischen Protobulgaren im Lichte einiger archäologischer Denkmäler. *Praehistorische Zeitschrift* 60, no. 1 (1985): 70–92.

Aldcroft, Derek Howard. *The European Economy 1914–2000.* London: Routledge, 2001.

———. *Europe's Third World: The European Periphery in the Interwar Years.* Aldershot: Ashgate, 2006.

Aleksandrov, Emil. *Kultura i lična vlast: az rabotich s Ljudmila Živkova.* Sofia: Izdat. Slănce, 1991.

Aleksov, Bojan. "Habsburg Confessionalism and Confessional Policies in Bosnia and Herzegovina." In *WechselWirkungen: Austria-Hungary, Bosnia-Herzegovina, and the Western Balkans, 1878–1918,* edited by Clemens Ruthner et al., 83–121. New York: Peter Lang, 2015.

———. "One Hundred Years of Yugoslavia: The Vision of Stojan Novaković Revisited." *Nationalities Papers* 39, no. 6 (2011): 997–1010.

a-Levi, Sa'adi Besalel. *A Jewish Voice from Ottoman Salonica: The Ladino Memoir of Sa'adi Besalel a-Levi.* Edited by Aron Rodrigue and Sarah Abrevaya Stein. Translated by Isaac Jerusalmi. Stanford, CA: Stanford University Press, 2012.

Anastassiadou, Meropi. *Salonique 1830–1912: Une ville ottomane à l'âge des Réformes.* Leiden: Brill, 1997.

———. "Yanni, Nikola, Lifder et les autres: le profil demographique et socio-professionnel de la population orthodoxe de Salonique à la veille des 'Tanzimat.'" *Südost-Forschungen* 53 (1994): 73–130.

Ancel, Jean. *The History of the Holocaust in Romania.* Translated by Yaffah Murciano. Lincoln: University of Nebraska Press, 2011.

Anderson, M. S. *The Eastern Question, 1774–1923: A Study in International Relations.* London: St. Martin's Press, 1966.

Andraş, Carmen. "Europe and / or Orient: British Travel Literature and the Recognition of Cultural Confluences in Inter-War Romania." *Anuarul Institutului de Cercetări Socio-Umane "Gheorghe Şincai" al Academiei Române* 11 (2008): 91–105.

Andrić, Ivo. *The Bridge on the Drina.* Translated by Lovett F. Edwards. London: George Allen and Unwin, 1959.

Angelow, Jürgen. "Der 'Kriegsfall Serbien' als Willenstherapie: Operative Planung, politische Mentalitäten und Visionen vor und zu Beginn des Ersten Weltkrieges." *Militärgeschichtliche Zeitschrift* 61 (2002): 315–36.

Anscombe, Frederick F. "The Balkan Revolutionary Age." *Journal of Modern History* 84, no. 3 (2012): 572–606.

Antonić, Zdravko, and Nikola Tasić. *Istorija Beograda.* Belgrade: Balkanološki Institut SANU, 1995.

Appadurai, Arjun. *Modernity at Large: Cultural Dimensions of Globalization.* Minneapolis: University of Minnesota Press, 1996.

Argyropoulos, Roxane. "Les Lumières françaises dans la pensée grecque moderne: Réception et réaction." *Balkan Studies* 2 (2000): 3–9.

Armitage, David, and Sanjay Subrahmanyam, eds. *The Age of Revolutions in Global Context, c. 1760–1840*. Houndmills: Palgrave Macmillan, 2010.

Aronsson, Peter, and Gabriella Elgenius. *National Museums and Nation-Building in Europe, 1750–2010: Mobilization and Legitimacy, Continuity and Change*. Milton Park: Routledge, 2014.

Ascherson, Neal. *Black Sea*. New York: Hill and Wang, 1995.

"Asien und Europa, eine politische Parallele." *Politisches Journal: nebst Anzeige von gelehrten und andern Sachen* 1 (1827): 483–89.

Atanasova, Ivanka N. "Lyudmila Zhivkova and the Paradox of Ideology and Identity in Communist Bulgaria." *East European Politics and Societies* 18, no. 2 (2004): 278–315.

Athanassoglou-Kallmyer, Nina M. *French Images from the Greek War of Independence (1821–1830): Art and Politics under the Restoration*. New Haven, CT: Yale University Press, 1989.

Atsiz, Bedriye. "Das Albanerbild der Türken nach osmanischen Chroniken des 15.–16. Jahrhunderts." *Münchner Zeitschrift für Balkankunde* 1 (1978): 15–25.

Attanassoff, Velko. "Bosnia and Herzegovina: Islamic Revival, International Advocacy Networks and Islamic Terrorism." *Strategic Insight* 6, no. 5 (May 2005).

———. "Islamic Revival in the Balkans." MA thesis, Naval Postgraduate School, Monterey, 2006.

Austin, Robert C. *Founding a Balkan State: Albania's Experiment with Democracy, 1920–1925*. Toronto: University of Toronto Press, 2012.

Baćević, Ljiljana, ed. *Jugoslavija na kriznoj prekretnici*. Belgrade: Institut društvenih nauka, 1991.

Baer, Marc. "Globalization, Cosmopolitanism, and the Dönme in Ottoman Salonica and Turkish Istanbul." *Journal of World History* 128, no. 2 (2007): 141–70.

Baernreither, Joseph Maria. *Fragmente eines politischen Tagebuches: Die südslawische Frage und Österreich-Ungarn vor dem Weltkrieg*. Berlin: Verlag für Kulturpolitik, 1928.

Baeva, Iskra, and Evgenia Kalinova. *Bãlgarskite prechodi: 1939–2010*. Sofia: Paradigma, 2010.

Bairoch, Paul. *Commerce extérieur et développement économique de l'Europe au XIXe siècle*. Paris: Mouton, 1976.

Bairoch, Paul, and Richard Kozul-Wright. "Globalization Myths: Some Historical Reflections on Integration, Industrialization and Growth in the World Economy." *UNCTAD Discussion Paper* 113 (March 1996): 1–32.

Bajamonti, Julije. *Storia della peste che regno in Dalmazia negli anni 1783–1784*. Venice: Presso Vincenzio Formaleoni, 1786.

Bajić, Aleksandra. *Bogovi starih slovena*. Belgrade: Pešić i sinovi, 2008.

———. *Slovenski bogovi na Balkanu*. Belgrade: Pešić i sinovi, 2006.

Bakić-Hayden, Milica. "Nesting Orientalism: The Case of Former Yugoslavia." *Slavic Review* 54, no. 4 (Winter 1995): 917–31.

Balch, Emily Greene. *Our Slavic Fellow Citizens*. New York: Charities Publication Committee, 1910.

Baleva, Martina. *Bulgarien im Bild: Die Erfindung von Nationen auf dem Balkan in der Kunst des 19. Jahrhunderts*. Cologne: Böhlau, 2012.

———. "Nationalmythos Batak: Die Dekonstruktion eines Bildes und die Folgen." *Kritische berichte—Zeitschrift für Kunst- und Kulturwissenschaften* 36, no. 2 (2008): 21–31.

Baleva, Martina, and Ulf Brunnbauer, eds. *Batak—ein bulgarischer Erinnerungsort: Ausstellung.* Sofia: Iztok-Zapad, 2007.

Ballantyne, Tony and Antoinette Burton. "Empires and the Reach of the Global." In *A World Connecting, 1870–1945,* edited by Emily S. Rosenberg, 285–431. Cambridge, MA: Belknap Press of Harvard University Press, 2012.

Balta, Sebastian. *Rumänien und die Großmächte in der Ära Antonescu, 1940–1944.* Stuttgart: Franz Steiner, 2005.

Banac, Ivo. *With Stalin against Tito: Cominformist Splits in Yugoslav Communism.* Ithaca, NY: Cornell University Press, 1988.

Barkey, Karen. *Empire of Difference: The Ottomans in Comparative Perspective.* Cambridge University Press, 2008.

Barlas, Dilek, and Yonca Köksal. "Turkey's Foreign Policy towards Bulgaria and the Turkish Minority (1923–1934)." *Southeast European and Black Sea Studies* 14, no. 2 (2014): 175–93.

Barleti, Marin. *The historie of George Castriot, surnamed Scanderbeg, King of Albanie.* Translated by Z. I. Gentleman. London: William Ponsonby, 1596.

Barth, Heinrich. *Reise durch das Innere der Europäischen Türkei von Rustchuk über Philippopel, Rilo (Monastir), Bitolia und den Thessalischen Olymp nach Saloniki im Herbst 1862.* Berlin: Dietrich Reimer, 1864.

Bartl, Peter. *Albanien: Vom Mittelalter bis zur Gegenwart.* Regensburg: Pustet, 1995.

Bartlett, William, and Ivana Prica. *The Variable Impact of the Global Economic Crisis in South East Europe.* London: LSEE, 2012.

Bartolović, Dragan. *Džemal Bijedić i njegovo vrijeme.* Mostar: Univerzitet Džemal Bijedić, 1985.

Bartov, Omer, and Eric D. Weitz. *Shatterzone of Empires: Coexistence and Violence in the German, Habsburg, Russian, and Ottoman Borderlands.* Bloomington: Indiana University Press, 2013.

Bartulović, Niko. *Od Revolucionarne Omladine do Orjune: Istorijat jugoslovenskog omladinskog pokreta.* Split: Direktorijum Orjune, 1925.

Bashford, Alison. "Nation, Empire, Globe: The Spaces of Population Debate in the Interwar Years." *Comparative Studies in Society and History* 49, no. 1 (2007): 170–201.

———. *Nova istorija srpskog naroda.* Belgrade: Naš Dom-L'age d'Homme, 2000.

Batinić, Jelena. *Women and Yugoslav Partisans: A History of World War II Resistance.* Cambridge University Press, 2015.

Bauer, Franz Alto. *Eine Stadt und ihr Patron: Thessaloniki und der Heilige Demetrios.* Regensburg: Schnell & Steiner, 2013.

Baumgart, Winfried. "Die 'Orientalische Frage'—redivivus? Große Mächte und kleine Nationalitäten 1820–1923." In *Neue Politische Geschichte,* edited by Dan Diner, 33–55. Tel Aviv: Institut für Deutsche Geschichte, 1999.

————. *Europäisches Konzert und nationale Bewegung: Internationale Beziehungen 1830–1878.* 2nd ed. Paderborn: Schöningh, 2007.

Bayly, Christopher A. "'Archaic' and 'Modern' Globalization in the Eurasian and African Arena, c. 1750–1850." In *Globalization in World History,* edited by A. G. Hopkins, 47–73. New York: Norton, 2002.

————. *The Birth of the Modern World, 1789–1914: Global Connections and Comparisons.* Malden, MA: Blackwell, 2004.

Beaujour, Louis-Auguste Félix. *A View of the Commerce of Greece, Formed After an Annual Average, from 1787 to 1797.* Translated by Thomas Hartwell Horne. London: H. L. Galabin, 1800.

Bechev, Dimitar. *Rival Power: Russia's Influence in Southeast Europe.* New Haven, CT: Yale University Press, 2017.

Becker, Christoph, Hans Hopfinger, and Albrecht Steinecke. *Geographie der Freizeit und des Tourismus: Bilanz und Ausblick.* 3rd ed. Munich: Oldenbourg, 2007.

Beckert, Sven. *Empire of Cotton: A Global History.* New York: Knopf, 2014.

Beer, Mathias. *Flucht und Vertreibung der Deutschen: Voraussetzungen, Verlauf, Folgen.* Munich: C.H. Beck, 2011.

Behschnitt, Wolf Dietrich. *Nationalismus bei Serben und Kroaten, 1830–1914: Analyse und Typologie der nationalen Ideologie.* Munich: Oldenbourg, 1980.

Belaj, Vitomir. *Hod kroz godinu: Mitska pozadina hrvatskih narodnih običaja i vjerovanja.* Zagreb: Golden marketing, 1998.

————. "Postati kršćaninom kao proces." *Studia Ethnologica Croatica* 21 (2009): 9–25.

Belegu, Mentar. "La révolution de juin 1924: un événement marqué pour l'Albanie et les Balkans." *Studia Albanica* 3, no. 2 (1966): 53–66.

Bell, John D. *Peasants in Power: Alexander Stamboliski and the Bulgarian Agrarian National Union, 1899–1923.* Princeton University Press, 1977.

Benbassa, Esther. *Die Geschichte der sephardischen Juden: Von Toledo bis Saloniki.* Translated by Lilli Herschhorn. Bochum: Winkler, 2005.

————. "Les relais nationalistes juifs dans les Balkans au XIXe siècle." In *Transmission et passages en monde juif,* edited by Esther Benbassa, 403–34. Paris: Publisud, 1997.

Benedek, Wolfgang, et al., eds. *Transnational Terrorism, Organized Crime and Peace-Building: Human Security in the Western Balkans.* Basingstoke: Palgrave Macmillan, 2010.

Bengtson, Hermann. *Philipp und Alexander der Große: Die Begründer der hellenistischen Welt.* Munich: Callwey, 1985.

Benjamin, Lya. *Evreii din România între anii 1940–1944.* Bucharest: Editura Hasefer, 1993–1998.

Benthall, Jonathan, and Jérôme Bellion-Jourdan. *The Charitable Crescent: Politics of Aid in the Muslim World.* London: I.B. Tauris, 2004.

Benz, Wolfgang, ed. *Dimension des Völkermords: Die Zahl der jüdischen Opfer des Nationalsozialismus.* Munich: Oldenbourg, 1991.

Benz, Wolfgang, and Werner Bergmann, eds. *Handbuch des Antisemitismus: Judenfeind-schaft in Geschichte und Gegenwart.* Vol. 3: *Begriffe, Theorien, Ideologien.* Munich: K.G. Saur, 2010.

Beograd u sećanjima. Belgrade: Srpska književna zadruga, 1977.

Berend, Ivan T. "Balkan Economic Development." *Economic History Review* 37, no. 2 (1984): 268–73.

———. *Central and Eastern Europe, 1944–1993: Detour from the Periphery to the Periphery.* Cambridge University Press, 1996.

———. *An Economic History of Nineteenth-Century Europe: Diversity and Industrializa-tion.* Cambridge University Press, 2013.

———. *From the Soviet Bloc to the European Union: The Economic and Social Transfor-mation of Central and Eastern Europe since 1973.* Cambridge University Press, 2009.

Berend, Iván T., and György Ránki. *Economic Development in East-Central Europe in the 19th and 20th Centuries.* New York: Columbia University Press, 1974.

———. *The European Periphery and Industrialization, 1780–1914.* Budapest: Akadémiai Kiadó, 1982.

———. "Polen, Ungarn, Rumänien und Albanien 1914–1980." In *Europäische Wirtschafts- und Sozialgeschichte vom Ersten Weltkrieg bis zur Gegenwart,* edited by Wolfram Fischer et al., 769–846. Stuttgart: Klett-Cotta, 1987.

Berghahn, Volker Rolf. *Der Erste Weltkrieg.* Munich: C.H. Beck, 2006.

Bergholz, Max. *Violence as a Generative Force: Identity, Nationalism, and Memory in a Balkan Community.* Ithaca, NY: Cornell University Press, 2016.

Berindei, Dan. "Die revolutionären Ereignisse von 1821 in den Rumänischen Fürstentümern." *Southeastern Europe* 3, no. 2 (1976): 153–66.

———. *L'année révolutionnaire 1821 dans les pays roumains.* Bucharest: Éditions de l'Académie de la République Socialiste de Roumanie, 1973.

Berković, Svjetlan. "Vanjska politika Dubrovačke republike." *Politička misao* 46, no. 4 (2009): 203–20.

Bernard, Sara. "The Return of the Gastarbeiter in Socialist Yugoslavia 1965–1991." PhD diss., University of Regensburg, 2015.

Bieber, Florian. *Post-War Bosnia: Ethnicity, Inequality and Public Sector Governance.* Houndmills: Palgrave Macmillan, 2006.

Biermann, Rafael. *Lehrjahre im Kosovo: Das Scheitern der internationalen Krisenprävention vor Kriegsausbruch.* Paderborn: Ferdinand Schöningh, 2006.

Bijedić, Džemal. *Samoupravljanje kao zahtjev i praksa.* Vol. 2. Sarajevo: Oslobođenje, 1981.

Bilandžić, Dušan. *Historija Socijalističke Federativne Republike Jugoslavije: glavni procesi.* Zagreb: Školska knjiga, 1978.

Bilandžić, Dušan, and Radovan Vukadinović. *Osnovne društvene promjene u Jugoslaviji (1945–1973).* Zagreb: Školska knjiga, 1973.

Biondich, Mark. *The Balkans: Revolution, War, and Political Violence since 1878.* Oxford University Press, 2011.

Birri-Tomovska, Kristina. *Jews of Yugoslavia, 1918–1941: A History of Macedonian Sephards.* Bern: Peter Lang, 2012.

Bîrsan, Christina. *Dimitrie Cantemir and the Islamic World.* Translated by Scott Tinney. Istanbul: Isis Press, 2004.

Bjelajac, Mile. "Novi (stari) zapleti oko uzroka prvog svetskog rata pred obeležavanje 100. godišnjice." *Tokovi istorije* 1 (2013): 15–62.

Bjelić, Dušan I., and Obrad Savić. *Balkan as Metaphor: Between Globalization and Fragmentation.* Cambridge, MA: MIT Press, 2002.

Blandiana, Ana. "Meine Heimat DIN A4." In *Heimat: Abbruch—Aufbruch— Ankunft,* edited by Ingeborg Szöllösi, 71–80. Halle: Mitteldeutscher Verlag, 2014.

Bled, Jean-Paul. *François-Ferdinand d'Autriche.* Paris: Tallandier, 2012.

Blinkhorn, Martin. *Fascism and the Right in Europe, 1919–1945.* Harlow: Longman, 2000.

———, ed. *Fascists and Conservatives: The Radical Right and the Establishment in Twentieth-Century Europe.* London: Unwin Hyman, 1990.

Boban, Ljubo. *Sporazum Cvetković-Maček.* Belgrade: Institut društvenih nauka, 1965.

Bochmann, Klaus. "Der Patriotismusbegriff im 19. Jahrhundert." In *Geschichte politisch-sozialer Begriffe in Rumänien und Moldova,* edited by Vasile Dumbrava, 42–60. Leipziger Universitätsverlag, 2010.

———, ed. *Dimitrie Cantemir: Fürst der Moldau, Gelehrter, Akteur der europäischen Kulturgeschichte.* Leipziger Universitäts-Verlag, 2008.

Bockman, Johanna. *Markets in the Name of Socialism: The Left-Wing Origins of Neoliberalism.* Stanford, CA: Stanford University Press, 2011.

Boeckh, Katrin. *Von den Balkankriegen zum Ersten Weltkrieg: Kleinstaatenpolitik und ethnische Selbstbestimmung auf dem Balkan.* Munich: Oldenbourg, 1996.

Bogdanović, Jelena, ed. *On the Very Edge: Modernism and Modernity in the Arts and Architecture of Interwar Serbia (1918–1941).* Leuven: Leuven University Press, 2014.

Boia, Lucian. *Fallstricke der Geschichte: Die rumänische Elite von 1930 bis 1950.* Translated by Larisa Schippel. Berlin: Frank & Timme, 2014.

Bojičić-Dželilović, Vesna, et al. *Civil Society and Transitions in the Western Balkans.* Basingstoke: Palgrave Macmillan, 2013.

Bojović, Boško I. *Kraljevstvo i svetost: Politička filozofija srednjovekovne Srbije.* Belgrade: Službeni list SRJ, 1999.

Bokovoy, Melissa K. "A Separate Road to Collectivization: The Communist Party of Yugoslavia's Agrarian Policy, 1941–1949." PhD diss., University of Michigan, 1991.

Boli, John, and George M. Thomas, eds. *Constructing World Culture: International Nongovernmental Organizations since 1875.* Stanford, CA: Stanford University Press, 1999.

Bombelles, Joseph T. "Federal Aid to the Less Developed Areas of Yugoslavia." *East European Politics and Society* 5, no. 3 (1991): 439–65.

Bono, Salvatore. *Piraten und Korsaren im Mittelmeer: Seekrieg, Handel und Sklaverei vom 16. bis 19. Jahrhundert.* Translated by Achim Wurm. Stuttgart: Klett-Cotta, 2009.

Boogert, Maurits H. van den. *The Capitulations and the Ottoman Legal System: Qadis, Consuls, and Beratlıs in the 18th Century.* Leiden: Brill, 2005.

Boom, Henk. *Der große Türke: Süleyman der Prächtige: Sein Leben, sein Reich und sein Einfluss auf Europa.* Berlin: Parthas, 2012.

Borgolte, Michael. *Europa entdeckt seine Vielfalt: 1050–1250.* Stuttgart: UTB, 2002.

Born, Robert. "Römer und / oder Daker: Zur symbolischen Funktionalisierung der Antike in Rumänien von 1918 bis 1989." In *Neue Staaten—neue Bilder? Visuelle Kultur im Dienst staatlicher Selbstdarstellung in Zentral- und Osteuropa seit 1918,* edited by Arnold Bartetzky et al., 257–71. Cologne: Böhlau, 2005.

Borojević, Rajka. *Iz Dubca u svet.* Belgrade: Etnografski muzej, 2006.

Borst, Arno. *Barbaren, Ketzer und Artisten: Welten des Mittelalters.* Munich: Piper, 1988.

———. *Die Katharer.* Vienna: Karolinger Verlag, 2012.

Bose, Sumantra. *Bosnia after Dayton: Nationalist Partition and International Intervention.* Oxford University Press, 2002.

Bošković, Ruđer Josip. *Reise von Konstantinopel, durch Romanien, Bulgarien, und die Moldau nach Lemberg in Pohlen.* Leipzig, 1779.

Boškovska, Nada. "Die Entführung der Miss Stone: Der Balkan im Blickfeld der westlichen Welt." *Historische Anthropologie* 16, no. 3 (2008): 420–42.

Boué, Ami. *Die europäische Türkei.* Vol. 1. Vienna: F. Tempsky, 1889.

———. *La Turquie d'Europe ou observations sur la géographie, la géologie, l'histoire naturelle, la statistique, les moeurs, les coutumes, l'archéologie, l'agriculture, l'industrie, le commerce, les gouvernements divers, le clergé, l'histoire et l'état politique de cet empire.* Paris: A. Bertrand, 1840.

Bougarel, Xavier. "From 'Young Muslims' to the Party of Democratic Action: The Emergence of a Panislamist Trend in Bosnia-Herzegovina." *Islamic Studies* 36, no. 2–3 (1997): 533–49.

———. "Islam, a 'Convenient Religion'? The Case of the 13th SS Division Handschar." In *Combatants of Muslim Origin in European Armies in the Twentieth Century: Far from Jihad,* edited by Xavier Bougarel et al., 137–59. London: Bloomsbury, 2017.

———. *Islam and Nationhood in Bosnia-Herzegovina: Surviving Empires.* London: Bloomsbury, 2018.

———. "Islam et politique en Bosnie-Herzégovine: Le Parti de l'action démocratique." PhD diss., Institut d'études politiques, 1999.

Bougarel, Xavier, and Nathalie Clayer. *Le nouvel islam balkanique: les musulmans, acteurs du post-communisme, 1990–2000.* Paris: Maisonneuve et Larose, 2001.

Bougarel, Xavier, Alexander Korb, Stefan Petke, and Franziska Zaugg. "Muslim SS Units in the Balkans and the Soviet Union." In *The Waffen-SS: A European History,* edited by Jochen Böhler and Robert Gerwarth, 252–83. Oxford University Press, 2017.

Bowen, John. "Beyond Migration: Islam as a Transnational Public Space." *Journal of Ethnic and Migration Studies* 30, no. 5 (2004): 879–94.

———. *A New Anthropology of Islam.* Cambridge University Press, 2012.

Boyar, Ebru, and Kate Fleet. *A Social History of Ottoman Istanbul.* Cambridge University Press, 2010.

Božić-Bužančić, Danica. *Južna Hrvatska u europskom fiziokratskom pokretu: Pokret za obnovu gospodarstva, gospodarske akademije, ogledni vrtovi i poljodjelske škole druge polovice XVIII. i početka XIX. stoljeća.* Split: Književni Krug, 1995.

———. *Privatni i društveni život Splita u osamnaestom stoljeću.* Zagreb: Školska knjiga, 1982.

Bracewell, Wendy. *The Uskoks of Senj: Piracy, Banditry, and Holy War in the Sixteenth-Century Adriatic.* Ithaca, NY: Cornell University Press, 1992.

Bracewell, Wendy, and Alex Drace-Francis, eds. *Balkan Departures: Travel Writing from Southeastern Europe.* New York: Berghahn Books, 2009.

Bradley, John, et al. *Regional Aid and Convergence: Evaluating the Impact of the Structural Funds on the European Periphery.* Aldershot: Avebury, 1995.

Bratianu, Georges Ioan. *La Mer Noire: des origines à la conquête ottomane.* Munich: Societas academica Dacoromana, 1969.

Braude, Benjamin, and Bernard Lewis, eds. *Christians and Jews in the Ottoman Empire: The Functioning of a Plural Society.* Vol. 1. New York: Holmes & Meier, 1982.

Braudel, Fernand. *Civilization and Capitalism, 15th–18th Century.* Vol. 3: The Perspective of the World. Translated by Siân Reynolds. New York: Harper and Row, 1982.

———. *The Mediterranean and the Mediterranean World in the Age of Philip II.* 2 vols. Translated by Siân Reynolds. New York: Harper and Row, 1972.

Bren, Paulina, and Mary Neuburger, eds. *Communism Unwrapped: Consumption in Cold War Eastern Europe.* Oxford University Press, 2012.

Brenner, Michael. *Geschichte des Zionismus.* Munich: C.H. Beck, 2002.

Brewer, David J. *The Flame of Freedom: The Greek War of Independence 1821–1833.* London: J. Murray, 2001.

Brier, Robert, ed. *Entangled Protest: Transnational Approaches to the History of Dissent in Eastern Europe and the Soviet Union.* Osnabrück: Fibre Verlag, 2013.

Brnardic, Teodora Shek. "Exchange and Commerce: Intercultural Communication in the Age of Enlightenment." *European Review of History* 16, no. 1 (2009): 79–99.

Brown, Keith. *Loyal unto Death: Trust and Terror in Revolutionary Macedonia.* Bloomington: Indiana University Press, 2013.

Brubaker, Rogers. *Grounds for Difference.* Cambridge, MA: Harvard University Press, 2015.

Brummett, Palmira. "Ottoman Expansion in Europe, ca. 1453–1606." In *The Cambridge History of Turkey,* vol. 2, edited by Suraiya Faroqhi and Kate Fleet, 44–73. Cambridge University Press, 2012.

Brunnbauer, Ulf. *"Die sozialistische Lebensweise": Ideologie, Gesellschaft, Familie und Politik in Bulgarien (1944–1989).* Vienna: Böhlau, 2007.

———. "Dimitrovgrad: Eine sozialistische Stadt in Bulgarien." In *Urbanisierung und Stadtentwicklung in Südosteuropa vom 19. bis zum 21. Jahrhundert,* edited by Thomas Bohn and Marie-Janine Calic, 197–219. Munich: Otto Sagner, 2010.

———. "Families and Mountains in the Balkans: Christian and Muslim Household Structures in the Rhodopes, 19th–20th Century." *History of the Family* 7, no. 3 (2002): 327–50.

———. *Gebirgsgesellschaften auf dem Balkan: Wirtschaft und Familienstrukturen im Rhodopengebirge (19./20. Jahrhundert).* Vienna: Böhlau, 2004.

———. "Gesellschaft und gesellschaftlicher Wandel in Südosteuropa nach 1945." In *Geschichte Südosteuropas: Vom frühen Mittelalter bis zur Gegenwart,* edited by Konrad Clewing and Oliver Jens Schmitt, 651–702. Regensburg: Pustet, 2011.

———. *Globalizing Southeastern Europe: Emigrants, America, and the State since the late 19th Century.* Lanham, MD: Lexington Books, 2016.

Brunnbauer, Ulf, and Stefan Troebst, eds. *Zwischen Amnesie und Nostalgie: Die Erinnerung an den Kommunismus in Südosteuropa.* Cologne: Böhlau, 2007.

Buchenau, Klaus. *Auf russischen Spuren: Orthodoxe Antiwestler in Serbien, 1850–1945.* Wiesbaden: Harrassowitz, 2011.

———. *Orthodoxie und Katholizismus in Jugoslawien, 1945–1991: Ein serbisch-kroatischer Vergleich.* Wiesbaden: Harrassowitz, 2004.

Buda, Octavian. "Black Death at the Outskirts of the Ottoman, Russian, and Habsburg Empires: The Epidemics in Phanariot Bucharest (1711–1821)." In *Medicine within and between the Habsburg and Ottoman Empires: 18th–19th Centuries,* edited by Teodora Daniela Sechel, 109–28. Bochum: Dieter Winkler, 2011.

Budak, Neven. "Die Gegenreformation in Kroatien." In *Reformation und Gegenreforma-tion im Pannonischen Raum,* 353–63. Eisenstadt: Burgenländisches Landes-museum, 1999.

———, ed. *Etnogeneza Hrvata.* Zagreb: Nakladni zavod Matice Hrvatske, 1995.

———. *Hrvatska povijest srednjeg vijeka.* Zagreb: Školska knjiga, 2006.

Bulmuş, Birsen. *Plague, Quarantines, and Geopolitics in the Ottoman Empire.* Edinburgh University Press, 2012.

Burbank, Jane, and Frederick Cooper. *Empires in World History: Power and the Politics of Difference.* Princeton University Press, 2010.

Burghardt, Peter. "Tango-Duell im Nebel." In *Die Fußballweltmeisterschaften 1930–1950,* 35–41. Munich: Süddeutsche Zeitung WM-Bibliothek, 2005.

Burgwyn, Howard J. *Empire on the Adriatic: Mussolini's Conquest of Yugoslavia, 1941–1943.* New York: Enigma, 2005.

Burks, Richard Voyles. *The Dynamics of Communism in Eastern Europe.* Princeton University Press, 1961.

Bushkoff, Leonard. "Marxism, Communism, and the Revolutionary Tradition in the Balkans, 1878–1924: An Analysis and an Interpretation." *East European Quarterly* 1, no. 4 (1968): 371–401.

Cabanes, Bruno. *The Great War and the Origins of Humanitarianism, 1918–1924.* Cambridge University Press, 2014.

Čajkanović, Veselin. *Stara srpska religija i mitologija.* Belgrade: Srpska književna zadruga, 1995.

Calic, Marie-Janine. "Der Stabilitätspakt für Südosteuropa." *Aus Politik und Zeitge-schichte* (March 23, 2001): 9–16.

———. "Ethnic Cleansing and War Crimes." In *Confronting the Yugoslav Controversies: A Scholars' Initiative,* edited by Charles Ingrao and Thomas A. Emmert, 114–51. West Lafayette, IN: Purdue University Press, 2009.

———. *Geschichte Jugoslawiens.* Munich: C.H. Beck, 2014.

———. *A History of Yugoslavia.* West Lafayette, IN: Purdue University Press, 2019.

———. *Krieg und Frieden in Bosnien-Hercegovina: Ursachen, Konfliktstrukturen, internationale Lösungsversuche.* Frankfurt: Suhrkamp, 1996.

———. "Kriegstreiber Serbien? Die Südslawen und der Erste Weltkrieg: Eine Richtigstellung." *Osteuropa* 64, no. 2–4 (2014): 43–58.

———. *Sozialgeschichte Serbiens, 1815–1941: Der aufhaltsame Fortschritt während der Industrialisierung.* Munich: Oldenbourg, 1994.

Calinescu, Matei. "The 1927 Generation in Romania: Friendships and Ideological Choices (Mihail Sebastian, Mircea Eliade, Nae Ionescu, Eugene Ionesco, E. M. Cioran)." *East European Politics and Societies* 15, no. 3 (2002): 649–77.

Calmès, Albert. *La situation économique et financière de l'Albanie: annexe au rapport présenté au Conseil par le Comité financier de la Commission économique et financière provisoire sur sa huitième session, Genève, Septembre 1922.* Geneva: Société des Nations, 1922.

Camariano, Nestor. *Alexandre Mavrocordato, le grand drogman: Son activité diplomatique 1673–1709.* Thessaloniki: Institute for Balkan Studies, 1970.

Campus, Eliza. *Ideea federală în perioada interbelică.* Bucharest: Editura Academiei Române, 1993.

Canapa, Marie-Paule. "L'islam et la question des nationalités en Yougoslavie." In *Radicalismes islamiques,* edited by Olivier Carré and Paul Dumont, 100–161. Paris: L'Harmattan, 1986.

Candea, Virgil. "Les intellectuels du sud-est européen au XVIIe siècle." *Revue des études sud-est européennes* 8, no. 2 (1970): 181–230.

Cardini, Franco. *Europa und der Islam: Geschichte eines Mißverständnisses.* Munich: C.H. Beck, 2010.

Carlson, W. Bernard. *Tesla: Inventor of the Electrical Age.* Princeton University Press, 2013.

Casagrande, Thomas. *Die volksdeutsche SS-Division "Prinz Eugen": Die Banater Schwaben und die nationalsozialistischen Kriegsverbrechen.* Frankfurt: Campus Verlag, 2003.

Casale, Giancarlo. *The Ottoman Age of Exploration.* Oxford University Press, 2010.

———. "Sokollu Mehmed Pasha and the Spice Trade." In *The Arab Lands in the Ottoman Era,* edited by Jane Hathaway, 63–91. Minneapolis: Center for Early Modern History, 2009.

Casanova, Giacomo Chevalier de Seingalt. *History of My Life.* Vols. 11–12. Translated by Willard R. Trask. Baltimore: Johns Hopkins University Press, 1997.

Casanova, José. "Religion in Modernity as Global Challenge." In *Religion und die umstrittene Moderne,* edited by Michael Reder and Matthias Rugel, 1–16. Stuttgart: Kohlhammer, 2010.

———. "Religion, the New Millennium, and Globalization." *Sociology of Religion* 62, no. 4 (2001): 415–41.

Case, Holly. *Between States: The Transylvanian Question and the European Idea during World War II.* Stanford, CA: Stanford University Press, 2009.

———. "The Strange Politics of Federative Ideas in East-Central Europe." *Journal of Modern History* 85, no. 4 (2013): 833–66.

Čavoški, Jovan. "Constructing Nasser's Neutralism: Egypt and the Rise of Nonalignment in the Middle East." In *The Regional Cold Wars in Europe, East Asia, and the Middle East: Crucial Periods and Turning Points,* edited by Lorenz M. Lüthi, 88–107. Washington, DC: Woodrow Wilson Center Press, 2015.

Çelebi, Evliya. *Im Reiche des Goldenen Apfels: Des türkischen Weltenbummlers Evliyâ Çelebî denkwürdige Reise in d. Giaurenland u. in d. Stadt. u. Festung Wien anno 1665.* Translated by Richard F. Kreutel. Graz: Styria, 1967.

Çelebi, Evliya, Robert Dankoff, and Sooyong Kim. *An Ottoman Traveller: Selections from the Book of Travels of Evliya Çelebi.* London: Eland, 2010.

Čelić, Džemal. *Sarajevo i okolica: Povijest, kultura, umjetnost, prirodne znamenitosti, turizam.* Zagreb: Privredni vjesnik, 1990.

Central Intelligence Agency. *Balkan Battlegrounds: A Military History of the Yugoslav Conflict, 1990–1995.* 2 vols. Washington, DC: Office of Russian and European Analysis, 2002.

Cernovodeanu, Paul. "Démètre Cantemir vu par ses contemporains (le monde savant et les milieux diplomatique européens)." *Revue des études sud-est européennes* 11, no. 4 (1973): 637–56.

Cernovodeanu, Paul, and Ion Stanciu. "The Romanians and the American Civil War." *Revue Roumaine d'Histoire* 19, no. 4 (1980): 599–625.

Chaconas, Stephen. *Adamantios Korais: A Study in Greek Nationalism.* New York: AMS Press, 1968.

Chirot, Daniel. *The Origins of Backwardness in Eastern Europe: Economics and Politics from the Middle Ages until the Early Twentieth Century.* Berkeley: University of California Press, 1989.

———. *Social Change in a Peripheral Society: The Creation of a Balkan Colony.* New York: Academic Press, 1976.

Chojnacki, Sven. *Wandel der Gewaltformen im internationalen System 1946–2006.* Osnabrück: Deutsche Stiftung Friedensforschung, 2008.

Ćirković, Sima M. *Kosovska bitka kao istorijski problem.* Novi Sad: Vojvođanska akademija nauka i umetnosti, 1992.

Čizmić, Ivan. "Emigration from Croatia, 1880–1914." In *Overseas Migration from East-Central and Southeastern Europe, 1880–1940,* edited by Julianna Puskás, 143–67. Budapest: Akadémiai Kiadó, 1990.

Clark, Christopher M. *The Sleepwalkers: How Europe Went to War in 1914.* London: Allen Lane, 2012.

Clarke, James F. "Reporting the Bulgarian Massacres: 'The Suffering in Bulgaria' by Henry O. Dwight and the Rev. J. F. Clarke (1876)." *Southeastern Europe* 4, no. 2 (1977): 278–96.

Clavin, Patricia. *Securing the World Economy: The Reinvention of the League of Nations, 1920–1946.* Oxford: Oxford University Press, 2013.

Clayer, Nathalie. "Netzwerke muslimischer Bruderschaften in Südosteuropa." Europäische Geschichte Online (EGO). Last modified April 26, 2012. http://www.ieg-ego.eu/clayern-2011-de.

———. *Religion et nation chez les albanais: XIXe–XXe siècles.* Istanbul: Isis Press, 2002.

————. "Transnational Connections and the Building of an Albanian and European Islam in Interwar Albania." *Transnational Islam in Interwar Europe: Muslim Activists and Thinkers,* edited by Götz Nordbruch and Umar Ryad, 45–66. New York: Palgrave Macmillan, 2014.

Clewing, Konrad. "Der Völkerbund und Albanien 1920–1923: Eine Genfer Quelle zu Südalbaniens Regionalproblemen." *Münchner Zeitschrift für Balkankunde* 10–12 (1996): 259–318.

————. "Staatensystem und innerstaatliches Agieren im multiethnischen Raum: Südosteuropa im langen 19. Jahrhundert." In *Geschichte Südosteuropas: Vom frühen Mittelalter bis zur Gegenwart,* edited by Konrad Clewing and Oliver Jens Schmitt, 432–553. Regensburg: Pustet, 2011.

Clissold, Stephen. *Yugoslavia and the Soviet Union.* London: Oxford University Press, 1975.

Clogg, Richard, ed. *Movement for Greek Independence 1770–1821.* London: Macmillan, 1976.

Çolak, Yilmaz. "Ottomanism vs. Kemalism: Collective Memory and Cultural Pluralism in 1990s Turkey." *Middle Eastern Studies* 42, no. 4 (July 2006): 587–602.

Coller, Ian. "East of Enlightenment: Regulating Cosmopolitanism between Istanbul and Paris in the Eighteenth Century." *Journal of World History* 21, no. 3 (2010): 447–70.

Čolović, Ivan. *Smrt na Kosovu polju: Istorija kosovoskog mita.* Belgrade: Biblioteka XX vek, 2016.

Conrad, Sebastian. *Globalgeschichte: Eine Einführung.* Munich: C.H. Beck, 2013.

Cornwall, Mark. "Serbia." In *Decisions for War, 1914,* edited by Keith M. Wilson, 55–97. New York: St. Martin's Press, 1995.

Ćosić, Stjepan. *Dubrovnik nakon pada Republike.* Dubrovnik: Academia Scientiarum et Artium Croatica, 1999.

Costa-Foru, Constantin. *Aus den Folterkammern Rumäniens.* Vienna: Kulturpolitischer Verlag, 1925.

Costantini, Emanuela. *Nae Ionescu, Mircea Eliade, Emil Cioran: antiliberalismo nazionalista alla periferia d'Europa.* Perugia: Morlacchi, 2005.

Cotrugli, Benedetto. *O trgovini i o savršenu trgovcu.* Zagreb: Jugoslavenska akademija znanosti i umjetnosti, 1985.

Crampton, R. J. *Bulgaria.* Oxford: Oxford University Press, 2010.

————. *Bulgaria, 1878–1918: A History.* Boulder: East European Monographs, 1983.

————. *A Concise History of Bulgaria.* Cambridge University Press, 2000.

Crowley, Roger. *Empires of the Sea: The Siege of Malta, the Battle of Lepanto, and the Contest for the Center of the World.* New York: Random House, 2008.

Čubrilović, Vasa. *Istorija Beograda.* Belgrade: Prosveta, 1974.

————. *Istorija političke misli u Srbiji XIX veka.* Belgrade: Prosveta, 1958.

Ćurčić, Slobodan. *Architecture in the Balkans: From Diocletian to Suleyman the Magnificent, c. 300–1550.* New Haven, CT: Yale University Press, 2010.

Ćurčin, Milan. *Ivan Meštrović: A Monograph.* London: Williams and Norgate, 1919.

Curta, Florin. *The Making of the Slavs: History and Archaeology of the Lower Danube Region, ca. 500–700.* Cambridge University Press, 2001.

Čuvalo, Ante. *The Croatian National Movement 1966–1972.* New York: Columbia University Press, 1990.

Cvijić, Jovan. *Balkansko poluostrvo.* Belgrade: Srpska akademija nauka i umetnosti, 1987.

Cvjetković, Marko. "Telegrafska i telefonska služba u Crnoj Gori." *Istorijski Zapisi* 12, no. 1/2 (1956): 165–90.

Dabčević-Kučar, Savka. *'71: hrvatski snovi i stvarnost.* Zagreb: Interpublic, 1997.

Dadić, Žarko. "Natural Sciences." In *Croatia in the Late Middle Ages and the Renaissance,* edited by Ivan Supičić, 741–56. Zagreb: Školska knjiga, 2008.

Daele, Jasmien van. *ILO Histories: Essays on the International Labour Organization and Its Impact on the World during the Twentieth Century.* Bern: Peter Lang, 2010.

Dalos, György. *Aufruhr im Kommunismus.* Erfurt: Landeszentrale für politische Bildung Thüringen, 2015.

Daniel, Ute. "Der Krimkrieg 1853–1856 und die Entstehungskontexte medialer Kriegsberichterstattung." In *Augenzeugen: Kriegsberichterstattung vom 18. zum 21. Jahrhundert,* edited by Ute Daniel, 40–67. Göttingen: Vandenhoeck & Ruprecht, 2006.

Danilović, Rajko. *Upotreba neprijatelja: politička suđenja 1945–1991 u Jugoslaviji.* Valjevo: Valjevac, 1993.

Dankoff, Robert. *An Ottoman Mentality: The World of Evliya Çelebi.* Leiden: Brill, 2006.

Darwin, John. *After Tamerlane: The Rise and Fall of Global Empires, 1400–2000.* New York: Bloomsbury Press, 2008.

Daskalov, Roumen. "Agrarian Ideologies and Peasant Movements in the Balkans." In *Entangled Histories of the Balkans,* edited by Roumen Daskalov and Diana Mishkova, 280–353. Vol. 2: *Transfers of Political Ideologies and Institutions.* Leiden: Brill, 2014.

———. "Bulgarian-Greek Dis/Entanglements." In *Entangled Histories of the Balkans,* edited by Roumen Daskalov and Tchavdar Marinov, 149–239. Vol. 1: *National Ideologies and Language Politics.* Leiden: Brill, 2013.

———. *Debating the Past: Modern Bulgarian History: From Stambolov to Zhivkov.* Budapest: Central European University Press, 2011.

———. "Ideas about, and Reactions to Modernization in the Balkans." *East European Quarterly* 31, no. 2 (1997): 141–80.

———. *The Making of a Nation in the Balkans: Historiography of the Bulgarian Revival.* Budapest: Central European University Press, 2004.

Daskalova, Krasimira. *Gramotnost, knižnina, čitateli, četene v Bălgarija.* Sofia: LIK, 1999.

Davenport, Richard A. *The Life of Ali Pasha of Tepeleni, Vizier of Epirus: Surnamed Aslan, or the Lion.* London: Thomas Tegg and Son, 1837.

David, Thomas. *Nationalisme économique et industrialisation: l'expérience des pays d'Europe de l'Est (1789–1939).* Geneva: Librairie Droz, 2009.

Davidova, Evguenia. *Balkan Transitions to Modernity and Nation-States: Through the Eyes of Three Generations of Merchants (1780s–1890s)*. Leiden: Brill, 2012.

Davis, Robert. "The Geography of Slaving in the Early Modern Mediterranean, 1500–1800." *Journal of Medieval & Early Modern Studies* 37, no. 1 (2007): 57–74.

De Franco, Chiara. *Media Power and the Transformation of War*. Houndmills: Palgrave Macmillan, 2012.

De Grazia, Victoria. *Irresistible Empire: America's Advance through Twentieth-Century Europe*. Cambridge, MA: Belknap Press of Harvard University Press, 2005.

de la Brosse, Renaud. *Political Propaganda and the Plan to Create a 'State for all Serbs': Consequences of Using the Media for Ultra-Nationalist Ends*. The Hague: Office of the Prosecutor of the International Criminal Tribunal for the Former Yugoslavia, 2003.

Deanović, Mirko. "Đuro Matijašević o prilikama u Dubrovniku na početku XVIII vijeka." *Građa za povijest književnosti Hrvatske* 11/12 (1933): 145–60.

Dedijer, Vladimir. *Novi prilozi za biografiju Josipa Broza Tita*. 3 vols. Zagreb: Mladost, 1980–84.

———. *The Road to Sarajevo*. New York: Simon and Schuster, 1966.

———. *Tito Speaks: His Self Portrait and Struggle with Stalin*. London: Weidenfeld and Nicolson, 1954.

Dedijer, Vladimir, and Antun Miletić. *Genocid nad Muslimanima, 1941–1945: zbornik dokumenata i svjedočenja*. Sarajevo: Svjetlost, 1990.

Deletant, Dennis. *Ceaușescu and the Securitate: Coercion and Dissent in Romania, 1965–1989*. Armonk: M.E. Sharpe, 1995.

———. *Romania under Communist Rule*. Iași: Center for Romanian Studies, 1999.

Demandt, Alexander. *Alexander der Große: Leben und Legende*. Munich: C.H. Beck, 2009.

"Der Prozeß gegen die Attentäter von Sarajewo (vom 12.–23. Oktober 1914) Aktenmäßig dargestellt von Professor Pharos." *Archiv für Strafrecht und Strafprozess* 64, no. 5–6 (1917): 385–418.

Despot, Andrea. *Amerikas Weg auf den Balkan: Zur Genese der Beziehungen zwischen den USA und Südosteuropa 1820–1920*. Wiesbaden: Harrassowitz, 2010.

Detrez, Raymond. "Pre-National Identities in the Balkans." In *Entangled Histories of the Balkans*, edited by Roumen Daskalov and Tchavdar Marinov, 13–65. Vol. 1: *National Ideologies and Language Politics*. Leiden: Brill, 2013.

———. "Relations between Greeks and Bulgarians in the Pre-Nationalist Era: The Gudilas in Plovdiv." In *Greece and the Balkans: Identities, Perceptions and Cultural Encounters since the Enlightenment*, edited by Dimitris Tziovas, 30–43. Aldershot: Ashgate, 2003.

Deusch, Engelbert. *Das k.(u.)k. Kultusprotektorat im albanischen Siedlungsgebiet in seinem kulturellen, politischen und wirtschaftlichen Umfeld*. Vienna: Böhlau, 2009.

Dialetis, Dimitris, Kostas Gavroglu, and Manolis Patiniotis. "The Sciences in the Greek-Speaking Regions during the 17th and 18th Centuries: The Process of Appropriation and the Dynamics of Reception and Resistance." In *The Sciences in the European Periphery during the Enlightenment*, edited by Kostas Gavroglu, 41–71. Dordrecht: Springer, 1999.

Dimaras, Konstantinos Theséos. *La Grèce aux temps des Lumières.* Geneva: Droz, 1969.

Dimitrijević, Sergije. *Socijalistički radnički pokret u Srbiji: 1870–1918.* Belgrade: Nolit, 1982.

Dimitrov, Theodore D. *La Bulgarie et la Société des Nations.* Geneva: International Documentation on Macedonia, 1986.

Dimitrov, Vesselin. "Bulgarian Neutrality: Domestic and International Perspectives." In *European Neutrals and Non-Belligerents during the Second World War,* edited by Neville Wylie, 192–216. Cambridge University Press, 2002.

Dimou, Augusta. *Entangled Paths towards Modernity: Contextualizing Socialism and Nationalism in the Balkans.* Budapest: Central European University Press, 2009.

Dinić, Kosta. *Srpska pisma iz Konga.* Belgrade: MAU, 1994.

Dinkel, Jürgen. *Die Bewegung Bündnisfreier Staaten.* Berlin: De Gruyter Oldenbourg, 2015.

Dinzelbacher, Peter, ed. *Europäische Mentalitätsgeschichte: Hauptthemen in Einzel-darstellungen.* Stuttgart: Alfred Kröner Verlag, 2008.

Ditrych, Ondrej. "'International Terrorism' as Conspiracy: Debating Terrorism in the League of Nations." *Historical Social Research* 38, no. 1 (2013): 200–210.

Djilas, Aleksa. *The Contested Country: Yugoslav Unity and Communist Revolution, 1919–1953.* Cambridge, MA: Harvard University Press, 1991.

Djilas, Milovan. *Jahre der Macht: Im jugoslawischen Kräftespiel, Memoiren 1945–1966.* Munich: Deutscher Taschenbuch Verlag, 1992.

Djokić, Dejan. *Elusive Compromise: A History of Interwar Yugoslavia.* London: Hurst, 2007.

Djordjević, Dimitrije. "Projects for the Federation of South-East Europe in the 1860s and 1870s." *Balcanica* 1 (1970): 119–45.

Dnevnik pobeda: Srbija u balkanskim ratovima 1912–1913. Belgrade: Filip Višnjić, 1988.

Dobreva, Doroteja. "Bulgarien auf der Pariser Weltausstellung 1900: Bilder von Eigenem und Fremdem in den zeitgenössischen publizistischen Debatten über die Ausstellung." In *Fremdes Europa? Selbstbilder und Europa-Vorstellungen in Bulgarien (1850–1945),* edited by Petar Petrov, Katerina Gehl, and Klaus Roth, 101–52. Berlin: LIT Verlag, 2007.

Dobrinsky, Rumen, and Peter Havlik. *Economic Convergence and Structural Change: The Role of Transition and EU Accession.* Research Report 395. Vienna Institute for International Economic Studies, 2014.

Dojnov, Stefan. "Bălgarite i Părvoto srăbsko văstanie." *Istoričeski Pregled* 26, no. 5 (1970): 51–74.

Donauschwäbisches Zentralmuseum. *Johnny Weissmüller: Ausstellung zum 100. Geburtstag.* Ulm: Donauschwäbisches Zentralmuseum, 2004.

Donia, Robert J. "Bosnia and Herzegovina: The Proximate Colony in the Twilight of Empire." *Godišnjak Centra za balkanološka ispitivanja* 42 (2013): 197–201.

———. *Sarajevo: A Biography,* London: Hurst, 2006.

Dorian, Emil. *The Quality of Witness: A Romanian Diary, 1937–1944.* Translated by Mara Soceanu Vamos. Philadelphia: Jewish Publication Society of America, 1982.

Douglas, R. M. *Orderly and Humane: The Expulsion of the Germans after the Second World War.* New Haven, CT: Yale University Press, 2013.

Drace-Francis, Alex. *The Making of Modern Romanian Culture: Literacy and the Development of National Identity.* London: Tauris Academic Studies, 2006.

———. "The Prehistory of a Neologism: 'South-Eastern Europe.'" *Balkanologie* 3 (1999): 117–27.

———. "Zur Geschichte des Südosteuropakonzepts bis 1914." In *Europa und die Grenzen im Kopf,* edited by Karl Kaser et al., 275–86. Klagenfurt: Wieser, 2003.

Dragojlović, Dragoljub. *Istorija filozofske misli u Srba epohe feudalizma.* Novi Sad: Svetovi, 1998.

Dragomir, Elena. *Cold War Perceptions: Romania's Policy Change towards the Soviet Union, 1960–1964.* Newcastle: Cambridge Scholars, 2015.

Dragostinova, Theodora. *Between Two Motherlands: Nationality and Emigration among the Greeks of Bulgaria, 1900–1949.* Ithaca, NY: Cornell University Press, 2011.

Draşovean, Marius Florin. "Industria auto interbelică: istoria unei crize sau debutul unei modernizări." *Sfera Politicii* 133 (2009): 61–73.

Duchhardt, Heinz. *Barock und Aufklärung.* Munich: Oldenbourg, 2007.

———. *Der Wiener Kongress: Die Neugestaltung Europas 1814/15.* Munich: C.H. Beck, 2013.

Dučić, Jovan. *Grof Sava Vladislavić: Jedan Srbin diplomata na dvoru Petra Velikog i Katarine I.* Belgrade: Štampar Makarije, 1999.

———. *Rapoarte diplomatice din Bucureşti: 1937–1939.* Bucharest: Universal Dalsi, 1998.

Duijzings, Ger, ed. *Global Villages: Rural and Urban Transformations in Contemporary Bulgaria.* London: Anthem Press, 2013.

Dülffer, Jost. *Europa im Ost-West-Konflikt 1945–1991.* Munich: Oldenbourg, 2010.

Dülffer, Jost, Martin Kröger, and Rolf-Harald Wippich. *Vermiedene Kriege: Deeskalationen von Konflikten der Großmächte zwischen Krimkrieg und Erstem Weltkrieg.* Munich: Oldenbourg, 1997.

Dulić, Tomislav. *Utopias of Nation: Local Mass Killing in Bosnia and Herzegovina, 1941–42.* Uppsala: Uppsala Universitet, 2005.

Dumbrava, Vasile, ed. *Geschichte politisch-sozialer Begriffe in Rumänien und Moldova.* Leipziger Universitätsverlag, 2010.

Dumont, Paul. "The Social Structure of the Jewish Community of Salonica at the End of the Nineteenth Century." *Southeastern Europe* 5, no. 2 (1979): 33–72.

Dušković, Vesna. *Srbija na svetskoj izložbi u Parizu 1900.* Belgrade: Etnografski muzej, 1995.

Duţu, Alexandru. *European Intellectual Movements and Modernization of Romanian Culture.* Translated by Adriana Ionescu-Parau. Bucharest: Editura Academiei Republicii Socialiste România, 1981.

———. *Humanisme, baroque, lumières: L'exemple roumain.* Bucharest: Editura Academiei Republicii Socialiste România, 1984.

Duţu, Alexandru, Edgar Hösch, and Norbert Oellers, eds. *Brief und Briefwechsel in Mittel- und Osteuropa im 18. und 19. Jahrhundert.* Essen: Hobbing, 1989.

Džaja, Srećko M. *Die "Bosnische Kirche" und das Islamisierungsproblem Bosniens und der Herzegowina in den Forschungen nach dem Zweiten Weltkrieg.* Munich: R. Trofenik, 1978.

———. *Konfessionalität und Nationalität Bosniens und der Herzegowina: Voremanzipatorische Phase 1463–1804.* Munich: Oldenbourg, 1984.

Džambo, Jozo. *Buchwesen in Bosnien und Herzegowina (1800–1878): Zum Problem der Lesersoziologie.* Frankfurt: Peter Lang, 1985.

———. *Die Franziskaner im mittelalterlichen Bosnien.* Werl: Dietrich-Coelde-Verlag, 1991.

———. "Milena Preindlsberger-Mrazović—eine Publizistin zwischen Folklore und Modernität." In *Frauenbildung und Emanzipation in der Habsburgermonarchie— der südslawische Raum und seine Wechselwirkung mit Wien, Prag und Budapest,* edited by Vesela Tutavac and Ilse Korotin, 173–213. Vienna: Praesens Verlag, 2016.

Džihić, Vedran. *Ethnopolitik in Bosnien-Herzegowina: Staat und Gesellschaft in der Krise.* Baden-Baden: Nomos, 2010.

Dzino, Danijel. *Becoming Slav, Becoming Croat: Identity Transformations in Post-Roman and Early Medieval Dalmatia.* Leiden: Brill, 2010.

Eckel, Jan. "The Rebirth of Politics from the Spirit of Morality: Explaining the Human Rights Revolution of the 1970s." In *The Breakthrough: Human Rights in the 1970s,* edited by Jan Eckel and Samuel Moyn, 226–59. Philadelphia: University of Pennsylvania Press, 2014.

Eichholtz, Dietrich. *Deutsche Politik und rumänisches Öl (1938–1941): Eine Studie über Erdölimperialismus.* Leipziger Universitätsverlag, 2005.

Eisermann, Daniel. *Der lange Weg nach Dayton: Die westliche Politik und der Krieg im ehemaligen Jugoslawien 1991 bis 1995.* Baden-Baden: Nomos, 2000.

Ekmečić, Milorad. *Stvaranje Jugoslavije 1790–1918.* Vol. 2. Belgrade: Prosveta, 1989.

Elbern, Stephan. *Rom—Eine Biografie: Menschen und Schicksale von Romulus bis Mussolini.* Mainz: Nünnerich-Asmus Verlag, 2013.

Eldem, Edhem. "Capitulations and Western Trade." In *The Cambridge History of Turkey,* vol. 3, edited by Suraiya Faroqhi and Kate Fleet, 281–335. Cambridge University Press, 2012.

Eldem, Edhem, Daniel Goffman, and Bruce A. Masters. *The Ottoman City between East and West: Aleppo, Izmir, and Istanbul.* Cambridge University Press, 1999.

Eliade, Mircea. *Erinnerungen 1907–1937.* Frankfurt: Insel-Verlag, 1987.

———. *File despre Nae Ionescu.* Bucharest: Criterion, 2008.

———. *Indisches Tagebuch: Reisenotizen 1928–1931.* Munich: Diederichs, 1996.

Elliott, John Huxtable. *The Old World and the New 1492–1650.* Cambridge University Press, 1992.

Emiralioğlu, M. Pinar. *Geographical Knowledge and Imperial Culture in the Early Modern Ottoman Empire.* Burlington, VT: Ashgate, 2014.

Erdem, Y. Hakan. *Slavery in the Ottoman Empire and Its Demise, 1800–1909.* New York: St. Martin's Press, 1996.

Erlich, Vera St. *Family in Transition: A Study of 300 Yugoslav Villages.* Princeton University Press, 1966.

Ersoy-Hacısalihoğlu, Neriman. "Textile Trade in Bulgaria in the Mid-Nineteenth Century and the Gümüşgerdan Family." In *Living in the Ottoman Ecumenical Community: Essays in Honour of Suraiya Faroqhi,* edited by Vera Costantini and Markus Koller, 181–200. Leiden: Brill, 2008.

Eurostat. *Pocketbook on Candidate and Potential Candidate Countries.* Brussels: European Union, 2010.

Evropski pokret u Srbiji. *Spoljna politika Srbije: Strategije i dokumenta.* Belgrade, 2010.

Fabijanec, Sabine Florence. "Hygiene and Commerce: The Example of Dalmatian Lazarettos from the Fourteenth until the Sixteenth Century." *Ekonomska i ekohistorija: časopis za gospodarsku povijest i povijest okoliša* 4, no. 8 (2008): 115–33.

Fachot, Morand. "The Media Dimension in Foreign Interventions." *Policy Options* (January–February 2001): 50–55.

Fahrmeir, Andreas. *Revolutionen und Reformen: Europa 1789–1850.* Munich: C.H. Beck, 2010.

Faroqhi, Suraiya. "Ein Istanbuler Derwisch im 17. Jahrhundert, seine Familie und seine Freunde: Das Tagebuch des Seyyid Hasan." In *Selbstzeugnisse in der Frühen Neuzeit: Individualisierungsweisen in interdisziplinärer Perspektive,* edited by Kaspar von Greyerz, 113–128. Munich: Oldenbourg, 2007.

———. *Geschichte des osmanischen Reiches.* Munich: C.H. Beck, 2010.

———. *Kultur und Alltag im Osmanischen Reich: Vom Mittelalter bis zum Anfang des 20. Jahrhunderts.* Munich: C.H. Beck, 1995.

———. "The Ottoman Empire and the Islamic World." In *Empires and Encounters: 1350–1750,* edited by Wolfgang Reinhard, 221–388. Cambridge, MA: Belknap Press of Harvard University Press, 2015.

———. *The Ottoman Empire and the World around It.* London: I.B. Tauris, 2004.

Feichtinger, Johannes. "Komplexer k. u. k. Orientalismus: Akteure, Institutionen, Diskurse im und 20. Jahrhundert in Österreich." In *Orientalismen in Ostmitteleuropa: Diskurse, Akteure und Disziplinen vom 19. Jahrhundert bis zum Zweiten Weltkrieg,* edited by Robert Born and Sarah Lemmen, 31–63. Bielefeld: transcript, 2014.

Feichtinger, Johannes, Ursula Prutsch, and Moritz Csáky, eds. *Habsburg postcolonial: Machtstrukturen und kollektives Gedächtnis.* Innsbruck: StudienVerlag, 2003.

Feinstein, Charles H., Peter Temin, and Gianni Toniolo. *The European Economy between the Wars.* Oxford University Press, 1997.

Fejzić, Elvis. "Political Thought in Bosnia and Herzegovina during Austro-Hungarian Rule, 1878–1918." *East Central Europe* 39, no. 2–3 (2012): 204–36.

Ferluga, Jadran. *Byzantium on the Balkans: Studies on the Byzantine Administration and the Southern Slavs from the VIIth to the XIIth Centuries.* Amsterdam: A.M. Hakkert, 1976.

Fevziu, Blendi. *Enver Hoxha: The Iron Fist of Albania.* London: I.B. Tauris, 2016.

Fichtner, Paula S. *The Habsburg Monarchy, 1490–1848: Attributes of Empire.* New York: Palgrave Macmillan, 2003.

Filandra, Šaćir, ed. *Bošnjaci i moderna: Humanistička misao Bošnjaka od polovine XIX. do polovine XX. stoljeća.* Sarajevo: Bosanski kulturni centar, 1996.

———. *Bošnjačka politika u XX. stoljeću.* Sarajevo: Sejtarija, 1998.

Fine, John V. A. *The Ancient Greeks: A Critical History.* Cambridge, MA: Belknap Press of Harvard University Press, 1983.

———. *The Bosnian Church: Its Place in State and Society from the 13th to the 15th Century: A New Interpretation.* London: Saqi, 2007.

———. *The Early Medieval Balkans: A Critical Survey from the Sixth to the Late Twelfth Century.* Ann Arbor: University of Michigan Press, 1983.

———. *The Late Medieval Balkans: A Critical Survey from the Late Twelfth Century to the Ottoman Conquest.* Ann Arbor: University of Michigan Press, 1987.

———. *When Ethnicity Did Not Matter in the Balkans: A Study of Identity in Pre-Nationalist Croatia, Dalmatia, and Slavonia in the Medieval and Early-Modern Periods.* Ann Arbor: University of Michigan Press, 2006.

Fink, Carole. *Defending the Rights of Others: The Great Powers, the Jews, and International Minority Protection, 1878–1938.* Cambridge University Press, 2004.

Fink, Matthias. *Srebrenica: Chronologie eines Völkermords oder was geschah mit Mirnes Osmanović.* Hamburg: Hamburger Edition, 2015.

Fisch, Jörg. *Das Selbstbestimmungsrecht der Völker: Die Domestizierung einer Illusion.* Munich: C.H. Beck, 2010.

Fischer, Bernd Jürgen. *Albania at War, 1939–1945.* West Lafayette, IN: Purdue University Press, 1999.

———. *Balkan Strongmen: Dictators and Authoritarian Rulers of South Eastern Europe.* West Lafayette, IN: Purdue University Press, 2007.

Fischer, Wladimir. *Dositej Obradović als bürgerlicher Kulturheld: Zur Formierung eines serbischen bürgerlichen Selbstbildes durch literarische Kommunikation 1783–1845.* Frankfurt: Peter Lang, 2007.

Fišera, Vladimir Claude. "Communisme et integration supranationale: la revue 'La Fédération Balkanique' (1924–1932)." *Revue d'Histoire Moderne & Contemporaine* 34, no. 3 (1987): 497–508.

Fleet, Kate. "The Ottomans, 1451–1603." In *The Cambridge History of Turkey,* vol. 2, edited by Suraiya Faroqhi and Kate Fleet, 19–43. Cambridge University Press, 2012.

Fleischer, Cornell H. *Bureaucrat and Intellectual in the Ottoman Empire: The Historian Mustafa Âli (1541–1600).* Princeton University Press, 1986.

Fleming, Katherine, ed. *A Faithful Sea: The Religious Cultures of the Mediterranean, 1200–1700.* Oxford: Oneworld, 2007.

———. *The Muslim Bonaparte: Diplomacy and Orientalism in Ali Pasha's Greece.* Princeton University Press, 1999.

Flere, Sergej. "Nacionalna identifikacija i preferirana nacionalna identifikacija kod mladih: pitanje jugoslavenstva." *Migracijske teme* 4, no. 4 (1988): 439–53.

Fodor, Pál. *In Quest of the Golden Apple: Imperial Ideology, Politics, and Military Administration in the Ottoman Empire.* Istanbul: Isis Press, 2000.

Fontenay, Michel. "Routes et modalités du commerce des esclaves dans la Méditerranée des temps modernes (XVIe, XVIIe et XVIIIe siècles)." *Revue Historique* 308, no. 4 (2006): 813–30.

Foretić, Vinko. *Povijest Dubrovnika do 1808.* Zagreb: Nakladni zavod MH, 1980.

Fortis, Alberto. *Die Sitten der Morlacken.* Bern, 1775.

Frangakis-Syrett, Elena. "Market Networks and Ottoman-European Commerce, c. 1700–1825." *Oriente Moderno* 25, no. 1 (2006): 109–28.

Frank, Alison. "The Children of the Desert and the Laws of the Sea: Austria, Great Britain, the Ottoman Empire, and the Mediterranean Slave Trade in the Nineteenth Century." *American Historical Review* 117, no. 2 (2012): 410–44.

Frazee, Charles A. *Catholics and Sultans: The Church and the Ottoman Empire, 1453–1923.* Cambridge University Press, 1983.

Freytag, Carl. *Deutschlands "Drang nach Südosten": Der Mitteleuropäische Wirtschaftstag und der "Ergänzungsraum Südosteuropa" 1931–1945.* Göttingen: V&R unipress, 2012.

Fried, Marvin. *Austro-Hungarian War Aims in the Balkans during World War I.* New York: Palgrave Macmillan, 2014.

Friedländer, Saul. *The Years of Extermination: Nazi Germany and the Jews, 1939–1945.* New York: HarperCollins, 2007.

Fryer, Charles. *The Destruction of Serbia in 1915.* Boulder: East European Monographs, 1997.

Fuhrmann, Horst. *Einladung ins Mittelalter.* 4th ed. Munich: C.H. Beck, 2009.

Gabucci, Ada. *Rom und sein Imperium.* Stuttgart: Theiss, 2005.

Gafencu, Grigore. *Vorspiel zum Krieg im Osten.* Zurich: Amstutz und Herdeg, 1944.

Gagnon, Valère P. *The Myth of Ethnic War: Serbia and Croatia in the 1990s.* Ithaca, NY: Cornell University Press, 2004.

Gall, Lothar. "Die europäischen Mächte und der Balkan im 19. Jahrhundert." In *Der Berliner Kongreß von 1878: Die Politik der Großmächte und die Probleme der Modernisierung in Südosteuropa in der zweiten Hälfte des 19. Jahrhunderts,* edited by Ralph Melville and Hans-Jürgen Schröder, 1–16. Wiesbaden: Franz Steiner, 1982.

Gandev, Hristo. "L'apparition des rapports capitalistes dans l'économie rurale de la Bulgarie du Nord-Ouest au cours du XVIII siècle." *Études Historiques* (1960): 207–20.

Gârleanu, Sava I. *Der Volksaufstand unter Tudor Vladimirescu (1821).* Bucharest: Wissenschaftlicher Verlag, 1968.

Gašić, Ranka. *Beograd u hodu ka Evropi: kulturni uticaji Britanije i Nemačke na beogradsku elitu 1918–1941.* Belgrade: Institut za savremenu istoriju, 2005.

Gatejel, Luminita. *Warten, hoffen und endlich fahren: Auto und Sozialismus in der Sowjetunion, in Rumänien und der DDR (1956–1989/91).* Frankfurt: Campus Verlag, 2014.

Gavrilova, Raina. *Bulgarian Urban Culture in the Eighteenth and Nineteenth Centuries.* Cranbury, NJ: Susquehanna University Press, 1999.

Gavrilović, Slavko, ed. *Istorija srpskog naroda.* Vol. 5/1: *Od prvog ustanka do Berlinskog Kongresa 1804–1878.* Belgrade: Srpska književna zadruga, 1981.

Genchev, Nikolaï. "The Bulgarian Cultural Revival." *Southeastern Europe* 8, no. 1–2 (1981): 97–116.

———. *Vŭzrozhdenskiiat Plovdiv.* Sofia: Iztok Zapad, 2007.

Gencheva, Yuliyana. "The International Children's Assembly 'Banner of Peace': A Case Study of Childhood under Socialism." *Red Feather Journal* 3, no. 1 (2012): 11–23.

Georgescu, Diana. "Excursions into National Specificity and European Identity: Mihail Sebastian's Interwar Travel Reportage." In *Under Eastern Eyes: A Comparative Introduction to East European Travel Writing on Europe,* edited by Wendy Bracewell and Alex Drace-Francis, 293–324. Budapest: Central European University Press, 2008.

Georgescu, Florian. *Bukarest: Historischer Überblick.* Bucharest: Verlag Meridiane, 1965.

Georgescu, Vlad. *Mémoires et projets de réforme dans les principautés Roumaines 1769–1830: Répertoire et textes inédits.* Bucharest: Association internationale d'études du Sud-Est européen, 1970.

———. *The Romanians: A History.* Translated by Alexandra Bley-Vroman. Columbus: Ohio State University Press, 1991.

Georgieva, Tsvetana. "Pomaks: Muslim Bulgarians." *Islam and Christian-Muslim Relations* 12, no. 3 (2001): 303–16.

Gerschenkron, Alexander. *Economic Backwardness in Historical Perspective: A Book of Essays.* Cambridge, MA: Belknap Press of Harvard University Press, 1962.

Gestrin, Ferdo. "Trgovina i seljačke bune u Sloveniji i Hrvatskoj u 16. stoljeću." *Radovi* 5, no. 1 (1973): 193–204.

Geyer, Michael and Charles Bright. "World History in a Global Age." *American Historical Review* 100, no. 4 (1995): 1034–60.

Ghobrial, John-Paul A. *The Whispers of Cities: Information Flows in Istanbul, London, and Paris in the Age of William Trumbull.* Oxford University Press, 2013.

Gianaris, Nicholas V. *The Economies of the Balkan Countries: Albania, Bulgaria, Greece, Romania, Turkey, and Yugoslavia.* New York: Praeger, 1982.

Gibbon, Edward. *The History of the Decline and Fall of the Roman Empire.* Vol. 1. London: W. Strahan and T. Cadell, 1776.

Gilboa, Eytan. "Global Communication and Foreign Policy." *Journal of Communication* 52, no. 4 (2002): 731–48.

Gimbutas, Marija. *The Slavs.* New York: Thames and Hudson, 1971.

Gingrich, Andre. "Kulturgeschichte, Wissenschaft und Orientalismus: Zur Diskussion des 'frontier orientalism' in der Spätzeit der k. u. k. Monarchie." In *Schauplatz Kultur—Zentraleuropa: Transdisziplinäre Annäherungen,* edited by Johannes Feichtinger, 279–88. Innsbruck: StudienVerlag, 2006.

Ginio, Eyal. "Aspects of Muslim Culture in the Ottoman Balkans: A View from Eighteenth-Century Salonica." In *Greece and the Balkans: Identities, Perceptions and Cultural Encounters since the Enlightenment,* edited by Dimitris Tziovas, 114–26. Aldershot: Ashgate, 2003.

————. "Migrants and Workers in an Ottoman Port: Ottoman Salonica in the Eighteenth Century." In *Outside In: On the Margins of the Modern Middle East,* edited by Eugen Rogan, 126–48. London: I.B. Tauris, 2002.

————. "Musulmans et non musulmans dans la Salonique ottomane XVIIIe siècle: L'affrontement sur les espaces et les lignes de démarcation." *Revue des mondes musulmans et de la Méditerranée* 107–110 (2005): 405–16.

————. "When Coffee Brought About Wealth and Prestige: The Impact of Egyptian Trade on Salonica." *Oriente Moderno* 25, no. 1 (2006): 93–107.

Giulianotti, Richard, and Roland Robertson. "Recovering the Social: Globalization, Football and Transnationalism." *Global Networks* 7, no. 2 (2007): 144–86.

Giurescu, Constantin C. *Geschichte der Stadt Bukarest.* Bucharest: Sport- und Touristikverlag, 1976.

Gi͡urova, Svetla and Nadi͡a Danova. *Kniga za bŭlgarskite khadzi.* Sofia: Akademichno izd-vo "Marin Drinov," 1995.

Glass, Hildrun. *Deutschland und die Verfolgung der Juden im rumänischen Machtbereich 1940–1944.* Munich: Oldenbourg, 2014.

Gligorijević, Branislav. *Kominterna, jugoslovensko i srpsko pitanje.* Belgrade: Institut za savremenu istoriju, 1992.

————. *Parlament i političke stranke u Jugoslaviji, 1919–1929.* Belgrade: Narodna knjiga, 1979.

Glišić, Venceslav. "Albanization of Kosovo and Metohija." In *Serbs and Albanians in the 19th and 20th Century,* edited by Andrej Mitrović, 293–308. Belgrade: Serbian Academy of Sciences and Arts, 1991.

Gobetti, Eric. *L'occupazione allegra: Gli italiani in Jugoslavia.* Rome: Carocci, 2007.

Goedde, Petra. "Global Cultures." In *Global Interdependence: The World After 1945,* edited by Akira Iriye, 537–678. Cambridge, MA: Belknap Press of Harvard University Press, 2014.

Goitein, Shlomo Dov Fritz. "From the Mediterranean to India: Documents on the Trade to India, South Arabia, and East Africa from the Eleventh and Twelfth Centuries." *Speculum* 29, no. 2 (1954): 181–97.

————. "Mediterranean Trade Preceding the Crusades: Some Facts and Problems." *Diogenes* 59 (1967): 47–62.

————. "The Unity of the Mediterranean World in the 'Middle' Middle Ages." *Studia Islamica* 12 (1960): 29–42.

Goldstein, Ivo, and Slavko Goldstein. *The Holocaust in Croatia.* Pittsburgh: University of Pittsburgh Press, 2016.

————. *Tito.* Zagreb: Profil, 2015.

Goldsworthy, Vesna. "Der Imperialismus der Imagination: Konstruktionen Europas und des Balkans." In *Europa und die Grenzen im Kopf,* edited by Karl Kaser et al., 253–74. Klagenfurt: Wieser, 2003.

————. *Inventing Ruritania: The Imperialism of the Imagination.* New Haven, CT: Yale University Press, 1998.

Golescu, Dinicu. *Aufzeichnung meiner Reise, die ich, Constandin Radovici aus Golești, im Jahre 1824, 1825, 1826 unternommen.* Bucharest: Kriterion, 1973.

Gollwitzer, Heinz, ed. *Europäische Bauernparteien im 20. Jahrhundert.* Stuttgart: Fischer, 1977.

Golopenţia, Sanda. "The Sociological School of Bucharest between Its Heyday and Suppression." *Revista Romana de Sociologie* 25, no. 5/6 (2014): 379–404.

Good, David F. "The Economic Lag of Central and Eastern Europe: Evidence from the Late Nineteenth-Century Habsburg Empire." Working Paper 93-7. Minneapolis: University of Minnesota Center for Austrian Studies, 1992.

Goodrich, Thomas D. *The Ottoman Turks and the New World: A Study of Tarih-i Hind-i Garbi and Sixteenth-Century Ottoman Americana.* Wiesbaden: Harrassowitz, 1990.

Goody, Jack.*The Interface between the Written and the Oral.* Cambridge University Press, 1987.

Goulding, Daniel J. *Liberated Cinema: The Yugoslav Experience, 1945–2001.* 2nd ed. Bloomington: Indiana University Press, 2002.

Gounaris, Basil. "Salonica." *Review (Fernand Braudel Center)* 16, no. 4 (1993): 499–518.

———. *Steam over Macedonia, 1870–1912: Socio-Economic Change and the Railway Factor.* Boulder: East European Monographs, 1993.

———. *Ta Valkania ton Hellēnōn: apo to diaphōtismo heōs tōn A' Pankosmio Polemo.* Thessaloniki: Epikentro, 2007.

Gradeva, Rossitsa. "Osman Pazvantoglu of Vidin: Between Old and New." In *War and Peace in Rumeli: 15th to Beginning of 19th Century,* edited by Rossitsa Gradeva, 11–50. Istanbul: Isis Press, 2008.

Graff, Michael, A. G. Kenwood, and A. L. Lougheed. *Growth of the International Economy, 1820–2015.* New York: Routledge, 2014.

Grandits, Hannes and Karin Taylor, eds. *Yugoslavia's Sunny Side: A History of Tourism in Socialism (1950s–1980s).* New York: Central European University Press, 2010.

Grant, Edward. "Cosmology." In *The Cambridge History of Science, Vol. 2: Medieval Science,* edited by David C. Lindberg and Michael H. Shank, 436–55. Cambridge University Press, 2013.

Grasshoff, Helmut. *A. D. Kantemir und Westeuropa.* Berlin: Akademie-Verlag, 1966.

Graziani, Giovanni. "Dependency Structures in COMECON." *Review of Radical Political Economics* 13, no. 1 (1981): 67–75.

Grdinić, Vladimir. *Ljekarništvo na tlu Hrvatske.* Zagreb: Nakladni zavod Matice Hrvatske, 1996.

Greble, Emily. *Sarajevo, 1941–1945: Muslims, Christians, and Jews in Hitler's Europe.* Ithaca, NY: Cornell University Press, 2011.

Greene, Molly. *Catholic Pirates and Greek Merchants: A Maritime History of the Mediterranean.* Princeton University Press, 2010.

Greenhalgh, Paul. *Fair World: A History of World's Fairs and Expositions, from London to Shanghai, 1851–2010.* Winterbourne: Papadakis, 2011.

Gries, Rainer. "Dramaturgie der Utopie: Kulturgeschichte der Rituale der Arbeiter-und-Bauern-Macht." In *Arbeiter im Staatssozialismus: ideologischer Anspruch und soziale Wirklichkeit,* edited by Peter Hübner, Christoph Klessmann, and Klaus Tenfelde, 191–214. Cologne: Böhlau, 2005.

Grišina, Ritta Petrovna. "Balkany v planach Kominterna (1924 god)." *Sovetskoe Slavjanovedenie* 5 (1994): 4–13.

Grmek, Mirko Dražen. "Medicine in Croatia." In *Croatia in the Late Middle Ages and the Renaissance,* edited by Ivan Supičić, 797–817. Zagreb: Školska knjiga, 2008.

Grmek, Mirko Dražen, and Žarko Dadić. "O astronomiji Ginu Gazulu i dubrovačkom traktatu o astrolabu." *Anali Historijskog Odjela Centra za Znanstveni Rad Jugoslavenske Akademije u Dubrovniku* 13–14 (1976): 53–94.

Gross, Mirjana. *Die Anfänge des modernen Kroatien: Gesellschaft, Politik und Kultur in Zivil-Kroatien und -Slawonien in den ersten dreißig Jahren nach 1848.* Vienna: Böhlau, 1993.

———. *Izvorno pravaštvo: Ideologija, agitacija, pokret.* Zagreb: Golden Marketing, 2000.

Gross, Stephen G. *Export Empire: German Soft Power in Southeastern Europe, 1890– 1945.* Cambridge University Press, 2015.

Grottian, Walter. *Das sowjetische Regierungssystem: Die Grundlagen der Macht der kommunist- ischen Parteiführung. Leitfaden und Quellenbuch.* Wiesbaden: Vieweg + Teubner Verlag, 1965.

Grubiša, Damir. "Forms of Government in the Renaissance: Uniqueness of the Dubrovnik Model." *Politička misao* 47, no. 4 (2010): 161–78.

Gruner, Wolf D. *Der Wiener Kongress 1814/15.* Stuttgart: Reclam, 2014.

Grunert, Heiner. *Glauben im Hinterland: Die Serbisch-Orthodoxen in der habsbur- gischen Herzegowina 1878–1918.* Göttingen: Vandenhoeck & Ruprecht, 2016.

Gruzinski, Serge. *Quelle heure est-il là-bas? Amérique et islam à l'orée des temps modernes.* Paris: Editions du Seuil, 2008.

Gudea, Nicolae, and Thomas Lobüscher. *Dacia: Eine römische Provinz zwischen Karpaten und Schwarzem Meer.* Mainz: Verlag Phillip von Zabern, 2006.

Gumz, Jonathan E. *The Resurrection and Collapse of Empire in Habsburg Serbia, 1914–1918.* Cambridge University Press, 2009.

Gündisch, Konrad. "'Saxones' im Bergbau von Siebenbürgen, Bosnien und Serbien." In *Die Deutschen in Ostmittel- und Südosteuropa,* edited by Gerhard Grimm and Krista Zach, 119–32. Munich: Verlag Südostdeutsches Kulturwerk, 1996.

Gvozden, Vladimir. *Jovan Dučić putopisac: Ogled iz imagologije.* Novi Sad: Svetovi, 2003.

Gyimesi, Sándor. "Motive und Probleme der Industrialisierung in den Staaten Südosteu- ropas bis zum Ersten Weltkrieg." In *Industrialisierung und gesellschaftlicher Wandel in Südosteuropa,* edited by Roland Schönfeld, 11–19. Munich: Südosteuropa- Gesellschaft, 1989.

Habibi, Anila. "Das autoritäre Regime Ahmed Zogus und die Gesellschaft Albaniens 1925–1939." In *Autoritäre Regime in Ostmittel- und Südosteuropa, 1919–1944,* edited by Erwin Oberländer et al., 349–78. Paderborn: Ferdinand Schöningh, 2001.

Hadžijahić, Muhamed, Mahmud Traljić, and Nijaz Šukrić. *Islam i Muslimani u Bosni i Hercegovini.* Sarajevo: Starješinstvo Islamske zajednice u SR Bosni i Hercegovini, 1977.

Hagen, Gottfried. "Das Fremde im Eigenen: Mehmed Aşiqs Reisen über den osmanischen Balkan." In *Bilder vom Eigenen und Fremden aus dem Donau-Balkan-Raum: Analysen literarischer und anderer Texte,* edited by Wolfgang Dahmen and Gabriella Schubert, 121–41. Munich: Südosteuropa-Gesellschaft, 2003.

———. "The Order of Knowledge, the Knowledge of Order: Intellectual Life." In *The Cambridge History of Turkey,* vol. 2, edited by Suraiya Faroqhi and Kate Fleet, 407–56. Cambridge University Press, 2012.

———. "Ottoman Understandings of the World in the Seventeenth Century." In *An Ottoman Mentality: The World of Evliya Çelebi,* edited by Robert Dankoff, 215–56. Leiden: Brill, 2006.

Hajdarpasic, Edin. *Whose Bosnia? Nationalism and Political Imagination in the Balkans, 1840–1914.* Ithaca, NY: Cornell University Press, 2015.

Hajdu, Ada. "The Pavilions of Greece, Serbia, Romania and Bulgaria at the 1900 Exposition Universelle in Paris." In *Balkan Heritages: Negotiating History and Culture,* edited by Maria Couroucli and Tchavdar Marinov, 47–76. Farnham: Ashgate, 2015.

Hall, Richard C. *The Balkan Wars 1912–1913: Prelude to the First World War.* London: Routledge, 2000.

———. *War in the Balkans: An Encyclopedic History from the Fall of the Ottoman Empire to the Breakup of Yugoslavia.* Santa Barbara, CA: ABC-CLIO, 2014.

Hamburger Institut für Sozialforschung, ed. *Verbrechen der Wehrmacht: Dimensionen des Vernichtungskrieges 1941–1944.* Hamburg: Hamburger Edition, 2002.

Handžić, Adem "The Origins and Development of Bijeljina in the 16th Century." *Prilozi za orijentalnu filologiju* 36 (1986): 277–312.

Hannick, Christian. "Die byzantinischen Missionen." In *Kirchengeschichte als Missionsgeschichte,* edited by Knut Schäferdiek et al., 279–359. Munich: Kaiser, 1978.

Harbova, Margarita. "L'espace culturel de la ville balkanique entre l'orient et l'europe (d'après l'exemple de la ville de Plovdiv, XVIIIe–XIXe siècles)." *Études Balkaniques* 38, no. 1 (2002): 128–43.

Hasluck, Frederick William. *Christianity and Islam under the Sultans.* 2 vols. Oxford University Press, 1929.

Hassiotis, I. K. "Thessaloniki under Ottoman Domination: The Early Period (16th Century to 1830)." In *Queen of the Worthy: Thessaloniki History and Culture,* edited by I. K. Hassiotis, 136–55. Thessaloniki: Paratiritis, 1997.

Haumann, Heiko. *Dracula: Leben und Legende.* Munich: C.H. Beck, 2011.

Hausberger, Bernd, ed. *Globale Lebensläufe: Menschen als Akteure im weltgeschichtlichen Geschehen.* Vienna: Mandelbaum, 2006.

Hecker, Hans. *Russische Universalgeschichtsschreibung: Von den Vierziger Jahren des 19. Jh. bis zur sowjetischen Weltgeschichte (1955–1965).* Munich: Oldenbourg, 1983.

Heer, Caspar. *Territorialentwicklung und Grenzfragen von Montenegro in der Zeit seiner Staatswerdung (1830–1887).* Frankfurt: Peter Lang, 1981.

Hegyi, Klára, and Vera Zimányi. *Muslime und Christen: Das Osmanische Reich in Europa.* Budapest: Corvina, 1988.

Hehn, Paul N. *A Low Dishonest Decade: The Great Powers, Eastern Europe, and the Economic Origins of World War II, 1930–1941.* New York: Continuum, 2002.

Heinen, Anton. *Islamic Cosmology: A Study of as-Suyūṭī's al-Hay'a as-Sanīya fī l-Hay'a as-Sunnīya.* Wiesbaden: Franz Steiner, 1982.

Heinen, Armin. "Der Hitler-Stalin-Pakt und Rumänien." In *Hitler-Stalin-Pakt 1939: das Ende Ostmitteleuropas?* edited by Erwin Oberländer, 98–113. Frankfurt: Fischer-Taschenbuch-Verlag, 1989.

———. *Die Legion "Erzengel Michael" in Rumänien—Soziale Bewegung und politische Organisation: Ein Beitrag zum Problem des internationalen Faschismus.* Munich: Oldenbourg, 1986.

———. *Rumänien, der Holocaust und die Logik der Gewalt.* Munich: Oldenbourg, 2007.

Helmedach, Andreas. *Das Verkehrssystem als Modernisierungsfaktor: Straßen, Post, Fuhrwesen und Reisen nach Triest und Fiume vom Beginn des 18. Jahrhunderts bis zum Eisenbahnzeitalter.* Munich: Oldenbourg, 2002.

Helmedach, Andreas, and Markus Koller. "Gewaltgemeinschaften: Von der Spätantike bis ins Jahrhundert." In *Gewaltgemeinschaften,* edited by Winfried Speitkamp, 231–49. Göttingen: V&R unipress, 2013.

Herbert, Ulrich. *Geschichte Deutschlands im 20. Jahrhundert.* Munich: C.H. Beck, 2014.

Herbst, Natalja. "Women in Socialist Yugoslavia in the 1950s: The Example of Rajka Borojević and the Dragačevo Women's Cooperative." In *Doing Gender—Doing the Balkans: Dynamics and Persistence of Gender Relations in Yugoslavia and the Yugoslav Successor States,* edited by Roswitha Kersten-Pejanić, 209–20. Munich: Sagner, 2012.

Hering, Gunnar. "Die Osmanenzeit im Selbstverständnis der Völker Südosteuropas." In *Die Staaten Südosteuropas und die Osmanen,* edited by Hans Georg Majer, 355–80. Munich: Südosteuropa-Gesellschaft, 1989.

———. *Die politischen Parteien in Griechenland 1821–1936.* Munich: Oldenbourg, 1992.

———. *Ökumenisches Patriarchat und europäische Politik: 1620–1638.* Wiesbaden: Franz Steiner, 1968.

Herman, Edward S., and David Peterson. "CNN: Selling Nato's War Globally." In *Degraded Capability: The Media and the Kosovo Crisis,* edited by Philip Hammond and Edward S. Herman, 111–22. London: Pluto Press, 2000.

Herzog, Christoph. "Aufklärung und Osmanisches Reich: Annäherung an ein historiographisches Problem." *Geschichte und Gesellschaft* Sonderheft 23 (2010): 291–321.

Hetzer, Armin. *Geschichte des Buchhandels in Albanien: Prolegomena zu einer Literatur-soziologie.* Wiesbaden: Harrassowitz, 1984.

Heuberger, Valeria. "Politische Institutionen und Verwaltung in Bosnien und der Hercegovina 1878–1918." In *Die Habsburgermonarchie 1848–1918.* Vol. 7 / 2: Verfassung und Parlamentarismus, edited by Helmut Rumpler and Peter Urbanitsch, 2383–425. Vienna: Österreichische Akademie der Wissenschaften, 2000.

Heuser, Beatrice. *Western "Containment" Policies in the Cold War: The Yugoslav Case, 1948–53.* London: Routledge, 1989.

Heyer, Friedrich. *Die orientalische Frage im kirchlichen Lebenskreis: Das Einwirken der Kirchen des Auslands auf die Emanzipation der orthodoxen Nationen Südosteuropas 1804–1912*. Wiesbaden: Harrassowitz, 1991.

Hildermeier, Manfred. *Geschichte Russlands*. Munich: C.H. Beck, 2013.

Hillgruber, Andreas. *Hitler, König Carol und Marschall Antonescu: Die deutsch-rumänischen Beziehungen, 1938–1944*. Wiesbaden: Franz Steiner, 1954.

Hinrichs, Uwe, ed. *Handbuch der Südosteuropa-Linguistik*. Wiesbaden: Harrassowitz, 1999.

Hirschon, Renée, ed. *Crossing the Aegean: An Appraisal of the 1923 Compulsory Population Exchange between Greece and Turkey*. New York: Berghahn Books, 2003.

Hitchins, Keith. *A Concise History of Romania*. Cambridge University Press, 2014.

Hixson, Walter L. *Parting the Curtain: Propaganda, Culture, and the Cold War, 1945–1961*. New York: St. Martin's Press, 1998.

Hoare, Marko Attila. *The Bosnian Muslims in the Second World War: A History*. Oxford University Press, 2013.

———. *Genocide and Resistance in Hitler's Bosnia: The Partisans and the Chetniks, 1941–1943*. Oxford University Press, 2006.

———. "The Partisans and the Serbs." In *Serbia and the Serbs in World War Two*, edited by Sabrina P. Ramet and Ola Listhaug, 201–21. New York: Palgrave Macmillan, 2011.

Hobsbawm, Eric. *The Age of Extremes: A History of the World, 1914–1991*. New York: Pantheon Books, 1994.

———. *The Age of Revolution 1789–1848*. New York: Vintage Books, 1996.

———. *Bandits*. New York: New Press, 2000.

Hockenos, Paul. *Homeland Calling: Exile Patriotism and the Balkan Wars*. Ithaca, NY: Cornell University Press, 2003.

Hoerder, Dirk. "Migrations and Belongings." In *A World Connecting, 1870–1945*, edited by Emily S. Rosenberg, 435–589. Cambridge, MA: Belknap Press of Harvard University Press, 2012.

Hoffmann, David L. *Stalinist Values: The Cultural Norms of Soviet Modernity, 1917–1941*. Ithaca, NY: Cornell University Press, 2003.

Holland, Henry. *Travels in the Ionian Isles, Albania, Thessaly, Macedonia etc. during the Years 1812 and 1813*. London: Longman, Hurst, Rees, Orme, and Brown, 1815.

Höllmann, Thomas O. *Die Seidenstraße*. Munich: C.H. Beck, 2004.

Hopf, Claudia. *Sprachnationalismus in Serbien und Griechenland: Theoretische Grundlagen sowie ein Vergleich von Vuk Stefanović Karadžić und Adamantios Korais*. Wiesbaden: Harrassowitz, 1997.

Höpken, Wolfgang. "'Modern Wars' and 'Backward Societies': The Balkan Wars in the History of Twentieth-Century European Warfare." In *The Wars of Yesterday: The Balkan Wars and the Emergence of Modern Military Conflict, 1912–13*. New York: Berghahn, 2018.

———. "Schrittmacher der Moderne? Urbanisierung und städtische Lebenswelten in den Metropolen Südosteuropas im 19. und frühen 20. Jahrhundert." In *Die europäische Stadt im 20. Jahrhundert: Wahrnehmung—Entwicklung—Erosion,* edited by Friedrich Lenger and Klaus Tenfelde, 61–104. Cologne: Böhlau, 2006.

———. "Strukturkrise oder verpasste Chance? Zum Demokratiepotential der südosteuropäischen Zwischenkriegsstaaten Bulgarien, Jugoslawien und Rumänien." In *Ostmitteleuropa zwischen den beiden Weltkriegen (1918–1939): Stärke und Schwäche der neuen Staaten, nationale Minderheiten,* edited by Hans Lemberg, 73–127. Marburg: Herder-Institut, 1997.

Hopkins, A. G., ed. *Globalization in World History.* New York: Norton, 2002.

Hoppe, Hans-Joachim. "Politik und Geschichtswissenschaft in Bulgarien 1968–1978." *Jahrbücher für Geschichte Osteuropas* 28, no. 2 (1980): 243–86.

Hoptner, Jacob. *Yugoslavia in Crisis, 1934–1941.* New York: Columbia University Press, 1962.

Horden, Peregrine and Nicholas Purcell. *The Corrupting Sea: A Study of Mediterranean History.* Oxford: Blackwell, 2000.

Horn, Gerd-Rainer, and Padraic Kenney, eds. *Transnational Moments of Change: Europe 1945, 1968, 1989.* Lanham, MD: Rowman and Littlefield, 2004.

Hösch, Edgar. "Das sogenannte 'griechische Projekt' Katharinas II: Ideologie und Wirklichkeit der russischen Orientpolitik in der zweiten Hälfte des 18. Jahrhunderts." *Jahrbücher für Geschichte Osteuropas* 12, no. 2 (1964): 168–206.

———. *Geschichte der Balkanländer: Von der Frühzeit bis zur Gegenwart.* Munich: C.H. Beck, 2008.

———. *Geschichte des Balkans.* Munich: C.H. Beck, 2004.

———. "Kritische Bemerkungen zum gegenwärtigen Stand der Bogomilen-Forschung." In *Kulturelle Traditionen in Bulgarien,* edited by Reinhard Lauer and Peter Schreiner, 103–15. Göttingen: Vandenhoeck & Ruprecht, 1989.

Hoško, Franjo Emanuel. *Biskup Vrhovac između baroka i liberalizma.* Zagreb: Kršćanska sadašnjost, 2007.

Hristov, Hristo. "Athos and the Exploit of Paisij of Hilendar." *Bulgarian Historical Review* 1 (1973): 31–48.

Hristov, Todor. *Otvăd identičnostta.* Berlin, 2007.

Hroch, Miroslav. *Das Europa der Nationen: Die moderne Nationsbildung im europäischen Vergleich.* Göttingen: Vandenhoeck & Ruprecht, 2005.

———. "From National Movement to the Fully-Formed Nation: The Nation-Building Process in Europe." *New Left Review* 198, no. 1 (1993): 3–20.

———. *In the National Interest.* Prague: Charles University, 1996.

———. "National Movements in the Habsburg and Ottoman Empires." In *The Oxford Handbook of the History of Nationalism,* edited by John Breuilly, 175–98. Oxford University Press, 2013.

Hubatsch, Walther. *Hitlers Weisungen für die Kriegführung, 1939–1945: Dokumente des Oberkommandos der Wehrmacht.* Koblenz: Bernard & Graefe, 1983.

Huber, Valeska. *Channelling Mobilities: Migration and Globalisation in the Suez Canal Region and Beyond, 1869–1914.* Cambridge University Press, 2013.

Hubka, Gustav von. *Die österreichisch-ungarische Offiziersmission in Makedonien 1903–1909.* Vienna: F. Tempsky, 1910.

Huntington, Samuel P. *The Third Wave: Democratization in the Late Twentieth Century.* Norman: University of Oklahoma Press, 1991.

Iacob, Bogdan C. "From Periphery to Cardinal Borderland: The Balkans in UNESCO." *C. A. S. Working Papers Series* (2015).

———. "Is It Transnational? A New Perspective in the Study of Communism." *East Central Europe* 40, no. 1–2 (2013): 114–39.

Iacobescu, Mihai. "Inițiative si preocupari ale României la societatea națiunilor în anii 1920–1933." *Anuarul Institutului de Istorie si Arheologie "A. D. Xenopol."* 18 (1981): 333–52.

Ianeva, Svetlana. "The Commercial Practices and Protoindustrial Activities of Haci Hristo Rachkov, a Bulgarian Trader at the End of the Eighteenth to the Beginning of the Nineteenth Century." *Oriente Moderno* 25, no. 1 (2006): 77–91.

———. "Main Characteristics of and Changes in Industrial Activity in the Central Balkans during 'the Long Nineteenth Century.'" In *The Economic Development of Southeastern Europe in the 19th Century,* edited by Edhem Eldem and Socrates Petmezas, 197–224. Athens: Alpha Bank, 2011.

Ibroscheva, Elza. "The Unbearable Lightness of Advertising: Culture, Media and the Rise of Advertising in Socialist Bulgaria." *Consumption, Markets & Culture* 16, no. 3 (2013): 290–310.

Ignjatović, Aleksandar. "Images of the Nation Foreseen: Ivan Meštrović's Vidvodan Temple and Primordial Yugoslavism." *Slavic Review* 73, no. 4 (2014): 828–58.

Ilić-Agapova, Marija. *Ilustrovana istorija Beograda.* Belgrade: Biblioteka opštine grada, 1933.

Inalcik, Halil. "Ottoman Methods of Conquest." *Studia Islamica* 2 (1954): 103–29.

Inalcik, Halil, and Donald Quataert, eds. *An Economic and Social History of the Ottoman Empire, 1300–1914.* Volume 1: 1300–1600. Cambridge University Press, 1994.

———. *An Economic and Social History of the Ottoman Empire, 1300–1914.* Volume 2: 1600–1914. Cambridge University Press, 1994.

Ingrao, Charles W., Nikola Samardžić, and Jovan Pesalj. *The Peace of Passarowitz, 1718.* West Lafayette, IN: Purdue University Press, 2011.

Innerhofer, Ian. "Post-War Economies (South East Europe), 1914–1918." *International Encyclopedia of the First World War.* Last modified April 12, 2017. http://dx.doi.org /10.15463/ie1418.10353.

International Commission on the Holocaust in Romania. *Final Report.* Iași: Polirom, 2005.

International Commission to Inquire into the Causes and Conduct of the Balkan Wars. *The Other Balkan Wars: A 1913 Carnegie Endowment Inquiry in Retrospect.* Washington, DC: Carnegie Endowment for International Peace, 1993.

Institutul central de statistică. *Recensământul general al populației României din 29 Dec. 1930.* Bucharest, 1938.

Ionescu, Ghiţa. *Communism in Rumania, 1944–1962.* London: Oxford University Press, 1964.

Iordan, Constantin. "Relations interbalkaniques (juillet–novembre 1939): Une perspective historique." *Revue des études sud-est européennes* 29, no. 1–2 (1991): 79–86.

Iorga, Nicolae. *Essai de synthèse de l'histoire de l'humanité.* Paris: J. Gamber, 1926.

Iosa, Ioana. *Bucarest: L'emblème d'une nation.* Rennes: Presses universitaires de Rennes, 2011.

Iriye, Akira. *Cultural Internationalism and World Order.* Baltimore: Johns Hopkins University Press, 1997.

———. *Global Community: The Role of International Organizations in the Making of the Contemporary World.* Berkeley: University of California Press, 2002.

Isaković, Alija, and Ivan Lovrenović, eds. *Putopisi.* Sarajevo: Svjetlost, 1985.

Islam, Syed Manzurul. *The Ethics of Travel: From Marco Polo to Kafka.* Manchester University Press, 1996.

Israel, Jonathan I. *Enlightenment Contested: Philosophy, Modernity, and the Emancipation of Man, 1670–1752.* Oxford University Press, 2008.

Izetbegović, Alija. *The Islamic Declaration.* Sarajevo: Bosna, 1990.

Jackson, George D. *Comintern and Peasant in East Europe, 1919–1930.* New York: Columbia University Press, 1966.

Jackson, Marvin R. "Comparing the Balkan Demographic Experience, 1860 to 1970." *Journal of European Economic History* 14, no. 2 (1985): 223–72.

Jakelic, Slavica. *Collectivistic Religions: Religion, Choice, and Identity in Late Modernity.* Farnham: Ashgate, 2010.

Jakir, Aleksandar. *Dalmatien zwischen den Weltkriegen: Agrarische und urbane Lebenswelt und das Scheitern der jugoslawischen Integration.* Munich: Oldenbourg, 1999.

Jakovina, Tvrtko. *Treća strana Hladnog rata.* Zagreb: Fraktura, 2011.

Jalal, Ayesha. "Islam's Contemporary Globalization, 1971–1979." In *The Shock of the Global: The 1970s in Perspective,* edited by Niall Ferguson et al., 319–36. Cambridge, MA: Belknap Press of Harvard University Press, 2010.

James, Harold. *The End of Globalization: Lessons from the Great Depression.* Cambridge, MA: Harvard University Press, 2002.

Jančeva, Irena G. *Etnologija na văzroždenskija Plovdiv vărchu periodičnija pečat.* Plovdiv: Plovdivsko Univ. Izdat, 1996.

Janev, Igor. *Odnosi Jugoslavije sa UNESCO-m: istorijski i kulturološki aspekti.* Belgrade: Institut za političke studije, 2010.

Janjatović, Petar. *Ilustrovana ex YU rock enciklopedija: 1960–2000.* Belgrade: Petar Janjatović, 2001.

Janković, Branimir. *The Balkans in International Relations.* New York: St. Martin's Press, 1988.

Janos, Andrew C. *East Central Europe in the Modern World: The Politics of the Borderlands from Pre- to Postcommunism.* Stanford, CA: Stanford University Press, 2000.

Janz, Oliver. *14—Der Große Krieg.* Bonn: Bundeszentrale für politische Bildung, 2013.

Jarnut, Jörg, and Matthias Wemhoff, eds. *Vom Umbruch zur Erneuerung? Das 11. und beginnende 12. Jahrhundert: Positionen der Forschung.* Munich: Fink, 2006.

Jelavich, Barbara. *Russia's Balkan Entanglements, 1806–1914.* Cambridge University Press, 1991.

Jelavich, Charles, and Barbara Jelavich. *The Establishment of the Balkan National States, 1804–1920.* Seattle: University of Washington Press, 1977.

Jelić-Butić, Fikreta. *Ustaše i Nezavisna Država Hrvatska 1941–1945.* Zagreb: Liber Školska knjiga, 1977.

Jennings, Christian. *Flashpoint Trieste: The First Battle of the Cold War.* Lebanon, NH: ForeEdge, 2017.

Jezernik, Božidar. *Wild Europe: The Balkans in the Gaze of Western Travellers.* London: Saqi, 2004.

Jireček, Konstantin. *Das Fürstenthum Bulgarien, seine Bodengestaltung, Natur, Bevölkerung, wirthschaftliche Zustände, geistige Cultur.* Leipzig: G. Freytag, 1891.

———. *Geschichte der Serben.* Vol. 1. Gotha: F.A. Perthes, 1911.

———. *Geschichte der Serben.* Vol. 2–1. Gotha: F.A. Perthes, 1918.

Jovanović, Jadranka. *Jugoslavija u Organizaciji Ujedinjenih Nacija: 1945–1953.* Belgrade: Institut za savremenu istoriju, 1985.

Jovanović, Slobodan. *Vlada Aleksandra Obrenovića: Knjiga druga (1897–1903).* Belgrade: Izdavačka knjižarnica Gece Kona, 1931.

Jovanovic, Zlatko. "'All Yugoslavia Is Dancing Rock and Roll': Yugoslavness and the Sense of Community in the 1980s Yu-Rock." PhD diss., University of Copenhagen, 2014.

Jović, Dejan. "Communist Yugoslavia and Its 'Others.'" In *Ideologies and National Identities: The Case of Twentieth-Century Europe,* edited by John Lampe and Mark Mazower, 277–302. Budapest: Central European University Press, 2006.

Judt, Tony. *Postwar: A History of Europe.* New York: Penguin, 2005.

Jugosloveni o društvenoj krizi (istraživanje javnog mnjenja 1985. godine). Belgrade: Izdavački centar Komunist, 1989.

Jurić, Šime. "Prilozi biografiji Ivana Gazulića." *Anali Historijskog instituta u Dubrovniku* VIII–IX (1962): 447–79.

Juzbašić, Dževad: *Politika i privreda u Bosni i Hercegovini pod austrougarskom upravom.* Sarajevo: Akademija nauka i umjetnosti Bosne i Hercegovine, 2002.

Kačavenda, Petar, and Đoko Tripković, eds. *Jugoslovensko-sovjetski sukob 1948. godine.* Belgrade: Institut za savremenu istoriju, 1999.

Kacza, Thomas. *Fan Stylian Noli (1882–1965): Albanischer Bischof und revolutionärer Demokrat.* Bad Salzuflen, 2011.

Kadare, Ismail. *The Siege.* Translated by David Bello. New York: Canongate, 2008.

Kadić, Ante. "Ruđe Bošković on American Independence." In *Essays in South Slavic Literature,* edited by Ante Kadić, 52–63. New Haven, CT: Yale Center for International and Area Studies, 1988.

Kadum, Vladimir. "O životu Ruđera Boškovića, njegovu znanstvenom i filozofskom radu." *Metodički ogledi* 14, no. 1 (2007): 19–36.

Kaelble, Hartmut. *Kalter Krieg und Wohlfahrtsstaat: Europa, 1945–1989.* Bonn: Bundeszentrale für Politische Bildung, 2011.

———. *Wege zur Demokratie: von der Französischen Revolution zur Europäischen Union.* Stuttgart: Deutsche Verlags-Anstalt, 2001.

Kafadar, Cemal. *Between Two Worlds: The Construction of the Ottoman State.* Berkeley: University of California Press, 1995.

Kaiser, Timothy. "Archaeology and Ideology in Southeast Europe." In *Nationalism, Politics, and the Practice of Archaeology,* edited by Philip L. Kohl and Clare Fawcett, 99–119. Cambridge University Press, 1995.

Kaiser, Wolfgang. "Politik und Geschäft: Interkulturelle Beziehungen zwischen Muslimen und Christen im Mittelmeerraum. In *Akteure der Außenbeziehungen: Netzwerke und Interkulturalität im historischen Wandel,* edited by Hillard von Thiessen and Christian Windler, 295–317. Cologne: Böhlau, 2010.

Kaldor, Mary. *Global Civil Society: An Answer to War.* Cambridge: Polity Press, 2003.

———. *New and Old Wars: Organized Violence in a Global Era.* Stanford, CA: Stanford University Press, 1999.

Kaltchas, Nicholas Stavrou. *Introduction to the Constitutional History of Modern Greece.* New York: Columbia University Press, 1940.

Kalyvas, Stathis N. *The Logic of Violence in Civil War.* Cambridge University Press, 2006.

———. "'New' and 'Old' Civil Wars: A Valid Distinction?" *World Politics* 54, no. 1 (2001): 99–118.

Kamberović, Husnija. *Džemal Bijedić: politička biografija.* Mostar: Muzej Herce-govine, 2017.

———. *Prema modernom društvu: Bosna i Hercegovina od 1945 do 1953. godine.* Tešanj: Centar za kulturu i obrazovanje, 2000.

Kanitz, Felix. *Das Königreich Serbien und das Serbenvolk von der Römerzeit bis zur Gegenwart.* Leipzig: Bernh. Meyer, 1904.

Kann, Robert A. *Geschichte des Habsburgerreiches 1526 bis 1918.* Vienna: Böhlau, 1990.

Kantakuzenos, Alexandros. *Briefe eines Augenzeugen der griechischen Revolution vom Jahre 1821.* Halle: Rengersche Verlagsbuchhandlung, 1824.

Kanzleiter, Boris, and Krunoslav Stojaković, eds. *"1968" in Jugoslawien: Studentenpro-teste und kulturelle Avantgarde zwischen 1960 und 1975.* Bonn: Dietz, 2008.

Kappeler, Andreas. *Russland als Vielvölkerreich: Entstehung, Geschichte, Zerfall.* Munich: C.H. Beck, 1992.

Karaberopoulos, Dimitrios, ed. *Rhigas Velestinlis: Die Revolutionsschriften.* Translated by Antonios Gavalas. Athens: Wissenschaftliche Studiengesellschaft Pheres-Velestino-Rhigas, 2010.

Karakasidou, Anastasia N. *Fields of Wheat, Hills of Blood: Passages to Nationhood in Greek Macedonia, 1870–1990.* Chicago: University of Chicago Press, 1997.

Karaman, Igor. *Hrvatska na pragu modernizacije (1750–1918).* Zagreb: Naklada Ljevak, 2000.

———. *Industrijalizacija građanske Hrvatske: 1800–1941.* Zagreb: Naprijed, 1991.

Karanovich, Milenko. *The Development of Education in Serbia and Emergence of Its Intelligentsia (1838–1858).* Boulder: East European Monographs, 1995.

Karavelov, Liuben. *Amerika—onaĩa obetovana zemĩa.* Sofia: Literaturen Forum, 2012.

———. *Zapiski za Bŭlgariĩa i za bŭlgaretĩe.* Sofia: Sibiĩa, 1995.

Karčić, Fikret. *The Bosniaks and the Challenges of Modernity: Late Ottoman and Habsburg Times.* Sarajevo: El-Kalem, 1999.

Karčić, Harun. "Islamic Revival in Post-Socialist Bosnia and Herzegovina: International Actors and Activities." *Journal of Muslim Minority Affairs* 30, no. 4 (2010): 519–34.

Karić, Vladimir. *Srbija: Opis zemlje, naroda i države.* Belgrade: Kraljevsko-srpska drž. štamparija, 1887.

Karpat, Kemal H. *An Inquiry into the Social Foundations of Nationalism in the Ottoman State: From Social Estates to Classes, from Millets to Nations.* Princeton, NJ: Center of International Studies, 1973.

Kasaba, Reşat. *The Ottoman Empire and the World Economy: The Nineteenth Century.* Albany: State University of New York Press, 1988.

Kaser, Karl. *Balkan und Naher Osten: Einführung in eine gemeinsame Geschichte.* Vienna: Böhlau, 2011.

———. "Economic Reforms and the Illusion of Transition." In *Central and Southeast European Politics since 1989,* edited by Sabrina P. Ramet, 91–110. Cambridge University Press, 2010.

———. *Familie und Verwandtschaft auf dem Balkan: Analyse einer untergehenden Kultur.* Vienna: Böhlau, 1995.

———. *Freier Bauer und Soldat: Die Militarisierung der agrarischen Gesellschaft und der kroatisch-slawonischen Militärgrenze (1535–1881).* Vienna: Böhlau, 1997.

———. *Hirten, Kämpfer, Stammeshelden.* Vienna: Böhlau, 1992.

———. "Household and Family Contexts in the Balkans." *History of the Family* 1, no. 4 (1996): 375–86.

Kasson, John F. *Houdini, Tarzan, and the Perfect Man: The White Male Body and the Challenge of Modernity in America.* New York: Hill and Wang, 2001.

Katsiardi-Hering, Olga. "Migrationen von Bevölkerungsgruppen in Südosteuropa vom 15. Jahrhundert bis zum Beginn des 19. Jahrhunderts." *Südost-Forschungen* (2000–2001) 59–60, 125–48.

———. "Southeastern European Migrant Groups between the Ottoman and the Habsburg Empires." In *Encounters in Europe's Southeast: The Habsburg Empire and the Orthodox World in the Eighteenth and Nineteenth Centuries,* edited by Harald Heppner and Eva Posch, 135–62. Bochum: Winkler, 2012.

Katsiardi-Hering, Olga, and Maria A. Stassinopoulou. "The Long 18th Century of Greek Commerce in the Habsburg Empire: Social Careers." In *Social Change in the Habsburg Monarchy,* edited by Harald Heppner, Peter Urbanitsch, and Renate Zedinger, 191–213. Bochum: Winkler, 2011.

Katus, László. "Die Magyaren." In *Die Habsburgermonarchie 1848–1918.* Vol. 3/1: Die Völker des Reiches, edited by Adam Wandruszka and Peter Urbanitsch, 410–88. Vienna: Österreichische Akademie der Wissenschaften, 1980.

Kavalski, Emilian. "The Balkan America? The Myth of America in the Creation of Bulgarian National Identity." *New Zealand Slavonic Journal* 38, no. 1 (2004): 131–58.

Keisinger, Florian. *Unzivilisierte Kriege im zivilisierten Europa? Die Balkankriege und die öffentliche Meinung in Deutschland, England und Irland 1876–1913.* Paderborn: Ferdinand Schöningh, 2008.

Kemal Bey, Ismail. *The Memoirs of Ismail Kemal Bey.* London: Constable and Company, 1920.

Kenney, Padraic. *1989: Democratic Revolutions at the Cold War's End: A Brief History with Documents.* Boston: Bedford / St. Martin's, 2010.

———. "Opposition Networks and Transnational Diffusion in the Revolutions of 1989." In *Transnational Moments of Change: Europe 1945, 1968, 1989,* edited by Gerd-Rainer Horn and Padraic Kenney, 207–23. Lanham, MD: Rowman and Littlefield, 2004.

Kerner, Robert Joseph, and Harry Nicholas Howard. *The Balkan Conferences and the Balkan Entente, 1930–1935: A Study in the Recent History of the Balkan and Near Eastern Peoples.* Berkeley: University of California Press, 1936.

Kessler, Wolfgang. "Buchproduktion und Lektüre in Zivilkroatien und -slawonien zwischen Aufklärung und Nationaler Wiedergeburt 1767–1748: Zum Leseverhalten in einer mehrsprachigen Gesellschaft." *Archiv für Geschichte des Buchwesens* 16 (1976): 339–790.

———. "Die gescheiterte Integration: Die Minderheitenfrage in Ostmitteleuropa 1919–1939." In *Ostmitteleuropa zwischen den beiden Weltkriegen (1918–1939): Stärke und Schwäche der neuen Staaten, nationale Minderheiten,* edited by Hans Lemberg, 161–88. Marburg: Herder-Institut, 1997.

———. *Politik, Kultur und Gesellschaft in Kroatien und Slawonien in der ersten Hälfte des 19. Jahrhunderts: Historiographie u. Grundlagen.* Munich: Oldenbourg, 1981.

Kia, Mehrdad. *Daily Life in Istanbul.* Santa Barbara, CA: Greenwood Press, 2011.

Kiel, Machiel. "The Incorporation of the Balkans into the Ottoman Empire, 1353–1454." In *The Cambridge History of Turkey,* vol. 2, edited by Suraiya Faroqhi and Kate Fleet, 138–91. Cambridge University Press, 2012.

Kieser, Hans-Lukas. "Djihad, Weltordnung, 'Goldener Apfel': Die osmanische Reichsideologie im Kontext west-östlicher Geschichte." In *Imperialismus in Geschichte und Gegenwart,* edited by Richard Faber, 183–204. Würzburg: Königshausen & Neumann, 2005.

Kilzer, Katharina. "'Ich kann alles—ich bin der Autor': Interview mit Ana Blandiana." In *Gedächtnis der Literatur: Erinnerungskulturen in den südosteuropäischen Ländern nach 1989,* edited by Edda Binder-Iijima et al., 273–98. Ludwigsburg: Pop, 2010.

———. "Literarisches Werk und soziales Engagement: Erinnerung als Auftrag bei Ana Blandiana." In *Gedächtnis der Literatur: Erinnerungskulturen in den südosteuropäischen Ländern nach 1989,* edited by Edda Binder-Iijima et al., 167–93. Ludwigsburg: Pop, 2010.

King, Charles. *The Black Sea: A History.* Oxford University Press, 2004.

———. *NDH i Italija: Političke veze i diplomatski odnosi.* Zagreb: Naklada Ljevak, 2001.

Kissoudi, P. "Sport, Politics and International Relations in the Balkans: The Balkan Games from 1933 to 1935." *International Journal of the History of Sport* 25, no. 13 (2008): 1814–35.

Kitromilides, Paschalis M. *Adamantios Korais and the European Enlightenment.* Oxford: Voltaire Foundation, 2010.

———. "Athos and the Enlightenment." In *An Orthodox Commonwealth: Symbolic Legacies and Cultural Encounters in Southeastern Europe,* edited by Paschalis M. Kitromilides, 257–72. Aldershot: Ashgate Variorum, 2007.

———. *The Enlightenment as Social Criticism: Iosipos Moisiodax and Greek Culture in the Eighteenth Century.* Princeton University Press, 1992.

———. *Enlightenment, Nationalism, Orthodoxy: Studies in the Culture and Political Thought of South-Eastern Europe.* Aldershot: Variorum, 1994.

Klaić, Nada. *Povijest Hrvata u srednjem vijeku.* Zagreb: Globus, 1990.

Klaniczay, Gábor, Michael Werner, and Ottó Gecser, eds. *Multiple Antiquities, Multiple Modernities: Ancient Histories in Nineteenth Century European Cultures.* Frankfurt: Campus Verlag, 2011.

Klemenčić, Matjaž. "Images of America among Slovene and Other Yugoslav Migrants." In *Distant Magnets. Expectations and Realities in the Immigrant Experience, 1840–1930,* edited by Dirk Hoerder and Horst Rössler, 199–221. New York: Holmes and Meier, 1993.

Klick, Donna J. "A Balkan Nuclear Weapon-Free Zone: Viability of the Regime and Implications for Crisis." *Journal of Peace Research* 24, no. 3 (June 1987): 111–24.

Klimke, Martin, and Joachim Scharloth, eds. *1968 in Europe: A History of Protest and Activism, 1956–1977.* New York: Palgrave Macmillan, 2008.

Klose, Fabian. *Menschenrechte im Schatten kolonialer Gewalt: Die Dekolonisierungskriege in Kenia und Algerien 1945–1962.* Munich: Oldenbourg, 2009.

Köbsch, Wieland. *Die Juden im Vielvölkerstaat Jugoslawien 1918–1941: Zwischen mosaischer Konfession und jüdischem Nationalismus im Spannungsfeld des jugoslawischen Nationalitätenkonflikts.* Berlin: LIT Verlag, 2013.

Kočev, Nikolaj C. *Christijanstvoto prez IV—načaloto na XI vek: problemy na pronikvaneto i utvărždavaneto mu na Balkanskija poluostrov.* Sofia: Izdat. Chejzăl, 1995.

———. *Filosofskata misăl văv Vizantija IX–XII v.* Sofia: Izdat. Nauka i Izkustvo, 1981.

Kocka, Jürgen. *Geschichte des Kapitalismus.* Munich: C.H. Beck, 2013.

Kočović, Bogoljub. *Žrtve Drugog svetskog rata u Jugoslaviji.* London: Veritas Foundation Press, 1985.

Kofman, Jan. "Economic Nationalism in East-Central Europe in the Interwar Period." In *Economic Nationalism in East-Central Europe and South America: 1918–1939= Le Nationalisme économique en Europe du Centre-Est et en Amérique du Sud,* edited by Henryk Szlajfer, 191–249. Translated by Maria Chmielewska-Szlajfer and Piotr Goc. Geneva: Librairie Droz, 1990.

Kogălniceanu, Mihail. *Esquisse sur l'histoire, les moeurs et la langue des Cigains connus en France sous le nom de Bohémiens: suivie d'un recueil de sept cents mots cigains.* Berlin: Behr, 1837.

Koken, Paul, Theodore N. Constant, and Seraphim G. Canoutas. *A History of the Greeks in the Americas, 1453–1938.* Ann Arbor, MI: Proctor, 1995.

Köksal, Yonca. "Transnational Networks and Kin States: The Turkish Minority in Bulgaria, 1878–1940." *Nationalities Papers* 38, no. 2 (2010): 191–211.

Kolar, Othmar. *Rumänien und seine nationalen Minderheiten 1918 bis heute.* Vienna: Böhlau, 1997.

Kolarov, Simeon. *Plovdiv.* Sofia Press Agency, 1968.

Kolev, Valery. "Krajat na 'turskoto robstvo' v sledosvoboždenska Bălgarija." *Istoričeski pregled,* no. 5 / 6 (2008): 88–102.

Koliopoulos, John. *Brigands with a Cause: Brigandage and Irredentism in Modern Greece, 1821–1912.* Oxford: Clarendon Press, 1987.

———. "Greek Foreign Policy and Strategy, 1939–1941." *Balkan Studies* 29, no. 1 (1988): 89–98.

Koller, Markus. "Die osmanische Geschichte Südosteuropas." *Europäische Geschichte Online (EGO).* Last modified December 3, 2010. http://www.ieg-ego.eu/kollerm-2010-de.

———. "The Penjez: Some Remarks on a Merchant Family in Eighteenth-Century Ottoman Bosnia." In *Merchants in the Ottoman Empire,* edited by Suraiya Faroqhi and Gilles Veinstein, 179–92. Paris: Peeters, 2008.

Koller, Markus, and Kemal H. Karpat, eds. *Ottoman Bosnia: A History in Peril.* Madison: University of Wisconsin Press, 2004.

Koller, Markus, and Peter Mario Kreuter. "Südosteuropa im Zeichen imperialer Herrschaft: Das Osmanische Reich vom 16. bis zum 18. Jahrhundert." In *Geschichte Südosteuropas: Vom frühen Mittelalter bis zur Gegenwart,* edited by Konrad Clewing and Oliver Jens Schmitt, 214–92. Regensburg: Pustet, 2011.

Konstantinou, Evangelos, ed. *Ausdrucksformen des europäischen und internationalen Philhellenismus vom 17.–19. Jahrhundert.* Frankfurt: Peter Lang, 2007.

Korade, Mijo, Mira Aleksić, and Jerko Matoš. *Jesuits and Croatian Culture.* Zagreb: Most, 1992.

Korb, Alexander. "Genocide in Times of Civil War: Popular Attitudes towards Ustaša Mass Violence, Croatia 1941–1945." In *The Holocaust and European Societies: Social Processes and Social Dynamics,* edited by Frank Bajohr and Andrea Löw, 127–45. London: Palgrave Macmillan, 2016.

———. *Im Schatten des Weltkriegs: Massengewalt der Ustaša gegen Serben, Juden und Roma in Kroatien 1941–1945.* Hamburg: Hamburger Edition, 2013.

Körbler, Đuro. "Istraga protiv mladića Nikole Remedellija zbog bezvjerstva 1776. godine." *Građa za povijest književnosti Hrvatske* 7 (1912): 1–45.

Kosanović, Bogdan. *Sava Vladislavić-Raguzinski u svom i našem vremenu.* Belgrade: Svet knjige, 2009.

Koselleck, Reinhart. "Über die Theoriebedürftigkeit der Geschichtswissenschaft." In *Theorie der Geschichtswissenschaft und Praxis des Geschichtsunterrichts,* edited by Werner Conze, 10–28. Stuttgart: Klett, 1972.

Kosev, Konstantin. *Istoriĭa na aprilskoto vŭstanie.* Sofia: Univ. izd-vo "Sv. Kliment Okhridski," 1996.

———. "The Uprising of April, 1876: The Summit of the Bulgarian National Revival." *Southeastern Europe* 4, no. 2 (1977): 143–68.

Kostić, Mita. "Kult Petra Velikog među Rusima, Srbima i Hrvatima u XVIII veku." *Istorijski časopis* 8 (1958): 83–106.

————. "Volter kod Srba." *Glas SAN* 240, no. 5 (1960): 49–68.

Kostovicova, Denisa, and Marlies Glasius. *Bottom-Up Politics: An Agency-Centred Approach to Globalization.* New York: Palgrave Macmillan, 2012.

Kotsakis, Kostas. "The Past Is Ours: Images of Greek Macedonia." In *Archaeology under Fire: Nationalism, Politics and Heritage in the Eastern Mediterranean and Middle East,* edited by Lynn Meskell, 44–67. London: Routledge, 1998.

Kovačević, Desanka. *Trgovina u srednjovjekovnoj Bosni.* Sarajevo: Naučno društvo NR Bosne i Hercegovine, 1961.

Kovačević-Kojić, Desanka. *Srednjovjekovna Srebrenica XIV–XV vijek.* Belgrade: Srpska akademija nauka i umetnosti, 2010.

Kovtun, Dmitriy. "Boosting Job Growth in the Western Balkans." IMF Working Paper WP/14/16. Washington, DC, 2014.

Kralj, Dejan. "Balkan Minds: Transnational Nationalism & the Transformation of South Slavic Immigrant Identity in Chicago, 1890–1941." PhD diss., Loyola University Chicago, 2013.

Kraljačić, Tomislav. *Kalajev režim u Bosni i Hercegovini (1882–1903).* Sarajevo: Veselin Masleša, 1987.

Kramer, Alan. *Dynamic of Destruction: Culture and Mass Killing in the First World War.* Oxford University Press, 2007.

Krasić, Stjepan. "Apothecary Activity in Dubrovnik Dominican Monastery from XVIIth to the beginning XIXth Century." *Acta Medico-Historica Adriatica* 9, no. 1 (2011): 19–32.

————. *Ivan Dominik Stratiko.* Split: Književni Krug, 1991.

Kreiser, Klaus. *Der Osmanische Staat 1300–1922.* Munich: Oldenbourg, 2010.

————. *Geschichte Istanbuls: Von der Antike bis zur Gegenwart.* Munich: C.H. Beck, 2010.

————. *Istanbul: Ein historischer Stadtführer.* Munich: C.H. Beck, 2013.

Kreiser, Klaus, and Christoph K. Neumann. *Kleine Geschichte der Türkei.* Bonn: Bundeszentrale für Politische Bildung, 2005.

Krekić, Bariša. "Contributions of Foreigners to Dubrovnik's Economic Growth in the Late Middle Ages." *Viator* 9 (1978): 375–94.

————. "Italian Creditors in Dubrovnik (Ragusa) and the Balkan Trade, Thirteenth through Fifteenth Centuries." In *The Dawn of Modern Banking,* 241–54. New Haven, CT: Yale University Press, 1979.

————. "On the Latino-Slavic Cultural Symbiosis in Late Medieval and Renaissance Dalmatia and Dubrovnik." In *Dubrovnik: A Mediterranean Urban Society, 1300–1600,* edited by Bariša Krekić, 312–32. Aldershot: Ashgate, 1997.

Kreutel, Richard F., ed. *Kara Mustafa vor Wien: Das türkische Tagebuch der Belagerung Wiens 1683, verfasst vom Zeremonienmeister der Hohen Pforte.* Graz: Styria, 1977.

Kreuter, Mario. *Der Vampirglaube in Südosteuropa: Studien zur Genese, Bedeutung und Funktion. Rumänien und der Balkanraum.* Berlin: Weidler, 2001.

Krizman, Bogdan. *Ante Pavelić i ustaše.* Zagreb: Globus, 1978.

Krleža, Miroslav, et al., eds. *Enciklopedija Jugoslavije.* Zagreb: Jugoslav. Leksikograf. Zavod, 1990.

Krstić, Tijana. *Contested Conversions to Islam: Narratives of Religious Change in the Early Modern Ottoman Empire.* Stanford, CA: Stanford University Press, 2011.

———. "Illuminated by the Light of Islam and the Glory of the Ottoman Sultanate: Self-Narratives of Conversion to Islam in the Age of Confessionalization." *Comparative Studies in Society and History* 51, no. 1 (2009): 35–63.

———. "Of Translation and Empire: Sixteenth-Century Ottoman Imperial Interpreters as Renaissance Go-Betweens." In *The Ottoman World,* edited by Christine Woodhead, 130–42. London: Routledge, 2012.

Krug, Wilhelm Traugott. *Krug's gesammelte Schriften: Theologische Schriften.* Braunschweig: Verlag Friedrich Vieweg, 1834.

Krumeich, Gerd. *Juli 1914: Eine Bilanz.* Paderborn: Ferdinand Schöningh, 2013.

Krunisanje srpskih vladara: 8 vekova manastira Žiča. Izložba se priređuje povodom jubileja Osam vekova manastira Sveta Žiča u Kraljevdana, dana Opštine Kraljevo. Belgrade: Istorijski Muzej Srbije, 2007.

Krušelj, Željko. *Franjo Tuđman.* Zagreb: Globus, 1991.

Küçük, Bekir Harun. "Early Enlightenment in Istanbul." PhD diss., University of California, San Diego, 2012.

Kulić, Vladimir. "An Avant-Garde Architecture for an Avant-Garde Socialism: Yugoslavia at EXPO '58." *Journal of Contemporary History* 47, no. 1 (2012): 161–84.

Kuljić, Todor. *Tito: sociološkoistorijska studija.* Zrenjanin: Kulturni Centar Zrenjanina, 2012.

Kuran, Aptullah. *Sinan: The Grand Old Master of Ottoman Architecture.* Washington, DC: Institute of Turkish Studies, 1987.

Kurmuş, Orhan. "The Cotton Famine and Its Effects on the Ottoman Empire." In *The Ottoman Empire and the World-Economy,* edited by Huri İslamoğlu-İnan, 160–77. Cambridge University Press, 1987.

Kurto, Nedžad. *Sarajevo 1462–1992.* Sarajevo: OKO, 1997.

Kurtynova-D'Herlugnan, Liubov. *The Tsar's Abolitionists: The Slave Trade in the Caucasus and Its Suppression.* Leiden: Brill, 2010.

Kusturica, Emir. *Der Tod ist ein unbestätigtes Gerücht: Mein bisheriges Leben.* Translated by Mascha Dabić. Munich: Knaus, 2011.

Kutleša, Stipe. "Ima li mjesta Bogu u znanosti? Primjer Boškovićeve teorije sila." *Nova prisutnost: časopis za intelektualna i duhovna pitanja* 10, no. 2 (2012): 165–78.

Kutz, Magnus-Sebastian. *Öffentlichkeitsarbeit in Kriegen: Legitimation von Kosovo-, Afghanistan- und Irakkrieg in Deutschland und den USA.* Wiesbaden: Springer VS, 2014.

Laignel-Lavastine, Alexandra. *Cioran, Eliade, Ionesco: l'oubli du fascisme; trois intellectuels roumains dans la tourmente du siècle.* Paris: PUF, 2002.

Lambert, Malcolm D. *The Cathars.* Malden, MA: Blackwell, 1998.

———. *Medieval Heresy: Popular Movements from Bogomil to Hus.* New York: Holmes and Meier, 1977.

Lampe, John R., and Marvin R. Jackson. *Balkan Economic History, 1550–1950: From Imperial Borderlands to Developing Nations.* Bloomington: Indiana University Press, 1982.

Landau, Jacob M. *Pan-Turkism: From Irredentism to Cooperation.* Bloomington: Indiana University Press, 1995.

Landes, David S. *The Wealth and Poverty of Nations: Why Some Are So Rich and Some So Poor.* New York: Norton, 1998.

Lane, Ann. *Britain, the Cold War and Yugoslav Unity, 1941–1949.* Brighton: Sussex Academic Press, 1996.

Langewiesche, Dieter. *Nation, Nationalismus, Nationalstaat in Europa.* Munich: C.H. Beck, 2000.

Larner, John. *Marco Polo and the Discovery of the World.* New Haven, CT: Yale University Press, 1999.

Lascaris, M. "La révolution grecque vue de Salonique: Rapports des consuls de France et d'Autriche (1821–1826)." *Balcania* 6 (1943): 145–68.

Latham, A. J. H. *The Depression and the Developing World, 1914–1939.* London: Croom Helm, 1981.

Latham, Michael E. *Modernization as Ideology: American Social Science and "Nation Building" in the Kennedy Era.* Chapel Hill: University of North Carolina Press, 2000.

Latić, Nedžad. *Boja povijesti: Izetbegovićeve godine 1983–2003.* Sarajevo: Bosančica-print, 2003.

Lazarević, Branko. *Sabrana dela.* Belgrade: Zavod za Udžbenike, 2007.

Lee, Eun-Jeung. *Guild Dynamics in Seventeenth-Century Istanbul: Fluidity and Leverage.* Leiden: Brill, 2004.

Lees, Lorraine M. *Keeping Tito Afloat: The United States, Yugoslavia, and the Cold War.* University Park: Pennsylvania State University Press, 1997.

Leezenberg, Michiel. "The Oriental Origins of Orientalism: The Case of Dimitrie Cantemir," In *The Making of the Humanities,* edited by Rens Bod, Jaap Maat, and Thijs Weststeijn, 243–63. Vol. 2: *From Early Modern to Modern Disciplines.* Amsterdam University Press, 2012.

Legrand, Émile, ed. *Documents inédits concernant Rhigas Vélestinlis et ses compagnons de martyre tirés des archives de Vienne en Autriche et p. p. Émile Legrand, Prof. à l'Éc. nat. d. Langues orient.* Paris, 1892.

Lemberg, Hans. "Zur Entstehung des Osteuropabegriffs im 19. Jahrhundert vom 'Norden' zum 'Osten' Europas." *Jahrbücher für Geschichte Osteuropas* 33, no. 1 (1985): 48–91.

Lemny, Stefan: "Die rumänische Aufklärung: Mit einer Grundlagenbibliographie." *Das achtzehnte Jahrhundert: Zeitschrift der Deutschen Gesellschaft für die Erforschung des achtzehnten Jahrhunderts* 19, no. 1 (1995): 36–57.

———. *Les Cantemir: L'aventure européenne d'une famille princière au XVIIIe siècle.* Paris: Complexe, 2009.

Lenger, Friedrich. *Metropolen der Moderne: Eine europäische Stadtgeschichte seit 1850.* Munich: C.H. Beck, 2013.

Leonhard, Jörn. *Die Büchse der Pandora: Geschichte des Ersten Weltkriegs.* Munich: C.H. Beck, 2014.

Lešić, Josip. *Istorija pozorišta Bosne i Hercegovine.* Sarajevo: OOUR Izdavačka djelat-nost, 1985.

Leuștean, Lucian. *Orthodox Christianity and Nationalism in Nineteenth-Century South-eastern Europe.* New York: Fordham University Press, 2014.

Levene, Mark. *Genocide in the Age of the Nation State.* London: I.B. Tauris, 2005.

Levy, Avigdor. *The Sephardim in the Ottoman Empire.* Princeton, NJ: Darwin Press, 1992.

Lewis, Bernard. *Cultures in Conflict: Christians, Muslims, and Jews in the Age of Discovery.* Oxford University Press, 1995.

———. "Der Westen aus der Sicht des Islam: Ein historischer Überblick." In *Europa und die Grenzen im Kopf,* edited by Karl Kaser et al., 287–302. Klagenfurt: Wieser, 2003.

———. *Istanbul and the Civilization of the Ottoman Empire.* Norman: University of Oklahoma Press, 1963.

———. *The Muslim Discovery of Europe.* 2nd ed. New York: Norton, 2001.

Libal, Wolfgang. *Balkan.* Munich: Prestel, 1987.

Lilie, Ralph-Johannes. *Byzanz: Geschichte des oströmischen Reiches 326–1453.* Munich: C.H. Beck, 2005.

Lilova, Dessislava. "Barbarians, Civilized People and Bulgarians: Definition of Identity in Textbooks and the Press (1830–1878)." *CAS Sofia Working Paper Series* 3 (2011): 1–25.

Little Global Cities: Streifzüge durch Sarajevo. Bielefeld: Kerber, 2014.

Liu, Yong. *Sino-Romanian Relations: 1950's–1960's.* Bucharest: Institutul Național pentru Studiul Totalitarismului, 2006.

Livezeanu, Irina. *Cultural Politics in Greater Romania: Regionalism, Nation Building & Ethnic Struggle, 1918–1930.* Ithaca: Cornell University Press, 1995.

Ljubić, Sime. "Izvještaj gos. la Maire, francezkoga konsula u Koronu, u Dubrovačkoj republiki." *Starine* 18 (1881): 39–118.

Ljušić, Radoš. *Knjiga o Načertaniju: nacionalni i državni program Kneževine Srbije (1844).* Belgrade: Beogradski izdavačko-grafički zavod, 1993.

Llewellyn-Smith, Michael. "Greece and Europe: Progress and Civilization, 1890s–1920s." In *Europe in Modern Greek History,* edited by Kevin Featherstone, 17–25. London: Hurst, 2014.

Lory, Bernard. "Immigration et intégration sociale à Plovdiv au XIXe siècle." *Revue du Monde Musulman et de la Méditerrannée* 66, no. 1 (1992): 95–103.

Loth, Wilfried. "States and the Changing Equations of Power." In *Global Interdependence: The World after 1945,* edited by Akira Iriye, 11–199. Cambridge, MA: Belknap Press of Harvard University Press, 2014.

Love, Joseph LeRoy. *Crafting the Third World: Theorizing Underdevelopment in Rumania and Brazil.* Stanford, CA: Stanford University Press, 1996.

———. "Theorizing Underdevelopment: Latin America and Romania, 1860–1950." *Estudos Avançados* 4, no. 8 (1990): 62–95.

Lowry, Heath W. *Fifteenth Century Ottoman Realities: Christian Peasant Life on the Aegean Island of Limnos.* Istanbul: Eren, 2002.

———. *The Shaping of the Ottoman Balkans, 1350–1550: The Conquest, Settlement & Infrastructural Development of Northern Greece.* Istanbul: Bahçeşehir University Publications, 2008.

Lozovan, E. "D. Cantemir et l'expansion russe au Caucase (1722–1724)." *Revue des Études Roumaines* 13 (1974): 91–105.

Lubonja, Fatos. "Between the Glory of a Virtual World and the Misery of a Real World." In *Albanian Identities: Myth and History,* edited by Stephanie Schwandner-Sievers and Bernd J. Fischer, 91–103. Bloomington: Indiana University Press, 2002.

Lucic, Iva. "In the Service of the Nation: Intellectuals' Articulation of the Muslim National Identity." *Nationalities Papers* 40, no. 1 (2012): 23–44.

Luetić, Josip. *Brodari i pomorci Dubrovačke republike.* Zagreb: Nakladni zavod Matice hrvatske, 1997.

———. *O pomorstvu Dubrovačke Republike u XVIII. stoljeću.* Zagreb: Jugoslavenska akademija u Zagrebu, 1959.

———. *Pomorci i jedrenjaci Republike Dubrovačke.* Zagreb: Nakl. zavod Matice hrvatske, 1984.

Lungu, Dov B. "The European Crisis of March–April 1939: The Romanian Dimension." *International History Review* 7, no. 3 (1985): 390–414.

———. *Romania and the Great Powers, 1933–40.* Durham, NC: Duke University Press, 1989.

Lydall, Harold. *Yugoslav Socialism: Theory and Practice.* Oxford University Press, 1984.

Macartney, C. A. *The Habsburg Empire, 1790–1918.* New York: Macmillan, 1969.

MacGahan, Januarius Aloysius. *The Turkish Atrocities in Bulgaria: Letters of the Special Commissioner of the "Daily News."* London: Bradbury, Agnew & Co., 1876.

Machedon, Luminita, and E. R. Scoffham. *Romanian Modernism: The Architecture of Bucharest, 1920–1940.* Cambridge, MA: MIT Press, 1999.

Maclean, Fitzroy. *Josip Broz Tito: A Pictorial Biography.* London: Macmillan, 1980.

———. "Tito: A Study." *Foreign Affairs* 28, no. 2 (1950): 231–46.

MacMillan, Margaret. *Peacemakers: The Paris Conference of 1919 and Its Attempt to End War.* London: J. Murray, 2001.

Maddison, Angus. *Die Weltwirtschaft: Eine Millenniumsperspektive.* Paris: OECD, 2004.

———. *The World Economy: Historical Statistics.* Paris: OECD, 2003.

Magaš, Branka. *Croatia through History: The Making of a Modern State.* London: Saqi Books, 2007.

Mager, Kōstas. *Historia tou Hellēnikou typou.* Athens: A. Dēmopoulos, 1957.

Maier, Charles S. "Leviathan 2.0: Inventing Modern Statehood." In *A World Connecting, 1870–1945,* edited by Emily S. Rosenberg, 29–282. Cambridge, MA: Belknap Press of Harvard University Press, 2012.

———. "'Malaise': The Crisis of Capitalism in the 1970s." In *The Shock of the Global: The 1970s in Perspective,* edited by Niall Ferguson et al., 25–48. Cambridge, MA: Belknap Press of Harvard University Press, 2010.

Majstorović, Stevan. *Cultural Policy in Yugoslavia.* Paris: UNESCO, 1972.

Majuru, Adrian. *Stadt der Verlockungen: Das vormoderne Bukarest zwischen Orient und Europa.* Berlin: Frank & Timme, 2014.

Makarenko, Tamara. "The Crime–Terror Continuum: Tracing the Interplay between Transnational Organised Crime and Terrorism." *Global Crime* 6, no. 1 (2004): 129–45.

———. *Europe's Crime-Terror Nexus: Links between Terrorist and Organized Crime Groups in the European Union.* Brussels: European Parliament, 2012.

Makrides, Vasilios. *Die religiöse Kritik am kopernikanischen Weltbild in Griechenland zwischen 1794 und 1821: Aspekte griechisch-orthodoxer Apologetik angesichts naturwissenschaftlicher Fortschritte.* Frankfurt: Peter Lang, 1995.

Malcolm, Noel. *Bosnia: A Short History.* New York: New York University Press, 1996.

———. *Kosovo: A Short History.* New York: New York University Press, 1998.

Mandaville, Peter. "Transnational Muslim Solidarities and Everyday Life." *Nations and Nationalism* 17, no. 1 (2011): 7–24.

Manela, Erez. *The Wilsonian Moment: Self-Determination and the International Origins of Anticolonial Nationalism.* Oxford University Press, 2007.

Maner, Hans-Christian. "Die 'rumänische Nation' in den Konzeptionen griechisch-katholischer und orthodoxer Geistlicher und Intellektueller Siebenbürgens im 18. und 19. Jahrhundert." In *Nationalisierung der Religion und Sakralisierung der Nation im östlichen Europa,* edited by Martin Schulze Wessel, 75–88. Stuttgart: Franz Steiner, 2006.

———. *Parlamentarismus in Rumänien (1930–1940): Demokratie im autoritären Umfeld.* Munich: Oldenbourg, 1997.

Manoschek, Walter. *"Serbien ist judenfrei": Militärische Besatzungspolitik und Judenvernichtung in Serbien 1941/42.* Munich: Oldenbourg, 1995.

Mansfield, Edward D., and Jack L. Snyder. *Electing to Fight: Why Emerging Democracies Go to War.* Cambridge, MA: MIT Press, 2005.

Mantran, Robert. *Istanbul dans la seconde moitié du XVIIe siècle: Essai d'histoire institutionnelle, économique et sociale.* Paris: Maisonneuve, 1962.

Marčeva, Ilijana I. *Todor Živkov—pätjat käm vlastta: politika i ikonomika v Bălgarija, 1953–1964 g.* Sofia: Inst. po Istorija, 2001.

Mark, James, Péter Apor, Radina Vučetić, and Piotr Osęka. "'We Are with You, Vietnam': Transnational Solidarities in Socialist Hungary, Poland and Yugoslavia." *Journal of Contemporary History* 50, no. 3 (2015): 393–464.

Marković, Predrag. *Beograd i Evropa 1918–1941.* Belgrade: Savremena administracija, 1992.

Marković, Todor. "Ljuben Karavelov u srpskoj književnosti." *Srpski književni glasnik* 24, no. 5 (1910): 347–59.

Marković, Zdenka. *Pjesnikinje starog Dubrovnika.* Zagreb: Jugoslavenska akademija znanosti i umjetnosti, 1970.

Marrus, Michael R.: *The Unwanted: European Refugees in the Twentieth Century.* Oxford University Press, 1999.

Massino, Jill. "From Black Caviar to Blackouts: Gender, Consumption, and Lifestyle in Ceauşescu's Romania." In *Communism Unwrapped: Consumption in Cold War Eastern Europe,* edited by Paulina Bren and Mary Neuburger, 226–49. Oxford University Press, 2012.

Matković, Stjepan. "Hrvatska percepcija Balkanskih ratova." *Istorijski zapisi* 1–2 (2013): 69–83.

Matkovski, Aleksandar. *Gjurčin Kokaleski.* Skopje, 1959.

Matsch, Erwin. *Internationale Politik: 1919–1939.* Vol. 1: *Eine Welt im Gipsverband: 1919–1932.* Vienna: Böhlau, 2005.

Matuz, Jozsef. *Das Osmanische Reich: Grundlinien seiner Geschichte.* Darmstadt: Wissenschaftliche Buchgesellschaft, 1990.

Mayerhofer, Lisa. *Zwischen Freund und Feind: Deutsche Besatzung in Rumänien 1916–1918.* Munich: Martin Meidenbauer, 2010.

Mazower, Mark. *After the War Was Over: Reconstructing the Family, Nation, and State in Greece, 1943–1960.* Princeton University Press, 2000.

———. *The Balkans: A Short History.* New York: Modern Library, 2002.

———. *Governing the World: The History of an Idea.* New York: Penguin, 2012.

———. *Greece and the Inter-War Economic Crisis.* Oxford University Press, 1991.

———. *Inside Hitler's Greece: The Experience of Occupation, 1941–44.* New Haven, CT: Yale University Press, 1993.

———. *Salonica, City of Ghosts: Christians, Muslims and Jews 1430–1950.* London: HarperCollins, 2004.

McCarthy, Justin. *Death and Exile: The Ethnic Cleansing of Ottoman Muslims, 1821–1922.* Princeton, NJ: Darwin Press, 1995.

McClellan, Woodford. *Svetozar Marković and the Origins of Balkan Socialism.* Princeton University Press, 1964.

McGowan, Bruce. *Economic Life in Ottoman Europe: Taxation, Trade, and the Struggle for Land, 1600–1800.* Cambridge University Press, 1981.

Meininger, Thomas A. *The Formation of a Nationalist Bulgarian Intelligentsia, 1835–1878.* New York: Garland, 1987.

———. "The Journalists and Journalism of the Bulgarian Revival." *Southeastern Europe* 3, no. 1 (1976): 19–31.

———. "The Social Stratification of the Bulgarian Town in the Third Quarter of the Nineteenth Century." *Southeastern Europe* 5, no. 2 (1979): 73–104.

Mellish, Liz. "The Koprivshtitsa Festival: From National Icon to Globalized Village Event." In *Global Villages: Rural and Urban Transformations in Contemporary Bulgaria,* edited by Ger Duijzings, 153–71. London: Anthem Press, 2013.

Merdjanova, Ina. *Rediscovering the Umma: Muslims in the Balkans between Nationalism and Transnationalism.* Oxford University Press, 2013.

Michail, Eugene. "Western Attitudes to War in the Balkans and the Shifting Meanings of Violence, 1912–91." *Journal of Contemporary History* 47, no. 2 (2012): 219–39.

Mihailović, Konstantin. *Memoirs of a Janissary.* Translated by Benjamin Stolz. Ann Arbor: University of Michigan Press, 1975.

Mihailović, Srećko, ed. *Deca krize: omladina Jugoslavije krajem osamdesetih.* Belgrade: Institut društvenih nauka, 1990.

Milata, Paul. *Zwischen Hitler, Stalin und Antonescu: Rumäniendeutsche in der Waffen-SS.* Cologne: Böhlau, 2007.

Milenković, Toma. "Međunarodna organizacija rada i Jugoslavija (1919–1929)." *Istorija 20. veka* 4, no. 1–2 (1986): 7–41.

Millo, Anna. "The Creation of a New Bourgeoisie in Trieste." In *Social Change in the Habsburg Monarchy*, edited by Harald Heppner, Peter Urbanitsch, and Renate Zedinger, 215–27. Bochum: Winkler, 2011.

Milo, Paskal. "Albania and the Balkan Entente." *Balkan Studies* 39, no. 1 (1998): 91–122.

Milutinović, Zoran. *Getting over Europe: The Construction of Europe in Serbian Culture.* Amsterdam: Rodopi, 2011.

———. "Oh, to Be a European! What Did Rastko Petrović Learn in Africa?" In *Under Eastern Eyes,* edited by Wendy Bracewell and Alex Drace-Francis, 267–91. Budapest: Central European University Press, 2008.

Milward, Alan S. *The European Rescue of the Nation-State.* London: Routledge, 2000.

Minehan, Philip B. *Civil War and World War in Europe: Spain, Yugoslavia and Greece, 1936–1949.* New York: Palgrave Macmillan, 2006.

Minkov, Anton. *Conversion to Islam in the Balkans: Kisve Bahası Petitions and Ottoman Social Life, 1670–1730.* Leiden: Brill, 2004.

Miović, Vesna. *Dubrovačka diplomacija u Istambulu.* Zagreb: Hrvatska akademija znanosti i umjetnosti, 2003.

———. *Dubrovačka Republika u spisima namjesnika Bosanskog Ejaleta i Hercegovačkog Sandžaka.* Dubrovnik: Državni arhiv, 2008.

———. *The Jewish Ghetto in the Dubrovnik Republic (1546–1808).* Dubrovnik: HAZU, 2005.

Mirković, Miroslava. *Moesia Superior: Eine Provinz an der mittleren Donau.* Mainz: Verlag Philipp von Zabern, 2007.

Mishkova, Diana. "Balkan Liberalisms: Historical Routes of a Modern Ideology." In *Entangled Histories of the Balkans,* edited by Roumen Daskalov and Diana Mishkova, 99–198. Vol. 2: *Transfers of Political Ideologies and Institutions.* Leiden: Brill, 2014.

———. "In Quest of Balkan Occidentalism." *Tokovi istorije* 1–2 (2006): 29–62.

———. "Literacy and Nation-Building in Bulgaria 1878–1912." *East European Quarterly* 28, no. 1 (1994): 63–93.

Mišković, Nataša. *Basare und Boulevards: Belgrad im 19. Jahrhundert.* Vienna: Böhlau, 2008.

Mitchell, Richard P. *The Society of the Muslim Brothers.* Oxford University Press, 1993.

Mitić, Ilija. *Dubrovačka država u međunarodnoj zajednici: Od 1358. do 1815.* Zagreb: Matica hrvatska, 1988.

Mitrović, Andrej. *Srbija u Prvom svetskom ratu.* Belgrade: Stubovi kulture, 2004.

Mitrović, Marija. "Turkish Foreign Policy towards the Balkans: The Influence of Traditional Determinants on Davutoğlu's Conception of Turkey–Balkan Relations." GeT MA Working Paper Series. Berlin: Humboldt University, 2014.

Mladenović, Božica. *Porodica u Srbiji u prvom svetskom ratu.* Belgrade: Istorijski Institut, 2006.

Moisuc, Viorica. "Orientation dans la politique extérieure de la Roumanie après le pacte de Munich." *Revue Roumaine d'Histoire* 5, no. 2 (1966): 327–40.

Mojić, Dušan. "Evolucija kulta Josipa Broza Tita 1945–1990: analiza štampe." *Srpska politička misao* 2, no. 1 (1995): 133–55.

Mojsov, Lazo. *Dimensions of Non-Alignment.* Belgrade: Jugoslovenska stvarnost, 1981.

Moldt, Dirk. *Deutsche Stadtrechte im mittelalterlichen Siebenbürgen: Korporationsrechte—Sachsenspiegelrecht—Bergrecht.* Cologne: Böhlau, 2009.

Mommsen, Wolfgang J. *Der Erste Weltkrieg: Anfang vom Ende des bürgerlichen Zeitalters.* Bonn: Bundeszentrale für Politische Bildung, 2004.

Montagu, Lady Mary Wortley. *Letters of the Right Honourable Lady Mary Wortley Montagu.* London: Theophilus Barrois, 1816.

Moore, Barrington. *Social Origins of Dictatorship and Democracy: Lord and Peasant in the Making of the Modern World.* Boston: Beacon Press, 1966.

Moore, Wilbert Ellis. *Economic Demography of Eastern and Southern Europe.* Geneva: League of Nations, 1945.

Morand, Paul. *Bucarest.* Paris: Plon, 1990.

Moravenov, Konstantin D. *Pametnik za plovdivskoto khristiĭansko naselenie v grada i za obshtite zavedeniĭa po proiznosno predanie: podaren na Bŭlgarskoto chitalishte v Tsarigrad 1869.* Sofia, 1884.

More, Robert Jasper. *Under the Balkans: Notes of a Visit to the District of Philippopolis in 1876.* London: Henry S. King & Co., 1877.

Morgan, Michael Cotey. "The Seventies and the Rebirth of Human Rights." In *The Shock of the Global: The 1970s in Perspective,* edited by Niall Ferguson et al., 237–50. Cambridge, MA: Belknap Press of Harvard University Press, 2010.

Moritsch, Andreas. "Die Bauernparteien bei den Kroaten, Serben und Slowenen." In *Europäische Bauernparteien im 20. Jahrhundert,* edited by Heinz Gollwitzer, 359–402. Stuttgart: Fischer, 1977.

Müller, Andreas E. *Berg Athos: Geschichte einer Mönchsrepublik.* Munich: C.H. Beck, 2005.

Müller, Joseph Franz. "Darstellung der Pestseuche in Rumelien in den Jahren 1837 und 1838." *Medicinische Jahrbücher des königl. kaiserl. Österreichischen Staates* 25 (1841): 32–45, 191–200.

Munck, Gerardo L., Jeff Skalnik, and Carol Leff. "Modes of Transition and Democratization: South America and Eastern Europe in Comparative Perspective." *Comparative Politics* 29, no. 3 (1997): 343–62.

Mungiu-Pippidi, Alina. "Romanian Political Intellectuals before and after the Revolution." In *Intellectuals and Politics in Central Europe,* edited by András Bozóki, 73–99. New York: Central European University Press, 1999.

Münkler, Herfried. *Die neuen Kriege.* Hamburg: Rowohlt, 2002.

Münkler, Marina. *Marco Polo: Leben und Legende.* Munich: C.H. Beck, 1998.

Murgasova, Zuzana, et al. *The Western Balkans: 15 Years of Economic Transition.* Washington, DC: International Monetary Fund, 2015.

Murgescu, Bogdan. *România și Europa: Acumularea decalajelor economice (1500–2010).* Iași: Polirom, 2010.

Nagy-Talavera, Nicholas M. *Nicolae Iorga: A Biography.* Iași: Center for Romanian Studies, 1998.

Nauright, John, and Charles Parrish, eds. *Sports around the World: History, Culture, and Practice.* Santa Barbara, CA: ABC-CLIO, 2012.

Nayhauss, Hans Christoph Graf von. "Mircea Eliades Indisches Tagebuch: Auf der Suche nach der indischen Seele." In *Der Gott der Anderen: Interkulturelle Transformationen religiöser Traditionen,* edited by Ernest W. B. Hess-Lüttich and Arupon Natarajan, 69–87. Frankfurt: Peter Lang, 2009.

Nećak, Dušan. *Hallsteinova doktrina in Jugoslavija: Tito med Zvezno Republiko Nemčijo in Nemško Demokratično Republiko.* Ljubljana: Znanstveni inštitut Filozofske fakultete, 2002.

Nejkow, Peter. *Unruhiger Balkan: Erinnerungen eines ehemaligen bulgarischen Diplomaten.* Berlin: Verlag der Nation, 1963.

Nenadović, Prota Mateja. *Memoari.* Belgrad, 1988.

———. *The Memoirs of Prota Matija Nenadović.* Translated by Lovett F. Edwards. Oxford: Clarendon Press, 1969.

Nenezić, Dragan S. *Jugoslovenske oblasti pod Italijom 1941–1943.* Belgrade: Vojnoistorijski institut vojske Jugoslavije, 1999.

Neuburger, Mary. *Balkan Smoke: Tobacco and the Making of Modern Bulgaria.* Ithaca, NY: Cornell University Press, 2013.

———. "'Kebabche,' Caviar, or Hot Dogs? Consuming the Cold War at the Plovdiv Fair 1947–72." *Journal of Contemporary History* 47, no. 1 (2012): 48–68.

———. "To Chicago and Back: Aleko Konstantinov, Rose Oil, and the Smell of Modernity." *Slavic Review* 65, no. 3 (2006): 427–45.

Newman, Edward. "The 'New Wars' Debate: A Historical Perspective is Needed." *Security Dialogue* 35, no. 2 (2004): 173–89.

Nicholas Titulescu, the European Statesman of the United Nations. Paris: Editrice Nagard, 1982.

Nicol, Donald MacGillivray. *Byzantium and Venice: A Study in Diplomatic and Cultural Relations.* Cambridge University Press, 1988.

———. *The Last Centuries of Byzantium, 1261–1453.* Cambridge University Press, 1993.

Nicolaidy, B. *Les Turcs et la Turquie contemporaine; itinéraire et compte-rendu de voyages dans les provinces ottomanes avec cartes détaillées.* 2 vols. Paris: F. Sartorius, 1859.

Niedermaier, Paul. *Städte, Dörfer, Bauwerke: Studien zur Siedlungs- und Baugeschichte Siebenbürgens.* Cologne: Böhlau, 2008.

Nielsen, Christian Axboe. *Making Yugoslavs: Identity in King Aleksandar's Yugoslavia.* Toronto: University of Toronto Press, 2014.

Nikolaidis, Efthymios. *Science and Eastern Orthodoxy: From the Greek Fathers to the Age of Globalization.* Baltimore: Johns Hopkins University Press, 2011.

Nikolić, Kosta. *Tito govori što narod misli: Kult Josipa Broza Tita 1944–1949.* Belgrade: Službeni List SCG, 2006.

Njagulov, Blagovest. "Early Socialism in the Balkans: Ideas and Practices in Serbia, Romania and Bulgaria." In *Entangled Histories of the Balkans,* edited by Roumen Daskalov and Diana Mishkova, 199–280. Vol. 2: *Transfers of Political Ideologies and Institutions.* Leiden: Brill, 2014.

Noble, Thomas F. X., ed. *From Roman Provinces to Medieval Kingdoms*. New York: Routledge, 2006.

Noli, Fan Stylian. *George Castrioti Scanderbeg: 1405–1468*. New York: International Universities Press, 1947.

North, John. *Astronomy and Astrology*. Cambridge University Press, 2013.

Novak, Grga. "Kultura u Dubrovniku oko 1775. godine." *Prilozi za književnost, jezik, istoriju i folklor* 2, no. 2 (1922): 189–95.

Novak, Maja. "Dubrovnik u drugoj polovici 18. stoljeća." *Anali historijskog odjela centra za znanstveni rad JAZU u Dubrovniku* 15–16 (1978): 137–78.

Novak, Slobodan Prosperov. *Dubrovnik Revisited*. Zagreb: Sveučilišna naklada Liber, 1987.

———. *Slaveni u renesansi*. Zagreb: Matica hrvatska, 2009.

Novaković, Stojan. *Selo*. Belgrade: Srpska književna zadruga, 1965.

Obolensky, Dimitri. *The Byzantine Commonwealth: Eastern Europe 500–1453*. New York: Praeger, 1971.

Obradović, Marija. *"Narodna demokratija" u Jugoslaviji, 1945–1952*. Belgrade: INIS, 1995.

O'Donnell, J. S. *Albania under Enver Hoxha: A Coming of Age*. New York: Columbia University Press, 1995.

Oeldemann, Johannes. *Die Kirchen des Christlichen Ostens: Orthodoxe, orientalische und mit Rom unierte Ostkirchen*. Regensburg: Topos plus, 2006.

Office for South East Europe. *Report on Activities of the European Commission/World Bank Office for South East Europe 2002*. Brussels, 2003.

Okey, Robin. *Taming Balkan Nationalism*. Oxford University Press, 2007.

Okuka, Miloš. *Eine Sprache - viele Erben: Sprachpolitik als Nationalisierungsinstrument in Ex-Jugoslawien*. Klagenfurt: Wieser, 1998.

Oldson, William O. *A Providential Anti-Semitism: Nationalism and Polity in Nineteenth Century Romania*. Philadelphia: American Philosophical Society, 1991.

Olshausen, Eckart. "Raum—Antike." In *Europäische Mentalitätsgeschichte: Hauptthemen in Einzeldarstellungen,* edited by Peter Dinzelbacher, 681–95. Stuttgart: Alfred Kröner Verlag, 2008.

Omerika, Armina. *Islam in Bosnien-Herzegowina und die Netzwerke der Jungmuslime (1918–1983)*. Wiesbaden: Harrassowitz, 2014.

Onasch, Konrad. *Einführung in die Konfessionskunde der orthodoxen Kirchen*. Berlin: De Gruyter, 1962.

Opfer, Björn. *Im Schatten des Krieges: Besatzung oder Anschluss—Befreiung oder Unterdrückung? Eine komparative Untersuchung über die bulgarische Herrschaft in Vardar-Makedonien 1915–1918 und 1941–1944*. Münster: LIT Verlag, 2005.

Oprea, Ion M. *Nicolae Titulescu's Diplomatic Activity*. Translated by Andrei Bantas. Bucharest: Academy of the Socialist Republic of Romania, 1968.

Organizacioni komitet XIV zimskih olimpijskih igara. *U znaku Sarajeva: Kako su XIV zimske olimpijske igre opisane u jugoslovenskoj štampi i JRT*. Sarajevo, 1984.

Orlić, Olga. "The Curious Case of Marco Polo from Korčula: An Example of Invented Tradition." *Journal of Marine and Island Cultures* 2 (2013): 20–28.

Ornea, Z. *The Romanian Extreme Right: The Nineteen Thirties*. Translated by Eugenia Maria Popescu. Boulder: East European Monographs, 1999.

Osăceanu, Victor G. *Pagini de diplomaţie romanească: România şi societatea naţiunilor.* Craiova: Aius, 2009.

Oşca, Alexandru. *O fereastră în cortina de fier România: declaraţia de independenţă din aprilie 1964.* Focşani: Ed. Vrantop, 1997.

Osterhammel, Jürgen. "Europamodelle und imperiale Kontexte." *Journal of Modern European History* 2, no. 2 (2004): 157–82.

———. *The Transformation of the World: A Global History of the Nineteenth Century.* Translated by Patrick Camiller. Princeton: Princeton University Press, 2014.

Osterhammel, Jürgen, and Niels P. Petersson. *Geschichte der Globalisierung: Dimensionen, Prozesse, Epochen.* Munich: C.H. Beck, 2006.

Ostrogorski, Georgije. "Vizantija i južni sloveni." *Jugoslovenski istorijski časopis* 1 (1963): 3–13.

Ostrogorsky, Georg. *Byzantinische Geschichte 324–1453.* Munich: C.H. Beck, 2006.

Outram, Dorinda. *The Enlightenment.* Cambridge University Press, 2005.

Overy, Richard J. *The Origins of the Second World War.* 4th ed. London: Routledge, 2017.

Özveren, Y. Eyüp. "A Framework for the Study of the Black Sea World, 1789–1915." *Review (Fernand Braudel Center)* 20 (1997): 77–113.

Özyurt, Senol. *Die Türkenlieder und das Türkenbild in der deutschen Volksüberlieferung vom 16. bis zum 20. Jh.* Munich: Fink, 1972.

Pach, Zsigmond Pál. "Colony or Periphery? The Position of East-Central Europe at the Dawn of Modern Times." *Aula* 13, no. 2 (1991): 191–98.

———. *Die ungarische Agrarentwicklung im 16.–17. Jahrhundert: Abbiegung vom westeuropäischen Entwicklungsgang.* Budapest: Akadémiai Kiadó, 1964.

———. "Diminishing Share of East-Central Europe in the 17th Century International Trade." *Acta Historica Academiae Scientiarum Hungaricae* 16, no. 3/4 (1970): 289–306.

———. *Hungary and the European Economy in Early Modern Times.* Aldershot: Variorum, 1994.

———. "Levantine Trade Routes to Hungary 15th–17th Centuries." *Acta Historica Academiae Scientiarum Hungaricae* 33, no. 1 (1987): 57–65.

Paić-Vukić, Tatjana. *Svijet Mustafe Muhibbija, sarajevskoga kadije.* Zagreb: Srednja Europa, 2007.

Paisy, Hilendarski. *A Slavo-Bulgarian History.* Translated by Krasimir Kabakchiev. Sofia: St. Kliment Ohridski University Press, 2000.

Palairet, Michael. *The Balkan Economies c. 1800–1914.* Cambridge University Press, 1997.

Palotás, Emil. "Die wirtschaftlichen Aspekte in der Balkanpolitik Österreich-Ungarns um 1878." In *Der Berliner Kongress von 1878: Die Politik der Großmächte und die Probleme der Modernisierung in Südosteuropa in der zweiten Hälfte des 19. Jahrhunderts,* edited by Ralph Melville and Hans-Jürgen Schröder, 271–85. Wiesbaden: Franz Steiner, 1982.

Pamuk, Şevket. "The Decline and Resistance of Ottoman Cotton Textiles 1820–1913." *Explorations in Economic History* 23, no. 2 (1986): 205–25.

———. "Estimating and Explaining Economic Growth in Nineteenth-Century Southeastern Europe and Eastern Mediterranean." In *The Economic Development of Southeastern Europe in the 19th Century,* edited by Edhem Eldem and Socrates Petmezas, 225–50. Athens: Alpha Bank, 2011.

Pamuk, Şevket, and Jeffrey G. Williamson. "Ottoman De-Industrialization, 1800–1913: Assessing the Magnitude, Impact, and Response." *Economic History Review* 64, no. 1 (2011): 159–84.

Panagiotou, Ritsa, and Anastasios Valvis. *How Is the Sovereign Debt Crisis Affecting Greece's Relations with the Balkan Countries and Greece's Standing in the Region?* Athens: ELIAMEP, 2014.

Pantelić, Dušan. *Beogradski pašaluk pred Prvi Srpski Ustanak.* Belgrade: Naučna knjiga, 1949.

Pantić, Dragomir. "Nacionalna distanca građana Jugoslavije." In *Jugoslavija na kriznoj prekretnici,* edited by Ljiljana Baćević, 168–86. Belgrade: Institut društvenih nauka, 1991.

———. "Prostorne, vremenske i socijalne koordinate religioznosti mladih u Jugoslaviji." In *Deca krize: omladina Jugoslavije krajem osamdesetih,* edited by Srećko Mihailović, 203–38. Belgrade: Institut društvenih nauka, 1990.

Panzac, Daniel. *The Barbary Corsairs: The End of a Legend, 1800–1820.* Translated by Victoria Hobson. Leiden: Brill, 2005.

———. *La peste dans l'Empire ottoman: 1700–1850.* Leuven: Peeters, 1985.

———. "Plague and Seafaring in the Ottoman Mediterranean in the Eighteenth Century." In *Trade and Cultural Exchange in the Early Modern Mediterranean: Braudel's Maritime Legacy,* edited by Maria Fusaro, Colin Heywood, and Mohamed-Salah Omri, 45–68. London: Tauris, 2010.

Papadakis, Aristeides. "The Historical Tradition of Church-State Relations under Orthodoxy." In *Eastern Christianity and Politics in the Twentieth Century,* edited by Pedro Ramet, 37–58. Durham, NC: Duke University Press, 1988.

Papadrianos, Iōannēs A. *Hē Hellēnikē palingenesia tou 1821 kai hē Valkanikē tēs diastasē.* Komotēnē: Dēmokriteio Panepistēmio Thrakēs, 1996.

Papakonstantinou, Katerina. "Transport and Communication in Southeastern Europe in the Nineteenth Century: The Impact on Trade." In *The Economic Development of Southeastern Europe in the 19th Century,* edited by Edhem Eldem and Socrates Petmezas, 349–95. Athens: Alpha Bank, 2011.

Papazoglou, Avraam. "I Thessaloniki kata ton Maio tou 1821." *Makedonika* 1 (1940): 417–28.

Papulia, Basilike F. *Ursprung und Wesen der "Knabenlese" im Osmanischen Reich.* Munich: Oldenbourg, 1963.

Parker, Charles H. *Global Interactions in the Early Modern Age, 1400–1800.* Cambridge University Press, 2010.

Parusheva, Dobrinka. "La vie quotidienne 'à la française' dans les Balkans, XIXe–début du XXe siècle." *Études Balkaniques* 2–3 (2001): 130–34.

Parvev, Ivan. *Habsburgs and Ottomans between Vienna and Belgrade (1683–1739).* Boulder: East European Monographs, 1995.

Pašić, Nikola. *Sloga Srbo-Hrvata.* Belgrade: Vreme knjige, 1995.

Patterson, Patrick Hyder. *Bought and Sold: Living and Losing the Good Life in Socialist Yugoslavia.* Ithaca, NY: Cornell University Press, 2011.

Paulmann, Johannes. "Grenzüberschreitungen und Grenzräume: Überlegungen zur Geschichte transnationaler Beziehungen von der Mitte des 19. Jahrhunderts bis in die Zeitgeschichte." In *Geschichte der internationalen Beziehungen: Erneuerung und Erweiterung einer historischen Disziplin,* edited by Eckart Conze, Ulrich Lappenküper, and Guido Müller, 169–96. Cologne: Böhlau, 2004.

———. "The Straits of Europe: History at the Margins of a Continent." *Bulletin of the German Historical Institute Washington* 52 (Spring 2013): 7–28.

Paulová, Milada. *Tajný výbor Maffie a spoluprace s Jiňoslovany v letech 1916–1918.* Prague: Academia, 1968.

Pavešković, Andjelko. "Putopisac Marco Polo." *Politički godišnjak* 23 (1998): 38–66.

Pavlowitch, Stevan K. "Society in Serbia, 1791–1830." In *Balkan Society in the Age of Greek Independence,* edited by Richard Clogg, 137–56. Totowa: Barnes and Noble, 1981.

Pearson, Sevan Philippe. "Muslims' Nation-building Process in Socialist Bosnia and Herzegovina in the 1960s." *Nations and Nationalism* 24, no. 2 (2018): 432–52.

———. "Wem gehört Bosnien? Die Nationalitätenpolitik der Kommunisten Bosnien und Herzegowinas 1943–1974." PhD diss., University of Lausanne, 2016.

Pedersen, Susan. "Back to the League of Nations." *American Historical Review* 112, no. 4 (2007): 1091–117.

Pedrotty, Kate Meehan. "Yugoslav Unity and Olympic Ideology at the 1984 Sarajevo Winter Olympic Games." In *Yugoslavia's Sunny Side: A History of Tourism in Socialism (1950s–1980s),* edited by Hannes Grandits and Karin Taylor, 335–63. New York: Central European University Press, 2010.

Peković, Slobodanka. "Ženski časopisi u Srbiji na početku 20. veka." *Slavica Tergestina* (May 2004): 11–12, 123–37.

Pentzopoulos, Dimitri. *The Balkan Exchange of Minorities and Its Impact upon Greece.* Paris: Mouton, 1962.

Peričić, Šime. "Oskudica i glad u Dalmaciji u XIX i početkom XX stoljeća." *Radovi: Razdio povijesnih znanosti* 13, no. 1 (1980): 1–32.

Perinić Lewis, Ana, and Pavao Rudan. "'Došlo je doba svjetlosti! Stratiko je u Hvaru!': biskup prosvjetitelj Ivan Dominik Stratiko o Hvaranima." *Rad Hrvat. akad. znan. umjet. Razred druš. znan.* 48 (2011): 83–100.

———. "Spectemur Agendo: prepoznaje nas se po našem delovanu! Prosvjetiteljski rad biskupa Ivana Dominika Stratika i liječnika Julija Bajamontija na otoku Hvaru." *Rad Hrvat. akad. znan. i umjet. Razred za druš. znan.* 49 (2012): 57–118.

Perović, Latinka. *Između anarhije i autokratije: Srpsko društvo na prelazima vekova (XIX–XXI).* Belgrade: Helsinški odbor za ljudska prava u Srbiji, 2006.

———. *Srpski socijalisti 19. veka: prilog istoriji socijalističke misli.* Belgrade: Službeni list SRJ, 1995.

Péteri, György. "Sites of Convergence: The USSR and Communist Eastern Europe at International Fairs Abroad and at Home." *Journal of Contemporary History* 47, no. 1 (2012): 3–12.

Petković, Ranko. *Nesvrstanost i Jugoslavija na pragu XXI veka.* Zagreb: Školska knjiga, 1989.

Petranović, Branko. *Balkanska federacija 1943–1948.* Belgrade: Zaslon, 1991.

Petrescu, Alexandra. "Entrepreneurial Tourism in Romania: A System-Stabilizing Factor?" In *"Schleichwege": Inoffizielle Begegnungen sozialistischer Staatsbürger zwischen 1956 und 1989,* edited by Włodzimierz Borodziej, Jerzy Kochanowski, and Joachim von Puttkamer, 115–33. Cologne: Böhlau, 2010.

———. "Les liens entre le Conseil National des Femmes Roumaines et le Conseil International des Femmes, 1921–1971." *Studia Politica* 2 (2007): 373–93.

Petrescu, Dragos. "Community Building and Identity Politics in Gheorghiu-Dej's Romania (1956–64)." In *Stalinism Revisited: The Establishment of Communist Regimes in East-Central Europe,* edited by Vladimir Tismaneanu, 401–22. Budapest: Central European University Press, 2009.

Petrişor, Vasile. "Marea demonstraţie de la 1 mai 1939, expresie a poziţiei antifasciste, antirăzboinice şi antirevizioniste a României, în contextul European al epocii." *Anale de Istorie* 31, no. 2 (1985): 56–70.

Petrović, Aleksandar. *Rakovica: Socijalno-zdravstvene i higijenske prilike.* Belgrade: Štamp. Centralnog higijenskog zavoda, 1935–1939.

Petrović, Dragan. *Istorija industrije Beograda: Razvoj i razmeštaj industrije Beograda u XIX i XX veku.* Belgrade: Srpsko Geografsko Društvo, 2006.

Petrović, Vladimir. "Josip Broz Tito's Summit Diplomacy in the International Relations of Socialist Yugoslavia 1944–1961." *Annales* 24, no. 4 (2014): 577–92.

———. *Titova lična diplomatija.* Belgrade: Institut za savremenu istoriju, 2010.

Petzer, Tatjana, and Angela Richter. *"Isochimenen": Kultur und Raum im Werk von Isidora Sekulić.* Munich: Sagner, 2012.

Pezo, Edvin. *Zwangsmigration in Friedenszeiten? Jugoslawische Migrationspolitik und die Auswanderung von Muslimen in die Türkei (1918 bis 1966).* Munich: Oldenbourg, 2013.

Philliou, Christine May. *Biography of an Empire: Governing Ottomans in an Age of Revolution.* Berkeley: University of California Press, 2011.

———. "Communities on the Verge: Unraveling the Phanariot Ascendancy in Ottoman Governance." *Comparative Studies in Society and History* 51, no. 1 (2009): 151–81.

Piketty, Thomas. *Capital in the Twenty-First Century.* Translated by Arthur Goldhammer. Cambridge, MA: Belknap Press of Harvard University Press, 2014.

Pinson, Marc. "Ottoman Colonization of the Circassians in Rumili after the Crimean War." *Études Balkaniques,* no. 3 (1972): 71–85.

Pipa, Arshi. "Fan Noli as a National and International Albanian Figure." *Südost-Forschungen* 43 (1984): 241–70.

Pippidi, Andrei. *Bucureşti: istorie şi urbanism.* Iaşi: Do-Mino R, 2002.

———. *Byzantins, Ottomans, Roumains: Le sud-est européen entre l'héritage impérial et les influences occidentales.* Paris: Champion, 2006.

———. *Visions of the Ottoman Empire in Renaissance Europe.* New York: Columbia University Press, 2012.

Pirjevic, Jože. *Tito and His Comrades.* Madison: University of Wisconsin Press, 2018.

Pitz, Ernst. *Die griechisch-römische Ökumene und die drei Kulturen des Mittelalters: Geschichte des mediterranen Weltteils zwischen Atlantik und Indischem Ozean, 270–812 A.D.* Berlin: Akademie Verlag, 2001.

Plaschka, Richard Georg. *Avantgarde des Widerstands: Modellfälle militärischen Widerstands im 19. und 20. Jahrhundert.* Vol. 1. Vienna: Böhlau, 2000.

Plaschka, Richard Georg, Anna Maria Drabek, and Birgitta Zaar, eds. *Eisenbahnbau und Kapitalinteressen in den Beziehungen der österreichischen mit den südslawischen Ländern.* Vienna: Österreichische Akademie der Wissenschaften, 1993.

Pleština, Dijana. *Regional Development in Communist Yugoslavia: Success, Failure, and Consequences.* Boulder: Westview Press, 1992.

Pocock, J. G. A. *Barbarism and Religion.* Cambridge University Press, 1999.

Podskalsky, Gerhard. *Griechische Theologie in der Zeit der Türkenherrschaft (1453–1821).* Munich: C.H. Beck, 1988.

Pohl, Walter. *Die Awaren: Ein Steppenvolk im Mitteleuropa, 567–822 n. Chr.* Munich: C.H. Beck, 1988.

Polanyi, Karl. *The Great Transformation.* New York: Farrar and Rinehart, 1944.

Polexe, Laura. *Auf engen Pfaden: Die rumänischen Freiwilligen in den internationalen Brigaden im spanischen Bürgerkrieg.* Stuttgart: ibidem, 2009.

———. *Netzwerke und Freundschaft: Sozialdemokraten in Rumänien, Russland und der Schweiz an der Schwelle zum 20. Jahrhundert.* Göttingen: V&R unipress, 2011.

Political and Economic Planning (PEP). *Economic Development in S.E. Europe: Including Poland, Czechoslovakia, Austria, Hungary, Roumania, Yugoslavia, Bulgaria and Greece.* London: Oxford University Press, 1945.

Polo, Marco, et al. *The Book of Ser Marco Polo, the Venetian: Concerning the Kingdoms and Marvels of the East.* Cambridge University Press, 2010.

Pomeranz, Kenneth. *The Great Divergence: China, Europe, and the Making of the Modern World Economy.* Princeton University Press, 2000.

Pop, Ioan Aurel. *Romanians and Romania: A Brief History.* Translated by Alexandra Dumitrescu and Ioana Nan. Boulder: East European Monographs, 1999.

Pop, Ioan Aurel, Ioan Bolovan, and Susana Andea. *History of Romania: Compendium.* Cluj-Napoca: Romanian Cultural Institute, 2006.

Popović, Marko. "Srednjovekovna epoha." In *Istorija privatnog života Srba,* edited by Marko Popović, Miroslav Timotijević, and Milan Ristović, 19–170. Belgrade: Clio, 2011.

Popović-Obradović, Olga. *Parlamentarizam u Srbiji od 1903. do 1914. godin.* Belgrade: Službeni list SRJ, 1998.

Populari Think Tank. *A Political Romance: Relations between Turkey and Bosnia and Herzegovina.* Sarajevo, 2014.

Porter, Roy. *The Enlightenment.* Atlantic Highlands, NJ: Humanities Press International, 1990.

Portmann, Michael. *Die kommunistische Revolution in der Vojvodina 1944–1952: Politik, Gesellschaft, Wirtschaft, Kultur.* Vienna: Akademie der Wissenschaften, 2008.

Poulton, Hugh. *Who Are the Macedonians?* Bloomington: Indiana University Press, 2000.

Preindlsberger-Mrazović, Milena. *Bosnische Volksmärchen*. Innsbruck: A. Edlinger, 1905.

Prelog, Milan. *Povijest Bosne u doba osmanlijske vlade*. Zagreb: Fortuna, 2009.

Pridham, Geoffrey, and Tom Gallagher, eds. *Experimenting with Democracy: Regime Change in the Balkans*. London: Routledge, 2000.

Prilozi historiji Sarajeva: radovi sa Znanstvenog Simpozija Pola Milenija Sarajeva, održanog 19. do 21. marta 1993. godine. Sarajevo: Institut za istoriju, 1997.

Prodan, David. *Supplex Libellus Valachorum: Aus der Geschichte der rumänischen Nationsbildung, 1700–1848*. Cologne: Böhlau, 1982.

Proeva, Nade. *Studii za antičkite Makedonci*. Skopje: Macedonia prima, 1997.

Prokesch von Osten, Anton. *Denkwürdigkeiten und Erinnerungen aus dem Orient*. Stuttgart: Hallberger, 1836.

Prošić-Dvornić, Mirjana. *Odevanje u Beogradu u XIX i početkom XX veka*. Belgrade: Stubovi kulture, 2006.

Protić, Milan. "The Ideology of the Serbian Radical Movement 1881–1903: Sources, Characteristics, Developments." PhD diss., University of California, Santa Barbara, 1988.

———. *Uspon i pad srpske ideje*. Belgrade: Balkanološki institut, 1994.

Prpic, George J. *South Slavic Immigration in America*. Boston: Twayne, 1978.

Prügel, Roland. *Im Zeichen der Stadt: Avantgarde in Rumänien, 1920–1938*. Cologne: Böhlau, 2008.

Prusin, Alexander Victor. *Serbia under the Swastika: A World War II Occupation*. Urbana: University of Illinois Press, 2017.

Purić, Božidar. *Naši iseljenici*. Belgrade: Izdanje knjižarnice S.V. Cvijanovića, 1929.

Purivatra, Atif. *Nacionalni i politički razvitak Muslimana*. Sarajevo: Svjetlost, 1969.

Pušić, Radosav. *Kapija od žada: putopisi Srba o Kini 1725–1935*. Belgrade: Biblioteka Grada Beograda, 1998.

Puskás, Julianna. *From Hungary to the United States (1880–1914)*. Translated by Maria Bales. Budapest: Akadémiai Kiadó, 1982.

Pyrros, Dionysios. *Periigisis istoriki kai viografia Dionysiou Pyrrou tou Thettalou*. Athens, 1864.

Quataert, Donald. *The Ottoman Empire 1700–1922*. Cambridge University Press, 2005.

Radelić, Zdenko. *Hrvatska u Jugoslaviji 1945.–1991. od zajedništva do razlaza*. Zagreb: Školska knjiga, 2006.

Radonić, Jovan. *Đurađ Kastriot Skenderbeg i Arbanija u XV veku*. Belgrade: Srpska kraljevska akademija, 1942.

Radtke, Bernd. *Weltgeschichte und Weltbeschreibung*. Stuttgart: Franz Steiner, 1992.

Rădulescu, Mihai Sorin. "About the Romanian Aristocracy between the Two World Wars." *New Europe College Yearbook* 1 (1996): 339–65.

Ragep, Jamil F. "Islamic Culture and the Natural Sciences." In *The Cambridge History of Science, Vol. 2: Medieval Science,* edited by David C. Lindberg and Michael H. Shank, 27–61. Cambridge University Press, 2013.

Rajak, Svetozar. "No Bargaining Chips, No Spheres of Interest: The Yugoslav Origins of Cold War Non-Alignment." In *The Non-Aligned Movement and the Cold War: Delhi—Bandung—Belgrade,* edited by Nataša Mišković, 146–79. London: Routledge, 2014.

Ramet, Pedro. *Yugoslavia in the 1980s.* Boulder: Westview Press, 1985.

Ramet, Sabrina P. *Central and Southeast European Politics since 1989.* Cambridge University Press, 2010.

———. *Rocking the State: Rock Music and Politics in Eastern Europe and Russia.* Boulder: Westview Press, 1994.

———. *Social Currents in Eastern Europe: The Sources and Consequences of the Great Transformation.* 2nd ed. Durham, NC: Duke University Press, 1995.

Ramet, Sabrina P., and Ola Listhaug, eds. *Serbia and the Serbs in World War Two.* New York: Palgrave Macmillan, 2011.

Ranke, Leopold von. *Die serbische Revolution: Aus serbischen Papieren u. Mitteilungen. Mit e. Charte v. Serbien.* Hamburg, 1829.

Ránki, György. *Economy and Foreign Policy: The Struggle of the Great Powers for Hegemony in the Danube Valley, 1919–1939.* Boulder: East European Monographs, 1983.

Raphael, Lutz. *Imperiale Gewalt und mobilisierte Nation: Europa 1914–1945.* Munich: C.H. Beck, 2014.

Rass, Christoph. *Institutionalisierungsprozesse auf einem internationalen Arbeitsmarkt: Bilaterale Wanderungsverträge in Europa zwischen 1919 und 1974.* Paderborn: Ferdinand Schöningh, 2010.

Rauchensteiner, Manfried. *The First World War and the End of the Habsburg Monarchy: 1914–1918.* Translated by Alex J. Kay and Anna Güttel-Bellert. Vienna: Böhlau, 2014.

Rautman, Marcus Louis. *Daily Life in the Byzantine Empire.* Westport, CT: Greenwood Press, 2006.

Redžić, Enver. *Muslimansko autonomaštvo i 13. SS divizija: autonomija Bosne i Hercegovine i Hitlerov Treći Rajh.* Sarajevo: Svjetlost, 1987.

Reeb, Hans-Joachim. "Öffentlichkeit als Teil des Schlachtfeldes." In *Krieg als Medienereignis II: Krisenkommunikation im 21. Jahrhundert,* edited by Martin Löffelholz, 197–213. Opladen: VS Verlag für Sozialwissenschaften, 2004.

Reinhard, Wolfgang. Introduction to *Empires and Encounters: 1350–1750,* edited by Wolfgang Reinhard, 3–52. Cambridge, MA: Belknap Press of Harvard University Press, 2015.

———. *Geschichte der Staatsgewalt: Eine vergleichende Verfassungsgeschichte Europas von den Anfängen bis zur Gegenwart.* Munich: C.H. Beck, 2002.

Reinkowski, Maurus. "Das Osmanische Reich—ein antikoloniales Imperium?" *Zeithistorische Forschungen/Studies in Contemporary History* 3, no. 1 (2006): 34–54.

———. *Die Dinge der Ordnung: Eine vergleichende Untersuchung über die osmanische Reformpolitik im 19. Jahrhundert.* Munich: Oldenbourg, 2005.

Reis, Piri. *Baḥrīje: Das türkische Segelhandbuch für das Mittelländische Meer vom Jahre 1521.* Berlin: Walter de Gruyter, 1926.

Reiss, Rodolphe A. *Šta sam video i proživeo u velikim danima onima koji se nisu vratili. Saopštenje jednog prijatelja iz teških vremena.* Belgrade: Mladost Turist, 1997.

Republički zavod za statistiku. *Materijalni i društveni razvoj Socijalističke Republike Bosne i Hercegovine 1947–1984.* Sarajevo, 1986.

Reynolds, Diana. "Kavaliere, Kostüme, Kunstgewerbe: Die Vorstellung Bosniens in Wien 1878–1900." In *Habsburg postcolonial: Machtstrukturen und kollektives Gedächtnis,* edited by Johannes Feichtinger, Ursula Prutsch, and Moritz Csáky, 243–57. Innsbruck: StudienVerlag, 2003.

Reynolds-Cordileone, Diana. "Displaying Bosnia: Imperialism, Orientalism, and Exhibitionary Cultures in Vienna and Beyond: 1878–1914." *Austrian History Yearbook* 46 (2015): 29–50.

Riedel, Sabine. *Die Erfindung der Balkanvölker: Identitätspolitik zwischen Konflikt und Integration.* Wiesbaden: VS Verlag für Sozialwissenschaften, 2005.

Ristović, Milan D. *U potrazi za utočištem: jugoslovenski Jevreji u bekstvu od holokausta 1941–1945.* Belgrade: Službeni list SRJ, 1998.

Rittberger, Volker, and Bernhard Zangl. *Internationale Organisationen: Politik und Geschichte.* Opladen: Leske + Budrich, 2003.

Roberts, Joanne. "Romanian—Intellectual—Jew: Mihail Sebastian in Bucharest, 1935–1944." *Central Europe* 4, no. 1 (2006): 25–42.

Rodogno, Davide. *Against Massacre: Humanitarian Interventions in the Ottoman Empire, 1815–1914: The Emergence of a European Concept and International Practice.* Princeton University Press, 2012.

———. *Il nuovo ordine mediterraneo: Le politiche dell'Italia fascista in Europa 1940–1943.* Turin: Bollati Boringhieri, 2003.

Rogel, Carole. "The Wandering Monk and the Balkan National Awakening." *Études Balkaniques* no. 1 (1976): 114–27.

Rogers, Clifford J. *The Oxford Encyclopedia of Medieval Warfare and Military Technology.* Oxford University Press, 2010.

Röhl, John C. G. *The Kaiser and his Court: Wilhelm II and the Government of Germany.* Translated by Terence F. Cole. Cambridge University Press, 1994.

Roksandić, Drago. *Triplex confinium, ili, O granicama i regijama hrvatske povijesti 1500–1800.* Zagreb: Barbat, 2003.

Rolf, Malte. "Einführung: Imperiale Biographien. Lebenswege imperialer Akteure in Groß- und Kolonialreichen (1850–1918)." *Geschichte und Gesellschaft* 40, no. 1 (2014): 5–21.

Rosandić, Ružica, and Vesna Pešić. *Ratništvo, patriotizam, patrijarhalnost.* Belgrade: Centar za Antiratnu Akciju, 1994.

Rosenberg, Emily S. "Transnational Currents in a Shrinking World." In *A World Connecting, 1870–1945,* edited by Emily S. Rosenberg, 815–996. Cambridge, MA: Belknap Press of Harvard University Press, 2012.

————, ed. *A World Connecting, 1870–1945*. Cambridge, MA: Belknap Press of Harvard University Press, 2012.

Rostás, Zoltán. "A Sociological School from a Communicational Perspective: The Case of Dimitrie Gusti's Monographic School." *Acta Universitatis Sapientiae, Social Analysis* 1, no. 1 (2011): 83–97.

Rothenberg, Gunther E. *The Military Border in Croatia, 1740–1881: A Study of an Imperial Institution*. Chicago: University of Chicago Press, 1966.

Rothman, E. Natalie. *Brokering Empire: Trans-Imperial Subjects between Venice and Istanbul*. Ithaca, NY: Cornell University Press, 2012.

Rothschild, Joseph. *East Central Europe between the Two World Wars*. Seattle: University of Washington Press, 1974.

Roudometof, Victor. "Transnationalism and Globalization: The Greek Orthodox Diaspora between Orthodox Universalism and Transnational Nationalism." *Diaspora* 9, no. 3 (2000): 361–97.

Roudometof, Victor, Alexander Agadjanian, and Jerry G. Pankhurst, eds. *Eastern Orthodoxy in a Global Age: Tradition Faces the Twenty-First Century*. Walnut Creek, CA: AltaMira Press, 2005.

Roudometof, Victor, and Vasilios Makrides. *Orthodox Christianity in 21st Century Greece: The Role of Religion in Culture, Ethnicity, and Politics*. Farnham: Ashgate, 2010.

Roudometof, Victor, and Roland Robertson. *Nationalism, Globalization, and Orthodoxy: The Social Origins of Ethnic Conflict in the Balkans*. Westport, CT: Greenwood Press, 2001.

Rozen, Mina, ed. *Homelands and Diasporas: Greeks, Jews and Their Migrations*. London: I.B. Tauris, 2008.

Rucker-Chang, Sunnie. "The Turkish Connection: Neo-Ottoman Influence in Post-Dayton Bosnia." *Journal of Muslim Minority Affairs* 34, no. 2 (2014): 152–64.

Rumeli und Bosna geographisch beschrieben von Mustafa Ben Adalla Hadschi Chalfa, aus dem Türkischen übersetzt von Joseph von Hammer. Vienna, 1812.

Rumpler, Helmut. *Eine Chance für Mitteleuropa: Bürgerliche Emanzipation und Staatsverfall in der Habsburgermonarchie*. Vienna: Ueberreuter, 1997.

Rumpler, Helmut, and Peter Urbanitsch, eds. *Die Habsburgermonarchie 1848–1918*. Vol. 8 / 2: *Politische Öffentlichkeit und Zivilgesellschaft: Vereine, Parteien und Interessenverbände als Träger der politischen Partizipation*. Vienna: Österreichische Akademie der Wissenschaften, 2006.

Runciman, Steven. *The Great Church in Captivity: A Study of the Patriarchate of Constantinople from the Eve of the Turkish Conquest to the Greek War of Independence*. Cambridge University Press, 1968.

————. *The Medieval Manichee: A Study of the Christian Dualist Heresy*. Cambridge University Press, 1955.

Rusev, Borislav. "Bulgarskite poštenski službi prez balkanskata vojna 1912–1913 godina." *Voennoistoričeski Zbornik* 58, no. 6 (1989): 140–48.

Rusinow, Dennison I. *The Yugoslav Experiment 1948–1974*. Berkeley: University of California Press, 1977.

Sadat, Deena R. "Rumeli Ayanlari: The Eighteenth Century." *Journal of Modern History* 44, no. 3 (1972): 346–63.

Sageman, Marc. *Turning to Political Violence: The Emergence of Terrorism.* Philadelphia: University of Pennsylvania Press, 2017.

Şahin, Kaya. *Empire and Power in the Reign of Süleyman: Narrating the Sixteenth-Century Ottoman World.* Cambridge University Press, 2013.

Said, Edward. *Orientalism.* New York: Pantheon Books, 1978.

Samardžić, Radovan, ed. *Kosovo i Metohija u srpskoj istoriji.* Belgrade: Srpska književna zadruga, 1989.

———. *Mehmed Sokolović.* Belgrade: Narodna knjiga, 1982.

Samuelsson, Kurt. *Religion and Economic Action: A Critique of Max Weber.* New York: Harper and Row, 1961.

Sanader, Mirjana. *Dalmatia: Eine römische Provinz an der Adria.* Mainz: Verlag Philipp von Zabern, 2009.

Sanders, Irwin Taylor. *Balkan Village.* Lexington: University Press of Kentucky, 1949.

Sapelli, Giulio. *Southern Europe since 1945: Tradition and Modernity in Portugal, Spain, Italy, Greece and Turkey.* London: Longman, 1995.

Savić, Milivoje M. *Zanati i industrija u prisajedinjenim oblastima i zanati u starim granicama Kraljevine Srbije.* Belgrade: Štamparija "Dositije Obradović," 1914.

Schachner, Lukas Amadeus. "Kirche, Mönche, Heilige." In *Pracht und Alltag in Byzanz (Katalog zur Ausstellung in der Kunst- und Ausstellungshalle der Bundesrepublik Deutschland Bonn, April–September 2009),* 32–39. Mainz: Hirmer Verlag, 2009.

Schanes, Daniela. *Serbien im Ersten Weltkrieg: Feind- und Kriegsdarstellungen in österreichisch-ungarischen, deutschen und serbischen Selbstzeugnissen.* Frankfurt: Peter Lang, 2011.

Scheer, Tamara. "Manifestation österreichisch-ungarischer Besatzungsmacht in Belgrad (1916–1918)." In *Der Erste Weltkrieg auf dem Balkan: Perspektiven der Forschung,* edited by Jürgen Angelow, 211–39. Berlin: be.bra wissenschaft verlag, 2011.

Scheuermann, Martin. *Minderheitenschutz contra Konfliktverhütung? Die Minderheiten-politik des Völkerbundes in den zwanziger Jahren.* Marburg: Verlag Herder-Institut, 2000.

Schierup, Carl-Ulrik. *Migration, Socialism, and the International Division of Labour: The Yugoslavian Experience.* Aldershot: Avebury, 1990.

Schilling, Heinz. "Das konfessionelle Europa: Die Konfessionalisierung der europäischen Länder seit Mitte des 16. Jahrhunderts und ihre Folgen für Kirche, Staat, Gesellschaft und Kultur." In *Konfessionalisierung in Ostmittel-europa: Wirkungen des religiösen Wandels im 16. und 17. Jahrhundert in Staat, Gesellschaft und Kultur,* edited by Joachim Bahlcke and Arno Strohmeyer, 13–62. Stuttgart: Franz Steiner, 1999.

———. "Nationale Identität und Konfession in der europäischen Neuzeit." In *Nationale und kulturelle Identität: Studien zur Entwicklung des kollektiven Bewußtseins in der Neuzeit,* edited by Bernhard Giesen, 192–252. Frankfurt: Suhrkamp, 1991.

Schlarp, Karl-Heinz. *Wirtschaft und Besatzung in Serbien 1941–44: Ein Beitrag zur nationalsozialistischen Wirtschaftspolitik in Südosteuropa.* Stuttgart: Franz Steiner, 1986.

Schmider, Klaus. "Auf Umwegen zum Vernichtungskrieg? Der Partisanenkrieg in Jugoslawien, 1941–1944." In *Die Wehrmacht: Mythos und Realität,* edited by Rolf-Dieter Mueller and Hans-Erich Volkmann, 901–22. Munich: Oldenbourg, 1999.

———. *Partisanenkrieg in Jugoslawien 1941–1944.* Hamburg: Mittler, 2002.

Schmidt-Neke, Michael. "Skanderbegs Gefangene: Zur Debatte um den albanischen Nationalhelden." *Südosteuropa* 58, no. 2 (2010): 273–302.

Schmitt, Jens Oliver. *Das venezianische Albanien (1392–1479).* Munich: Oldenbourg, 2001.

———. *Die Albaner: Eine Geschichte zwischen Orient und Okzident.* Munich: C.H. Beck, 2012.

———. *Kosovo: Kurze Geschichte einer zentralbalkanischen Landschaft.* Vienna: Böhlau, 2008.

———. *Skanderbeg: Der neue Alexander auf dem Balkan.* Regensburg: Pustet, 2009.

———. *Südosteuropa und die Adria im späten Mittelalter.* Brăila: Editura Istros, 2012.

Schnytzer, Adi. *Stalinist Economic Strategy in Practice: The Case of Albania.* Oxford University Press, 1982.

Schödl, Günter. *Kroatische Nationalpolitik und "Jugoslavenstvo": Studien zu nationaler Integration und regionaler Politik in Kroatien-Dalmatien am Beginn des 20. Jahrhunderts.* Munich: Oldenbourg, 1990.

Scholem, Gershom. *Sabbatai Sevi: The Mystical Messiah, 1626–1676.* Princeton University Press, 1973.

Schöllgen, Gregor. *Das Zeitalter des Imperialismus.* Munich: Oldenbourg, 2000.

———. *Imperialismus und Gleichgewicht: Deutschland, England und die orientalische Frage 1871–1914.* Munich: Oldenbourg, 1984.

Schramm, Gottfried. *Ein Damm bricht: Die römische Donaugrenze und die Invasionen des 5.–7. Jahrhunderts im Lichte von Namen und Wörtern.* Munich: Oldenbourg, 1997.

Schraud, Franz von. *Geschichte der Pest in Sirmien in den Jahren 1795 und 1796.* Pesth: Trattner, 1801.

Schreiber, Gerhard. "Deutschland, Italien und Südosteuropa: Von der politischen und wirtschaftlichen Hegemonie zur militärischen Aggression." In *Das Deutsche Reich und der Zweite Weltkrieg,* vol. 3, edited by Militärgeschichtliches Forschungsamt, 278–414. Stuttgart: Deutsche Verlags-Anstalt, 1984.

Schroeder, Paul W. "The Nineteenth-Century International System: Changes in the Structure." *World Politics* 39, no. 1 (1986): 1–26.

Schultz, Helga. *Europäischer Sozialismus—immer anders.* Berlin: Berliner Wissenschafts-Verlag, 2014.

Schulz, Oliver. *Ein Sieg der zivilisierten Welt? Die Intervention der europäischen Großmächte im griechischen Unabhängigkeitskrieg (1826–1832).* Berlin: LIT Verlag, 2011.

Schulze, Hagen. *Staat und Nation in der europäischen Geschichte.* 2nd ed. Munich: C.H. Beck, 2004.

Schulze, Reinhard. *Islamischer Internationalismus im 20. Jahrhundert: Untersuchungen zur Geschichte der islamischen Weltliga.* Leiden: Brill, 1990.

Schwab-Trapp, Michael. *Kriegsdiskurse: Die politische Kultur des Krieges im Wandel 1991–1999.* Opladen: Leske + Budrich, 2002.

Schwartz, Michael. *Ethnische "Säuberungen" in der Moderne: Globale Wechselwirkungen nationalistischer und rassistischer Gewaltpolitik im 19. und 20. Jahrhundert.* Munich: Oldenbourg, 2013.

Schwoebel, Robert. *The Shadow of the Crescent: The Renaissance Image of the Turk (1453–1517).* Nieuwkoop: B. de Graaf, 1967.

Sebastian, Mihail. *Journal, 1935–1944.* Translated by Patrick Camiller. Chicago: Ivan R. Dee, 2000.

Seckendorf, Martin. *Die Okkupationspolitik des deutschen Faschismus in Jugoslawien, Griechenland, Albanien, Italien und Ungarn (1941–1945).* Berlin: Hüthig, 1992.

Seewann, Gerhard. *Geschichte der Deutschen in Ungarn.* Vol. 1: *Vom Frühmittelalter bis 1860.* Marburg: Herder-Institut, 2012.

———. *Geschichte der Deutschen in Ungarn.* Vol. 2: *1860 bis 2006.* Marburg: Herder-Institut, 2012.

Seidl, Johannes, and Angelika Ende, eds. *Ami Boué: Autobiographie—Genealogie—Opus.* Melle: Wagener Edition, 2013.

Seidl, Wolf. *Bayern in Griechenland: Die Geburt des griechischen Nationalstaats und die Regierung König Ottos.* Munich: Prestel, 1981.

Seitz, Robert, and Bernhard Müller. *Albanien: Land im Umbruch.* Ulm: Gerhard Hess, 1994.

Sekelj, Laslo. *Yugoslavia: The Process of Disintegration.* New York: Columbia University Press, 1993.

Šešelj, Vojislav. *Šta da se radi.* London: Naša Reč, 1985.

Seton-Watson, R. W. *The Southern Slav Question and the Habsburg Monarchy.* London: Constable & Co., 1911.

Sharp, Alan. *Consequences of Peace: The Versailles Settlement: Aftermath and Legacy, 1919–2010.* London: Haus, 2010.

———. *The Versailles Settlement: Peacemaking after the First World War, 1919–1923.* Basingstoke: Palgrave Macmillan, 2008.

Shea, Jamie. "Die Kosovo-Krise und die Medien: Reflexionen eines NATO-Sprechers." *S und F: Vierteljahresschrift für Sicherheit und Frieden* 18, no. 3 (2000): 208–17.

Shepherd, Ben. *Terror in the Balkans: German Armies and Partisan Warfare.* Cambridge, MA: Harvard University Press, 2012.

Shimizu, Akiko. *Die deutsche Okkupation des serbischen Banats 1941–1944: Unter besonderer Berücksichtigung der deutschen Volksgruppe in Jugoslawien.* Münster: LIT Verlag, 2003.

Siemann, Wolfram. "Asyl, Exil und Emigration." In *Demokratiebewegung und Revolution 1847–1849: Internationale Aspekte und europäische Verbindungen,* edited by Dieter Langewiesche, 70–91. Berlin: Springer-Verlag, 1998.

Siraisi, Nancy G. *Medieval & Early Renaissance Medicine: An Introduction to Knowledge and Practice.* Chicago: University of Chicago Press, 1990.

Siupiur, Elena, and Daniel Cain. "La culture et les élites de la communauté bulgare en Roumanie." *Études Balkaniques* 13, no. 1 (2006): 35–44.

Sjöberg, Örjan. *Rural Change and Development in Albania.* Boulder: Westview Press, 1991.

Skala, Karolj. "From Bošković's Fundamental Theory in Natural Philosophy to Generic Technical Innovations of Tesla." *Periodicum Biologorum* 115, no. 1 (2013): 9–14.

Skenderović, Robert. "Kuga u Požegi i Požeškoj kotlini 1739. godine." *Scrinia Slavonica* 3, no. 3 (2003): 157–70.

Skerlić, Jovan. *Istorijski pregled srpske štampe 1791–1911.* Belgrade: Izd. Srpskog novinarskog udruženja, 1911.

Skopetea, Eli. *"Uzor-kraljevina" i velika ideja: pojavni oblici nacionalnog problema u Jeladi.* Belgrade: Filip Višnjić, 2005.

Skran, Claudena M. *Refugees in Inter-War Europe: The Emergence of a Regime.* Oxford University Press, 1995.

Slatarski, W. N. *Geschichte der Bulgaren: Von der Gründung des bulgarischen Reiches bis zur Türkenzeit (679–1396).* Leipzig: I. Parlapanoff, 1918.

Sluga, Glenda. *Internationalism in the Age of Nationalism.* Philadelphia: University of Pennsylvania Press, 2013.

Smirnova, N. D. "Albania's 'Red Bishop' Fan Noli." *Novaia i noveishaia istoriia* 3 (1973): 32–56.

Smith, Bonnie G., ed. *The Oxford Encyclopedia of Women in World History.* Oxford University Press, 2008.

Snyder, Timothy, and Katherine Younger, eds. *The Balkans as Europe, 1821–1914.* Rochester, NY: University of Rochester Press, 2018.

Sojčić, Tvrtko P. *Die "Lösung" der kroatischen Frage zwischen 1939 und 1945: Kalküle und Illusionen.* Stuttgart: Franz Steiner, 2008.

Šoljić, Ante. "O ranoj renesansi u Dubrovniku." *Anali Zavoda za povijesne znanosti Hrvatske akademije znanosti i umjetnosti u Dubrovniku* 40 (2002): 127–46.

Solonari, Vladimir. *Purifying the Nation: Population Exchange and Ethnic Cleansing in Nazi-Allied Romania.* Washington, DC: Woodrow Wilson Center Press, 2010.

Sonne, Wolfgang. "Die Hauptstadt als Bild des Staates: Planungen des frühen 20. Jahrhunderts im internationalen Vergleich." In *Neue Staaten—neue Bilder? Visuelle Kultur im Dienst staatlicher Selbstdarstellung in Zentral- und Osteuropa seit 1918,* edited by Arnold Bartetzky et al., 13–31. Cologne: Böhlau, 2005.

Soulis, Georgios Ch. "I Thessaloniki kata tas archas tis ellinikis epanastaseos." *Makedonika* 2 (1953): 583–89.

Sowards, Steven W. *Austria's Policy of Macedonian Reform.* Boulder: East European Monographs, 1989.

Sparks, Mary. "The Good Woman of Sarajevo." *History Today* 63, no. 12 (2013): 20–26.

Spaskovska, Ljubica. *The Last Yugoslav Generation: The Rethinking of Youth Politics and Cultures in Late Socialism.* Manchester University Press, 2017.

Sperber, Manès. *Wie eine Träne im Ozean: Romantrilogie.* Munich: dtv, 2000.

Spiliotis, Susanne-Sophia. "Die Metaxas-Diktatur in Griechenland 1936–1941: ein faschistoides Regime?" In *Autoritäre Regime in Ostmittel- und Südosteuropa, 1919–1944,* edited by Erwin Oberländer et al., 403–30. Paderborn: Ferdinand Schöningh, 2001.

———. *Transterritorialität und nationale Abgrenzung: Konstitutionsprozesse der griechischen Gesellschaft und Ansätze ihrer faschistoiden Transformation, 1922/24– 1941.* Munich: Oldenbourg, 1998.

Spoerer, Mark. *Zwangsarbeit unter dem Hakenkreuz: Ausländische Zivilarbeiter, Kriegsgefangene und Häftlinge im Deutschen Reich und im besetzten Europa 1939–1945.* Stuttgart: Deutsche Verlags-Anstalt, 2001.

Špoljarić, Stjepan. *Rudjer Bošković u službi diplomacije Dubrovačke Republike.* Zagreb: Diplomatska akademija, 2011.

Stachel, Peter. "Der koloniale Blick auf Bosnien-Herzegowina in der ethnographischen Popularliteratur der Habsburgermonarchie." In *Habsburg postcolonial: Machtstrukturen und kollektives Gedächtnis,* edited by Johannes Feichtinger, Ursula Prutsch, and Moritz Csáky, 261–70. Innsbruck: StudienVerlag, 2003.

———. "Halb-kolonial und halb-orientalisch? Dalmatien als Reiseziel im 19. und frühen 20. Jahrhundert." In *Zwischen Exotik und Vertrautem: zum Tourismus in der Habsburgermonarchie und ihren Nachfolgestaaten,* edited by Peter Stachel and Martina Thomsen, 165–99. Bielefeld: transcript, 2014.

Stamenovitch, Christa. *L'émigration yougoslave (serbo-croato-slovène).* Paris: A. Pédone, 1930.

Standish, M. J. Alex. "Enver Hoxha's Role in the Development of Socialist Albanian Myths." In *Albanian Identities: Myth and History,* edited by Stephanie Schwandner-Sievers and Bernd J. Fischer, 115–24. Bloomington: Indiana University Press, 2002.

Stassinopulou, Maria A. *Weltgeschichte im Denken eines griechischen Aufklärers: Konstantinos Michail Koumas als Historiograph.* Frankfurt: Peter Lang, 1992.

Statistički godišnjak Jugoslavije. 35 vols. Belgrade: Zavod, 1968–2002.

Stauber, Reinhard. *Der Wiener Kongress.* Vienna: Böhlau, 2014.

Stavrianos, Leften Stavros. *Balkan Federation: A History of the Movement toward Balkan Unity in Modern Times.* Hamden: Archon Books, 1964.

———. *The Balkans since 1453.* New York: New York University Press, 2000.

Stefanov, Nenad. "'Message in a Bottle': Yugoslav Praxis Philosophy, Critical Theory of Society and the Transfer of Ideas between East and West." In *Entangled Protest: Transnational Approaches to the History of Dissent in Eastern Europe and the Soviet Union,* edited by Robert Brier, 109–26. Osnabrück: Fibre Verlag, 2013.

Steger, Manfred B. *Globalization: A Very Short Introduction.* Oxford University Press, 2003.

Steindorff, Ludwig. *Kroatien: Vom Mittelalter bis zur Gegenwart.* Regensburg: Pustet, 2007.

Steiner, Zara. *The Triumph of the Dark: European International History, 1933–1939.* Oxford University Press, 2011.

Stephenson, Paul. *Byzantium's Balkan Frontier: A Political Study of the Northern Balkans, 900–1204.* Cambridge University Press, 2000.

Stergiou, Andreas. "Der Antikommunismus in Griechenland." *Jahrbuch für historische Kommunismusforschung* (2011): 101–18.

Stipetić, Vladimir. "The Beginning of Scientific Economic Thought in Croatia." In *Croatia in the Late Middle Ages and the Renaissance,* edited by Ivan Supičić, 819–27. Zagreb: Školska knjiga, 2008.

Stoianovich, Traian. "The Conquering Balkan Orthodox Merchant." *Journal of Economic History* 20, no. 2 (1960): 234–313.

Stojan, Slavica. *U salonu Marije Giorgi Bona.* Dubrovnik: Academia Scientiarum et Artium Slavorum Meridionalium, 1996.

———. *Vjerenice i nevjernice: žene u svakodnevici Dubrovnika: 1600–1815.* Zagreb: HAZU, 2003.

Stojančević, Vladimir. "Prvi srpski ustanak prema Bugarskoj i Bugarima." *Istorijski Glasnik* 1, no. 1 (1954): 121–47.

Stojanović, Dubravka. *Kaldrma i asfalt: Urbanizacija i evropeizacija Beograda 1890–1914.* Belgrade: Udruženje za društvenu istoriju, 2008.

———. "Rural against Urban: Anti-Urban Discourse and Ideology in Early Twentieth Century Serbia." *Ethnologia Balkanica* 9 (2005): 65–79.

———. *Srbija i demokratija, 1903–1914: Istorijska studija o "zlatnom dobu srpske demokratije."* Belgrade: Udruženje za društvenu istoriju, 2003.

Stojković, Andrija B. K. *Životni put Dositeja Obradovića: od šegrta i kaluđera do filozofa prosvetitelja i Karađorđevog ministra prosvete.* Belgrade: Beletra, 1989.

Stokes, Gale. *Politics as Development: The Emergence of Political Parties in Nineteenth-Century Serbia.* Durham, NC: Duke University Press, 1990.

———. "The Social Origins of East European Politics." *Eastern European Politics and Societies* 1, no. 1 (1987): 30–74.

Stollberg-Rilinger, Barbara. *Die Aufklärung: Europa im 18. Jahrhundert.* Stuttgart: Reclam, 2011.

Storfa, Joachim-Peter. *Die politischen Schriften des Mihai Eminescu.* Vienna: WUV-Universitätsverlag, 1995.

Stoye, John. *The Siege of Vienna.* London: Collins, 1964.

Strachan, Hew. *The First World War: A New History.* London: Simon and Schuster, 2014.

Štraus, Ivan. *Arhitektura Jugoslavije 1945–1990.* Sarajevo: Svjetlost, 1991.

Strauss, Johann. "Ottoman Rule Experienced and Remembered: Remarks on Some Local Greek Chronicles of the Tourkokratia." In *The Ottomans and the Balkans: A Discussion of Historiography,* edited by Fikret Adanir and Suraiya Faroqhi, 193–221. Leiden: Brill, 2002.

Strong, Frederick. *Greece as a Kingdom, or, a Statistical Description of that Country from the Arrival of King Otto, in 1833, Down to the Present Time: Drawn up from Official Documents and Other Authentic Sources.* London: Longman, Brown, Green, and Longmans, 1842.

Stulli, Bernard. *Židovi u Dubrovniku.* Zagreb: Jevrejska općina, 1989.

Subotić, Irina. *Likovni krog revije "Zenit" (1921–1926).* Ljubljana: Znanstveni Inšt. Filoz. Fak., 1995.

Suciu, I. D. "The Echo in Romania of the USA Civil War." *Revue Roumaine d'Histoire* 4, no. 5 (1965): 739–63.

Sugar, Peter F. *Industrialization of Bosnia-Hercegovina: 1878–1918.* Seattle: University of Washington Press, 1963.

———. *Southeastern Europe under Ottoman Rule 1354–1804.* Seattle: University of Washington Press, 1977.

Sunajko, Goran. "Juraj Križanić između Augustina i Hobbesa." *Politička misao* 49, no. 1 (2012): 152–68.

Sundhaussen, Holm. *Der Einfluss der Herderschen Ideen auf die Nationsbildung bei den Völkern der Habsburger Monarchie.* Munich: Oldenbourg, 1973.

———. "Der Wandel in der osteuropäischen Agrarverfassung während der frühen Neuzeit: Ein Beitrag zur Divergenz der Entwicklungswege von Ost- und Westeuropa." *Südost-Forschungen* 49 (1990): 15–56.

———. "Eliten, Bürgertum, politische Klasse? Anmerkungen zu den Oberschichten in den Balkanländern des 19. und 20. Jahrhunderts." In *Eliten in Südosteuropa: Rolle, Kontinuität, Brüche in Geschichte und Gegenwart,* edited by Wolfgang Höpken and Holm Sundhaussen, 5–30. Munich: Südosteuropa-Gesellschaft, 1998.

———. *Geschichte Serbiens: 19.–21. Jahrhundert.* Vienna: Böhlau, 2007.

———. "Geschichte Südosteuropas als Migrationsgeschichte: Eine Skizze." *Südost-Forschungen* 65–66 (2006): 422–77.

———. "Jugoslawien." In *Dimension des Völkermords: Die Zahl der jüdischen Opfer des Nationalsozialismus,* edited by Wolfgang Benz, 311–30. Munich: Oldenbourg, 1991.

———. "Nation und Nationalstaat auf dem Balkan: Konzepte und Konsequenzen im 19. und 20. Jh." In *Der Balkan: Eine europäische Krisenregion in Geschichte und Gegenwart,* edited by Jürgen Elvert, 77–90. Stuttgart: Franz Steiner, 1997.

———. *Sarajevo: Geschichte einer Stadt,* Vienna: Böhlau, 2014.

———. "Südosteuropäische Gesellschaft und Kultur vom Beginn des 19. bis zur Mitte des 20. Jahrhunderts." In *Geschichte Südosteuropas: Vom frühen Mittelalter bis zur Gegenwart,* edited by Konrad Clewing and Oliver Jens Schmitt, 345–425. Regensburg: Pustet, 2011.

———. *Wirtschaftsgeschichte Kroatiens im nationalsozialistischen Großraum 1941–1945: Das Scheitern einer Ausbeutungsstrategie.* Stuttgart: Deutsche Verlags-Anstalt, 1983.

Supek, Ivan. *Ruđer Bošković: Vizionar u prijelomima filozofije, znanosti i društva.* Zagreb: Jugoslavenska akademija znanosti i umjetnosti, 1989.

Surugiu, Romina. "Nae Ionescu on Democracy, Individuality, Leadership and Nation: Philosophical (Re)Sources for a Right-Wing Ideology." *Journal for the Study of Religions and Ideologies* 8, no. 23 (2009): 68–81.

Šuvar, Stipe. *Nacije i međunacionalni odnosi u socijalističkoj Jugoslaviji.* Zagreb: Naše teme, 1970.

Svoronos, Nikos. *Le commerce de Salonique au XVIII siècle.* Paris: Presses universitaires de France, 1956.

Szabo, Agneza. "Uzroci i posljedice političkih demonstracija u Hrvatskoj 1903. godine." *Časopis za suvremenu povijest* 37, no. 3 (2005): 597–608.

Szlajfer, Henryk, ed. *Economic Nationalism in East-Central Europe and South America: 1918–1939= Le Nationalisme économique en Europe du Centre-Est et en Amérique du*

Sud. Translated by Maria Chmielewska-Szlajfer and Piotr Goc. Geneva: Librairie Droz, 1990.

Tadić, Jorjo. "Johannes Gazulus, dubrovački humanista XV veka." *Zbornik filozofskog fakulteta u Beogradu* 8, no. 1 (1964): 429–54.

Tagore, Rabindranath. *Nationalism.* San Francisco: Book Club of California, 1917.

Tanasković, Darko. *Neoosmanizam: doktrina i spoljnopolitička praksa.* Belgrade: Službeni Glasnik, 2010.

Tanović, Bakir. *Historija Bosne u okviru Osmanskog Carstva.* Sarajevo: Svjetlost, 2010.

Ţăranu, Liviu. *România în Consiliul de Ajutor Economic Reciproc: 1949–1965.* Bucharest: Editura Enciclopedică, 2007.

Tasić, Milutin. *Znamenite srpske žene.* Belgrade: Bookland, 2010.

Teichova, Alice. "Bilateral Trade Revisited: Did the Southeast European States Exploit National Socialist Germany on the Eve of the Second World War?" In *Modern Age—Modern Historian: In Memoriam György Ránki (1930–1988),* edited by Ferenc Glatz, 193–209. Budapest: Institute of History of the Hungarian Academy of Sciences, 1990.

———. "East-Central and South-East Europe, 1919–39." In *The Cambridge Economic History of Europe.* Vol. 8: *The Industrial Economies: The Development of Economic and Social Policies,* edited by Peter Mathias and Sidney Pollard, 887–983. Cambridge University Press, 1989.

———. *Kleinstaaten im Spannungsfeld der Großmächte: Wirtschaft und Politik in Mittel- und Südosteuropa in der Zwischenkriegszeit.* Munich: Oldenbourg, 1988.

Teply, Karl. *Türkische Sagen und Legenden um die Kaiserstadt Wien.* Vienna: Böhlau, 1980.

Tesla, Nikola. *My Inventions: The Autobiography of Nikola Tesla.* Edited by Ben Johnston. Williston, VT: Hart Brothers, 1982.

———. "The Transmission of Electrical Energy without Wires As a Means for Furthering Peace." *Electrical World and Engineer* (January 7, 1905): 21–24.

Tezcan, Baki. *The Second Ottoman Empire: Political and Social Transformation in the Early Modern World.* Cambridge University Press, 2010.

Thamer, Hans-Ulrich. *Die Französische Revolution.* Munich: C.H. Beck, 2013.

Ther, Philipp. *Die dunkle Seite der Nationalstaaten: "Ethnische Säuberungen" im modernen Europa.* Göttingen: Vandenhoeck & Ruprecht, 2011.

———. *Die neue Ordnung auf dem alten Kontinent: Eine Geschichte des neoliberalen Europa.* Berlin: Suhrkamp, 2014.

Therborn, Göran. *Die Gesellschaften Europas 1945–2000.* Translated by Andreas Wirthensohn. Frankfurt: Campus Verlag, 2000.

Thiersch, Friedrich Wilhelm. *De l'état actuel de la Grèce et des moyens d'arriver à sa restauration.* 2 vols. Leipzig: F.A. Brockhaus, 1833.

Tihon, Anne. *Science in the Byzantine Empire.* Cambridge University Press, 2013.

Tismaneanu, Vladimir, ed. *Promises of 1968: Crisis, Illusion, and Utopia.* Budapest: Central European University Press, 2011.

———. *The Revolutions of 1989.* London: Routledge, 1999.

———. *Stalinism for All Seasons: A Political History of Romanian Communism.* Berkeley: University of California Press, 2003.

Titulescu, Nicolae, George G. Potra, and C. I. Turcu. *Romania's Foreign Policy, 1937.* Bucharest: Encyclopaedic Publishing House, 1994.

Todorov, Nikolaj. *The Balkan City, 1400–1900.* Seattle: University of Washington Press, 1983.

———. *Balkanski izmerenija na Grăckoto văstanie ot 1821 godina: prinosăt na bălgarite.* Sofia: Izd-vo na Otechestveniia front, 1984.

———. "La participation des Bulgares à l'insurrection hétairiste dans le principautés danubiennes." In *Society, the City, and Industry in the Balkans, 15th–19th Centuries,* edited by Nikolaj Todorov, 49–96. Aldershot: Ashgate, 1997.

Todorova, Maria. *Bones of Contention: The Living Archive of Vasil Levski and the Making of Bulgaria's National Hero.* Budapest: Central European University Press, 2009.

———. "The Course and Discourses of Bulgarian Nationalism." In *Eastern European Nationalism in the Twentieth Century,* edited by Peter F. Sugar, 55–102. Washington, DC: American University Press, 1995.

———. "Historische Vermächtnisse als Analysekategorie: Der Fall Südosteuropa." In *Europa und die Grenzen im Kopf,* edited by Karl Kaser et al., 227–52. Klagenfurt: Wieser, 2003.

———. *Imagining the Balkans.* Oxford University Press, 1997.

———. "Situating the Family of Ottoman Bulgaria within the European Pattern." *History of the Family* 1, no. 4 (1996): 443–59.

Toledano, Ehud R. "Late Ottoman Concepts of Slavery (1830s–1880s)." *Poetics Today* 14, no. 3 (1993): 447–506.

———. *The Ottoman Slave Trade and Its Suppression: 1840–1890.* Princeton University Press, 1983.

Tomasevich, Jozo. *The Chetniks.* Stanford, CA: Stanford University Press, 1975.

———. *War and Revolution in Yugoslavia, 1941–1945: Occupation and Collaboration.* Stanford, CA: Stanford University Press, 2001.

Topik, Steven C., and Allen Wells. "Commodity Chains in a Global Economy." In *A World Connecting, 1870–1945,* edited by Emily S. Rosenberg, 593–812. Cambridge, MA: Belknap Press of Harvard University Press, 2012.

Toth, Helena. "Biographien, Netzwerke und Narrative: Transnationale Aspekte des politischen Exils nach 1848." In *Vergessene Vielfalt: Territorialität und Internationalisierung in Ostmitteleuropa seit der Mitte des 19. Jahrhunderts,* edited by Steffi Marung and Katja Naumann, 137–65. Göttingen: Vandenhoeck & Ruprecht, 2014.

Tóth, István György. *Literacy and Written Culture in Early Modern Central Europe.* Budapest: Central European University Press, 2000.

Trencsényi, Balázs, Maciej Janowski, Monika Baár, Maria Falina, and Michal Kopeček. *A History of Modern Political Thought in East Central Europe.* Oxford University Press, 2016.

Trencsényi, Balázs, and Michal Kopeček, eds. *Discourses of Collective Identity in Central and Southeast Europe (1770–1945): Texts and Commentaries.* Vol. 1: *Late Enlightenment.* Budapest: Central European University Press, 2006.

————. *Discourses of Collective Identity in Central and Southeast Europe (1770–1945): Texts and Commentaries*. Vol. 2: *National Romanticism*. Budapest: Central European University Press, 2007.

Trendafilov, Vladimir. "The Formation of Bulgarian Countercultures: Rock Music, Socialism, and After." *East Central Europe* 38, no. 2/3 (2011): 238–54.

Trgovčević, Ljubinka. "South Slav Intellectuals and the Creation of Yugoslavia." In *Yugoslavism: Histories of a Failed Idea, 1918–1992*, edited by Dejan Djokić, 222–37. London: Hurst, 2003.

Trhulj, Sead. *Mladi Muslimani*. Zagreb: Globus, 1990.

Tripalo, Miko. *Hrvatsko proljeće*. Zagreb: Globus, 1989.

Trivellato, Francesca. *The Familiarity of Strangers: The Sephardic Diaspora, Livorno, and Cross-Cultural Trade in the Early Modern Period*. New Haven, CT: Yale University Press, 2009.

————. *Mussolini, Makedonien und die Mächte, 1922–1930: Die "Innere Makedonische Revolutionäre Organisation" in der Südosteuropapolitik des faschistischen Italien*. Cologne: Böhlau, 1987.

Trotsky, Leon. *The Balkan Wars 1912–13: The War Correspondence of Leon Trotsky*. Edited by George Weissman and Duncan Williams. Translated by Brian Pearce. New York: Monad Press, 1980.

Tsoutsoumpis, Spyros. *A History of the Greek Resistance in the Second World War: The People's Armies*. Manchester University Press, 2016.

Tucović, Dimitrije. *Srbija i Arbanija*. Belgrade: Radnička štampa, 1914.

Tunçer, Ali Coşkun. *Sovereign Debt and International Financial Control: The Middle East and the Balkans, 1870–1914*. Basingstoke: Palgrave, 2015.

Turczynski, Emanuel. *Die deutsch-griechischen Kulturbeziehungen bis zur Berufung König Ottos*. Munich: Oldenbourg, 1959.

————. "Gestaltwandel und Trägerschichten der Aufklärung in Ost- und Südosteuropa." In *Die Aufklärung in Ost- und Südosteuropa: Aufsätze, Vorträge, Dokumentationen*, edited by Erna Lesky et al., 23–49. Cologne: Böhlau, 1972.

————. *Konfession und Nation: Zur Frühgeschichte der serbischen und rumänischen Nationsbildung*. Düsseldorf: Schwann, 1976.

————. "The Role of the Orthodox Church in Adapting and Transforming the Western Enlightenment in Southeastern Europe." *East European Quarterly* 9, no. 4 (1975): 415–40.

————. *Sozial- und Kulturgeschichte Griechenlands im 19. Jahrhundert: Von der Hinwendung zu Europa bis zu den ersten Olympischen Spielen der Neuzeit*. Mannheim: Bibliopolis, 2003.

————. *Von der Aufklärung zum Frühliberalismus: Politische Trägergruppen und deren Forderungskatalog in Rumänien*. Munich: Oldenbourg, 1985.

————. "Zur periodischen Entwicklung der Aufklärung in Russland, Ost- und Südosteuropa." In *Serta Slavica: In memoriam Aloisii Schmaus*, edited by Wolfgang Gesemann, 710–21. Munich: Trofenik, 1971.

Turnock, David. "Railways and Economic Development in Romania before 1918." *Journal of Transport Geography* 9 (2001): 137–50.

Tziovas, Dimitris, ed. *Greek Diaspora and Migration since 1700: Society, Politics, and Culture.* Aldershot: Ashgate, 2009.

UN Office on Drugs and Crime (UNODC). *Crime and Its Impact on the Balkans and Affected Countries.* Vienna: United Nations, 2008.

———. *The Illicit Drug Trade through South-Eastern Europe.* Vienna: United Nations, 2014.

Vakalopoulos, Apostolos E. *A History of Thessaloniki.* Thessaloniki: Institute for Balkan Studies, 1963.

Valentić, Mirko, and Lovorka Čoralić, eds. *Povijest Hrvata: od kraja 15. st. do kraja prvoga svjetskog rata.* Zagreb: Školska knjiga, 2005.

Valérien, Harry. *Olympia 84: Los Angeles—Sarajevo.* Munich: Südwest-Verlag, 1984.

Van Hengel, Guido. "'Up in Flames': Gavrilo Princip and the City." *Prilozi* 43 (2014): 89–97.

Vangeli, Anastas. "Nation-Building Ancient Macedonian Style: The Origins and the Effects of the So-Called Antiquization in Macedonia." *Nationalities Papers* 39, no. 1 (2011): 13–32.

Vanino, Miroslav. *Isusovci i hrvatski narod.* Zagreb: Filozofsko-teološki institut Družbe Isusove, 2005.

Vaporis, N. M. *Witnesses for Christ: Orthodox Christian Neomartyrs of the Ottoman Period, 1437–1860.* Crestwood, NY: St. Vladimir's Seminary Press, 2000.

Varićak, Vladimir. "Ulomak Boškovićeve korespondencije." *Rad Jugoslavenske akademije znanosti i umjetnosti* (1912): 163–383.

Varlik, Nükhet. "Conquest, Urbanization and Plague Networks in the Ottoman Empire, 1453–1600." In *The Ottoman World,* edited by Christine Woodhead, 251–63. London: Routledge, 2012.

Vasdravellis, Ioannis. "Fototypisis kai epanekdosis dyo tourkikon engrafon ek Veroias anaferomenon eis tin epanastasin tou 1821." *Makedonika* 12 (1972): 296–302.

Vasdravellis, John. *The Greek Struggle for Independence: The Macedonians in the Revolution of 1821.* Translated by Photeine P. Bourboulis. Thessaloniki: Institute for Balkan Studies, 1968.

———. *Piracy on the Macedonian Coast during the Rule of the Turks.* Translated by T. F. Carney. Thessaloniki: Hetaireia Makedonikōn Spoudōn, 1970.

Veinstein, Gilles. "Sokollu Mehmed Pasha." In *The Encyclopaedia of Islam,* edited by E. van Donzel et al., 706–11. 2nd ed. Leiden: Brill, 1997.

Velculescu, Cătălina. "Die rumänischen Kopisten zwischen Schrifttum und Mündlichkeit." *Revue Roumaine d'Histoire* 22, no. 4 (1983): 303–7.

Velichi, Constantin N. *La Roumanie et le mouvement révolutionnaire bulgare de libération nationale, (1850–1878).* Bucharest: Editura: Academiei Republicii Socialiste România, 1979.

———. "Romanian-Bulgarian Relations during the Bulgarian Revival, 1762–1878." *Southeastern Europe* 5, no. 1 (1978): 75–87.

Velikonja, Mitja. *Religious Separation and Political Intolerance in Bosnia-Herzegovina.* Translated by Rang'ichi Ng'inja. College Station: Texas A&M University Press, 2003.

Velimirović, Danijela. "Odevanje i moda: ka novoj politici stila." In *Privatni život kod Srba u dvadesetom veku,* edited by Milan Ristović, 342–61. Belgrade: Clio, 2007.

Veliz, Fernando. *The Politics of Croatia-Slavonia 1903–1918: Nationalism, State Allegiance and the Changing International Order.* Wiesbaden: Harrassowitz, 2012.

Veloudis, Georg. *Alexander der Große: Ein alter Neugrieche.* Munich: Heimeran, 1969.

Venturi, Franco, and Stuart Woolf. *Italy and the Enlightenment: Studies in a Cosmopolitan Century.* Translated by Susan Corsi. London: Longman, 1972.

Verdery, Katherine. *National Ideology under Socialism: Identity and Cultural Politics in Ceauşescu's Romania.* Berkeley: University of California Press, 1991.

———. "What Was Socialism and Why Did It Fall?" In *The Revolutions of 1989: Rewriting Histories,* edited by Vladimir Tismaneanu, 63–85. London: Routledge, 1999.

Vezenkov, Alexander. "Das Projekt und der Skandal 'Batak.'" *Südosteuropa* 2 (2010): 250–72.

Vickers, Miranda. *The Albanians: A Modern History.* London: I.B. Tauris, 1995.

Vidojković, Dario. *Von Helden und Königsmördern: Das deutsche Serbienbild im öffentlichen Diskurs und in der Diplomatie von 1878 bis 1914.* Wiesbaden: Harrassowitz, 2015.

Vlachopoulou, Anna Stamatia. "Die lokalen Auslöser für die Griechische Revolution von 1821: Die Peloponnes während der zweiten Turkokratie (1715–1821)." PhD diss., University of Munich, 2012.

Vlad, Laurenţiu. *Imagini ale identităţii naţionale: România şi expoziţiile universale de la Paris, 1867–1937.* Bucharest: Meridian, 2001.

Vodušek Starič, Vera. *Kako su komunisti osvojili vlast, 1944–1946.* Zagreb: Naklada Pavičić, 2006.

Vogel, Detlef. "Das Eingreifen Deutschlands auf dem Balkan." In *Das Deutsche Reich und der Zweite Weltkrieg,* edited by Militärgeschichtliches Forschungsamt, 417–511. Vol. 3. Stuttgart: Deutsche Verlags-Anstalt, 1984.

Vojnović, Kosto. "Crkva i država u dubrovačkoj republici." *Rad Jugoslavenske akademije znanosti i umjetnosti* 120 (1894): 32–142.

———. "Crkva i država u dubrovačkoj republici." *Rad Jugoslavenske akademije znanosti i umjetnosti* 121 (1895): 1–91.

Vossen, Joachim. *Bukarest—die Entwicklung des Stadtraums: Von den Anfängen bis zur Gegenwart.* Berlin: Reimer, 2004.

Vranicki, Predrag. *Geschichte des Marxismus.* Frankfurt: Suhrkamp, 1983.

Vučetić, Radina. *Koka-kola socijalizam: amerikanizacija jugoslovenske popularne kulture šezdesetih godina XX veka.* Belgrade: Službeni glasnik, 2012.

———. "Yugoslavia, Vietnam War and Antiwar Activism." *Tokovi istorije* 2 (2013): 165–80.

Vučković, Čedomir. *Nesvrstanost u misli i delu Tita.* Belgrade: Rad, 1977.

Vučo, Nikola. *Agrarna kriza u Jugoslaviji 1930–1934.* Belgrade: Prosveta, 1968.

Vuković, Boris. *Povijest hrvatskog turizma.* Zagreb: Prometej, 2005.

Wachtel, Andrew Baruch. *The Balkans in World History.* Oxford University Press, 2008.

——. *Making a Nation, Breaking a Nation: Literature and Cultural Politics in Yugoslavia.* Stanford, CA: Stanford University Press, 1998.

Wallerstein, Immanuel. *The Modern World-System I: Capitalist Agriculture and the Origins of the European World-Economy in the Sixteenth Century.* New York: Academic Press, 1974.

——. *The Modern World-System II: Mercantilism and the Consolidation of the European World-Economy, 1600–1750.* New York: Academic Press, 1974.

——. *The Modern World-System IV: Centrist Liberalism Triumphant, 1789–1914.* New York: Academic Press, 1974.

Walters, F. P. *A History of the League of Nations.* Oxford University Press, 1965.

Wasow, Ivan. *Im Schoße der Rhodopen: Wanderungen durch Bulgarien.* Berlin: Rütten & Loening, 1982.

Weber, Claudia. *Auf der Suche nach der Nation: Erinnerungskultur in Bulgarien von 1878–1944.* Berlin: LIT Verlag, 2006.

Weck, René de. *Journal de guerre (1939–1945): Un diplomate suisse à Bucarest.* Lausanne: SHSR, 2001.

Weinbaum, Alys Eve, et al., eds. *The Modern Girl around the World: Consumption, Modernity, and Globalization.* Durham, NC: Duke University Press, 2008.

Weinberg, Gerhard L. *Hitler's Foreign Policy 1933–1939: The Road to World War II.* New York: Enigma, 2010.

Weiner, Robert. "Albanian and Romanian Deviance in the United Nations." *East European Quarterly* 7, no. 1 (1973): 65–90.

——. *Romanian Foreign Policy and the United Nations.* New York: Praeger, 1984.

Weithmann, Michael W. *Die Donau: Geschichte eines europäischen Flusses.* Cologne: Böhlau, 2012.

Weitz, Eric D. *A Century of Genocide: Utopias of Race and Nation.* Princeton University Press, 2003.

Westad, Odd Arne. *The Global Cold War: Third World Interventions and the Making of Our Times.* Cambridge University Press, 2007.

Wheeler, Nicholas J. *Saving Strangers: Humanitarian Intervention in International Society.* Oxford University Press, 2000.

White, Charles. *Three Years in Constantinople: Or, Domestic Manners of the Turks in 1844.* 3 vols. London: Henry Colburn, 1846.

Wiedemann, Felix. "Orientalismus, Version: 1.0." Docupedia-Zeitgeschichte. Last modified April 19, 2012. http://docupedia.de/zg/Orientalismus?oldid=106462.

Wilkes, John. *The Illyrians.* Cambridge: Blackwell, 1992.

Williams, Eric Eustace. *Capitalism and Slavery.* Chapel Hill: University of North Carolina Press, 1944.

Williamson, Samuel R. Jr. *Austria-Hungary and the Origins of the First World War.* New York: St. Martin's Press, 1991.

Wirsching, Andreas. *Der Preis der Freiheit: Geschichte Europas in unserer Zeit.* Bonn: Bundeszentrale für Politische Bildung, 2012.

Wolff, Larry. *Inventing Eastern Europe: The Map of Civilization on the Mind of the Enlightenment.* Stanford, CA: Stanford University Press, 1994.

Woodhouse, Christopher M. *Rhigas Velestinlis: The Proto-Martyr of the Greek Revolution.* Limni: Denise Harvey, 1995.

Woodward, Susan L. *Balkan Tragedy: Chaos and Dissolution after the Cold War.* Washington, DC: Brookings Institution, 1995.

World Bank. *Transition: The First Ten Years: Analysis and Lessons for Eastern Europe and the Former Soviet Union.* Washington, DC: World Bank, 2002.

Wraza, Sofroni von. *Leben und Leiden des sündigen Sofroni.* Translated by Norbert Randow. Leipzig: Insel-Verlag, 1972.

Wurm, Heidrun. *Der osmanische Historiker Ḥüseyn b. Ǧaʿfer, genannt Hezārfenn, und die Istanbuler Gesellschaft in der zweiten Hälfte des 17. Jahrhunderts.* Freiburg: Schwarz, 1971.

Yeomans, Rory, ed. *The Utopia of Terror: Life and Death in Wartime Croatia.* Rochester, NY: University of Rochester Press, 2015.

———. *Visions of Annihilation: The Ustasha Regime and the Cultural Politics of Fascism, 1941–1945.* Pittsburgh: University of Pittsburgh Press, 2013.

Zaharia, Edgar A. "Liuben Karavelov: Bulgarian Apostle of Balkan Federation." PhD diss., University of Arizona, 1984.

Zaimova, Raia. "L'histoire du Moine Paissij (1762) dans le contexte europeen." *Études Balkaniques* 36, no. 2 (2000): 31–35.

Zakić, Mirna. *Ethnic Germans and National Socialism in Yugoslavia in World War II.* Cambridge University Press, 2017.

Žanić, Ivo. *Smrt crvenog fiće.* Zagreb: Studio grafičkih ideja, 1993.

Zaugg, Franziska. *Albanische Muslime in der Waffen-SS: Von "Großalbanien" zur Division "Skanderbeg."* Paderborn: Ferdinand Schöningh, 2016.

Zechlin, Egmont. "Die türkischen Meerengen—ein Brennpunkt der Weltgeschichte." *Geschichte in Wissenschaft und Unterricht* 17, no. 1 (1966): 1–33.

Zeiler, Thomas W. "Opening Doors in the World Economy." In *Global Interdependence: The World after 1945,* edited by Akira Iriye, 203–361. Cambridge, MA: Belknap Press of Harvard University Press, 2014.

Zelepos, Ioannis. *Die Ethnisierung griechischer Identität, 1870–1912: Staat und private Akteure vor dem Hintergrund der "Megali Idea."* Munich: Oldenbourg, 2002.

———. *Kleine Geschichte Griechenlands: Von der Staatsgründung bis heute.* Munich: C.H. Beck, 2014.

———. *Orthodoxe Eiferer im osmanischen Südosteuropa: die Kollyvadenbewegung (1750–1820) und ihr Beitrag zu den Auseinandersetzungen um Tradition, Aufklärung und Identität.* Wiesbaden: Harrassowitz, 2012.

Zeman, Mirna. *Reise zu den 'Illyriern': Kroatienstereotype in der deutschsprachigen Reiseliteratur und Statistik (1740–1809).* Munich: Oldenbourg, 2013.

Žerjavić, Vladimir. *Population Losses in Yugoslavia, 1941–1945.* Zagreb: Hrvatski Institut za povijest, 1997.

Zhivkova, Lyudmila T. *Lyudmila Zhivkova: Her Many Worlds, New Culture and Beauty, Concepts and Action.* New York: Pergamon Press, 1986.

Zielinski, Michael. *Die neutralen und blockfreien Staaten und ihre Rolle im KSZE-Prozess.* Baden-Baden: Nomos, 1990.

Ziemann, Daniel. *Vom Wandervolk zur Großmacht: Die Entstehung Bulgariens im frühen Mittelalter (7. bis 9. Jh.).* Vienna: Böhlau, 2007.

Zilfi, Madeline C. "The Kadizadelis: Discordant Revivalism in Seventeenth-Century Istanbul." *Journal for Near Eastern Studies* 45, no. 4 (1986): 251–69.

Zirojević, Olga. "Kosovo in the Collective Memory." In *The Road to War in Serbia: Trauma and Catharsis,* edited by Nebojša Popov and Drinka Gojković, 189–212. Budapest: Central European University Press, 2000.

———. "Mehmed Pascha Sokolli im Lichte jugoslawischer Quellen und Überlieferungen." *Journal of Ottoman Studies* 4 (1984): 55–67.

Živojinović, Dragoljub R. *Kralj Petar I Karadordević: U otadžbini 1903–1914. godine.* Belgrade: Zavod za udžbenike, 2003.

Zub, Alexandru. *Mihail Kogălniceanu 1817–1891: Un fondateur de la Roumanie moderne.* Bucharest: Editura Științifică și enciclopedică, 1978.

———. *Mihail Kogălniceanu: Istoric.* Iași: Editura Universității "Alexandru Ioan Cuza," 2012.

Acknowledgments

I would like to thank Jozo Džambo, Mariana Hausleitner, Nataša Mišković, Mary C. Neuburger, and Ioannis Zelepos for their helpful suggestions. I am particularly grateful to Hildrun Glass, Gerhard Seewann, and Anna Vlachopoulou for reading parts of the manuscript, and above all to Daniel Bussenius and Christian Deubner for reading through all of it. The comments from two anonymous readers were invaluable to the final version. I owe an additional debt of gratitude to Włodzimierz Borodziej and Joachim von Puttkamer; their support for my yearlong residence at the Imre Kertész Kolleg in Jena allowed me to complete the manuscript in a timely way. Not least, I express my thanks to Elizabeth Janik for her skillful and thorough translation, as well as to Harvard University Press and the Verlag C. H. Beck for their unfailingly friendly and enthusiastic support.

Index